D1824280

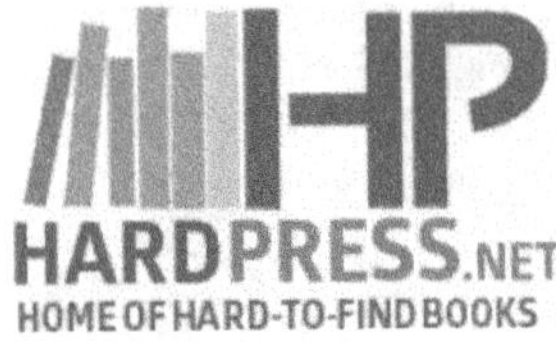

The Monthly Review, Or, Literary Journal

by Ralph Griffiths

Address:
HardPress
8345 NW 66TH ST #2561
MIAMI FL 33166-2626
USA
Email: info@hardpress.net

Princeton University Library
32101 064253949

Dei
Sub Numine
Viget

THE MONTHLY REVIEW; OR, LITERARY JOURNAL:

From July to December, 1771.

WITH

AN APPENDIX

Containing the Foreign Literature.

By SEVERAL HANDS.

VOLUME XLV.

LONDON:

Printed for R. Griffiths:

And Sold by T. Becket and P. A. De Hondt, in the Strand.

M,DCC,LXXII.

TABLE

TO THE

TITLES, AUTHORS NAMES, &c. of the BOOKS and PAMPHLETS contained in this Volume.

N. B. For REMARKABLE PASSAGES, see the INDEX, at the End of the Volume.

BRITISH PUBLICATIONS.

*** For the CONTENTS of the FOREIGN articles, see the last page of this Table.

Forsyth's

Reflec-

CONTENTS of the FOREIGN ARTICLES, in the APPENDIX to this Volume.

THE

THE

MONTHLY REVIEW,

For JULY, 1771.

ART. I. *Poems*, by the Reverend Mr. Cawthorn, late Master of Tunbridge School. 4to. 6 s. sewed. Bladon, &c. 1771.

THE late Mr. Cawthorn had a lively imagination, and an early turn for poetry; but his judgment was not equal to his fancy, and his most finished productions discover an incorrectness of taste. Nothing, therefore, can excuse his Editor for introducing any juvenile productions, though he has apologised for some of these as such, because he was, by that means, laying his Author under every disadvantage. Mr. Cawthorn formed himself upon Pope, as a model of heroic verse; and it is saying much for him, that he sometimes wrote like his master. But he could not long maintain Pope's easy elegance, nor keep up to the free and unwearied spirit that he breathed.

We will, however, do him all the justice that his remains require. He gives us the following traits of a military friend, whose death is the subject of the poem from which they are extracted:

'O blest with all that youth can give to please,
The form majestic, and the mien of ease,
Alike empower'd by nature, and by art,
To storm the rampart, and to win the heart;
Correct of manners, delicate of mind,
With spirit humble, and with truth refin'd;
For public life's meridian sunshine made
Yet known to ev'ry virtue of the shade;
In war while all the trumps of fame inspire,
Each passion raving, and each wish on fire;
At home, without or vanity, or rage;
As soft as pity, and as cool as age.'

His poem on the Regulation of the Passions has merit in many places, and the concluding images of the ensuing extract are beautiful and just:

 'Plea-

'Pleasure, my friend! on this side folly lies;
It may be vig'rous, but it must be wise:
And when our organs once that end attain,
Each step beyond it is a step to pain.
For ask the man whose appetites pursue
Each loose Roxana of the burning stew,
Who cannot eat till luxury refine
His tutor'd taste, and teach him how to dine;
Who cannot drink till Spain's rich vintage flow,
Mix'd with the coolness of December's snow:
Ask him, if all these ecstasies that move
The pulse of rapture, and the rage of love,
When wine, wit, woman, all their pow'rs employ,
And ev'ry sense is lost in ev'ry joy,
E'er fill'd his heart, and beam'd upon his breast
Content's full sunshine, with the calm of rest?
No——virtue only gives fair peace to shine,
And health, O sacred temperance! is thine.
Hence the poor peasant, whose laborious spade,
Rids the rough crag of half its heath and shade,
Feels in the quiet of his genial nights
A bliss more genuine than the club at White's:
And has in full exchange for fame and wealth
Herculean vigour, and eternal health.

'Of blooming genius, judgment, wit, possess'd,
By poets envied, and by peers caress'd;
By royal mercy sav'd from legal doom,
With royal favour crown'd for years to come,
O hadst thou, Savage! known thy lot to prize,
And sacred held fair friendship's gen'rous ties;
Hadst thou, sincere to wisdom, virtue, truth,
Curb'd the wild sallies of impetuous youth;
Had but thy life been equal to thy lays,
In vain had envy strove to blast thy bays;
In vain thy mother's unrelenting pride
Had strove to push thee helpless from her side;
Fair competence had lent her genial dow'r,
And smiling peace adorn'd thy evening hour:
True pleasure would have led thee to her shrine,
And ev'ry friend to merit had been thine.
Blest with the choicest boon that heav'n can give,
Thou then hadst learnt with dignity to live,
The scorn of wealth, the threats of want to brave,
Nor sought from prison a refuge in the grave.

'Th' immortal Rembrant all his pictures made
Soft as their union into light and shade:
Whene'er his colours wore too bright an air,
A kindred shadow took off all the glare;
Whene'er that shadow, carelessly embrown'd,
Stole on the tints, and breath'd a gloom around,

Th' at

Th' attentive artiſt threw a warmer dye,
Or call'd a glory from a pictur'd ſky;
Till both th' oppoſing powers mix'd in one,
Cool as the night, and brilliant as the ſun.

'Paſſions, like colours, have their ſtrength and eaſe,
Thoſe too inſipid, and too gaudy theſe:
Some on the heart, like Spagnoletti's throw
Fictitious horrors, and a weight of woe;
Some, like Albano's, catch from ev'ry ray
Too ſtrong a ſunſhine, and too rich a day;
Others, with Carlo's Magdalens, require
A quicker ſpirit, and a touch of fire,
Or want, perhaps, though of celeſtial race,
Correggio's ſoftneſs, and a Guido's grace.

'Wou'dſt thou then reach what Rembrant's genius knew,
And live the model that his pencil drew,
Form all thy life with all his warmth divine,
Great as his plan, and faultleſs as his line;
Let all thy paſſions, like his colours, play,
Strong without harſhneſs, without glaring, gay:
Contraſt them, curb them, ſpread them, or confine,
Ennoble theſe, and thoſe forbid to ſhine;
With cooler ſhades ambition's fire allay,
And mildly melt the pomp of pride away;
Her rainbow-robe from vanity remove,
And ſoften malice with the ſmile of love;
Bid o'er revenge the charities prevail,
Nor let a grace be ſeen without a veil:
So ſhalt thou live as heav'n itſelf deſign'd,
Each pulſe congenial with th' informing mind,
Each action ſtation'd in its proper place,
Each virtue blooming with its native grace,
Each paſſion vig'rous to its juſt decree,
And the fair whole a perfect ſymmetry.'

In his eſſay on Taſte, many of our modern follies are ridiculed with no leſs propriety than poetry:

'Hence all our ſtucco'd walls, Moſaic floors,
Palladian windows, and Venetian doors,
Our Gothic fronts, whoſe Attic wings unfold
Fluted pilaſters tipp'd with leaves of gold,
Our maſſy cieling, grac'd with gay feſtoons,
The weeping marbles of our damp ſalons,
Lawns, fring'd with citr ns, amaranthine bow'rs,
Expiring myrtles, and unop'ning flow'rs.
Hence the good Scotſman bids th' anana blow
In rocks of cryſtal, or in Alps of ſnow;
On Orcus' ſteep extends his wide arcade,
And kills his ſcanty ſunſhine in a ſhade.

'One might expect a ſanctity of ſtyle,
Auguſt and manly in an holy pile,
And think an architect extremely odd
To build a playhouſe for the church of God:
Yet half our churches, ſuch the mode that reigns,
Are Roman theatres, or Grecian fanes;
Where broad arch'd windows to the eye convey
The keen diffuſion of too ſtrong a day;
Where, in the luxury of wanton pride,
Corinthian columns languiſh ſide by ſide,
Clos'd by an altar, exquiſitely fine,
Looſe and laſcivious as a Cyprian ſhrine.

'Of late, 'tis true, quite ſick of Rome and Greece,
We fetch our models from the wiſe Chineſe:
European artiſts are too cool, and chaſte,
For Mand'rin only is the man of taſte;
Whoſe bolder genius, fondly wild to ſee
His grove a foreſt, and his pond a ſea,
Breaks out——and, whimſically great, deſigns
Without the ſhackles or of rules, or lines:
Form'd on his plans, our farms and ſeats begin
To match the boaſted villas of Pekin.
On ev'ry hill a ſpire-crown'd temple ſwells,
Hung round with ſerpents, and a fringe of bells:
Junks and balons along our waters ſail,
With each a guilded cockboat at his tail;
Our choice exotics to the breeze exhale,
Within th' incloſure of a zigzag rail;
In Tartar huts our cows and horſes lie,
Our hogs are fatted in an Indian ſtye,
On ev'ry ſhelf a Joſs divinely ſtares,
Nymphs laid on chintzes ſprawl upon our chairs;
While o'er our cabinets Confucius nods,
'Midſt Porcelain elephants, and China gods.'

To avoid theſe follies, he adviſes us to follow Nature in our improvements:

'Examine Nature with the eye of Taſte:
Mark where ſhe ſpreads the lawn or pours the rill,
Falls in the vale, or breaks upon the hill;
Plan as ſhe plans, and where her genius calls,
There ſink your grottos, and there raiſe your walls.'

Mr. Cawthorn had given us an idea of moral œconomy from painting. In another of his poems he draws the ſame idea from mſic:

'A coxcomb once in Handel's parlour found
A Grecian lyre, and try'd to make it ſound;
O'er the fine ſtops his awkward fiſt he flings,
And rudely preſſes on th' elaſtic ſtrings:

Awaken'd

Awaken'd difcord fhrieks, and fcolds, and raves,
Wild as the diffonance of winds and waves,
Loud as a Wapping mob at midnight bawls,
Harfh as ten chariots rolling round St. Paul's,
And hoarfer far than all th' ecftatic race
Whofe drunken orgies ftunn'd the wilds of Thrace.

'Friend! quoth the fage, that fine machine contains
Exacter numbers and diviner ftrains,
Strains fuch as once could build the Theban wall,
And ftop the mountain torrent in its fall:
But yet, to wake them, rouze them, and infpire,
Afks a fine finger, and a touch of fire,
A feeling foul whofe all expreffive pow'rs
Can copy Nature as fhe finks or foars;
And, juft alike to paffion, time, and place,
Refine correctnefs into eafe and grace.
He faid—and, flying o'er each quiv'ring wire,
Spread his light hand, and fwept it on the lyre.
Quick to his touch the lyre began to glow,
The found to kindle, and the air to flow,
Deep as the murmurs of the falling floods,
Sweet as the warbles of the vocal woods:
The lift'ning paffions hear, and fink, and rife,
As the rich harmony or fwells, or dies;
The pulfe of avarice forgets to move,
A purer rapture fills the breaft of love;
Devotion lifts to heav'n a holier eye,
And bleeding pity heaves a fofter figh.

'Life has its eafe, amufement, joy, and fire,
Hid in itfelf as mufic in the lyre;
And, like the lyre, will all its pow'rs impart
When touch'd and manag'd by the hand of art:
But half mankind, like Handel's fool, deftroy,
Through rage and ignorance, the ftrain of joy,
Irregularly will their paffions roll
Through nature's fineft inftrument, the foul:
While men of fenfe, with Handel's happier fkill,
Correct the tafte, and harmonize the will,
Teach their affections like his notes to flow,
Not raif'd too high, nor ever funk too low;
Till ev'ry virtue, meafur'd and refin'd,
As fits the concert of the mafter-mind,
Melts in its kindred founds, and pours along
Th' according mufic of the moral fong.'

His Abelard to Eloifa contains many ftrong lines, much paffion, and animated expreffion; but the hand of the perfect mafter was wanting to difpofe the colours, and chaftife the piece *.

* We remember to have firft feen it in the Poetical Calendar. See Rev. vol. xxviii. p. 488.

☞ An anonymous Writer, in the St. James's Chronicle of April 25, has informed the public, that the first poem in this collection is *not* Mr. Cawthorn's, but was written probably before Mr. C. was born. It is, says he, the acknowledged production of Mr. Pitt, the translator of Virgil and Vida, and is to be found at p. 120 of the Poems published by him in 1727.—We have not Mr. Pitt's Poems (which is a scarce book) to refer to on this occasion; but we take the fact for granted, especially as no defence hath yet, that we know of, been made against this charge of unfair dealing, by the Editor of Mr. C.'s Poems.

ART. II. *The Heresy and Heretic of the Scriptures completely described*; that Description honestly improved; and to the Censure of the Public modestly submitted. By the Author of the Triumphs of Jehovah. 8vo. 1 s. 6 d. Buckland. 1771.

THE Writer of this pamphlet gives us no other information concerning himself than what the title-page declares, that he was the author of a performance called the *Triumphs of Jehovah*. Whatever merit * there might be in that publication, the singularity of its title would, we apprehend, disgust a number of readers, rather than recommend either that or the present work to their regard. Nevertheless, it must be said of the Treatise before us, that it is sensible and candid, and discovers a great share of attention and diligence, in endeavouring to investigate and explain a subject which must be acknowledged to have some considerable difficulty.

For a brief view of the plan here pursued, and the interpretation adopted, we will transcribe a summary of the work, which is given at the end of the third chapter. 'It appears in the first place,' says the Author, 'that heresy hath relation to sentiment, and that an heretic is a dogmatist, or a man who hath taken up a peculiar set of opinions. But this account is only general and introductory, and observed for the sake of distinction of ideas, and precision, and not as the very subject described in scripture. But upon this ground it is next observed, that the heresy properly intended in scripture is error in the faith, and a reception of religious doctrines opposite to those we are taught in the gospel, and an heretic is one who believes and propagates such doctrines. This notion is essential to heresy, and the character of an heretic But this is not the whole of the account; it includes more. Accordingly, it is further observed, that wickedness is connected with heresy, and impiety doth always

---

* The Reader is referred to our opinion of this wild and fanciful performance, Rev. vol. xxix. p. 463.

inmix

inmix in the character of the heretic. So that hereſy is error in the faith, deriving from the wicked luſts of the heart; and the heretic is the man who adopts ſuch error in gratification, and at the ſolicitation of ſome or other corrupt affection. Theſe two things then, error and luſt, and the laſt conſidered as the riſe of the firſt, exhauſt the ſubject of hereſy, as laid down in ſcripture, and fill up the character of an heretic.'

In ſupport of the firſt part of this account, that hereſy, in general, denotes ſentiment, and not fact, it is ſaid, 'The *Greek* verb (αιρεω) the root of theſe terms, ſignifies, among other notions, *to think or judge, to be of opinion*, as ſome of the lexicographers render. What then can (αἱρεσις) *hereſy*, in the firſt place denote, but *ſentiment* and *opinion*? This muſt be its primary idea, as it is a regular deduction from its root. And from hence, in a very eaſy connection, derives the idea of *ſect* or party, becauſe nothing ſo readily divides people into ſects as their opinions.'

His next aſſertion is, that the hereſy of ſcripture means—miſtaken ſentiments in divine matters: this is the ſubject of the ſecond chapter, where he conſiders and illuſtrates ſome texts of ſcripture, with a little criticiſm, as under the former head.

The third chapter takes a ſurvey of the different explications which have been given of the word hereſy. Among which the laſt-mentioned opinion is one that, within the preſent century, greatly drew the attention of enquiring perſons: 'This ſays (in the words of our Author) the adoption of doctrines in religion, contrary to the inward perſuaſions of the mind, is the very hereſy enquired after; and that man is, by ſcripture-rule, an heretic, who eſpouſes ſentiments he knows to be falſe, and that are the reverſe of his convictions. This opinion was agitated and debated ſome years ago, between two learned and ingenious gentlemen *, and it is by no means our deſign, adds the Author, to interfere in that conteſt.'

This Writer rejects the foregoing interpretation, together with the others that are mentioned; and in regard to the laſt, he thinks it ſufficient to obſerve, that 'it can never anſwer the end intended, or be the means to diſcover hereſy and heretics, in caſe it be ill-founded, and built on an entire miſtake of the expreſſion *ſelf-condemned*, uſed by the apoſtle, Tit. iii. 11. concerning an heretic.' That it is ſo our Author endeavours to make appear in another part of the pamphlet, where this paſſage of ſcripture is ſaid to come regularly under examination, each part of

* The curious Reader will find the ſubject of *Hereſy* diſcuſſed in a very maſterly manner, in the celebrated controverſy between Foſter and Stebbing, in which the former, particularſy, diſcovered a liberality of ſentiment, which will long endear his memory to thoſe who are ſincere well-wiſhers to the natural rights of the human mind.

the text is there closely considered, and, this clause, Αυτοκατάκριτος, rendered in our translation *self-condemned*, is particularly canvassed, and upon the whole it is concluded, that it 'describes, not the act of the heretic, but that of his judges. They, being well-assured of his revolt from the Christian faith, and of the rise of it in wicked lusts, and that from his own temper and practice, pronounce sentence against him as an heretic convict, and separate him from the Christian community.' But we must acknowledge, that the criticism and explication here proposed, appear to us rather precarious and unsatisfactory.

The third chapter is principally employed in establishing the farther part of the sentiment here advanced, that 'whatever error in the faith is the offspring of wicked lusts and carnal affections, doth for that reason become heresy.' The passages of scripture here produced, it must be owned, appear to give some probability and strength to the description which is given of an heretic, though we cannot consider it as altogether new: the quotations which we find in the title-page, from Bp. Taylor's Liberty of Prophecy, and from Austin, *de utilitate Credendi*, as mentioned in Foster's first Letter to Stebbing, do each of them seem to point at somewhat of the same kind with that which is here proposed.

In the two last chapters, some observations are made concerning the admonition of an heretic, &c. with other reflections, for the farther elucidation of the doctrine here delivered. The Writer infers, that 'popery is real heresy, and the pope of *Rome* the chief of all heretics. And this,' says he, 'being the plain truth, we are satisfied we not only may, but that we must, and are in duty bound to renounce the religion of *Rome*, to separate from the pope of *Rome*, and hold no Christian communion with him.' It is also inferred, from the rule here laid down, that we should 'forbear any imputation of heresy on account of mere differences in opinion,'—and that 'we must pay more regard to temper and affections, in judging of heresy, than to doctrines and opinions.' On the whole, here are several pertinent and useful remarks on an intricate question, but how near the Author approaches to the exact and full meaning of the scripture-expressions, we pretend not to determine.

Art. III. Dossie's *Memoirs of Agriculture*, Vol. II. *concluded.*

In the Review for last month, we gave our Readers a view of the first five papers in the present collection, preceded by a brief notice of the Editor's prefatory address to the public: we now proceed to Article VI. containing Sir Digby Legard's comparison of the drill and broad-cast husbandry of wheat.

We

We find many passages of this account which deserve censure, but shall pass over all such as seem not particularly to call for it. We have all possible personal esteem for Sir D. Legard, but must think him a prejudiced devotee to a fanciful system. He owns the subject to be very interesting to the public, and therefore will not only *forgive* but *applaud* our endeavour to throw *light* on what he owns to be *dark*.

First fallacy. Sir D. Legard says, " It *cannot* be urged that the riches of the soil were exhausted, because the four acres in question do not comprehend that particular acre first mentioned." P. 63. But does this evasion prove that repeated horse-hoeing crops of wheat do not *exhaust* the ground? Surely no such thing. Is it not evident, from the whole cast of Sir D. Legard's own experiments, that successive horse-hoeing crops are in general worse than preceding, unless when more seed is given, or additional ground is taken into the account, or some other advantages are thrown into the driller's scale?

Second fallacy. Sir D. Legard states the expences	l.	s.	d.
of four acres drilled - - -	13	5	6
And the product - - - -	15	11	3
So that the clear profit is - - - -	2	5	9

But the tenth of the product to the parson is not deducted, viz. 1 l. 11 s. 1½ d. or about 3 s. 8 d. per acre.—Nay, this is not a clear profit; for town rates, interest of money employed, &c. &c. should be deducted. In short, it is reduced to a mere nothing, or worse than nothing *.—*N. B.* In this experiment, which seems so advantageous to drillers, only one ploughing is given, and that rated only at 6 s. though Mr. Young has publicly avowed, that he would not undertake to sustain the expence of the best drill instruments known, for 2 s. 6 d. per acre.

Third fallacy. Sir D. Legard states the profit by	l.	s.	d.
three acres drilled at - - -	12	10	6
That profit by two acres broad-cast at -	6	16	0

* In order to give an experiment *usefully* and *fairly*, tythe and town-charges should be deducted exactly, or the *clear profit* can never be known; and when particular instances are given as encouragements to particular modes of culture, without such deduction, a gross deceit is committed. A man might as well calculate his *profit* on a *rent of favour*. Wherever tythe is not compounded for, it ought to be understood to be *taken* in *kind*. If Sir D. Legard should answer, that his land is exempt from tythe; this circumstance proves his estate so much better than it would be if subject, as lands generally are, to tythe: but this circumstance *suppressed*, it is right to conclude the contrary, as any person, not exempt, who went on Sir D. Legard's plan, would find his parson seize a tenth part of his sheaves.

These

These profits thus set by each other, give a specious advantage of superiority to the drill husbandry. But examine the matter to the bottom, and the profits on equal quantities are - - - -

l.	s.	d.
8	6	6
6	16	0

or 4l. 3s. 3d. by the drill, and 3l. 8s. by the broad-cast; or 15s. 3d. more by the drill.—But then look to the difference of management. Three-fourths of the broad-cast were on the sod after once ploughing (see p. 67); and the other fourth was on a wheat stubble. What wretched management! The drilled was on oat stubble, twice ploughed since harvest. What a difference! The crop of the *broad-cast* coming so near that of the *drilled*, is one of the strongest encomiums on the former method: beside, there appears no evidence of probability that the expences of the two methods are justly stated.—Who can believe that the expence of ploughing, &c. the broad-cast can be 1 l. 6 s. by the acre, and that of the drilled only 1 l. 4 s.? The whole is a string of fallacies.

Fourth fallacy. Sir D. Legard pretends that the *broad-cast* must want manure as much as the *drilled* ground, because the crop is a *large* and consequently *exhausting* one, p. 70. Is not the *indemnifying* manure then to be charged in proportion to the crop? Why then is the charge on both portions made equal? Plainly to make the broad-cast husbandry appear to disadvantage! Because the drilled husbandry exhausts the ground, must the broad-cast be equally condemned?—Is it not evident that a better crop of barley might justly be expected after the wheat on swarth than the wheat had been?—What will the candid Mr. *Howman* say to these facts? Will he exhort Sir D. Legard to carry on his experiments of both cultures?—His experiment in 1764, his last in the drill way, is liable to many of the same censures. Nothing convincing, or fair, can be deduced from it, in favour of the drill.

Fifth fallacy. Sir D. Legard makes a table of recapitulation, the last column of which can only serve to lead people into a sadly mistaken notion of the superior advantage of the *drill method*, by shewing that to produce sometimes as high as twenty-fold, nay twenty-one-fold, nay twenty-four-fold, in horse-hoed crops. But what is this *produce* towards stating the real *profit?* Is it not palpable, that if *horse-hoeing* produce twenty fold, and *(cæteris paribus)* broad-cast only ten-fold, yet if a little more than twice the quantity be sown on the same ground, the profit is greater by the latter method?

Sixth fallacy. Sir D. Legard states, in this table of recapitulation, only a single experiment of *broad-cast* husbandry, taken from a neighbour, the circumstances of which might be so different from those of the drilled, that perhaps no comparison could be be justly made of them; at least it does not appear that it could, and the maxim, "*De* non apparentibus, *et* non-existentibus, *eadem est ratio*," is universally allowed.—Praised be the accuracy of Mr. Young in his comparisons!—Yet not content with this single instance of his own chusing as he found it, Sir D. Legard deducts from the profit of it nearly 45 s. or 2 l. 5 s. per acre for manure, as though this single crop should be charged with what was rather a benefit to the succeeding. Will not honest Mr. *Howman*'s candour blush at his baronet's disingenuity? However, having tricked up the state of the crops to his own *fancy* and *purpose*, Sir Digby finds the *medium acreable* produce of one method to be 5 l. and of the other to be only 2 l. 15 s. little more than half as much! The Reader, who has seen how sanguine an advocate Sir D. Legard is for drilling, will naturally conclude that this superiority is made to fall on the side of the drillers. But to say the truth, *strange* as it is, it neither falls on the *one* side or the *other*: for, by an unaccountable *capriccio*, Sir D. Legard jumbles together the *broad-cast* and *hand-hoed* drilled crops, and contrasts with them the *horse-hoed!* He boasts of his *generosity* to the *broad-cast husbandmen*, as giving them great advantage by their alliance with the *hand-hoeing drillers*, as expending less seed, and getting greater crops than the broad-cast men. Knights-errant love to extol *their adversaries*, in order to magnify the glory of themselves when conquerors. Thus our worthy Knight omenizes, that, with all these gratuitous advantages, he will foil his *antagonists*.

And now, Reader, how does he effect this victory? He states the expence of an horse-hoed crop annually at 1 l. 8 s. then he makes the annual produce to be 1 quarter 3 bushels, or 11 bushels, and hence concludes, that the net profit yearly of an acre will be a moidore.—Now to this part of the comparison it may be justly objected, first, that it does by no means appear that 1 l. 8 s. per acre is not too low an expence; and, secondly, that probably 11 bushels (though a poor crop) is more than can be reasonably depended on, as a series of experiments lead us to conclude that successive crops fail by degrees.

As to the other part of the comparison, we must, in compliment to the honour of Sir D. Legard as a gentleman, suppose him not designedly to misrepresent; but as we have seen such inaccuracies above in his account, we may be allowed to deny an implicit assent to his stating the particulars of *produce* and *expences*. On comparing his two states, we find that the *new husbandry* (i. e. horse-hoeing) gives for four years a neat profit of 5 l. 8 s. per acre, and the *old* (broad-cast and hand-hoeing) gives only 4 l. 12 s. or a difference of 16 s. or 4 s. per annum.—Mr. Howman however has observed, that this is *impracticable husbandry*, and we observe that Sir D. Legard rates the

the land on which his experiments were made only at 12 s. per acre, whereas it was let when in grass at 16 s. so that he has just as much loss by ploughing *at all*, as he supposes himself to have advantage by preferring horse-hoeing to any other method. All this is said on admission of his own stating an impracticable scheme. How much more is justly objectable to his partial decision we have pointed out to the judicious Reader †. —It is however too remarkable to be omitted, that Sir Digby closes his memoir by pretending to make his conclusion *general*. Here, says he, turnip, barley, and clover husbandry is admitted; but on stiff clays, &c. this culture cannot be used; *therefore* my conclusion against the old husbandry is stronger, see p. 75. But, on the contrary, such soils admit the culture of cabbages; and Sir D. Legard allows not a farthing profit by a turnip crop; so that, we presume, the impartial Reader will deduce a consequence directly contrary to Sir Digby's.

To close our review of this article (which would need an apology were it not of *vast* importance) Mr. Young seems to have shewn, that, upon the whole, in the scale of utility, the three methods of culture stand thus: 1. broad-cast; 2. hand-hoeing;

† In mere justice to the argument we have undertaken, and to the public, we must add, that there is another *gross fallacy* in stating the crops in the two methods. It is this; deduction is made of the full expence of the manure of the wheat crop in the old husbandry; and again a deduction of the full expence of the manure in the turnip crop; that is, a deduction of the full expence of manure is twice made in one course of four crops, so that the profit of the turnip crop is reduced to nothing: and all this is effected with seeming propriety, by an artful arrangement of the crops; that is, by placing, first, the wheat crop, then the turnip crop, then the barley, and last the clover.—We must beg leave to ask the worthy Baronet whether, after a wheat crop, so manured as he supposes, the ground is not able to bear another crop without fresh manure? And, whether a compleat manuring for turnips, and two ameliorating crops, and only one exhausting crop, the ground cannot bear wheat without manuring?—'Tis now well known that one of the most profitable courses for such land as is in question is, 1. turnips; 2. barley; 3. clover; and, 4. wheat. By this means only one manuring is expended, and as good, or nearly as good, a crop of wheat is obtained, as after a fallow and manuring.—Was it not sufficient, in order to depreciate the old husbandry, to deem turnips an unprofitable crop, and to reckon clover profitable only by 10 s. per acre? Was it necessary also to charge a fresh manuring for wheat? We will venture to assert, that ground which, after so full a manuring for turnips as to exhaust all the profit of the crop, and such slight profit as attends the barley and clover, will not bear wheat, is not worth cultivating at all, and ought not to be brought as an example in stating the profits of any general methods of culture.

3. horse-

3. horſe-hoeing; and Nature ſpeaks loudly her ſuffrage for this order: but Sir D. Legard reverſes it!

Art. VII. contains accounts of the utility of burnet, from Meſſrs. *Jarvis*, *Siſſon*, and *Barber*; the laſt of whom adds obſervations on the *turnip* and *Anjou* cabbages. Mr. Jarvis repreſents burnet as much liked by, and good for ſheep and lambs, and beſt when ſown with barley. We agree with him. Mr. Doſſie obſerves, that burnet may be ſowed *profitably* on the lea for fallow for turnips.

Mr. Siſſon ſowed 14 lb. of burnet on an acre, and next year reaped 23 buſhels of ſeed. Mr. Doſſie remarks that an acre of burnet gives by two crops of ſeed in a ſeaſon 10 quarters; and refers to p. 207 of the former volume of this work.

Mr. Barber aſſerts, that *burnet* improves land from 6 s. to 20 s. per acre; and that though all ſheep do not like it at firſt, they will at laſt. He has ſowed 60 acres of it, and ſuppoſes it prevents the rot in ſheep. He thinks the low-rooted ſort of turnip-cabbage preferable to the reſt of that kind, but prefers the Anjou cabbage to all other.—We have quite oppoſite accounts of this laſt ſort.

This article concludes with a certificate of the ſucceſs of ſowing burnet on Mr. Barber's lands, where it appears to be a good ſpring food for ſheep; and that it ſhould be ſown thick.

Art. VIII. is a very accurate and judicious diſſertation on *cole-ſeed*, by Mr. Doſſie, to ſhew its difference from *rape*, and various methods of culture, as a winter and ſpring food for cattle and ſheep.

Mr. Doſſie ſhews, that even *Miller* has confounded *rape* and *cole-ſeed*. He obſerves that the *former* is called *bunias*, *bunias ſylveſtris*, *napus ſylveſtris*, and *napus flore luteo*: in Engliſh, *navew gentle*, or *wild navew*, and is a ſpecies of *wild turnip*: [*braſſica*, in modern botaniſts, includes both *cabbages* and *turnips*] and has leaves more or leſs jagged. The latter is of the *cabbage kind*, a *wild colewort*, called *braſſica avenſis*, *ſylveſtris*, *rubra minor*, *crambe*, *colſa*; in Engliſh, *field colewort*. He adds, that only within the memory of man was this latter brought from Flanders, as a harder ſpecies for oil, and bearing more herbage. There are three ſorts, viz. the *white*, *warm*, and *cold*. The laſt *only* is cultivated in England; but, Mr. Doſſie ſays, the *warm* thrives on *poorer ſoils*. He obſerves that the cole-ſeed requires land either *naturally* or *artificially* rich, well pulveriſed, and laid dry; that the quantity of ſeed for an acre is half a peck; and that the plants are generally *hoed*; that ſmall ſnails, black fly, black canker [a ſmall worm], green caterpillar, and ſmut, are enemies to cole-ſeed, and may be oppoſed, in a certain degree, with ſucceſs. He adviſes that the plants for ſeed ſtand at the diſtance of two feet.

In

In the fens, the preparation for this plant is solely by paring and burning. Mr. Dossie well advises to lay the heaps of sods in quincunx, and to burn them as soon as dry, and spread the ashes as soon as burnt, and to plough them in immediately.—He observes, that cole-seed feeds sheep as quickly again as turnips do, and should not be fed after Candlemas if intended for seed. He advises to mow the stumps to prevent their rotting. The *green fly*, enemy of the tender pods, can only be opposed by smoaking of the field. Mr. Dossie fixes the criterion for the proper time of cutting, viz. when some pods grow brownish; and then gives an exact description of the cutting and threshing of the seed as practised in the fenny countries. He makes the medium produce of an acre to be 28 bushels. He then gives the Flanders method of transplantation of cole-seed, which, in our opinion, is more expensive, and less certain of success. The Flanderkins stack the reaps not yet dry, to *ferment*, and afterwards thresh them. Mr. Dossie well observes, that it seems a prudent experiment to try the quantity of oil produced by a given quantity of cole-seed stacked, with that which is threshed when unstacked; and we apprehend that it would be so. Mr. Dossie observes, that cole-seed cakes, when powdered and mixed with bran, will be eaten by cattle; and that an acre in Flanders is computed, at an average, worth 8 l. 10 s.

Art. IX. presents us with Mr. *Reynolds*'s brining of corn to prevent smut, and also his account of the causes of smut.

Mr. Reynolds, in the postscript to his letter of November 9, owns, that the learned are not agreed how the smut is *conveyed* and *increased*, nor does he pretend to say any thing certain. He is here modest; but in his letter of November 20, he takes it for *granted* that *insects* are the cause of *smut*. Much may be said on both sides. But, on a supposition that Mr. Reynolds has hit upon the true *cause*, let us *examine* how far he has discovered the *remedy* of this *disease*. This is a simple steeping of the seed in brine formed by *lime* and *salt and water*. Mr. Reynolds affirms, that he *never* had any *black wheat* from seed *thus steeped*. Let us suppose both the Gentleman's *honesty* and *accuracy*. Our duty to the public obliges us to say, that this evidence is not satisfactory to impartial judges; for it is certain that steeps of the same nature as this, have been sometimes used, in *all* parts of the kingdom, without *any* success of this sort, as the voice of the public attests. The fair conclusion seems to be, that Mr. Reynolds may have had the good luck to escape the smut, from soil, &c. But let us attend the process. This brine causes the light seeds to swim; and they being taken away, it is concluded that the evil is taken away. Now, in order to evince this point, let us ask Mr. Reynolds, Are these *light* seeds which

which he calls *deformed, ſmutty* ones? No; at the moſt they are ſuppoſed only to be *ſmutted*, or to have contracted ſome of the *ſmutty* ſubſtance. This all the ſeed which grew together may as juſtly be ſuppoſed to have contracted; and therefore, abſtractedly from the conſideration of their being *light* and *unlikely* to produce a vigorous ſtem, they ought no more to be given to the poultry than all the reſt of the ſeed. If we conſult our ſenſes we ſhall find that the ſtems are as vigorous as any, till the ear is attacked by the ſmut. This ſeems a ſtrong preſumption that the cauſe of the ſmut is not in the ſeed *ſown*, but in ſomething in the air, viz. inſects, &c. If any ſtronger is deſired, it ſeems deduced from the well known circumſtance that ſome ears are ſmutty, while others from the ſame root are not; nay, that parts of the ſame ear are differently affected.—Let Mr. Reynolds ſow his light ſeeds, and ſee if they all bring up *ſmutty* ears. This will be one ſtep to prove his *hypotheſis*. In the mean time the Reader will remember, that *Tenterden* ſteeple is not the true cauſe of the *Goodwin* ſands.

In Art. X. a very ſenſible and modeſt correſpondent (who ſigns himſelf A. B.) communicates to Mr. Doſſie, obſervations on *pines*, *firs*, and *larches*.

He adviſes to plant them out when four feet high, at the diſtance of four or ſix feet; to thin them gradually, and, at the end of 20 years, to leave the beſt for timber, diſtant four yards, that is 240 on an acre. He refers to the plantations at Woodburn, for theſe trees thriving on a *dry ſand*. He believes theſe trees to come to perfection in 50 or 60 years.—As to the real value of Engliſh deal, we can aſſure this worthy Gentleman that it is *very trifling*, on our own experience, as a floor laid at conſiderable expence, about 20 years ago, is now quite worm-eaten, though the trees grew on good ſound ſoil. Reaſon ſhews that ſuch ſoils as the foreign firs naturally grow on, viz. *ſandy*, muſt be the propereſt. We apprehend that our good Engliſh ſoils give them too much ſpongineſs. Mr. Doſſie's note on this point is very ſenſible.—A. B. has ſeen a larch tree, planted in 1737, at the time of his writing, five feet in circumference and 60 high; yet he does not find the growth of the larch ſo ſuperior to that of the fir as Mr. *Harte* repreſents it: and Mr. Doſſie adds a note, which ſhews the Scotch fir to be a quicker grower in thickneſs.—A. B. recommends the Weymouth *pine* as hardy, bearing removal, growing well, and not nice in ſoil; and adviſes the Society to appoint a perſon to collect, in America, ſeeds of trees and plants likely to be naturalized with us.

Art. XI. contains obſervations on the contents of Count *Ginanni*'s Treatiſe on Italian Diſeaſes of growing Corn.

The

The Observator reduces the principal diseases to four, viz: the *blight*, the *loose smut*, the *bag smut*, and the *mildew*; and shews, that the Count's cures in the first case are trifling, &c. He thinks whatever gives vigour to the stem, without too great luxuriancy, a good preventive in this case. As to the second distemper, the Count does not mention that of *small animals*, to which cause *alone* Mr. Reynolds, in Art. IX. of this volume, ascribes it. The Observator patronizes Mr. Reynolds's scheme. It is *possible* that this evil may proceed from the *seed*; but we know his remedy frequently unavailing. The Count, on this head, also produces little of probable remedy. As to the third disease, he proposes, among other remedies, lime-water; but owns it to be, what we have esteemed it in Art. IX. no *certain* or absolute preventive. Our *Observator* is its sanguine advocate. The Count's advice to pick out all *smutted ears*, appears to us, as to the Observator, impracticable in large fields.—Both the Count and his Observator maintain that the last disease arises from insects. The Count thinks them communicated by the seed and *infectious*; but the Observator, with whom we agree, thinks otherwise.—The Count enumerates the less formidable diseases, to review which may be less worth our while. His Observator seems to do him justice, when he represents him as a man of more reading than *experience*; or, we may add, true philosophy.—We apprehend this Observator to be Mr. Dossie, and we mean to praise him.

Art. XII. contains numerous experiments for rearing and fattening hogs, by A. Young, Esq.—This is his prize discourse: for which see Review, vol. xli. page 70.

Mr. Dossie adds several useful notes to this essay; and particularly recommends the *conglomerated potatoe*.—*N. B.* Mr Young values the dung of 90 swine fatted at 30 l. Mr. Dossie affirms that, a *few years* ago, hog's dung in Yorkshire was *thrown away* as *noxious*. We know the North, and Yorkshire, well, and have lived about half a century, and never heard of such barbarism. From our earliest memory it was highly esteemed.

Art. XIII. contains, 1. Rules for making good bread; 2. Preserving yeast; 3. Making leaven; and, 4. Making bread from ingredients cheaper than corn. As to the first and second heads, we have no room to dwell upon them: we believe the second is well known. The third is said to be a nice point, gained only by experience. As to the fourth, we know bread of potatoes to be excellent, and that of turnips not despicable.

Art. XIV. gives the management of the *true* or *palmated rhubarb* introduced into Great Britain. The Author of this account, who is (we apprehend) Mr. Dossie, informs us that Dr. *Mouncy*, an English physician residing in Russia, obtained seeds

ſeeds of this beſt kind of rhubarb from the Royal Academy of Sciences at Peterſburgh, and ſent them into England; and from theſe Mr. Engliſh of Hampſtead raiſed plants, from which, at the end of ſix years, he ſent ſpecimens of the roots to the Society, &c. and they having examined theſe, propoſed a premium for the cultivation. He then gives an account of it from Linnæus, and adds all that Mr. Bell (in his narrative of his journey from Peterſburgh to Pekin) has wrote about its condition in *Mungal Tartary*; and concludes with directions for cultivating this plant, and drying the root.

Art. XV. preſents us with an account of a ſpecies of potatoe, called the *conglomerated*, from its growing like *cluſters*, or the *Bedfordſhire*, for its being firſt cultivated largely in that county.—*N. B.* It was alſo early cultivated in Northumberland, and planted in Sion garden.

From the memoirs of Mr. *Howard* of Cardington in Bedfordſhire, &c. this potatoe appears to be recommended by its *weight*, *ſolidity*, and *ſweetneſs*, and by its producing a greater crop on leſs rich ground. It ſeems, however, that it is not generally liked, and that its ſize occaſions its burſting on the outſide, whether roaſted or boiled, before it is ſufficiently cooked near the heart: but it appears to be good for cattle and ſwine. We ſuppoſe Mr. Doſſie to be the author of this account.

Art. XVI. gives a liſt of the machines and models in the repoſitory of the Society, divided into four claſſes; 1ſt, thoſe ſubſervient to manufactures; 2d, to works by mills, cranes, water, carriages, &c. 3d, to agriculture; 4th, to chemiſtry.

Some Readers perhaps may think (what we ſuggeſted with reſpect to the former volume, viz.) that Mr. Doſſie has made too free with the treaſure-houſe of the Society; but many perſons, doubtleſs, beſide thoſe who have ſolicited this publication, will be glad to know whither they may have recourſe to ſee improvements they want. Mr. Doſſie has added many uſeful notes, to give a general idea of ſeveral principal machines; and he promiſes prints, &c. of them.

Art. XVII. exhibits the Rev. Mr. *Lambe*'s obſervations on the culture and uſe of *Timothy-graſs*, *bird-graſs*, *burnet*, *turnip-cabbage*, and *turnip-rooted cabbage*.

From this memoir, and Mr. Doſſie's notes, we learn, that *Timothy-graſs* ſuits wet ſoils; that *bird graſs* has a fine verdure; that burnet falls off in a few years, yet is good for ſheep; that turnip-cabbage will not ſtand keen froſts; but that turnip-rooted-cabbage is likely to ſupply its place.

We always rejoice to ſee clergymen intereſt themſelves in the cauſe of agriculture, as their education and ſituation, render their labours of this kind likely to be uſeful. We have in this volume Mr. Howman and Mr. Lambe.

 Art.

Art. XVIII. lays before us three letters of Mr. *Jeffard* to the Society, &c. in praise of the turnip-rooted-cabbage, which he shews to produce 44 tons of food per acre.—*N. B.* Mr. Dossie, in a note, candidly warns the Reader not to depend so intirely on the encomiums bestowed on this plant in Art. XVII. and XVIII. as to cultivate largely, till due experiment of the soil is made, as it sometimes strikes only a tap-root.

Art. XIX. Two letters of Mr. *Chambers* give an account to the Society, of the success of sowing *turnips* with *beans*, and of a crop of spring wheat.—We are far from acquiescing with Mr. Chambers in his account that the *shading* of the beans alone preserves the turnips from the fly, we cannot agree with Mr. Dossie that it is even a *partial* means.

Art. XX. and last, favours the public with Mr. Dossie's own *dissertation on the murrain*; a work of which we entertain (as we hinted above) a very high opinion; insomuch that should the pestilence of the murrain invade us (and the late accounts tell us that it continues its progress among our neighbours the Dutch) we should *certainly* treat our own cattle in the manner prescribed by Mr. Dossie, which seems highly rational. We judge him perfectly faultless in treating this subject *scientifically*, and especially as he writes chiefly to the upper class of mankind, who are to see to the execution of acts of parliament, orders of council, &c. and may be supposed fitted by education to understand him: and (as he observes in the preface) since he opposes received opinions, he therefore may reasonably be expected to give *reasons*.—We are at some loss how to institute our review of this piece, which, if published *alone*, would have found with us an exact discussion. But as it stands at the end of an ample work, which has obtained the space of a large article already, we believe we must bestow on it only a slighter review, repeating, however, that we think this article, on account of the importance of the subject, and the probability that we may be again visited by the destroyer, more worth the attention of the public than all the others in this volume.—He promises to give this dissertation more at large. In the mean time we hope much of the *essence* of this powerful treatise may be contained in the following short *compass*.

Mr. Dossie thinks that as *the contagious distemper among the horned cattle* appears, by its symptoms, to be what was called formerly the *murrain*, this name should be resumed. He speaks, 1st, of the *manner* and *periods* of its former appearance, both here and in other places, and refers, in his note, to Authors ancient and modern who have wrote of it. 2dly, He states the different *susceptibility* of the cattle according to their weakness, whether *natural* or *accidental*, (viz. that of sex, colour, pregnancy, poverty, and danger) to be in proportion

tion to the same causes; also to the moisture of soil, to winds, and badness of provisions. 3dly, He considers the conveyance of the contagion, and observing, that no proof exists of the air immediately conveying it, he ascribes it to contact, immediate or mediate, of the infected body. 4thly, He examines the *means* hitherto proposed for *preventing* or *curing* the distemper, viz. *fumigations*, rubbings with sulphur, mundifications, antiseptics, bleedings, purgings; and thinks them all so far from being *useful*, that many of them are *hurtful*; and that *inoculation* is pernicious, as it does not secure from the distemper's return, is very dangerous, and keeps the *infection* stirring. He judiciously observes, that the great failure of physicians, on this subject, seems to have been, the not calculating such a method of cure that the *probability* of *recovery* is likely to answer the certainty of expence. He then, 5thly, states all the symptoms in the several stages of the distemper with great exactness, and shews how, in *strong* cattle, the leven of the virus is overcome and expelled by the natural animal ferments, and the contrary in *weak* ones. 6thly, From the *symptoms* which he justly considers as *indications* of cure, he wisely deduces the true method of cure, viz. to assist the *force of nature*, first, by medicines 'astringent, febrifuge, grumous parts of vegetables, and vinous liquors,' viz. *tormentil root*, *carroway seeds*, *ale*, and *geneva*: secondly, by corn, and when the appetite declines, meal. He also advises how to carry the order of council into *prudent execution.*

Art. IV. *A Dissertation on Miracles, designed to shew, that they are Arguments of a divine Interposition, and absolute Proofs of the Mission and Doctrine of a Prophet.* By Hugh Farmer. 8vo. 6 s. sewed. Cadell. 1771.

SO great a number of learned and elaborate treatises have been written upon miracles, that many of our Readers will be disposed to consider the subject as entirely exhausted, or will imagine, at least, that nothing farther can be said upon it, that is very necessary or important. But the persons who form this opinion will, we believe, upon a diligent examination of the matter, find themselves to be mistaken. Indeed, the notion that it is scarce possible to advance any thing which is new, is a false one, with regard almost to every object of knowledge and science. The continued cultivation of human reason, and a free and accurate discussion of nice and difficult questions, cannot fail either of producing fresh discoveries, or of setting what is already known in a clearer and more striking point of view. Even the multitude of books that have been published on a subject, may render a farther enquiry into it extremely desirable and useful, in order to disentangle it from the errors which have been mixed with it, and to bring men back to the ſimplicity of truth.

This is particularly the caſe with reſpect to miracles. Were we to conſult the natural dictates of the underſtanding, we could ſcarce doubt but that miracles muſt proceed from God alone, and that they are deciſive teſtimonies of the divine authority of the perſons by whom they are wrought. Theſe plain and obvious principles have, however, been ſtrangely obſcured and perverted, not only by the ſubtleties of ſcepticiſm, but by the falſe reaſonings, and abſurd ſuppoſitions, of Chriſtian writers. Divines of the greateſt eminence, and who in other reſpects have done ſignal ſervice to the intereſts of revelation, have fallen into conſiderable miſtakes in relation to the true nature and deſign of miracles, and eſpecially with regard to the beings who have been ſuppoſed capable of performing them. It became, therefore, highly neceſſary to re-examine the ſubject; to clear it from the embarraſſments in which it has been involved; and to place it in that juſt and proper point of light in which it is exhibited by the genuine dictates of reaſon and the concurrent repreſentations of ſcripture. This hath been done, in a very ſatisfactory manner, in the ingenious and learned work before us, which we ſcruple not to pronounce to be one of thoſe ſubſtantial and durable treatiſes that will always be conſidered as a valuable and important acquiſition to the cauſe of ſacred literature.

'What is attempted, ſays Mr. Farmer, in the following ſheets, is, to refute thoſe principles of demoniſm which have done ſo much diſcredit to the argument drawn from miracles in favour of the Jewiſh and Chriſtian revelations. Without entering into an examination of the peculiar nature and circumſtances of the ſcripture miracles, I conſider only *the general queſtion*, Whether miracles are, in themſelves, evidences of a divine interpoſition, and conſequently (when properly applied) certain proofs of the divine original of a ſupernatural revelation? Nor is it merely the credit of revelation that is concerned in this queſtion, but the honour alſo of the general adminiſtration of divine providence, and the common intereſts of piety and virtue.'

The preſent performance opens with ſome preliminary conſiderations; in the firſt ſection of which the nature of miracles is explained, and ſhewn to conſiſt in their contrariety to thoſe general rules by which the viſible world is governed, or to the common courſe of events in it.

'That the viſible world, ſays our Author, is governed by ſtated general rules, commonly called the laws of nature; or that there is an order of cauſes and effects eſtabliſhed in every part of the ſyſtem of nature, ſo far as it falls under our obſervation, is a point which none can controvert. Effects produced by the regular operation of the laws of nature, or that are conformable to its eſtabliſhed courſe, are called *natural*. Effects contrary to this ſettled conſtitution and courſe

course of things, I esteem *miraculous*. Were the constant motion of the planets to be suspended, or a dead man to return to life, each of these would be a miracle, because repugnant to those general rules by which this world is governed at all other times.

'All miracles pre suppose an established system of nature, within the limits of which they operate, and with the order of which they disagree. The creation of the world at first, therefore, though an immediate effect of divine omnipotence, would not come under this denomination. It was different from, but not contrary to, that course of nature, which had not hitherto taken place. And miracles may be said to disagree with, or to be contrary to, the general rules and order of the natural system, not only when they *change* the former qualities of any of the constituent parts of nature (as when water, for example, is converted into wine) or when they *controul* their usual operation and effects (as when fire, without losing its properties, does not burn combustible materials; or a river is divided in its course, the water still preserving its gravity) but also when they *supersede* (as they always do) the usual operation of natural causes. For effects produced in the pre-established system of nature, without the assistance of natural causes, are manifest variations from, or contradictions to, the order and usual course of things in that system. That a man should be enabled to speak a new language, which he never learnt in a natural way, and that his body should be supported without food, are events evidently contrary to the ordinary course of things, and to that constitution of divine providence which renders mankind dependent upon their own study and application for the knowledge of languages, and upon food for sustenance. We do not affirm, that miracles do universally and necessarily imply a proper *suspension* of the laws of the natural world, so as that they should cease to produce their usual effects: the human mind may receive new knowledge in a supernatural manner, without any suspension of its present powers. Nevertheless, the supernatural communication of new knowledge to the human mind, is contrary to the general rules by which the human system is governed, or to that connection which God has established between our acquisition of knowledge, and the proper exercise of our rational faculties.'

After clearing this account from objections, Mr. Farmer goes on to observe, that most writers, in defining a miracle, seem to place it, not in *the effect produced*, but in the *cause*, or at least include the latter in their definition.

'A *miraculous effect*, like every *common appearance*, has its own proper specific nature, distinguishing it from all others of a different kind, separate from the consideration of its cause. And it is the operation or effect alone, which is affirmed to be contrary to that established order and disposition of things, commonly called the course of nature: the real invisible agent by whom the effect is produced, though he acts out of his usual sphere, exerts only his natural powers. The contrariety or conformity of the event itself to those laws by which this world is governed in the course of God's general providence, is that alone which denominates and constitutes it a proper miracle or not.'

From the description which our ingenious Author has given of the nature of miracles, he draws four conclusions, the third of which is as follows:

'Before we can pronounce with certainty any effect to be a true miracle, it is necessary—that the common course of nature be in some degree first understood. In all those cases in which we are *ignorant* of nature, it is impossible to determine what is or is not a deviation from it, or to distinguish between miracles and natural effects. Even a real miracle cannot be admitted as such, or carry any conviction, to those who are not assured that the event is contradictory to the course of nature. On the other hand, in all cases in which the course of nature is *understood*, it will be easy to determine whether any particular event be contrary or conformable to it, that is, whether it be a real miracle. Miracles therefore are not, what some represent them, appeals to our ignorance; they suppose some antecedent knowledge of nature, *without* which, it is owned, no proper judgment can be formed concerning them; though *with* it, their reality may be so apparent as to prevent all dispute or hesitation. *Every sensible deviation from or contradiction to the known laws of Nature, must be an evident and incontestible miracle.*'

The design of the second section of the first chapter, is to prove that miracles are not impossible to the power of God; that they are not necessarily repugnant to our ideas of his wisdom and immutability; and that they do not imply any inconsistency in the divine conduct, or any defect or disturbance of the laws of Nature. In shewing that miracles are not repugnant to our ideas of the divine wisdom, the learned Writer observes, that frequent miraculous interpositions might, indeed, argue a defect in those general laws by which the world is governed; to the regular execution of which laws we owe our ideas of order and harmony, our rational expectations of success in all our undertakings, and our strongest convictions of wise counsel in the frame and government of the universe.

'Consequently, says he, it must appear highly improbable, that variations from those laws should take place, unless upon some special and urgent occasions. Yet whoever reflects on the boundless extent and duration of the divine government, will easily perceive that nothing can be more absurd, as well as arrogant, than for man, a creature whose faculties are so limited, and who is but of yesterday, to presume to determine that no fit occasion for extraordinary interposals can ever occur in that administration, the plan of which transcends his comprehension. By what principles of reason can it be demonstrated, that he who reigns from eternity to eternity, never formed any designs except such as may be accomplished by the present establishment and structure of the universe?—It would be difficult to prove that God may not, in certain circumstances, have *greater reasons* for varying from his stated rules of acting, than for adhering to them. And whenever this is the case, and the end proposed is proportionable to the means of accomplishing it, the miracles are worthy of a divine interposition.'

In the third and last section of the preliminary considerations, Mr. Farmer examines into the different causes to which miracles have been ascribed; and, at the conclusion of the chapter, sets before his Readers the following view of his own scheme, and the point he hath undertaken to establish.

'It will now, perhaps, be enquired, "If miracles are neither the effects of natural causes, nor of superior created intelligences, acting from themselves alone; and if it cannot be proved that they do universally and necessarily require the exertion of infinite power, to what cause are they to be ascribed?" I answer, they are always to be ascribed to *a divine interposition:* by which I mean, that they are never wrought but either immediately by God himself, or by such other beings as he commissions and empowers to perform them. Miracles may not require a degree of power absolutely *incommunicable* to any created agent; and yet God may never *actually communicate* a miraculous power to any creature, or do it only where he directly authorizes its use. Now whether God works the miracles himself alone, or whether he enables and commissions others to work them, there is equally a divine interposition: and in either case every purpose of religion will be secured; for whatever God authorizes and empowers another to do, is, in effect, done by God, and is as manifestly a declaration of his will, as what he does immediately himself. He can no more authorize another to act, than he can himself act, in opposition to his own nature, or in confirmation of imposture.

'The point then which I shall undertake to establish, is this, "that miracles are the peculiar works of God, or such as can never be effected without *a divine interposition*, in the sense of the phrase already explained." This point we shall endeavour to establish both by reason and revelation. And should we succeed in this attempt, there will then be no difficulty in shewing that miracles are, in themselves, certain proofs of the divinity of the mission and doctrine of the performer, and the most effectual methods of recommending him to the regard of mankind.'

The second chapter contains the arguments that may be drawn from reason, to prove that miracles are never effected without a divine interposition; and, in the first section of this chapter, it is shewn that the same considerations which manifest the existence of superior created intelligences, do much more strongly conclude against their acting out of their proper sphere. From the *diversity of creatures*, and the *gradual ascent* from the lowest to the highest order of existence, observable here on earth, it has been inferred, that the scale of beings is continued upwards above man, and that there are numberless species of creatures superior to him, as we know there are of such as are inferior to him. This reasoning, according to our Author, has not, perhaps, all that force in it, which its having been uncontroverted might lead us to suppose. Should it, however, be granted, that the scale of beings in our planet is a conclusive proof, not only of a like gradation of beings elsewhere, but also of there being in the universe creatures as much superior to man, as man is to the meanest reptile: still, he observes, the same kind of reasoning which proves there are such beings, proves, at the same time, that they have a certain limited sphere of action appointed them by God. For how various soever the powers of different species of creatures here on earth may be, they are all under particular laws, and have bounds circumscribed to their activity, which they are not able to transgress: and the rule of analogy teaches us to conclude the same concerning all other beings.

'If we may judge of the conduct of Providence in unknown instances, by those which fall under our observation: He, *who has set bounds to the Sea, which it cannot pass, and says to its proud waves, Hitherto shall ye come, but no farther*, has bounded the power, and fixed the state of all the creatures which he hath made, not excepting those of the noblest order. And therefore whatever their natural powers may be, and however freely they may be allowed to use them, they are limited and determined to such purposes as God has appointed, and cannot possibly be extended beyond the sphere assigned them by the Creator. And yet no sooner is it proved (or thought to be so) that probably there are, in some portion of the universe, beings superior to man, than it seems to be taken for granted, that they have the liberty of an unbounded range over the whole creation, that their influence extends over this earthly globe, in particular, and that they stand in the same relation to man, as man himself does to inferior creatures. But though there be a strict connexion between the different orders of creatures on this earth, who all belong to the same system, yet none of them have any possible communication from this lower world with the inhabitants of different systems; none of them are able to traverse the universe, or to pass the bounds of their proper dwelling. And this must be the case in other systems, supposing them to be regulated by the same laws which take place in our own. Their inhabitants may have larger capacities than mankind, and a wider province assigned them, and yet have no more power over us than we have over them; they may have no communication with us, nor any influence beyond the limits of their own globe.

'If, continues Mr. Farmer, we wave the argument from what is called the scale of being, and appeal to the unbounded power and goodness of God, or to the astonishing magnificence of the universe, in proof of the existence of creatures of a higher order than man: still these arguments, however conclusive, will not prove that they are not under the continual government and controul of God, or that they have not all their proper department: for not to alledge that the power and goodness of God, though strictly infinite, and though they have (without doubt) displayed themselves in the production of more noble orders of beings than mankind, are not, however, exerted to the utmost in every, or in *any*, single effect, it is certain they are never exercised but under the direction of unerring wisdom, by which

which all things are framed in the most exact proportions: and, as to the universe, it is no less distinguished by its perfect order and harmony, than by its grandeur and extent. To what purpose then is it to plead, that we know not what degrees of power God may have communicated to created beings? Can it be shewn that they are subject to no laws, that their influence is unconfined and reaches to all the systems of the universe?'

It is the opinion of that justly celebrated writer Dr. Clarke, that to deny created spirits the *natural* power of working miracles, is saying, *they have no power naturally to do any thing at all.* But our ingenious Author observes, that Dr. Clarke's reasoning proceeds upon these two principles, that superior natures have the *same sphere of action* assigned them with those inferior to them; and that they enjoy the *very same powers and privileges.*

'The former of these, says he, is destitute of proof, and the latter is contradicted by the wise order and œconomy of Providence. Has man the strength or swiftness of brute animals? Can he fly in the air, or dive into the ocean? How much soever man may excel the brutes, he has not the same organs and powers of action, and his operations must therefore be quite different from theirs. The same may be true of *angels* compared with men. Their capacities may be more noble than ours, and they may move in a much more exalted sphere, without being able to do every thing which man is capable of doing.—The consideration of their possessing powers superior to mankind, will not create any proof, or even the lowest degree of presumption, that they have any power over this earthly globe, or are capable of disturbing the laws by which it is governed.'

Should it be said, "that allowing that superior created beings have only a limited sphere of action assigned them; yet how does it appear that this lower world itself is not their appointed sphere, and that they have not a power of interposing to work miracles upon this earthly globe?"

To this question an answer is given at large in the next section, in which it is shewn that there is no proper evidence of the truth of any miracles but such as might have God for their author. The supposition of the power of any created agent to work miracles, in this lower world, without a divine commission, is contradicted by the observation and experience of all ages; there being, in fact, no proper evidence of the truth of any miracles, but such as may fitly be ascribed to the Deity. All the facts appealed to, in proof of the miraculous agency of evil spirits, are either *not supernatural*, or *not real.* Several general reasons are likewise alledged for rejecting all miracles that could not have God for their author; after which, Mr. Farmer adds the following observations:

'Now, says he, if there be no sufficient reason to believe that any superior spirits, acting without the order of God, have ever, from the beginning of the world to this day, performed a single miracle upon our earthly globe, how void of all foundation must be the ascribing to them a miraculous power? Were they possessed of such

such a power, it is natural to suppose they would have exerted it *frequently*, especially as it may so easily be made subservient to the purposes of malevolence and impiety. What miseries of every kind might not wicked spirits, from a principle of envy and hatred, introduce amongst mankind? And if good spirits enjoyed an equal liberty of doing good offices to men, what a theatre of contention would our globe have been between spirits of such opposite dispositions and designs: and therefore, if, in a long succession of ages, there has been no appearance of any such contest between virtuous and wicked spirits; if no motives whatever have excited the one or the other to exert a miraculous power, so much as *once*, is it not a natural inference that they do not possess it? With regard to God, indeed, reason informs us, that he who established the course of nature, can change it at pleasure, even whether he has already done so or not. But the case is different as to other beings, whose powers and operations are only to be known (in a natural way) by observation and experience. God is manifest in every part of nature; but who can point out the effects of other spirits, and their operations on the universe? And if we see no effects of their agency on this earthly globe; if no such effects have ever been seen, there can be no ground from reason to ascribe it to them. It is as repugnant to the observation and experience of all ages, to ascribe to evil spirits a miraculous power, as it is to ascribe life to the inanimate, or speech to the brute creation.'

We could with pleasure follow our sagacious and learned Writer through the third and fourth sections of the second chapter, in which he endeavours to prove that, as the laws of Nature are ordained by God, and essential to the order and happiness of the world, it is impossible he should delegate to any of his creatures a power of working miracles, by which those divine establishments may be superseded and controuled, and that the ascribing such a power to any superior beings besides God, and those immediately commissioned by him, subverts the foundation of natural piety, and is a fruitful source of idolatry and superstition: but we shall only transcribe the conclusion of the fourth section.

'Most melancholy is it to reflect how much the general principle we are here opposing, viz. the power of Satan to work miracles, and the various superstitions grounded upon it, have contributed, in all ages, and in all nations, to the disquiet and corruption of the human race, and to the extinction of rational piety. This consideration alone, were there no other, should check the zeal of Christians to maintain an opinion—so destructive to our virtue and happiness, and which the wisest Heathens, from principles of benevolence and piety, earnestly wished and laboured to extirpate.

'In a word, if we entertain just and honourable sentiments of the constitution of the universe, and its all-wise and benevolent Author, can we believe that he has subjected us to the pleasures and disposal of superior beings, many of whom are supposed to be as capricious and malevolent as they are powerful? Has God put our very life, and the whole happiness of it, into such hands? This some maintain

tain he has done; and this he must have done, if he has granted them the power of working miracles at pleasure: an opinion which cannot fail to rivet Heathens in their idolatry, and Christians in the most detestable superstitions.'

The intention of the fifth section is to shew, that, if miracles were performed in favour of false doctrines, mankind would be exposed to frequent and unavoidable delusion.

'If,' says our judicious Author, after some previous remarks, 'miracles, by their own natural influence, are calculated to procure immediate credit to the doctrine they attest; if they constitute an evidence adapted to the common sense and feelings of mankind; if they make an impression which scarce any resistance can totally prevent or efface: it is an easy and obvious inference from hence, that if they were performed in favour of false doctrines, the generality of mankind would be necessarily exposed to frequent delusion: and those would be the least able to resist the impression of miracles, who had the strongest sense of God upon their minds, the most honourable apprehensions of his natural and moral government, and were the most fearful of incurring his displeasure, by rejecting any revelation of his will.

'Here it will be objected, "That if miracles were wrought to confirm falsehood, the nature of the *doctrine* might serve to guard us against being deceived, and direct us to ascribe the works to some evil agent, who was *permitted* to perform them for the *trial* of mankind." In answer to this objection, it might perhaps be sufficient to observe, that what some call God's *permitting*, would be in reality *empowering* and *commissioning* evil spirits to work miracles. For God's removal of the restraint or disability which those spirits are under at all other times, amounts to his giving them both a power and a commission to work miracles on this particular occasion. And this God cannot do in confirmation of falsehood.

'But much stress being laid on this objection, we will offer some farther observations upon it. The most arbitrary and unnatural suppositions, when they have been long made, are thought at last to have some foundation to support them, and require the same notice to be taken of them as if they had. It is not true, in fact, that any miracles have ever been performed in support of error, on purpose to try our faith: at least, no sufficient evidence appears of the truth of any such miracles; nor do the ends of the divine goverument seem to require that mankind should be exposed to this particular trial. The temptations which occur in the ordinary course of Providence, are abundantly sufficient to exercise our virtue; and it is quite needless that miracles should be wrought, merely to put it to a farther proof. Now if reason cannot shew that mankind *ought to be*, and experience convinces us that they never *have been*, exposed to the delusion of false doctrines inforced by miracles, the notion that they may be so must be considered as a mere fiction. Besides, how unlike would such a trial be to those ordained by God? The latter arise from passions planted in our nature for the most valuable purposes, and from the most useful and necessary relations of life. But our adversaries suppose miracles may be atchieved with no other view than

as

as *mere* matter of trial to mankind, which is repugnant to all our knowledge of the divine dispensations. Not to observe, that errors inforced by miracles, would, very frequently at least, constitute a trial rather of the understanding, than of the heart; and in this respect, likewise, it would differ from those to which God has subjected mankind.

'To convince us more fully that no miracles can ever accompany a false doctrine, merely for the trial of mankind, I would observe, that they are not capable of answering this end, upon the principles of those by whom it is assigned. Were a false doctrine to be attested by miracles, it must be asserted, either that the falsehood of it was discerned, or that it was not. If the falsehood of the doctrine was discerned, and it was at the same time known that the miracles attesting it might and must be performed by some evil agent: in this case, where would be the trial? The miracles, it would be allowed, were no evidence of the truth or divinity of the doctrine, and contained no recommendation of it, or motive to embrace it; nay, they could only serve to furnish an invincible prejudice against it, on account of the known malevolence of their author. If, on the other hand, the falsehood of the doctrine was not and could not be discerned, the miracles attending it being considered only as proofs of the interposition of some superior being, the mind must be thrown into a state of perplexity and suspence about the author of the works, and remain void of all inducement either to embrace or reject the doctrine. And consequently here also there would be no trial at all. We are never more in danger of charging God foolishly, than when we judge of him, not by what he has done, but by what we presume it becomes him to do. It might convince us how little a way bare speculation can carry us in all researches into the nature and government of God, to find the strongest minds, when trusting to speculation alone, ascribing to him unworthy measures, and inventing designs and ends for them, which they are not adapted to answer. The very scheme which assigns the trial of mankind, as the end of God's permitting miracles to be performed in confirmation of error, does itself shew it could not be promoted by them. Now whoever calls upon us to believe, that miracles may be wrought without any necessity, and even without any use, demands our assent to what contradicts all our ideas of divine wisdom, and the whole course of the divine dispensations, as well as the several reasons before urged to shew that no variations from the established laws of Nature can take place, except when they are dispensably necessary to promote the most important purposes of God's administration.'

After offering several other arguments to prove that God cannot subject mankind to the delusion they would necessarily be exposed to, if miracles were wrought in favour of false doctrines, Mr. Farmer comes to the sixth and last section of the second chapter; the business of which is to evince, that, if miracles may be performed without a divine interposition, and in support of falsehood, they cannot be authentic credentials of a divine mission, and criterions of truth. There are two cases in which miracles are considered as evidences of a divine mission,

sion, by some who plead that such works may, on other occasions, be performed without the order of God. It is urged, first, "That in case of a contest between two opposite parties working miracles for a victory, the party which works the *most* and *greatest* miracles, may reasonably be supposed to be assisted by the Supreme Being;" and, secondly, "That such miracles only are to be ascribed to God as are performed for an end not unworthy of him." It is clearly shewn, by our learned Writer, that these two suppositions by no means remove the difficulty; and we shall present our Readers with part of what he has advanced concerning the judging of miracles by the doctrine.

'It is necessary, says he, to observe farther, that the making the doctrine the test of the divinity of the miracles, is, to make the doctrine the rule of judging concerning the miracle, not the miracle the rule of judging concerning the doctrine. The proper and immediate design of miracles is, to establish some truth unknown before, and such as is not demonstrable by reason, or capable of other evidence besides that of miracles; to prove, for example, the mission of the prophet by whom they are performed, and the divine original of his message or doctrine, and to engage men to receive and comply with it, however contrary it may be to their prejudices and passions. But, according to some learned men, the doctrine must first be examined without passion or prejudice, and then employed to prove the divinity of the miracles. But is not this repugnant to the proper use and intention of miracles? It is making the whole force of the proof to depend upon the doctrine to be proved. It is of importance to add, that miracles are intended more especially for the conviction of the ignorant and unlearned, who are easily imposed upon by the sophistry of science, and the specious disguises of error, as well as utterly disqualified to determine by abstract reasonings concerning the absolute necessity, or the fitness and propriety of special divine interpositions. It is necessary therefore that miracles, when they are offered as evidences of a divine commission, should contain in their own nature a clear demonstrative proof of their divine original: for otherwise their special design could not be answered. It is quite unnatural to suppose, that the doctrine must first establish the divinity of the miracles, before the miracles can attest the divinity of the doctrine; and it is absurd to expect that a new revelation and offensive truths (which are not received without reluctance, even where there is a prior conviction of the divinity of the miracles attesting them) should themselves effectually engage men to ascribe those works to God which might be performed by numberless other invisible agents.

'Now can it be imagined that God will ever allow superior beings to work miracles in support of falsehood, if hereby he would destroy the proof from these works of his own immediate interposition, and put it out of his own power to employ them as certain credentials of a divine mission? Miracles (under which term I comprehend those of *knowledge* as well as *power*) being the *only* means whereby God can assure

assure the world of the truth of a new revelation, he must have reserved the use of it to himself alone, without ever parting with it to serve the purposes of his rivals and opposers.'

Though we have extended this article to a considerable length, we are under no apprehension that our Readers will be displeased with us, because the subject is peculiarly important, and because our ingenious Author's reasonings upon it are uncommonly clear, just, and forcible.

[*To be concluded in our next.*]

ART. V. *The History of Great Britain, from the first Invasion of it by the Romans under Julius Cæsar.* Written on a new Plan. By Robert Henry, D. D. one of the Ministers of Edinburgh. Vol. I. 4to. 1 l. 1 s. in boards. Cadell. 1771.

THE advancement of a free people in civilization and refinement, and the struggles between liberty and ambition, which they exhibit in the different periods of their history, are objects the most interesting to mankind. Those works, of consequence, which entertain and instruct us the most, are the histories of Greece and of Rome. In modern times, the transactions and revolutions which have taken place in our own island, have been thought the most important and engaging; and our Author, struck with their dignity and variety, has made them the subject of his researches and reflections. Of the design and plan of his performance he gives the following account.

'The chief design,' says he, 'of this work is,—To give the Reader a concise account of the most important events which have happened in Great Britain, from the first Invasion of it by the Romans under Julius Cæsar, to the present times; together with a distinct view of the religion, laws, learning, arts, commerce and manners of its inhabitants, in every age between these two periods. It is intended to draw a faithful picture of the characters and circumstances of our ancestors from age to age, both in public and in private life; to describe, in their genuine colours, the great actions which they performed, and the disgraces which they sustained; the liberties which they enjoyed, and the thraldom to which they were subjected; the knowledge, natural, moral, and religious, with which they were illuminated, and the darkness in which they were involved; the arts which they practised, and the commerce which they carried on; the virtues with which they were adorned, and the vices with which they were infected; the pleasures and amusements in which they delighted, and the distresses and miseries to which they were exposed; not omitting even their fleeting fashions, and ever-changing customs and modes of life, when they can be discovered. This, it is hoped, will give the Reader as clear, full, and just ideas of Great Britain, and of its inhabitants, in every

every age, as can reaſonably be deſired, or, at leaſt, as can now be obtained from the faithful records of hiſtory.

'To accompliſh this very extenſive deſign, within as narrow limits as poſſible, the Author has endeavoured to expreſs every thing in the feweſt and plaineſt words; to avoid all digreſſions and repetitions; and to arrange his materials in the moſt regular order, according to the following plan:

'The whole work is divided into ten books. Each book begins and ends at ſome remarkable revolution, and contains the hiſtory and delineation of the firſt of theſe revolutions, and of the intervening period. Every one of theſe ten books is uniformly divided into ſeven chapters, which do not carry on the thread of the hiſtory, one after another, as in other works of this kind; but all the ſeven chapters of the ſame book begin at the ſame point of time, run parallel to one another, and end together; each chapter preſenting the Reader with the hiſtory of one particular object. For example:

'The firſt chapter of each book contains the civil and military hiſtory of Great Britain, in the period which is the ſubject of that book. The ſecond chapter of the ſame book contains the hiſtory of religion, or the eccleſiaſtical hiſtory of Britain in the ſame period. The third chapter contains the hiſtory of our conſtitution, government, laws, and courts of juſtice. The fourth chapter comprehends the hiſtory of learning and learned men, and the chief ſeminaries of learning. The fifth chapter contains the hiſtory of the arts, both uſeful and ornamental, neceſſary and pleaſing. The fixth chapter is employed in giving the hiſtory of commerce, of ſhipping, of money or coin, and of the prices of commodities. The ſeventh and laſt chapter of the ſame book contains the hiſtory of the manners, virtues, vices, remarkable cuſtoms, language, dreſs, diet, and diverſions of the people of Great Britain, in the ſame period. This plan is regularly and ſtrictly purſued from the beginning to the end of this work: ſo that each of the ten books of which it conſiſts, may be conſidered as a complete work in itſelf, as far as it reaches; and alſo as a perfect pattern and model of all the other books.

'To render this plan ſtill more perfectly regular and uniform in all its parts, the Author has diſpoſed the materials of all the chapters of the ſame number, in all the ten books, in the ſame order, as far as the ſubjects treated of in theſe chapters would permit. For example, the arts, which are the ſubject of the fifth chapter of every book, are diſpoſed one after another in the the ſame order of ſucceſſion, in all the fifth chapters through the whole work. The ſame may be ſaid of all the other chapters, whoſe ſubjects are capable of being diſpoſed in a regular order and arrangement. By this means, as every book is a perfect model of of all the other books of this work, so every chapter is also a perfect model of all the other chapters of the same number. It is thought unnecessary to attempt to carry order and regularity of method further than this. It is even imagined, that any endeavour to do this would defeat its own design, by rendering the plan too intricate and artificial.'

From the comprehensive nature of our Author's method and arrangement, we should think it impossible, that any facts or observations of importance should escape his attention. Accordingly, the first volume of his work, which is now offered to the public, will be allowed to be full of erudition, and to contain many curious particulars concerning Britain while a Roman province, that are not generally to be met with in our historians.

The detail, which it gives of the civil and military history of this island, from the invasion of Cæsar to the arrival of the Saxons, is exact and circumstantial. In his account of Druidism, our Author has also the merit of minuteness and precision; but perhaps he has not sufficiently attended to the spirit and policy of that system of religion. It constitutes a very considerable part of the government of the Britains; and it is remarkable that its importance, in this respect, engaged the Romans to take violent measures to abolish it.

The remarks that are made on the constitution and laws of the British nations, form not, it may be thought, the least important division of the publication before us. It is liable, however, to several exceptions. We cannot, for example, agree with our historian, when he supposes, that the ancient Germans and Britains were strangers to the law of primogeniture; and that the custom of Gavelkind directed universally their succession to land. On this head he has probably been led into error by following too implicitly the authority of Sir Henry Spelman and Lambard. His opinion, he founds, with these antiquaries, on the following passage from Tacitus:—*Heredes successoresque sui cuique liberi: et nullum testamentum: Si liberi non sunt, proximus gradus in possessione, fratres, patrui, avunculi.* There is here, however, no mention of the equal partition of land implied in Gavelkind; and the same intelligent Author has, in another place of his admirable work, asserted, in the strongest terms, that the Germans were governed in succession by the rule of primogeniture. His words are:—*Inter familiam, et penates, et jura successionum, equi traduntur, excipit filius, non* UT CETERA MAXIMUS NATU, *sed prout ferox bello et melior* *.

On the different heads of the learning, commerce, arts, and manners of the ancient Britains, our Author has presented

* De Mor. Germ. c. 32.

many

many interesting and useful observations to his Reader, and it is to be wished that historians were generally attentive to extend their inquiries beyond sieges and battles, and the policy and disputes of princes.

As a specimen of the execution and value of the present performance, we shall extract a part of the account which it gives of the civil government of the Romans in Britain.

'As soon,' says our historian, 'as some of the British nations in the south-east corner of this island had submitted to Claudius, the Romans began to practise here their usual arts for securing, improving, and enlarging their acquisitions. With this view they formed alliances with the Iceni, the Dobuni, the Brigantes, and perhaps with some other British nations. From these alliances the Romans derived many advantages. They prevented these powerful nations from forming a confederacy with the other British states, in defence of their common liberty, and for expelling the ambitious invaders of their country, before they had obtained a firm footing: they also gained a plausible pretence of obtruding their commands upon them on all occasions, under the appearance of friendly advices; and if these were not observed, of quarrelling with them, and reducing them to subjection. This was sooner or later the fate of all the allies of that ambitious and artful people, as well as of those in Britain.

'It was with the same interested views that the Emperor Claudius and his successors heaped such uncommon favours on Cogidunus, king of the Dobuni, who had early and warmly embraced their cause against that of his country. This prince was not only permitted to retain his own dominions, but some other states were put under his government, to make the world believe that the Romans were as generous to their friends, as they were terrible to their enemies. "For (as Tacitus honestly confesseth) it was a custom which had been long received and practised by the Romans, to make use of kings as their instruments in establishing the bondage of nations, and subjecting them to their authority." The honours and favours which they bestowed on Cogidunus, and other kings who embraced their cause, were dangerous and deceitful, much greater in appearance than in reality. They had no longer any authority of their own, but were wholly subservient to, and dependant upon, the Roman emperors, whose lieutenants they were, and by whom they might be degraded at pleasure. This was the case of Cogidunus, as appears from the inscription quoted below *. This very

* Neptuno et Minervæ templum pro salute domus divinæ, ex auctoritate Tiberij Claudij, Cogidubni regis, legati Augusti in Britannia,

very remarkable inscription, which was found at Chichester A. D. 1723, shews, among many other curious particulars, that Cogidunus, king of the Dobuni, had assumed the name of Tiberius Claudius, in compliment to the emperor Claudius; and that he had been appointed imperial legate, in which capacity he governed that part of Britain which was subjected to his authority.

' In order still further to secure their conquests, the Romans, as soon as it was possible, planted a colony of their veteran soldiers and others at Camulodunum, which had been the capital of Cunobelinus, agreeable to their constant practice of colonizing wherever they conquered. From this practice the Romans derived many great advantages. The soldiers were thereby rendered more eager to make conquests, of which they hoped to enjoy a share: their veterans were at once rewarded for their past services, at a very small expence; and engaged to perform new services in defence of the state, in order to preserve their own properties: the city of Rome, and other cities of Italy, were relieved from time to time of their superfluous inhabitants, who were dangerous at home, but useful in the colonies: the Roman language, laws, manners, and arts, were introduced into the conquered countries, which were thereby improved and adorned, as well as secured and defended. For the capital of every Roman colony was Rome in miniature, and governed by similar laws and magistrates, and adorned with temples, courts, theatres, statues, &c. in imitation of that great capital of the world. The sight of this magnificence charmed the conquered nations, and reconciled them to the dominion of a people by whom their several countries were so much improved and beautified. This further contributed to accustom these nations to the Roman yoke, by engaging them to imitate the magnificence and elegance, the pleasures and vices of the Romans, which rivetted their chains, and made them fond of servitude. As the Romans enlarged their conquests in Britain, they planted new colonies in the most convenient places, for preserving and improving these conquests; as at Caerleon, at Lincoln, at York, and at Chester.

' Still further to secure their conquests, and to gain the affections of those Britons who had submitted to their authority, the Romans, according to their usual policy in other countries, made London and Verulamium *municipia* or free cities; bestowing on their inhabitants all the valuable privileges of Roman citizens. By this means these two places were, in a few years,

---

nia, collegium fabrorum, et qui in eo a sacris sunt de suo dedicaverunt donante aream Pudente, Pudentini filio.

Hors. Brit. Rom. N° 76. p. 192. 332.

crowded

crowded with inhabitants, who were all zealous partizans of the Roman government. Both these facts are demonstrated by what happened to these two cities in the great revolt under Boadicia. The revolted Britons poured like a torrent upon London and Verulamium, on account of their attachment to the Romans, and destroyed no fewer than seventy thousand of their inhabitants, which is a sufficient proof of their populousness.

'By these arts, and by others of a military nature which shall be hereafter mentioned, the Romans preserved, and, by degrees, enlarged that small province which they formed in the south-east parts of Britain in the reign of Claudius. The government of this province was committed, according to custom, to a president or imperial legate. The authority of these presidents of provinces, under the first Roman emperors, was very great. They had not only the chief command of the forts, garrisons, and armies within their provinces, but they had also the administration of justice, and the direction of all civil affairs in their hands. For by the Roman laws, all the powers of all the different magistrates of the city of Rome were bestowed upon every president of a province, within his own province: and, which was still more extraordinary, he was not obliged to exercise those powers according to the laws of Rome, but according to the general principles of equity, and in that manner which seemed to him most conducive to the good of his province. The presidents of provinces had also a power to appoint commissioners, to hear and determine such causes as they had not leisure to judge of and determine in person. These extraordinary powers with which the presidents of provinces were invested, were no doubt frequently abused, to the great oppression of the provincials. This appears to have been very much the case in Britain before Julius Agricola was advanced to the government of this province. For that excellent person employed his first winter in redressing the grievances of the provincial Britons, which had been so great, that they had occasioned frequent revolts, and had rendered a state of peace more terrible to them than a state of war. The emperor Hadrian abridged this exorbitant power of the presidents of provinces, by an edict which he promulgated A. D. 131. This was called the perpetual edict, and contained a system of rules by which the provincial presidents were to regulate their conduct in their judicial capacity, in order to render the administration of justice uniform in all the provinces of the empire.

'The only officer who was in any degree independent of the president of the province, was the imperial procurator, who had the chief direction in the collection and management of the imperial revenues. This officer often acted as a spy upon the governor of the province, and informed the emperor of any

 thing

thing he had observed wrong in his conduct. At other times these officers agreed too well in deceiving the emperor, and in plundering and oppressing the provincials. "Formerly (said the discontented Britons before their great revolt) we were subject only to one king, but now we are under the dominion of two tyrants; the imperial president, who insults our persons, and the imperial procurator, who plunders our goods: and the agreement of these two tyrants is no less pernicious to us than their discord." Though this was the language of violent discontent, and therefore probably too strong, yet we have reason to believe, that when a perfectly good understanding subsisted between these two officers, they sometimes agreed to enrich themselves at the expence of the subjects, especially in those provinces that were at a great distance from the seat of empire.—

'The Roman emperors, from time to time, created new officers to assist them in the management of their prodigious empire, and made frequent changes in the distribution of the civil power. It would be very improper to enter upon a minute detail of all these changes; but that one which was made by Constantine the Great was so considerable in itself, and so much affected the political state of Britain, that it merits a place in this section. That renowned emperor, having obtained the dominion of the whole Roman empire, by a series of glorious victories over all his rivals, divided it into the four prefectures of the East, of Illyricum, of Italy, and of Gaul; over each of which he established a prefect, who had the chief authority in the civil government of his own prefecture. Each of these prefectures were subdivided into a certain number of dioceses, according to its extent and other circumstances; and each of these dioceses was governed under the prefect by an officer who was called the vicar of that diocese. The prefecture of Gaul comprehended the three dioceses of Gaul, Spain, and Britain, which last was governed under the prefect of Gaul by an officer called the vicar of Britain, whose authority extended over all the provinces in this island. The vicar of Britain resided chiefly at London, and lived in great pomp. His court was composed of the following officers, for transacting the business of his government, a principal officer of the agents, a principal secretary, two chief auditors of accounts, a master of the prisons, a notary, a secretary for dispatches, an assistant, under-assistants, clerks for appeals, serjeants, and inferior officers. Appeals might be made to him from the governors of the provinces, and from him to the prefect of Gaul. The title of the vicar of Britain was *Spectabilis* (his Excellence), and the ensigns of his order were, a book of instructions in a green cover, and five castles on the triangular form of the island, representing the five provinces under his jurisdiction. Each of the five provinces in Britain had a para particular governor, who resided within the province, and had a court composed of a competent number of officers for dispatching the several branches of business. The governors of the two most northerly provinces, Valentia and Maxima Cæsariensis, which were most exposed to danger, were of consular dignity; but those of the other three were only stiled presidents. By the vicar of Britain, and these five governors of provinces, with their respective officers, all civil affairs were regulated, justice was administered, and the taxes and public revenues of all kinds were collected.

'Though ambition was long the reigning passion of the Romans, they were far from being inattentive to their interests, but studied how to gain wealth, as well as glory, by their conquests. When nations first submitted to their authority, they often obliged them to pay a certain stipulated sum of money, or quantity of corn annually, by way of tribute, leaving them for some time in the possession of their other privileges; and these nations were called tributaries Thus Julius Cæsar imposed a certain annual tribute on the British states, which made their submissions to him, though he hath not mentioned either the nature or quantity of that tribute. But the Romans did not commonly continue long to treat those nations which had submitted to them with this indulgence, but on one pretence or other they soon reduced them into provinces, and subjected them to a great variety of taxations, which were levied with much severity. To this state were the British nations reduced by the Emperor Claudius and his successors, which makes it necessary to give a very brief account of some of the chief taxes which the Romans imposed upon their provinces, and particularly on this island.

'One of the chief taxes which the Romans imposed on their provincial subjects, was a certain proportion of the produce of all their arable lands, which may not improperly be called a land-tax. This proportion varied at different times, and in different places, from the fifth part to the twentieth, though the most common proportion was the tenth. This tax was imposed upon the people of Britain, with this additional hardship. that the farmers were obliged by the publicans to carry their tithe-corn to a great distance, or to pay them some bribe, to be excused from that trouble. This great abuse was rectified by Agricola, though the tax itself was still exacted and even augmented. When the Romans had occasion for corn to supply the city of Rome or their armies, this tax was levied in kind; but when they had not, it was paid in money, according to a certain fixed rate. They exacted a still higher proportion, commonly a fifth part, of the produce of orchards, perhaps because less labour was required in their cultivation. The produce of this

this land-tax became so great in Britain, by the improvements that were made in agriculture, that it not only supplied all the Roman troops in this island with corn, but afforded a considerable surplus for exportation.

'The Romans also imposed a tax, in all the provinces of their empire, on pasture grounds, or rather on the cattle that grazed in them. This tax was called *Scriptura* (the writing) because the collectors of it visited all the pastures, and took an exact list of all the cattle of different kinds in writing, and demanded a certain sum for each beast according to an established rate. This tax proved very oppressive to the Britons, when it was first imposed by the emperor Claudius, and for some time after. For, as they abounded in cattle, it amounted to a great sum, and being destitute of money to pay the tax, they were obliged either to sell some of their cattle at a disadvantage, or to borrow money from the wealthy Romans at an exorbitant interest. The famous Seneca alone is said to have lent the distressed Britons, on this occasion, the prodigious sum of three hundred and twenty thousand pounds; and, that his demanding it with rigour, at a time when they were not able to pay, pushed them on, among other things, to the great revolt under Boadicia. This tax was sometimes taken in kind, when they needed cattle for their armies. Nor were meadows exempted from taxation; for a certain proportion of their produce (most probably the tenth) was exacted, in order to provide forage for the cavalry.

'The Romans, not contented with these impositions on lands of different kinds, extracted taxes from the very bowels of the earth, and obliged the proprietors of mines of all kinds of metal to pay a certain proportion of their profits to the state. Gold mines were commonly seized by the emperors, wrought at their expence, and for their profit; but the proprietors of mines of silver, copper, iron, lead, &c. were permitted to work them for their own benefit, upon paying the tax which was imposed upon them, which seems to have been the tenth part of what they produced. The revenue arising from the mines, in some provinces, was prodigious. The silver mines near New-Carthage in Spain are said to have employed forty thousand men, and to have yielded a revenue of twenty-five thousand drachmæ, or 600 l. of our money, a day to the Romans. This industrious people had not been long in Britain before they discovered and wrought mines of gold, silver, and other metals to so much advantage, that they yielded them an ample reward for their toils and victories, though we know not the particular sum.'

Our historian, throughout the whole of the present volume, has very exactly referred to the sources from which he has gathered

thered his information. Thofe materials which could not be inferted with propriety in the body of his performance, he has annexed to it in the form of an appendix. It clearly appears to us, that he has made truth the end of his enquiries; and that on no occafion has he facrificed it to ingenuity and ornament. His induftry and candour are highly worthy of approbation. In regard to compofition, his work has not attained, in our opinion, that mafterly polifh which diftinguifhes the more eminent productions of the prefent age; but his ftyle, it may be obferved, though fometimes feeble and carelefs, cannot juftly be cenfured as either mean or obfcure.

ART. VI. *Memoirs of Great Britain and Ireland. From the Diffolution of the laft Parliament of Charles* II. *until the Sea-battle off La Hogue.* By Sir John Dalrymple, Bart. 4to. 18 s. boards. Edinburgh, 1771. Cadell, London.

IT is fomewhat unfortunate, that the Author of thefe Memoirs, fhould, in the very introduction to his work, give his fanction to an opinion, which owes its foundation to the prejudice and art of thofe hiftorians, who have defended the prerogative of our monarchs. He has fuppofed, that the title of the Duke of Normandy to the crown of England, was by conqueft *; and that we are indebted for our freedom to the ufurpations of the people on the privileges of our kings. But it appears, from the tapeftry, which was found in the Cathedral of Bayeux, and from other monuments of our hiftory, that Duke William was called to the fucceffion by the deftination of Edward, with confent of the great council of the nation; and that Harold was fent to Normandy to inform him of this circumftance; an office, which that nobleman would have refufed, if the meffage had proceeded folely from the Confeffor. His invafion of the kingdom, it has been faid, was hoftile. His quarrel, however, was not with the nation, but with Harold. The victory of Haftings was obtained over the perfon of this ufurper, not over the rights of the people; and William received the crown with its inherent properties, and fubject to the laws.

There are other fentiments and opinions in our Author's introduction, which are alfo liable to exception; and, in general, he has expreffed himfelf in it, with a degree of obfcurity, from which an intelligent reader muft conclude, that he poffeffes not

* An acquifition of territory by any means, is implied in the word *conqueft*; and an acquifition by purchafe or fucceffion, and not by victory, is the fenfe in which it is moft frequently ufed in ancient records and hiftories. See Cook's Argument. Anti-Norm. n. 30, 31, 32.

a very accurate knowlege of the English history. Our historians, even those of greatest merit, have written under the influence of the spirit of party; and have been either advocates for the people or the prerogative. Truth was not the object of their inquiries; and while consulted by men, whose undistinguishing vivacity has not permitted them to perceive the scope and tendency of their compositions, they prove a source of confusion and error. It has been thus with our Author. He has not allowed for the pertinacious obstinacy of the Panegyrists of the people, nor for the low servility of those of the crown. Relations, disguised with art, he has considered as authentic; and he now feels the impressions of a republican ardour, and now classes himself with the adorers of monarchy.

The same want of system and of discernment, which disgraces his preliminary reviews, is apparent in his memoirs. He affects to be enamoured of liberty, and yet scruples not to bestow commendation on James II; and while he enumerates the arbitrary acts of that prince, his narration excites neither the horror nor the indignation of his readers. He has not even been able to point out the characteristical features, which distinguished this unfortunate monarch.

The courage of James has not unfrequently been insisted upon by historians; but if he had possessed this quality, would he have trusted to the elevation of the host for protection against the Prince of Orange, or would he have fled from a throne, under the ruins of which he should rather have perished? His sincerity has sometimes been a topic of panegyric; but was he sincere in those frequent promises, which he made to the nation, of preserving its civil and religious liberties? He was skilled, it has been urged, in naval affairs; but his skill was that of a subaltern. His ambition made him aim at subverting the laws of his country; and his vanity and obstinacy did not allow him to conceal his views, or to foresee the danger which threatened him. He had the weakness and the virtues of a Monk; not the policy and the talents of a great King.

It is in vain also, that we seek in our historian for a just portrait of King William. Dazzled with the eulogiums which have been lavished on him by the friends of the revolution, or struck with the severity with which his memory has been treated by the partisans of the house of Stuart, he has exhibited nothing decisive with regard to him. If we were disposed to draw the character of this prince, we should ascribe to him more judgment than genius. He had not the talent of invention; but he could decide with singular propriety concerning projects that were laid before him. He was rather obstinate, we should think, than firm; and his sullenness and reserve, though accounted wisdom by the Dutch, were possibly the consequences

of

of a temper, suspicious and distrustful. He understood the balance of power, and was skilled in the policy and views of foreign courts; but, perhaps, he had little knowlege of the domestic affairs of the country he was called to govern. His military qualities have been much extolled; but he was, doubtless, greatly indebted for his success to the weakness of James, and to the peculiarity of his situation. It is no unmeaning reproach, which has been frequently repeated against him, that he never undertook a siege, which he did not raise, and never fought a battle, which he did not lose.

But if our historian has hesitated to pronounce concerning the characters of those personages whom it most concerned him to delineate; he has freed himself from this objection in regard to those of others, whose insignificance required, that he should either have passed them over in silence, or have described them transiently in the course of his narration. To Lord Dundee, in particular, he has given the utmost importance; and one must smile, to find, That the hero of a book on the revolution, is a Scots Lord, who followed the fortunes of King James.

The anecdotes with which our Author has loaded his performance, are often frivolous and suspicious; and there is a disgusting puerility in the frequent allusions he has made to the history of Greece and of Rome. He discovers a propensity to wonder and admiration, which never degrades the productions of cultivated and superior men. The morality which he inculcates, supposes that honour and noble birth are inseparable; and that individuals of high quality can alone possess those virtues, which give a dignity to human nature. His political reflexions are neither uncommon nor profound; for, when he finds it difficult to account, by natural causes, for any train of events, he has the sagacity to impute them to the operations of the Deity. On this head, he cannot justly be charged with giving way to ingenuity and refinement: nor in the course of his performance, has he exhibited any *new* views of his subject. But perhaps this objection ought not to be applied to him, as he has observed in his preface, That he was under a necessity of publishing his papers, before he had collected his materials.

The specimen, which we shall lay before our readers, from the present publication, is the account, which it gives of the manners of the Scots Highlanders; and this we have selected, because, it appears to us to be written with an accuracy and care, which our Author has preposterously refused to objects, more important and worthy of attention:

'The Highlanders, says he, were composed of a number of tribes called *Clans*, each of which bore a different name, and lived upon the lands of a different chieftain. The members of every tribe were tied one to another, not only by the feudal, but by by the patriarchal bond: for while the individuals which composed it were vassals or tenants of their own hereditary chieftain, they were also all descended from his family, and could count exactly the degree of their descent: and the right of primogeniture, together with the weakness of the laws to reach inaccessible countries, and more inaccessible men, had, in the revolution of centuries, converted these natural principles of connexion betwixt the chieftain and his people, into the most sacred ties of human life. The castle of the chieftain was a kind of palace, to which every man of his tribe was made welcome, and where he was entertained according to his station in time of peace, and to which all flocked at the sound of war. Thus the meanest of the clan, knowing himself to be as well-born as the head of it, revered in his chieftain his own honour; loved in his clan his own blood; complained not of the difference of station into which fortune had thrown him, and respected himself: the chieftain in return bestowed a protection, founded equally on gratitude, and the consciousness of his own interest. Hence the Highlanders, whom more savage nations called Savage, carried, in the outward expression of their manners, the politeness of courts without their vices, and, in their bosoms, the high point of honour without its follies.

'In countries where the surface is rugged, and the climate uncertain, there is little room for the use of the plough; and, where no coal is to be found, and few provisions can be raised, there is still less for that of the anvil and shuttle. As the Highlanders were, upon these accounts, excluded from extensive agriculture and manufacture alike, every family raised just as much grain, and made as much raiment as sufficed for itself; and nature, whom art cannot force, destined them to the life of shepherds. Hence, they had not that excess of industry which reduces man to a machine, nor that total want of it which sinks him into a rank of animals below his own.

'They lived in villages built in vallies and by the sides of rivers. At two seasons of the year, they were busy; the one in the end of spring and beginning of summer, when they put the plough into the little land they had capable of receiving it, sowed their corn, and laid in their provision of turf for the winter's fuel; the other, just before winter, when they reaped their harvest: the rest of the year was all their own for amusement or for war. If not engaged in war, they indulged themselves in summer in the most delicious of all pleasures to men in a cold climate and a romantic country, the enjoyment of the sun, and of the summer views of nature; never in the house during the day, even sleeping often at night in the open air, among the mountains and woods. They spent the winter in the chace, while the sun was up; and in the evening, assembling altogether

altogether round a common fire, they entertained themſelves with the ſong, the tale, and the dance: but they were ignorant of ſitting days and nights at games of ſkill or of hazard, amuſements which keep the body in inaction, and the mind in a ſtate of vicious activity!

'The want of a good, and even of a fine ear for muſic, was almoſt unknown among them; becauſe it was kept in continual practice, among the multitude from paſſion, but by the wiſer few, becauſe they knew that the love of muſic both heightened the courage, and ſoftened the tempers of their people. Their vocal muſic was plaintive, even to the depth of melancholy; their inſtrumental either lively for briſk dances, or martial for the battle. Some of their tunes even contained the great, but natural, idea of a hiſtory deſcribed in muſic: the joys of a marriage, the noiſe of a quarrel, the ſounding to arms, the rage of a battle, the broken diſorder of a flight, the whole concluding with the ſolemn dirge and lamentation for the ſlain. By the loudneſs and artificial jarring of their war inſtrument, the bagpipe, which played continually during action, their ſpirits were exalted to a phrenzy of courage in battle.

'They joined the pleaſures of hiſtory and poetry to thoſe of muſic, and the love of claſſical learning to both. For, in order to cheriſh high ſentiments in the minds of all, every conſiderable family had a hiſtorian who recounted, and a bard who ſung the deeds of the clan, and of its chieftain: And all, even the loweſt in ſtation, were ſent to ſchool in their youth; partly becauſe they had nothing elſe to do at that age, and partly becauſe literature was thought the diſtinction, not the want of it the mark, of good birth.

'The ſeverity of their climate, the heighth of their mountains, the diſtance of their villages from each other, their love of the chace, and of war, with their deſire to viſit, and be viſited, forced them to great bodily exertions. The vaſtneſs of the objects which ſurrounded them, lakes, mountains, rocks, cataracts, extended and elevated their minds: for they were not in the ſtate of men who only know the way from one market town to another. Their want of regular occupation led them, like the ancient Spartans, to contemplation, and the powers of converſation: powers, which they exerted in ſtriking out the original thoughts which nature ſuggeſted, not in languidly repeating thoſe which they had learned from other people.

'They valued themſelves without undervaluing other nations. They loved to quit their own country to ſee and to hear, adopted eaſily the manners of others, and were attentive and inſinuating wherever they went: but they loved more to return home, to repeat what they had obſerved; and, among other things, to relate with aſtoniſhment, that they had been in the midſt of great

great ſocieties, where every individual made his ſenſe of independence to conſiſt in keeping at a diſtance from another. Yet they did not think themſelves entitled to hate or deſpiſe the manners of ſtrangers, becauſe theſe differed from their own. For they revered the great qualities of other nations; and only made their failings the ſubject of an inoffenſive merriment.

'When ſtrangers came among them, they received them, not with a ceremony which forbids a ſecond viſit, not with a coldneſs which cauſes repentance of the firſt, not with an embarraſſment which leaves both the landlord and his gueſt in equal miſery, but with the moſt pleaſing of all politeneſs, the ſimplicity and cordiality of affection; proud to give that hoſpitality which they had not received, and to humble the perſons who had thought of them with contempt, by ſhewing how little they deſerved it.

'Having been driven from the low countries of Scotland by invaſion, they, from time immemorial, thought themſelves entitled to make repriſals upon the property of their invaders; but they touched not that of each other: ſo that, in the ſame men, there appeared, to thoſe who did not look into the cauſes of things, a ſtrange mixture of vice and of virtue. For, what we call theft and rapine, they termed right and juſtice. But, from the practice of theſe repriſals, they acquired the habits of being enterprizing, artful, and bold.

'An injury done to one of a clan, was held to be an injury done to all, on account of the common relation of blood. Hence the Highlanders were in the habitual practice of war; and hence their attachment to their chieftain and to each other, was founded upon the two moſt active principles of human nature, love of their friends, and reſentment againſt their enemies.

'But the frequency of war tempered its ferocity. They bound up the wounds of their priſoners, while they neglected their own; and, in the perſon of an enemy, reſpected and pitied the ſtranger.

'They went always compleatly armed: a faſhion, which by accuſtoming them to the inſtruments of death, removed the fear of death itſelf; and which, from the danger of provocation, made the common people as polite, and as guarded in their behaviour, as the gentry of other countries.

'From theſe combined circumſtances, the higher ranks and the lower ranks of the Highlanders alike joined that refinement of ſentiment, which, in all other nations, is peculiar to the former, to that ſtrength and hardineſs of body, which, in other countries, is poſſeſſed only by the latter.

'To be modeſt as well as brave; to be contented with the few things which nature requires; to act, and to ſuffer without complaining;

complaining; to be as much aſhamed of doing any thing inſolent or injurious to others, as of bearing it when done to themſelves; and to die with pleaſure, to revenge affronts offered to their clan or their country: theſe they accounted their higheſt accompliſhments.

'Their Chriſtianity was ſtrongly tinctured with traditions derived from the ancient bards of their country: for they were believers in Ghoſts: they marked the appearances of the heavens, and by the forms of the clouds, which in their variable climate were continually ſhifting, were induced to gueſs at preſent, and to predict future events; and they even thought that to ſome men the divinity had communicated a portion of his own preſcience. From this mixture of ſyſtem, they did not enter much into diſputes concerning the particular modes of Chriſtianity; but every man followed, with indifference of ſentiment, the mode which his chieftain had aſſumed. Perhaps to the ſame cauſe it is owing, that their country is the only one of Europe, into which perſecution never entered.

'Their dreſs, which was the laſt remains of the Roman habit in Europe, was well ſuited to the nature of their country, and ſtill better to the neceſſities of war. It conſiſted of a roll of light woollen, called a plaid, ſix yards in length, and two in breadth, wrapped looſely around the body, the upper lappet of which reſted on the left ſhoulder, leaving the right arm at full liberty; a jacket of thick cloth, fitted tightly to the body; and a looſe ſhort garment of light woollen, which went round the waiſt and covered the thigh. In rain, they formed the plaid into folds, and laying it on the ſhoulders, were covered as with a roof. When they were obliged to lie abroad in the hills in their hunting parties, or tending their cattle, or in war, the plaid ſerved them both for bed and for covering; for, when three men ſlept together, they could ſpread three folds of cloth below, and ſix above them. The garters of their ſtockings were tied under the knee, with a view to give more freedom to the limb; and they wore no breeches, that they might climb mountains with the greater eaſe. The lightneſs and looſeneſs of their dreſs, the habit they had of going always on foot, never on horſeback, their love of long journies, but above all, that patience of hunger, and every kind of hardſhip, which carried their bodies forward, even after their ſpirits were exhauſted, made them exceed all other European nations in ſpeed and perſeverance of march. Montroſe's marches were ſometimes ſixty miles in a day, without food or halting, over mountains, along rocks, through moraſſes. In encampments, they were expert at forming beds in a moment, by tying together bunches of heath, and fixing them upright in the ground: an art, which,

as

as the beds were both ſoft and dry, preſerved their health in the field, when other ſoldiers loſt theirs.

'Their arms were a broad ſword, a dagger called a durk, a target, a muſquet, and two piſtols: ſo that they carried the long ſword of the Celtes, the pugio of the Romans, the ſhield of the ancients, and both kinds of modern fire arms, altogether. In battle, they threw away the plaid and under garment, and fought in their jackets, making thus their movements quicker, and their ſtrokes more forcible. Their advance to battle was rapid, like the charge of dragoons: when near the enemy, they ſtopped a little to draw breath and diſcharge their muſquets, which they then dropped on the ground: advancing, they fired their piſtols, which they threw almoſt at the ſame inſtant, againſt the heads of their opponents: and then ruſhed into their ranks with the broad ſword, threatening, and ſhaking the ſword as they ran on, ſo as to conquer the enemy's eye, while his body was yet unhurt. They fought not in long and regular lines, but in ſeparate bands, like wedges condenſed and firm; the army being ranged according to the clans which compoſed it, and each clan according to its families; ſo that there aroſe a competition in valour of clan with clan, of family with family, of brother with brother. To make an opening in regular troops, and to conquer, they reckoned the ſame thing; becauſe in cloſe engagements, and in broken ranks, no regular troops could withſtand them. They received the bayonet in the target, which they carried on the left arm; then turning it aſide, or twiſting it in the target, they attacked with the broad ſword the enemy incumbered and defenceleſs; and, where they could not wield the broad ſword, they ſtabbed with the durk. The only foes they dreaded were cavalry; to which many cauſes contributed: the novelty of the enemy; their want of the bayonet to receive the ſhock of horſe; the attack made upon them with their own weapon the broad ſword; the ſize of dragoon horſes appearing larger to them, from a compariſon with thoſe of their own country; but, above all, a belief entertained univerſally among the lower claſs of Highlanders, that a war-horſe is taught to fight with his feet and his teeth.

'Notwithſtanding all theſe advantages, the victories of the Highlanders have always been more honourable for themſelves, than of conſequence to others. A river ſtopped them, becauſe they were unaccuſtomed to ſwim: a fort had the ſame effect, becauſe they knew not the ſcience of attack: they wanted cannon, carriages, and magazines, from their poverty and ignorance of the arts: they ſpoke an unknown language; and therefore could derive their reſources only from themſelves. Although their reſpect for their chieftains gave them, as long as they continued in in the field, that exact habit of obedience, which only the excessive rigour of discipline can secure over other troops; yet, as soon as the victory was gained, they accounted their duty, which was to conquer, fulfilled, and ran many of them home to recount their feats, and store up their plunder; and, in Spring and harvest, more were obliged to retire, or leave their women and children to die of famine: their chieftains too were apt to separate from the army, upon quarrels and points of honour among themselves and with others.'

It remains for us to observe, that in the style and manner of our Author, we perceive few of those qualities, which ought to distinguish historical compositions; no power of expression or language, no exact proportion of parts, no diversity of narration. Unimpassioned and cold, he gives his facts in an artless and negligent succession; incidents following incidents without selection or choice; and his work displaying little of that vigour and exertion of mind, for which the great historians of antiquity, and some few of the moderns, are so justly celebrated.

ART. VII. *Essays and Dissertations on various Subjects relating to human Life and Happiness.* 12mo. 2 Vols. 7 s. bound. Dilly. 1771.

THE fifteen first papers in these volumes, under the name of Essays, we are informed, were published in the Bath Chronicle, in the year 1766. Of these, therefore, it is sufficient to say, that they are of a serious and moral turn. The Dissertations are now first published, and treat of the following subjects: On *Conscience*——*Experience*——*Providence*——*Happiness*——*Desire*——*Education*——*Death*——*Immortality*.

The Author of these papers appears to be a man of sense and benevolence, yet we cannot avoid thinking his disquisitions too elaborate, his distinctions and subdistinctions too numerous and intricate, to please such Readers as expect a clear elucidation of points on which men of the greatest talents have differed. If any new information is to be now expected in philosophical inquiries, it will more probably be gained, rather by simplifying the consideration of them, than by entering into scholastic labyrinths, in which men of the most fertile genius are the most liable to be bewildered, and the least likely to find their way consistently out again.

As we have neither time or room to trace our Author through all his branches of investigation on the before-mentioned subjects, which we are sorry to observe rather tired than informed us, or to compare passages with each other; for this reason we premised

premised the above general remark, as applicable to the whole, and shall subjoin only some incidental observations, on two or three particulars, where the Writer appeared to us more obviously to overshoot the object he aimed at.

As a specimen, however, of his manner of treating his subjects, we shall give the general divisions under which *conscience* is considered. He observes, that conscience 'may be thus briefly defined; a reflex principle within us necessarily or involuntarily determining us to approve of some of our actions and affections as good, and disapprove of the contrary as evil, in a moral and religious sense, as we shall afterwards see; in which view, the questions that naturally arise with respect to it are as follows:

'1. What *relation* it bears to the *other powers* of the mind?

'2. What *qualities* in actions and affections determine it to approve or disapprove of them?

'3. What *ends* or purposes it answers in the human constitution?

'4. How far its *province* or office properly extends, and about what objects it is exercised?

'5. Wherein the regard due to it consists, and how far its judgment *justifies*?

'6. How we may know when it is properly exercised, and this regard paid to it?'

Each of these is branched out into a number of subordinate heads, which may shew the Writer's abilities as a casuist, but will hardly enable the Reader to *feel* his obligations to his fellow-creatures more sensibly than he did before.

We have happily, however, a single canon, of an old date, suited to all capacities, and applicable to all circumstances, which no rational being can misapply, unless perhaps to his own prejudice, by extending it to objects who forfeit their pretensions to it;—an error not often committed. It is conveyed home to every breast in these few simple words, *All things whatsoever ye would that men should do to you, do ye even so to them; for this is the law and the prophets.* This test of conscience no sincere mind can mistake, no bad one pervert, while he professes to act by it; whereas a designing man may frame distinctions to elude more complex rules of conduct. If ever words were worthy of an inspired teacher, these are; not for their mysteriousness, but for such simplicity, that every one bound to obey the precept is capable of understanding it, and of *feeling* the obligation to it, without the aid of a commentator.

But, notwithstanding our Author treats so largely of conscientious obligations, he denies that—'we have any such relation to inferior and irrational beings, that our conduct toward them

them can be justly denominated matter of conscience.' We are however of a quite contrary opinion: for though the brute creation is not comprehended in our Saviour's precept quoted above, yet, so far as we are concerned with the animals around us, subject to like feelings with ourselves, a moral regard is clearly due to them. We indeed use some for food, we render others subservient to us by their labour; we keep some for our recreation; we destroy others that are noxious to us, either by their depredations on our property, or for their poisonous qualities, when they come in our way. But tenderness may be observed under all these circumstances, and holy writ, in divers places, comes in aid of common sense, to exhort us to such a conduct. Indeed, a man so void of sympathy, as to behave with wanton cruelty toward his beast, or to any animal, is not likely to act mercifully by mankind, and may be safely declared void of *Conscience*.

The Dissertation on Providence contains no new illustrations of that mysterious subject of inquiry; though difficulties may appear very easily accounted for, as indeed they are, by laying down a set of dogmas as first principles, and by concluding that every thing not clearly explicable by them must nevertheless be conformable to them. But it is not every pen that is qualified to write of what no human being can thoroughly comprehend.

The Author appears too full, too complicated, in his Dissertation on Happiness, to give a general abstract idea of human happiness, or the best means of attaining it. He indeed says—' The result of all is, that the highest happiness of men consists in the resemblance and favour, or enjoyment of God.' This he amplifies greatly; but had he been treating of the *duty* of man as a sincere Christian, he might then truly say—his highest *duty* was to resemble God, taking that resemblance to consist in a pure unspotted life, and in the practice of those virtues which are attributed to the divine Author of Nature in the utmost perfection: how to *enjoy* God, or to be conscious of being *favoured* by him, no man will presume to determine, till arrived at a certain degree of enthusiasm. But a philosophical dissertation on human happiness having a scope as wide as human nature, a persuasion of the truths of the Christian revelation (a detail of the chief points of which he enters into, as a necessary ingredient of human happiness), however much it may and will contribute to the happiness of a pious Christian, cannot be understood as part of the happiness of mankind generally; this persuasion making no part of the happiness of those nations who are either ignorant of the gospel dispensation, or who do not acknowledge it.

In the following passage, indeed, the Author may be supposed to address himself to his fellow Christians :

'If you would have your ease and happiness in this life durable and steady, you must build it upon a durable and steady foundation, such as you are sure God has put always in your own power, and enabled you to secure. It cannot therefore be any outward attainments, such as power, wealth, and human applause, nor even any personal advantages of health, strength, wit, beauty, and the like ; for these are all precarious, and may fail you, after you have done your utmost to secure them ; but the only sure foundation of happiness and joy, is to have God approving you, through your own conscience, or the reason of your own mind, calmly and impartially reviewing itself, and testifying that you are rightly affected or disposed with respect to God and man, and have endeavoured to regulate your life accordingly, in the use of these advantages, abilities, and opportunites, which God has given you, or seriously repented and implored his pardon through Christ, where you came short.'

Not to insist upon the dispute among Christians, whether the utmost efforts of human righteousness can be understood to *co-operate* with the Messiah in the great work of human redemption *, it may be observed, so far as concerns our temporal happiness, that men of a pious turn of mind may set as light as they please by the comforts and conveniences of life, in comparison with our future expectations ; yet, while we are in the body, our happiness or unhappiness will in great measure depend on the presence or absence of worldly advantages ; and it is right that things should be so constituted. Riches can never be placed in worthier hands than in those of a sincere Christian ; and he is justified in exerting all *laudable* endeavours to obtain them : a nation of philosophers, or of self-denying zealots, would soon become a poor, spiritless, barbarous, and contemptible people. Nor is it to be inferred from this, that the art of contentment, or a calm resignation to the adverse dispensations of Providence, are hereby condemned. No such thing. While it is our duty to exercise our industry and emulation in all honest avocations, these prove the sweetest consolations to support us under unavoidable calamities ; but they are perverted when employed to relax our minds and bodies from those objects and pursuits, in the midst of which divine Providence has placed us.

Were we to consider happiness abstractedly, it might be defined *prolonged pleasure*, or *uninterrupted satisfaction*, a situation which is not to be found permanent on a changeable earth. But,

* James ii. 10.

to

to use the word in a looser sense, adapted to human circumstances, no general definition or description can be given of it, as each man's pleasure or happiness is as various as each individual's organical constitution and turn of mind. Nor are any one man's desires always the same; his body undergoes a progressive alteration, and hence the pleasures of life are various in its different stages; even variety itself constitutes one of our chief gratifications. Our only inquiry then should be, What species of happiness is the most rational? But every man's system of notions, and plan of conduct, are rational to himself; and those who, from a depraved turn of mind, cannot suit their taste to the result of the inquiry, will not find their happiness in conforming to it. Even Mr. Pope's *health*, *peace*, *and competence*, are no farther universal ingredients, than as *competence* will afford every one the means of living according to his particular humour. We have only to ascertain what this *competence* is; but this may prove as difficult a point to determine, to general satisfaction, as any of the rest. Here then our inquiry must drop, and we shall end it with the following happy couplet from the Ethic poet:

> Fix'd to no spot is happiness sincere;
> 'Tis no where to be found,——or ev'ry where.

The Author's general idea of prayer is happily conceived, though it may not meet with general approbation:

'Doubt not therefore the efficacy of *Prayer*, through the mediation of your Redeemer; scripture declares, reason testifies, and experience confirms it.

'Not that we can inform God of any thing he knew not before, or move him to act otherwise than he has determined, and sees agreeable to the eternal rules of right and equity, but as it evidences the feelings of our own minds, and tends to establish them in a humble and firm dependance on his providence, conformity to his will, and resemblance of *these* * perfections we adore, so far as they are communicable to us.'

These sentiments are rational, and consistent with the immutability of the divine Author of Nature, a perfection always enumerated among the attributes of the Deity, though Christians are too apt to forget it, in their more particular discourses and writings. We should with great pleasure have found this gentleman's notions, in every other particular, equally philosophical, and conformable to the standard of common sense.

* North British writers commonly put these for those, and sometimes *vice versa*.

Art. VIII. Concluſion *of our Account of the Farmer's Letters,* Vol. II. See Review for May.

IN letter I. of the ſecond part of his work, on the Improvement of uncultivated lands, the Author divides moors into *dry* and *wet*, as the two great indexes of the two general diſtinctions of culture. He divides dry moors again into what is called in the North *white land* (a fine light, ſound loam, which he juſtly thinks moſt highly improvable, and equal to what is lett in cultivated countries at 15 s. per acre) and black earth mixed with white ſandy grit, and covered with *ling* (or heath) which is worſe.

He obſerves that one party of men, much the larger, deem all theſe moors highly improvable; and another, much ſmaller, that they are not profitably ſo improvable; and he declares himſelf, from much obſervation, of the former opinion; as we alſo do.

He ſpeaks firſt of the buildings to be erected on tracts of moor to be improved; and aſſerts that the grit ſtone, eaſily formed into a kind of brick, is found almoſt every where in the moors, and reduces the price of building incredibly; and that the hard *whin ſtone* is not commonly found; but lime ſtone often. Our experience confirms all theſe aſſertions; but then impartiality obliges us to add, that coals to burn the laſt ſtone to lime, are, in many places, ſo diſtant from it, as to make the expence of burning lime very conſiderable, though ſeldom in ſuch degree as to diſcourage ſenſible men from cultivation.

Mr. Young thinks that the houſe, &c. for a ſmall farm may be built in the North of ſtone and ſlate for 50 l. We, ſpeaking from much experience, are of a different opinion, as the timber ſufficient for a ſlate covering generally comes dear, being uſually led from ſome diſtance.—He rates the cutting, carrying, and *laying* of the ſtones at only 5 s. 6 d. per rood, that is ſeven yards long, and five foot high: we judge this rate to be conſiderably below the average.

Our Farmer adviſes to incloſe by double walls, diſtant 20 yards, that part of the moor which adjoins to the *uncultivated* country, and to plant the fir tribe. This we think a great improvement; but muſt add, that double walls are ſo expenſive, that few men, who ſeek immediate profit, will be at this great expence at firſt.

Letter II. opens with Mr. Y.'s approbation of paring and burning moors. He obſerves that the enemies of this practice urge mere reaſoning againſt experience. We apprehend that the fault of theſe diſputants lies not in *reaſoning*, but in reaſoning *not right*. Experience and true reaſoning are ever *at union*.

Our Author well obſerves, that very ſhallow ſoils are proved to have been pared and burned many times in the memory of old men,

men, and, by tradition, long before their time, without having their thickneſs impaired. He adds, that if the paring diminiſhed the ſtaple of the land, by this time land which was of ſix inches ſtaple deep, would have no ſtaple, whereas it has its old.

Mr. Y. doubts whether the continuance of the ſame depth of ſtaple be occaſioned by the crops, produced by paring, returning part of themſelves, or by the turf (which conſiſts of roots and bulbs) being alone reduced to aſhes; though he thinks the latter the true caſe.—We apprehend, that if earth be converted to aſhes, as theſe mix with and open the *under earth*, nothing is loſt from the ſtaple.

The Farmer ſhews, however, clearly, how much cheaper manuring of ground is by theſe aſhes produced by burning, than manuring by aſhes brought; that 500 buſhels will be produced by an acre burned, the coſt 16 s. or 18 s. and that the ſame quantity brought may coſt 12 l. 10 s.—This laſt account, we think, muſt certainly be much exaggerated.

Mr. Y. thinks the ſpeedineſs of bringing waſte land into culture, *almoſt inſtantly*, is the grand point of paring and burning.—We agree with him that it is a *grand point*.

To the objection againſt paring and burning, viz. that "the wind blows away the aſhes," he gives ſeveral anſwers; firſt, that the aſhes are little moved by the wind; ſecondly, that all but ſlovens ſpread and plough them in hot; and, thirdly, this objection holds againſt manuring with ſoot and lime.—We think the ſecond and third anſwers good, but the firſt not at all ſo; as experience ſhews that the aſhes may be moſt violently carried away by the wind, ſo that the ploughing them in, quickly, is eſſential to good huſbandry.

Mr. Y. reckons the deſtruction of ling, &c. a great advantage of paring.—It certainly deſtroys ling, to a certain depth; but *how deep* is the great queſtion.—He thinks 1 l. per acre is a ſufficient average price for paring, burning, and ſpreading.—We think it exceſſive, as we know, from conſiderable experience, that an acre may be pared for about 10 s. and the burning will be done for much leſs; the ſpreading is uſually 6 d. Mr. Y. ſpeaks of pared ground which bears, firſt, turnips, and then five, ſix, or ſeven crops of *meſlin*, *oats*, *barley big*, and well laid. We are, perhaps, as well acquainted with the North as our Author, yet never heard of an inſtance of this kind, unleſs he means with ſeveral limings, &c.

In letter III. he obſerves, that chymiſts give to lime ſuch qualities as appear to agree with the nature of moors; he ſhews how lime converts the ſoil into food for plants; and that, in order to make *liming* a profitable practice, either, firſt, the limeſtone ſhould be found on the eſtate to be improved, or, ſecondly, that the ſtone ſhould be got from neighbouring lands; or, thirdly,

thirdly, the lime purchased near hand.—He thinks that not one moory estate in an hundred wants all these conveniences. We fear, and know, that many of those estates want them in the North, if coal be essential to lime burning *.

Mr. Y. owns his ignorance of improvement of moors without lime, by paring and burning; but we believe that much land is improved by the ashes alone. We agree with him that few large tracts of moors are without such stone as will burn to lime: but we intirely disagree with him in thinking that the moors give *no tracts of former culture.* On the contrary, if Mr. Y. were as well acquainted with the North, by a six months tour, as those who have dwelt there many years, he would know that there are, in many considerable tracts, the marks of former culture, perhaps as perfect as the present. This is a point of great consequence, and will have due notice in the sequel.

Letter IV. opens with a prevailing sentiment of *Northern* improvers, "that lands gained from the moors are better for pasture and meadow than for arable." Mr. Y. however observes, that crops on these lands indicate no such matter. He justly condemns the husbandry of the Northern farmers, who, after paring, &c. take five or six crops, as *execrable!* He advises to take only two *corn* crops, and with the latter, oats, to sow grass seeds! He also rightly recommends to improve a certain quantity of land every year, as by this method winter food of all kinds will be secured, and the teams have constant employ. Having noted, that turnips have commonly been the first crop with success, Mr. Y. recommends cabbages, by Mr. Scroope's and the Earl of Darlington's example. We think, however, that in general, a mixture of both these crops may be most advantageous. We approve his advice to contract for as many articles of improvement as can be done *by the great*, as teams and servants are very expensive.

Letter V. which is a long one of about 60 pages, opens with a state of expences. Mr. Y. advises, rightly, if other circumstances coincide, to carry on, every year, building and other improvements sufficient for such a farm as is lett in the country improved to most advantage. He advises his improver to buy a large flock of sheep to fold on the land to be improved; and we think the scheme a very good one; as we also judge it to be, to mend the breed of the moor ewes by a better ram, yet to keep them pretty nearly to their original hardiness. We agree with Mr. Y. that it is a great advantage to finish the paring, &c. in April, to have time for tillage. But we think the nature of the moors in the North, and the climate, such as seldom will render the turf fit to burn in that season. He advises to plough the ground pared and burned, twice, for cab-

* But we know it is not so.

bages,

bages, and we agree with him.—He juſtly ſuppoſes the turnips might be made much more valuable by hoeing; but we muſt think 3 l. 10 s. per acre for the *unhoed* far too great an average price. Mr. Y. however thinks that 50 or 60 acres of turnips will, in winter, ſerve 1000 ſheep, with good feed. On the ſtate of expences and product of the firſt year, we muſt obſerve, that we have never heard of unhoed turnips at 5 l. or 6 l. per acre; but Mr. Y. declares it is *no* unuſual thing. "*Sit penes auctorem fides.*"—His calculation, which may be very juſt, is, that a flock of 1000 ſheep, in 340 days (leſs than a year) will ſufficiently manure, by folding, 68 acres. A great advantage indeed!

In the ſecond year, we ſuppoſe 7 quarters of oats per acre beyond the average product, as we alſo think the profit of 7 s. 6 d. per head of ſheep, when we conſider the chances of death. We wiſh that 150 l. improvement of 60 oxen, by winter keeping on turnips and ſtraw, be not far too much, when we conſider the chances of diſtempers, which may ſink, and more than ſink, all the product, and of death, which muſt be a conſiderable deduction from the product of the whole.

Our Author ſtates the ſaving of expence by leading lime in a broad wheeled waggon; viz. that ſix horſes bring only three chaldron in a narrow wheeled one, and eight in a broad wheeled one bring ſeven; but Mr. Y. muſt conſider that many hills in the North are ſuch that, probably, no eight horſes in the world will raiſe ſeven chaldrons. Let him remember his etymology of *Scare-Nick!*

In the third year we think Mr. Y. allows amply for draining on dry moors; but as laſt year we could not be ſatisfied that oxen bought at 6 l. would leave the profit he eſtimated, ſo we are now unſatisfied that 100 oxen, bought at 700 l. will be improved to 1015. However, we own ourſelves leſs experienced in this branch of huſbandry.

Mr. Y. now comes to the letting of his firſt farm, and ſays, that as the common improvements of moors is to 15 s. ſo this of his may, for its completeneſs, be worth 20 s. per acre. Of this fact we have ſome doubt. The new buildings will certainly tempt tenants to promiſe a great rent, but if the ground cannot produce the rent, it muſt remain unpaid.——He reckons land lett for 80 l. per annum what one may *mortgage* or *ſell* for 2000 l. But, ſay Mr. Y. what he will to the contrary, it is obvious that people will ſcruple to buy the *new* like *old* farms, becauſe this point is certain, that there is room to doubt whether this ſoil will continue of the ſame value? a point which we ſhall inſiſt on in the ſequel.

On ſtating accounts at the end of the fourth year, Mr. Y. ſhews that the improver has nearly 3000 l. in hand, 240 acres of improved land unlett, and all his live and dead ſtock.

 Mr.

Mr. Y. foresees that many of his Readers will exclaim, "*Credat Judæus Apella!*" Therefore to open the eyes of *unbelief* he asserts, first, that the waste moors in the North of England, and in Scotland, are immense; secondly, that all the operations of improvement are well known, and commonly practised in those countries; thirdly, that the prices which he allows for the several works will always bring men; fourthly, that the soil is fairly described; and, fifthly, that 'tis allowed by all men to be very improvable. We agree with him in all these points, and in a sixth, viz. that land thus improved will *never want* tenants. However we have, in passing, *impartially* observed, that the profits seem stated too high.

Mr. Y. also reproaches gentlemen improvers with carrying on designs of this sort by methods too slow, and not on a connected plan. But in defence of this caution we could observe many things, which will suggest themselves to every one who thinks. He justly regards a flock of sheep to *fold*, as an essential of this kind of improvement: but we can by no means agree with him, that it is clear that various parts of the moors which *seem* never to have a fold, have never known it.—On the contrary we must own it our firm opinion, that vast tracts of moors, which now appear to injudicious eyes never to have been cultivated, have formerly been cultivated, and well cultivated, and probably with sheep; so that whether they have relapsed into their former condition through mere neglect, or from some *inherent defect* in the soil, is the great point to be inquired into.

To the objection started by a man advised to commence improver, "I cannot spare the money proposed," Mr. Y. angrily answers by another question, "Cannot you borrow it?"—This question may *silence*, but will not *satisfy*.

Mr. Y. being thus got into the high way of improvement, proceeds at a swift rate. He acquires a new farm of 120 l. a year, or more than 3000 l. in value every year. At the end of the seventh year his improver has above 10,000 l. in hand, and cultivates 360 acres more in the eighth year. Mr. Y. foresees an obstacle to his career, viz. that men will be wanting for such vast undertakings. He affirms, however, that if his improver employs 100 men this year, he may be assured of 150 the next, and so on.—But may we not be permitted to whisper in his ear, that the men in a certain country are a certain number, and that if they are collected by high prices, the whole country from whence they are drawn, must suffer by the want of them, and in a very considerable degree. Besides, how will men, thus amassed, corrupt one another; and how licentious will they grow?

At

At the end of the eighth year Mr. Y. finds himſelf to have caſh in hand to the amount of betwixt 14 or 15,000 l. and at the end of the ninth, betwixt 16 and 17,000 l.

And now, in the tenth year, he is ſo moderate as to content himſelf with incloſing *only* two farms of 120 acres each, and running a plantation round the improved ſquare of two miles each ſide. He incloſes this plantation with a wall; an expence, which although prodigious to a man of a middling fortune, is yet a *mere nothing* to one that gains thouſands of pounds in a year! The plantation itſelf is *only* 160 acres, and will require *not quite* 80,000 trees.—Men of ſlow imaginations would meet with *ſome ſmall* difficulties in finding this quantity of firs, pines, &c. But Mr. Y. having many hundreds of pounds in his pockets, with his pen conjures up, and then plants them, at once!

At the end of the tenth year, he has almoſt 24,000 l. in pocket. He now mortgages or ſells his land, and has above 60,000 l. neat profit. As ſome curious man may happen to ſuggeſt that the original value of the land ſhould be deducted, Mr. Y. anſwers, '’Tis a nothing.' But that he may appear as generous as rich, he gives you 160 acres of wood for this nothing. He concludes his letter by eſtimating the 62,000 l. raiſed in eleven years, nearly as equal to 6000 per annum, and all the product of 3147 l. 'but this matter is *ſo very unuſual.*' It is indeed! If any one intends to be an improver, on Mr. Y.'s plan, and enjoys his 62,000 l. beforehand, he would probably ſay to his friends who ſhould *endeavour* to moderate his hopes,

> ——“ *Pol me occidiſtis, amici,*
> *Non ſervaſtis, ait, cui ſic extorta voluptas,*
> *Et demtus per vim menti gratiſſimus error!*”
>
> Hor.

In letter VI. Mr. Y. inſiſts upon his principles as *indubitable*, viz. that the kind of land is univerſally allowed very improvable; that as to its anſwering the expence, it is well known that he has allowed prices above the mark; and that the rate of 20 s. per acre for the improved graſs is moderate. In anſwer to the queſtion, “If ſuch improvements here ſtated can be made, how can the proprietors neglect them?” He aſks, “How can men who keep from 5000 to 40,000 ſheep, never think of folding, although the loſs by this neglect is prodigious?” We think this laſt queſtion a good anſwer to the former. But we deem not ſo of Mr. Y.'s other queſtion, viz. “Why don't they improve their breed at the trifling expence of buying a few good tups?” For while the feed continues bad, it is rather a loſs than gain to attempt to improve the carcaſs of the ſheep, which infallibly degenerates to a ſize ſuited to its feed, and in the mean time thrives not.—Indeed, the knowledge of a ſhep-herd

herd is not Mr. Y.'s *fort*; and he elſewhere owns it. Mr. Y. is *very eloquent* on the uſes to which a father of a family may comfortably apply 60,000 l. and we think needleſsly.—He then obſerves, that preceding writers on agriculture have ſaid ſo little on improvement of moors, that it might be contained in two pages.

We own this ſeems to be a very great reproach to them all, and is to us in a particular manner *aſtoniſhing*, as we are ourſelves fully convinced that this part of huſbandry has been, long ago, much practiſed in ſeveral countries, and we believe with ſucceſs, at leaſt for a time. Hence it appears to us one of the *moſt curious* and *moſt important* deſiderata, why this branch of ancient huſbandry ſhould have fallen ſo much into oblivion, that a ſpirited inquirer into the ancient ſtate of the moors, in 'a Six Months Tour,' cannot diſcover any marks of their priſtine culture. We have, however, ſeen it in a thouſand inſtances, and only remain in doubt, whether the relapſe of the land into its ancient ſtate be the effect of bad culture or defect of the ſoil to continue improved. This appears to be ſo important an inquiry that we hope ſuch of our Readers as love agriculture (and none elſe will read our review of this work) will forgive our frequently ſuggeſting this inquiry.

Mr. Y. now reduces the value of the improved graſs land to 12 s. per acre, and ſhews that even, on this ſuppoſition, the improver on his plan may have 30,000 l. in pocket at the end of the above term. For our part, we believe that 12 s. per acre is too low a rent for much improved moor land, and we fear 20 s. is too high a rent on an average. We apprehend that in this, as in moſt caſes, truth lies betwixt the diſputants.

The VIIth letter begins with a propoſal of improvement upon a *larger* ſcale, which we are *heartily* ſorry for; ſince, as we apprehend, that ſuch improvements as have been *already* diſplayed, are in the main *feaſible*; ſo, on the other hand, we fear that the enlarging the proſpect of them beyond the *preſent horizon*, will diſguſt almoſt all whom he invites. Extremes run into one another; and he who promiſes too much, diſcourages. "*Quid dignum tanto*," &c. ſays Horace, who well knew human nature. Let the world, Mr. Y. try your former ſcheme of improvement, and when they ſucceed in that, they will be ready to work on your larger plan; or rather, they will not want your new plan. They will be *planners* themſelves.

Mr. Y. however, by his enlarged ſcale, gets nearly 10,000 l. into pocket at the end of his third year, and betwixt 15 and 16,000 l. at the end of his fourth. At the end of his fifth year he has above 20,000 l. in caſh, which runs up faſt towards 30,000 l. at the end of the 6th year; and at the cloſe of the ſeventh exceeds 40,000 l.; at the end of the eighth year amounts to to almoſt 75,000 l. and at the cloſe of the ninth is betwixt 140,000 l. and 150,000 l. neat profit from 10,000 l. ſtock! Nay, he has much more profit by his plantations, &c. &c. But our pen is wore out with tranſcribing!—Some people may object (as a difficulty attending this ſcheme of getting 150,000 l. nay 175,000 l. in nine years) that 5000 acres, neceſſary to work theſe wonders, are not to be found contiguous. But Mr. Y. aſſures his readers, on his word, that nobles, nay gentlemen, poſſeſs waſte moors of ten times the number, viz. 50,000.—Happy England! Why ſhould we run to the deſerts of America?

Our Farmer proceeds to ſhew, that although it is much better to plant waſte grounds with *firs* and *pines* than with *nothing*, yet 'tis *forty times* more advantageous to reduce it to corn and graſs land. This may be true; but when he aſſerts that "in a *rich*, *populous*, *induſtrious* kingdom, *every inch* of ſoil ſhould be applied to *feeding* MAN," we ſee not this verified in England! We ſtand aſtoniſhed at Mr. Y.'s picture of "a kingdom where coal is to be had in *every* village." We have travelled through many counties of this kingdom, and in how few have we ſeen coals in any village! In how many villages, and market and borough towns, cannot coals be obtained at any price! How great a part of this kingdom depends upon wood only for fuel! How entirely, almoſt, do the villages of the extenſive north-riding of Yorkſhire (which Mr. Y. juſtly conſiders as one great ſeat of theſe improvements) want coals! By the bye, it is this want of coals which makes lime ſo dear in many parts of that riding, as to diſcourage the improvement of moors.

Mr. Y. concludes this letter with an aſſertion that aſtoniſhes us above meaſure, viz. "the immenſity of the profit is *nearly* the ſame to thoſe who would hire theſe moors [as to the proprietors."] What reaſon can be plauſibly aſſigned in ſupport of this paradox?—'Rent is too trifling to calculate."—What then?—Be the original rent ever ſo trifling, will any man give Mr. Y. any thing like nearly the ſame money on mortgage of his *leaſehold* as of his *freehold* equally improved?—What inadvertency! If it could be ſhewn that the projected improvement would laſt only a certain number of years, and that the leaſe is commenſurate to that term, the value of the leaſehold and freehold would be nearly the ſame, and much leſs than Mr. Y. calculates; but while the improvements are ſuppoſed *perennial*, the caſe is as different as can be imagined.

In letter VIII. Mr. Y. propoſes to examine the leaſt extent of improvement of moor which can *profitably* be undertaken. On this plan we ſhall obſerve a few things, viz. 1ſt, that the profit of keeping, *one* year, on graſs, two years old Scotch heifers, ſeems ſtated unreaſonably high at 40 s. per acre; for, in the firſt

firſt place, heifers ſo young can ſeldom be bought at any price, the Scotchmen wiſely keeping them till they ſell at a better: ſecondly, they ſeldom *feed*, but *grow in carcaſe*, and weigh ill at three years old. 2dly, ſeven quarters of oats per acre ſeems too great an average crop; and, 3dly, 40 loads of compoſt, led by the team *every* day, ſeems too great a taſk, as the diſtance muſt be various.

Mr. Y. ſhews that, on his plan of improvement, the leaſt ſum of money with which a man ſhould begin, is nearly 1800 l. and hence he accounts for ſo few improvements being carried on ſucceſsfully. Indeed he judiciouſly obſerves, that turnips, oats, &c. are wanting in ſucceſſion; and as double cropping ruins land, a want of improving new land every year, ruins all.

Upon the whole, on Mr. Y.'s calculation, a man with moor enough and betwixt 1700 l. and 1800 l. in his pocket, by improving 20 acres every year, may, in 15 years' time, have a clear profit of above 2000 l. beſides the ſtock, or fee-ſimple of 300 acres, worth 300 l. per ann. or 9000 l. more.

Letter IX. begins with an aſſurance that 'he who, on the *data* of improving a grit-ſtone moor, begins to improve a lime-ſtone moor, ſoil the ſame, will prove a great loſer.'—This appears to us amazing, if the coals be no further diſtant in the latter caſe than the lime in the former. But Mr. Y. has his *data* from the very ingenious Mr. Scroope.

One of Mr. Scroope's *data*, however, we are aſtoniſhed at, viz. that "all expences of burning lime are 3 s. 10 d. per chaldron." We know that the price of getting up lime-ſtones, where eaſieſt to be come at, breaking them and filling the kiln, that is, mixing the coals and broken ſtones, is 2 s. Now it is inconceivable how the coals ſhould only coſt 1 s. 10 d. for a chaldron. We know of no coals nearer Mr. Scroope's than the biſhopric of Durham, and a chaldron of coals will only burn three or four chaldrons of lime.—We know that in ſome parts of the North-riding, Mr. Scroope's country, the very getting up of a chaldron of coals coſts 8 s.. ſo that on the whole it ſeems that the main expence of the burning of lime, the coals, is omitted. If he who burns lime with his own ſtone can purchaſe coals as cheap as the grit-ſtone improver purchaſes lime, and leads from an equal diſtance, he has a very conſiderable advantage over him; for if a chaldron of coals burns four chaldrons of lime, he ſaves three-fourths of the leading. Four chaldrons of lime coſt 1 l. 12 s. in the one caſe; in the other caſe coals coſt 8 s. and burning four chaldrons of lime 16 s. ſo that one fourth of the money expended, and three fourths of the leading, are ſaved. How conſiderable all this!—But if inſtead of 4 s. per chaldron getting up ſtones, &c. be reckoned only 2 s. how much more is the advantage!

We

We must, however, think Mr. Y.'s ſtate of the expence of lime at 4 s. the chaldron greatly below the truth; and this miſcalculation is conſiderable, when near 500 chaldrons are laid on every year's improvement. We are alſo much miſtaken if he could hire labourers to fill and ſpread five chaldrons of lime for 1 s. 6 d. Would not the man who ſhould fill and ſpread this quantity, work a hard day's work, and be ill paid? The rating of tithe alſo at 2 s. per acre, on ſuch improved ground, ſeems much too low. What clergyman would take 2 s. for his tenth part of cabbages, ſuppoſed worth 6 l. or 8 l.? All this is ſelf deluſion!——Mr. Y. makes the improvement of ſtock by 30 acres of cabbages and 40 of turnips, to be 300 l. The tenth part of this ſum is 30 l. whereas the tithe of 70 acres, at 2 s. is only 7 l. not a fourth of 30 l. What a difference!

In the ſecond year there is ſome great miſtake about ſeed for 60 acres of oats, charged only 3 l. *i. e.* 1 s. per acre *. In p. 267 expence ſhould be ſet againſt 3092, &c. not againſt 362, &c. which is the balance of expence and product. But Mr. Y. means by the expence, the ſurplus of diſburſements above receipts. He makes the total ſum requiſite for this improvement 5260 l. &c. and at the end of the fourth year finds 6260 l. in his pocket; at the end of the fifth nearly 10,000 l. at the end of the ſixth nearly 13,000 l. at the end of the ſeventh nearly 17,000 l. at the end of the eighth above 23,000 l. at the end of the ninth almoſt 35,000 l. and at the end of the tenth almoſt 40,000 l. and by ſale of ſtock and land this ſum is made up 104,122 l. And now Mr. Y. aſſures his improver that he has calculated his advantages much too low!

Mr. Y. obſerves, that by his management, a gentleman who owes 95,000 l. need only add the odd 5000 l. to his debt, and follow our Author in the enchanting agricultural walk; and in a few years he will have all his debts paid, with 100,000 l. in his pocket! We remember a common ſubject of a theme at ſchool, "*Multa fidem promiſſa levant.*"

Mr. Y. is very ſolicitous to remove all fear of wanting hands. 'High wages will bring them, and conſtant employ keep them.' Be it ſo. He inſtances turnpikes, navigations, &c. But do not theſe inſtances prove the damage by draining an already cultivated country of *neceſſary hands?*

Mr. Y. affirms that, in Northumberland *alone*, are ſix hundred thouſand acres of moor-land, and in Weſtmoreland, Cumberland, Durham, Yorkſhire, and Derby, three millions!

His Xth letter propoſes to improve ſuch lands as Yorkſhire wolds, plains in Wiltſhire, heaths in Norfolk, &c. When

* It ſeems, according to other allowances, 30 l.

theſe

these light, shallow, hazel loams are covered with rubbish, he would pare and burn them; when clear, only plough them up. *N. B.* He omits consideration of their culture by lime, as that manure seems unfit where richness is wanting. The grand improvement he proposes is *sainfoine*, and he proceeds on the experiments of Sir Digby Legard. The improvement is from 1 s. to 10 s. per acre. Mr. Y. thinks the best disposition of a farm on this land is, to have two-thirds sainfoine, one of them for hay, and the other for pasture; the remainder for *turnips* and *barley* alternately: the *former* worth 30 s. per acre, the *latter* amounting to 3 quarters *.

Mr. Y. supposes rent, tithe, and town charges of 150 acres only 12 l. But what clergyman, not an ideot, will be content with his pittance of this sum? If he knows the land can be raised to 10 s. per acre, by sainfoine, will he not expect 1 s. per acre, or 7 l. 10 s. for the 150 acres? If it produce 3 quarters of barley, or 2 l. 8 s. will not he expect 4 s. 6 d. per acre?

He shews that 2483 l. &c. are requisite to cultivate 450 acres of this land; and that at the end of the third year the improver will have in hand 2760 l. &c. at the end of the fourth 4192 l. at the end of the fifth 5249 l. &c. at the end of the sixth 6019 l. at the end of the seventh 8347 l. at the end of the eighth 11,248 l. at end of the ninth 13,492 l. the end of the tenth 25,437 l. and at the end of the eleventh his neat profit is 44,914 l. Mr. Y. observes, first, that the seed of *sainfoine* sometimes fails, and, in that case, a crop of turnips must be taken, and sainfoine sown again; and, secondly, that after 20 years it will be necessary to renew the sainfoine by sowing again.

Letter XI. considers the cultivation of soils which cover *marle*, *fat chalk*, and *clay*. Mr. Y. advises his improver, having raised his necessary buildings and fences, to lay on every acre 200 loads (each 15 bushels) of the marle, &c. and avows that the land will lett, at an average, for 10 s. per acre, the original rent 1 s. 6 d.

This is a kind of improvement which makes a quick return, so that at the end of the second year Mr. Y. reckons that the improver who has laid out 1565 l. will have cash in hand 2338 l. at the end of the third year 4225 l. at the end of the fourth year 5559 l. at the end of the fifth 8367 l. at the end of the sixth 11,680 l. at the end of the seventh 20,686 l. and at the end of the eighth 92,218 l. besides 740 acres of plantation which cost 4300 l. So that from expending 1690 l. is gained about 100,000 l. in eight years. This profit needs no encomium: but Mr. Y. sees it will be thought to want defence,

* Mr. Young transposes the *words*, but we follow the *sense*.

and therefore he endeavours to ſhew that he has laid the expences too high, and that 10 s. an acre is not too high rent to be expected. He dwells much on the good ſtate of the buildings, fences, &c.——But we have before ſaid, that theſe will certainly allure a tenant, but not enable him to pay a neat rent. We believe marle a *good* and *laſting* manure; but we apprehend its kinds to be ſo various, that we muſt ſuppoſe its profits as various; and we have no very high opinion of clays, at leaſt till mixed and mellowed with oppoſite ſoils. Mr. Y. avers, that he can point to *many* parts of England where ſeveral hundred thouſands of acres, thus to be improved, may be met with. We rejoice at the news, for the ſake of the public, as we have hitherto thought that the *true profitable* fat marle is not commonly to be found. We ſuppoſe, if it can be thus abundantly found, that is the moſt *profitable* ſort of improvement. Mr. Y. endeavours to ſhew that the ill ſucceſs of farmers who marle, ſhould not be urged to diſcourage improvers. He *candidly* owns, however, that the improver muſt *mortgage* his improved farms as faſt as poſſible, or he will be obliged to raiſe *greater* ſums than any ſenſible man would think of raiſing, "nay, that all the *preceding immenſe* profits will vaniſh *at once!*" This is bad news: for how muſt the improver be ſure of an opportunity of mortgaging his farm? Will not *monied men* chuſe to ſee how theſe new farms anſwer to the tenants, before they hazard their caſh?

Letter XII. diſplays the improvements to be made on ſuch tracts as Enfield Chace, Epping-Foreſt, New Foreſt, &c. by which he apprehends that the rent may be raiſed from 2 s. 6 d. to 20 s. an acre. This we honeſtly believe very eaſy.—He obſerves, that the ſhrubs, &c. would ſell to an advantage, and not only fill the covered drains, but go conſiderably towards making the hedges, which alſo we are convinced of.—He recommends planting of cabbages on this new-improved ſoil, unfit for turnips, and, we think, judiciouſly. However, we doubt of the reality of 320 acres of cabbages in the firſt year, giving to the ſtock nearly 2000 improvement. Perhaps, all things conſidered, Mr. Y.'s product of 1600 quarters of barley from 320 acres is not extravagant. He makes about 7500 l. the ſum requiſite for carrying on this great improvement.

On this plan he has caſh in hand at the end of the third year, 15.702 l. at the end of the fourth 24,181 l. at the end of the fifth 33,245 l. at the end of the ſixth 52,289 l. at the end of the ſeventh 74,365 l. at the eighth 87,000 l and at the end of the ninth 178,965 l. and have beſides in hand 5120 acres, with all ſtock, which will bring him in 9369 l.! We fear this ſtate of accounts will remind his readers of the celebrated *Perſian glaſs-man* in the Spectator.

But

But not yet content, Mr. Y. ſhews, that, in the tenth year, the income will be 200,000 l. and that at the end of the twelfth year, the neat profit is above 600,000 l. He alſo thinks this profit very moderate; and that it is impoſſible this undertaking ſhould fail of ſucceſs!

The laſt Letter diſplays the advantages of this improvement, not to the individual, but the public.—This point, of great importance, will be ſo obvious to any man of ſenſe, that we will not enter into our Author's detail, but refer the Reader who wants conviction of the truth of this conſequence of Mr. Y.'s ſuppoſed improvements, to the Letter itſelf; which, we ſuppoſe, will afford much entertainment to any true patriot, who believes that the value of Mr. Y.'s improvements will be only a tenth of what he ſtates it to be.

In p. 402, he adviſes landlords who are too timorous to execute works like theſe propoſed, to lend money on them to men of ſkill.—We are fully convinced, that moſt of Mr. Y.'s propoſed improvements are very likely to be attended with conſiderable advantages (eſpecially the laſt), and therefore wiſh that timorous landlords of waſte grounds may meet with men of undoubted *integrity*, as well as *ſkill* and *induſtry*, to whom they may *prudently* and *profitably* lend money on ſuch plans. But we apprehend, that the landlord, who is too timid to expend his money with his own hand, under his own eye, will be more cautious of lending it to projectors, however rational.——We wiſh, however, that all landlords would conſider, that the money lent being expended on the lender's ground, he is put almoſt immediately into poſſeſſion of land-ſecurity, as Mr. Y. obſerves; and adds a caution, that ſecurity for expending the money lent on the land, be taken.

The Farmer juſtly laments, that *utility* is not put on the ſame foot as *beauty*, and that a *maſter-improver* is not encouraged equally with a *maſter of ornamental diſpoſition of grounds.*—In the two laſt pages he deſcribes ſuch a *maſter-improver*, a picture which we apprehend to be no bad reſemblance of himſelf.

Mr. Y. has, in this work, opened a new *world* to the ſearcher into nature; and therefore we will make no apology to our Readers for the *length* of this review, or to our Author for the *freedom* of it.—We have *avoided* all *verbal* criticiſm, but we beg leave to remind Mr. Y. that we have paſſed over ſuch inaccuracies, that we muſt ſay, not only *Prician*'s head, but that of *common ſenſe* is broke by them.

[*N. B. For Implement, p.* 374, *l.* 1. read *Improvement.*]

Hints

ART. IX. *Hints for improving the Kingdom of Ireland, in a Letter to his Excellency George Lord Viscount Townshend, Lord Lieutenant of Ireland.* By A Lover of his Country. Dublin printed. 1771. One Sheet.

WE are induced to take notice of this little publication, both by a motive of *civility* *, and a much better, that of *compassion*. We doubt not that all the great facts here asserted can be proved; and on that supposition we know not whether we ought more to *wonder* or to *pity*.

The Letter-writer affirms, that Ireland, notwithstanding the advantages of a free constitution, excellent soil, and tolerable population, is the most uncultivated part of the British empire, or perhaps all Europe; upon the whole, not much better than Hounslow-heath, &c. Indeed, the instances which follow are strong in point, viz. 1. not one waggon or cart in a farmer's stock, but one-horse cars, with wheels not three feet high, and quite solid; 2. not one public waggon; 3. in 100 miles from the south to Dublin, only four corn-fields in blade on November 11th; and in the forwardest counties much arable land unsown; 4. fences made only to last one year; and, 5. lands universally laid to grass without seeds.

The Writer affirms, that flax-husbandry is scarcely known out of the province of Ulster; and concludes, from the *data* of Essays published by the Dublin Society in 1732, that the county of Limerick would yield a clear profit of 10 l. per acre, and contains 375,320 acres; so that the profit would be 3,753,200 l. per annum,—nearly equal to half the rental of the kingdom.

Our Letter-writer proceeds to shew the consequence of this wretched husbandry, viz. the misery of the labouring poor, equal to that of any poor on earth; and which would be still greater, were it not for potatoes. He assures us that the yeomanry are but by one degree less miserable, although their markets are as good as the English, and labour is much lower.

His advice to his countrymen, to sit down content under the restrictions of trade which England lays on them, and to cultivate those branches which she allows, is certainly judicious.

He apprehends, and (we think) with justice, that the foundation of *Irish misery* lies in the first English settlers not considering themselves as colonists, and therefore not planting and inclosing their respective territories; and he justly laments the non-continuance of those improvements by the grantees, which are mentioned in the statute as the foundation of grants by Elizabeth.

---

* See the Correspondence at the end of this month.

In oppoſition to Sir William Petty's notion, that "*manufacture* is preferable to *agriculture*," our Letter-writer ſhews, from Mr. Young, that a leſs number of people produce by agriculture 83,237,651 l. than thoſe who by manufactures produce 27 millions: a difference of *above* † three to one in favour of agriculture!

We mean not to undertake the defence of Mr. Young's calculations. But it is evidently abſurd for any nation to cultivate *manufactures* till they have made a good progreſs in *agriculture*.

Our Letter-writer obſerves that the Dutch, by judicious huſbandry, make their lands pay 7 l. per acre, according to Sir William Petty, and 10 l. per acre, according to Sir Richard Weſton: whereas Mr. Young eſtimates the produce of ours only at 2 l. 10 s. and the Letter-writer hopes we may improve to the ſtandard of the Dutch.

We, on the contrary, hope no ſuch thing; but are convinced that the value of the Dutch lands, in a great meaſure, depends on the ſmall extent of their country, and conſequently on the nearneſs of all parts of them to water. Certainly, however, inland navigations, if properly conducted, promiſe great advances of the real value of lands.

Our Letter-writer obſerves, that the bounty on exportation of corn has not had the ſame effect in Ireland as in England, and thinks the true reaſon to be, that it is given at a price under the market. He declaims on the advantages of the bounty on exportation of corn, and we agree with him in general, but are convinced that prudence dictates bounds to that bounty.

The Letter-writer notes the uniformity of half arable and half paſture in England which Mr. Young found, and thinks that ſuch a diviſion in Ireland would not defeat the legiſlature's views. This point we apprehend to require much more diſquiſition than a letter of one ſheet admits. We agree with him however in thinking that the obſervation of a judicious courſe of crops might very properly be made a qualification of receiving the bounty.

The Writer has a period, at the ſenſe of which we can only gueſs. We apprehend it to be, that the bounty paid on the exportation of corn by England, has been more than 72,433 l.; and he thinks a third part of that ſum, expended in the ſame manner in Ireland, would make it a flouriſhing kingdom.

Another means of improvement which the Letter-writer wiſhes, is the diſtribution of premiums for the flax-huſbandry, in aid of the bounty granted by parliament, and we own, as the Iriſh have great advantages of water, all encouragement to that huſbandry ſeems *rational*.

† The Letter-writer ſays *almoſt*; but he ſhould have ſaid *above*.

On

On Mr. Young's assertion, that sheep are *four times* more profitable on *inclosed* than *open* ground, our Letter-writer concludes, that '*inclosing* is an *improvement* worth at least 10 s. per acre, which amounts in the whole kingdom to five millions per annum.' We know the improvement is considerable, but dare not maintain it to be equal to this state of it.

The Letter-writer thinks that two millions would inclose the whole kingdom of Ireland, that is, finish the inclosure with quick hedges. We see no *data* on which to ground that conclusion; yet agree with him, that whatever the expence be, it would be amply repaid. On comparing the two kingdoms, we say—"*Facies non una, nec diversa tamen*—" and we may add, "*Qualem decet esse sororum!*"

Art. X. *A Review of the History of Job; wherein the principal Characters, Transactions, and Incidents in that Book are considered with Attention; also, Enquiry made, whether they are countenanced by Reason, Nature, and Truth, or are in Reality supported other Parts of Scripture-History. With an Appendix, containing Remarks on that generally misapplied Passage, Chap.* xii. *Ver.* 12. By a private Gentleman. 8vo. 2 s. sewed. Buckland, &c. 1771.

THERE is, we believe, no book of scripture that is, upon the whole, so difficult as the Book of Job. It is certain there is none that hath afforded greater occasion for critical speculations and enquiries, or concerning which more elaborate dissertations and treatises have been written. Several of the most eminent and learned authors of our own country have distinguished themselves upon the subject, within not many years past; and yet there will still be found room for new observations.

The Writer of the present tract hath delivered, with great plainness and modesty, the remarks of a sensible and thoughtful man on the history of Job. His design is, to prove, from what light the history itself affords, connected with some chronological accounts in other parts of scripture, the reality of the person of Job; nearly the time in which he lived, and the country he inhabited; the authenticity of his history; to offer a probable conjecture with regard to the writer of it; and to answer, in the course of the work, some objections to the truth of the story. This is the plan laid down by our Author; but he doth not strictly adhere to it, and, indeed, he considers the doing so as a matter of little or no consequence; though, perhaps, several of his Readers may be of a different opinion.

He begins with stating his sentiments concerning the general intention of the history of Job, which he believes to be as follows, 1st, To justify the conduct of the all-wise infinite Being, who always sees things as they are, and who, in every of his providential dispensations, intends the best good of all his creatures. 2dly, To shew, that men frequently mistake characters; and in consequence thereof, as frequently draw erroneous and false conclusions, prejudicial to themselves and others. 3dly, That afflictions in the present state, simply considered, are no proof of the displeasure of the Almighty, but occasionally are quite the contrary. 4thly, As a general lesson, by shewing, that the behaviour of Job, considered as a man, was, upon the whole, agreeable to truth, reason, and nature.

In discussing these particulars, our Author introduces some observations in favour of the conduct of Job's wife. He is inclined to think, that if she actually made use of the word *barec*, it was not in the sense usually put upon it in this place. 'For if,' says he, 'the word means not only to bless, but to salute, or give the knee (and there are but four more places in all the Bible where it can be supposed to have an opposite meaning—), I should imagine she had so high an opinion of her husband's innocence, that she might mean to advise him, seeing, notwithstanding his uprightness, he was thus amazingly afflicted——*to go and kneel, or bow down before God, and plead, or, as it were, expostulate with him concerning the reason of these dreadful calamities,—even though he should die.* If this sense of her expressions be allowed, it will justify *Job*'s wise rebuke for her inconsiderateness, while, as he still possessed his soul in submissive patience, crying out, "Thou speakest as a rash, thoughtless, or foolish woman; what, *shall we receive good at the hand of God, and shall we not receive evil?*" Indeed, it should seem, that God himself did not behold her as an impious or blasphemous woman; inasmuch as we find, from the sequel of the history, she was made a great instrument in *Job*'s future and remarkable prosperity; she becoming, after the great calamity, the mother of seven sons, and three most beautiful daughters. I say, she was their mother, because we have no intimation that *Job* had any other wife.'

Our Author has endeavoured to shew, that, even in the places where the word *barec* has been almost undoubtedly thought to signify *curse*, it may admit of a contrary meaning; after which he proceeds to enquire who was the writer of the history; and, having here considered and expressed his disapprobation of the opinions of several learned men, he proposes his own, which is, that Elihu was the first penman of the book of Job. He supposes, however, that Moses might be the translator of it, and

give

give it the sublimity of diction, and the other poetical ornaments with which it every where abounds. The reasons assigned for ascribing it originally to Elihu are, 1st, His being the youngest of all the persons mentioned as having any acquaintance with Job and his story, so that he might probably outlive Job, and could ascertain the circumstances recorded in the xliid chapter. 2dly, His being well-acquainted with the several particulars of Job's history. 3dly, His amiable character, and remarkable modesty, which fitted him for relating facts as they really happened. And, 4thly, His being little more than a spectator, whose mind was not disturbed or distressed; by which means he was much better qualified than even Job himself, to examine and recollect the different circumstances of the affliction, the complaint, the dialogue, accusation, defence, and other incidents which compose this very remarkable story.

But the chief design of the present performance is to prove the reality of the person of Job, and the truth of the facts related concerning him, the objections to which opinion are very distinctly considered, and, in our apprehension, successfully removed. We shall, however, with regard to this part of the work, only take notice of the interpretation which is given of the dialogues carried on between Jehovah and Satan, in the two first chapters. These dialogues our Author supposes to be only a poetical picture or representation of contrasted characters, beautifully drawn and highly finished. 'If,' says he, 'this part of the history was to be divested of its poetical representation, the matter of Satan, in plain language, would run thus: Job was a virtuous and good man, one who walked uprightly, fearing God and avoiding evil: his possessions were very large, and so much increased, that he became greater than his neighbours, which prosperity was the occasion of some very envious *adversary*, who did not thrive as he did, not only to view him with a jealous eye, but openly to accuse him, and exclaim, in the following manner: "*Doth Job serve God for nought? is not his substance increased in the land? yet this pretended fear of God, and perfect uprightness, is nothing more than dissimulation and gross hypocrisy. As things are now with him, he may very well appear as one that avoids evil; for he has no occasion to use art, craft, or fraud in his dealings, seeing the work of his hand is blessed. But did he fall under any remarkable calamity, or meet with heavy losses in his substance, he would soon discover the wickedness of his heart; for then he would appear quite a different person before God, nor, as he does now, would he be seen to bless God to his face.*"

'This,' continues the Writer, 'is no unfair representation of the matter,—and when it is said, "So went Satan forth from the presence of the Lord, and smote Job with sore boils from the sole of his foot unto his crown;" I am persuaded it should be be considered only as a poetical description of the disease, which really happened to Job by permission of divine providence.'

The place of Job's habitation was, according to our Author, beyond a doubt, in or about the borders of Idumea, in the land which received its name from Uz, the son of Dishan.

No little pains are taken, in the present enquiry, to prove that Job's three friends were base hypocrites, and, in fact, his bitter enemies. Though we acknowledge that what is said in support of this opinion is ingenious, and even forcible, we do not, however, entirely agree with it. At the same time, we go farther than Mr. Peters, and think that they were not only mistaken in their sentiments, but very criminally severe and uncharitable in their treatment of Job.

Our Author has judiciously selected a variety of circumstances, in order to determine the age in which Job lived; and as, on the one hand, he vigorously opposes the notion of Dr. Warburton, that Ezra was the writer of the history; so he contends, on the other hand, that the Book of Job could not be the oldest book in the world. 'Perhaps,' says he, 'it may be the most ancient Arabian regular history; and also the oldest poetical one, wearing the dramatic form; but I think, in any other view, it is not to be so accounted.' Upon the whole, he appears to have shewn, with the greatest degree of probability, that Job lived a considerable time later than Abraham. Indeed, if the opinion be right, that Eliphaz, Job's friend, was the eldest son of Esau, it follows that Job, who seems to have been a much younger man than Eliphaz, must have been co-temporary with the children and grandchildren of Jacob.

Toward the conclusion of this performance, a conjecture is offered, why the three daughters of Job are mentioned by name in the last chapter, and not his seven sons; and several reasons are alledged to prove, that Jobab, a great-grandson of Esau, was not, as some have maintained, the same person with Job.

The design of the appendix is to shew, that the words, "*With the Ancient is wisdom, and in Length of Days understanding,*" relate to God, and not to man.

After a careful review of the present publication, we are clearly of opinion, that the Author hath collected together, with no little sagacity and judgment, a multitude of arguments, which very sufficiently confirm his grand proposition, 'That the history of Job is true.'

MONTHLY

MONTHLY CATALOGUE, For JULY, 1771.

MEDICAL.

Art. 11. *Impartial Remarks on the Suttonian Method of Inoculation.* Interspersed with Cases, Observations, and Remarks, on both the natural and artificial Small-Pox. In a Letter to Dr. Glass. By Nicholas May, junior, Surgeon at Plymouth. 8vo. 2 s. 6 d. Tilley, Wheble, &c.

THIS is a bulky pamphlet which contains nothing new on the subjects in question.—The Author endeavours to prove the following propositions, viz. that the Suttons do not possess any particular *nostrum*, which renders their practice more successful:—but that their success arises from the *small quantity* of matter which is used in the operation.

The truth of the first of these propositions is now pretty generally acknowledged; but the truth of the second is by no means ascertained; and the following history, which is related by our Author, is a strong argument that this is not the case:

'A middle-aged lady, of considerable fortune and distinction, in this neighbourhood, was inoculated by Mr. Sutton, who resided entirely at her house during the necessary period, in order the better to conduct the whole of the process, so highly consequential to his credit, and the safety of his patient.—Every injunction, respecting medicine, diet, air, &c. was most strictly complied with; and, as usual, at the expected time a small number of pustules made their appearance, which were pronounced by Mr. Sutton to be genuine, and to contain a sufficient quantity of matter, so as to prevent any future ill consequence, often *supposed* to exist in default of a larger crop. Some few days (I am informed about four) after the eruption had been completed, the lady was prevailed on to drink a little wine, and also to make use of a little high-seasoned or rich sauce, in order to raise her spirits, much dejected with fears lest so inconsiderable a number of eruptions might not sufficiently secure her from a future attack of a distemper she had ever much dreaded. Much about this time Dr. Colwell, an eminent physician of this town, after visiting a patient in that neighbourhood, paid the lady a friendly visit, to inquire after her health, and congratulate her, on her present happy state and approaching recovery. The Doctor assured her that the pustules looked very kindly, and gave her every possible encouragement. But, notwithstanding all the counter-persuasions of both the Doctor and her operator, she grew more and more dejected; nay, at length, almost despondent; intimating that she found herself much out of order, and believed that she should never get the better of it. From constant exclamations like these, Mr. Sutton became very uneasy and alarmed, and truly not without reason: for it must be confessed that his situation was very distressing. It was now thought necessary, for the satisfaction of all parties, to call in further assistance.

'Late in the evening of the second day from Dr. Colwell's last visit, Mr. Sutton's servant came to town to the Doctor's house, in great haste, and desired the Doctor to go with him to visit the lady with the utmost expedition.—The Doctor found her much indisposed, with the appearance of a pretty plentiful eruption, when, at their unanimous request, she became intirely his patient. Dr. Colwell says, the pustules in her face only, being numbered, were found to be about *three hundred*, and throughout the rest of the body they were as numerous as could well be, to allow them *distinct*; and that they were more like the effects of an infection taken in the natural way, than those of inoculation.—She got very well through the disease.—But though a much larger quantity of matter was now determined from the centre to the circumference, by means of a much more considerable number of pustules than usually attend this operator's method; and though incrustation and exsiccation were both kindly and regular; yet, after all, considerable abscesses, produced by the matter still floating with the humours, were nevertheless consequent, and required the assistance of chirurgical treatment.'

Art. 12. *Observationes Huxhamii, &c.* i. e. Huxham's Observations on the Air and epidemic Diseases, from the Year 1749 to the End of the Year 1752. Vol. III. Published from his Father's Manuscript, by J. Cor. Huxham, A. M. R. S. S. &c. 8vo. 2s. sewed. Hinton.

There can be no doubt with respect to these being the genuine observations of Dr. Huxham.—Had the Doctor however intended them for the public, he would probably have completed another ten years †, and have published them during his life.—The truth appears to be this,—the Doctor found that a third volume would be little more than a repetition of what had been already given in the two preceding volumes.

Art. 13. *Elements of Therapeutics.* By Andrew Duncan, M. D. Of the Royal College of Physicians at Edinburgh. 8vo. 4 s. Edinburgh printed, and sold in London by Richardson and Co. 1770.

These elements are divided into two parts; the first treats of Therapeutics in general: the second of the particular classes of medicines.

The first of these parts was read in one lecture, and is here published as then delivered:—the Author's intention is, to investigate that plan upon which the prosecution of this subject may be conducted with the greatest advantage. Here Dr. Duncan appears to possess considerable abilities, and to have taken great pains with his subject, but his manner of expressing himself is sometimes perplexed, and will, we apprehend, for the most part, prove rather irksome to such of his readers as have a taste for good writing.

The second part treats of particular classes, and is intended as a text to the succeeding lectures. Here our Author acquits himself much more agreeably, and has drawn up a clear, useful, and comprehensive syllabus.——The following is a list of the classes.——

† Each of the former volumes contains a series of observations for ten years.

1. Emetics.

1. Emetics. 2. Cathartics. 3. Diaphoretics. 4. Epispastics. 5. Diuretics. 6. Expectorants. 7. Errhines. 8. Sialagogues. 9. Blood-letting. 10. Emmenagogues. 11. Anthelmintics. 12. Lithontriptics. 13. Antacids. 14. Antalkalins. 15. Attenuants. 16. Inspissants. 17. Antiseptics. 18. Astringents. 19. Emollients. 20. Corrosives. 21. Demulcents. 22. Stimulants. 23. Sedatives. 24. Antispasmodics.

NOVELS.

Art. 14. *The Palinode:* or, The Triumphs of Virtue over Love. A sentimental Novel. In which are painted to the Life the Characters and Manners of some of the most celebrated Beauties in England. By M. Treyssac De Vergy. 12mo. 2 Vols. 5 s. sewed. Woodfall and Evans.

This novel is by much the most decent and unexceptionable that has fallen from the pen of Monf. De Vergy. If it were not for one or two passages which are rather too voluptuous, we could almost venture to recommend it to our fair countrywomen. The scenes between Rambler and Mrs. Guery have singular delicacy, and discover, that the Author is no mean proficient in the study of the female mind.

Art. 15. *The generous Husband*; or, The History of Lord Lelius and the fair Emilia. Containing likewise the genuine Memoirs of Asmodei. the pretended Piedmontese Count, from the Time of his Birth, to his late ignominious Fall in Hyde-park. 12mo. 2 s. 6 d. Wheble. 1771.

This wretched production has no kind of merit to plead in its favour. It talks of love, but with an insipidity and languor that render it, in the highest degree, disgusting.

Art. 16. *Letters to Eleonora.* 12mo. 2 Vols. 5 s. sewed. Becket.

These Letters attempt to express the natural sentiments of love, and to exhibit a lively and genuine portrait of that passion. They speak not, however, to the heart. Their Author has preposterously ventured to impress his Reader with sensations and emotions which he himself did not feel.

Art. 17. *Jessy*; or, The Bridal-day. Written by a Lady, after the Manner of the late Mr. Richardson, (Author of Clarissa, &c.) but *not revised* by that celebrated Writer. 12mo. 2 Vols. 4 s. sewed. Noble. 1771.

Circumstances of distress are here collected for the purpose of moving the passions; but they appear with so little choice or propriety, that they produce a very contrary effect. To imitate, with any degree of success, the manner of Richardson, it is necessary to possess some proportion of his genius.

Art. 18. *The Marriage*: or, History of four well-known Characters. Translated from the celebrated French Novel of the same Title. By Thomas Marten, A. M. 12mo. 2 Vols. 5 s. sewed. Wheble. 1771.

The progress of love in an unexperienced mind, with the caprices of that passion, are described in this performance, with more exactness than delicacy. It does not seem to us that the original merited a translation.

Art.

Art. 19. *Miss Melmoth*; or, The New Clarissa. 12mo. 3 Vols. 9s. Lowndes. 1771.

The good-natured and benevolent Reader will receive more pleasure from the perusal of this work, than the critic. The former, whose *heart* must been *rent* by the cruel fate of the first Clarissa, will be delighted with the better fortune of her amiable name-sake; while the latter will be less benignly employed in marking the inferiority of the new production, which, like other imitations, is certainly inferior to the original.

The New Clarissa, however, is a performance of considerable merit; and might, had the old one never been written, have possessed a greater share of the public favour than it is now likely to obtain, under the unfortunate circumstance of *comparison*.

Art. 20. *The unguarded Moment*. 12mo. 2 Vols. 5s. sewed. Almon. 1771.

This publication, unexceptionable in its moral, is not so with regard to execution. It can boast of no elegance of expression; and the incidents it describes are often extravagant and improbable.

Art. 21. *The Noble Family*. In a Series of Letters. By Mrs. Austin. 12mo. 3 Vols. 9s. Pearch. 1771.

This novel is replete with business and incident; but it wants nature and probability; and its Author is little acquainted with the art of composition.

THEATRICAL.

Art. 22. *The Man of Family*: a Sentimental Comedy. By the Author of the Placid Man, and Letters from Altamont in the Capital to his Friends in the Country. 8vo. 1s. 6d. Cadell. 1771.

An imitation of the *Pere de Famille* of Diderot, and designed for the closet. Its Author imagines, *that it not only will bear a near inspection, but, like a good picture, will improve upon a closer examination*. We are however of a very different opinion. The Reader, whom it entertains, must, we apprehend, be destitute of taste, and little acquainted with real life. It displays no vivacity of dialogue, and its characters are neither marked with precision, nor sustained with propriety. It substitutes dulness for delicacy, and trite maxims of morality for exalted sentiments. The talents of its Author are better calculated for composing a sermon than a comedy.

RELIGIOUS and CONTROVERSIAL.

Art. 23. *A Letter to a modern Defender of Christianity*. To which is added, A Tract on the Ground and Nature of Christian Redemption. 12mo. 1s. Nicoll. 1771.

Although the Writer of this Letter is a follower of William Law and of Jacob Behmen, we do not find many of those unaccountable and inexplicable phrases and expressions with which some productions of this kind have abounded. An advertisement at the beginning observes, that 'It is needless to say any thing of the original composition of the following letter, or of the person to whom it was several years ago addressed. It has been since considerably altered; and with an application as strictly just as the first, is published in this new form, not as an occasion of controversy, but for the sake of those who desire

desire to be delivered from the mazes of human opinion, and restored to the simplicity and purity of their first created life.'

We are not particularly informed, either in the advertisement, or in the Letter itself, for what person it is immediately intended, but the very first paragraph, we suppose, is thought to afford a sufficient criterion for pointing him out to the Reader: 'Whilst I was lately reading,' it is said, 'your idolized productions, The old great Work without Beginning, Middle, or End, and The new little one that ends in nothing, I could not suppress the wonder which almost every page excited, that one of our common nature should live till your time of day, and entertain of himself and his writings an opinion so different from the rest of mankind, and so repugnant to every principle of truth and piety.' A note which we meet with in the farther part of the book expresly mentions the present bishop of Gloucester, and his *doctrine of grace*. Several of the reflections here delivered, however just they may be, appear to be more severe and sarcastical than is perfectly consistent with that humility and meekness which writers of this stamp plead greatly for. In one part of this work we observe, that the author whom it attacks is placed in the rank with Tindal; and Wollaston also is brought in as one of the party: after which our Correspondent proceeds as follows: 'Now, if you have a mind to know how it comes to pass, that such defenders of religion as yourself, such oppugners as Tindal, and such blunderers as Wollaston, have in one sense never done Christianity good or harm, I will tell you, you have all set out upon a wrong foundation, &c.'

Whatever truth there may be in *some* of this Author's observations, it is most certainly unpardonable in him to join the term *blunderer* with the respectable name of *Wollaston*, and might persuade his readers to pay no farther attention to his work. There is a degree of acuteness and good sense in his observations, but his expressions are sometimes mean, and a mixture of *mysticism* or of *Quakerism* runs throughout the whole Letter: possibly, if his meaning was fully explained, it might appear that he intends nothing more, as to his views of religion, than is intended by every serious and well-disposed mind. We find some strange remarks in one place upon the scriptures, or the *written word*, for the writing of which he tells us, our Saviour gave no orders: he allows that the apostles intended the glory of God and the good of mankind, by their narratives, 'but how,' says he, 'that glory and good have been hitherto served, let the present scene of things, and the annals of former ages declare; how they may be served, seems not as yet to have appeared.' He seems to think that it had been as happy, nay happier, for the world, if these scriptures had not been published, for 'God would not,' he concludes, 'have left himself without witness,—there might then have been,' he adds, 'apostles, evangelists, teachers of God's own sending, in *the Spirit*, as well as *the name* of Christ, whilst a pretence to free enquiry could never have sprung up. But, alas! as soon as mankind unhappily got hold of a book to call the gospel, giving out, that in it was some rule of faith, and in it was contained all things necessary to salvation;—then did they (with respect to themselves) forestall the goodness of God, putting Antichrist in the place of his Son;—then was the mantle of Christ put upon the rudiments of this world;

world;—mankind explaining his words,—and losing by that means *the spirit* and *power* thereof.' Surely we may say, upon this, how near do enthusiasm and fanaticism approach to popery and infidelity!

Art. 24. *Three Sermons preached on particular Occasions*: viz. The first on the 29th of November 1759, being the Day appointed for a general Thanksgiving for the Conquest of Quebec, &c. The second at a Visitation, held the 20th of April 1761. The third against *with-holding of Bread-corn*, on the 17th of August 1766. By John Sampson, M. A. Rector of Croscombe in Somersetshire, and late Fellow of Merton College. 8vo. 1 s. 6 d. Wilkie. 1771.

Few discourses of this kind are utterly destitute of something good and useful; those now before us appear to be on the whole ingenious and sensible, though sometimes superficial, and rather inconclusive in respect to the inferences which are drawn from some parts of the subjects. One particular we could not avoid remarking, as singular in a *Protestant* minister, though it should be thought to discover a benevolent mind. It is in the sermon on the conquest of Quebec, where he recommends it to his auditors 'to implore Almighty God—that he would receive those into his mercy, who were (says he) slain in this just and necessary war.'

Art. 25. *Reflections upon the Study of Divinity*. To which are subjoined, Heads of a Course of Lectures. By Edward Bentham, D. D. King's Professor of Divinity, and Canon of Christ-church, Oxford. 8vo. 1 s. 6 d. White, &c. 1771.

It hath been a frequent complaint, with regard to the famous and learned universities of Oxford and Cambridge, that the public professorships have been too much converted into sinecures, and that there is a deficiency of public lectures. A disposition to remove this complaint seems to have prevailed of late years, and perhaps we are, in some measure, indebted for it to the admirable effects which have been produced by the Vinerian institution. Archbishop Secker, who had a great concern for the honour and good conduct of the clergy, was solicitous that divinity might be taught to better advantage than had usually been done; and, for this purpose, he engaged Dr. Bentham to accept the office of King's professor of that science, in Oxford. The doctor has here presented the heads of his course of lectures to the public, together with a number of observations on the study of divinity, and the method to be pursued by a tutor in communicating its principles, and by a student in gaining an acquaintance with it. The reflections are, most of them, judicious, and shew the Author's close attention to every branch of theology. The plan is very extensive, and, if well-filled up, would make a more compleat body of divinity than has yet appeared. It cannot be doubted but that the students who are formed upon this scheme must be qualified for becoming useful ministers in their respective parishes. They will have a greater stock of knowledge than is commonly met with, and will possess a degree of rationality and moderation far superior to what we see in the methodistical part of the clergy. At the same time, this course of lectures does not seem calculated to produce

duce perſons who will be animated with the daring zeal of a Blackbourne, or riſe even to the gentle and charming liberality of a Jortin. Without indulging to a ſpirit of innovation and novelty, Dr. Bentham's pupils will probably continue in a peaceful ſubjection to eſtabliſhed doctrines and conſtitutions; and ſuch, we apprehend, are the very kind of clergymen that would be moſt agreeable to the temper and views of the late archbiſhop Secker.

Art. 26. *Free Thoughts upon a Free Enquiry into the Authenticity of the firſt and ſecond Chapters of St. Matthew's Goſpel.* Addreſſed to the anonymous Author. With a ſhort prefatory Defence of the Purity and Integrity of the New-Teſtament Canon. By Theophilus. 8vo. 1 s. Wilkie.

This is the production, not only of a ſenſible Writer, but of one who entertains the moſt enlarged views with regard to the doctrines of the New Teſtament. We cannot, therefore, but think that he is more diſconcerted at the Free Enquiry than might be expected from a perſon of ſo liberal a turn of ſentiment. The cauſe of truth will bear the ſtricteſt ſcrutiny; and could it even be proved, that the two firſt chapters of St. Matthew are ſpurious, the purity and integrity of the goſpel canon would ſtill be maintained, according to the very idea of the ſubject laid down by Theophilus himſelf, viz. ' That no one truth in the New-Teſtament code, on which the principle, ſpirit, and power of that revelation ſuſtains its divine authority, can be ſuppoſed to come within the power of man to change or alter; or, in other words, that there is no one ſanctifying, ſaving truth, which can be taken from, or changed in that volume.' We do not make theſe remarks as concurring in opinion with the Author of the Free Enquiry. On the contrary, we think it highly probable that the firſt and ſecond chapters of St. Matthew are authentic, and that his hiſtory was originally written in the Greek language.

As to the thoughts here offered by Theophilus, many of them are judicious and important, and tend, in no inconſiderable degree, to remove ſeveral of the difficulties ſtarted in the work to which the pamphlet before us is an anſwer.

Of the *Free Enquiry*, which has given birth to theſe *Free Thoughts*, our Readers will find an account in the Review for April.

Art. 27. *The Authenticity of the firſt and ſecond Chapters of St. Matthew's Goſpel vindicated.* In Anſwer to a Treatiſe, intitled, ' A Free Enquiry into the Authenticity,' &c. 8vo. 6 d. Wilkie.

This little piece, which is written with remarkable candour, comes directly to the point in debate. In our account of the Free Enquiry, we obſerved, that the Author of it had been more ſucceſsful in ſtating the internal than the external evidence relative to his ſubject. The truth of this remark is abundantly manifeſt in the preſent performance; the Writer of which hath brought ſeveral conſiderable arguments to ſupport the authenticity of the two firſt chapters of St. Matthew. He has rendered it almoſt certain that the Ebionite goſpel was only a tranſlation from the Greek, and has ſhewn, that the Free Enquirer is miſtaken in ſome of his authorities. In ſhort, that gentleman will find this tract to be worthy of his very ſerious attention.

MISCEL-

MISCELLANEOUS.

Art. 28. *De Vita et Moribus Johannis Burtoni*, S. T. P. *Etonensis. Epistola Edwardi Bentham*, S. T. P. R. *ad Reverendum admodum Robertum Lowth*, S. T. P. *Episcopum Oxeniensem*, 8vo. 6 d. White, &c. 1771.

The general character of the late Dr. Burton cannot have been unknown to our learned Readers, and we have several times had occasion to mention his writings in the course of our Review. A more particularly account of him may, however, be acceptable to many persons; and such an account is now presented to the public by Dr. Bentham, partly from private affection and gratitude, and partly with a view of exhibiting to the clergy an useful and laudable example.

From the narrative here given it appears, that Dr. Burton was long an eminent tutor at Oxford, that he always retained a peculiar fondness for academical exercises, and was a great friend to improvements in the discipline of the university. It is much to his honour that he introduced Locke, and other modern philosophers, into the schools. In a number of respects beside, his life and conduct were deserving of notice and applause;—but, for particulars, we must refer to the tract itself, which cannot fail of being entertaining to such as love to be acquainted with the peaceful employments of men who have been devoted to literary studies.

Art. 29. *Oratio Harveii Instituto habita in Theatro Collegii Regalis Medicorum Londinensis, festo Sancti Lucæ, Oct.* 18. 1770. 4to. 1 s. Johnston.

A flowery declamation, in which we are told, what we have been often told before by the learned college, viz. that Linacre was the Mæcenas of the age in which he lived. The orator is Dr. Relhan.

Art. 30. *Animadversions upon Elements of Criticism:* calculated equally for the Benefit of that celebrated Work, and the Improvement of English Stile. With an Appendix on Scotticism. By James Elphinston. 8vo. 2 s. 6 d. sewed. Owen. 1771.

The Author of this publication does not seem to be unacquainted with the principles of the English language; and his animadversions may answer, in some measure, the ends he proposed by them. We must observe, however, that he appears to us to have conceived too high an opinion of the work he has criticised, which, with regard to composition, in particular, is extremely defective: it no where attains to the praise of elegance; and it every where abounds with grammatical inaccuracies, and colloquial impurities.

Art. 31. *The elementary Principles of Tactics*; with new Observations on the military Art. Written originally in French by Sieur B——, Knight of the military Order of St. Lewis, and translated by an Officer of the British Army. 8vo. 6 s. Hooper. 1771.

This appears to be the work of an ingenious and intelligent officer. It traces to their source many errors in the present system of tactics in Europe: and suggests a method by which they may be remedied. The remarks, which it offers on the military discipline and arrangements of the Greeks and Romans, have particular merit.

Art.

Art. 32. *A new and accurate Description of all the direct and cross Roads in Great Britain.* By D. Patterson, Assistant to the Quarter-master general of his Majesty's Forces. 8vo. 1 s. 6 d. sewed. Carnan. 1771.

Several improvements are here made on the former publications of this kind; the new roads, and the alterations in the old ones, being especially noticed: but we have yet seen no road-book on a plan sufficiently intelligible, and easy for common use. They are all, indeed, so intricate, that many, who may want to consult them, find it a very difficult matter to comprehend the scheme of the work, so as, on immediate inspection, to gain the information they may occasionally want. We apprehend the dictionary-form would prove more generally useful; in which every circumstance relating to each town or city might be simply comprehended in one article, without farther reference or deduction.

Art. 33. *Travels into France and Italy*, in a Series of Letters to a Lady. 12mo. 2 Vols. 5 s. sewed. Becket and De Hondt. 1771.

The disagreeable affectation of taste and *virtu*, which runs through these volumes, is too frequently characteristic of our travellers. The compliments too which the Author pays to the Lady, to whom he addresses his Letters, are too frequent, and too insipid, to be any recommendation to them. There are Readers, however, to whom, on the whole, this performance may not be unacceptable.

SERMONS.

I. *The Nature of the Christian Covenant considered.* In a Discourse on Gal. v. 5, 6. intended as a Confutation to the pestilential and novel Doctrines propagated and taught by certain itinerant Missionaries called Methodists; who are now dispersing, in the most artful Method, through this Kingdom, as the Author is advised of by his Diocesan the Bishop of Exeter. By the Rev. H. Land, A. M. late Fellow of Oriel College, Oxford, and Rector of Clare Portion in the Church of Tiverton. 8vo. 6 d. Robinson and Roberts.

II. *A Discourse upon Friendship*, before the Corporation of Liverpool. By the Rev. William Hunter, Fellow of Brazen-Nose College, Oxford, and Minister of St. Paul's, Liverpool. 8vo. 6 d. Cadell. 1771.

III. *A Sermon on the Millenium*, or Reign of Saints for a thousand Years. By Joseph Greenhill, A. M. Rector of East Horsley and East Clandon, in Surry. 4to. 6 d. Wilkie. 1771.

IV. *To* LIVE *is* CHRIST, *to* DIE *is* GAIN. On the Death of the Rev. Mr. George Whitefield, at Newbury Port. By Jonathan Parsons, A. M. Minister of the Presbyterian Church there. To which are added, An Account of his Interment, the Speech over his Grave by the Rev. Mr. Jewet; and some Verses to his Memory, by the Rev. Thomas Gibbons, D. D. Portsmouth, New Hampshire, printed. London reprinted. Buckland.

V. *The Folly, Sin, and Danger of conforming to the World.* Preached at a monthly Exercise, at the Rev. Mr. Reynolds's Meeting-place, near Cripplegate, March 21, 1771. By Samuel Stennet, D. D. 6 d. Buckland, &c.

CORRE-

CORRESPONDENCE.

From Dublin we have received the following addrefs, the civility of which deferves that attention we have endeavoured to exprefs in the review of the '*Letter to Lord Townfhend**,' which came with it, as we underftand, from the Author, who is (we dare fay) what he ftyles himfelf, a *Lover of his country.*

"Gentlemen,

"The very inconfiderable figure this country has made in the republic of letters, is, no doubt, the reafon you *never* touch at it in your literary peregrinations. –

"Juft as this reafon may be, I wifh it may not, in its confequence, prove a difcouragement to literature. The love of fame was planted in the human breaft for very wife purpofes, which you do not (I am fure) wifh to obftruct; and yet may not your inattention to this country have that operation? How many may expect to receive immortality at your hands, who could not hope for it from their fellow-citizens?

"The facts ftated in the *fmall* compofition which I fend you, are *little*, if *at all*, known in England, notwithftanding it cannot be denied, that they deferve the attention of every one that wifhes well to the intereft of the Britifh empire, but particularly of the Society for the encouragement of arts, who have fo laudably extended their encouragement to this *much-neglected* country.

"The obvious means you have of recommending defigns of this kind to public attention, is the beft apology that can be made for this communication.

"I am, (Gentlemen), your obedient fervant,

"A LOVER OF HIS COUNTRY."

We affure this worthy gentleman, that we heartily wifh our ability to recommend, effectually, defigns of the fort which is here communicated, were at all proportioned to our inclination. But, alas! "*Patriæ cecidêre manus!*"

We behold, with *filial* concern, the horrid uncultivated waftes on the bofom of our fruitful mother, England. A gentleman, whom our Correfpondent frequently praifes, has made the tour of this kingdom, and ftrenuoufly recommends the cultivation of thefe waftes. We gave our humble fuffrage for that *great* and *good* work of improvement, as we heartily give it to this which is now propofed by our Correfpondent.

And, as true friends to the cultivation of every part of the Britifh empire, we earneftly recommend to the defigners of fuch public fpirited plans, not to promife too great things. We know that the fuppofed extravagancies of Mr. Young's fcheme have hurt its reception. "*Moderata durant*" be our motto.

---

* See page 65 of this month's Review.

THE MONTHLY REVIEW,

For AUGUST, 1771.

ART. I. *The History of England, from the Accession of James I. to the Elevation of the House of Hanover.* By Catherine Macaulay. Vol. V. From the Death of Charles I. to the Restoration of Charles II. 4to. 15 s. Boards. Dilly. 1771.

THOSE of the female sex, who have been ambitious of reputation in the republic of letters, have generally distinguished themselves by their vivacity and imagination. Topics, which require investigation and labour, have been thought too serious and important to engage their attention. It has been conceived, that they are inferior in capacity to men, and that wisdom is an enemy to beauty. The narrowness, however, of understanding objected to them, is not to be ascribed to nature, but to the want of cultivation; and it must be allowed, that our fair Historian has acquitted herself with a degree of ability and merit, which has not always been attained by those who have treated of English affairs.

The great objects of her attention, in the volume before us, are the abolition of monarchy, by the commons, after the execution of Charles I.; the establishment and acts of the republic; the usurpation of Cromwell; and the state of parties and events, to the restoration.

While England continued under the republican form, it rose to a state of singular prosperity and grandeur; and the spirited Writer dwells with much triumph on this interesting period of our history.

'Never, says she, did the annals of humanity furnish the example of a government, so newly established, so formidable to foreign states as was at this period * the English commonwealth. To republics the object of envy, to monarchs of hate,

* 1651.

to both of fear, it was assiduously courted by all the powers of Europe. London was full of ambassadors to endeavour for their respective superiors to excuse former demerits, to renew former treaties, and to court stricter alliances with England. Nor did the multiplicity of foreign negociations, the conduct of war, or the attention necessary to guard their country from the attempts of its domestic foes, occasion its magnanimous parliament, actuated with the true spirit of heroic patriotism, to neglect any part of the minutiæ of interior government. Excellent laws, to preserve, in the fullest enjoyment of religious freedom, the purity of religious sentiment, to correct the morals and the manners of the people, without infringement of their political rights, to guard the poor from the miseries of undeserved poverty, to protect society in general from the impositions, fraud, and rapacity of individuals, to secure and extend the commerce of the country, were enacted; whilst subjects of reformation in the system and practice of the English law, and in every part of police, were from time to time agitated in this illustrious assembly.——

'In all the annals of recorded time, continues our Historian, never had fortune reared so tall a monument of human virtue as were the atchievements of this assembly. In the short space of twelve years, an established tyranny of more than five hundred they had entirely subdued; in the form of government built on its ruins, they had recalled the wisdom and glory of ancient times. One revolted nation they had reduced to former obedience, another they had added to the English empire. The United Provinces were humbled to a state of accepting any imposed terms; and the declared enmity of the several courts and states of Europe was turned to humble and earnest solicitations for friendship and alliance. At this full period of national glory, when both the domestic and foreign enemies of the country were dispersed and every where subdued; when England, after so long a subjection to monarchical tyranny, bad fair to outdo in the constitution of its government, and consequently in its power and strength, every circumstance of glory, wisdom, and happiness related of ancient or modern empire; when Englishmen were on the point of attaining a fuller measure of happiness than had ever been the portion of human society; the base and wicked selfishness of one trusted citizen disappointed the promised harvest of their hopes, and deprived them of that liberty, for which, at the expence of their blood and treasure, they had so long and so bravely contended.'

In her detail of the conduct and views of Cromwell, it appears to us that our Historian has entered very deeply into his character; and we cannot but agree with her in opinion, that to his fortune and success, more than to his ability, he is

4 indebted

indebted for the eulogiums with which he has been loaded by the English historians. Her review of his administration is clear and spirited, and the portrait she has drawn of him is executed with great energy of expression: and these, as they form not the least original or interesting part of the volume before us, we shall submit to the examination of our Readers.

'The hyperbolical praises, she observes, bestowed by his partizans on the unhappy Charles, have been fully refuted by several pens; but the yet-more-exalted commendations lavished on his fortunate successor Cromwell, have, from an odd concurrence of circumstances, met with little contradiction. Did facts allow us to give credit to the exaggerations of panegyrists, the power and reputation which England acquired by the magnanimous government of the republican parliament, entirely flowed from the unparalleled genius and virtue of the hero Cromwell: Cromwell imprinted throughout all Europe a terror of the English name: Cromwell was the conqueror of the Dutch: he retrieved the honour of his country in the business of Amboyna, and prescribed a peace to that insolent republic on his own terms: Cromwell was the scourge of the piratical states; the scourge of the house of Austria; every court in Europe trembled at his nod; he was the umpire of the North, the support of the reformed religion, and the friend and patron of that warlike Protestant monarch the king of Sweden. In regard to his domestic government, Cromwell was ever ready to attend to complaints and redress grievances; Cromwell administered the public affairs with frugality; filled Westminster-hall with judges of learning and integrity; observed the strictest discipline in his army; was the support of religious liberty, and a benefactor to the learned: under the administration of Cromwell every branch of trade flourished: in his court a face of religion was preserved, without the appearance of pomp, or needless magnificence: he was simple in his way of living, and easy and modest in his deportment.

'False as is this representation to the true character of the usurper, it has been adopted by that party among us who call themselves Whigs, as a mortifying contrast to the principles, administration, and conduct of the Stewart line; and the Royalists of all denominations are well pleased to give to the government of an individual a reputation, which was alone due to the republic, and to conceal from the multitude the truth of facts, which must discover to vulgar observation that eternal opposition to the general good of society which exists in the one, with the contrary spirit which so evidently shone forth in the other. Historians, either from prejudice or want of attention, have in general given into these ill-founded encomiums so prodigally

digally bestowed on the usurper; but a just narration of the transactions of those times shews, that it was under the government of the parliament the nation gained all its real advantages, and that the maritime power they had raised and supported, with the skill and bravery of the commanders they had placed over the naval force, was the sole means by which Cromwell supported the reputation of his government.

'Excepting the Dutch, whom the parliament had totally subdued, with the Danes and Portuguese, whom they had brought to a state of humiliation, the usurper found the English commonwealth at peace with all the powers of Europe, and in the sole possession of the Spanish trade, a great source of national wealth. The Spaniards, who had paid great court to the parliament, were equally warm in their professions to Cromwell, and would have entered into a close union with him on the easy terms of his remaining neuter during their contention with France. This was the plan pursued by the parliament, and the obvious interest of England; but the usurper sacrificing both the glory and the welfare of his country to the security of his own establishment, after having made a shameful peace with the Dutch, on terms lower than they had offered and the parliament had refused, he, for the sake of procuring money to support his despotism, made war with Spain without previous declaration, whilst he was amusing them with the hopes of a treaty; entered into a league offensive and defensive with the French court, on the reason of removing his rivals the Stewart family from so near a neighbourhood, and to please the English fanatics, his only fast friends, and pamper a vain-glorious appetite by the reputation of being the protector of the Protestant interest. Could he have brought the Dutch into his destructive measures, he would have assisted the Swedish monarch in acquiring a power which would have laid all Europe at the mercy of Sweden and France.

'The domestic administration of the usurper was a greater opposition to the liberty of his country, than his foreign transactions to her security and interest as a state. The models or rules of his government were of his own making; and though he changed them according to his pleasure or conveniency, he never abided by the directions of any. He ruled entirely by the sword, burthened the people with the maintenance of an army of thirty thousand men, and more grossly violated their right to legislation by their representatives than had any other tyrant who had gone before him. The power he delegated to his major-generals superseded the established laws of the country. He threatened the judges, and dismissed them from their office when they refused to become the instruments of his arbitrary will; imprisoned lawyers for pleading in a legal manner the cause of their clients; packed juries; eluded the redress of Habeas Corpus; and kept John Lilbourn in confinement after an acquittance by the verdict of a jury. In the point of religious liberty, the usurper, as it served his purposes, encouraged and oppressed all the different sectaries, not excepting the Papists; and if he was liberal to men of learning, it was with a view to make use of their talents for his own peculiar advantage. Some face of decency in his court, and continuance of that familiarity to his inferiors by which he had effected his ambitious purposes, were absolutely necessary to the preservation of his power; but so far was he from preserving, or even affecting, that simplicity of appearance particularly useful in a supreme governor, that, when only in the character of general of the army of the commonwealth, he lived in a kind of regal state at Whitehall. By his parlimentary interest, he prevented the sale of the royal palaces, with a view to possess them when he had compassed his intended usurpation; and that he never appeared in public without an ostentatious parade and pomp, and lived in high state and magnificence, is confirmed by authentic records, with the testimony of all parties. On the dissolution of the republican government, there were five hundred thousand pounds in the public treasury; the value of seven hundred thousand pounds in the magazines; the army was three or four months pay in advance, the maritime power was sufficiently strong to enable England to give law to all nations; and the trade of the country in so flourishing a condition that nine hundred thousand a year had been refused for the customs and excise. On the death of the usurper, notwithstanding the money he had arbitrarily levied on the people, the aid afforded him by a convention of his own nomination which he termed a parliament, the vast sums he had raised by decimating the cavaliers, the sums paid by the Dutch, the Portuguese, and the Duke of Tuscany, with the treasure he at different times had taken from the Spaniards, the state was left in debt, the army in arrear, and the fleet in decay! To these national evils was added the loss of a great part of the Spanish trade, with the foundation of that greatness in the French monarchy, which is to this day formidable to the liberty of England.

'Such were the fruits of a government carried *on on* the principles of public good, and of that œconomy preserved by the parliament; and such the mischief to society, when the lusts of an individual are to be supplied from the public stock, and the general good of the community sacrificed to particular interest. The aggrandizement of the French monarchy, to which Cromwell so essentially contributed, was no less fatal to

G 3 the

the intereſt of the reformed, which he affected to protect, than oppoſite to the welfare and ſecurity of England. To ſum up the villany of his conduct in a few lines——He deprived his country of a full and equal ſyſtem of liberty, at the very inſtant of fruition; ſtopped the courſe of her power, in the midſt of her victories; impeded the progreſs of reformation, by deſtroying her government and limiting the bounds of her empire; and, by a fatal concurrence of circumſtances, was enabled to obſtruct more good, and occaſion more evil, than has been the lot of any other individual.

'It is ſaid that Cromwell was exemplary in the relative duties of a ſon, a huſband, and a father; and the whole of his private conduct has been allowed by all parties to have been decent, though his mirth often degenerated into buffoonery, and the pleaſures of his table bordered on licentiouſneſs. If, as a citizen and magiſtrate, his character has been attacked by a few of the judicious, there are none who doubt the almoſt ſupernatural abilities of a man, who, from a private ſtation, could attain to the ſummit of ſplendor and power. The accidental occurrences of life, ſo frequently favourable to fools and madmen, are never taken into the account of great fortune. Fairfax, though his underſtanding is allowed by all parties to have been weak, had he poſſeſſed a heart as corrupt as Cromwell's, might have taken the advantage his military command gave him, to tyrannize over a people unſettled in their government, ignorant of their true happineſs, and divided both in their political and religious opinions. Fairfax, without abilities to be of eminent ſervice to his country, was too honeſt to do it a real injury. The ſelfiſh Cromwell let no opportunity ſlip to turn to his particular advantage the victories gained on the ſide of liberty, and eſtabliſh a perſonal intereſt on the ruins of the public cauſe. That he was active, eager, and acute; that he was a maſter in all the powers of grimace and the arts of hypocriſy, is obvious in every part of his conduct: but theſe qualities are no proof of extraordinary abilities; they are to be met with daily in common life, and never fail of ſucceſs equal to their opportunities. The ſagacity and judgment of Cromwell, in that point where his peculiar intereſt was immediately concerned, will appear very deficient, if we conſider the ſacrifice he made of thoſe durable bleſſings which muſt have attended his perſon and poſterity from acting an honeſt part, in the eſtabliſhing the commonwealth on a juſt and permanent baſis, and the obvious danger of thoſe evils he incurred for the temporary gratification of reigning a few years at the expence of honour, conſcience, and repoſe.

'Cromwell,

'Cromwell, both by the male and the female line, was descended from families of good antiquity; and though it does not appear he was a proficient in any of the learned sciences, yet his father, notwithstanding his circumstances were narrow, was not sparing in the article of education. An elevated sense of religion, which took place in his mind after a licentious and prodigal course, recommended him to the reformers of the age, and was the cause of his promotion to a seat in parliament; and the grimace of godliness, when the reality was extinguished by the fumes of ambition, with his signal military talents, at length lifted him to the throne of empire. Notwithstanding that perfection in the science of war to which he attained, he was upwards of forty when he commenced soldier; a circumstance not to be forgotten, as it is the only splendid part of his character. He usurped the government five years; died at the age of fifty-nine; married Elizabeth the daughter of Sir James Bouchier; and had issue two sons and four daughters.'

An enumeration of the causes which induced the English to bear with impatience the tyranny of the Tudor line, which made them oppose the arbitrary measures of James, which conducted them to national liberty and glory, and then disposed them to submit to monarchy, concludes the present publication.

The same political principles which our Author has inculcated in the former parts * of her work, are here warmly insisted upon, and have led her, on some occasions, to disguise facts, and to depart from that impartiality which is the chief quality of an historian. But the detestation she expresses against every mode of tyranny, and the commendation she bestows on liberty and equal laws, render her performance extremely useful, and acceptable, in a country where there is a perpetual and necessary opposition between the interest of the crown and that of the people. In her manner she is more diffuse than concise; and her style is rather forcible than elegant.

ART. II. *Reflections on the English Language, in the Nature of Vaugelas's Reflections on the French; being a Detection of many improper Expressions used in Conversation, and of many others to be found in Authors. To which is prefixed, a Discourse addressed to his Majesty.* 8vo. 2 s. sewed. Bell.

THE discourse to his Majesty contains a proposal for the establishment of an academy in London, of the same kind with the academy of *Belles Lettres* at Paris, as a means of remov-

---

* For our account of the former volumes, see Reviews for Nov. and Dec. 1763; for March 1765; for April and Sept. 1767; and for May 1769.

ing the incorrectneſſes and barbariſms with which our language, both oral and written, abounds; and recommends it to his Majeſty's conſideration, whether 'there might not be found out a much more expeditious method of teaching languages than any hitherto practiſed, and at the ſame time much leſs unpleaſant to the learner.' The Author complains, and with too much reaſon, that 'the generality of boys, who paſs five, ſix, or ſeven years at ſchool, are ſo very imperfect, even in the Latin tongue (not to ſpeak of the Greek) at their coming away, that they might almoſt as well be entirely ignorant of it. When they are grown up, they know ſtill leſs of it than at their leaving the ſchool, becauſe not underſtanding it well enough, when they come away, to comprehend a Latin author with eaſe, ſo as to read him with any *ſort of* pleaſure, they entirely neglect the language from that time, and conſequently forget ſome part even of the little they once knew. *Some few* indeed, who are fond of books, and have a good deal of leiſure, purſue the ſtudy of it after leaving the ſchool, and come to underſtand it well. But the number of theſe is very ſmall.'

The reaſon of their learning ſo little, he ſays, is that, properly ſpeaking, they are not taught, but are left, in a manner, to find out every thing themſelves. 'The grammar, ſays he, with which they begin, conſiſts of dry rules, which young boys don't well underſtand even when they have learnt them by heart: for, in ſhort, theſe rules are delivered in a conciſe and obſcure way, not well adapted to the capacity of children: and yet a conſiderable time is commonly ſpent in thus learning them by heart.—This is called *a Foundation.*

'After this, a dictionary and one of the eaſieſt Latin authors are put into their hands. By the help of this dictionary, and of the confuſed knowledge they have of the rules they have gone through, they are to render this author into Engliſh; and a few lines are given for every leſſon: in which leſſon, after *hammering* their brains about it for an hour or two, even your bright boys are commonly very imperfect; and, as to your dull ones, they have little or no conception of the meaning of the writer.

'When they have gone through a part of this book, a more difficult one is given them, with which they make almoſt as dreadful work as with the firſt: for, though by this time they know a very ſmall matter more of the language than they did, yet the ſuperior difficulty of the ſtyle is perhaps equal, or nearly equal, to that additional knowledge.

'In this manner they paſs from one author to a more difficult one, for five, ſix, ſeven years, or more, till they have gone through the moſt difficult ones of all: and then, truly, they

they are supposed to be Latin scholars. And yet their knowledge of the language, after all this time painfully spent, is superficial and confused.'

As a better method of teaching Greek and Latin, the Author proposes that the scholars should be divided into three classes, and that the lowest class should be told even the minutest things. He then explains himself by the two first lines of Virgil: 'the master, says he, first reads to the scholars these two lines:

Arma virumque cano, Trojæ qui primus ab oris
Italiam, Fato profugus, Lavinaque venit
Littora.

'Then he gives the general sense of them in English. *I sing of arms, and of the man, the first who, impelled by a decree of heaven, having left the coasts of Troy, sailed to Italy and the Lavinian shore.* He then construes them word by word. *Cano I sing of, arma arms, que and, virum the man, qui who, primus the first, profugus being driven, fato by heaven, or destiny, venit came, ab oris from the coasts, Trojæ of Troy, in Italiam to Italy (the preposition* IN *is here supposed) que and, Lavina littora the Lavinian shores.* Then he tells them what part of speech each word is, and what its office is, and declines the nouns and conjugates the verbs. *Cano is a verb active of the third conjugation. It is the first person singular of the present tense of the indicative mood. Arma is a noun substantive of the third declension and of the neuter gender. It is in the accusative case of the plural number. This word has no singular number. The nominative case is arma, the genitive armorum, the dative armis. Que is a conjunction copulative between arma and virum. Virum is a noun substantive of the second declension. It is the accusative case of the singlar number. The nominative is vir, the genitive viri, the dative viro, &c.*

'In this manner he explains every word, and then proceeds to the next sentence.'

He is convinced, he says, that boys thus instructed would learn more in one year, than they learn by the common method in four! but it must be remarked, that if the boys in his first class have not learnt grammar, he will not be understood when he tells them that *cano* is a *verb active of the first conjugation*; and that if they have, this information will in a great degree be unnecessary. The Author indeed proposes that the boys of the inferior class should get *a few* of the grammar rules every night, but says, that there is no necessity for boys to have gone through any part of their grammar *before* they begin to read authors, and that they may enter on both at once. However, whether the learning of grammar is, or is not necessary, to the learning of a language, it is certainly necessary that a boy should have

have learnt grammar whom it is intended to instruct by the technical terms of the science. A boy who is told that *cano* is a *verb active* of the *first conjugation*, will be dismissed with very little advantage to a night task in which he is, for the first time, to learn a few grammar rules; and perhaps there is no absurdity in the present method of teaching Latin and Greek more gross, than that of delivering instructions in a technical language which has not been learnt.

If our Author's method of teaching particular languages is adopted, a general knowledge of grammar, as a science common to all languages, and a familiar acquaintance with its terms and their meaning, seems to be an essential qualification for admittance into his lowest class.

In teaching the second class he thinks it will be sufficient to say, that such a word is a verb neuter of such a conjugation; that it is such a tense of such a mood, without mentioning the person or number; that such a word is a noun substantive of such a declension, and that it is in the ablative case, without going through all the preceding cases; and he proposes that to the third class the master should only construe without mentioning the parts of speech.

When the master has gone through the lesson, it is proposed that the scholars should sit down and consider it; and, after a proper time, be called out again to construe it, when they are to do every thing that the master did before.

As this is the only part of our Author's discourse to the King, which seems to deserve attention, we proceed to his reflections on the English language: he tells us in his preface, that 'he must be a *great dunce* that does not *easily attain* to the knowledge of the rules of grammar.' But if this is true, what need is there for this Author's reflections? And what right has he to suppose that any of them are *new*? They would be precluded by the knowledge of grammar, and, according to his account, this knowledge, by all but great dunces, may be easily obtained; so that whether his reflections are just or not, he may well be asked, 'Why he has given himself this trouble?' If we were of the same opinion with this Author concerning the facility of obtaining the knowledge of grammar, we should here close our account of his work; but, on the contrary, we are of opinion that the perfect and habitual knowledge of grammar is very difficult to acquire, and therefore very rarely possessed: for this reason we shall extract some of the passages which indicate faults that have been committed by good writers, and exhibit instances in which grammar has been ignorantly violated by men who have not only been distinguished for genius but learning.

As

As follow used for *as follows*.

' Some good writers (among others Addison) express themselves in this manner, *The articles were as follow.—The circumstances of the affair are as follow.—The conditions of the agreement are as follow.*

' I conceive this expression to be wrong, and that *as follows* ought to be here used, and not *as follow*. What deceives these writers is, that the preceding substantive is in the plural number. But this substantive is by no means a nominative case to *follow* or *follows*. Neither is there any intervening pronoun between this substantive and this verb, that is relative to the former, and serves as a nominative to the latter. If the verb *follow* or *follows*, have any nominative, it is the pronoun *It*, which is supposed, and is here unrelative, as in many other cases: in these, for instance; *It is very hot weather,—It is cold.*

' The sense then is, *The articles were as it here follows.—The circumstances of the affair are as it here follows.—The conditions of the agreement are as it here follows.* Consequently *follows* ought to be used, and not *follow*. Indeed, if the word *such* preceded the *as*, *follow* would be right, and not *follows*; because *such as* would be equivalent to *these which.*——

The words *ago* and *since*.

' These two words are not to be used together. *It is not above two months ago since he left the university.—It is three years ago since his father died.*—These expressions don't make sense; the word *since* being equivalent to *ago that*.

' The proper expressions are, *It is not above two months ago that he left the university.—It is not above two months since he left the university. It is three years ago that his father died.—It is three years since his father died.*——

To *set*. To *sit*.

' These two verbs are continually confounded in more than one tense, and give occasion to innumerable instances of false English. Even people of very good education misemploy them.

' The first of them, which has several different significations, does not change in any of the tenses, let the signification of the word be what it will. We say, *What time do you set out?—He set out yesterday for Bath.—I shall set somebody to watch them.*

' *Set* is likewise used with the auxiliaries. *A dog was set at me—He is now set about it in good earnest—He has set down his load—I ought to have set the trees some time ago—They being so violently set against each other, there is no probability of a reconciliation.*

' As to the verb *To sit*, its preterperfect is *sat*, which is also used with the auxiliaries. *He sat down—When we had sat there some time, we removed—Having sat with us about an hour, they left us.*

' This

'This verb is ſometimes uſed not as a neuter, but as a verb active, with an accuſative caſe following it. *I'll ſit me down—She ſat her down—They ſat themſelves down.*

'But it is to be obſerved that the verb is active, and governs an accuſative only when we ſpeak of perſons ſeating *themſelves*, and not in mentioning their cauſing *others* to ſit. Therefore ſuch expreſſions as theſe—*I'll ſit you down—He ſat her down—They ſat us down*—are not proper.

'*To ſeat* is a regular verb. *Seated*, which is the preterperfect, is uſed with the auxiliaries. *He ſeated himſelf—When we had ſeated ourſelves—She was ſeated—They being ſeated.*'

Whom.

This word is ſometimes uſed by good writers for *who*:

The king of dykes, than *whom* no ſluice of mud
With deeper ſable blots the ſilver flood.

Pope's Dunciad.

In this paſſage the laws of grammar require *who* inſtead of *whom*, for the word is in the ſame caſe with ſluice, which is a nominative.

Him, her, me, them.

'Some inferior writers ſeem to think they ſhew an extraordinary correctneſs by uſing an accuſative caſe where a verb active follows, as ſuppoſing it to be governed by that verb. For example, inſtead of *It was not he they attacked—It was not we they ſlandered*—they would ſay *It was not him they attacked—It was not us they ſlandered*—imagining *him* and *us* to be accuſatives governed reſpectively by the verbs *attacked* and *ſlandered.* But they write falſe Engliſh. Theſe pronouns ought to be in the nominative caſe, as following the verb *was*. There is indeed an accuſative (viz. *whom*, or *that*) governed by *attacked* and *ſlandered*. But this accuſative is ſuppoſed, the regular way of ſpeaking being this—*It was not he, whom* (or *that*) *they attacked—It was not we, whom* (or *that*) *they ſlandered.*'

Neither, either.

Theſe adjectives are frequently made plural when they ſhould be ſingular, as,

Are either of thoſe two men relations of your's? No, neither of them *are*. Inſtead of, *Is* either of thoſe two men relations of your's? No, neither of them *is*.

'We find in many authors (and, among others, in Swift) the expreſſion of *The manner of it is thus.*

'The word *thus* ſignifies *in this manner*. It ſhould ſeem therefore as though *The manner of it is thus* were as much as to ſay *The manner of it is in this manner*; which is nonſenſe.

'It is better to ſay *The manner of it is this.*'

Swift

Swift says 'the rents of land in Ireland may be computed *to* two millions;' but he should have said computed *at*.

He also, and many others on his authority, use the word *both* improperly. He says, 'The goddess Minerva had heard of one Arachne, a young virgin very famous for spinning and weaving. They *both* met upon a trial of skill.'

The word *both* is not only superfluous here but absurd. It might be imagined that the author thought Minerva could meet Arachne, without Arachne's meeting Minerva.

It is equally absurd to say that A. and B. are *both* equal in capacity.

Mussulman is not compounded of *Mussul* and *man*, any more than German is compounded of Ger and man, or Ottoman of Otto and man, it is therefore as absurd to make Mussulman plural by writing it Mussulmen, as German and Ottoman plural by writing them Ottomen and Germen.

The words *the reason of*, and the word *because*, should never be used in the same sentence, as in the following: '*the reason of* my desiring to see you was *because*, &c.'

Adjectives are often used adverbially, as the word antecedent in the following note on Cicero's letters:

'This is evident from a letter to Atticus, written about four years *antecedent* to the fact of which I am speaking.' *Antecedent* thus joined to *written* is used adverbially; but *antecedent* is not an adverb.

A preposition is often omitted, as in the following: 'His compliance can by no means be considered in the favourable light which he here represents it.' To make this passage grammar, the word *in* should be repeated after *light*.

Only. Not only. Neither. Either.

'There are innumerable instances of the wrong placing these words.

'*Only*, by not being in its proper place, gives a sense not intended. *Not only*, *neither* and *either*, by being out of their places, make nonsense.

'*Theism*, says my Lord Shaftesbury, *can only be opposed to polytheism* or *atheism*.

'He ought to have said *Theism can be opposed only to polytheism or atheism*: for his meaning is, that polytheism and atheism are the only things to which theism can be opposed. But his words don't imply this: for *theism can only be opposed to polytheism or atheism* signifies that theism is not capable of any thing, except of being opposed to polytheism or atheism; which is a quite different sense. Besides, it makes a false assertion: for, though it may be true that polytheism and atheism are the only species of belief to which theism can stand in opposition, yet there

there are many other things of which theiſm is capable. It is capable of influencing a man's conduct. It is capable of gaining him the good will of another in the ſame, or of exciting the averſion of thoſe in a different way of thinking. In ſhort, there is no ſaying of how many things it is capable.

'*He was not only an eye-witneſs of thoſe affairs, but had a great ſhare in them.* Biographical Dictionary.

'*He was neither learned in the languages, nor philoſophy.* Ibid.

'The proper way of ſpeaking is, *He not only was an eye-witneſs of thoſe affairs, but had a great ſhare in them.* The *not only* ought to precede the *was*, not to follow it.—*He was learned neither in the languages nor in philoſophy. Learned* ought to precede *neither*.

'When we ſay, *He was not only an eye-witneſs of thoſe affairs, but had a great ſhare in them*, the ſenſe of the word *was*, by this word's being put before the *not only*, is brought forward to the *but had a great ſhare in them.* It is therefore the ſame as if we ſaid, *He was not only an eye-witneſs of thoſe affairs, but alſo he was had a great ſhare in them*; which is nonſenſe.

'So likewiſe in the other ſentence, *He was neither learned in the languages, nor philoſophy*; by putting *neither* before *learned*, the word *philoſophy*, which ought to be oppoſed only to *the languages*, becomes oppoſed to *learned in the languages*; whereby we ſay, *He neither was learned in the languages, nor was he philoſophy*; which alſo is nonſenſe.'

Lord Bolingbroke ſays, '*They ſpeak not only of the law, but refer to many of the facts related in the Pentateuch.* By putting *ſpeak* before *not only*, he has brought forward the ſenſe of this word, *ſpeak*, to the latter part of the ſentence, and made nonſenſe, for it is as though he ſaid, *They ſpeak not only of the law. They likewiſe ſpeak refer to many of the facts related in the Pentateuch.*

'If a man ſays *I ſpeak not only of him, but of all his companions*, here the word *ſpeak* is rightly placed before the *not only*, becauſe the *all his companions* ſtands oppoſed to the *him*; for which reaſon the ſenſe of the word, *ſpeak*, ought to be brought forward to the latter part of the ſentence, the meaning of the ſpeaker being this, *I ſpeak not of him only. I likewiſe ſpeak of all his companions.*'

Other obſervations occur in this little book which are worthy of notice; many no doubt will deſpiſe them, but among theſe there will be found not a few who have committed, and are continually committing, the faults they were intended to prevent. The Author himſelf has by no means given an example of the correctneſs and propriety which he recommends to others, as we ſhall prove by a few quotations from his work.

In his diſcourſe to the King, he ſays, 'My firſt propoſal is that you would take *it* into conſideration, whether *it* might not be be proper to establish an academy.' The first of these *its* is superfluous, and both inelegant. He should have written, ' take into consideration the propriety of establishing.'

He uses the phrases *as I take it*, and *I look upon it*, to express his opinion; and *pitching upon*, to express his choice. He speaks of reading a Latin author with any *sort* of pleasure, and thus confounds *kind* with *degree*. He uses the expression, ' *hammering their brains*,' to express perplexed and difficult application. He uses the barbarous phrase *some few*, and the word *hold* for *continue*; he says ' a teacher should shew a learner every, even the minutest circumstance, *without any more to do*;' he hopes that a school may be established upon a *something-like* principle with *what* he has here *gone upon*. He frequently uses the word *whatsoever*, when it is a mere expletive, and not only useless but inelegant. ' The prints, says he, may be sold to any painter or sculptor *whatsoever*:' he uses absolute terms relatively, ' however difficult or *impossible*, says he, it might be.' The impropriety of using the word *impossible* with *however* in this sentence is the more gross, as the word difficult fixes it to its absolute meaning. In another place he says Wilks is a man of *most infinite* vanity. He sometimes leaves words that should be expressed, to be understood, as in the following sentence: ' 'Tis an egregious mistake many pretended judges of painting *lie under*, that copies are always known for such:' the word *which* is wanting between *mistake* and *many*: *'tis*, is also a barbarous contraction of *it is*; and the phrase *lie under*, is ' a vile phrase:' so is, *gave him to understand*, instead of, informed him. Though he supposes that the *s*, which is sometimes used at the end of our genitives, instead of the word *of* before them, is a contraction of *his*, he uses both *of* and the *s*: ' those portraits, says he, pass for originals *of* Vandyke'*s*:' but he should have written either Vandyke's originals, without the *of*; or originals of Vandyke, without the *s*. After a long period he repeats the words that began it with an *I say*, which is making one inelegance necessary by another. He uses the word *as* with *also*. ' Whether my taste, says he, be so good as is requisite for what I have undertaken, *as also* whether I am sufficiently acquainted with the idioms of the tongue, must be left to be decided by the work itself:' instead of *as also*, he should have written *and*, or *as well as*. He uses *when* and *where* improperly in the following and other instances: ' It will undoubtedly be thought strange *when* I declare'—' a circulating library *where* I subscribe.' It is the *declaration* that will be thought strange, but this sense is not grammatically expressed by the words *it* will be thought strange *when*: if this Author's employment had been the subscribing papers of any kind, and he had opened an office at the circulating library, he might with

with propriety have diftinguifhed that library by calling it 'the library *where* I fubfcribe;' but as that is not the cafe, he fhould have written *to which* inftead of *where*.

We hope that in thefe ftrictures we have concurred in his general defign of reforming the language, and therefore that he will confider this article as a neceffary appendix to his book.

Art. III. *The Hermit of Warkworth; a Northumberland Ballad; in three Fits, or Cantos.* 4to. 2s. 6d. Davies, &c. 1771.

WE have obferved that *fimplicity*, though naked, is not poor: we may add, her nakednefs is that of a grace, not that of a beggar. Her motion, her air, her attitude, muft breathe of genuine nature, but of nature in her faireft form. Whatever improvements nature can acquire, they are ftill a part of herfelf, becaufe fhe only could purfue or point them out. What fhe gains, fhe gains not at the expence of her original characteriftic of fimplicity. It attends her polifhed as well as her uncultivated ftate. She grows more fair, more animated, more interefting; but it is not thus that her fimplicity is loft. It derives an advantage from her cultivation, which at the fame time it returns; as light and fhade reciprocally fet off each other.

The truth of thefe obfervations is apparent in the progrefs of the fine arts. Rude, though fimple in their early ftate, *Mufic* confifted of meafures without paffion; *Painting*, of figures without expreffion or animation; and *Poetry*, of numbers without melody or elegance: we fhall at prefent confine ourfelves to the confideration of the latter.

For fome time there has prevailed among us a fafhionable but falfe tafte of imitating the vernacular fimplicity of the old ballad-poets. As if poetry had, contrary to its fate in other nations, with us arrived at perfection almoft as foon as it was born, the rude efforts of our anceftors are now to be confidered as beauties and patterns of compofition. This is partly owing to an uninformed love of fimplicity, which miftakenly follows it in its rude inftead of its improved principles; and partly to an enthufiaftic fondnefs and veneration for antiquity. Truth and tafte united have no chance in the conteft with enthufiafm. Whatever its objects may be, whether the peculiarities of antiquity, or any other, ftill they are beauties which it beholds through one flattering medium. What fhould we think of the tafte of thofe who would affert that the original *Nut brown Maid* is fuperior in point of compofition to that of Prior? Yet fuch there are, mifled by the love of antiquity, or miftaken in the idea of fimplicity.

What

What but ſuch principles could have led the learned Author of this performance into the dull meaſure, and ſometimes too (ſorry we are ſo to ſay) into the duller language of Sternhold? —To trim ſuch bays!—To contend for ſuch honours!—How unworthy the ambition!

It is true the Hermit of Warkworth contains many good lines, many ſtanzas that may be read with ſatisfaction, and here and there a poetical, though rarely an original, image. But what ſhall we ſay of ſuch verſes as the following?

And, oh! to ſave him from his foes
  It was his grandſire's care.

* *

Nor long before the brave old earl
  At Bramham loſt his life.

* *

Cheer up, my ſon, thou ſhalt her ſee,
  As ſoon as thou canſt ride.

* *

Sir Bertram from his ſick-bed roſe,
  His bride he would go ſee.

* *

And he would tend him on the way,
  Becauſe his wounds were green.

Theſe lines will ſufficiently ſhew with what juſtice we condemn that ſtyle of writing which leads even men of genius into ſuch vulgarities of expreſſion. It is certain that no ſerious poetry will bear them. What then can be ſaid for their admiſſion into pathetic compoſitions? Nature is never more beautiful than in her mournful attire. Her dreſs is eaſy and ſimple, never coarſe or vulgar. Elegant in diſtreſs, like Cleopatra when ſhe received Auguſtus, ſhe inſpires at the ſame time affection and compaſſion.

To be weak, or to be low, is frequently the fate of this ballad poetry. Of the former we have an inſtance in the following lines, particularly the laſt:

This way and that he drives the ſteel,
  And keenly pierces through.

The latter will be felt when we read,

Now cloſing faſt on every ſide,
  They hem Sir Bertram round.

The former, when

Lord Percy mark'd their gallant mien,
  And thus his friend addreſſ'd.

In the following stanza, both:

It chanc'd that on that very morn
Their chief was prisoner ta'en;
Lord Percy *bad us soon exchang'd*,
And strove to soothe my pain.

Though the Author of this poem has in general *succeeded* in imitating the ancient ballad-style, and bestowed much more labour upon it than it deserved, he has sometimes made a sort of medley of it by falling into the modern metaphor and mode of expression. Thus,

They rais'd my heart to *that pure source*
Whence heavenly *comfort flows*.

And again,

No more the slave of human pride,
Vain hope, and sordid care.
* *
To spend the tranquil hour
* *
This sweet, sequester'd vale I chose.

This, indeed, it must have been difficult to avoid; and when a good expression occurred to the poet, he must, with reason, have thought it hard to substitute a worse, even whilst he might think it expedient to write with a more antiquated air.

We do not give ourselves the consequence to expect that the Author should alter what we here call faults, in his future editions; or that he should hereafter abandon a species of poetry, the *revival* of which we cannot but condemn. We give this public criticism in support of public taste, indifferent as to the reception it may meet with from the person whom it most concerns. In the following stanzas, however, there is a fault, which the Author, we presume, will think it proper to correct, if not for our sakes, at least for his own:

Nor far from hence, where yon full stream
Runs winding down the lea,
Fair Warkworth *lifts her lofty towers*,
And overlooks the sea.

Those towers, alas! *now lie forlorn*,
With noisome weeds o'erspread,
Where feasted lords and courtly dames,
And where the poor were fed.

Beside the obvious blunder marked in italics, the two last lines breathe strongly of the bathos.

Having pointed out what, in the perusal of this poem, we thought most exceptionable, it is necessary we should do the Author the justice to give some connected passage, in which he may

may ſpeak for himſelf. For this purpoſe we ſhall ſelect the moſt intereſting part, the concluſion of the hermit's tale.

This hermit, who relates his ſtory to a noble pair, whom accident had brought to his cell, was originally Sir Bertram, a knight of great renown. By his perſonal merit and valour he had won the heart of a fair lady. After he had proved the helmet ſhe had preſented to him, with great honour to himſelf, in a bloody battle with the Scots, and recovered from the wounds he had received, *as ſoon as he could ride*, he ſet out accompanied by his brother, to wait upon her, but found that ſhe had, ſometime before, left her father's caſtle, with an intent to viſit him. Suſpecting that ſhe had been carried off by the Scots, Sir Bertram and his brother go in queſt of her.

Now, brother, we'll our ways divide,
  O'er Scottiſh hills to range;
Do thou go north, and I'll go weſt;
  And all our dreſs we'll change,

Some Scottiſh carle hath ſeized my love,
  And borne her to his den;
And ne'er will I tread Engliſh ground
  Till ſhe is reſtored agen.

The brothers ſtrait their paths divide,
  O'er Scottiſh hills to range;
And hide themſelves in queint diſguiſe,
  And oft their dreſs they change.

Sir Bertram clad in gown of grey,
  Moſt like a Palmer poor,
To halls and caſtles wanders round,
  And begs from door to door.

Sometimes a Minſtrel's garb he wears,
  With pipes ſo ſweet and ſhrill;
And wends to every tower and town;
  O'er every dale and hill.

One day as he ſate under a thorn
  All ſunk in deep deſpair,
An aged Pilgrim paſs'd him by,
  Who mark'd his face of care.

All Minſtrels yet that ever I ſaw,
  Are full of game and glee:
But thou art ſad and woe-begone!
  I marvel whence it be!

Father, I ſerve an aged lord,
  Whoſe grief afflicts my mind;
His only child is ſtol'n away,
  And fain I would her find.

The Hermit of Warkworth.

Cheer up, my fon; perchance (he faid)
Some tidings I may bear;
For oft when human hopes have fail'd,
Then heavenly comfort's near.

Behind yon hills fo fteep and high,
Down in a lowly glen,
There ftands a caftle fair and ftrong,
Far from th'abode of men.

As late I chanc'd to crave an alms
About this evening hour,
Me-thought I heard a lady's voice
Lamenting in the tower.

And when I afk'd, what harm had hap'd,
What lady fick there lay?
They rudely drove me from the gate,
And bade me wend away.

Thefe tidings caught Sir Bertram's ear,
He thank'd him for his tale;
And foon he hafted o'er the hills,
And foon he reach'd the vale.

Then drawing near thofe lonely towers,
Which ftood in dale fo low,
And fitting down befide the gate,
His pipes he 'gan to blow.

Sir Porter, is thy lord at home
To hear a Minftrel's fong?
Or may I crave a lodging here,
Without offence or wrong?

My lord, he faid, is not at home
To hear a Minftrel's fong:
And fhould I lend thee lodging here
My life would not be long.

He play'd again fo foft a ftrain,
Such power fweet founds impart,
He won the churlifh Porter's ear,
And moved his ftubborn heart.

Minftrel, he fay'd, thou play'ft fo fweet,
Fair entrance thou fhould'ft win;
But, alas, I'm fworn upon the rood
To let no ftranger in.

Yet, Minftrel, in yon rifing cliff
Thou'lt find a fheltering cave;
And here thou fhalt my fupper fhare,
And there thy lodging have.

All day he fits befide the gate,
And pipes both loud and clear:
All night he watches round the walls,
In hopes his love to hear.

The firft night, as he filent watch'd,
All at the midnight hour,
He plainly heard his lady's voice
Lamenting in the tower.

The fecond night the moon fhone clear,
And gilt the fpangled dew;
He faw his lady through the grate,
But 'twas a tranfient view.

The third night wearied out he flept
Till near the morning tide;
When ftarting up, he feiz'd his fword,
And to the caftle hy'd.

When, lo! he faw a ladder of ropes
Depending from the wall;
And o'er the mote was newly laid
A poplar ftrong and tall.

And foon he faw his love defcend
Wrapt in a tartan plaid;
Affifted by a fturdy youth
In highland garb y-clad.

Amaz'd, confounded at the fight,
He lay unfeen and ftill;
And foon he faw them crofs the ftream,
And mount the neighbouring hill.

Unheard, unknown of all within,
The youthful couple fly,
But what can fcape the lover's ken?
Or fhun his piercing eye?

With filent ftep he follows clofe
Behind the flying pair,
And faw her hang upon his arm
With fond familiar air.

Thanks, gentle youth, fhe often faid;
My thanks thou well haft won:
For me what wiles haft thou contriv'd?
For me what dangers run?

And ever fhall my grateful heart
Thy fervices repay:—
Sir Bertram could no farther hear,
But cried, Vile traitor, ftay!

Vile traitor! yield that lady up!—
And quick his fword he drew.
The ftranger turn'd in fudden rage,
And at Sir Bertram flew.

With mortal hate their vigorous arms
Gave many a vengeful blow:
But Bertram's ftronger hand prevail'd,
And laid the ftranger low.

Die, traitor, die!—A deadly thruſt
  Attends each furious word.
Ah! then fair Iſabel knew his voice,
  And ruſh'd beneath his ſword.

O ſtop, ſhe cried, O ſtop thy arm!
  Thou doſt thy brother ſlay!—
And here the Hermit paus'd, and wept:
  His tongue no more could ſay.

At length he cried, Ye lovely pair,
  How ſhall I tell the reſt?
Ere I could ſtop my piercing ſword,
  It fell, and ſtabb'd her breaſt.

Wert thou thyſelf that hapleſs youth?
  Ah! cruel fate! they ſaid.
The Hermit wept, and ſo did they:
  They ſigh'd; he hung his head.

O blind and jealous rage, he cried,
  What evils from thee flow?
The Hermit paus'd; they ſilent mourn'd;
  He wept, and they were woe.

Ah! when I heard my brother's name,
  And ſaw my lady bleed,
I rav'd, I wept, I curſt my arm,
  That wrought the fatal deed.

In vain I claſp'd her to my breaſt,
  And clos'd the ghaſtly wound;
In vain I preſs'd his bleeding corpſe,
  And rais'd it from the ground.

My brother, alas! ſpake never more,
  His precious life was flown.
She kindly ſtrove to ſooth my pain,
  Regardleſs of her own.

Bertram, ſhe ſaid, be comforted,
  And live to think on me:
May we in heaven that union prove,
  Which here was not to be!

Bertram, ſhe ſaid, I ſtill was true;
  Thou only hadſt my heart:
May we hereafter meet in bliſs!
  We now, alas! muſt part.

For thee, I left my father's hall,
  And flew to thy relief,
When, lo! near Chiviot's fatal hills
  I met a Scottiſh chief,

Lord Malcolm's ſon, whoſe proffer'd love,
  I had refus'd with ſcorn;
He ſlew my guards and ſeiz'd on me
  Upon that fatal morn:

And in those dreary hated walls
He kept me close confin'd;
And fondly sued, and warmly press'd
To win me to his mind.

Each rising morn increas'd my pain,
Each night increas'd my fear;
When wandering in this northern garb
Thy brother found me here.

He quickly form'd this brave design
To set me captive free;
And on the moor his horses wait,
Ty'd to a neighbouring tree.

Then haste, my love, escape away,
And for thyself provide;
And sometime fondly think on her,
Who should have been thy bride.

Thus pouring comfort on my soul
Even with her latest breath,
She gave one parting fond embrace,
And clos'd her eyes in death.

Amongst other little affectations of antiquity, we would recommend it to the Author to discard the obsolete word *Fits*, used for parts or cantos; which, surely, has no propriety in a poem that plainly speaks itself of modern date.

ART. IV. *Armine and Elvira; a Legendary Tale: In Two Parts.* 4to. 2 s. Murray.

THIS poem, somewhat similar, in the subject, to the Hermit of Warkworth, is, in the style and execution, very different. The ingenious Author has adopted the simplicity of our ancient poetry, but has judiciously rejected its rudeness and poverty of language. He has adorned his little work with the elegance of polished expression, and with all the splendor of metaphorical beauty. The flowers that TIME has gathered in his passage, he has preferred to the weeds of his uncultivated state, without worshipping his wrinkles, or staining himself with his rust; whatever he has ripened, whatever he has meliorated, he has made his own. This is discernable on the very opening of the poem:

A Hermit on the banks of Trent,
Far from the world's bewildering maze,
To humbler scenes of calm content
Had fled from brighter, busier days.

If haply from his guarded breast
Had stol'n the unsuspected sigh,
And Memory, an unbidden guest,
With former passions fill'd his eye;

Then

Then pious hope and duty prais'd
  The wisdom of th' UNERRING SWAY:
And whilst his eye to heaven he rais'd,
  Its silent waters sunk away.

There is not within our knowledge, perhaps not in poetry, a more striking beauty than that which the two last lines exhibit. And, so far at least as we are able to recollect, the idea has the merit of being totally new.

The first part of this poem is chiefly preceptive, and conveys much sensible and liberal instruction in the Hermit's address to his only son:

Complete Ambition's wildest scheme;
  In power's most brilliant robes appear,
Indulge in Fortune's golden dream,
  Then ask thy heart if peace be there.

No: it shall tell thee, peace retires,
  If once of her lov'd friends depriv'd,
Contentment calm, subdued desires,
  And happiness that's self deriv'd.

The following apostrophe to Fortune is equally spirited and elegant:

O Fortune, at thy crowded shrine
  What wretched worlds of suppliants bow!
For ever hail'd thy power divine!
  Forever breath'd the serious vow!

With tottering pace and feeble knee,
  See Age advance in shameless haste!
The palsy'd hand is stretch'd to thee,
  For wealth he wants the power to taste.

See led by Hope the youthful train!
  Her fairy dreams their hearts have won.
She points to what they shall not gain,
  Or dearly gain—to be undone.

And some of the tender offices of Pity are no less elegantly described:

——— Though Fortune's frown deny
  With wealth to bid the sufferer live,
Yet Pity's hand can oft supply
  A balm she never knew to give.

Can oft with lenient drops asswage
  The wounds no ruder hand can heal,
When grief, despair, distraction rage,
  While death the lips of love shall seal,

Ah then, his anguish to remove,
  Depriv'd of all his heart holds dear,
How sweet the still surviving love
  Of Friendship's smile, of Pity's tear!

6 It

It is impoſſible to read the inſtructions young Armine receives to cultivate the ſocial virtues, without finding the heart better for them :

——— He oft would cry,
From theſe, my ſon, O ne'er depart,
Theſe tender charities that tie
In mutual league the human heart.

Be thine thoſe feelings of the mind
That wake at honour's, friendſhip's call,
Benevolence, that unconfin'd
Extends her liberal hand to all.

By ſympathy's untutor'd voice
Be taught her ſocial laws to keep ;
Rejoice if human heart rejoice,
And weep if human eye ſhall weep.

The heart that bleeds for others' woes
Shall feel each ſelfiſh ſorrow leſs ;
His breaſt, who happineſs beſtows,
Reflected happineſs ſhall bleſs.

Each ruder paſſion ſtill withſtood
That breaks o'er Virtue's ſober line,
The tender, noble, and the good
To cheriſh and indulge be thine.

The Hermit's next precepts inſtruct his ſon to guard againſt the paſſion of Love :

Ah ! then the ſoft contagion fly,
And timely ſhun th' alluring bait.
The riſing bluſh, the downcaſt eye
Proclaim'd—the precept was too late.

Here the tale begins. Raymond, an ancient Earl, of high military power and reputation, has an only daughter named Elvira, whoſe beauty is thus charmingly deſcribed :

By Nature's happieſt pencil drawn,
She wore the vernal morning's ray :
The vernal morning's bluſhing dawn
Breaks not ſo beauteous into day.

Her breaſt, impatient of controul,
Scorn'd in its ſilken chains to lie ;
And the ſoft language of the ſoul
Flow'd from her never ſilent eye.

The bloom that open'd on her face
Well ſeem'd an emblem of her mind :
Where ſnowy innocence we trace
With bluſhing modeſty combin'd.

This

This distinguished beauty, when,

On Sherwood's old heroic plain,
Her Armine bore the prize away,

became the object of his affections, and, at the same time, conceived an unconquerable passion for him. Armine, not knowing the dignity of his birth, had long languished in distant and hopeless silence; or, if he spoke, it was in this plaintive strain;

Then go, fallacious hope! adieu!
The flattering prospect I resign;
And bear from my deluded view
The bliss that never must be mine!

Thus the tale proceeds:

Twice twelve revolving moons had past
Since first he caught the fatal view,
Unchang'd by time, his sorrows last,
Uncheer'd by hope, his passion grew.

That passion to indulge he sought
In Raymond's groves the deepest shade,
There Fancy's haunting spirit brought
The image of his long-lov'd maid.

But hark! What more than mortal sound
Steals on Attention's raptur'd ear?
The voice of Harmony around
Swells in wild whispers soft and clear.

Can human hand a tone so fine
Sweep from the string with touch profane?
Can human lip with breath divine
Pour on the gale so sweet a strain?

'Tis she the source of Armine's woe;
'Tis she whence all his joy must spring.
From her lov'd lips the numbers flow,
Her magic hand awakes the string.

Now, Armine! now thy love proclaim;
Thy instant suit the time demands.
Delay not;—tumult shakes his frame!
And lost in extacy he stands!

The lover in this perplexing situation

She sees, nor unalarm'd retires.

Stay, sweet illusion! stay thy flight!
'Tis gone:—Elvira's form it wore—
Yet, one more glimpse of short delight!
'Tis gone! to be beheld no more!

Fly loitering feet!—the charm pursue
That plays upon my hopes and fears!
Hah! no illusion mocks my view!
'Tis she—Elvira's self appears.

And

And ſhall I on her ſteps intrude?
Alarm her in theſe lonely ſhades?
O ſtay, fair nymph! no ruffian rude
With baſe intent your walk invades.

Far gentler thoughts—his faultering tongue,
By humble diffidence reſtrain'd,
Paus'd in ſuſpence—But thus ere long,
As love impell'd, its power regain'd.

Far gentler thoughts that form inſpires;
With me far gentler paſſions dwell;
This heart hides only blameleſs fires,
Yet burns with what it fears to tell.

The faultering voice that fears controul,
Bluſhes that inward fires declare,
Each tender tumult of the ſoul
In ſilence owns Elvira there.

He ſaid; and as the trembling dove
Sent forth t'explore the watery plain,
Soon fear'd her flight might fatal prove,
And ſudden ſought her ark again,

His heart recoil'd, as one that rued
What he too haſtily confeſt,
And all the riſing ſoul ſubdued
Sought refuge in his inmoſt breaſt.

Nothing but the moſt conſummate knowledge of the operations of the human heart could have ſuggeſted this image ſo beautiful in itſelf, ſo admirably beautiful in the compariſon. Comparative imagery is the ſoul of poetry, one of thoſe ſtriking and eſſential graces, without which there can be nothing perfect or excellent. How happy the Author of Armine and Elvira is in this reſpect we have already ſeen, and ſhall further ſee, if we proceed only to the next ſtanza:

The tender ſtrife Elvira ſaw
Diſtreſt, and as ſome parent mild,
When arm'd with words and looks of awe,
Melts o'er the terrors of her child;

Reproof prepar'd and angry fear
In ſoft ſenſations dy'd away,
They felt the force of Armine's tear,
And fled from pity's riſing ſway.

That mournful voice, that modeſt air,
Young ſtranger, ſpeak the courteous breaſt,
Then why to theſe rude ſcenes repair
Of ſhades the ſolitary gueſt?

And who is ſhe whoſe fortunes bear
Elvira's melancholy name?
O may thoſe fortunes prove more fair
Than hers who ſadly owns the ſame!

Ah,

Ah; gentle maid, in mine ſurvey
  A heart, he cried, that's your's alone!
Long has it own'd Elvira's ſway,
  Though long unnotic'd and unknown.

On Sherwood's old heroic plain
  Elvira grac'd the feſtal day:
There foremoſt of the youthful train
  Her Armine bore the prize away.

There firſt that form my eyes ſurvey'd,
  With future hopes that fill'd my heart;
But, ah! beneath that frown they fade,
  Depart; vain, vanquiſh'd hopes depart!

He ſaid; and on the ground his eyes
  Were fix'd abaſh'd: th' attentive maid
Loſt in the tumult of ſurprize,
  The well remember'd youth ſurvey'd.

The tranſient colour went and came,
  The ſtruggling boſom ſunk and roſe;
The trembling tumults of her frame
  The ſtrong conflicting ſoul diſcloſe.

The time, the ſcene ſhe ſaw with dread,
  Like Cynthia ſetting, glanc'd away;
But ſcatter'd bluſhes as ſhe fled,
  Bluſhes that ſpoke a brighter day.

The alchymiſts, in the reign of Charles the Firſt, pretended to have diſcovered an elixir which was an abſolute antidote to mortality. Had this poem no other merit, the laſt quoted ſtanza alone would ſave it from periſhing. The beauties of it are too ſtriking to require pointing out, too excellent to be equalled by praiſe.

The lover retires for the evening to a ſhepherd's cottage; where

——— Hope, the lover's downy bed,
  A ſweeter charm than ſlumber brought.

But when

The ſcanty pane the riſing ray
  On the plain wall in diamonds threw,
The lover hail'd the welcome day,
  And to his favourite ſcene he flew.

There ſoon Elvira bent her way,
  Where long her lonely walks had been,
Nor leſs had the preceding day,
  Nor Armine leſs endear'd the ſcene.

The *ſcanty pane*, &c. is extremely picturesque, but Nature is deſcribed in a more intereſting manner in the following ſtanza, which all who know the ſentiments of a heart that has felt the tender paſſion, will acknowledge to be a true copy:

Oft,

Oft, as ſhe paſs'd, her riſing heart
Its ſtronger tenderneſs confeſs'd;
And oft ſhe linger'd to impart
To ſome ſafe ſhade her ſecret breaſt.

A ſhort ſoliloquy, which has equal beauty and propriety, is interrupted by the appearance of the lover:

But oh, the favour'd youth appears;
In penſive grief he ſeems to move:
My heart forbodes unnumber'd fears;
Support it Pity, Virtue, Love!

Unconſcious of the dignity of his birth, he pleads only in favour of natural attachments, and the merit of real affection. To which,

Think not, ſhe ſaid, by forms betray'd,
To humbler worth my heart is blind;
For ſoon ſhall every ſplendor fade,
That beams not from the gifted mind.

After mutual explanations, the ſituation of Elvira is deſcribed in the following maſterly ſtrokes:

Elvira bluſh'd the warm reply,
(To love a language not unknown)
The milder glories fill'd her eye,
And there a ſofter luſtre ſhone.

The yielding ſmile that's half ſuppreſt,
The ſhort, quick breath, the trembling tear,
The ſwell tumultuous of her breaſt
In Armine's favour all appear.

The reſt of the ſcene becomes extremely intereſting, and is ſupported with great ſpirit:

Reſpectful to his lips he preſt
Her yielded hand—In haſte away
Her yielded hand ſhe drew diſtreſt,
With looks that witneſs'd wild diſmay.

" Ah whence, fair excellence, thoſe tears?
What terror unforeſeen alarms?"
" See, where a father's frown appears,
She ſaid, and ſunk into his arms *."

My daughter! heavens! it cannot be—
And yet it muſt—O dire diſgrace!
Elvira have I liv'd to ſee
Claſp'd in a peaſant's vile embrace?

This daring guilt let death repay—
His vengeful arm the javelin threw;
With erring aim it wing'd its way,
And far, by Fate averted, flew.

* Of this there is a very beautiful repreſentation in the vignet on the title-page, deſigned and engraved by Taylor.

Elvira

Elvira breathes——her pulses beat,
  Returning life illumes her eye;
Trembling a father's view to meet,
  She spies a reverend hermit nigh.

Your wrath, she cries, let tears asswage—
  Unheeded must Elvira pray?
O let an injur'd father's rage
  This hermit's sacred presence stay!

Yet deem not, lost in guilty love,
  I plead to save my virgin fame!
My weakness Virtue might approve,
  And smile on Nature's holy flame.

O welcome to my hopes again,
  My son, the raptur'd hermit cries,
I sought thee sorrowing on the plain,
  And all the father fill'd his eyes.

Art thou, the raging Raymond said,
  Of this audacious boy the sire?
Curse on the dart that idly sped,
  Nor bade his peasant soul expire.

His peasant soul! indignant fire
  Flash'd from the conscious father's eye—
A gallant earl is Armine's sire;
  And know, proud chief, that earl am I.

Though here within the hermit's cell,
  I long have liv'd unknown to fame;
Yet crouded camps and courts can tell,
  Thou too hast heard of Egbert's name.

Hah! Egbert! he whom tyrant rage
  Forc'd from his country's bleeding breast?
The patron of my orphan age,
  My friend, my warrior stands confest!

But why?—The painful story spare;
  That prostrate youth, said Egbert, see;
His anguish asks a parent's care,
  A parent, once who pitied thee.

Raymond, as one who, glancing round,
  Seems from some sudden trance to start,
Snatch'd the pale lovers from the ground,
  And held them trembling to his heart.

Joy, gratitude, and wonder, shed
  United tears o'er Hymen's reign,
And Nature her best triumph led,
  For Love and Virtue join'd her train.

There is no name prefixed to this beautiful poem; but from the advertisements it appears to be written by the Rev. Mr. Cartwright, Fellow of Magdalen College, Oxford.

ART. V.

ART. V. *Review of the third Volume of Mr.* Gaillard's *History of the Rivalship between France and England.* See our last Appendix. (Article concluded.)

MR. Gaillard considers the remainder of the reigns of Louis IX. and Henry III. as the time in which the French monarchy strengthened itself by the management of a wise and just King, and that of England degenerated towards democracy, by the mismanagement of a weak and unjust one.

It is certain that Henry's inconstancy and servitude to ministers, was as pernicious to England as his father's impetuosity. The slave of Hubert de Burgh, he violated the two charters: the slave of the Bishop of Winchester (a foreigner) he punished Hubert de Burgh barbarously and *unconstitutionally*, and suffered that prelate traiterously to slay the great Earl of Pembroke, his brother-in-law, [and head of the *just* malecontents] whose father had gained him the crown. He had, however, so much virtue as to feel some remorse.

On the remonstrance of the Archbishop of Canterbury, he gives up the Bishop of Winchester, reinstates Hubert de Burgh, is the slave of the Bishop of Valence, invites his half brothers into England, promises to dismiss foreigners, gains money, breaks his word, gives his sister unwillingly in marriage to the Earl of Leicester, and then disgraces that favourite. What a series of follies!—Hence the famous statutes of Oxford to confirm the charters, with twelve barons named by the King, and as many by the parliament (Leicester at their head) to *conserve* them. The King and Prince Edward swear to observe them.

The Popes Alexander IX. and Urban IV. annul these statutes, and Henry goes to war with the barons.

The offered mediation of Louis is accepted by Henry and the barons; and here Mr. G. harangues, very floridly indeed, on the honour and equity of Louis. But how does he determine? He re-establishes the charters, and annuls the statutes of Oxford. The barons refuse to acquiesce in this decree, and Mr. G. assures us, that all Europe called them, from this moment, *rebels.* But the barons justly pleaded, that Henry's frequent breaches of faith had made the conservators appointed by the statutes necessary; and they were *certainly so* during Henry's reign.

Leicester is slain at the battle of Evesham, [which Prince Edward gains] and his prisoner Henry remounts the throne.

Mr. G. seems too severe on the Earl of Leicester, and Grosthead * (Bishop of Lincoln) his director, as friends of liberty. The commons now possessed seats in parliament.

* This prelate was, in effect, a Protestant, and Author of many excellent pieces against Popery, *Papistarum Malleus.*

He

He paints Louis as the arbiter of Europe, determining the rights of the pretenders to Flanders, and refusing the empire for his Relation; while Henry suffers Pope Alexander IV. to pillage England, under pretence of giving the crown of Sicily to his second son, Edmund.

Urban IV. gives the same crown to Charles Duke of Anjou, Louis's brother. Mr. G. is sensible how incompatible with the *just* policy, for which he has celebrated Louis, was his assisting his brother in this *iniquitous* expedition. The excuses, (such as the feudal rights of the Popes, the prospect of an English prince's gaining that crown if a French one did not, the ambition of the Count and Countess of Anjou, &c.) which Mr. G. adduces, are, indeed, miserable ones!

It must be confessed, however, that Louis seems not so ambitious of gaining the county of Provence to the crown of France, as he might have been expected to be, with his plausible pretensions.

It must be acknowledged, also, that while Mr. G. confesses and bemoans the weakness of Louis in crusading, he paints the virtues of his private life in such strong colours as *seduces* cool judgment, and almost *forces* us to think that he *was* a saint. 'His marriage with Margaret of Provence, says he, was the union of two heavenly souls!' Marriages of Kings and Queens are so rarely the effects of choice, that we must seldom expect in them either happiness or fidelity.

This Louis's dying advice to his son has been so esteemed, that one of his descendants said, "It was the noblest inheritance which he left his family."

His weak rival, Henry, who seemed born to be governed, and whose ruling passion was fear, outlived him only two years. According to our Author, Louis far outrivaled him in *rational* piety. Our Author justly makes it a characteristic of Henry's weak reign, that his courtiers were obliged, through want of their wages, to be the associates of highwaymen!

Philip the Hardy was with his father in Africa when he died, and our Edward I. in Palestine (both on crusades) when his father expired. Edward paid his homage to Philip, and they lived as friends, notwithstanding some interesting occurrences; and this fact confirms the good effects of the treaty of Abbeville and of Amiens, A. D. 1279.

Yet Edward would not assist Philip in his expedition against Arragon (the crown of which was given him by Pope Martin IV.) in which he dies.

Edward eclipsed Philip in the art of government, but stained his laurels, gained in Wales (which he totally subdued) by his cruelty towards Lluellin, the prince of that country.

Edward

Edward does homage to Philip the Handsome; assumes the character of mediator betwixt France and Castile, and effects a treaty, by which the former loses the kingdom of Arragon, and part of the kingdom of Sicily.

By art Edward now obtains an acknowledgment of his sovereignty over Scotland; but Philip, taking advantage of quarrels betwixt the English and French subjects, cites Edward to his court of peers; and, on his non-appearance, confiscates his provinces in France; and, by an artifice, contrives to gain possession of Guienne. Mr. G. acknowledges the French fraud, and also that by which Philip imprisoned the Count of Flanders, Edward's chief ally.

The flame of war being thus kindled, Edward reduces John King of Scotland, Philip's grand ally. But Pope Boniface VIII. chosen by himself *arbiter*, or rather *judge*, over these rival Kings, condemns Philip to restore Guienne, &c. to Edward, and Flanders to the Count; and, on his disobedience to this award, formally deposes him from the throne of France, and gives it first to Edward, and then to the Emperor Albert *.

Philip having imprisoned the Count of Flanders and his sons, oppresses the Flemings, who revolt, and, with 25,000 artisans of Ghent and Bruges, beat 50,000 Frenchmen, at the battle of Courtray, or the *Spurs* ‡.

Edward, however, makes a definitive treaty with Philip, A. D. 1303, by which he recovers Guienne, &c. and the peace is confirmed by a double marriage, viz. of Edward and his eldest son with two French princesses. Allies on both sides are sacrificed!

Mr. G. is far from being so dazzled with Philip's splendor, as not to see in him the features of a tyrant. On the contrary, he paints them all to the very life, and shews him as *miserable* as a tyrant ought to be!—An impartial Englishman will as honestly confess the tyrant in Edward, who exercised his cruelty on Scotland, and on her brave son William Wallace.

Philip gains over the Flemings the sea-fight at Zuriczee, and in person that of Mons; which is followed by a peace, and the releasement of the Count of Flanders, &c.

The conclusion of these wars affords a strong instance in favour of Mr. G.'s main argument in this work.

---

* The quarrel betwixt Boniface and Philip makes one of the most diverting parts of the history of the times; and all who love to hear two fish-women scold, may find amusement in it.

‡ The Flemings hung up 500 pairs of gilt spurs, taken from French gentlemen in this battle, in the Cathedral of Courtray. They took in all 4000.

Edward, in pursuit of the heroic Robert Bruce, dies of a dysentery. Mr. G. says justly of him, that 'he did more *harm* by his *manners*, than *good* by his *laws*.'

Philip survived his rival (both in virtues and vices) seven years, but in peace. Having oppressed his subjects by financiers, who debased the coin, &c. he died penitent.

In the reigns of these rivals, the third estate in France, and the commons in England, gained a fixed footing. Happy æra in the annals of liberty! Switzerland also now became free.

Edward II. maintained peace * with the three sons of Philip the Handsome, viz. Louis Hutin, Philip the Long, and Charles the Handsome.

These Kings of France were governed by an uncle, and by financiers. Edward was governed by favourites; first by Gaveston, whom he loaded with riches and honours, and was obliged to banish as the encourager and object of his vices. The barons (Earl of Lancaster at their head) execute the minion at his third return; and the Earl recommends Spenser, who becomes the favourite, and brings his patron, Lancaster, ignominiously to the scaffold †, after an unsuccessful insurrection.

Queen Isabel, ill used by the Spensers, and involved in an intrigue with Mortimer, goes to France to effect peace betwixt Charles and Edward in appearance, but in reality to gain her brother's protection for her lover, who escapes thither from prison and death.

Isabel now sails for England with 3000 men, destroys the Spensers, and keeps the King prisoner till he is deposed by parliament, murthered, &c.

Charles survives not long his peace with Edward III.

Mr. G. observes, that here ends the first epoch of the rivalship betwixt the two nations, and that all the past horrors are but a prelude to the subsequent, in which the object of contest will be the whole kingdom, as hitherto it has been only some particular provinces. The mutual *hate* and *envy* of the nations may be supposed to rise in proportion.

To this history Mr. G. subjoins a *recapitulation*, or general view of the success of the two nations in war; with the characters of their Kings, and the national characters.

The French, says he, had imprudently suffered the Normans to gain possession of England, and it was become their business

---

* Excepting in a *fracas* of no moment, in the reign of Charles the Handsome.

† He was dressed in a capuchin, &c. This was a species of cruelty, we think, scarce paralleled.

to

to recover Normandy. The English wanted to aggrandize themselves in France, and France longed to chace them from her bosom.

Louis the Fat begins this work; Louis the Young overturns it, and gives to England half of France. Philip the August recovers almost all, and Louis the Lion follows the plan. St. Louis forms a new one, viz. '*to create peace by equity.*' Philip the Hardy respects this plan of his father's; but Philip the Handsome resumes the old one of expulsion. His three sons maintain peace. This is in the main a just recapitulation.

From the time of John, and Philip the August, England lost ground in France; and, at the death of Edward II. she possessed Guienne and Ponthieu in France,—pretty nearly equal to Normandy, which William the Conqueror possessed: so that, in effect, war had gained nothing by all the blood and gold it had wasted. What a confirmation of Mr. G.'s principal position!

If Philip I. had hindered William I. from gaining England, there would have been no English power in France. If Louis the Young had not divorced Eleanor, the English would not have possessed half of France: and if John had not assassinated his nephew, they would not have lost most of those provinces.

The faults * of the French raised the English power in France; the crimes of a King of England almost overturned, and would have destroyed it, but for new faults of the French. The moderation of St. Louis gave peace for thirty-five years. The pride of Edward I. and Philip the Handsome rekindled war: and what was gained by it? Nothing!—His following characters are, in general, just, *viz.*

The *voluptuous* Philip I. was not worthy to rival William I. and as he was less *severe* and *violent* than William Rufus, so he was less *formidable*.

Louis the Fat and Henry I. were well matched rivals; but while the latter *oppressed* his people, the former *freed* his subjects.—Louis the Young would not, perhaps, have been quite eclipsed by Stephen, but was by Henry II.

Philip the August and Richard I. had great talents and great passions. The former was a King, the latter an hero, but an afflicted one, and he therefore interests our compassion. Philip the August was the chastiser of John.

Henry III. was the weak rival of Louis VIII. (who lived not long enough to afford grounds for an accurate judgment of him) and too weak to be the rival of St. Louis, who was a great

* Mr. G. distinguishes *faults* from *crimes*, and means only by *faults* defects in policy.

 man

man and a great King, incomparably greater than Henry II. as calm reason is incomparably superior to impetuous passion.

Edward I. and Philip the Hardy were pretty equal friends Edward, and Philip the Handsome, were nearly equal rivals in the field.

Edward II. was, by his vices, inferior to his brothers-in-law, the sons of Philip the Handsome.——

Such is Mr. G.'s review of the sovereigns of both nations, in the period of which he has written. We agree not with him in some pourtraits, for we think Philip the August as worthless a wretch as John; and Henry II. as great a King as Louis the Saint.

Mr. G. seems more just in giving the character of our nation than of our Kings. He regards the English as a people whose hearts were not enslaved by the three first Norman princes, but he thinks they contracted a melancholy, the effect of *just hate restrained by weakness.* He judges, that from the civil wars, under Stephen, we derived that fierceness which is allowed to make a part of our character.

He acknowledges, that under Henry II. the nation resumed its *natural magnanimity,* displayed its *talents, virtues,* &c. He thinks that under Richard we became soldiers, and that the splendor of his arms flattered us so much, that we forgave his tyranny. Here we must be allowed to add, that the barbarity and treachery of Philip the August toward this Richard, seems to have contributed much to the hatred which the English bore the French. Under John we vindicated (according to Mr. G. and *truth)* the rights of men; and a love of liberty, perhaps a little too violent, became the standing national character.—Henry I. contributed to confirm this spirit. But Edward I. by turning the nation's martial ardour towards Wales and Scotland, made *turbulent citizens* become *good soldiers.* No wonder that a nation, whose character was thus formed, carried its opposition to Edward II. into excess.—In short, Mr. G. thus accounts for our national character of *solidity, reflection,* and *melancholy.*

He affirms that in France, from Louis the Fat to Philip the Handsome, the *people's liberty* increased with the *authority of the King*; and hence he accounts for the gaiety which is now their *national characteristic.* But he observes, that the oppressions under Philip the Handsome shewed the people to be capable of a resentment which nothing but that Prince's dying repentance disarmed.

When Mr. G. asserts, that the French become rivals of the English in the *love of liberty,* we smile.

In his last chapter Mr. G. gives the state of letters in the two nations during the period of this history; and it is a very agreeable part of his work.

He

He begins with an *eulogium* on reason and philosophy, as the only means of making mankind happy.

He remarks, that it is no wonder that the ancient history of every nation is full of fables, when the first historians of *almost every* nation were *poets.*

He observes that Arthur protected the bards, and they immortalized him; that Clovis continued a *barbarian*, but Chilperick was a *fine Genius* and a *divine*, yet a barbarian and a ridiculous one. His instances are, that he made placards for admission of the double letters ‡ of the Greeks into the French alphabet; and that Gregory of Tours convicts him of Sabellianism.

Under the *heptarchy*, and the Merovingian race of Kings, we had Gildas, and venerable Bede; the French had Gregory of Tours, the father of their history: Alcuin, born in England but formed in Italy, contributed to the happiness of France under Charlemagne. He was the *most knowing* and *most amiable* of men (according to Mr. G.) and formed that academy in the palace of Charlemagne, of which the King and courtiers were members.

As Charlemagne changed the face of France, so Alfred soon after changed that of England. He was an *inventive genius*, and could have been any thing; but, happily for the public, he chose to be a *great King*. To shew us how slow is the improvement of reason, Mr. G. observes, that Charlemagne and Louis the Debonnaire were afraid of *eclipses* and *comets.*

When Alfred undertook the restoration of learning in England, scarce a priest could be found who understood the easiest Latin: this was partly the effect of the ravages of the Danes.

He placed, as a master, in the monastery of Malmsbury, John Scot (called Erigena) born in England, but by descent of the Scots in Ireland. He was a fine genius, philosopher, and divine. He had studied Greek at Athens, was master of the Eastern tongues, had travelled through Italy and France, and was, by his conversation, so dear to Charles the Bald, that he made him lie in his chamber. Yet he was a follower of *Pelagius* (who was born in England in the time of the Saxons) on the subject of grace, and a *sacramentary*, or disbeliever of the *real presence* *. He considers Berenger, a Frenchman, as author of *the Disbelief of the Real Presence,* and as confuted by Lanfranc, Archbishop of Canterbury.

Mr. G. observes, that England produced few heretics and heresies; and he ascribes this purity, to her being employed in the

‡ Means Mr. Gaillard Φ, X, Ψ?

* Another expression of transubstantiation.

 pursuit

pursuit of *civil liberty*. He owns that France produced many heretics, viz. *Manicheans*, *Albigenses*, *Vaudois*, &c †

He has a very just remark, viz. that William the Conqueror's endeavour to introduce his Norman French as the current language into England, was a great check to the progress of our learning, as our scholars were thereby induced to write in Latin: a language in which, it being unnatural to them, they could not so well express themselves, while the French writers improved their mother tongue.

He observes, that the famous Doctors of that age *assumed* or *obtained* proud titles for their scholastic learning. Alexander Hales, born at Glocester but educated at Paris, was called the *irrefragable* Doctor. John Duns, a Scot, bred at Oxford but finished at Paris, was called the *subtle* Doctor. William Ockham (his scholar and rival) was called the *singular* Doctor.

Among the French, Alan Lille was called the *universal* Doctor. Francis de Mayrons was stiled the *illumined* Doctor. Vincent de Beauvais was Author of the *Grand Mirrour*; and Hugh de St. Cher made the first Concordance of the Bible. All these were Doctors of *Trivium* and *Quadrivium* ‡.

Mr. G. enumerates the English and French historians, who, in this period, wrote in Latin; and he notes that Ville Hardouin was the first historian who wrote in French; and that Joinville will be read, in his Life of St. Louis, for his language.

He observes, justly, that we have nothing before the fourteenth century which can be paralleled with the *Romance of the Rose*, or, as it was long styled emphatically, the *French Romance*.

He concludes the third volume of his work by an observation, that through the cloud of ignorance, in the times under question, shine two great men, Gorbert, and Roger Bacon, both monks, but assigned to opposite fates. The former was raised, from the obscurity of his cell, to the papal see, by the name of Silvester II. The latter was buried in a prison, on the complaint of his whole order, by his ignorant general, who mounted the papal chair with the name of Nicholas IV.

---

† All these names were given to the Protestants of those days.

‡ The *Trivium* was the knowledge of *grammar*, *rhetoric*, *logic*; the *Quadrivium* was the knowledge of *arithmetic*, *geometry*, *astronomy*, *music*. On such a plan as this was the scheme of university education with us laid. After three years, in which the three first sciences were learnt, our youth, or boys, took the degree of A. B. after the completion of the seven they were men, and took the degree of A. M.

Gorbert

Gorbert made clocks, and constructed a sphere, in the tenth century. The consequence was, as some historians say, he was raised to the papal throne for his great philosophy; as were others by a pact with the devil.

Bacon had the knowledge of *microscopes*, *telescopes*, *mirrors*, *gunpowder*, and proposed to Pope Clement IV. in A. D. 1267, that reformation of the Calendar which was adopted by Pope Gregory XIII. 300 years after. He wrote to prove that there was no such thing as conjuring, and was condemned as a conjurer!

We are now arrived at the conclusion of this work; to which the Author has made some additions, corrections, &c. in which we find little or nothing worth the attention of a Reviewer. The principal addition is a summary of what Mr. Brequigny has collected from MSS. in the Tower of London concerning the reclaiming of Provence, by Margaret of France and Eleanor of England.

ART. VI. *Aretin: A Dialogue on Painting.* From the Italian of Lodovico Dolce. 8vo. 4 s. sewed. Elmsley, &c.

DOLCE was born in 1508, and died in 1568: he was contemporary with Michael Angelo; with Titian and Raphael Urban; with Aretin, Ariosto, Tasso, Sannazarius, and some others, who were not all of them contemporaries with each other.

He held a considerable rank among the literati of his time; one of his performances is a tragedy called Marianna, which was acted with the greatest applause: he translated Euripedes, Horace, and Cicero, into his native language; and among his original productions, which are very numerous, this dialogue is said to have been eminently distinguished.

It is generally believed that some thoughts, which Raphael, who died when Dolce was about twelve years old, had reduced to writing, were put into his hands to methodize, and that he made these the ground-work of his dialogue: it is also supposed by some that Aretin assisted in the composition.

The Translator has inserted small extracts from various authors, by way of note at the bottom of the page, to shew how far their sentiments and those of his Author differ, or coincide.

The speakers in the dialogue are Fabrini and Aretin. Fabrini asserts, that Michael Angelo was superior as a painter to all others, particularly to Raphael. Aretin on the contrary maintains, that Raphael was superior to Angelo; this difference of opinion brings on a dispute, in which Aretin professes 'to explain what painting is, and what are the duties and office of a painter, a painter, to treat of the importance of painting in general, to draw a parallel between the two masters in question, and to speak of the relative merit of others, especially of Titian.'

Painting is defined to be 'the imitation of Nature,' and he is said to be the greatest master whose works approach nearest to the original. From this principle is drawn the following conclusion: 'any man of good natural abilities, and nice discernment, is sufficiently qualified to judge completely of painting.'

Much time is spent in shewing the usefulness and importance of painting, which might well have been spared: painting, like beauty, is pleasing to man in consequence of an instinct or sense; and in virtue of the pleasure which it gives, by this instinct or sense, and not of any usefulness discovered and approved by the understanding, it will be always in high estimation.

The Reader, after a cheerless journey through 70 pages, finds the subject divided into three heads,—Invention, Design, and Colouring: 'Invention, says the Author, is the history or fable, and the order or disposition of the figures of a picture. Design is the contour or outline; the form, the attitudes and actions of the figures. Colouring is the natural distribution of the teints, or a faithful representation of the colours, and the lights and the shades, as they are painted and represented to us by nature, in a boundless variety of manners suitable to the subject, whether animate, inanimate, or vegetable, and the infinite gradations and intermixtures between these. To these may be *added*, expression and grace, which respect the whole, and are the highest accomplishments of the art.'

The Author proceeds to treat of these particulars separately. Under the head of Invention he says, that 'order and propriety ought strictly to be observed in it. For instance, says he, Christ, or St. Paul, preaching, are not to be painted naked, nor cloathed in a mean and ordinary habit, nor represented in any manner unsuitable or unbecoming the dignity and lustre of their characters; but from the gesture and the whole air of the person of Christ, to impress an idea of the most amiable, the most perfect of human beings; manifesting by his countenance and action, his universal benevolence and love to mankind, so far as the beams of divinity, and the emanations of a perfect soul, can be expressed by the face of man; emitting a radiant glory around his head, reflected by the atmosphere on the faces, persons, and other objects immediately surrounding him, in a judicious and pleasing manner: and in the person and action of St. Paul, to express that dignity, that force, that divine energy, with which he was inspired, and was known to deliver himself. These are subjects that require the sublimest invention and ex-

pression

pression that the most elevated imagination can conceive, and which none but a Raphael can execute.—It was said, and not without reason, to Donatello, who had made a wooden crucifix, that he had put a peasant upon the cross; although in modern times few have equalled, none surpassed Donatello in sculpture, M. Angelo excepted. So in the painting of Moses, the artist must represent in him the majesty of a sovereign, the dignity of a lawgiver, and the air of a commander. And on all occasions he must have a strict regard to the difference that distinguisheth man from man, and one nation from another, their different ranks, qualities, habits, arms, customs, and manners in different ages, points of time, and places. In painting one of Cæsar or Alexander's battles, it would be very improper to arm the soldiers according to the custom of the present times; or in a modern battle, to draw up the forces after the manner of the ancients; as it would be ridiculous to paint Cæsar with a Turkish turban upon his head, or a cap like ours or those now worn at Venice.'

He proceeds thus: 'In invention, the painter should always, in the first place, carefully consider the nature and climate of the country where the scene or action he proposes to represent is known, supposed or feigned to have happened; whether fertile or barren; the nature of its productions, animal and vegetable; the natural appearances also of the country; whether mountainous or abounding in hills or plains, or whether a desart; or amply supplied with water, pouring down in torrents and broken cascades, or flowing in rapid and transparent rivers and smaller streams, or gliding slowly in dull and ousey meanders. The nature also and character of the inhabitants, who in all countries are suited to the climate and the soil, and likewise to the structure of their buildings.' And the more accurate the painter is in these respects, the more pleasing and learned he will appear. The least error against the Costume is seldom passed over without censure. Then what shall we say of the painter who presumed to represent the miracle of Moses striking the rock in the desart, and the plenteous gushing out of the water, to the great astonishment and relief of the half famished Jews, who, according to this man's representation, appeared to be placed in a fertile country, abounding with little hills and vales, with trees and plenty of herbage, where neither water nor fruits could be conceived to be wanting?——

'The disposition of the figures in an historical work is still more essential, as the principal group ought to attract the eye so forcibly, as to engage the whole of your attention, till you have fully contemplated the composition, and the characters that compose it. On observing the works of the greatest masters, nothing seems more easy, and yet in the execution there is is nothing so difficult. It is easy to say, the first characters of the history or fable ought to possess the place of the principal group; but the difficulty lies in distinguishing and preserving a proper pre-eminence and subordination among these and the rest of the figures that compose the picture; and the difficulty will necessarily encrease in proportion to the number or multitude of the figures.'

The Author proceeds to give some directions for Design, which he defines to be 'the form or outlines, the attitudes and action of the figures of a picture.

'In this, says he, the painter is to take especial care to give easy and graceful attitudes, and proper and expressive action to all the figures; to draw the outlines of the body, and all its component parts, with the utmost accuracy and precision, giving them strength, energy, and force, according to the subject, or all the elegance and grace that can be found in the most perfect and beautiful nature; and not imitate, but correct and supply, any imperfections, disproportions, or defects, he may at any time observe or discover in nature.

'For the least distortion, disproportion, or unnatural appearance, in the representation of any of his figures, would debase, if not totally destroy, the merit even of the finest invention.'

Surely these instructions to painters are something like the precepts of virtue and religion which Hodge leaves with his boy when he first puts him under the butler in the 'squire's family; "be a good boy, and serve God." Both the artist and the boy are rather reminded of their duty than taught it. The Author might just as well have given one general precept, "paint a fine picture," as direct his artist to draw his outlines with the utmost accuracy and precision, giving them, united with strength, all the grace that can be found in the most perfect and beautiful nature.

Our Author however proceeds to some more practical and particular instructions, and gives the proportions of the several parts of the human body to each other, which we shall not transcribe, as they are to be found, with other rudiments of the art, in almost every drawing book which is sold at the print-shops, as first lessons for beginners.

He proceeds to give some useful cautions against copying the antique with too minute an exactness, and exaggerating beauties into defects. We have, says he, a painter, who having observed that the ancients, for the most part, designed their figures light and slender, has exceeded the bounds, and rendered his figures ridiculous, and others, by an imitation equally injudicious, have stretched the necks of their figures, especially of their women, to an enormous length.

6 Other

Other inſtructions there are which it is ſtrange that any man ſhould think it worth his while to write; as that 'if the painter is to repreſent Samſon, he muſt not give him the ſoftneſs and delicacy of Ganymede, and that if he is to paint Ganymede he muſt not give him the nerves and robuſtneſs of Samſon.'

He then recommends variety, and gives ſome precepts leſs obvious, and therefore more uſeful. The artiſt, he ſays, ſhould vary not his heads only, but his hands, feet, bodies, attitudes, and every other particular; obſerving, very juſtly, that in Nature ſcarce any two men can be found who do not conſiderably differ from each other, and therefore that no two figures ſhould be exactly alike in a picture. Yet he cautions againſt the practice of ſome painters, who, when they have painted a youth, conſtantly place an old man or a child by his ſide; contraſt a girl by an old woman, a profile with a full face, and never repreſent a figure with his back towards the ſpectator without another ſeen in full front at his elbow.

The artiſt is admoniſhed to be ſparing of what is called foreſhortening: it is, he ſays, difficult to execute, and has ſeldom a pleaſing effect.

In what he ſays about drapery we can find little to ſelect, for why ſhould we repeat after him that an apoſtle muſt not be put in a ſhort coat, nor a captain in a robe with long ſleeves; that the plaits of velvet are of one kind, and thoſe of armozeen of another, and that care ſhould be taken to adapt plaits of all kinds to their right places?

Under the article *Colouring* the Author obſerves, that it conſiſts principally in the contraſt between light and ſhade, with a middle tint which blends one extreme with the other, and makes the figures appear round, and either near or at a diſtance. But all the rules which he gives may be reduced to this, 'colour after Nature;' do not give the fleſh of an old woman the ſame hue with that of a girl, nor diſtinguiſh lips and cheeks, like ſonnetteers, by vermillion and coral.

The ſpeakers in dialogue are always well-bred perſons, who take every opportunity to compliment each other, and alternately expreſs the utmoſt ſatisfaction in the ſentiments that are reciprocated between them: this harmony and good breeding are very remarkable in Fabrini and Aretin; and, however ſhort Aretin's inſtructions may fall of the Reader's expectation, Fabrini finds them ſatisfactory in the higheſt degree. 'What you have already ſaid, ſays he, ſeems to me quite ſufficient, not only for perfectly judging, but even for painting.—Among all that you have ſaid two things pleaſe me highly: the firſt, that pictures ſhould affect the ſpectators; the other, that the painter muſt be born ſo.' Who but Fabrini would think an artiſt enlightened by being told that he ſhould make ſuch pictures as would

would affect the spectators? or that to facilitate the learning painting as an art, it was of importance to be told that it was the gift of Nature?

The rest of the book consists principally of a defence of Aretin's opinion, that Raphael was superior to Michael Angelo; but it seems to be absurd in a comparison between these great masters with respect to ability in their art, to object against Angelo his having drawn naked figures in the church of St. Peter at Rome; this, however, is the subject of a long contest between them. Fabrini is, at length, wholly a convert to Aretin's opinion; and the dialogue is concluded by some account of the respective excellencies of several other painters, particularly Leonardo da Vinci, Julio Romano, Corregio, Parmegiano, Andrea del Sarto, and especially Titian, upon whom there is an elaborate encomium, with a short account of some of his principal works. We cannot say that we think with the Translator, that 'this work will be peculiarly useful to every student in painting,' nor 'acceptable to every gentleman who is desirous of attaining a competent knowledge of the art:' it may, however, furnish the curious and speculative with amusement, by shewing in what estimation those artists, who are now become the standards of merit in painting, stood with the connoisseurs of their own age, and in particular what were then considered as their distinguishing excellencies and defects, when put in comparison with each other.

ART. VII. *A Dissertation on the Gout, and all chronic Diseases, jointly considered, as proceeding from the same Causes; what those Causes are; and a rational and natural Method of Cure proposed. Addressed to all Invalids.* By William Cadogan, Fellow of the College of Physicians. 8vo. 1 s. 6 d. Dodsley. 1771.

INdolence, intemperance, or vexation, are considered by Dr. Cadogan, as the causes of all or most chronic diseases; and one or more of these causes acting daily upon the body, must in the strong and vigorous produce the gout, and in the weaker habits, rheumatism, cholic, stone, palsy, and any or all of the nervous and hysterical class.

Before our Author proceeds to discuss these three heads, he makes some short, but not altogether satisfactory, observations, to prove,—that the gout is not hereditary,—that it is not periodical,—and that it is not incurable.—But without entering further into this part, we shall proceed to give our Readers an abstract of what is said concerning the three great causes above enumerated.

The effects of *indolence* are, obstructions in the smaller orders of vessels; the capillaries are closed into fibres; perspiration is diminished,

minished, and what should be thrown off in this form, becomes putrid and acrimonious.

Intemperance and its effects are thus described by Dr. Cadogan: 'Now let us compare this simple idea of temperance with the common course of most men's lives, and observe their progress from health to sickness. For I fear we shall find but very few who have any pretensions to real temperance. In early youth we are insensibly led into intemperance by the indulgence and mistaken fondness of parents and friends wishing to make us happy by anticipation. Having thus exhausted the first degrees of luxury before we come to the dominion of ourselves, we should find no pleasure in our liberty did we not advance in new sensations, nor feel ourselves free but as we abuse it. Thus we go on till some friendly pain or disease bids, or rather forces us to stop. But in youth all the parts of our bodies are strong and flexible, and bear the first loads of excess with less hurt, and throw them off soon by their own natural vigour and action, or with very little assistance from artificial evacuation. As we grow older, either by nature in due time, or repeated excesses before our time, the body is less able to free itself, and wants more aid from art. The man however goes on taking daily more than he wants, or can possibly get rid of, he feels himself replete and oppressed, and, his appetite failing, his spirits sink for want of fresh supply. He has recourse to dainties, sauces, pickles, provocatives, of all sorts. These soon lose their power; and though he washes down each mouthful with a glass of wine, he can relish nothing. What is to be done? Send for a physician. Doctor, I have lost my stomach; pray give me, says he, with great innocence and ignorance, something to give me an appetite; as if want of appetite was a disease to be cured by art. In vain would the physician, moved by particular friendship to the man, or that integrity he owes to all men, give him the best advice in two words, *quære sudando*, seek it by labour. He would be thought a man void of all knowledge and skill in his profession, if he did not immediately, or after a few evacuations, prescribe stomachics, bitter spicy infusions in wine or brandy, vitriolic elixirs, bark, steel, &c. By the use of these things the stomach, roused to a little extraordinary action, frees itself, by discharging its crude, austere, coagulated contents into the bowels, to be thence forwarded into the blood. The man is freed for a time, finds he can eat again, and thinks all well. But this is a short-lived delusion. If he is robust, the acrimony floating in the blood will be thrown out, and a fit of gout succeeds; if less so, rheumatism or cholic, &c. as I have already said. But let us suppose it to be the gout, which if he bears patiently, and lives moderately, drinking no Madeira or brandy to keep it out of his stomach, nature will relieve him in a certain time, and the gouty acrimony concocted and exhausted by the symptomatic fever that always attends, he will recover into health; if assisted by judicious, mild, and soft medicines, his pains might be greatly assuaged and mitigated, and he would recover sooner. But however he recovers, it is but for a short time; for he returns to his former habits, and quickly brings on the same round of complaints again and again, all aggravated by each return, and

and he less able to bear them; till he becomes a confirmed invalid and cripple for life, which, with a great deal of useless medication, and a few journies to Bath, he drags on, till, in spite of all the doctors he has consulted, and the infallible quack medicines he has taken, lamenting that none have been lucky enough to hit his case, he sinks below opium and brandy, and dies long before his time. This is the course I have lived to see many take, and believe it to be the case of more whom I have never heard of, and which any one may observe in the circle of his acquaintance: all this chain of evils is brought on and accumulated by indolence and intemperance, or mistaken choice of diet. How easily might they have been remedied, had the real causes been known and attended to in time.'

Vexation, our Author says, is not so common a cause of the gout as either indolence or intemperance. Its effects, however, whether proceeding from anger, envy, resentment, discontent, or sorrow, are very prejudicial. It injures the action of the stomach, prevents nourishment, disturbs the circulation, destroys sleep, and renders the secretions and excretions irregular.

'Whoever vexes long, must certainly want nourishment; for, besides the disturbed state of the stomach, its broken appetite and bad digestion, from whence what supply there is must come, not only ill-prepared but vitiated into the blood; there can be no sleep in this state of mind: the perturbed spirit cannot rest; and it is in sleep that all nourishment is performed, and the finer parts of the body, chafed and worn with the fatigue of the day, are repaired and restored to their natural vigour. While we are awake this cannot so well be done; because the incessant action of the body or mind, being always partial and irregular, prevents that equal distribution of the blood to all parts alike, from which each fibre and filament receives that share or portion that suits it best. In sleep, when it is quiet and natural, all the muscles of the body, that is, all its active powers that are subject to our will, are lulled to rest, composed and relaxed into a genial temporary kind of palsy, that leaves not the least obstruction or hindrance of the passage of the blood to every atom. Accordingly the pulse is always slower and more equal, the respiration deeper and more regular, and the same degree of vital warmth diffused alike through every part; so that the extremities are equally warm with the heart.

'Vexation operating in this manner upon the organs of digestion and concoction, and disturbing and obstructing the natural progress of nutrition, must often produce diseases similar to those of long-continued intemperance; its first effect being indigestion with all its symptoms, wind, eructation, heart-burn, hiccup, &c. It is no wonder therefore it should sometimes bring on a fit of gout, which, as I have said, is manifestly a disease of crudity and indigestion; and often the gout in the stomach and bowels. Indeed most cold crude cholics are of this kind. Schirrous concretions will also be formed in the spleen, liver, glands of the mesentery, and throughout the whole system of the belly. Many of these indurated tumors will appear outwardly, so as to be felt by the hand; these in time will degenerate

generate into cancers and cancerous ulcerations, and many fatal evils, not the least of which, in my opinion, is, that the patient will suffer a long time before he dies.'

Dr. Cadogan next proceeds to the method of cure:—' and, continues he, if there be any truth or weight in what I have said, the remedies are obvious: activity, temperance, and peace of mind.'

After giving the following account of the proper manner of treating the gout during the fit, he then points out how these three grand remedies are to be managed, so as to prevent a return, and establish the patient in perfect health.

'Let us suppose the case of a man from forty to fifty years of age, who has had at least twenty fits of gout; by which most of his joints have been so clogged and obstructed, as to make walking, or any kind of motion, very uneasy to him: let him have had it sometimes in his stomach, a little in his head, and often all over him, so as to make him universally sick and low-spirited, especially before a regular fit has come to relieve him. This I apprehend to be as bad a case as we need propose, and that it will not be expected that every old cripple, whose joints are burnt to chalk, and his bones grown together and united by anchilosis, who must be carried from his bed to his table and back again, should be proposed as an object of medication and cure; and yet even he might perhaps receive some relief and palliation in pain, if he has any great degree of it, which is not very common in this case. Let us therefore suppose the first example.

'If the point be to assuage the violent raging of a present paroxysm; this may be safely done by giving some soft and slowly-operating laxative, neither hot nor cold, but warm, either in small doses repeated so as to move the patient once or twice in twenty four hours, or, by a larger dose, oftener in less time, according to the strength and exigency. This may be followed by a few lenient obsorbent correctors of acrimony, or even gentle anodynes: proper cataplasms may also be safely applied to the raging part, which often assuage pain surprizingly; with as much mild and spontaneously-dissolving nourishment as may keep the spirits from sinking too low: but I would wish them to sink a little, and exhort the patient to bear that lowness with patience and resignation, till nature, assisted by soft and succulent food, can have time to relieve him. This easy method of treating a fit of the gout would answer in any age; and if the patient was young and vigorous, and the pain violent, there could be no danger in taking away a little blood. Thus in two or three days time I have often seen a severe fit mitigated and made tolerable; and this is a better way of treating it with regard to future consequences, than bearing it with patience, and suffering it to take its course: for the sooner the joints are relieved from distension and pain, the less danger there is of their being calcined and utterly destroyed. But instead of this, the general practice is quite the reverse. Oh! keep up your spirits, they cry; keep it out of your stomach at all events; where, whenever it rages in a distant part, it is not at all inclined to come. As you cannot eat, you must drink the more freely: so they take cordials, strong wines, and rich spoon meats.

By

By urging in this manner, a great fever is raised, the pain enraged and prolonged; and a fit, that would have ended spontaneously in less than a week, protracted to a month or six weeks, and when it goes off at last, leaves such obstruction and weakness in the parts, as cripple the man ever after. All this I hope will be fairly and candidly understood; for there is doubtless a great variety of gouty cases, but no case that will not admit of medical assistance judiciously administered.'

Dr. Cadogan then points out the various means of exercise, and afterwards lays down his regimen of *temperance*.

'While we are thus endeavouring to resolve all old obstructions, to open the fine vessels, and strain and purify the blood, and by degrees to enable the man to use a certain degree of exercise or labour every day; great care must be taken in the choice of his diet, that no new acrimony be added to the old, to thwart and frustrate this salutary operation. His food must be soft, mild, and spontaneously digesting, and in moderate quantity, so as to give the least possible labour to the stomach and bowels; that it may neither turn sour, nor bitter, nor rancid, nor any way degenerate from those qualities necessary to make good blood. Such things are, at first, new-laid eggs boiled so as not to harden the white creamy part of them, tripe, calves feet, chicken, partridge, rabbits, most sorts of white mild fish, such as whiting, skate, cod, turbot, &c. and all sorts of shell fish, particularly oysters raw. Very soon he will be strong enough to eat beef, veal, mutton, lamb, pork, venison, &c. but these must all be kept till they are tender, and eaten with their own gravies without any compounded sauces or pickles whatever: instead of which, boiled or stewed vegetables, and sallads of lettuce and endive, may be used: and the luxury that is not unwholsome may be allowed, light puddings, custards, creams, blanc-manger, &c. and ripe fruits of all kinds and seasons. But because * wine undoubtedly produces nine in ten of all the gouts in the world, wine must be avoided, or taken very sparingly, and but seldom. How is this to be done? Can a man used to it every day, who thinks he cannot live without it, and that his existence depends upon it, leave it off safely? If he thinks he

* 'I have made what inquiries I could upon this capital article from living witnesses; for I do not always pin my faith upon books, knowing it to be no uncommon thing for authors, instead of framing their system from observation and experience, to wrest and explain both to support their opinions. I have been assured by a physician who practised above thirty years in Turkey, that from the Danube to the Euphrates he had never seen a gouty Turk. I have also been informed by some of our ministers who had resided many years at Constantinople, that the gout, and other diseases of the same class, were not uncommon at court; but the courtiers, it seems, were not as good Mahometans as those who lived in the country; for they drank wine, drams, liqueurs of all sorts, without restraint.

'I have also been very credibly informed, that the Gentoos or Marratas, a people of India living in the most temperate simplicity, chiefly upon rice, have no such thing as the gout, or indeed any other chronic disease among them.'

he must die of the experiment, doing it all at once, he may do it by degrees, and drink but half the quantity of yesterday till he has brought it to nothing. But the danger of attempting it in this manner is, that it will never be done; and, like a procrastinating sinner, he will for ever put off his penitential resolution till to-morrow. If he did it all at once, I would be hanged if he died of the attempt; he would be uneasy for three or four days, that's all. He may change his liquor, and drink a little good porter, and, by degrees, come to small beer, the wholsomest and best of all liquors, except good soft water. But I do not mean that this rigorous abstinence from wine is to last for life, but only during the conflict with the disease. As soon as he has recovered health and strength to use exercise enough to subdue it, he may safely indulge once a week, or perhaps twice, with a pint of wine for the sake of good humour and good company, if they cannot be enjoyed without it; for I would not be such a churl as to forbid, or even damp, one of the greatest joys of human life.—

'He must never lose sight, however, of the three great principles of health and long life, Activity, Temperance, and Peace of Mind. With these ever in view, he may eat and drink of every thing the earth produces, but his diet must be plain, simple, solid, and tender, or in proportion to his consumption; he must eat but of one thing or two at most at a meal, and this will soon bring him to be satisfied with about half his usual quantity; for all men eat about twice as much as they ought to do, provoked by variety: he must drink but little of any liquor, and never till he has done eating: the drier every man's diet is, the better. No wine oftener than once or twice a week at most; and this must be considered as a luxurious indulgence. If he be sometimes led unawares into a debauch, it must be expiated by abstinence and double exercise the next day, and he may take a little of my magnesia and rhubarb as a good antidote: or if he cannot sleep with his unusual load, he may drink water, and with his finger in his throat throw it up. I have known some old soldiers by this trick alone, never taking their dose to bed with them, live to kill their acquaintance two or three times over. One moderate meal a day is abundantly sufficient; therefore it is better to omit supper, because dinner is not so easily avoided. Instead of supper, any good ripe fruit of the season would be very salutary, preventing costiveness, and keeping the bowels free and open, and cooling, correcting, and carrying off the heats and crudities of his indigestion.

'His activity need be no more than to persevere in the habit of rubbing all over, night and morning, for eight or ten minutes, and walking three or four miles every day, or riding ten, or using any bodily labour or exercise equivalent to it. In bad weather I can see no great evil in throwing a cloak round his shoulders and walking even in the rain; the only difficulty is to summon resolution enough to venture out; and a little use would take off all danger of catching cold, by hardening and securing him against the possibility of it upon that and all other occasions. If he dares not risque this, some succedaneum must be used within doors; more especially when bad weather continues any time. I recommend it to all men to wash their

 feet

feet every day, the gouty in particular, and not to lie a bed above seven hours in summer, and eight in winter.——

'Some perhaps may be reasonable enough to observe and say. This plan of yours is very simple; there is nothing marvellous in it; no wonderful discovery of any the latent powers of medicine: but will a regimen so easy to be complied with as this, cure the gout, stone, dropsy, &c.? Will it repair broken constitutions and restore old invalids to health? My answer is, that if I may trust the experience of my whole life, and above all the experience I have had in my own person, having not only got rid of the gout, of which I have had four severe fits in my younger days, but also immerged from the lowest ebb of life, that a man could possibly be reduced to by cholic, jaundice, and a complication of complaints, and recovered to perfect health; which I have now uninterruptedly enjoyed above ten years: I say, if I may rely upon all this, I may with great safety pronounce and promise that the plan here recommended, assisted at first with all the collateral aids of medicine peculiar to each case, correcting many an untoward concomitant symptom, pursued with resolution and patience, will certainly procure to others the same befits I received from it, and cure every curable disease. If this be thought too much to promise, I beg it may be considered, that a life of bad habits produces all these diseases: nothing therefore so likely as good ones long continued to restore or preserve health.'

The general doctrines here inculcated are so very useful, and deserve so much to be attended to, that we forbear to make any observations upon some few parts which are less conclusive and less satisfactory.

Art. VIII. *A short Ramble through some Parts of France and Italy.* By Lancelot Temple, Esq. 12mo. 1 s. 6 d. sewed. Cadell. 1771.

'SQUIRE Temple was sick, and would take no more physic; and his three physicians, after debating whether they should stew him at Buxton, or boil him at Caldas, or freeze him at Pyrmont, at last sentenced him to a sea-voyage. They were certainly right. It is plain that his disorder was of the atrabilious kind; for he quarrels with every thing he meets with. The first object of his wrath is his very good friend the sea, which he calls 'mad, savage, tyger-and-leopard-like.' He then sees the coast of Spain and Portugal, and calls it 'naked, barren, and uncomfortable.' Next he observes Mount *Singe*, and from thence takes an opportunity to abuse the poor *Ape*, calling it the most detestable of all animals. He then beholds the mountains of Granada, and calls them 'stern, savage, and inhospitable.' Presently Genoa comes in view, which he had heard called *superb*, but would not allow it to be so. Here he takes an opportunity to call the gentlemen who frequent the coffeehouses in England, 'a parcel of ill-bred boobies,' and says

says that the English ladies 'turn up their noses.' At Genoa he goes to the *Palazzo Durazzi* to see the paintings; and though there was a croud of people, 'not one, says he, of the WHOLE HERD, EXCEPT MYSELF, and perhaps two or three more, who were lost in the MOB, had the decency to pull off his hat as the lady of the house past.'

From Genoa he goes to Florence, visits the Grand Duke's collection, and calls the celebrated Venus a celestial prude. Arrived at Rome, he goes to St. Peter's, and calls Bernini's stairs, *conceited* screws of stairs; his Evangelists, *clumsy* Evangelists; and prophesies that St. Peter's will fall, and make a horrible *crush* before its *natural* time. In the *Capella Sistina*, he quarrels with the devil, calls Michael Angelo an ass for giving him long sharp ears, and thinks he would as well become a chancellor's wig, and a blue cockade. This quarrel with his infernal majesty puts him out of all patience. He calls aloud for a house-painter's brush dipt in whiting, to dash out all the insipid, DIRTY MOB of unmeaning figures that disgrace the side-walls of the *Capella Sistina*.

His rage is still violent. 'Often in the churches, says he, you cannot see the bottom of a fine picture for tall candles and crucifixes. What is still more *tantalizing* and *provoking*, you cannot see the first-rate pictures for a great glaring window, so that they might as well be packt up and deposited in a warehouse or a lumber-garret.'

He next vents his spleen on the 'base, thievish, cowardly scratches of Gothic envy,' visible in some of the pictures; sees the celebrated Cartons, finds them *clumsily* copied, calls them *bungled* imitations, and quarrels with Raphael for chusing an *unnatural* subject. The *Torso* he terms a *deplorable* fragment; the Antinous an *insipid* young man. He has seen many women whom he liked better than the *Venus*. Tiberius, whom some travellers have thought like our Charles the Second, has a flat head, and an air of vacancy that means nothing either genial or good-natured. Messilina he could not very well see, for an *impertinent* window: however, she was *not so handsome* as you would expect. Nero is a mere vulgar ruffian, aiming at your throat.

As to the people of Italy 'there are more *bad* than good, and a great majority of indifferents.' Of the Pope's dominions we have the following agreeable picture; they consist of 'a large extent of flat, melancholy, idle desart, whose rich soil, for want of cultivation, exhales such a putrid malignant vapour, that in the heats of July and August it is reckoned almost mortal to travellers; while the few inhabitants lead an anxious, miserable life, under perpetual apprehensions of a malignant fever, which is only not quite pestilential.'—Can this be that

Campania of which Florus ſays, "*Nihil mollius cælo, nihil uberius terra, nihil hoſpitalius mare?*" The following is perhaps one of the moſt curious inſtances of ſplenetic pleaſure that any language exhibits:

'" At Marſeilles my GREAT AMUSEMENT was to obſerve the POOR GALLEY-SLAVES induſtriouſly plying their different occupations, every one in his own booth upon the keys, a very ENTERTAINING walk! As far as I underſtand phyſiognomy, very few of thoſe *unhappy* people looked worſe than the *common run* of mankind!'

'Squire Temple now vents his rage againſt France: 'That part of Provence and Dauphiny, through which the road runs from Marſeilles to Lyons, has a meagre, hungry look, and is in general a naked ſkeleton of a country.—The olive is an uncomfortable creature to look at, not much more genial than the willow.'

Making all expedition to ſhun his own ſociety, in which he was certainly right, our Traveller arrives at Paris; where, he obſerves, the houſes of the nobility contribute nothing towards the embelliſhment of the place, but dead walls; meets with nothing ſo chearful or *riant* as he expected; finds the common dwelling-houſes gloomy, unfiniſhed, and ſlovenly, with heavy, old-faſhioned furniture; and imputes this to the want of frequent fires, which have ſo *good* an *effect* in London. In the Louvre all is ſtraggling and imperfect: a building ſtill advancing with a loitering progreſs, and likely to remain a dirty, duſty, uncomfortable, embarraſſing object of imperfection, without any reaſonable proſpect of its ever being finiſhed, or much regretted, perhaps, if it never ſhould. A building carried on at a great expence, for the reception of Kings that poſſibly enough will never paſs a night at Paris.' Such is the very curious picture that ſpleen has exhibited of the glory of France! Now for the Thuilleries.

'The Thuilleries is a ſpot not quite ſo agreeable as I expected to find it. One end is a melancholy grove of tall trees, divided into walks; but it does not appear that there is ever any verdure below. The other, next the buildings, is an inſipid, naked parterre, diverſified with whimſical, trifling flower-knots.'

When Mr. Temple comes to ſpeak of the ornamental architecture of gardens, he is perfectly outrageous. He cannot endure the ſplendour of ſuch objects. They turn his brain. Hear how he raves—'you muſt have a temple of *Concord*, truly! Of *Fortitude*, to be ſure! Of *public Spirit*, an't pleaſe heaven! Of the *Muſes*, of *Taſte* above all things in the world!—And perhaps a temple of *Friendſhip* to the memory of one who at heart deſpiſed you.' Excellent, inimitable picture of ſpleen! but

but let us hear him further—' I would down with all these unmeaning, impertinent childish ornaments in a great hurry! I would not bombard 'em because they may supply materials, &c.' Gracious and merciful! But what, gentle Reader, do you suppose that this *good-humoured* Traveller proposes as a substitute for your garden ornaments? Why; a gardener's house, a number of cottages, a hen-house, a bee-house, a dairy, and a larder. And so good b'ye to you!

ART. IX. *A Letter written by a Country Clergyman to Archbishop Herring, in the Year* 1754. 8vo. 1 s. Payne, &c. 1771.

THIS is a serious well written pamphlet, urging in a close and animated manner, some attempt toward that alteration in the present forms of the church of England, which has been for many years earnestly desired by many of the most judicious, pious, and worthy men, among both the clergy and laity. It may possibly be thought that, in some instances, the Writer has expressed himself with too great a degree of severity, considering the several obstacles which must be surmounted for accomplishing the end proposed; yet it will be allowed that, in the general, he discovers a spirit of candour and modesty, while he exerts a natural and (on the whole) a becoming fervor, on a point, which, he is persuaded, is of very great importance, and which, if there be any thing in virtue and religion, we apprehend, must be regarded as such, by all sober and reflecting persons.

The Editor has neither communicated to the public his own name, nor that of the Author; but we are acquainted, by an advertisement prefixed, that the original of this letter was lately found among the papers of a gentleman who was formerly about the person of the great prelate to whom it is addressed; that it was inclosed in a cover directed to his Grace, stamped with the mark of the post-office from whence it was dispatched, and might possibly have been put into the hands of the person in whose custody it was found, with a view of his publishing something by way of animadversion on its contents.

The Editor observes, that the policy of the church, about this time, took a turn to the peaceable counsels of STIFELING, and he therefore conjectures, that all contentious operation upon this letter had been countermanded. Such motives having, he says, no weight with him for suppressing it, it is now offered to the public, 'rather (he adds, with some asperity) as a matter of curiosity, than with any expectation that the church, or the pillars which support her, should be either the better or the worse for it.'

The subject has been repeatedly canvassed,—by some, with the utmost moderation,—by others, with greater energy of expres-

 sion;

ſion; but it does not appear that theſe renewed addreſſes have been ſufficient to rouze the attention of thoſe whoſe peculiar office it is to forward the good work of reformation. We cannot then wonder that the application ſhould be frequently revived; and as there is no reaſon to ſuppoſe that the ſtate of church affairs is much altered for the better during the few years which have elapſed ſince the date of this letter; it may with propriety be, at this time, offered to the public notice. But as we have often declared our ſentiments on this topic, in the courſe of our remarks on the different treatiſes which it hath occaſioned, we ſhould have diſmiſſed the preſent performance (the authenticity of which we conclude there is no cauſe to call in queſtion) without any farther extenſion of the article; was it not, that, beſide the merit which the Letter has in itſelf, the peculiar circumſtances with which it is attended, may probably excite a curioſity in many of our Readers to know ſomewhat more of its contents; on which account we ſhall preſent them with a few extracts, though the pamphlet certainly appears to the greateſt advantage when regularly peruſed in that order aſſigned to each part of it by the Writer.

The Clergyman, having mentioned the *Free and Candid Diſquiſitions*, together with the *Eſſay on Spirit*, and the Writers who ſeconded that performance, in relation to the Athanaſian controverſy, obſerves, that the Archbiſhop was not wholly unmindful of the caſe, as appears by the ſecond page of Mr. Knowles's anſwer to the above-mentioned *Eſſay*: 'An anſwer, he ſays, by no means ſatisfactory even to the *Athanaſians* themſelves, ſome of whom have been heard to ſay, that it was neither worthy of the cauſe he pretends to vindicate, nor of your Grace's patronage.' After this reflection, our Author gives an account of the ſtate of himſelf and his brethren in theſe words:

'In the mean time, the truly conſcientious clergy are anxious and diſcouraged. The arguments offered againſt this Creed, and many other things which occur in our daily miniſtrations, are plauſible, and for ought we know, may be juſt and ſolid. I ſay, my Lord, for ought we know; for your Grace needs not be told, that a large majority of us have not given, nor indeed are *made capable* of giving matters of this nature, that previous deliberation which is neceſſary to form a competent judgment upon them, before our entrance into the miniſtry. And, to that ſo many parochial duties and family cares ſucceed, that I am afraid we of the inferior claſs, who are doomed to bear *the burden and heat of the day*, have but little leiſure, and leſs means, to acquire this kind of learning by our own induſtry. In theſe circumſtances, and with this ſlender proviſion, it is our misfortune to be called, by unavoidable occaſions, into a variety of companies, where, with great freedom, our church forms are

are brought into debate, as well by the members of our own communion, as Dissenters and adversaries of different denominations; many of whom, however, bating the reproach of an invidious name, appear to be men of candour, probity, and good sense, sufficient to intitle their sentiments and observations to a very serious consideration.

'In this situation we naturally look up toward our superiors, for such aids and instructions as men of inferior talents and limited provinces do, from time to time, require. And I beg leave to assure your Grace, there never was an emergency when we had more occasion.

'And yet, alas! so it is, that very little of this instruction is to be had in proportion to our necessities.

'Our Bishops and Archdeacons charges, when we are favoured with them, which is but seldom, are commonly short and general; consisting chiefly of declamatory encomiums on our own system, and reflections on the principles of the adversary; of political observations which we understand not, and allusions to facts we never heard of; with, perhaps, some few gentle directions concerning our conduct, which, if they had the least experience of the condition, abilities, commerce, and connexions of the inferior clergy, their Lordships would know to be impracticable.'

In a farther part of this pamphlet, in which the Creed of Athanasius, as *imposed* upon the members of our church, is particularly alluded to, this Writer proceeds as follows:

'The church requires them to denounce, with their own mouths, eternal perdition upon themselves and all others who do not believe the contents of the Athanasian Creed. They cannot be made to understand that the contents of this Creed are conformable to the gospel of Christ. On the other side, they *are* made to understand, by plain arguments, that there is great probability the Athanasian doctrine is *not* conformable to the doctrine of the gospel. The church still persists in requiring them to believe and denounce as above, without affording them any new lights to their understandings. Is this a state for a reasonable creature to acquiesce in? Is this the method in which the fathers of the church should treat those souls for whom Christ died? Is this the way to *support the weak*, and to *comfort the feeble-minded?*

'This conduct of the church of *England*, my Lord, I call unreasonable, nay I call it unchristian. And I should call it unreasonable and unchristian, if the church of *England* were *Arian* and should deal the same measure to the *Athanasians*. Whilst churches and churchmen forsake the spirit, the simplicity, the charity, the edification of the gospel, and betake themselves to the *cunning craftiness* of worldly politics, they may be Athanasians, Arians, Socinians, Papists, Episcopalians, Presbyterians

byterians, Anabaptists, Quakers, Methodists, or whatever else you please to call them, but *Christians* they cannot be.

'The gospel says, *Prove all things, hold fast that which is good.* The policy of the church says, " Hold fast all things good and bad, right and false. The church of England is a compact body, and has the law on her side. Adhere to the establishment as such with all your heart and soul, and if there be ever so many remonstrants against particular defects, superfluities, or corruptions, answer them not a word. They must comply or starve."

'O my Lord! did the Protestants set up upon these principles? Had there been one Protestant in the world if these principles had prevailed?

'For, that I may not be mistaken by your Grace, the remonstrants I mean to plead for are those only who are so upon Protestant principles; who have no other view in calling for a reform, than to have the government, the discipline, and the worship of the church reduced to and regulated by the genuine principles of the Christian religion. In how many instances the church of *England* is said, and, I am afraid, proved to have deviated from and counteracted these principles, your Grace has no occasion to be informed by me.

'It is in vain to say, as some would pretend, that these remonstrances are no more than the clamours and cant of some discontented or some fanatical spirits. The treatises that have been written to solicit a review of our church affairs, shame this pretence even to ridicule. They demonstrate to all impartial and disinterested judges, that, let the station and influence of the authors be what it will, there are but few better or wiser men in the three kingdoms.'

In the course of his reflections our Author has occasion to remark, that the corruption of manners observable among the laity, has been sometimes greatly attributed to the negligence or ill examples of the public teachers of religion. We are by no means disposed to join in indiscriminate reflections on any body of men, much less on the clergy of our church, whose office and circumstances entitle them to respect, and many of whom are, without doubt, persons of very respectable characters. But so far as the following reflections are just they ought to be made public, that some effectual remedy may be applied by these who have the power for this purpose. After having mentioned the censure which has been passed upon our ministers, the Letter-writer thus proceeds:

'An heavy charge, my Lord, upon the clergy! But how shall we acquit ourselves? Shall we say, or should we be believed in saying, that the clergy do their duty in all respects? That they are, in general, laborious, faithful, and vigilant in the pastoral

paſtoral care; patient and gentle towards all men; modeſt, humble, and condeſcending, to the poor as well as the rich; contented with their ſtation, and unambitious of wealth and power; *in all things approving themſelves as the miniſters of God, and enſamples to the flock, in word, in converſation, in charity, in ſpirit, in faith, in purity?*—If this be true, it can hardly be true too that the flock of God, having thus their portion of ſpiritual food in due ſeaſon, ſhould profit ſo little under the miniſtry of ſuch paſtors. Lay the two facts together, and the plain conſequence will be, that our office is abſolutely uſeleſs, and that the public might very well ſpare the millions that are expended upon a particular order of men, under the notion of rewarding a ſervice they cannot poſſibly perform, namely, that of making the individuals of a community better than they would be otherwiſe for all the purpoſes of civil ſociety.

'But let God be true, and every man who makes theſe inferences, a liar. The premiſes are falſe, and the concluſion is impious; inaſmuch as the reflection ſuggeſted in it would fall not upon the clergy, but upon the Chriſtian religion itſelf, which will never be found to have fallen ſo far ſhort in its influence, where the means of knowledge and edification it affords have been duly and faithfully diſpenſed.

'The alternative then is, that the clergy are ſlothful and ſecular, either unfit for the office they have undertaken, or unconcerned about the faithful diſcharge of it. And ſo, upon examination, we find it.

'The collective body of the clergy, excepting a very inconſiderable number, conſiſts of men whoſe lives and ordinary occupations are moſt foreign to their profeſſion. We find among them all ſorts of ſecular characters; courtiers, politicians, lawyers, merchants, uſurers, civil magiſtrates, ſportſmen, muſicians, ſtewards of country 'ſquires, and tools of men in power, and even companions of rakes and infidels: not to mention the ignorant herd of poor curates, to whom the inſtruction of our common people is committed, who are accordingly, in religious matters, the moſt ignorant common people that are in any Proteſtant, if not in any Chriſtian ſociety upon the face of the earth.

'There are to be found among the clergy of our church, geniuſes who are fit for almoſt any thing but the particular character and function they have undertaken, or rather into which they have been driven; and I am much miſtaken if a college of Apoſtles would not find a large majority of us much fitter for ſomething elſe.'

Some farther pages are employed in reflections of this kind; and in ſeveral brief conſiderations in reſpect to the meaſures which ſhould be taken by the governors of the church, for the correction of theſe evils; after which the Letter-writer proceeds:

'For

'For the honour of the calling, however, and to preserve all possible reverence for our superiors, I am willing to suppose that every kind and degree of Christian discipline would be faithfully administered by them, if their hands were not unhappily tied up by the nature of our present ecclesiastical constitution.

'But then, my Lord, I fear it will be difficult to acquit them on another hand, either before God or man, if it be true, that knowing and seeing, as they needs must, the tendency of this constitution, to countenance secularity, hypocrisy, and prevarication in the clergy, and all manner of vice and licentiousness among the people, as well as to give strength and encouragement to impiety and infidelity, they not only are content to have it so, but do all they can to keep it so.

'That the frame of our church affairs is so contrived as in too many cases to defeat all the good ends of a Christian ministry, needs no great depth of penetration to discover.

'A non-resident incumbent is not only nonsense in terms, but a character so utterly inconsistent with the duties of the ministerial calling, that let him preach his four sermons in so many years, instead of so many months, like an angel, the very circumstance of turning his back upon his flock as soon as this piece of drudgery is over, and his rents in his pocket, and leaving them to a poor curate, is sufficient to convince the first of his parishioners that dips into *Paul's* epistles to *Timothy* and *Titus*, that this man cannot possibly be in earnest.

'The subscription of so many ministers, every year, to articles of religion, which many of them understand not, and many others of them believe not (both of which have been publicly charged upon them, in print, very lately) affords such suspicions of impenetrable stupidity, voracious avarice, and prostituted conscience in the subscribers, as will unanswerably fix upon the church of England, as long as this state of things shall last, all that odium and contempt which reasonable and upright men have for arbitrary impositions, and mean and sordid submissions to them.

'The abominable oppressions and partialities of our spiritual courts, supported, many of them, by no law, and contrary (most of them) to the genius of our civil policy, as well as to the plainest precepts of the gospel, are the curse of the poor, the jest of the rich, and the abhorrence of the wise and good even among the clergy themselves.

'And, if to this we add the strange expressions, and childish ordinances in our public worship, so different from the spirit and simplicity of the piety and devotion prescribed in the gospel of Christ, and without all authority but the dreams and impositions of fantastical and factious men, who can wonder that infi-

delity

delity should spread and flourish among us, under this hopeful cultivation of its prejudices against the Christian religion?

'Is it astonishing that such a set of men as the *Methodists* should arise, and attempt to awaken the drowsy heads, and alarm the stupified hearts of our people, immersed, as they are, in all the secular security into which the doctrines and examples of their own pastors may, with too much probability, be supposed to have thrown them?

'Who that considers, that there has not been one argument offered against a review of our church affairs, which would not have operated at the Reformation with equal truth and force in favour of Popery.—Who, I say, that considers this, will be surprized at the numbers which are said to be daily dropping from us into that horrid abyss of impiety and superstition?'

In this manner our Author manifests the necessity of a reform, at the same time allowing that it is a work full of difficulties; but proceeds, nevertheless, to urge an attempt towards it:

'To whom then, says he, shall we look for the beginnings of so great a blessing, with so much propriety, as to the Prelate at the head of our national church? A Prelate of the greatest piety; a Prelate of distinguished principles in favour of truth and liberty; a Prelate of known contempt for the sordid accumulation of wealth; a Prelate of the most amiable and engaging humility, and upon whom the prospect of losing either his riches or his power in a righteous cause will make no impression; in a word, a Prelate, who having an heart to pity, and an hand to relieve every human complaint, cannot be supposed to turn a deaf ear, or an indifferent eye, to the distresses of the most grievous, and therefore of the most moving nature, the distresses of conscientious ministers of God's word, struggling in bonds, and labouring under burdens, which they can neither bear without the most galling anguish of mind, nor break and cast off without ruin to themselves and families, and scandal to the society, which they would wish to see perpetually flourishing in *true* honour, and *deservedly* a name and a praise in all the earth.

'Pardon me, my good Lord, if I should affirm that, in the present situation of things, and whilst your Grace is in possession of your present station and talents, no consideration, relating merely to the secondary and subordinate articles of human happiness, will excuse your Grace at the great day of account, for neglecting or postponing the care of those things which respect the endless felicity of mankind. It is the souls of the people of England that are your Grace's province. To your Grace's charge these are committed by your God and your king, and permit me most humbly to suggest to your Grace, the very little merit there will be in your Grace's attention to affairs of the

 greatest

greatest secular importance, whilst these poor souls are wandering in the paths of darkness and deceit, of disorder and confusion, for want of any assistance that might be afforded them by your Grace's pastoral endeavours.'

This writer assures his Grace, that his name and station should have been communicated, if the knowledge of them could have been supposed in the least degree to have contributed to the accomplishment of what he so earnestly pleads for; after which he thus finishes his letter:

'The man himself, my Lord, is a serious Christian, hastening, in the decline of life, to put off all his mortal connexions, not without eagerly wishing to see, ere he depart hence, some provision made for the succession of a more rational and righteous generation of his countrymen, than he fears the next will prove, without it.

'In the course of these reflections, the miserable state of the church, and your Grace's influence towards the amendment of it, could not escape his notice, though he had a notion that possibly neither of them might be so obvious to your Grace.—Pity, he thought, the one should continue to be estimated by no other measure than the false, partial, evasive and perjurious returns that are made to visitation books; or the idea of the other lessened by chimerical difficulties, raised and magnified by those who perhaps are afraid of nothing so much as to see your Grace shine forth in a province, where, though your Grace might not have so many of *their* compliments and adulations, your Grace would both have and deserve true honour, esteem and reverence from much better men: and if, by a hint of all this, your Grace might be prevailed with to try your strength in this field of true glory, he thought it were even a sin not to give it, though no other conveyance could be found for it than the meanest hand in the kingdom.

'These are the considerations which gave conception and and birth to these papers, upon which the writer implores the blessing of Almighty God, having nothing in view but his glory, and the advancement of the kingdom of Christ, and consequently an encrease of virtue and happiness among mankind. If he is in the wrong, it is not what he intends, and therefore can be no great loser by his mistake, being led into it by some of the plainest and clearest documents in the New Testament. On the other hand, if that book contains the rule of Christian life, he *must* be in the right; and in that case assures himself these papers, slight as they are, and whatever reception they may meet with from your Grace, shall not utterly perish. They may be consumed in the flames, rot in the dust, or be rendered unlegible by the moths, yet will the time come when they shall be raised from this state of obscurity and oblivion, and admitted

to

to bear their testimony, when and where it will be no objection to them that they were addressed to the first Prelate in *England*, by, My Lord, *your Grace's dutiful son and humble servant*,

A PRIVATE CLERGYMAN.'

**** Among the errors of the press observed in this pamphlet, there is one, in particular, where the Author mentions a country glazier as one character in which a clergyman may have appeared: he probably meant *a country grazier*.

ART. X. *The open Address of New Testament evidence: Or, three plain Monuments authenticating three Facts, on which the Divinity of our holy Religion has its Support. Humbly proposed to public* Consideration, *in an unthinking Age.* By Caleb Fleming, D.D. 8vo. 1s. 6d. Buckland. 1771.

WE are here presented with a sensible account and vindication of three institutions which peculiarly distinguish the gospel revelation: these institutions are the *Christian Sabbath*, *Baptism*, and the *Lord's Supper*. At the same time that the Author explains the nature and design of each, he considers them as affording a three-fold testimony to the divinity of the Christian doctrine, since, says he, these monuments, within the church, have had their existence ever since the facts had place, of our Lord's humiliation, resurrection, and exaltation.

The *Christian Sabbath* falls first under consideration, in which he proves its obligation, shews the intent and excellence of the appointment, and urges Christians to give it a suitable regard. In taking notice of the change of the day from the seventh to the first day of the week, for which suitable reasons are alledged, he seems to incline to an opinion mentioned in *Bedford's Scripture Chronology*, viz. that the seventh day from the creation, being the first day of Adam's life, was the first day of the week according to the Jewish computation, but the sabbath was altered from this day to the seventh in commemoration of their deliverance; and consequently (we suppose) that the day which Christians now observe is most conformable to the original institution. However, this is only a circumstance; the observance of a day of religious rest appears to have been divinely appointed, and Dr. F. remarks that 'The law of the sabbath essentially belongs to the system of the *divine moral*; and though we call it a law of the first table, yet, on our observation of it, greatly depends the regard we pay to the duties we owe both to God and man.' The farther reflections which are here presented in a rational manner, demand the sober thought of every Christian. The Author justly laments the present state of things among us in this particular: 'How shockingly faulty, says he, is our police!

lice! How shamefully little regard is shewn, even by our magistrates, to the religious observance of the weekly sabbath! All avenues to vice are set open, both within and all around this great city.' The great, the rich, the noble, the princely, are themselves exhibiting the most shocking spectacles of sabbath profanation, in open contempt of law, both human and divine. Nay, even card-tables are said to be common in the houses of families of rank and title; and what is more astonishing, in some card parties the Cleric is found! The consecrated priest thus desecrates and disgraces his function! In fact, the day which God has sanctified for religious rest, men impiously convert into a day of pleasure, or of loose gratification: a day of travelling, of banqueting, routs, of revelling and debauchery. Every where the common people are closely copying such enormous impieties; spending these holy days in all the dissipations and wantonnesses of pleasurable amusements, and in every depraving indulgence.

We would hope that one part of the above desciption is stretched a little too far; it is however certain, that this state of things calls for very serious attention.

Christian Baptism is the next subject of enquiry. As a theme for his dissertation, our Author fixes upon 1 Pet. iii. 21, 22. *The like figure whereunto baptism does now save us,* &c. In which text, considered in its connection with what is before said of Noah's deliverance in the time of the deluge, he supposes that Noah's salvation by water is to be regarded as the type, the antitype of which must be water-baptism: at the same time, says he, there was no saving causality either in the type or the antitype, but only an instrumentality. After which he farther explains the text in this manner, 'As all those taken into the ark with Noah were preserved from the general destruction, by the ark's being buoyant on the flood; so that which was made the instrument of destruction to a wicked world, was made salutary to Noah and his family; in resemblance of which, baptismal water now saves, as it separates the baptised from a world that lies in wickedness, and puts under the protection and guidance of the Saviour of mankind. Apostles will tell us, that the condition of the converted pagan, was as different from his former state, as light is from darkness, and as life is from death.'

Dr. Fleming proceeds to tell us what baptism does not do for us; as, 'that it cannot secure us of any saving benefit, since this must wholly depend upon our subsequent behaviour.' He farther shews what it can do; and here observes, that the direction in the original institution to baptize "*In* the name," seems to be generally mistaken: 'to me, says he, it appears evidently to intend that authority *in* or *by* which the apostles were to baptize, and not into which men were baptized.' To which he adds,

adds; 'Baptism does save, as it initiates into a divine constitution, at the head of which the Saviour of the world presides.' He vindicates the baptism of infants, and then, from observing what is added in the verses mentioned above, as the foundation of his discourse, concerning the resurrection and ascension of Christ, he concludes, that baptism is to be regarded as a 'monument erected in the Christian church, which should perpetually recognize a fact, of so high and important a nature, as that of the exaltation of Jesus to the seat of sovereign power! It puts, he says, the baptized into a constitution, or renders him the member of a body, over which the presiding head has a superiority given him to all other orders of beings, that can any way affect either the safety or the weal of man.—If the ends of baptism, it is added, are thus religiously kept in view, we become not only related, but united to him, and are joint heirs with him of eternal life.'

The acount which is given, in the next dissertation, of the *reason and end of the Lord's Supper*, is something peculiar, though rational and pious; but for a more particular view of it, we must refer our readers to the tract itself. From the reflections which are added toward the close of this work, we shall select the following, because it corresponds to one part of the proposal laid down in the title-page, leaving it to others to make such observations upon it as they think proper.

'We might now appeal, says our Author, to the modern deist, i. e. to the unbeliever in revelation, and defy his ability of confuting the three-fold testimony given to the divinity of the gospel dispensation, since these monuments, within the church, have had their existence ever since the facts had place of our Lord's humiliation, resurrection and exaltation. Jesus, the night in which he was betrayed, instituted the memorial of his crucifixion. When risen from the dead (after he had continued in *hades* the seventh day sabbath) by his resurrection he consecrates the weekly festival of the first day of the week sabbath: a day universally observed by Christians, in abrogation of the Jewish sabbath. And because Deity has exalted him to the right hand of power, and made him head over all things to the church of God, he has instituted baptism to recognize his Lordship, and to initiate into his kingdom; which monument remains *in high preservation* until this day.'

'Pray what sort of evidence will convince of the divinity of the gospel-system, if this will not? If these witnesses, which answer to the spirit, the water, and the blood, will not persuade, neither would miracle make the least impression on the infidel.'

There are some expressions of this Author which may appear a little uncouth, if not somewhat affected, as particularly the above which we have put into italics: but he writes like a serious, worthy man, who has the consciousness of sincerity, though he should in some instances be mistaken. His concluding words are, 'Thus I have finished the survey I proposed of the three institutions,—and have with integrity, and, I hope, with evidence, pleaded the cause of truth and religion. Do me the favour of an impartial, serious and close re-consideration,—and do yourselves the justice of a faithful and efficacious application.'

Art. XI. *Anecdotes of a Convent.* By the Author of Memoirs of Mrs. Williams *. 12mo. 3 vols. 7s. 6d. Becket and De Hondt. 1771.

IN the novel before us, we observe a degree of merit, rarely to be met with in publications of the same class. It discovers an enlarged acquaintance with the human heart, and exhibits a beautiful picture of real manners. The ingenious Author does not depart from the road of nature to excite surprize and wonder by bold and improbable fictions. The attention of the reader is kept up by other methods;—by characters delineated in just and expressive colours, by incidents conceived with propriety and taste, and by an interesting and artful arrangement. The work is complicated, without obscurity; and the different stories, which compose it, give it a variety highly engaging and delightful. We feel every situation it describes; and are alternately melted with tenderness, sunk in dejection, chearful through hope, and exulting with joy.

Miss Bolton, a young lady of immense fortune, is one of the principal characters in this performance. She is in love with Mr. Boothby, the son of her guardian; but her guardian, from a principle of rare delicacy, is averse to their marriage, and, on this account, sends his son abroad. Miss Bolton, however, discovers by accident the place of his residence, and addresses the following letter to him:

'Ever since the cruel moment, in which your father deceived us both, and separated you from your *Julia*, I have been unhappy. Do you remember, my *Harry*, that on the fatal day on which I lost you, how chearful we were, and how unsuspicious of the misfortune which then hung over our heads, and was in a few hours to fall, with all its weight, upon us? You cannot have so soon forgot, that you and I had been out together all the morning a fishing in the great canal; there, whilst seated by my side, how often did you swear that you would prefer a cottage with your *Julia*, to a throne without her; nay, generous as you were, you wished I had been less

---

* See Review, vol. xlii. p. 230: *Letters between an English Lady and her Friend at Paris.*

rich,

rich, that you might have had an opportunity of ſhewing the diſintereſtedneſs of your paſſion for me. How unneceſſary was ſuch a wiſh, my *Harry!* Did I ever doubt your worth, or the nobility of your ſentiments? Surely not, ſince I fancy nobody will ever draw your picture more amiable than it is pourtrayed in my breaſt: at this inſtant I ſee you at my feet, as you were on that fatal morning; your voice ſtill vibrates on my ear, as it did when you declared, that neither time nor abſence ſhould ever make you forget me, or ſhake your conſtancy. I promiſed, on my part, by all things ſacred, never to give my hand to any other man than my *Harry*, who ſo entirely poſſeſſed my heart. Sure ſome guardian angel, in pity of our innocence, knowing we were on the verge of being ſeparated, (perhaps for ever) urged us thus to plight our mutual vows of love and fidelity to each other: mine are written on the tablets of providence, never to be effaced; nor do I doubt the validity of yours: let us live then for one another, and truſt the event to time, and our invariable conſtancy.

'In the evening, when your father had taken you out, on pretence of viſiting a ſick friend in the neighbourhood, I ſat down to the organ, and began playing over your favourite tunes, counting the minutes, however, till your return; when, alas! towards night, I ſaw your father arrive alone. I aſked him, with precipitation, where you were? He anſwered, negligently, "I left him with a friend for a day or two." I looked chagrined, I believe, but made no reply, as I naturally ſuppoſed you would walk over and ſee us ſome part of the following day; the next day came, the day after, and the third, yet ſtill I had not ſeen you: On the fourth I loſt all patience, and aſked your father if you never was to return home? Yes, ſaid he, my dear, I hope ſo, but not yet; for *Harry*'s now of an age to go into the world, and to chuſe a profeſſion; it would, therefore, be doing him an injuſtice to keep him idling at home, when he ſhould be improving himſelf abroad; I have, therefore, ſent him to a gentleman of my acquaintance, who will, I hope, render him all the ſervice in his power, in whatever plan of life he ſhall himſelf chuſe to enter. But when will he come back? ſaid I, impatiently. I really don't exactly know, replied your father, but I fancy it will be ſome time firſt; for you are to conſider, Madam, that *Harry* is a younger brother, and muſt, therefore, make his own fortune, or go without one. I would hear no more, but, burſting into tears, left the room; ſince which time I never could learn from your obdurate father, where you were: accident gave me that information; I knew it but yeſterday, and to-day I write. O *Harry!* I have been very wretched, but ſhall be no longer ſo, ſince I have now the conſolation of correſponding with you; for I cannot doubt of your expedition in anſwering this. Direct to me at Mrs. *Pinup*'s, mantua-maker, in *New Bond-ſtreet*; I ſhall receive your letters ſafe, and without any danger of their falling into wrong hands. Adieu, my beloved *Harry*, depend on my unalterable fidelity; take care of your health, if you would preſerve the life of your ever faithful and affectionate

JULIA BOLTON.'

The following is the return to this letter:

'*Julia!* my lovely, my adorable *Julia!* what tranſports did your faithful *Harry* feel on the reception of your dear letter! Tranſports, as pure as they were violent; for I did not purchaſe them by the forfeiture of my word, ſince I know not by what means you found out my *addreſs*; but bleſſed be the hand that gave it you: your dear image, which I conſtantly wear on my breaſt, though it is painted in much livelier colours in my heart, has been my only conſolation ſince the fatal day of our ſeparation, *Julia*; the recollection of that day, when my father declared that I ſhould ſee you no more, unmans me, and my tears obſtruct my ſight; yet he gave ſuch reaſons for doing what I thought a cruel act, as obliged me to admire him, even whilſt I was a martyr to his juſtice: he ſhewed me to demonſtration, my angel, what I ought always to have known, preſumptuous as I was. How unworthy an offer I was making you, when I dared to propoſe myſelf! He ſhewed me how ungenerous it was in me to impoſe upon your tender and inexperienced heart, in order to rob you, by a connexion with myſelf, of thoſe advantages of rank, ſplendor, &c. to which your birth, fortune, and beauty, ſo juſtly intitled you: he proved to me—or at leaſt he tried to do ſo—that I loved with a paſſion not worthy of you; ſince I preferred ſelf-gratification to the honour and proſperity of the object beloved. True love, he urged, (and ſuch a one alone was worthy of being inſpired by Miſs Bolton) muſt neceſſarily be as diſintereſted and generous, as the ſource from whence it ſprung. "And could you, *Harry*, (ſaid my father in a pathetic tone) fancy you loved with this exalted paſſion, when, not being able to climb ſo high as the object of your adoration, you would have pulled her down to your level? Beſides, did you never once reflect on the diſhonour which you muſt inevitably have brought upon me by this match? What would the world have ſaid on the occaſion? Why certainly, that I was a villain, and had betrayed the truſt her noble father, the ſon of my patron and benefactor, Lord *Wanſworth*, had placed in me, with ſuch unbounded confidence. Know, *Harry*, that the hour which had united you clandeſtinely with my lovely ward, would have preceded but a few days that of your father's death; as I could not have ſurvived my honour, nor, indeed, the ſorrow I ſhould have felt, on ſeeing all my hopes of her future

future eſtabliſhment, in a manner worthy of her, defeated by the machinations of my own ſon." You ſeem affected at my diſcourſe, child, ſaid my father. I anſwered him by my tears. "Well, continued he, let virtue and honour be your guides; they will ſupport you in the conflict, and infallibly conquer an ill-judged paſſion; time and abſence will lend their aid to this neceſſary work; and, in the mean while, I intreat *Harry* as a friend, and command you as a father, never from henceforward to write a line, nor cauſe one to be wrote, to Miſs Bolton; as I intend to keep her totally ignorant of every circumſtance concerning you, except the ſtate of your health; that I will communicate to her, as I will her's to you, becauſe I would have you friends to each other, though not lovers." And now, my ſon, ſaid he, give me your hand, and promiſe me, upon your honour, that you will neither directly nor indirectly, give any information to *Julia*, of the place of your reſidence, either while you are in *England*, or when you ſhall be in *France*; even ſhould ſhe, by any extraordinary accident, find out your direction, and write to you, though, I think, I ſhall take ſuch precautions as will render it impoſſible; in that caſe, I inſiſt upon your immediately informing me of it, and I will inſtantly remove you out of her knowledge. Here he pauſed, as waiting for my anſwer; what could I do, but obey this beſt of fathers? I gave my word of honour to fulfil implicitely (as far as it was in my power) all his injunctions; and in conſequence of this promiſe, I have—how ſhall I tell it you, my *Julia!*—I have, by this poſt, wrote to my father, to inform him, that, by means unknown to me, you have diſcovered the place of my abode: thus I have put it out of my power ever to be bleſſed with another letter from you, as I am certain I ſhall inſtantly be removed from hence, as ſoon as my father receives my letter; therefore, I intreat you write no more to me, even ſhould you again find out where I am. Heaven! is it poſſible that your *Harry* ſhould intreat not to hear from the idol of his heart! his *Julia!* Yes, my charming girl, I will love you, as you deſerve to be beloved for yourſelf; be happy in a properer choice:—O! may the man you ſhall fix upon—Away, I cannot talk of him; my *Julia* my brain turns—I would procure *your* happineſs, Miſs Bolton, though eternal miſery to *myſelf* ſhould be the purchaſe. I will obey my father, though my life may be the ſacrifice; but I will never ceaſe to love my *Julia*, whilſt my pulſe beats, or my heart has one ſenſation left in it; to this I ſwear; record it, ye hoſt of angels; and, O! believe me, too generous, and too charming maid, that I am unalterably your faithful, but unfortunate friend and lover,

HENRY BOOTHBY.

These letters are given as a ſpecimen of the Author's manner: it muſt be obſerved, however, that we have ſelected them, not

becauſe

because we think them the beſt in the performance, but becauſe they are ſhort and detached, and ſuit the limits which we preſcribe to articles of this kind.

Art. XII. *The Life of Benvenuto Cellini: a Florentine Artiſt. Containing a Variety of courious and entertaining Particulars relative to Painting, Sculpture, and Architecture; and the Hiſtory of his own Time.* Written by himſelf in the Tuſcan Language, and tranſlated from the Original by Thomas Nugent, LL. D. F.S.A. 8vo. 2 Vols. 10 s. 6 d. Boards. Davies. 1771.

CELLINI lived about two centuries ago. He was bred a jeweller and goldſmith; but ſeems to have had an extraordinary genius for the fine arts in general. In proceſs of time he became eminent alſo for his ſkill in ſtatuary; and ſome of his productions in that branch are deemed moſt exquiſite. His admirable ſkill and taſte in all the various kinds of workmanſhip to which he applied his aſtoniſhing talents, brought him acquainted with the great artiſts who flouriſhed in that remarkable æra: as Michael Angelo, Julio Romano, &c. &c. And he was employed by popes, kings, and other princely patrons of genius—encouragers of every improvement of the ſciences and arts ſo highly cultivated in the days of Leo X. Charles V. and Francis I.

The original of this uncommon piece of biography was not, we are told, publiſhed till the year 1730. It was, probably, withheld ſo long from the public eye, on account of the exceſſive freedom with which the Author hath treated the characters of many eminent perſons, the heads of ſeveral great families in Italy, &c. The book, however, is now well known through most parts of Europe; and the wonder is, that it did not ſooner make its appearance in the Engliſh language.

With reſpect to the entertainment which the reader may expect to meet with in theſe memoirs, it may be ſufficient, briefly to obſerve, that many of Cellini's adventures are, really, (conſidered as matters of fact, not as efforts of invention) extraordinary and intereſting. He was a man of violent paſſions, high ſpirit, romantic, enterprizing; ſo that, as his indiſcretions were perpetually creating him enemies, his reſentments were continually impelling him, headlong, to ſome extravagance of conduct, in order to gratify his inordinate thirſt of vengeance. And it ſeems to have been owing merely to the partial reſpect paid to his rare talents, as an artiſt, that he, more than once eſcaped the hand of juſtice for the aſſaſſinations he committed in the tumults and frays in which he was ſo often engaged.

In other reſpects, Cellini appears to have been an honeſt, generous, charitable, and even pious man; but with ſtrange inconſiſtencie cies in his character: for, with all his ingenuity, his knowledge, and his licentiousness of conduct, he appears to have been the slave of superstition, and most egregiously the dupe of his own wild visionary fancies:—dealing with conjurors, conversing with angels, and falling into various other enthusiastic delusions, particularly during his imprisonment in the castle of St. Angelo, at Rome; from whence he escaped in a most surprizing manner, though he had the misfortune to be retaken.

On the whole, though Cellini is often intolerably minute and circumstantial in relating the most trifling incidents of his life, and of the works in which he was successively engaged, yet the many vicissitudes which he experienced will not fail to interest his readers in his various reverses of fortune;—and the anecdotes of other geniuses, his cotemporaries, will also contribute to the entertainment they will receive from this very singular performance: a performance which may, in some measure, though in a lower rank of life, be considered as a companion to the picture which the romantic Lord Herbert of Cherbury has given us of himself.

MONTHLY CATALOGUE,

For AUGUST, 1771.

POETICAL.

Art. 13. *Poems.* By a Lady. 12mo. 2 s. sewed. Walter. 1771.

THE following little poem, with the compliment annexed, will serve at once as a specimen of this Lady's abilities, and as a criticism on her book:

On Mr. Walpole's *House at Strawberry Hill.* Written in the Year 1760.

When Envy saw yon Gothic structure rise,
She view'd the fabric with malignant eyes;
With grief she gazes on the antique wall,
The pictur'd window and the trophied hall:
Through well rang'd chambers next she bends her way,
Gloomy, not dark, and chearful, though not gay:
Where to the whole each part proportion bears,
And all around a pleasing aspect wears.
Tow'rds Learning's mansion then her footsteps tend,
Where columns rise, and sculptor'd arches bend.
Here soothing Melancholy holds her seat,
And Contemplation seeks the lov'd retreat.
The garden next displays a magic scene
Of fragrant plants, and never-fading green.
Each various season various gifts bestows,
The woodbine, lilac, violet, and rose.
Hence in clear prospect to the *gazer's eye*,
Woods, hills, and streams, in sweet confusion lie.

The silver Thames, as he pursues his way,
Here seems to loiter, and prolong his stay.
These matchless charms her indignation move,
She weeps to find she cannot but approve.
Then sorely sighing from her canker'd breast,
Thus the curst fiend her impious woes exprest:

'Am I, in vain, a foe to all thy race?
'Twas I that wrought thy patriot-sire's disgrace.
Vainly I strove to blast his *honour'd* name,
Brighter it *shines*, restor'd to endless *fame*.
And must another Walpole break my rest?
Still must thy praises my repose molest?
'Tis thine by various talents still to please,
To plan with judgment, execute with ease:
With equal skill to build, converse, or write,
To charm the mind, and gratify the sight.
Ah, could I but these battlements o'erthrow!
And lay this monument of genius low!—
But vain the wish; for Art and Nature join
To add perfection to the fair design!
It must proceed; for so the Fates decree
But mark the sentence that's pronounc'd by me.
Thousands that view it shall the work despise;
And thousands more shall view it with my eyes.
Th' applause which thou so gladly wouldst receive,
The candid and the wise alone can give.
Taste, though much talk'd of, is confin'd to few;
They best can prize it who are most like you.

To the Authoress *of some Lines on Strawberry Hill.*

Mistaken fair one, check thy fancy's flight;
Nor let fond poetry misguide thy sight,
The sweet creation by thy pencil drawn,
Nor real in the fabric nor the lawn.
Less in the master is the picture true;
Enlarg'd the portrait, and improv'd the view.
A trifling, careless, short-liv'd writer, he
Nor Envy's topic can, nor object be.
Nor pasteboard walls, nor mimic towers are fit
To exercise her tooth, or Delia's wit.
No, 'twas Parnassus did her fancy fill,
Which the kind maid mistook for Strawberry-Hill:
Whilst Modesty persuaded her to place
Another on that mount, she ought to grace.

HOR. WALPOLE.

Art. 14. *The Pursuits of Happiness.* Inscribed to a Friend. 4to. 1 s. 6 d. Cadell. 1771.

Whether the inequalities of poetry, so common with modern poets, proceed from idleness, or from the imperfection of taste, we pretend not to determine. Possibly, both these causes may operate occasionally. We are sorry, however, that a poem such as this, which contains

tains many good lines, should be disgraced with many bad ones. The title too is improper. It ought rather to have been called *Sketches of Characters.*

Art. 15. *A Portrait*; most humbly addressed to his Royal Highness George Prince of Wales. 4to. 1 s. Wilkie. 1771.

A silly low-written character of Edward the Sixth, who

'Ne'er broke his word, nor left a debt unpaid.'

Art. 16. *The Wish*; a Poem. By a Gentleman of Cambridge. 4to. 1 s. Dodsley, &c. 1771.

A shocking wish! a vile wicked wish!

'Let Truth and Virtue, Lords and Commons bleed!'

Art. 17. *A Farewell to the Fleet at Spithead*; describing the wretched Situation of France; concluding with an Address to the Great, by their Example to make Virtue fashionable. Dedicated to Sir George Saville, without his Permission or Knowledge. By a Sea Officer. 4to. 1 s. 6 d. Kearsly.

A warning to every unthinking mortal in this nation to prepare for his latter end; as, according to this honest Tar's description of the ship Britannia, we shall very soon be at the bottom:

——— Shatter'd in her masts and sails
Her planks eat through, and sprung her beams,
Grown leaky by repeated gales,
Her oakhum spew'd from all her seams.

Art. 18. *Christianity unmasked; or, unavoidable Ignorance preferable to corrupt Christianity*; a Poem, in twenty-one Cantos. By Michael Smith, A. B. Vicar of South Mims, in Hertfordshire. 8vo. 4 s. sewed. Turpin. 1771.

The Author's professed design in this work is to place the principles of pure Christianity in so obvious a view, that they may the more easily be distinguished from the knaveries of Popery, the delusive ardours of Fanaticism, the destructive manners of Atheism, and from the baneful influence of all. He writes like a man of liberal sentiments, and attacks religious delinquents of various denominations with the weapons of Hudibrastic verse, in which he might have succeeded better, had his wit and humour been equal to his honesty and good sense.

DRAMATIC.

Art. 19. *Three Comedies*; *The Uneasy Man*, *The Financier*, and *The Sylph*. Freely translated from Messrs. St. Foix and Fagan. 8vo. 2 s. 6 d. sewed. Walter. 1771.

These three little comedies, or rather comic entertainments, are selected as instances of the pathetic, the genteel, and the humorous. We allow them to be such. They are much esteemed in France, and well translated into English.

Art. 20. *The Tobacconist*; a Comedy of Two Acts. Altered from Ben Johnson. 8vo. 1 s. Bell. 1771.

As the objects of the Alchymist's comic satire are no more, the play is, of course, heavy and uninteresting; and nothing could have kept it on the stage except the extraordinary humour and action of Garrick in the character of Drugger. It is now altered in favour of Weston, who has singular merit in that character. The added and

and altered scenes have a good deal of low vivacity, and that kind of wit which one may suppose to have been begotten by Punch on the body of the comic Muse. The piece concludes with that new old absurdity of making the actor address the audience at the same time in his play-character and in his own.

Art. 21. *Dido*; a Comic Opera. As it is performed at the Theatre Royal in the Hay-market. 8vo. 1 s. Davies. 1771.

The story of Æneas and Dido burlesqued. To say that it is the work of the Trevestier of Homer, will be sufficient to recommend it to the lovers of this species of low humour. The best scenes in his Dido, however, are not equal to the worst in his Homer.

Art. 22. *The Downfall of the Association*; a Comic Tragedy, of Five Acts. 8vo. 1 s. 6 d. Winchester, printed for the Author; and sold by Crowder, &c. in London. 1771.

The subject of this piece is the arbitrary and oppressive conduct of a set of country justices, *associated for the preservation of the game.* As a play, the piece has no great merit; but the Author expresses his hope that the public will candidly overlook its defects for the sake of the good design, and especially because '*every passage is attended with the strictest* TRUTH, *divested of all ornamental fiction.*'—If we credit this declaration, we must believe in the actual appearance of Justice *Quorum*'s ghost. Vid. Act V. Sc. IX.

NOVELS.

Art. 23. *The Expedition of Humphry Clinker.* By the Author of Roderick Random. 12mo. 3 Vols. 7 s. 6 d. sewed. Johnston, &c. 1771.

Some modern wits appear to have entertained a notion that there is but one kind of *indecency* in writing; and that, provided they exhibit nothing of a lascivious nature, they may freely paint, with their pencils dipt in the most odious materials that can possibly be raked together for the most filthy and disgustful colouring.—These nasty geniuses seem to follow their great leader, Swift, only in his obscene and dirty walks. The present Writer, nevertheless, has humour and wit, as well as grossness and ill-nature.—But we need not enlarge on his literary character, which is well known to the public. Roderick Random and Peregrine Pickle have long been numbered with the best of our English romances. His present work, however, is not equal to these; but it is superior to his Ferdinand Fathom, and perhaps equal to the Adventures of an Atom.

Art. 24. *Coquetilla*; *or, Envy its own Scourge*: Containing the Adventures of several great Personages. From a Manuscript late in the Possession of a Gentleman famous for his acquaintance with the great World. 12mo. 2 s. 6 d. Leacroft. 1771.

This novel is introduced to the public with great modesty; and, on that account, we are sorry that it cannot boast of more important claims to attention and favour.

Art. 25. *The Jealous Mother*; *or, Innocence triumphant.* 12mo. 2 Vols. 6 s. Robinson and Roberts. 1771.

In this performance we have nature, good sense, and tolerable composition. It is superior to the common run of publications of the same class.

Art. 26. *The Captives: or, the History of Charles Arlington, Esq; and Miss Louisa Somerville.* 12mo. 3 Vols. 7 s. 6 d. sewed. Vernor. 1771.

We are here presented with adventures that shock probability by their extravagance; while the history of them possesses no advantages of style or manner to recommend it.

Art. 27. *Cuckoldom Triumphant; or, Matrimonial Incontinence vindicated.* Illustrated with Intrigues public and private, ancient and modern. By a Gentleman of Doctors Commons. To which is added, a Looking Glass for each sex. 12mo. 2 Vols. 5 s. sewed. Thorn.

This impudent apology for matrimonial incontinence unites excessive dulness with obscenity, and is, in the highest degree, detestable.

Art. 28. *Cupid turned Spy upon Hymen; or, Matrimonial Intrigues in polite Life.* 12mo. 2 Vols. 5 s. Boards. Roson.

The foregoing worthless production, vamped with a new title-page.

MEDICAL.

Art. 29. *Incontestible Proofs of curing the Gout, and other Disorders, chronic and acute* (deemed incurable) *by mild and efficacious Medicines*, originally discovered, and chemically prepared, by Henry Flower, Gent. An American. The second Edition. 8vo. 6 d. Leage.

We have here some cases to prove the efficacy of Mr. Flower's medicines.

There is one thing which needs no proof, and with which we apprehend Mr. Flower is very well acquainted, viz. that an *unknown* medicine operates much more powerfully, at least on the imagination, than a *known* one.

Art. 30. *A candid and impartial State of the* FARTHER * *Progress of the Gout-Medicine of Dr.* LE FEVRE; being the Evidence of the Year 1770, and part of the Year 1771. By Edmund Marshall, M. A. Vicar of Charing, in Kent. 8vo. 2 s. Dilly, &c.

From this farther account, it appears, that the time fixed by Le Fevre for the perfect cure of the gout, has been compleated with the Rev. Mr. Marshall, and some others, and yet that they still continue to be afflicted with the gout.

From the Appendix, we learn, that Le Fevre has had fifty English patients; that twenty of these were so much dissatisfied and chagrined, as not to give themselves the trouble of writing to Mr. Marshall:—and as for the other thirty,—surely such a discouraging, lame, hobling set of witnesses were never before produced to give credit to a *gout-nostrum*.

We can readily believe Mr. Marshall, when he assures us, that this present treatise is published, 'expresly against the repeated desire of his friend Le Fevre.'—Le Fevre has had one very good harvest in England; and, had Mr. Marshall given no further evidence, might have had a chance for a second, or at least some good gleanings. But as the matter now stands, Marshall's defence is the strongest

* For Mr. M.'s former publication, see Review, vol. xliii. p. 65.

strongest evidence against Le Fevre; and from this evidence alone, we are convinced,—that Le Fevre is a quack,—and that the best apology which can be made for his reverend panegyrist, is, that he is very sanguine, and very credulous.

Art. 31. *An Essay on the Cure of the Gonorrhœa, or fresh contracted Venereal Infection, without the Use of internal Medicines.* By William Rowley, Surgeon. 8vo. 1 s. Newbery.

An injection, composed of quicksilver, mucilage of gum-arabic, and expressed oil of linseed, constitutes Mr. Rowley's method of cure.—But surely it was not necessary that Mr. Rowley should draw up a twelve-penny pamphlet, to make the world acquainted with this practice!

Art. 32. *The Practice of Physic in general, as delivered in a Course of Lectures on the Theory of Diseases, and the proper Method of treating them.* By Theophilus Lobb, M. D. Member of the College of Physicians in London, and F. R. S. Published from the Doctor's own MS. 8vo. 2 Vols. 9 s. Buckland. 1771.

Whether we consider the *physiology*, *pathology*, or *methodus medendi* of these lectures, we cannot esteem them as a very valuable present to the public.

Were we to speak Dr. Lobb's eulogy, we should say, that the Doctor appears to be much more distinguished by an honest and benevolent heart, than by his abilities as a lecturer on the theory and practice of medicine.

POLITICAL.

Art. 33. *Magna Charta, opposed to assumed Privilege*: Being a complete View of the late interesting Disputes between the House of Commons and the Magistrates of London; containing an Account of the whole Transactions, from the first arresting of the Printers, to the Enlargement of the Two illustrious Patriots from the Tower, May 8, 1771. With a Collection of the genuine Speeches made in Parliament, and the Arguments of the Counsel on the Habeas Corpus in the Courts of Exchequer and Common-pleas. Also all the authentic Addresses of the several Wards, Corporations, Grand Juries, &c. and the answers of the Lord-Mayor, Mr. Alderman Wilkes, and Mr. Alderman Oliver; with several original Papers, never before published. The Whole designed to perpetuate an *Æra* that will signally distinguish the Spirit and Independency of the Citizens, on the one Part, and the oppressive and arbitrary Proceedings of a corrupt House of Commons, on the other. 8vo. 3 s. Kearsly. 1771.

The title of this publication is so ample, that it is altogether unnecessary for us to give any account of its contents. It will be acceptable to those who are friends to liberty and the constitution.

Art. 34. *An Essay on the Character and Conduct of his Excellency Lord Viscount Townshend, Lord Lieutenant of Ireland, &c.* 8vo. 1 s. Dodsley.

A well-written defence of his Lordship's character and conduct.

MISCELLANEOUS.

Art. 35. *The Circles of Gomer*; or, an Essay towards an Investigation and Introduction of the English as an universal Language, upon

upon the first Principles of Speech, according to its Hieroglyphic Signs, Argrafic, Archetypes, and superior Pretensions to Originality; a Retrieval of original Knowledge; and a Re-union of Nations and Opinions on the like Principles, as well as the Evidence of ancient Writers; with an English Grammar, some Illustrations of the Subjects of the Author's late Essays, and other interesting Discoveries. By Row. Jones, Esq. 8vo. 5 s. Crowder. 1771.

A mystic in divinity is a dangerous *Ignis Fatuus* that will lead you through a deep fog into an inhospitable quagmire; but a cabalist in philology is an inoffensive being, to whom you may listen with as little danger as you would to a straw-crowned monarch through his iron-grate. However, this Writer's disorder is certainly not an hydrophobia, for he has made a Dictionary of more than 200 full octavo pages, and resolved every word into *spring water*.

Art. 36. *An Historical Collection of the several Voyages and Discoveries in the South Pacific Ocean.* Vol. II. Containing the Dutch Voyages. By Alexander Dalrymple, Esq. 4to *. Nourse, &c. 1771.

The first part of this Collection of Voyages was mentioned in the Review, vol. xliv. p. 290; and Mr. D. in the introduction to that volume, took so very ill a remark that we had incidentally made on a former occasion relating to this undertaking, that, to avoid any fresh cause of offence, we desire that the account above referred to, of the former volume, may be understood to be extended to this also, so far as relates to the general intention of the work.

This volume contains the voyages of Le Maire and Schouten, Abel Jansen Tasman, and Jacob Roggewein, as promised in the former part: to these the Compiler has added, remarks on the conduct of the discoverers in the tracks they made choice of; an investigation of what may be farther expected in the South Sea; a vocabulary of languages in some of the islands visited by Le Maire and Schouten; a chronological table of discoverers in the Southern Hemisphere and Pacific Ocean; and, lastly, an index to the two volumes.

We shall add nothing farther respecting this collection, than that the industrious care of Mr. D. in making himself master of what other voyagers have discovered in the Southern parts of the Pacific Ocean, added to his own experience, point him out as a person sufficiently qualified to be employed in any future voyages that may be undertaken for discovery in those latitudes.

Art. 37. *Summary and free Reflections on various Subjects.* 12mo. 2 s. Bladon. 1771.

This performance is composed after the manner of Montaigne; and, if it wants the wit and easy negligence which characterise that agreeable writer, it must be allowed that its Author has copied very successfully his incoherence and imperfections. The observations it contains are destitute of novelty, and expressed without taste or propriety.

* For the *price*, see the *head-title* to our article relating to the first volume.

Art. 38. *Pro and Con*; or the Opinionists: an ancient Fragment. Published for the Amusement of the curious in Antiquity. By Mrs. Latter. 12mo. 2 s. sewed. Lowndes. 1771.

The Author of this production mistakes for wit, the ravings of a deranged imagination.

Art. 39. *The Samians*; a Tale. 12mo. 1 s. 6 d. Dodsley. 1771.

Written in the false taste of the Arcadian, heroi-comi-tragi-pastoral stuff that now pesters France; and in that kind of style which we have so often condemned, prose titupping on a Parnassian poney.

Art. 40. *An Essay on the Mystery of tempering Steel*, extracted from the Works of the celebrated Monf. Reaumur. By J. Savigny. 8vo. 1 s. Kearsly.

Every body must acknowledge the merit of Monf. Reaumur, as an experimental philosopher. His hypothesis, in regard to the hardening and tempering of steel, is undoubtedly ingenious, and he has had the good fortune to meet with a very competent translator in Mr. Savigny *, whose practical knowledge of the subject is equally unquestionable.

RELIGIOUS and CONTROVERSIAL.

Art. 41. *The Christian's Companion in the Principles of Religion, and the Concerns of human Life*: or the Sum of the Christian Religion. Shewing what are those Things necessary to be *known*, *believed*, and *practised*, for the Attainment of *everlasting Salvation*. 8vo. 5 s. bound. Robinson and Roberts. 1771

Mr. William Jones, in a letter to the Editors of this book, after expressing his satisfaction in the publication, adds, 'To speak my mind freely, I think the common people may obtain much more information from such a work as this, and with much less labour and expence, than from bulky commentaries on the Bible, where the doctrines and precepts of Christianity are too much diffused for an ordinary reader to take a proper view of them.' We confess ourselves somewhat inclined to Mr. Jones's opinion, with respect to such performances as are judiciously and properly executed: that he supposes the present work to be such, is evident from his declaration that he can 'discover in it no symptoms of a party spirit, but instead of it a principle of unaffected love to God, and charity to men. If I knew, he adds, of any other work of the kind more generally useful as a *family book*, I would recommend that instead of this; but this at present is what I purpose to use in my own family, and I shall disperse some of them about my house, to lie in the way of strangers.'

We find in this publication a number of sensible observations and admonitions as to religion and morality: the whole is thrown into a systematical form, and that part which treats of God, his being and attributes, directed according to what many esteem, and some ironically term, the *orthodox* profession. It is particularly adapted, in some respects, for the assistance of those who attend upon the service of our national church, and has perhaps some tendency to promote an undue prejudice for its forms, and rites, and places of worship: but

* Of Pall-mall. He is famous for making excellent razors and pen-knives, of *cast* steel.

the greater part of the book may be perused to advantage by persons of any denomination. There is, however, one objection to systematical performances;—there is danger lest they should promote formality, rather than produce that rational and solid piety, that spirit of benevolence, and that real goodness of heart, which is the great design of the gospel, and to which, when suitably regarded, it most plainly and powerfully leads.

Art. 42. *The Church of England vindicated* from the Charge of absolute Predestination, as it is stated and asserted by the Translator of Jerome Zanchius, in his Letter to the Reverend Dr. Nowell. Together with some Animadversions on his Translation of Zanchius, his Letter to the Reverend Mr. John Wesley, and his Sermon on 1 Tim. i. 10. 12mo. 1s. Cabe. 1771.

This little book carries on a dispute, which, from the nature of the subject, and from what appears to be the disposition of the contending parties, may continue for a great while. The Author, we suppose, distinguishes between predestination and *absolute* predestination; for that the church of England does, in some sense, teach predestination, is not to be doubted. He is very unwilling (though a matter of trifling moment indeed) that our church should be thought Calvinistical. The debate cannot be greatly interesting in the present day, especially as numbers wish to see the foundation on which it rests wholly taken out of the way. We shall only observe, that we remember, the learned Bishop Burnet, in his comments upon the seventeenth article, which we imagine is the principal rule for determining the question, remarks, that this article seems to be framed according to St. Austin's doctrine; he allows that the Remonstrants may subscribe it without renouncing their opinion; further adding, on the other hand, that the Calvinists have less occasion for scruple, since the article does seem more plainly to favour them.

Art. 43. *A Letter to Mr. James Baine*, Minister in Edinburgh; occasioned by his Sermon, intitled the Theatre licentious and perverted; or Strictures upon the Doctrine lately insisted on against Samuel Foote, Esq; &c. on account of a late Representation of the Comedy called the Minor, at the Theatre Royal, Edinburgh. 8vo. 6d. Robinson and Roberts.

When people are disposed to wrangle, a lock of goat's wool may do as well as any other subject of contention.

Art. 44. Five Sermons on the following Subjects, *viz.* I. The Wonders of God in the Deep. II. Christ's Dominion over the Wind and Sea. III, IV. The Mystery of Divine Providence to be explained hereafter. V. God corrects, yet pardons his People. Preached at Yarmouth in Norfolk, on some Occasions of great Losses and Distresses by *the Sea*; and now published with a particular View to the Consolation of the many Sufferers by *the late hard Gale of Wind*. By Thomas Howe. 8vo. 1s. 6d. Dilly. 1771.

These discourses appear to be serious, sensible, practical, and very well suited to the immediate occasions which gave them rise. We observe one thing with much satisfaction in these sermons, which is, that some parts of them are addressed, and in very suitable terms,

 to

to sea-faring men; a very important and useful part of the community, but we fear too much neglected as to any moral or religious assistance and instruction, notwithstanding some kind of provision is made for it by authority.

Art. 45. *Free Thoughts on the Book of Common Prayer, and other Forms*; according to the Use of the Church of England. Humbly recommending an Abridgment, with other Alterations. 4to. 1s. Becket. 1771.

This writer is an advocate for an established form in public worship, as the most likely means of preserving decency and order. But surely he contradicts, if not his own judgment, yet the truth and matter of fact, when speaking concerning a different method, and referring, we suppose, to what is called extempore prayer, he roundly asserts; 'The impropriety of such supplications, and that especially in public assemblies, must be very plain and manifest to *every thinking and impartial person*:' allowing the strength of argument to lie on the other side, yet so very different is the real state of the case, from this representation, that, we suppose, even bigotry and prejudice must find itself obliged to acknowledge, that there have been, and are, *several* wise, juditious, and worthy persons, who have embraced that side of the question which is here so authoritatively condemned. But the observation was, perhaps, more the effect of haste than of design; for the performance is rather superficial and inaccurate, though it offers proposals and remarks which appear to be just and worthy of attention.

Our *Free Thinker* does not object to the doctrinal part of our liturgy; the Athanasian creed he is willing to receives as agreeable to the scriptures; but as it seems, he says, to be expressed in too abstruse articles for a mixed multitude, he thinks, it might be superseded by that of the apostles.

He concludes his reflections with a proposal that seems candid and reasonable: 'If the government, says he, should ever order the liturgy, and other forms of the church, to be altered and abridged, it might perhaps be prudent, to leave the old and new forms to be used at the discretion of the ministers and churches; (as in the case of the old and new version of the psalms:) whereby discontents and uneasinesses would be greatly avoided, and, in time, that form which was most perfect, would be universally received.—People's inclinations would not be forced, and their judgments would be allowed a calm and cool deliberation.'

It is observable, from this and many other instances, that persons of very different sentiments in several points of religion, do still unite in their desire of some alterations in our established forms for public worship; this may perhaps give us encouragement to hope that the request will not long continue to be treated with utter neglect.

Art. 46. *A short Review and Defence of the Authorities on which the Catholic Doctrine of the Trinity in Unity is grounded.* By Lawrence Jackson, B. D. Prebendary of Lincoln. 8vo. 2s. Hingeston. 1771.

Mr. Jackson sets out with giving us an account of heresy and heretics. 'Heresy, he says, is a departure from the Christian faith; that faith

faith which is delivered in the holy scriptures. A heretic is one who acknowledges his departure from the faith thus established, and so become αὐτοκατάκριτος, self-condemned as to the fact, and after admonition is to be ejected out of the church.'

But surely such a definition is vague and indeterminate: it may be supposed to include only infidels or unbelievers in general: or if it can be accommodated to any persons who believe the Christian revelation, it will still leave room for much wrangling and debate. Should the Prebendary be asked, whether the acknowledgement of a power in the church to decree rites and ceremonies, or that it has authority in matters of faith, is not a departure from the faith delivered in the scriptures, how would he disengage himself from the consequence? However, we will not wrangle with him upon the matter; only as he is, doubtless, a man of reading and learning, we suppose he must have known that different accounts, and those supported with probable arguments, have been given of heresy and heretics; it would not, therefore, have been unworthy of him to have delivered his opinion in a less confident and peremptory manner.

The arguments here collected in support of the doctrine in question are the same which have been often published; but Mr. Jackson tells us, that he thought it might be seasonable at this time to give a short, plain and popular review of them, for the benefit of the unlearned, who may not be able to extract them from more elaborate and voluminous discourses.

Each of the contending parties, on this subject, professes to bring their proofs and authorities from the scriptures; each of them also appears to be convinced, that those writings determine in favour of that side which they have embraced: we shall close the article with just observing, in consequence of this, that since the matter, after all, remains so debateable, the most probable truth is, that revelation has not intended to furnish us with clear and certain notions about it, and therefore the greater part of those volumes and treatises, to which it has given rise, are wholly unnecessary and useless.

Art. 47. *The New Birth*; as represented to the Congregation of Protestant Dissenters in St. Mary's Parish at Maldon in Essex. By the Reverend Rest Knipe. 12mo. 1 s. 6d. Buckland, &c. 1771.

The *reverend* Rest Knipe has collected together several remarks and reflections, which are to be met with in some old books of divinity on the subject of which he treats. It will not be requisite to offer any extracts from this performance; the general character of which we apprehend to be, that it is serious, but not solid; pious and well meant, but rather enthusiastical, mistaken, and discouraging. There are in it, no doubt, some good reflections and useful exhortations; and far be it from us to say any thing to prevent what beneficial tendency any persons may find in it to amend the heart, if it does not contribute to enlighten the understanding; since we allow, that some preachers and some writers may have been really serviceable in the former view, which in the latter have been greatly bewildered, confused, and even, in some respects, nonsensical; though it is not our intention to rank the present publication under the last mentioned denomination.

CORRESPONDENCE.

AS the Rev. Editor of Mr. Cawthorn's Poems appears to be affected by a paragraph added to our account of that publication, in the Review for last month, p. 6, we gladly take the first opportunity of publishing the following declaration, extracted from the Editor's letter to a friend.

——"An anonymous Writer, in the St. James's Chronicle for April 22, has asserted that the first piece in Mr. Cawthorn's Poems was not originally composed by him, but by Mr. Pitt, the translator of Virgil, &c.——As this assertion, if unnoticed, might be of prejudice to my character, I take the liberty of informing you, in my own vindication, that the poem in debate was really selected from a number of Mr. Cawthorn's juvenile pieces which are in my possession, in his own hand-writing: and what is more,—to this (as well as several others) he has affixed the place where, and the year, day, and age of his life when it was written. Now as it is very unusual for persons to insert, in a common-place-book, the time when they make any extracts from other writers; so I had not the least reason to suppose that the poem in question was copied, and especially as there are several others in the same collection, which (if we may believe Mr. Cawthorn) can belong to no other Author. For, at the close of one piece, which is called A MEDITATION, dated K. Lonsdale, Jan. 30, 1735, he says, "This essay, as well as the other "pieces of divine poetry, was composed in the hurry of imagina-"tion, without any regard to connexion: which is excusable in a "person whose judgment, by reason of his years, is deficient. I "chose rather this kind of poetry, since the pens of the most cele-"brated writers have been employed in other matters. They were "designed for my private amusement, and to unbend the mind when "engaged in works of not so agreeable a nature.

"CAWTHORN."

"These particulars will surely be thought sufficient to justify the Editor of Mr. Cawthorn's Poems, to every person of candour. I am, &c. Aug. 15, 1771.

"*P. S.* I should have taken earlier notice of the above-mentioned advertisement, but did not know of it till I saw it referred to in the last Monthly Review."

*** A Letter signed A. W. dated Wiltshire, Aug. 12, 1771, mentions certain publications, of which no account hath yet appeared in the Review. One or two of the books in his list will probably fall under notice, as opportunity offers, but the others will scarcely merit our attention. There are many catchpenny productions, in periodical numbers, and under obviously feigned names †; the very titles of which would take up too much of our room, and which, too, it would be quite unnecessary to insert, as a bare perusal of the advertisements and hand-bills relating to them, must sufficiently intimate, to every intelligent reader, that these are no other than the bastard productions of the press, conceived and hatched in Grubstreet.

† Collections of Voyages and Travels, Histories of England, Commentaries on the Bible, &c. &c.

THE

MONTHLY REVIEW,

For SEPTEMBER, 1771.

ART. I. *The present State of Music in France and Italy; or, the Journal of a Tour through those Countries, undertaken to collect Materials for a general History of Music.* By Charles Burney, Mus. D. 8vo. 5 s. sewed. Becket. 1771.

THE public are indebted for the information and entertainment, which they will undoubtedly receive from the perusal of this work, to a design long since formed by the ingenious Writer, of composing a general history of music. With that view he had for many years past been employed in collecting the necessary materials. Finding, however, that the preceding writers on this subject had done little more than servilely copy each other, so that 'he who reads two or three has the substance of as many hundred,' and animated with a laudable ambition to discover fresh matter, 'unpolluted by profane compilers and printers,' and thereby stamp some marks of originality on his intended work, he naturally cast his eye towards Italy, as to the fountain of musical knowledge, and the source of every thing that is sublime, beautiful, and refined in that elegant art. He accordingly undertook the present tour with a design to levy contributions in that fertile region both on the living and the dead; and he appears, from the present account, in consequence of his own unremitting ardour and assiduity, seconded by the distinguished countenance which he and his scheme every where received, from persons the most eminent both in rank and learning, to have returned home richly fraught with many valuable acquisitions,—the *spolia opima* of the land of harmony.

The Author prefaces the account of his tour with a just remark on the unaccountable silence of the numerous, and certainly not incommunicative travellers, who have hitherto visited that country, with regard to the subject of his inquiries. Scarce a single picture, statue, or building, of any consequence has been left undescribed; and yet the *Conservatorios* or musical schools in Italy, the operas, and the oratorios have scarce been mentioned by them; and though 'every library, he observes, is crowded with histories of painting and other arts, as well as with the lives of their most illustrious professors, music and musicians have been utterly neglected:' and yet not one of the liberal arts is so much cultivated in that country as at present, nor was music ever in such high estimation, or so well understood, throughout Europe; neither can the Italians now boast so incontestable a superiority over the rest of the world, in any thing so much as in their musical productions and performances. In Italy music still *lives*; while the other arts, for which that country is principally visited, speak only a *dead* language.

The Author commences his musical inquiries in France; where he omitted no opportunities of consulting the public libraries and the learned, with regard to the principal object of his journey, and of visiting the churches and other public places, in order to form a judgment of the *present state* of music in that country. In consequence of two former visits to that kingdom, and a thorough acquaintance with the French compositions, he was already well prepared for this enquiry.

He describes music, though the French 'talk and write so well, and so much, about it,' as still in its infancy in that country, with respect to the two great essentials of melody and expression; the last of which particularly, how successfully soever some French composers of great merit imitate the Italian style in their productions, is, to use the Author's strong phrase, '*notoriously hateful*' to all the people in Europe, except themselves. Even the purest and best compositions become gallicised, that is, contaminated by it, and as Dryden, he observes, said of M'Flecno's wit—

> "*Sound* passed through them no longer is the same,
> As food digested takes a different name."

Some idea of the feelings, and of the vitiated and unsettled taste of a French audience, may be collected from the following summary of the Author's account of an evening's performance at the *Concert spirituel*, a grand concert performed in the great hall of the Louvre. —*Ab uno omnes.*

The first piece was a *Motet*, or Latin hymn, chiefly made up of chorusses, performed with more force than feeling, and composed in the style of the old French opera. It met, however, with the most unbounded applause from the audience; though it appeared *detestable* to the Author. This piece was succeeded by a concerto on the hautbois, by Bezozzi, nephew to the two celebrated performers of that name at Turin. With this performance the Author was greatly delighted, and, in honour of the

the French, he acknowledges that it received likewise the applause of the audience. This honour, however, the Author considerably diminishes, by somewhat maliciously reminding us that these two equally applauded pieces, or, in other words, the Italian and French music in general, are as opposite as light and darkness; and by observing that the French do not like Italian music, but pretend to adopt and admire it through mere affectation. In short, from the whole of his account, they appear to us ridiculously vibrating between good and evil, with affectation and vanity in the opposite scales of the balance; but without a sufficient portion of true taste or genuine sensibility, to give a decisive cast to the scale.

After this high finished performance, Mademoiselle Delcambre, we are told, 'screamed out *Exaudi Deus*, with all the power of lungs she could muster; and was as well received as if Bezozzi had done nothing.' A concerto in the Italian style next succeeded, many parts of which Signior Traversa played with great delicacy, good tone, and facility of execution; but this was not so well relished as the ravishing screams of Mademoiselle Delcambre. He had not indeed the *honour* of being hissed, which M. Pagin, one of Tartini's best scholars, had received in the same place some years before, for daring to play in that style. It is one step at least towards reformation, the Author observes, to begin to tolerate what ought to be adopted. The countenances, however, of the audience, and their manner of receiving Signior Traversa's piece, plainly indicated how little they had felt it. Madame Philidor next sung a Motet of her husband's composition, who '*drinks hard at the Italian fountain*;' but though this, says the Author, 'was more *like* good singing and good music than any vocal piece that had preceded it, yet it was not applauded with that fury, which leaves not the least doubt of its having been felt.' The last piece was a Motet in grand chorus, with solo and duet parts between. A solo verse in it was bellowed out by the principal counter-tenor, with as much violence as if a knife had been all the time held at his throat. 'Though this, says the Author, wholly stunned me, I plainly *saw* by the smiles of ineffable satisfaction which were visible in the countenances of ninety-nine out of a hundred of the company, and *heard*, by the most violent applause that a ravished audience could bestow, that it was quite what their hearts felt, and their souls loved. *C'est superbe!* was echoed from one to the other through the whole house. But the last chorus, he adds, was a *finisher* with a vengeance!' He had frequently thought the choruses of our oratorios rather too loud and violent: but these are soft and soothing music compared with this violent clashing of contending sounds, which surpassed, in clamour, all the noises he had

 ever

ever heard in his life. This part of the Author's account reminds us of that given by M. D'Alembert, who humourously represents foreigners, after three hours sufferings at the French opera, rushing out of the house, with aching heads, and their hands clapped to their ears, fully determined never to enter the doors again *.

The Author very candidly gave the French music a fair hearing before he entered Italy, as he apprehended he might become too dainty, after long rioting on Italian luxuries, to judge favourably of it, on his return from thence. In his way home, however, he gave it a second hearing, and was, as he expected, much more disgusted with it than before. At Lyons he was present at an opera, the music of which really contained many pretty passages, but 'so ill sung, with so false an expression, and with such screaming, forcing, and trilling,' as quite made him sick. The disease, it seems, does not come on all at once, on descending the Alps, but, to use a musical term, *Crescendo*, or gradually. In Provence and Languedoc the tunes of the country are rather pretty, and are sung in a natural and simple manner. These airs are less wild than the Scots, as less ancient; but the Author is inclined to think that the melodies of these two countries are older than any now subsisting that were formed on the system of Guido, who flourished in the beginning of the 13th century. The Author finally qualifies the harsh things which he has been obliged to say of the French music, by owning that 'the French have as long known the mechanical laws of counter-point as any nation in Europe—that by means of M. Rameau's system, they are very good Judges of harmony;—that they have long been in possession of simple and agreeable Provençale and Languedocian melodies, to which they continue to adapt the prettiest words, for social purposes, of any people on the globe; that they have now the merit of imitating very successfully the music of the Italian burlettas, and of greatly surpassing the Italians, and, perhaps every other nation, in the *poetical* composition of these dramas.' He elsewhere adds, that the theatre, at Paris, is elegant and noble; that the dresses and decorations are fine; the machinery ingenious; and the dancing excellent: but these adjuncts, alas! are all objects for the eye; whereas an opera elsewhere is intended to gratify the ear; which will relish the delight of intrinsically good music, without the aid of these meretricious ornaments.

The Author entered Italy by the way of Turin, where, as well as in every other part of his tour, he was indefatigable in visiting the libraries, churches, and theatres, as well as the

* *Melanges de Litterature,* tome iv. p. 396.

most

most eminent professors, from whom he every where met with the most friendly reception, the utmost assistance, and even zeal, in procuring him information with regard to the different objects of his inquiries. As this city was the birth-place of David Rizio, he here endeavoured to determine the long disputed question, whether he was the Author of the Scots melodies generally attributed to him: but the result of his inquiries on this head is properly reserved for his general history; though it may be inferred from what has been already said in the preceding paragraph. Among the living performers he visited the two Bezozzi's abovementioned. The great merit of these brothers, and a striking singularity in their characters, induce us to transcribe our Author's relation of this visit, as a specimen of his style, and his masterly and feeling manner of characterizing performers.

We should premise that the eldest of these brothers is now seventy, and the youngest upwards of sixty. 'Their long and uninterrupted regard for each other, says the Author, is as remarkable as their performance.—They have so much of the *Idem velle & idem nolle* about them, that they have ever lived together in the utmost harmony and affection; carrying their similarity of taste to their very dress, which is the same in every particular, even to buttons and buckles. They are batchelors, and have lived so long, and in so friendly a manner together, that it is thought here, whenever one of them dies, the other will not long survive him.—The eldest plays the hautbois, and the youngest the bassoon, which instrument continues the scale of the hautbois, and is its true base. Their compositions generally consist of select and detached passages, yet so elaborately finished, that, like select thoughts or maxims in literature, each is not a fragment, but a whole. These pieces are in a peculiar manner adapted to display the powers of the performers; but it is difficult to describe their style of playing. Their compositions, when printed, give but an imperfect idea of it. So much expression! such delicacy! such a perfect *acquiescence* and agreement together, that many of the passages seem *heart-felt sighs breathed through the same reed.* No brilliancy of execution is aimed at; all are notes of meaning. The imitations are exact; the melody is pretty equally distributed between the two instruments; each *forte*, *piano*, *crescendo*, *diminuendo*, and *appoggiatura*, is observed with a minute exactness, which could be attained only by such a long residence and study together. The eldest has lost his under front teeth, and complained of age; and it is natural to suppose that the performance of each has been better: however, to me, who heard them now for the first time, it was charming. If there is any defect in so exquisite a performance, it arises from the *equal perfection* of the *two parts*; which distracts the attention, and renders it impossible to listen to both, when both have dissimilar melodies equally pleasing.'

The Author next visited Milan, and describes the present state of music in the churches, theatres, and *academias*, or private concerts, in that city, where it is much cultivated, and where, in consequence of very powerful recommendations, all the treasures of the Ambrosian library were laid open to him. Among these he mentions a beautiful and well preserved MS. Missal of the ninth century, and consequently written at least 200 years before the time of Guido, and before the lines used by that monk were invented. A specimen of this ancient notation, which consists principally of accents of different kinds placed over the words, will be given in his general history.

A description of the performance of the nuns, in one of the convents of this city, gives the Author an opportunity of bearing his testimony against loud accompaniments, which are too much practised in Italy, as well as against that 'jargon of different parts, and of laboured contrivance,' to which certainly the natural, simple, and touching graces of melody, both vocal and instrumental, are too frequently sacrificed. These may indeed give a pleasure of a *certain kind*, but that only to the learned and chosen few who are in the secret. The performance at the convent had neither of these defects, and accordingly meets with the warmest applause of our Author, whose judgment on this head is of the more weight, as it is that of one perfectly well acquainted with all that is to be effected by the learned intricacies of artificial harmony. With regard to the loudness of accompaniments, when joined with the voice particularly, the Author observes, and complains, that 'in the opera-house nothing but the instruments can be heard, unless when the *Baritoni* or base voices sing, who can contend with them; and that nothing but noise can be heard through noise:' so that a delicate voice is overwhelmed and absolutely suffocated in the harmonical crowd. In the entertainment of this day, one of the nuns sung alone. She had an excellent voice, 'full, rich, sweet, and flexible, with a true shake, and exquisite expression: it was delightful, and left nothing to wish, but duration.' She was accompanied only by an organ and harpsichord together, played on by another nun. 'The accompaniment, says the Author, of that instrument alone with the heavenly voice abovementioned, pleased me beyond description, and not so much by what it *did*, as by what it did *not* do.—— Upon such occasions, he adds, even harmony itself is an evil, when it becomes a sovereign instead of a subject. I know this is not speaking like a *Musician*; but I shall always give up the *profession*, when it inclines to pedantry; and give way to my feelings,

feelings, when they seem to have reason on their side. If a voice be coarse, or otherwise displeasing, the less it is heard the better; and then tumultuous accompaniments and artful contrivances may have their use: but a single note from such a voice as that I heard this morning, penetrates deeper into the soul, than the same note from the most perfect instrument on earth can do; which, at best, is but an imitation of the human voice.'

Though the Author set out with a full determination not to have 'his purpose turned awry by any other curiosity or inquiry;' to hear and see nothing but music, and to devote himself entirely to the service of Terpsichore; his love of science betrays him into a few transient infidelities, and we occasionally find him holding short dalliance with Urania and a few others of the sisterhood*. Among these stolen interviews we may reckon his visit to Father Beccaria, so advantageously known throughout Europe, by his enlarged views, and excellent writings on the subject of electricity. The Author was received with the most engaging cordiality by this good father, on the footing of an *Amateur*, which he translates a *Dabbler*, in electricity; and after an agreeable visit, in which they had much conversation on electrical matters, left 'this great and good man,' impressed with the highest respect and affection for him. We mention this interview principally on account of some anecdotes which exhibit the philosophical simplicity of character, and mode of living, of this ingenious ecclesiastic; who, 'through choice, lives up six pair of stairs, among his observatories, machines, and mathematical instruments; and there does every thing for himself, even to making his bed, and dressing his dinner.' This good father is so little acquainted with worldly concerns, particularly money matters, that he was quite astonished and pleased at the ingenuity and novelty of a letter of credit, which was accidentally produced before him during this visit, by the Author's banker; and could hardly comprehend how this letter should be *argent comptant*, ready money, throughout all Italy. He presented to the Author his last work, of which this is the first notice we have received, and which is intituled, *Experimenta, atque Observationes, quibus* ELECTRICITAS VINDEX *late constituitur atque explicatur.*

* Of these short excursions from his professed purpose we shall only cursorily mention his visit to Father Boscovich, who gratified him and some other visitants with the exhibition of some optical experiments; and to Father de la Torre, who presented him with some of his microscopic globules. We can scarce class with these his attention to statuary and painting, which he found of use to his future work; as from these he acquired his ideas and drawings of the instruments of the ancients, as well as of the early moderns.

At Bologna we find the Author visiting the celebrated female academician and electrician, the *Dotteressa*, Madame Laura Bassi, to whom the Abbé Nollet addresses two of his letters on electricity. From his relation of this visit we learn that, immediately after Dr. Franklyn's discovery of the identity of the electrical matter and lightning, Signior Bassi had caused conductors to be erected at the Institute; but that the people of Bologna, through an apprehension that the rods might rather invite than prevent the stroke, had obliged him to take them down: and though Benedict XIV. one of the most enlightened and enlarged of the Popes, a native, and in a particular manner the patron, as well as sovereign of Bologna, wrote a letter to recommend their being replaced; yet with all these titles to veneration, or, at least acquiescence, his Holiness's letter failed of reconciling the Bolognese to the use of electrical conductors, which accordingly have never since been reinstated.

While we are on the subject of the Author's excursions, and before we close our extracts for the present, we shall mention his visit at Ferney, and transcribe a part of the conversation which passed between him and M. Voltaire; as it may seem to require our notice, as Reviewers, in particular. In the course of this conference M. Voltaire enquired, 'What poets we had now?' and was answered, 'we had Mason and Gray.' 'They write but little, said he, and you seem to have no one who lords it over the rest, like Dryden, Pope, and Swift.' 'I told him, adds the Author, that it was, perhaps, one of the inconveniencies of periodical journals, however well executed, that they often silenced modest men of genius, while impudent blockheads were impenetrable, and unable to feel the critic's scourge: that Mr. Gray and Mr. Mason had both been illiberally treated by mechanical critics, even in news-papers; and added, that modesty and love of quiet seemed in these gentlemen to have got the better even of their love of fame.'

Though we generally treat, with that silent pity or contempt which they justly deserve, the ill-grounded complaints of interested and disappointed Authors; the candour and good sense of the present Writer, who beside is not a party in the question, induce us to say a word or two, in general, on the subject of the preceding paragraph; especially as, to a hasty reader of the foregoing quotation, we may seem to be involved in the same censure with the illiberal news-paper critics there complained of; or at least be considered as accessories in the guilt of sometimes depriving the public of valuable compositions, by silencing writers of merit, through the freedom of our remarks. With regard to this charge, so far as it may be thought to affect us, we can only express our sorrow that our occasional strictures should ever operate in a manner so contrary to our intentions. But we should ill discharge the task we have undertaken, of giving just characters of the numerous works which daily issue from the press, were we to confine ourselves within the limits mentioned by Horace, and, like the Authors of the Fescennine verses, be

Ad BENE DICENDUM *delectandumque redacti.*

We may very properly appeal, on this occasion, to the authority of our great forefather Bayle, one of the primitive Reviewers, who was charged with the contrary fault, of being too complaisant to Authors, and who seems to have made it a rule to censure none. Even this courtly predecessor of ours thus speaks of the liberty which ought to subsist in the *Commonwealth* (very properly so called) of letters. " *Cette republique*, says he, *est un etat extremement* libre. *On n'y reconnoit que l'empire de la verité & de la raison*; *& sous leurs auspices on fait la guerre* innocemment *à* QUI QUE CE SOIT †. How constantly, in the course of our critical *warfare*, we have fought under these respectable banners, must be left to the decision of the public. We pretend not to impeccability, nor would insinuate that, in the review of many thousand volumes, we have, in no instance, conducted ourselves irreproachably. We possibly have our splenetic fits—[the very nature of our occupation, or rather of the major part of the subjects on which it is exercised, tending to cast a gloom over us] and on some occasions are perhaps somewhat too delicate and fastidious: we acknowledge the ebullitions of a little subacid humour now and then; and are sometimes betrayed by a sudden flow of spirits, into a vein of waggery or levity, which may be thought unseemly, when applied to characters of distinguished eminence *: not to mention errors of judgment, inaccuracies, &c. which we have in common with all writers. For any such instances of fallability or frailty, we take the opportunity, once for all, of here entering our rightful claim to a little of that indulgence for ourselves, which, with all our imputed severity, we daily, though silently

† " This republic is a state of the utmost freedom; the members of which acknowledge no other sovereigns than Truth and Reason; and under their banners innocently wage war on their fellow-citizens, *of what rank soever.*"

* We shall appeal once more to an authority, equally respectable with the foregoing, on this subject. " The faults (says a distinguished moralist, as well as critic) of a writer of acknowledged excellence are more dangerous, because the influence of his example is more extensive; and the interest of learning requires that they should be discovered and *stigmatized*, before they have the sanction of antiquity conferred upon them, and become precedents of indisputable authority." Rambler, N° 93.

and

and unostentatiously, exercise towards others; sometimes through a, perhaps, pardonable unwillingness "to interrupt the dream of harmless stupidity," though at the expence of strict justice to the public. After all, we can only repeat our concern that the dunces should be so frequently callous to our reproofs, and men of genius sometimes so *tremblingly alive* to our criticisms.

In compensation however of the inconvenience abovementioned, we would just hint, on the other hand, that through our means modest merit is often drawn forth from the crowd, encouraged, and held up to more general and extensive notice; and that though our censures do not operate to the utter extinction of literary delinquencies, they are undoubtedly in a great measure conducive to the diminution of them. For though the critical shaft fails to pierce the hardened scribbler, cased in tenfold brass, and drops, a *telum imbelle sine ictu*, at his feet;—yet its very whizzing, nay the apprehension of it, often strikes the less callous *sensorium* of the wary printer, and operates with a most salutary, *preventive* efficacy on the master of the types. The number of literary criminals, nevertheless, is undoubtedly considerable: but so is that of the monthly culprits at the Old-Bailey. Accordingly, both the civil and critical *Sessions-papers* are crouded every month with fresh delinquents, and even with old and sturdy offenders, 'flagrant from the lash,' repeatedly, though unavailingly, applied: but it does not from thence follow that the wholesome severities and terrors of the law, and of the critic's scourge, are administered without effect.

[*To be concluded in our next.*]

ART. II. *The Roman History, from the Building of Rome to the Ruin of the Commonwealth. Illustrated with Maps and other Plates.* Vol. IV *. By N. Hooke, Esq. 4to. 18s. Boards. Cadell. 1771.

BEFORE six centuries had elapsed from the building of Rome, many causes united to corrupt the manners of the Romans. The wars, which the ambition of that people had led them to carry on in distant countries, had given a check to their republican ardour. The value, which was placed in being a citizen of Rome, wore away. The luxury and respect for riches, which the conquest of Asia introduced among them, laid them open to the intrigues of ambitious leaders. The love of their country and of liberty, which, in early times, had rendered them invincible, had no longer any influence on their conduct. The pernicious policy of Sylla had taught

* For our account of the 3d volume of this History, see Reviews for February and March, 1764.

the

the ſoldiers to receive and expect lands; and he had invented proſcriptions, which debaſed entirely the genius of his nation. Rome was prepared for ſlavery and a maſter; when Pompey and Cæſar, the two moſt diſtinguiſhed of her citizens, conceived the criminal ambition of overturning the liberties of their country. The contentions of theſe chiefs, with the ſucceeding revolutions and events, till the ſettlement of the empire on Auguſtus, are the ſubject of the preſent publication; and form a portion of hiſtory, the moſt important and intereſting, which the annals of any nation can preſent to us. Having formerly treated of the conqueſts and the greatneſs of the Romans, our Hiſtorian now ſets himſelf to trace the progreſs of their government from liberty to deſpotiſm.

In order to execute this taſk with the greater preciſion, he has enquired, with a minute attention, into the riſe and progreſs of the conteſt between Pompey and Cæſar. The former had returned twice to Rome in a condition to enſlave his country; but, being ambitious to owe his power to the gift of the people, he had, on theſe occaſions, diſbanded his troops. After the Mithridatic war, he ſeems to have been confident, that the growing diſorders of the ſtate would make it neceſſary for all parties to give him the ſole management of affairs; and it excited his utmoſt ſurprize, when he found that his meaſures met with oppoſition. His great enemy was Craſſus; and while his influence was employed againſt him, the ſenate could caſt the balance into the ſalutary ſcale. But Cæſar, perceiving that if they ſhould unite their intereſts, they would be irreſiſtible, he attempted to reconcile them. Craſſus was his particular friend, and he had ingratiated himſelf with Pompey, who thought that he might be uſeful to him from his influence with the people. The firſt triumvirate accordingly was formed; and Pompey did not perceive that he was governed by the policy of a competitor. It was the ambition of Craſſus to be ſent to the Parthian war, and he obtained it; Cæſar continued in the government of Gaul; and Pompey, though inveſted with the command of an army, and the management of Spain, remained in Italy, and directed the public tranſactions. This combination, however, did not laſt long. It was broken by the death of Craſſus. The pride of Pompey could not then bear a rival, and Cæſar could admit of no ſuperior. The death of Julia had alſo given a blow to their union; and Pompey, being careſſed by the ſenate, who truſted him with the whole power of the ſtate, and beginning to entertain a jealouſy of the military renown of Cæſar, thought of changing his politics. 'The empire, to uſe the words of our Author, was thrown as a kind of prize between two, and it was natural that they ſhould di-

4 vide,

vide, and head, respectively, the two permanent and distinct parties in the republic, the *Aristocracy* and the *People*.

Pompey having joined himself to the aristocracy, a resolution was formed to revoke Cæsar's command, and to appoint him a successor. But when this measure was proposed by Marcellus, the tribune Curio, whom Cæsar had bought over to his party, demanded that Pompey should be ordered, at the same time, to renounce his province of Spain, and to give up the command of his legions; and declared, that the one as well as the other ought to be reduced to the condition of private citizens. The senate, however, rejected his proposal, and the tribune, in return, interposed his negative. The debates on this occasion, and the different steps taken by the parties, are well explained by our Historian; who blames, and perhaps justly, the pride and insincerity of Pompey, and commends the moderation of Cæsar, who shewed a willingness to come to an accommodation. It is evident, at least, that Cæsar must have fallen a victim to his enemies, if he had renounced his command while Pompey retained his province and his legions.

Having shewn the grounds of the contest between Pompey and Cæsar, our Author proceeds to that famous decree of the Roman senate, by which Cæsar was ordered to disband his army before a certain day; and by which, in case of disobedience, he was declared an enemy to the state. He then relates the transactions of the civil war, till the flight of Pompey into Greece; and points out the policy and arts which were employed by the rival statesmen to bring over to their interests the more distinguished citizens, and those of consular rank. On this occasion he has taken an opportunity to inquire particularly into the principles and political conduct of Cicero, whose extensive influence made them extremely solicitous to have the sanction of his name and authority. But the reflections, which he has thrown out on this subject, rest not, in our opinion, on the most solid foundation; and we should think, that he has censured this great man with an asperity and keenness which are by no means to be justified. Because Cicero hesitated, for some time, before he could determine whether he ought to join himself to Pompey or to Cæsar, or whether he should preserve a neutrality, does he deserve to be termed weak, irresolute, and undecisive? The importance of the step he was to take required, surely, the most serious deliberation. Nor do we imagine that he ought to be condemned for the insincerity that appears in his familiar letters, and in those which he addressed to Atticus. Are we to blame him for writing in one strain to Cæsar, and in another to Atticus? Are we to judge of the behaviour of a politician by the standard of a severe morality? If our Historian

Historian had attended to the characters and the weaknesses of the persons he corresponded with, and to the views with which his letters were written, he would have found the key to the contradictory sentiments they exhibit, and might have learned that the principles and conduct of this illustrious Roman were uniform and consistent. In this case he would have acknowledged, that the arts and finesse he employed, while they marked his ability and good sense, did not derogate from his integrity.

It may be observed in general, that almost all historians have failed in the judgments they have given of those great men who have acted in difficult situations. Unaccustomed to perform any part in active scenes, they are unacquainted with the feelings of those who are busied in them; and while they form their opinions of statesmen and princes, by the criterion of a fancied perfection, they are frequently led to apply their censure, where they should have bestowed their approbation and panegyric. It is for this reason, that men of mere speculation and study are extremely unfit for historical compositions; and when we consider this circumstance, we cannot but think that the republic of letters never sustained such a loss as in that of those memorials which many of the greatest of the Romans left behind them concerning their own actions, and their own times. In the memoirs of Sylla and Augustus, and in those of Mæcenas and Agrippa, history would have appeared in its utmost dignity, and in its most instructive form. But while we censure Mr. Hooke as deficient in political sagacity, and ascribe the same fault to the generality of historians, our candour requires us, in particular, to make an exception with regard to the penetrating biographer of the Emperor Charles V. whose genius, it must be allowed, has surmounted the disadvantages of his situation, and who, in the retirement of a college, has been able to discuss the transactions of men, with the experience and discernment of an accomplished statesman.

Having related the events which followed the precipitate retreat of Pompey from Italy, with the reduction of Sardinia by Valerius, and that of Sicily by Curio, our Author proceeds to the operations of Cæsar in his Spanish expedition. This celebrated commander had here to act against an army greatly superior to his own, and conducted by two able leaders. These, however, he reduced, without hazarding a battle, to the necessity of disbanding their forces. He discovered, on this occasion, great conduct and address; and the incidents of this enterprize have been therefore described by Mr. Hooke, at considerable length, and with particular care.

He then turns his attention to the siege of Marseilles, the defeat of Cæsar's lieutenants in Illyricum, and Curio's unfortunate expedition into Africa; and having exhibited an ample narration

narration of these particulars, he proceeds to describe the famous campaign between Cæsar and Pompey before Dyrrachium and in Thessaly. The political and military skill which these illustrious competitors displayed at this time, he has examined with great candour and impartiality. He does not, with a multitude of Authors, derogate from the capacity of Pompey to add to that of Cæsar: abilities he allows to both, and the investigation of truth he has considered as a more important object than the finishing of a favourite character. It is, however, but an indifferent compliment which these Authors would pay to their hero, at the expence of his rival. For, where there is no equality in the parties, there can be no struggle or competition. It is a poor triumph which the man of distinguished talents obtains over an inferior, or one of ordinary capacity.

The account given by our Historian of Pompey's escape from the battle of Pharsalia, which terminated this famous campaign, and of his death in Egypt, is pathetic and interesting; and we must observe, to his honour, that after having offered a few reflections on the fortunes and capacity of this illustrious man, he has examined and confuted, in a great measure, the character which Dr. Middleton has given of him. This examination cannot be disagreeable to our Readers, and may give them an idea of his attention and acuteness.

'As this history, says he, includes a sort of critical examination of the life of Cicero, by Dr. Middleton, we will not scruple to present the Reader with the character, which this Writer has given of Pompey the Great, together with some short observations upon it.

"Pompey had early acquired the surname of *Great*, by that sort of merit, which, from the constitution of the Republic, necessarily made him *great*; a fame and success in war superior to what Rome had ever known in the most celebrated of her generals." [The surname of *Great*, according to Plutarch, was a compliment of Sylla, after the good services Pompey had done him in Italy, Sicily, and Africa. Though young Pompey had been bred to war in the camp of his father, a man of great military capacity, and had shewn his talents in the support of Sylla's party, he had not yet properly *acquired* or merited that surname by a success in war, *superior to what Rome had ever known*. Livy, or his abbreviator, says, that this surname was given him after his victories in Asia.] "He had triumphed at three several times over the three different parts of the known world, Europe, Asia, Africa; and, by his victories, had almost doubled the extent, as well as the revenues of the Roman dominion; for, as he declared to the people, on his return from the Mithridatic war, *he had found* the lesser *Asia the boundary, but left it the middle of their empire*." [If Pompey made this declaration, he was guilty of an unpardonable gasconade, for he added to the Roman empire only Pontus, Bithynia, and Syria: but, if he did not double the revenues of the Commonwealth, he greatly multiplied his own; for he received every month from Ariobarzanes, King of Cappadocia, alone, above

above 6393 l. which was almost all that poor King could raise. See *Ad. Att.* vi. 1.] " He was six years older than Cæsar; and, while Cæsar, immersed in pleasures, oppressed with debts, and suspected by all honest men, was hardly able to shew his head, Pompey was flourishing in the height of power and glory, and by the consent of all parties placed at the head of the Republic." [This is not a fair representation of the fortunes of these two men: Pompey was raised to all his power and wealth *against the will of the Senate*; who was ever envious and jealous of him: and Cæsar not only dared to shew his head, but was ever so much the darling of the city, that he carried every thing he stood for, by almost the unanimous votes of the people, notwithstanding the opposition of the same Senate.] " This was the post his ambition seemed to aim at, to be the first man in Rome; the leader, not the *tyrant of his country:* for he more than once had it in his power to have made himself the master of it without any risk, if his virtue, or his phlegm, at least, had not restrained him." [This is a groundless assertion. Pompey, after the Sertorian war, kept his army in Italy; and so did Crassus to check him; till they both disbanded their troops by agreement: neither of them dared *then* to act the tyrant. After the Mithridatic war, the opposition Cæsar and Metellus, who openly courted Pompey, met with, plainly shewed how jealous the city was of Pompey's power: and that same jealousy prevailed after his arrival, notwithstanding all the favour and credit his victories had procured him. He could not depend upon his army in an enterprize against his country, when he had no motive of revenge to stimulate them with, nor indeed any other that he could avow with common decency. Cæsar and Crassus were willing to associate with him against the *aristocracy*, but not to become his servants *.] " But he lived in a perpetual expectation of receiving, from the gift of the people, what he did not care to seize by force; and, by fomenting the disorders of the city, hoped to drive them to the necessity of creating him Dictator. It is an observation of all the historians, that, while Cæsar made no difference of power, *whether it was conferred or usurped*; *whether over those who loved, or those who feared him*; Pompey seemed to value none but what was *offered*; *nor to have any desire to govern, but with the good-will of the governed.*" [Velleius ii. 29, says indeed of Pompey, *Potentiæ quæ honoris causa ad eum deferretur, non ut ab eo occuparetur,*

* We must here observe, that we are by no means disposed to agree with our Author, in the strictures which he has made on the opinion of Dr. Middleton, which supposes, that Pompey had it more than once in his power to have enslaved his country. After the Sertorian war, his reputation was so great, and the soldiery were so much at his devotion, that Crassus must have been extremely unequal to the task of contending with him; and, after the Mithridatic war, there was no force in the empire that could be opposed to his veteran legions. It is to be remarked, however, that there is much darkness and obscurity in history, with regard to his life and transactions. It is a pity that we have lost the memoirs of his secretary, Theophanes of Mitylene, who, it is said, was a man of singular discernment and ability.

cupidissimus:

cupidissimus: but I do not see any difference between Pompey and Cæsar in this respect. As long as power was offered to Pompey, he did not undertake to seize it by an armed force; neither did Cæsar; but no sooner did Pompey foresee that Cæsar would become his equal, than he armed, illegally, the whole empire, to preserve his own superiority: and this is allowed by the same historian: *Civis in toga, nisi uti vereretur, ne quem haberet parem, modestissimus.* A power, maintained all along by the most open and scandalous bribery, cannot be deemed a power offered by the good-will of the governed: and a man who employs such means, in defiance of the laws, cannot, with any propriety, be called a man of integrity.] "What leisure he found from his wars he employed in the study of polite letters, and especially of eloquence, *in which he would have acquired great fame, if his genius had not drawn him to the more dazzling glory of arms.* Yet he pleaded several causes with applause, in the defence of his friends and clients; and some of them in conjunction with Cicero. His language was copious and elevated; his sentiments just; his voice sweet; his action noble and full of dignity. But his talents were better formed for arms than the gown; for though in both he observed the same discipline; a perpetual modesty, temperance, and gravity of outward behaviour; yet, in the licence of camps, the example was more rare and striking. His person was extremely graceful, and imprinting respect; yet with an air of reserve and haughtiness, which became the general better than the citizen. His parts were plausible rather than great; specious rather than penetrating; and his views of politics but narrow; for his chief instrument of governing was *dissimulation*; yet he had not always the art to conceal his real sentiments. As he was a better soldier than a statesman, so what he gained in the camp he usually lost in the city; and, though adored when abroad, was often affronted and mortified at home; till the imprudent opposition of the Senate drove him to that alliance with Crassus and Cæsar, which proved fatal both to himself and to the Republic. He took in these two not as the *partners*, but the *ministers* rather of his power." [They had more interest in the city than he, and he could not compass his ends without their assistance: they were therefore necessary allies, not ministers of his power.] "That, by giving them some share with him, he might make his own authority uncontroulable: he had no reason to apprehend that they could ever prove his rivals; since neither of them had any credit or character of that kind, which alone could raise them above the laws; a superior fame and experience in war, *with the militia of the empire at their devotion:* all this was purely his own; till, by cherishing Cæsar, and throwing into his hands the only things which he wanted, *arms and military command*, he made him at last too strong for himself, and never began to fear him till it was too late." [That Pompey helped Cæsar, during his triumvirate, will be easily granted; but that he owed all to Pompey is not true: and Pompey was at least as much indebted to Cæsar, as Cæsar to him. Would Pompey have condescended to marry the daughter of the man whom he suspected to have debauched his wife Mucia, the mother of Cnæus and Sextus Pompey, and whom, for this reason, during the civil war, he used to call Ægisthus, if his alliance had not been deemed

deemed absolutely necessary to support his credit: and indeed he could never have supported himself in that long reign of his during the Gallic war without Cæsar's interest. This is evident from the whole history of the times.] "Cicero warmly dissuaded both his union and his breach with Cæsar;" [So Cicero says in his second Philippic; but his letters shew that he greatly approved of the breach between Cæsar and Pompey, till the prospect was darkened, and the civil war was ready to break out with great advantage on Cæsar's side. If Cicero did not approve of their union at first, he cemented it afterwards, and was very subservient to the confederate chiefs. See his apologetic letter, cited vol. iii. p. 509.] "And, after the rupture, as warmly still, the thought of giving him battle: if any of these counsels had been followed, Pompey had preserved his life and honour, and the Republic its liberty." [*Pace opus est: ex victoria cum multa mala, tum certè tyrannus existet. Ad Att.* vii. 5. *Depugna, inquis, potius, quam servias: Ut quid? Si victus eris, proscribare? Si viceris, tamen servias? Ad Att.* vii. 7. *Hoc Cnæus noster cum antea nunquam, tum in hac causa minimè cogitavit; beata et honesta civitas ut esset. Dominatio quæsita ab utroque est.—Genus illud Sullani regni jampridem appetitur,* [*a Pompeio*] *multus, qui unà sunt, cupientibus. Ad. Att.* viii. 11. It appears then that Cicero was not of Dr. Middleton's opinion. He thought also that Pompey's victory would have been a very cruel one: *Tanta erat in illis crudelitas, ut non nominatim, sed generatim proscriptio esset informata; ut jam omnium judicio constitutum esset, omnium vestrum bona prædam esse illius victoriæ; vestrum planè dico: nunquam enim de te ipso, nisi crudelissimè, cogitatum est. Ad Att.* xi. 6.] "But he was urged to his fate by a natural superstition, and attention to those vain auguries with which he was flattered by all the Haruspices: he had seen the same temper in Marius and Sylla, and observed the happy effects of it: but they assumed it only out of policy, he out of principle. They used to animate their soldiers, when they had found a probable opportunity of fighting; but he, against all prudence and probability, was encouraged by it to fight to his own ruin." [I should think that Pompey was not altogether so credulous as Dr. Middleton makes him. Cicero, in his Letters, and Cæsar, in his Commentaries, assign other reasons for Pompey's confidence: and these reasons influenced not only Pompey, but Labienus and all the generals in his army, whom we cannot suppose to have been all addicted, in a great degree, to superstition.']

Cæsar, after the death of Pompey, engaged in the Alexandrian war; and we must, doubtless, agree with our Author in opinion, that he exhibited great military skill in the conduct of it. But we must confess, that we cannot conceive that he lay under any necessity of undertaking it. It served to retard his advancement to empire; and though several historians have justified his behaviour in this particular, we must think that he acted without his usual penetration. When, on his arrival at Alexandria, he was presented with the head and the ring of his rival, he ought immediately to have thought of opposing the

Pompeian chiefs, who had fled to Africa. But he was detained, it is said, by the Etesian winds. The Etesian winds, however, did not surely engage him to interfere in the quarrels of Ptolemy and Cleopatra, and make him bring upon himself a very hazardous war, at a time when he was totally unprepared for it. His impolitic delay, in so critical a season of his affairs, must be ascribed to some more powerful cause. We should imagine, that the charms of Cleopatra were the irresistible attraction which detained him. In this instance his passion for gallantry got the better of his ambition.

In recording the events of the African war, our Historian takes an opportunity, after having mentioned the surrendry of Utica, to examine particularly into the character of Cato; and he has favoured his Readers with several strictures upon it, in which there is a great deal of truth. But we must observe, that in delineating the characters of antiquity we ought not to judge of them by the manners or morality of our own times. Different ages, and different nations, have ways of thinking peculiar to them; and it is, accordingly, by different standards of purity or perfection, that they bestow their censure or approbation. When Cato destroyed himself, he acted in conformity to the maxims of his philosophy, and to the conduct which he had uniformly maintained. If he had survived the liberties of his country, he would have exposed himself to the greatest disgrace, in the opinion of a Roman; because he would have broken in upon that *decorum of life*, so Cicero calls it, which consisted in supporting a certain equality of behaviour. Nor can we agree with our Author in censuring his Cyprian expedition; which, indeed, if judged of by the notions of the present times, must have been extremely unjust. The ancient historians talk of this expedition as highly worthy of his virtues; and the ancient moralists have even extolled it as one of the most glorious atchievements of his life. Let us judge of a Roman by his own laws, and not apply to him laws by which he knew not how to act.

When Cæsar had put an end to the African war, he returned to Rome; and the honours, which were then decreed to him by the Senate, his triumphs, and his civil administration and clemency, are described by our Historian with his usual minuteness and accuracy. He then treats of the war in Spain against Pompey's sons; and having enumerated the consequences of their defeat, he passes to the consideration of the works which Cicero composed during his retreat at this time. On this last head he leads us to admire the universality of Cicero's talents; and we could have wished that he had found it consistent with his views to have examined his character as a

man

man of genius and ſcience, with as much attention as he has conſidered his conduct as a politician.

After Cæſar had arrived at empire, he employed his thoughts in forming many great deſigns, which, if his untimely death had not prevented their execution, would have contributed highly to the glory and advantage of the Roman empire. 'Being born, ſays our Author, for great atchievements, and paſſionately fond of glory, his continual ſucceſs was no inducement to him to enjoy the fruits of his labours, but became a ſpur to animate him to greater enterprizes. He grew inſenſible to preſent glory, that he might ſeek freſh honour; and, becoming in a manner his own rival, he was ambitious, by new enterprizes and exploits, to efface the ſplendor of his former ones.' Having given an account of the deſign he had conceived of avenging the defeat of Craſſus, by making war upon the Parthians, and of the other projects in which he intended to engage, Mr. Hooke exhibits a relation of the conſpiracy entered into againſt him by Brutus and Caſſius, in conſequence of which he was murdered in the Senate-houſe; and his deſcription of the death and character of this diſtinguiſhed Roman, while it will entertain our Readers, may enable them to form a concluſion concerning his merit as an Hiſtorian.

'As the intrigues, ſays he, of the conſpirators could not be conducted ſo ſecretly as not to give ſome cauſe of ſuſpicion, Cæſar, if we believe Plutarch, received information of their nightly meetings; and one day, when he was cautioned to be upon his guard againſt Antony and Dolabella, he anſwered, *It is not thoſe plump, jolly, curled fellows that I am afraid of; it is of the pale, meagre ones:* under which deſcription he glanced at Caſſius and Brutus. Brutus, in particular, adds the ſame hiſtorian, appeared formidable to him, on account of his courage, ſeverity, and natural impetuoſity: but, when he reflected on his *probity* and *honour*, his apprehenſions diſappeared; and, when he was adviſed not to truſt him too far, *What*, ſaid he, clapping his hand to his breaſt, *do you think that Brutus will not ſtay till this debilitated carcaſe has finiſhed its career!* Cæſar had reſolved to truſt to fortune, and was often heard to ſay, that he had rather die once by treachery than live always in fear of it; that he had lived long enough, and that, by his death, the empire would be a greater loſer than himſelf. The very night before his aſſaſſination, being at ſupper in Lepidus's houſe, he maintained, that the moſt eligible death was that which was leaſt expected.

'In the morning of the fatal day, we are told, that Cæſar, finding himſelf indiſpoſed, was inclined to put off the aſſembly; to which he is ſaid by Suetonius and Plutarch to have been likewiſe moved by many prodigies that had lately happened, and a dream that his wife Calpurnia had that very night, in which ſhe ſaw him ſtabbed in her boſom: but D. Brutus, by rallying thoſe fears as unmanly and unworthy of him, and alledging that his abſence would be interpreted as an affront to the assembly, drew him out against his will to meet his destined fate.

' M. Brutus and Cassius appeared according to custom in the Forum, sitting in their prætorian tribunals to hear and determine causes; where, though they had daggers under their gowns, they sat with the same calmness, as if they had nothing upon their minds; till the news of Cæsar's coming out to the Senate called them away to the performance of their part in the tragical act. Plutarch, who never fails to give us every circumstance that can make his relation more interesting, whether it be founded in good authority or not, tells us, that, when Cæsar came out of his house, a slave endeavoured to get near and speak to him; but, not having been able to pierce the crowd that attended him, he went into the house and desired Calpurnia to secure him till Cæsar's return, because he had something to communicate to him of the greatest importance. In the way to the Senate-house, Artemidorus, a Greek philosopher, put into his hands a paper containing a circumstantial account of the whole plot, and said to him: *Read this, and lose no time, for it concerns you much.* This man, who assisted several of Brutus's friends in the prosecution of their studies, had made several discoveries; but Cæsar, surrounded as he was by his courtiers, could not read the contents, and entered the Senate-house with the paper in his hand. Many circumstances gave the conspirators great alarms, and put their fortitude to the test. An acquaintance of Casca came up to him and said, *You thought to be very secret, but Brutus has acquainted me of the whole affair.* Just as Casca was going to make a reply, which would have discovered all, the other added; *What then, my Friend, are you on a sudden grown rich enough to stand for the edileship!* Casca shuddered at the danger he had escaped. M. Brutus himself had a most violent shock: word was brought him that his dearly beloved Porcia was at the point of death: for, as the moment of her husband's hazardous enterprize drew near, she was seized with a deadly panic. Brutus, however, shewed himself a true descendant of that hero who sacrificed his own children to the liberty of his country, and the same spirit over-ruled now in him every other affection. In fine, Cæsar arrives; and, as he came out of his litter, Popilius Lænas, a senator, made up to him and talked with him with much earnestness, and the Dictator seemed to give much attention to what he delivered. This Popilius, a little time before, had been with Brutus and Cassius, and said to them, *I wish your design may succeed, and I advise you not to defer it; for there are several private accounts of it.* The conspirators did not doubt, therefore, but that they were discovered and betrayed. An universal consternation reigned among our intrepid assassins; they looked at each other, and agreed by signs not to wait till they were seized, but to stab themselves in order to avoid the ignominy of a public execution: and already Cassius and some others had laid their hands to their poniards; when Brutus, observing that the gesture and attitude of Popilius was rather that of a supplicant than an accuser, perceived his error, and, by the serenity of his countenance, made the others understand that they had nothing to fear. At length Popilius kissed the Dictator's hand and withdrew.

' Cæsar

'Cæsar went forward, and a number of the conspirators surrounded and conducted him to the Curule chair: whilst two of them, Decimus and Trebonius, stopped Antony at the door of the Senate-house. As soon as he had taken his place, Tillius Cimber, who was to begin the attack upon his person, advanced nearer than the rest, as if he had some favour to request of him; and, laying hold of his gown, drew it over his shoulders, which was the sign agreed upon. *This*, said Cæsar, *is plain violence:* and he had scarcely pronounced these words, when he was wounded a little below the throat by one of the Casca's. He seized the assassin's arm and ran it through with his *style* for writing; and, endeavouring to rush forward, was stopped by another wound, which was afterwards judged to be the only mortal one he received. Finding himself surrounded on all sides with drawn daggers, he wrapped up his head in his toga, and spread it also over his legs, that he might fall the more decently; and so received three and twenty wounds, fetching a groan only on receiving the first, without uttering so much as one word.

'Thus fell Cæsar, in the 56th year of his age: a man, who, considered as a statesman and a captain, may justly challenge the first place in the registers of mankind. He was formed to excel in peace as well as in war; was provident in council, fearless in action, and executed what he had once resolved on with an amazing celerity. With the greatest nobleness of birth, of person, and of countenance, he joined every great quality that can exalt human nature, and give a man the ascendant in society. He was open, sincere, great, and magnanimous, in all his behaviour; faithful to his friends, and zealous to promote their interests; generous and liberal, even to profusion, to his dependents; and was distinguished for the most singular humanity and clemency in the midst of the greatest provocations and examples of cruelty and revenge. He was magnificent, polite, and, in respect to natural endowments, learning and eloquence, scarce inferior to any man. He was a most munificent patron of wit and learning, wheresoever he found them; and, from his love for those talents, could easily pardon such as had employed them against him. In all the military qualifications he had no superior; and no general ever acquired, to such a degree, the esteem and affection of his soldiers. In riding, in throwing the javelin, and in every exercise, he possessed a singular dexterity; and he was able to endure fatigue beyond all credibility. He used to march commonly at the head of his troops, bare-headed, both in foul and fair weather; and to swim over the rivers which obstructed his way. In his expeditions he was daring, but cautious; and never marched an army without using every possible precaution against surprises. He was never discouraged from any enterprize, nor retarded in the prosecution of it, by ill omens: he engaged in battle, not only after previous deliberation, but often on a sudden, when opportunities offered, after a march, or in stormy weather, when nobody could imagine he would move: and, on all occasions, he behaved with the greatest intrepidity and resolution; insomuch, that the serenity of his countenance was, often, in the most imminent dangers, the chief support of the courage of his troops. Just and impartial to his officers and soldiers, he treated them with an equal severity and indulgence; when the

 enemy

enemy was near, exacting the strictest discipline; but, on other occasions, excusing them from all duty, and leaving them to revel at pleasure. His soldiers, he used to boast, did not fight the worse for being perfumed. In his speeches to them, he called them always *Comrades*; and he ornamented their arms with gold and silver, that they might make the finer appearance, and be the more tenacious of them in battle. He loved them to that degree, that, when he heard of the disaster of his troops under Titurius Sabinus, he neither cut his hair nor shaved his beard, till he had revenged it upon the enemy; by which means he inspired them with a mutual affection for his person and an invincible bravery. They never mutinied during the whole course of the Gallic war; and, when they were guilty of it during the *civil* war, we have seen how quickly he brought them back to their duty, by his authority. In his civil capacity he was directed by great and extensive views: the acts of his consulship, which the Aristocracy so vigorously opposed, were all wise and tending to the public good: and, when he was master of the empire in quality of Perpetual Dictator, he discovered in all his undertakings the most general benevolence.'

In a succeeding number of our Review, we shall attend our Author from the death of Cæsar to the settlement of the empire on Augustus; and the strictures we shall offer on this period of his history, we shall accompany with some general remarks concerning his ability, and the degree of approbation to which we think he is entitled.

ART. III. *The First Book of the Lusiad, published as a Specimen of a Translation of that celebrated Epic Poem.* By William Julius Mickle, Author of the Concubine, &c. 8vo. 1 s. Oxford printed, and sold by Cadell, &c. in London.

ON the revival of letters a mistaken idea prevailed in the poetical department, with respect to theological machinery. The Christian was substituted for the Pagan theology, and the Trinity supplied the place of Jupiter, Apollo, and Mercury. The Venetian opera, one of the earliest species of revived poetry, was constructed on this principle; and in our own nation the first dramatic pieces were founded on the Christian system. But on the Continent, as well as, afterwards, in this island, it was soon discovered that Beings, which were the objects of mens serious fears, were by no means the proper objects of their amusement. The Pagan system was adopted for poetical operations, whether of the epic or dramatic kind; but, what rendered the matter, if possible, worse than before, it was only adopted in part. A preposterous medley of the Heathen mythology and the Christian divinity ensued; and Bacchus and Venus co-operated with Jesus Christ and the Holy Ghost.

Such is the powerful objection which rests against the Lusiad; an objection which neither the force of genius, nor the wealth

wealth of fancy it exhibits can ever render unconsequential; and we own that, under this predicament, whatever abilities the Translator might possess, we should not wish to see it in the English language. To be ignorant of the beauties of the Lusiad is of much less consequence to us as a people, than to see our religious system discredited by a fabulous use of its founder.

M. Duperron de Castera, who translated the Lusiad into French prose, very prudently omitted the Christian part of the machinery, and thereby avoided the offensive impropriety of this mixt theology. We are sorry to find that the ingenious Translator of this specimen does not proceed on the same principle, which would have rendered his work both less laborious and less exceptionable.

The merit of the Lusiad is altogether unquestionable. It has received the suffrage of the greatest names. Tasso has mentioned it in the most honourable terms; and Voltaire, though he has freely censured its imperfections, has not disallowed its due praise. It exhibits many marks of true genius, and strong fancy, lively paintings, and happy powers of description.

The following extract from Voltaire's Essay on the Epic poetry of the European nations, written by himself in English, while he was printing his Henriade in London, will give our Readers a farther idea of the Lusiad and its Author.

'While Trissino was clearing away the rubbish in Italy, which barbarity and ignorance had heaped up for ten centuries, in the way of the arts and sciences, Camoens in Portugal steered a new course, and acquired a reputation, which lasts still among his countrymen, who pay as much respect to his memory as the English to Milton.

'He was a strong instance of the irresistible impulse of nature, which determines a true genius to follow the bent of his talents in spite of all the obstacles which could check his course.

'His infancy lost amidst the idleness and ignorance of the court of Lisbon; his youth spent in romantic loves, or in war against the Moors; his long voyages at sea in his riper years; his misfortunes at court, the revolutions of his country, none of all these could suppress his genius.

'Emanuel, the second king of Portugal, having a mind to find a new way to the East Indies by the ocean, sent Vasco De Gama with a fleet, in the year 1497, to that undertaking, which, being new, was deemed rash and impracticable, and which of course gained him a great reputation when it succeeded.'

Camoens, who was born in 1517, and who afterwards pursued the track that Gama had opened, and made a voyage to the East Indies, 'wrote his poem,' called the Lusiad, on the subject of Gama's expedition, ' part on the Atlantic sea, and part on the Indian shore. I ought not to omit that in a shipwreck, on the coast of Malabar *, he swam ashore, holding up his poem in one hand, which otherwise had been perhaps lost for ever.

' Such a new subject, managed by an uncommon genius, could not but produce a sort of Epic poetry unheard of before. There no bloody *wars* are *fought*, no heroes wounded in a thousand different ways; no woman enticed away and the world overturned by her cause; no empire † founded; in short, nothing of what was deemed before the only subject of poetry.

' The poet conducts the Portuguese fleet to the mouth of the Ganges round the coasts of Africa. He takes notice of many nations who live upon the African shore. He interweaves, artfully, the history of Portugal. The simplicity of his subject is raised by some fictions of different kinds, which I think not improper to acquaint the Reader with.

' When the fleet is sailing in sight of the Cape of Good Hope, called then the Cape of Storms, a formidable shape appears to them, walking in the depth of the sea; his head reaches to the clouds; the storms, the winds, the thunder, and the lightening hang about him; his arms are extended over the waves. 'Tis the guardian of that foreign ocean, unplowed before by any ship. He complains of being obliged to submit to fate, and to the audacious undertaking of the Portuguese; and foretells them all the misfortunes they must undergo in the Indies. I believe that such a fiction would be thought noble and proper in all ages, and in all nations.

' There is another which perhaps would have pleased the Italians as well as the Portuguese, but no *other* nation *besides*. It is an enchanted island, called the Island of Bliss, which the fleet finds in *her* way home, just rising from the sea for their comfort and reward. Camoens describes that place, as Tasso did, some years after, his island of Armida. There a supernatural power brings in all the beauties, and presents all the pleasures which Nature can afford, and which the heart may wish for; a goddess enamoured with Vasco de Gama, carries him to the top of an high mountain, from whence she shews him all the kingdoms of the earth, and foretels the fate of Portugal.

' After Camoens hath given a loose to his fancy in the lascivious description of the pleasures which Gama and his crew en-

* This, says our Translator, is a mistake. It was at the mouth of the river Mehon in China.

† This too, as Mr. M. also observes, is an inadvertency; for the founding of the Portuguese empire in the East, is the principal subject of the poem.

joyed

joyed in the island, he takes care to inform the Reader, that he ought to understand by this fiction, nothing but the satisfaction which the virtuous man feels, and the glory which accrues to him by the practice of virtue. But the best excuse for such an invention is the charming style in which it is delivered, (if we believe the Portuguese) for the beauty of the elocution makes sometimes amends for the faults of the poets, as the colouring of Rubens makes some defects in his figures pass unregarded.'

Such is Voltaire's account of this celebrated poem, with the addition of some objections of the same nature with those we have made at the beginning of this article; but his strictures on the Island of Bliss are, in our opinion, both invidious and unjust.—As to the instances of bad English, which we have distinguished by the *Italic character*, the Reader who bears in mind that Voltaire wrote this Essay in a language foreign to him, will think them very pardonable.

As Mr. Mickle proposes to publish a translation of this poem by subscription, an extract from the specimen he has here given us will best shew our Readers how far he is entitled to their favour.

'Whilst thus in heav'n's bright palace Fate was weigh'd,
Right onward still the brave armada stray'd:
Right on they steer by Ethiopia's strand
And pastoral Madagascar's verdant land.
Before the balmy gales of cheerful spring,
With heav'n their friend, they spread the canvas wing;
The sky cerulean, and the breathing air,
The lasting promise of a calm declare.
Behind them now the Cape of Praso bends,
Another ocean to their view extends,
Where black-top't islands, to their longing eyes,
Lav'd by the gentle waves †, in prospect rise.
But GAMA (captain of the vent'rous band,
Of bold emprize, and born for high command,
Whose martial fires, with prudence close allied,
Secur'd the smiles of fortune on his side)
Bears off those shores which waste and wild appear'd,
And eastward still for happier climates steer'd:
When gathering round and blackening o'er the tide,
A fleet of small canoes the pilot spied;
Hoisting their sails of palm-tree leaves, inwove
With curious art, a swarming crowd they move:

† '*Lav'd by the gentle waves*——The original says, the sea shewed them new islands, which it encircled and laved. Thus rendered by Fanshaw,

Neptune disclos'd new isles which he did play
About, and with his billows danc't the bay.

Long

Long were their boats *, and sharp to bound along
Through the dash'd waters, broad their oars and strong:
The bending rowers on their features bore
The swarthy marks of Phaeton's † fall of yore;
When flaming lightnings scorch'd the banks of Po,
And nations blacken'd in the dread o'erthrow.
Their garb, *discover'd as approaching nigh,*
Was cotton strip'd with many a gaudy dye:
'Twas one whole piece beneath one arm confin'd,
The rest hung loose and flutter'd on the wind,
All, but one breast, above the loins was bare,
And swelling turbans bound their jetty hair:
Their arms were bearded darts and faulchions broad,
And warlike music sounded as they row'd.
With joy the sailors saw the boats draw near,
With joy beheld the human face appear:
What nations these, their wondering thoughts explore,
What rites they follow, and what God adore!

---

* '*Long were their boats, and sharp to bound along*—Fanshaw's translation of this passage may serve as a specimen of his usual manner:

For strait out of that isle which seem'd most neer
Unto the continent, Behold a number
Of little boats in company appeer,
Which (clapping all wings on) the long sea sunder!
The men are wrapt with joy, and, with the meer
Excess of it, can only look and wonder.
What nation's this (within themselves they say)
What rites, what laws, what king do they obey?

Their coming thus: in boats with fins, nor flat,
But apt t' o'er-set (as being pincht and long)
And then they'd swim like rats. The sayles, of mat
Made of palm leaves, wove curiously and strong,
The men's complexion, the self-same with that
HEE gave the earth's burnt parts (from heaven flung)
Who was more brave than wise; That this is true
The Po doth know and Lampetusa rue.

† '——*of Phaeton's fall*——The historical foundation of the fable of Phaeton is this. Phaeton was a young enterprising prince of Libya. Crossing the Mediterranean in quest of adventures he landed at Epirus, from whence he went to Italy to see his intimate friend Cygnus. Phaeton was skilled in astrology, from whence he arrogated to himself the title of the son of Apollo. One day in the heat of summer as he was riding along the banks of the Po, his horses took fright at a clap of thunder, and plunged into the river, where, together with their master, they perished. Cygnus, who was a poet, celebrated the death of his friend in verse, from whence the fable.

Vid. Plutar. in vit. Pyrr.

And

And now with hands and kerchiefs wav'd in air
The barb'rous race their friendly mind declare.
Glad were the crew, and ween'd that happy day
Should end their dangers and their toils repay.
The lofty masts the nimble youths ascend,
The ropes they haule, and o'er the yard-arms bend;
Already pointing to the island's shore,
A safe moon'd bay, with slacken'd sails they bore:
With cheerful shouts they furl the gather'd sail
That less and less flaps quivering on the gale;
The prows their speed stopt, o'er the surges nod,
The falling anchors dash the foaming flood;
When sudden as they stopt, the swarthy race
With smiles of friendly welcome on each face,
Alert and bounding, by the cordage climb:
Illustrious GAMA, with an air sublime,
Soften'd by mild humanity, receives,
And to their chief the hand of friendship gives,
Bids spread the board, and, instant as he said,
Along the deck the festive board is spread:
The sparkling wine in chrystal goblets glows,
And round the guests with cheerful welcome flows;
While thus the wine its sprightly glee inspires,
From whence the fleet, the swarthy chief enquires,
What seas they past, what *vantage* would attain,
And what the shore their purpose hop'd to gain?
From farthest west, the *Portingals* reply,
To reach the golden eastern shores we try.
Through that unbounded sea where billows roll
From the cold northern to the southern pole;
And by the wide extent, the dreary vast
Of Afric's bays, already have we past;
And many a sky have seen, and many a shore,
Where *but* sea-monsters cut the waves before.
To spread the glories of our monarch's reign,
For India's shore we brave the trackless main,
Our glorious toil, and at his nod would brave
The dismal gulphs of Acheron's black wave.
And now, in turn, your race, your country shew,
And what, for truth, of India's site you know.

'Rude are the natives here, the Moor reply'd,
Dark are their minds, and brute-desire their guide:
But we of alien blood and strangers here,
Nor hold their customs nor their laws revere.
From Abram's * race our holy prophet sprung,
An angel taught, and heav'n inspir'd his tongue;
His sacred rites and mandates we obey,
And distant empires own his holy sway.

* '*From Abram's race our holy prophet sprung*——Mohammed, who was descended from Ishmael, the son of Abraham by Hagar.

From

From isle to isle our trading vessels roam,
Mozambic's harbour our commodious home.
As then your sails for India's shores expand,
For sultry Ganges or Hydaspes' strand,
Here shall you find a pilot skill'd to guide
Through all the *dangers* of the *per'lous* tide,
Though wide-spread shelves, and cruel rocks unseen,
Lurk in the way, and whirlpools rage between.
Accept, mean while, what fruits these islands hold,
And to the regent let your wish be told.
Then may your caterers at will provide,
And all your various wants be here supplied.'

Mr. Mickle has, before this, given proofs of his poetical talents in Pollio, an elegy; and in the Concubine, a poem. We are of opinion, however, that in the specimen now published there are many lines that want the strengthening, and some that require the polishing hand.

Art. IV. *Observations concerning the Distinction of Ranks in Society.* By John Millar, Esq; Professor of Laws in the University of Glasgow. 4to. 9s. Murray. 1771.

THE study of human nature has been cultivated, with peculiar attention, by the greatest men in all ages; but the means employed by them to promote it, have not always been the same. It was not till of late, in particular, that they endeavoured to investigate the principles of human nature, by examining the sentiments of mankind in the different ages of society. As this philosophy took its rise in our own island *, we have reason to hope that it will here also receive its perfection.

By the history of society, taken in the most extensive sense of the phrase, we mean not the annals of particular nations under the different periods of their government; much less an account of the manners and customs which prevail among different nations whose circumstances are nearly the same; but a view of mankind in general, placed in all that variety of positions which occasions a diversity in their manners and way of thinking.

Were it possible that such an history should ever be completed, we might hope to obtain a more extensive knowledge of human nature than had formerly been aimed at: and this knowledge would not be more agreeable to our curiosity, than advantageous to our interest. After learning by history and observation the effect of different circumstances on the manners and sentiments of men, we might infer, from these circum-

* See Hobbes, Mandeville, Temple, Bolingbroke, Hume, &c.

stances,

stances, how, on all occasions, they would think and act, and thence learn to conduct ourselves with propriety in every possible situation.

This however, though a grand and fertile, is but a distant prospect. The almost infinite variety of objects about which mankind are employed, the circumstances, no less various, which influence their reasonings and feelings, and the striking dissimilitudes which prevail even among those societies where the resemblance is the nearest, these are powerful obstacles, which will long resist all our force and activity. If there are not two Tartar hordes, two American tribes, or two savage communities on the coast of Africa, among whom a very considerable difference does not take place, both in manners and conduct, what reason have we to expect a greater degree of analogy between the more improved societies of men, where the circumstances which occasion variety, and still more the combination of these circumstances, are vastly more numerous and powerful?

This consideration has led some learned men too hastily to determine that it is impossible to lay down fixed principles with regard to human conduct, or to arrive at any degree of science on a subject so intricate, so uncertain, and where the particulars are too dissimilar to admit of generalization. But many successful attempts by which customs seemingly the most capricious, and manners seemingly the most unnatural †, have been completely accounted for, and even traced up to the most powerful and best known principles in human nature, are sufficient to prove the fallacy of such an opinion, and to encourage us to proceed forward in the same field of investigation. It is of no importance that in many cases there should appear exceptions to the general principles established: these exceptions arise from particularities which have not been attended to; and as the properties of the square or the circle are not the less true for not agreeing to the physical squares or circles in the material universe, so neither can the truth of abstract political principles be affected by their disagreement with political combinations which were not in the supposition. But these principles, when firmly established, afford the best assistance for enabling us to find our way through all the mazes of human action, and to give a certain degree of regularity to what was before not only without form, but seemed incapable of receiving it.

The Author of the performance before us has pointed out the more common and obvious distinctions in the state of civil society, and shewn the influence of these distinctions on the manners, laws, and government of a people. He begins with the

† See Montesquieu, *passim*.

rudest and most barbarous circumstances in which mankind can exist; and traces them through their various successive improvements. In his preface, after making some remarks on the utility of such inquiries, and on the manner on which they ought to be conducted, he gives an analysis, or more properly the contents, of his work. Of the five chapters which follow, the first treats of the rank and condition of women in different ages; the second, of the jurisdiction and authority of a father over his children; the third, of the authority of a chief over the members of a tribe or village; the fourth, of the rise of a sovereign over an extensive society, and of the advancement of a people in civilization and refinement; the last, of the condition of servants in different parts of the world.

The chapter on the rank of women in different ages, is chiefly founded on two principles which are universally admitted. The first, that the rank of women in society depends on the different degrees of strength or weakness of the passion between the sexes. The second principle is expressed by Shakespeare, when he says, "The impediments in fancy's way are causes of mere fancy."

Taking these principles for granted, the Author observes, that in a rude and barbarous age the passions between the sexes can hardly arise to any considerable height. A savage, who is continually employed in acquiring the bare necessaries of life, who subsists precariously from day to day, and whose desires are neither cherished by affluence, nor inflamed by indulgence, will seldom bestow much attention on their gratification. In a society too, where most sources of distinction and consequently all rules of decorum are unknown, and where individuals live together in the coarsest familiarity, and give way to their natural propensities without hesitation, there can be no difficulty in gratifying the passion between the sexes. Hence, under these circumstances, the force of this passion is in a great measure weakened, and the women possessed of no other means of acquiring consideration, lose all the respect which arises from the refined sentiments of the men in the more improved ages of society. The husband exercises over them that authority which the strong assume over the weak: an authority exorbitant and boundless, and which frequently is exerted in the most dreadful manner. The Author illustrates this observation from the history of rude nations; and sufficiently proves that, among these nations, the wife is regarded as nothing more than the slave of her husband. There is an exception, indeed, to this general conclusion, in those countries where marriage is not properly established, and where the mother, having more connection with the children than the father who is unknown, avails herself of this circumstance to acquire distinction and importance.

But

But the first considerable alteration produced on the manners of a rude society, arises from the invention of taming and pasturing cattle. The profession of a shepherd is not so precarious as that of a huntsman, nor exposed to so many difficulties and dangers. Having acquired the necessaries of life, he begins to seek after its comforts and enjoyments. The passion between the sexes excites his attention, and the indolent tranquillity accompanying the pastoral way of life, naturally disposes him to indulge in it. The introduction of property in cattle, too, distinguishing individuals from one another, and elevating the richest members of the society above the rest, prevents that freedom of intercourse which took place in a ruder age, when strength, courage, and other personal accomplishments, were the only sources of distinction. If we add to this, the rivalship which naturally takes place among neighbouring great families, with the animosities and quarrels which frequently arise between them, we shall perceive a sufficient cause for the origin of those difficulties and dangers which are the soul of the passion between the sexes, and without which it can never arrive at any considerable height. In the age of shepherds, accordingly, we find a certain refinement and delicacy in this passion, and a proportional degree of respect paid to the female character.

The introduction of agriculture is the next improvement in society, after that of pasturage. It is easy to perceive that agriculture, by establishing the idea of land-property, must encrease the natural causes of distinction, and consequently of rivalship among mankind, and occasion a still higher degree of attention to be paid to the women. The Author illustrates this, by describing the manners of the Gothic nations who overran the Roman empire. He proves that the romantic gallantry by which they were distinguished, was chiefly owing to that distant reserve which naturally prevailed among haughty and independent families, and prevented the free intercourse between the sexes. The next change is produced by the progress of arts, manufactures, and government. This progress, while on the one hand it removes the obstacles to the free intercourse between the sexes, and thereby discredits all extravagance in love, tends, on the other, to augment the respect paid to the women, by affording them an occasion of distinguishing themselves, by their attention to the domestic virtues, which are now sought after and esteemed. The wife is neither considered as the slave nor as the idol of her husband, but as his friend and companion, who soothes and alleviates his misfortunes, who doubles all his joys, and who is capable of taking a part in the care and labour to which he is subjected. The circumstances of this age therefore naturally bestowing that rank on the

the women, which seems of right to become them, it is here that we are to expect the most perfect models of the female character. This is illustrated by the state of society, and manners of the women, in ancient Greece, and in some other countries.

A farther progress in arts, introducing opulence and luxury, the women begin to be esteemed on account of the talents and accomplishments which prevail in an elegant age, and which form the delight of a refined society. They are no longer confined to their houses and their families; they are introduced into all companies of pleasure, and act a principal part on the grand theatre of the world. Thus do the extremes of barbarity and refinement approach to one another, and the women now enjoy, from the esteem of the men, that same degree of liberty which they before possessed on account of their indifference.

Our Author, as we before mentioned, has divided what follows into four chapters. The three first however may, without impropriety, be run into one another, and considered under one view. They treat of the origin of authority among mankind, which always depends on the same principles, whoever be the persons that acquire it. These principles, which have often been taken notice of *, may be reduced to the four following, strength, courage, wisdom, and opulence, together with the force of custom and habit, which on all occasions have so much influence on human affairs.

According to these principles we may naturally suppose that, in a rude age, the authority of a father over his children will be unbounded. He not only enjoys, during their early years, the most absolute superiority in point of strength, a superiority which the force of custom will confirm and maintain, but in an age where the art of writing is unknown, and all kinds of knowledge are acquired only by experience, persons of advanced years must be regarded with the utmost veneration. Their words are listened to as so many oracles; their counsels are always conceived to be those of wisdom; and their commands are executed with the most punctual and implicit obedience. At a period too when arts and professions are unknown, children have no opportunity of leaving the houses of their fathers: they remain in his family, and are supported from the common stock, of which he is the sole manager and disposer. Hence all the principles which raise the authority of one man above another are united in establishing the power of a father over his children; and hence among all barbarous na-

* See Temple's Essay on Government, and Rousseau on the Inequality of Ranks among Men, &c.

tions

tions children are reduced into a state of dependence and servitude. It is easy to perceive that when the circumstances of society are changed, when knowledge is improved, when arts and professions are established, that the father must gradually be deprived of this exorbitant authority.

The Author illustrates this subject by the history of the Roman law, with regard to the power of fathers over their children. He explains the different branches of this power, which was the same with that exercised by masters over their slaves; and he describes at large the circumstances which led to the abolition of it.

The same circumstances which serve to raise a father above the several members of his family, elevate a chief, or leader, above a tribe or certain number of families. In the rudest age of society, when hunting and war are the sole occupations of men, it becomes necessary for each tribe to choose some person of superior talents to direct their common expeditions. When the members of each family lived separately by themselves, they were under the direction of their common parent; and now that different families have, for their mutual advantage, incorporated themselves together, they naturally establish the same form of government in the tribe which prevailed before in the family. Strength, agility, warlike skill, and address, are the talents which are required in their leader. When property in cattle, and still more, when landed property is introduced, the greatest share in both necessarily devolving on the chieftain, his influence will be prodigiously extended. He is regarded not only as their leader in war, but as their judge and legislator in time of peace, and from a natural propensity to believe that those are particularly favoured by the gods, for whom we ourselves have a great respect, he becomes the supreme conductor of their religious ceremonies. In this way is a country divided among a number of distinct tribes, over whom their respective chieftains exercise an authority similar to that of a father in his own family.

In the same manner that these leaders are established by the union of different families, a sovereign rises above the whole nation by the incorporation of the tribes which compose it. These tribes, living in a continual state of war and animosity, must weaken and distress each other. The leaders of such of them as have suffered the most from these dissentions, or originally were the least numerous, and the weakest, will submit to their more powerful neighbours, in order to acquire their assistance and protection. As we cannot suppose a perfect equality to prevail among the latter, those who are already the most distinguished, must naturally receive the greatest number of submissions. This will still more enhance their superiority, and,

 by

by degrees, instead of a vast number of small societies governed by inconsiderable chieftains, we shall have a smaller number of great ones under the subjection of more powerful leaders. This situation may continue while the nation is in no danger from abroad, or has no design to engage itself in foreign expeditions. But as soon as these are undertaken, it becomes necessary to have some one person to conduct their operations. The office of leading them forth to war devolves on the person who already possesses the greatest influence and authority. From the force of custom, from the natural ascendant he has acquired, and from the superiority of his talents, this person still continues, even in time of peace, to assume the lead in all matters of public concern. His neighbours, continually at variance among themselves, seldom venture to dispute with their acknowledged superior, and, when distressed by one another, naturally court his friendship and protection. In this manner does the king obtain the submissions of the greater barons, as they had before obtained the submissions of the smaller.

The Author supposes this to have been the progress of government among the northern nations who settled in the different provinces of the Roman empire. According to him the feudal system, which distinguished these nations, and which is commonly regarded as a singular phenomenon, naturally ought to take place in every society of men, living under similar circumstances. He ventures to go so far upon this subject as to point out institutions, of the same sort with those which prevailed among the Gothic nations, in several kingdoms of Africa and of the East Indies. But without examining the justness of this opinion, which would swell the present article beyond its due bounds, we shall mention the effects of improvement in arts, manufactures, and commerce, on the government of such a nation. Though a king be now established at the head of the whole society, he is far from enjoying that unlimited power which is assumed by some of the modern princes of Europe. The nobles indeed have submitted to his protection, yet still they have arms in their hands, and were they to turn them against their sovereign, he has no force sufficient to oppose them. But after the introduction of arts and manufactures, a variety of professions are established, and the greater part of the society, busied in lucrative employments, or enervated by luxury and wealth, become averse to a military life. Hence the necessity of mercenary armies, which being disciplined with great labour and expence, are naturally kept on foot, even in time of peace. These armies, raised under the immediate inspection of the prince, by whom also they are managed and supported, may throw a prodigious weight into the scale of government, and controul every sort of opposition on the part of the people. But

the

the progress of civilization, though in this view it tends to exalt the royal prerogative, yet in other respects is extremely favourable to liberty. The lower ranks of people, who formerly had not the means of subsisting but by attaching themselves to the service of some great man, may now acquire, by their labour, an independent and comfortable livelihood. The advancement of arts and luxury, while it gives an opportunity to the nobles, of dissipating their large fortunes, affords occasions to the industrious merchant, of rising to opulence and grandeur. From this fluctuation of property, family-distinctions lose their force, wealth becomes the great source of honours and respect; and as wealth is more generally diffused among all ranks of men, so does power, the natural concomitant of wealth, become more equally divided among the different members of the community.

In the last chapter of this performance, the Author considers the condition of servants in different parts of the world. In a rude age mankind are disposed to reduce into a state of servitude all those of their fellow-creatures who fall into their power. The titles of servant and slave are at this time synonymous. The rude notions of a savage naturally prompt him to believe that he makes the most of his advantage by depriving those who are subjected to him, of every degree of liberty. But it is remarkable that the same way of thinking should prevail in the more enlightened ages. A slave who is incapable of acquiring property, who, by all his activity and skill, can obtain but a bare subsistence, cannot possibly be supposed equally industrious in his employment with those who are continually excited by every motive of interest and emulation: his work, therefore, can never be so profitable to the community as that of a freeman. Notwithstanding this conclusion, than which nothing seems more obvious, the practice of servitude prevailed among all the nations of antiquity.

The Author next enquires how servitude happened to be abolished among the modern nations of Europe. His disquisition on this subject is extremely ingenious, and there are in it many very judicious remarks, which, however, our bounds will not permit us to transcribe. The performance, indeed, deserves to be read in the Author's own words. The manner in which it is written is agreeable; and the style is in general correct, without stiffness or affectation. From the short analysis of it which we have given, the learned Reader will perceive that this is one of those works which only could be produced in an age superior to prejudices, and guided by the spirit of a free and liberal philosophy.

ART. V. *The complete English Farmer; or, a practical System of Husbandry, founded upon natural, certain, and obvious Principles; in which is comprized a general View of the whole Art of Agriculture, exhibiting the different Effects of cultivating Land according to the Usage of the old and new Husbandry. The Whole exemplified by a Series of suitable Management from the first Apportionment of a Farm from the Waste, to the Time of perfecting it by proper Cultivation in every Part. To which are added, particular Directions for the Culture of every Species of Grain in common Use; and a new Method of Tillage recommended, partaking of the Simplicity of the old Husbandry, and of all the Advantages of the new. Illustrated with Plans of the necessary Buildings belonging to a Farm-House; and an Attempt to establish a Rule for constructing Barns, which may be applied to all Dimensions: Also accurate Delineations of some newly-invented farming Instruments.* By a Practical Farmer, and a Friend of the late Mr. JETHRO TULL, Author of *The Horse-hoeing Husbandry.* 8vo. 5 s. 6 d. Boards. Newbery. 1771.

IT has been observed, that a book with a verbose title, has seldom any thing else to recommend it. We would not apply this observation to our practical Farmer, who declares, in the beginning of his preface, that he means to comprize, in one small volume, all that is *necessary* to the farmer; yet cautions his reader against considering *too hastily* this work as a mere compilation. He bemoans the fate of husbandry, the writers upon which have been chiefly *mere theorists*, or *mere practisers*; yet exempts from this general charge his late ingenious friend Mr. J. Tull, the laborious Mr. A. Young, and the *elegant* Mr. W. Hart.

Our practical Farmer observes the necessity of adopting some *known theory* or *new hypothesis*, to which reference may be made, when we consider agriculture as an *art*; and he affirms that the *only theory* which has received the *sanction* of *modern approbation*, is his friend Mr. Tull's,—which he then explains.

He justly observes, that we might as well maintain that the art of navigation is imperfect, because hurricanes drive the mariner out of his course, as that the art of agriculture is imperfect, because bad seasons deprive us of good crops.

He derides Dr. Home's application of chemical experiments to establish a new theory of agriculture, and affirms that his work has given us no new manures, unless *oil of olives*, *spirits of hartshorn*, and *flour of brimstone* be such!

Indeed he seems to prove, by fair quotation, that Mr. Tull supposed *nitre*, *water*, *air*, and *fire*, to be included in that *earth* which he made *the food* of plants, and that Dr. Home has done him injustice in asserting or supposing the contrary.

Dr.

Dr. Home seems to have added, to Mr. Tull's principles, *oil* and *salt*, but to mean by salt, *nitre*.

As our practical Farmer has warned us against considering his work as a *mere compilation*, he cautions us, also, against the fruitless expectation of *many new discoveries*.

He now assures us, that he fully and frankly acquiesces in the principles of the *new* husbandry, but inclines to the practice of the *old*; and he assigns reasons for what he calls only a *seeming* contradiction, viz. that experiments in favour of the *new*, are, first, ouly in *small*; secondly, may be supposed made only on lands peculiarly fit for it; thirdly, that *exactness in expence* is neglected. He declares further, that he knows no farmer who has *grown rich* by the *new husbandry*, but that he has known gentlemen of small fortunes *hurt* by it, and believes Mr. Tull suffered by it. He honestly owns that the dearness of labour in England will make the *expence* of drill husbandry exceed the *profit*, and he shews the utter improbability that four inches in horse-hoed crops can equal seventy-two in the broad cast. He justly insists also on the expence of five or six ploughings, the necessity of these in rainy seasons, and the inconvenience, next to impossibility, of them in large concerns. The impossibility of these operations in clay soils, will affect two-thirds of the whole arable in England.

All we can say to these passages is, that our Author convinces us, that this contradiction is not *seeming* but *real*; and that he *gives up* the conclusion, yet *holds* the premises.

He is desirous, however, of shewing what the world owes to Mr. Tull; but we cannot allow several things which he ascribes to him, viz. the advantage of frequent ploughings, which was known long before him; the drilling of pease and sainfoin, which are found not equal to broad-casting; and the using less seed, which is found by Mr. Young's experiments not to be a *saving*, but a *loss*. Nor has Mr. Tull shewn dung to be *well saved*, as appears by the same experiments. The *drilling of beans* and *hoeing of turnips* seem to be the sole advantages which he has given to the farmer.

Mr. Tull's Friend now shews that fertility depends upon a proper temperature with regard to *heat* and *cold*, *moisture* and *dryness*; and that *chalk*, *clay*, and other manures, effect this.— He then gives the plan of his work, which will be seen as he proceeds.

The plan of our review of this work must be very different from that on which we proceeded in considering Mr. Young's Course of Experiments. We must take little or no notice of all the common things which our Farmer repeats; but when he advances any thing rather new, by way of confir-

 mation

mation, or confutation, of points not altogether common, we will examine it.

In chapter 1, (on inclosing, &c. a new farm) our Author well observes, that an *exact square* is *most commodious* and *least expensive*, as a *right-lin'd* form is the best for ploughing, and a square includes the greatest quantity that any given right lines can.

He advises to place quick fences in three rows; but we apprehend that in these the roots of the sets will entangle and prevent the growth of each other, and that one row of good plants will be found sufficient. He notes not the distance of the sets, which is a great omission.

He condemns the dry stone walls, as we have done in our review of the second part of the Farmer's Letters.

We join with him in thinking, that the method of forming a ridge above quicksets is pernicious, as it gives an inclination to the necessary moisture to drain off.

He recommends *turf* or *sod walls*, and calculates them at under 12d. per rood. But those who are well acquainted with the North, from whence he takes his notion, know that no good turf wall can be built for any thing like that expence, and that they are much more liable to accidents and disappointments than dry stone walls.

Sir Digby Legard's proposal of double stone walls is so unreasonably expensive, that we wonder not that our practical Farmer should disapprove, but that Sir Digby should ever propose them.

We approve what our Farmer has said against trees in hedge-rows; but we cannot allow a black-thorn fence to be even comparable to that of white thorn for bounds, although it will require less securing.

The expences of inclosing and planting are so various in different parts of the kingdom, that no general estimate can be made..

The dead hedge, which this Writer proposes to raise as a fence for his young oak, &c. is so utterly unequal to the purpose, that it is a disgrace to his avowed experience.

He rightly observes, that shortening the tap-root of young trees makes them grow *faster*, but it destroys the *heart* of them so much, that this practice should never be allowed in trees for timber.

Our Author assures us that elms thrive best in an *harsh* clay, tenacious of moisture. We have always observed, on the contrary, that they thrive best in a dry soil mixed with sand.

We wish our Farmer had explained, by a note, what tree he means by the *plane*: this name is vulgarly given to the *great maple*, which he seems not to mean. The true *platanus*, *plane-tree*, is not common nor successful in England.

His

His calculation of fencing, ſeems ſo much below the truth, that no deductions from it can be allowed; and his ſuppoſal that alders, willows, poplars, will, in 40 or 50 years time, be worth 20 s. each, is a wild hope. The advantageous time of cutting them is much earlier.

He juſtly explodes the cuſtom of polling trees; but we can by no means approve his ſcheme of planting five acres of ground near the homeſtead, for coppice (at 30 l. coſt, and loſs of the ſoil) for fire-wood, as the quick-hedges, if properly lop'd, will yield abundant ſupply.

We incline to our practical Farmer's judgment in the 2d chapter, to build his houſe, &c. near the center of his farm, although he be further from the public road; and we agree with him in thinking (chap. 3.) that in building of barns the threſhing floors are chiefly to be regarded, as moſt of the corn may be preſerved well in ſtacks.

The expence of buildings in ſmall farms is great; but we can ſcarcely conclude, with our Author, that they are ſuch, except in very ſmall farms indeed, as to reduce the profits of the landlord to little more than legal intereſt of his money expended.

In chap. 4, our Farmer gives a general calculation for a barn on theſe principles, viz. firſt, what corn the ground in tillage will yield; ſecondly, what number of men, in 40 weeks (allowing 12 for harveſt, &c.) will threſh that quantity. This is uſeful.

Our practical Farmer's 5th chapter, on buildings, contains numerous terms which the readers he deſigns them for, cannot poſſibly underſtand. The project of making the dairy a cellar, we muſt diſapprove, as it will almoſt certainly be damp, and attended with bad conſequences; and a room above-ground may be kept ſufficiently cool. Mr. Tull's Friend, however, cloſes this chapter with two methods of procuring *ſoft water*, which may be uſeful to ſuch as want that bleſſing. One is by mixing, in a large ciſtern, clay with the water, and then letting it ſtand to ſettle: the other is much more known, viz. the collecting by a pipe the rain which falls on the houſe, and conveying it into a pit, with a double floor of tiles laid in terras.

In the 6th chapter, on barns, we have only to obſerve, that although the floors of many barns are made with leſs coſtly wood than oak, and even ſome with plaiſter, and may be ſufficient for ſmall farms where little corn is threſhed, yet for large farms, good oak floors are cheapeſt. It muſt however be only in dear countries, and for very large farms, that 300 guineas, here ſpecified, can be prudently laid out in barns.

The ſcreens faſtened in the floor of the granary, with valves for ſweetening the grain (as recommended in chap. 7.) are an admirable contrivance.

Open ſheds furniſhed with racks (as recommended in chap. 8.) are of great uſe in winter, eſpecially for ſheep, whoſe carcaſes ſuffer much from the wet.

In his 9th chapter our Farmer adviſes that the Dutch elms, in his homeſtead of 20 acres, be defended with a *dead hedge*. But whoever conſiders that all the ſtock of the farm are to have acceſs to this homeſtead, and how little time a dead hedge will continue a good fence, will be tempted to conclude that our Farmer is not much practiſed in this branch. Indeed, ſcarce one of his trees in one thouſand, thus fenced, would come to perfection.

He thinks (chap. 10.) that if the new farm be adapted to grazing, the incloſures ſhould be ſmall; for in his opinion cattle delight in frequent change, and thrive much better by feeding in freſh paſture. This point however is as confidently oppoſed by a conſiderable party in the agricultural walk. "*Non noſtri eſt, tantas componere lites.*" We incline however to the practical Farmer, and think alſo with him, that incloſures of arable, leſs than 10 acres, loſe much by hedges, birds, &c. But we own we do not at all underſtand him when he ſays, that 'incloſures of more than 20 acres are hurtful to cattle in the cultivation.'

He adviſes the farmer to have fields *wet* and *dry* for cultivation in oppoſite ſeaſons. He thinks, too, that *barren* land ſhould not be incloſed with *fertile*. But ſurely no fence is requiſite to diſtinguiſh theſe oppoſite ſoils to the farmer's eye.

He makes the whole expences of theſe buildings, incloſures, &c. amount to above 2000 l. and as the whole 500 acres incloſed are only to give a rent of 200 l. per ann. and for a ſunk capital, the diſburſer may juſtly expect double intereſt, and legal intereſt is 5 l. per cent. we fear that his landlord will think that he verifies on a *large* farm what he ſaid of a *ſmall* one, viz. that 'he might as well (nay, better) put out his money on mortgage, and give up his 500 acres.'

In chapter 11, our Farmer attempts to ſhew, that the expence of buildings, &c. for a farm of 30 l. will riſe to 515 l. 15 s. which, at legal intereſt, amounts to 25 l. 15 s. Then he deducts 4 l. for land-tax, and concludes that only 5 s. remain. We are no friends to ſmall farms; but theſe calculations are very extravagant, as, (if it were quite neceſſary) we could eaſily ſhew. In the countries where new incloſures are generally made, materials and labour are very cheap, and the land-tax is low.

Our

Our Farmer (in chap. 12.) ſtates expences of ſtocking a farm ſo as to conclude that one of 200 l. per ann. will require 1500 l. We believe that in *many*, nay *moſt* counties, a prudent man, who will work in his youth, may do with a conſiderably leſs ſum; but as we know the loſs, both to individuals and the public, which ariſes from a farmer's overmatching himſelf with ground, we will not contribute to that evil.

In his 13th chapter he obſerves of oxen, that the beſt method of yoking them ſingle to exert their powers to moſt advantage, is in open collars and double harneſs, like that of horſes. We incline to think this may be the truth: but, when they are harneſſed two abreaſt, we apprehend that they muſt have yokes and bows. His advice to his young pupil to hire a ſervant accuſtomed to hoeing of turnips, is very proper.

Chapter 14, well deſcribes a good horſe, but ſtates his price at 18 or 20 guineas, which is below the preſent high markets.

Chapter 15, our Farmer ſeems juſtly to commend the ſwing-plough as the *moſt general* one, and thinks that the double ſwing-plough muſt be a very great improvement for light lands. So think we.

In chapter 16, our Farmer, treating of the variety of ſoils, gives the preference to that which reſembles freſh earth on a mole-hill, and wants no improvement; the next in value is the *hazely* or *marley*; the third *clayey*, which, with *chalk*, compoſes the *marley*; the fourth is the *chalky*; and the fifth the *ſandy*, which is improved by folding of ſheep; the ſixth *boggy* or *peaty*, for which our Farmer recommends *foul ſalt* (a manure few can come at) the ſeventh the *dry brown caking* ſoil; the eighth the *gravelly*; and his laſt appears to be what in the North is called *limeſtone ſoil*. But before this laſt he mentions a ſoil which Dr. Home calls *till*, hardly to be fertilized except by *lime*, *dung*, and *air*, aſſiſted by time. This is deſcribed as 'of a *red*, *grey*, or *yellow* colour, effervescing with vinegar and oil of vitriol diluted with water, and having an irony taſte.'

The 17th chapter enumerates how many things a farmer ſhould know, and deſerves to be read by that claſs of men to keep them modeſt. Our practical Farmer however (with a prejudice very natural to his profeſſion) thinks the *art of farming* 'the moſt difficult to be acquired of any art or calling to which the induſtry of man is applied.'

Chapter 18, ſhews, that he underſtands little of the practice of ſowing rye, who adviſes to ſow it on ſwarth broke up after Midſummer, that is, from the middle of Auguſt * to the middle of September. Our Author directs to plough for wheat till the

* Not October.

middle of November. His manner of turning down the ſwarth may contribute a little, and but a little, to a crop, and a ſoil peculiarly good may ſucceed. He ſuppoſes, however, that the ground on which he ſowed his turnips and rye on one earth, will be fit for barley and clover in ſpring. How different his expectations from thoſe of Virgil, in a much more favourable climate! "*Illa ſeges demum*, &c."

In Chap. 19, our Author approves Dr. Home's account of marle, viz. that it is a body compoſed of clay and lime by nature, ſo as no art can temper it. But is not lime a *factitious* body? However, its effects on land continue almoſt 20 years, and therefore it is well worthy of being ſearched for by the borer. Our Farmer alſo allows that Dr. Home has well diſtinguiſhed (as he knows by ſad experience) a kind of *falſe* marle, which injures land much, and is known by its making no efferveſcence with acids.

Our complete Farmer aſſerts, and, we think, with reaſon, that chalk warms cold land, cools hot, and fertilizes both. He calls lime, *chalk diveſted of its moiſture*; and, from Dr. Home, ſhews how it acts as a fertilizer, viz. 'by attracting oleaginous particles from earth and air, and reſtoring them when miſcible with water.' He denies, as we do, that lime fertilizes not the firſt crop, yet thinks that farmers who bring chalk to burn to lime from any diſtance, if they calculated all the expences, would *never lime* another acre. On the contrary, we *know* lime to be ſo neceſſary for ſome lands, that it can ſcarcely be bought too dear. But we muſt note, that *ſtone* lime is *incomparably* better than *chalk* lime, which our Author here ſpeaks of.

Chapter 20, on compoſts. We have here only two things to note, viz. firſt, that we think, with our Farmer, that woollen rags are become much too dear to be a profitable manure, and that old Markham is truly ridiculous when he pretends that a ſackful will manure an acre: ſecondly, we can ſee no reaſon why Mr. Tull's Friend ſhould call the addition of other manures to chalk, *abſurd*.

The 21ſt chapter ſhews, that no experiments yet prove that 'dung acts only as a divider of the ſoil,' as Mr. Tull maintained. Our Author's experiments confirm what we have long thought, that ſteeps in brine and lime do not prevent ſmutty corn. He mentions a pleaſant miſtake made by Dr. Home, about fertilizing with *ſods*, or a *ſod wall*, on which our neceſſary brevity allows us not to expatiate.

Chapter 22, our Farmer rightly owns, that variation in ſoil, ſituation, convenience, and ſeaſons, will require great variation in *cropping* of lands.

We cordially agree with him, that it is a *vulgar* (and, we add, *very pernicious*) error, that dung should not be laid on till the *l*ploughing; on the contrary, we maintain with him, that dung cannot be too much mixed with the earth before *s*wing.'

We as totally dissent from him when he prescribes only two *b*ushels of seed-wheat to the acre, being convinced by Mr. *Y*oung's experiments that this quantity is considerably too *li*ttle.

We however agree with him to save seed of the first crop of *c*lover, which must be much more vigorous than of the second, *t*hough the contrary *absurd* practice *generally* prevails. But we *ca*nnot approve our Farmer's taking a crop of oats after clover, *as* that requires a fallow, without which most land, well ma-*na*ged, will bring wheat after clover. We approve, however, *his* cropping a shallow soil with barley and sainfoin. We in-*cl*ine to think with him that a shallow soil is improper for pa-*r*ing, and that his method of *turning down* the swart, and cover-*i*ng it with the under mold, is preferable.

He approves Mr. Comber's method of paring off the swart of mossy pastures, burning it, and ploughing in the ashes. We believe that gentleman does not advise to *plough in the ashes*, but *merely to spread them*. The *Musæum Rusticum*, whither we suppose our Farmer to refer, is not at hand. But whatever be Mr. Comber's opinion, we apprehend that the ashes will penetrate sufficiently *without ploughing*, which will cut the roots of the grass, and retard the recovery of the *swart*. That candid cultivator, if we differ from him, will take our dissent in good part.

In chapter 23, our Author gives, from a treatise by Mr. North of Lambeth *, good rules for cultivating of willows or poplars on *marsh* ground, and justly exposes Rocque's cheating his customers, by selling the seed of *Foxtail* instead of *Timothy-grass*, which, he thinks, might suit marsh land, as also would *Flote-fescue*, which last grass we know to be a bauble.

The subject of the 24th chapter, 'the improvement of heath-ground,' is of such vast consequence to the public, that it ought not to be undertaken and treated by any writer in the *light* and *desultory* manner in which it is here considered. Our Farmer seems to have read nothing for the improvement of such ground but what Mr. Young advanced in his *Northern Tour*; to which he objects, that the garden of a turnpike-keeper is not a *sufficient instance*; and thinks, that 'if such soil were improvable, our ancestors would have improved it.' The wild Irish might as well conclude, that if a better way of harnessing horses than

* See Review, vol. xxii. p. 525.

by

by the tails could have been invented, their anceſtors wo have invented it. He tells us, however, that Sir D. Leg has *candidly* * acknowledged that the improvement of this k of ſoil is *much leſs profitable* than Mr. Young aſſerts. Sir Digby Legard and Mr. Young ſettle that account. But us not conclude, that if the improvement be not *ſo great* as Young thinks it, therefore it is not *great*.

Mr. Young has now publiſhed his concluſions on that ſu ject in the ſecond part of his *Farmer's Letters*, and we have viewed them, we hope, with ſome degree of accuracy. W know that there is great variety of expence both in incloſi *heath ſoils*, and in their real value, and therefore the profit incloſing them muſt be as various.

We are ſorry to be obliged, in juſtice to the public, to o ſerve that a *total condemnation* of the great incloſures of th kind in Glouceſterſhire, on ſuch vague report as our worth Farmer here adduces, is rather unbecoming one who profeſſ to have, and, we doubt not, really has, the advancement agriculture at heart.

His propoſal to make above 20 s. per acre annual rent of ſuc land, by planting it with Scotch firs, ſeems very unfeaſible, we have obſerved ſuch plantations not to ſucceed at all; an he ſeems to *forget entirely* that for this purpoſe the ground mu

---

* We were much puzzled by this aſſertion of our Author; for w had never heard of any writing of Sir Digby Legard's in which delivers any opinion of the value of improvements of the kind land here under queſtion.

At length we thought the Farmer muſt refer to Sir Digby Legard's letter to Mr. Young, publiſhed in the ſecond volume of the *Northern Tour*; but, in order to do juſtice to our Farmer, and to proceed upon *certain* ground, we uſed effectual means to know what writing of Sir Digby Legard's he here alludes to; and we are now aſſured, to our ſurprize, that he refers to the letter above-mentioned.

Thus he argues: 'Mr. Young ſtates the value of improvement of *heath* ground at 12 s. per acre (proper authorities are referred to): but Sir Digby Legard affirms, that he only made 8 l. per cent. by improvement of ſuch ground. Therefore he allows it not ſo much as Mr. Young would make it.'

To this argument we muſt give a ſhort, plain, and inconteſtable anſwer, viz. "Mr. Young ſpeaks of deep, rich, heathy ground, and Sir Digby Legard of as different ground as can well be imagined, viz. ſhallow, poor, limeſtone ſoil."

One ſpeaks of North-riding moors, and the other of Eaſt-riding wolds.

If our Farmer is that good ſort of man which we take him to be, he will candidly acknowledge his miſtake, and thank us for rectifying it.

be

: incloſed at the ſame expence as for corn and graſs ; and the cloſure is the main expence.

He affirms that ‘ he never knew land of this kind ſo managed Mr. Young adviſes, which was not reſtored of neceſſity to *unimproved* ſtate within a few years.’ We *know* much land this ſort, which, on the contrary, has been long preſerved excellent improvement, although we have known *ſome* thus lapſed. The brevity neceſſary to our Review allows us not reconcile *here* theſe *phenomena* ; and till we have an opportuty for it in another manner, we leave to our ingenious Farmer e pleaſure of thinking that his *forefathers*, and the preſent generation of *non-improvers*, were not and are not fools.

In Chap. 25, our Farmer combats Sir Digby Legard’s acunt of the improvements of the wolds. His objections are, ſt, he allows no part of the 70 acres of his farm for an meſtead ; ſecondly, he makes no allowance for fallows ; irdly, he makes none for loſſes ; fourthly, he over-rates his ops ; fifthly, he allows not land enough for his ſheep, horſes, c. Now there may be ſome force in *all* theſe objections ; yet rely great deductions may, on theſe accounts, be made from 14 l. 2 s. produce, and the farmer be able to pay 35 l. rent r his 70 acres. Our Farmer allows he may, but denies that e landholder will make 8 l. per cent. of his money thus laid t, when he has built an houſe, barn, &c. This point deves examination. Our practical Farmer concludes, from Sir igby Legard’s own premiſes, viz. that he makes only 8 l. per nt. on 300 acres cultivated by himſelf, and without charge theſe buildings. This ſeems concluſive againſt the baronet.

	l.	s.	d.
But Sir Digby Legard ſtates a farm-houſe, &c. for a farm of 70 acres to coſt - - - -	130	0	0
The incloſing with a ſingle fence (all that is neceſſary) - - - - -	150	0	0
-	280	0	0
The improving the land at a guinea per acre -	73	10	0
	353	10	0
Intereſt of this total at 4 l. per cent. - -	14	0	0
Rent - - - - - - - - -	35	0	0

Is not here ſufficient encouragement for improvement on r Digby Legard’s principles ?

In chapter 26, our Farmer aſſerts, that it is yet a queſtion whether incloſures are a benefit to the community ? We allow at the many incloſures already made, and yet making, muſt

be

be profitable in *various* degrees; and that so much iniquit committed in effecting several of them, that some may be v *little profitable* to single proprietors, nay, even perhaps *unpro able*. But a man who can doubt whether, on the who inclosures be profitable to the community, must surely shut eyes against the light.

Yet our Author, not content with this general assertion, supported by one single *fact* or *reason*, proceeds to declaim agai inclosures as *unjust* and indeed *unconstitutional*. He asserts, t William the Conqueror gave every *Englishman* an inherita of land, of which he could not be dispossessed but by *forc fraud*. Such an assertion will appear strange to any man ver in the *English* history. His notion, however, is, that this *Prince* (as he stiles the Conqueror) gave the *commons* to the *h bandmen*; so that, according to him, every man, not a men servant, became of right an *inheritor of land*; whereas it is n well known, that William the Conqueror gave knights f (double fees and half fees) to his knights, &c. and they to der tenants, and so on; and that these lords let certain la uncultivated remain for the use of their *tenants in common*, revocable on conditions, or at pleasure; and therefore no p man had more than a tenant right under some lord.—By grees the law-doctrines of settlements and provision of the p founded on statutes, grew up; and the improvements of co mons by inclosures, was a *natural* and *necessary* consequence improvements of other kinds; and it is an act of *real* tho not *intended* sedition in our honest Farmer, to excite the poor, this *licentious* age, to think themselves injured by the legislat who encourage enclosures.

Our Farmer, however, makes amends for this futile dec mation against inclosures, by an account of the managemen sheep in Spain; and draws a deduction from thence wh seems to deserve notice, viz. that 'due exercise keeps sheep exact temperature, improves their wool, &c.'—But we by no means agree with him, that the warmth of their cov ings contributes as much as their manure to the enriching of soil.

In the 27th chapter (on planting of coppices) our Far confesses, that the fence should be so good as to exclude h and rabbits; a circumstance which we only mention to s how much higher are the expences of effectual fencing yo wood, than what he talks of every now and then, viz. a *hedge*.

Chap. 28th. Here our Farmer finds work enough to be d by his pupil betwixt seed-time and harvest.

In chap. 29th he calculates, that fourteen men will cut do 290 acres of corn in five weeks, or thirty work-days.

this calculation we must observe, that it will be reasonable to expect sixty tolerable harvest days in the season, and therefore if the corn be sown so as not to be all ripe nearly together, the farmer may have more help from his own family, and not have occasion to hire so much as seven men for sixty days. Fewer carts, horses, &c. also will be wanting to lead in the corn; and as the latter part of harvest is sometimes better than the former, it is prudent *not* to have all his corn down nearly together.—In the same chapter our farmer informs us, that it is not yet decided whether the *old* or *new* husbandry should be preferred. We think this point decided against the new, and our Farmer seems (in a former chapter as well as this) to have assigned such reasons, which determine his own practice, as cannot be confuted. However, as the subject is of vast consequence to the publick, and cannot be too accurately discussed, we will attend to every thing that is said on either side of the question, in this chapter.

Our Farmer's first objection to the new husbandry is a complex one, viz. that five different workmen must be *taught* and *satisfied*, before a complete set of instruments for the drill husbandry can be effected; that then servants must be instructed and gratified, and that the expence and trouble of all this is excessive.

His second objection is, that the expence of horse-hoeing and hand-hoeing must be very great. He reckons six or eight horse-hoeings equal to three or four ploughings; and adds, that hand-hoeing the partitions where the corn grows, and the rows also, will enhance the expence amazingly; and this work is not to be done for want of hands, if the practice becomes general.

Let us now attend to Mr. Tull's assertions of the advantages of the *new* over the *old* husbandry, and our Farmer's observations.

1. "The old husbandman cannot fallow his ground early, for fear of killing the grasses necessary to his sheep."—*Observation:* "Is this a candid representation of the general practice of the best husbandmen?" We answer, By no means!

2. "The old husbandman, as *he sows late*, must not *sow dry*, lest winter kill his wheat; and *cannot sow wet*, because he sows under furrow."—*Obs.* "The reverse is found to be fact." We add, that the *old* husbandman, if a *good* one, need not sow late in general, but has the same advantages as the new one.

3. "The *old* husbandman in *light* lands *must not sow dry* for fear of poppies, &c."—*Obs.* "One would think he meant to say, *must not sow wet*." Honestly spoken, and shrewdly, by the Friend of Mr. Tull!

4. "The old husbandman's crop in *strong* land, if he sow early, whether *wet* or *dry*, will either be starved in *poor ground*, or

or lodge on *wet*."—*Obs.* "According to this account, the old husbandman could never have a good crop. But let experience testify."

5. "The old husbandman has frequently not time to plough all his ground when dry."—*Obs.* "He has grounds of different kinds; and besides, 'tis not essential to success that ground should be *ploughed dry*, and *sowed wet*."

6. "The old husbandman must either lose the benefit of deep ploughing, or incur the danger of burying his seed."—*Obs.* "The old husbandman ploughs deep when he fallows, and when he sows." Conclusive!

7. "The *old* husbandman sowing over furrow, must leave his corn exposed to cold winds, water, &c."—*Obs.* "Water will run from a *smooth* surface sooner than a *rough* one."

Mr. *Tull* now enumerates the advantages of the new husbandman.

1. "We can plough the two furrows for the next crop, immediately after the former is off."—*Obs.* "This is a great advantage." We add, This is no superiority over the old husbandman, who, if a *good* one, can always plough early enough.

2. "We need no fold, which could only *help* a single crop, and that *uncertainly*, and would lose us a crop which is better than that would be."—*Obs.* "Mr. *Tull* unjustly diminishes the advantages of the fold to sink the profits of the *old* husbandman, and inhance those of the *new*." Boldly and honestly observed by 'his Friend.'

3. "'We can *plough dry*, and *drill wet*."—*Obs.* "Mr. Tull's land was of a peculiar cast, or it would not have admitted of that maxim. Clay lands would not."

4. "The old husbandman fears that weeds will grow to *destroy* his crop. We hope that they will grow to destroy them."—*Obs.* "I am very apt to suspect that this observation is introduced for the sake of the *antithesis*."—Critically severe, but just, is our practical Farmer here; and in the same spirit he plays on Mr. *Tull*, and remarks, that "In the old husbandry the crop itself will sometimes destroy the weeds; in the new husbandry, the weeds, if not removed, will destroy the crop."

5. "We plant our wheat early, because we can soften our land by hoeing."—*Obs.* "Will the benefit of hoeing compensate for land unoccupied?" Experience answers No!

6. "We can plough *wet* or *dry*."—*Obs.* "This is an advantage." We add, That it is no such advantage but what an old husbandman, if attentive to seasons, may sufficiently catch.

7. "We can *plant* at what depth we please."—*Obs.* "Is there no danger of having *all* the seed picked up by vermin?"

We

We add, The old husbandman can sow at what depth he pleases.

8. "Our seed is well defended by our ridges from cold," &c.—*Obs.* "But being in so small a quantity, 'tis liable to be destroyed by a multitude of causes."

Our Farmer then shews us how far from profiting by his husbandry Mr. Tull was, with all his frugality.

The Friend of Mr. *Tull*, however, would persuade us, that the old husbandry has received improvements from the *new*. But to this we must deny our implicit assent. The expediency of pulverizing the earth by frequent ploughings, was known to good husbandmen long before Mr. *Tull* was born. On the contrary, the old husbandry has *suffered* much from the *new*; for the cultivators of the *old* have been over-persuaded to sow much less seed than they ought, as Mr. Young has shewn *decisively* in his course of experiments.

We must add, that it does not at all appear (as our Farmer would persuade us) that we should be less sparing of our labour than of the dung-cart; but we ought to be sparing of neither. *Dung* pulverizes as the *share* does, and carries nutriment to the corn also from other causes than its dividing power.

[*To be concluded in our next.*]

ART. VI. *Travels into North America; containing its Natural History, and a circumstantial Account of its Plantations and Agriculture in general, with the Civil, Ecclesiastical, and Commercial State of the Country, the Manners of the Inhabitants, and several curious and important Remarks on various Subjects.* By Peter Kalm, Professor of Œconomy in the University of Aobo in Swedish Finland, and Member of the Swedish Royal Academy of Sciences. Translated into English by John Reinhold Forster, F. A. S. Enriched with a Map, several Cuts for the Illustration of Natural History, and some additional Notes. 8vo. 3 Vols. 18 s. bound. Lowndes. 1771.

TRAVELS in North America, a country, for the most part, uncultivated, the face of which remains just as Nature forms it, inhabited by wild animals, and scattered tribes of Indians in the same rude state, promise no less entertainment to the Reader, from the novelty of the scenes, than journies through more cultivated countries. Beside which, those adventures prove most amusing to the peruser of them, that were least so to the traveller, whose difficulties we enjoy as much as travellers do the means of deliverance from them.

Mr. Kalm was sent into North America to make observations on natural history, manufactures, and arts, by the Royal Academy of Arts at Stockholm, assisted in the expences of the undertaking by the Swedish universities.

The summary of this tour is thus given in the Translator's preface:

'Professor Kalm having obtained leave of his Majesty to be absent from his post as professor, and having got a passport, and recommendations to the several Swedish ministers at the courts of London, Paris, Madrid, and at the Hague, in order to obtain passports for him in their respective states, set out from Upsala, the 16th of October 1747, accompanied by Lars Yungstroem, a gardener well skilled in the knowledge of plants and mechanics, and who had at the same time a good hand for drawing, whom he took into his service. He then set sail from Gothenburgh, the 11th of December, but a violent hurricane obliged the ship he was in to take shelter in the harbour of Groemstad in Norway, from which place he made excursions to Arendal and Christiansand. He went again to sea February the 8th, 1748, and arrived at London the 17th of the same month. He staid in England till August 15, in which interval of time he made excursions to Woodford in Essex, to little Gaddesden in Hertfordshire, where William Ellis, a man celebrated for his publications in husbandry lived, but whose practical husbandry Mr. Kalm found not to be equal to the theory laid down in his writings; he likewise saw Ivinghoe in Buckinghamshire, Eaton and several other places, and all the curiosities and gardens in and about London: at last he went on board a ship, and traversed the ocean to Philadelphia in Pensylvania, which was formerly called New Sweden, where he arrived September the 26th. The rest of that year he employed in collecting seeds of trees and plants, and sending them up to Sweden; and in several excursions in the environs of Philadelphia. The winter he passed among his countrymen at Raccoon in New Jersey. The next year, 1749, Mr. Kalm went through New Jersey and New York along the river Hudson to Albany, and from thence, after having crossed the lakes of St. George and Champlain, to Montreal and Quebec, he returned that very year against winter to Philadelphia, and sent a new cargo of seeds, plants, and curiosities to Sweden. In the year 1750, Mr. Kalm saw the western parts of Pensylvania and the coast of New Jersey; Yungstroem staid in the former province all the summer for the collection of seeds, and Prof Kalm, in the mean time, passed New York and the blue mountains, went to Albany, then along the river Mohawk to the Iroquois nations, where he got acquainted with the Mohawks, Oneidas, Tuskaroras, Onandagas and Kayugaws. He then viewed and navigated the great lake Ontario, and saw the celebrated fall at Niagara. In his return from his summer expedition, he crossed the blue mountains in a different place, and in October again reached Philadelphia.

'In the year 1751, the 13th of February, he went at Newcastle on board a ship for England, and after a passage subject to many dangers in the most dreadful hurricanes, he arrived March the 27th in the Thames, and two days after in London. He took passage for Gothenburgh, May the 5th, and was the 16th of the same month at the place of his destination, and the 13th of June he again arrived

rived at Stockholm, after having been on this truly useful expedition three years and eight months. He afterwards returned again to his place of professor at Aobo, where, in a small garden of his own, he cultivates many hundreds of American plants, as there is not yet a public botanical garden for the use of the university, and he, with great expectation, wishes to see what plants will bear the climate, and bear good and ripe seeds so far north. He published the account of his journey by intervals, for want of encouragement, and fearing the expences of publishing at once in a country where few booksellers are found, and where the Author must very often embrace the business of bookseller, in order to reimburse himself for the expences of his publication. He published in his first volume observations on England, and chiefly on its husbandry, where he, with the most minute scrupulousness and detail, entered into the very minutiæ of this branch of his business for the benefit of his countrymen; and this subject he continued at the beginning of the second volume. A passage cross the Atlantic ocean is a new thing to Swedes, who are little used to it, unless they go in the few East India ships of their country. Every thing therefore was new to Mr. Kalm, and he omitted no circumstance unobserved which are repeated in all the navigators from the earlier times down to our own age. It would be a kind of injustice to the public, to give all this at large to the reader. All that part describing England and its curiosities and husbandry we omitted. The particulars of the passage from England to Pensylvania we abridged; no circumstance interesting to natural history, or to any other part of literature, has been omitted. And from his arrival at Philadelphia, we give the original at large, except where we omitted some trifling circumstances, viz. the way of eating oysters, the art of making apple dumplings, and some more of the same nature, which struck that Swedish gentleman with their novelty.'

The work now published is not, however, the whole that the public may expect; for, in the preface to the third volume, we are farther informed by the Translator, that—' The Author, who, as far as I know, is still living, has not yet finished this work; these three volumes contain all that he has hitherto published relative to America; the journal of a whole year's travelling, and especially his expedition to the Iroquese, and fort Niagara, are still to come; which, as soon as they appear, if Providence spares my life and health, and if my situation allows of it, I will translate into English; and there are some hopes of obtaining the original from the Author. He likewise often promises, in the course of this work, to publish a great Latin work, concerning the animals and plants of North America, as far as he went through it; which would certainly make the small catalogue I could make, useless. It is likewise probable that the description of the animal kingdom will fall to the share of an abler pen than mine.'——He also mentions Mr. Kalm's partiality in favour of the French colonists, in comparing them with the English; an instance of which we shall notice in a proper place. This Mr. Forster naturally accounts for, from

 the

the political connections between the Swedes and the French, from the polite behaviour of the latter, and from his associating chiefly with the remains of the Swedish settlers, while he was in the English colonies.

These travels are detailed in the form of a journal. Hence it is, that though they are entertaining, and contain some curious hints of information respecting the places he passed through, they are by no means digested or methodized; the subjects being treated of just as they occurred to notice. This indeed is the natural form for travels; but with regard to the description of plants and other natural productions, it is imagined that some mode of classing them, as to the species, places, climate, and soil where they were found, might be more satisfactory to the naturalist. They contain also many minute remarks, which will seem trifling to an English reader when made on customs familiar to him; but as they were noted by a Swede as singularities, they give us an idea of his punctuality and veracity.

As our American provinces and their principal towns are well known to us, by the continual intercourse with them, and by accurate descriptions and histories, we shall, in our specimens of Mr. Kalm's performance, attend chiefly to such information as he affords, concerning subjects not commonly known or attended to: and in this view we stand a better chance of profiting by the remarks of an intelligent foreigner, than by those of a native.

The first volume describes the plants, animals, and other subjects of natural history which fell under the Author's observation in Pensylvania and New Jersey; the second consists of New Jersey, Albany, and part of his rout toward Montreal; the third, of Montreal, Quebec, and parts adjacent.

In the beginning of the second volume, he gives a terrible list of insects that infest North America,—mosquitoes, locusts, caterpillars, grass-worms, moths, fleas, crickets, bugs, mill-beetles or cock-roaches, and wood-lice; the very enumeration of which, with the accounts of their effects and depredations, are enough to make a human being shudder at the thoughts of venturing among such legions of vermin. But it is likely that they are not quite so formidable apart as they appear collectively on the muster; and, as cultivation takes place, they will retire westward, with the other inhabitants of wide unimproved hunting grounds.

To these are to be added the rattle-snake, and the black-snake; the former a very dangerous reptile, whose description is well known; of the latter our Author gives the following entertaining account:

'On

'On the road [from New Jersey northward] we ſaw a *black ſnake*, which we killed, and found juſt five feet long. Catesby has deſcribed it and its qualities, and alſo drawn it. The full-grown black ſnakes are commonly about five feet long, but very ſlender; the thickeſt I ever ſaw was, in the broadeſt part, hardly three inches thick; the back is black, ſhining, and ſmooth; the chin white and ſmooth; the belly whitiſh turning into blue, ſhining, and very ſmooth; I believe there are ſome varieties of this ſnake. One, which was nineteen inches long, had a hundred and eighty-ſix ſcales on the belly *(Scuta Abdominalia)* and ninety-two half ſcales on the tail *(Squamæ ſubcaudales)* which I found to be true, by a repeated counting of the ſcales. Another, which was ſeventeen inches and a half in length, had a hundred and eighty-four ſcales on the belly, and only ſixty-four half ſcales on the tail; this I likewiſe aſſured myſelf of, by counting the ſcales over again. It is poſſible that the end of this laſt ſnake's tail was cut off, and the wound healed up again.

'The country abounds with black ſnakes. They are among the firſt that come out in ſpring, and often appear very early if warm weather happens; but if it grows cold again after that, they are quite frozen, and lie ſtiff and torpid on the ground, or on the ice; when taken in this ſtate and put before a fire, they revive in leſs than an hour's time. It has ſometimes happened, when the beginning of January is very warm, that they come out of their winter habitations. They commonly appear about the end of March, old ſtyle.

'This is the ſwifteſt of all the ſnakes which are to be found here, for it moves ſo quick, that a dog can hardly catch it. It is therefore almoſt impoſſible for a man to eſcape it if purſued: but happily its bite is neither poiſonous nor any way dangerous; many people have been bit by it in the woods, and have ſcarce felt any more inconvenience than if they had been wounded by a knife; the wounded place only remains painful for ſome time. The black ſnakes ſeldom do any harm, except in ſpring, when they copulate; but if any body comes in their way at that time, they are ſo much vexed, as to purſue him as faſt as they can. If they meet with a perſon who is afraid of them, he is in great diſtreſs. I am acquainted with ſeveral people who have, on ſuch an occaſion, run ſo hard as to be quite out of breath, in endeavouring to eſcape the ſnake, which moved with the ſwiftneſs of an arrow after them. If a perſon thus purſued can muſter up courage enough to oppoſe the ſnake with a ſtick or any thing elſe, when it is either paſſed by him, or when he ſteps aſide to avoid it, it will turn back again, and ſeek a refuge in its ſwiftneſs. It is, however, ſometimes bold enough to run directly upon a man, and not to depart before it has received a good ſtroke. I have been aſſured by ſeveral, that when it overtakes a perſon, who has tried to eſcape it, and who has not courage enough to oppoſe it, it winds round his feet, ſo as to make him fall down; it then bites him ſeveral times in the leg, or whatever part it can get hold of, and goes off again. I ſhall mention two circumſtances, which confirm what I have ſaid. During my ſtay in New York, Dr. Colden told me, that in the ſpring, 1748, he had

 ſeveral

ſeveral workmen at his country ſeat, and among them one lately arrived from Europe, who of courſe knew very little of the qualities of the black ſnake. The other workmen ſeeing a great black ſnake copulating with its female, engaged the new-comer to go and kill it, which he intended to do with a little ſtick. But on approaching the place where the ſnakes lay, they perceived him, and the male in great wrath leaves his pleaſure to purſue the fellow with amazing ſwiftneſs; he little expected ſuch courage in the ſnake, and flinging away his ſtick, began to run as faſt as he was able. The ſnake purſued him, overtook him, and twiſting ſeveral times round his feet, threw him down, and frightened him almoſt out of his ſenſes; he could not get rid of the ſnake, till he took a knife and cut it through in two or three places. The other workmen were rejoiced at this ſight, and laughed at it, without offering to help their companion. Many people at Albany told me of an accident which happened to a young lady, who went out of town in ſummer, together with many other girls, attended by her negro. She ſat down in the wood, in a place where the others were running about, and before ſhe was aware, a black ſnake being diſturbed in its amours, ran under her petticoats, and twiſted round her waiſt, ſo that ſhe fell backwards in a ſwoon, occaſioned by her fright, or by the compreſſion which the ſnake cauſed. The negro came up to her, and ſuſpecting that a black ſnake might have hurt her, on making uſe of a remedy to bring his lady to herſelf again, he lifted up her cloaths, and really found the ſnake wound about her body as cloſe as poſſible; the negro was not able to tear it away, and therefore cut it, and the girl came to herſelf again; but ſhe conceived ſo great an averſion to the negro, that ſhe could not bear the ſight of him afterwards, and died of a conſumption. At other times of the year this ſnake is more apt to run away, than to attack people. However, I have heard it aſſerted frequently, that even in ſummer, when its time of copulation is paſt, it purſues people, eſpecially children, if it finds that they are afraid and run from her. Several people likewiſe aſſured me, from their own experience, that it may be provoked to purſue people, if they throw at it, and then run away. I cannot well doubt of this, as I have heard it ſaid by numbers of creditable people; but I could never ſucceed in provoking them. I ran always away on perceiving it, or flung ſomething at it, and then took to my heels, but I could never bring the ſnakes to purſue me: I know not for what reaſon they ſhunned me, unleſs they took me for an artful ſeducer.

'Moſt of the people in this country aſcribed to this ſnake a power of faſcinating birds and ſquirrels, as I have deſcribed in ſeveral parts of my journal. When the ſnake lies under a tree, and has fixed his eyes on a bird or ſquirrel above; it obliges them to come down, and to go directly into its mouth. I cannot account for this, for I never ſaw it done. However, I have a liſt of more than twenty perſons, among which are ſome of the moſt creditable people, who have all unanimouſly, though living far diſtant from each other, aſſerted the ſame thing; they aſſured me, upon their honour, that they have ſeen (at ſeveral times) theſe black ſnakes faſcinating ſquirrels and birds which

which sat on the tops of trees, the snake lying at the foot of the tree, with its eyes fixed upon the bird or squirrel, which sits above it, and utters a doleful note; from which it is easy to conclude with certainty that it is about to be fascinated, though you cannot see it. The bird or squirrel runs up and down along the tree continuing its plaintive song, and always comes nearer the snake, whose eyes are unalterably fixed upon it. It should seem as if these poor creatures endeavoured to escape the snake, by hopping or running up the tree; but there appears to be a power which withholds them: they are forced downwards, and each time that they turn back, they approach nearer their enemy, till they are at last forced to leap into its mouth, which stands wide open for that purpose. Numbers of squirrels and birds are continually running and hopping fearless in the woods on the ground, where the snakes lie in wait for them, and can easily give these poor creatures a mortal bite. Therefore it seems that this fascination might be thus interpreted, that the creature has first got a mortal wound from the snake, which is sure of her bite, and lies quiet, being assured that the wounded creature has been poisoned with the bite, or at least feels pain from the violence of the bite, and that it will at last be obliged to come down into its mouth. The plaintive note is perhaps occasioned by the acuteness of the pain which the wound gives the creature. But to this it may be objected that the bite of the black snake is not poisonous; it may further be objected, that if the snake could come near enough to a bird or squirrel to give it a mortal bite, it might as easily keep hold of it, or, as it sometimes does with poultry, twist round and strangle or stifle it. But the chief objection which lies against this interpretation, is the following account, which I received from the most creditable people, who have assured me of it. The squirrel being upon the point of running into the snake's mouth, the spectators have not been able to let it come to that pitch, but killed the snake, and as soon as it had got a mortal blow, the squirrel or bird destined for destruction, flew away, and left off their mournful note, as if they had broke loose from a net. Some say, that if they only touched the snake, so as to draw off its attention from the squirrel, it went off quickly, not stopping till it had got to a great distance. Why do the squirrels or birds go away so suddenly, and why no sooner? If they had been poisoned or bitten by the snake before, so as not to be able to get from the tree, and to be forced to approach the snake always more and more, they could however not get new strength by the snake being killed or diverted: therefore it seems that they are only *enchanted*, whilst the snake has its eyes fixed on them. However, this looks odd and unaccountable, though many of the worthiest and most reputable people have related it, and though it is so universally believed here, that to doubt it would be to expose one's self to general laughter.

The black snakes kill the smaller species of frogs, and eat them. If they get at eggs of poultry, or of other birds, they make holes in them, and suck the contents. When the hens are sitting on the eggs, they creep into the nest, wind round the birds, stifle them, and suck the eggs. Mr. Bartram asserted, that he had often seen this snake creep up into the tallest trees, after bird's eggs, or young

 birds,

birds, always with the head foremoſt, when deſcending. A Swede told me, that a black ſnake had once got the head of one of his hens in its mouth, and was wound ſeveral times round the body, when he came and killed the ſnake. The hen was afterwards as well as ever.

'This ſnake is very greedy of milk, and it is difficult to keep it out, when it is once uſed to go into a cellar where milk is kept. It has been ſeen eating milk out of the ſame diſh with children, without biting them, though they often gave it blows with the ſpoon upon the head, when it was overgreedy. I never heard it hiſſing. It can raiſe more than one half of its body from the ground, in order to look about her. It ſkins every year; and its ſkin is ſaid to be a remedy againſt the cramp, if continually worn about the body.'

The bull-frog may alſo be added as an harmleſs animal, to which we are ſtrangers, and of which we have the enſuing deſcription:

'Bull-frogs are a large ſpecies of frogs, which I had an opportunity of hearing and ſeeing to-day. As I was riding out, I heard a roaring before me; and I thought it was a bull in the buſhes, on the other ſide of the dyke, though the ſound was rather more hoarſe than that of a bull. I was however afraid, that a bad goring bull might be near me, though I did not ſee him; and I continued to think ſo till ſome hours after, when I talked with ſome Swedes about the *bull frogs*, and, by their account, I immediately found that I had heard their voice; for the Swedes told me, that there were numbers of them in the dyke. I afterwards hunted for them. Of all the frogs in this country, this is doubtleſs the greateſt. I am told, that towards autumn, as ſoon as the air begins to grow a little cool, they hide themſelves under the mud, which lies at the bottom of ponds and ſtagnant waters, and lie there torpid during winter. As ſoon as the weather grows mild, towards ſummer, they begin to get out of their holes, and croak. If the ſpring, that is, if the mild weather, begins early, they appear about the end of March, old ſtyle; but if it happens late, they tarry under water till late in April. Their places of abode are ponds, and bogs with ſtagnant water; they are never in any flowing water. When many of them croak together, they make an enormous noiſe. Their croak exactly reſembles the roaring of an ox or bull, which is ſomewhat hoarſe. They croak ſo loud, that two people talking by the ſide of a pond cannot underſtand each other. They croak all together; then ſtop a little, and begin again. It ſeems as if they had a captain among them: for when he begins to croak, all the others follow; and when he ſtops, the others are all ſilent. When this captain gives the ſignal for ſtopping, you hear a note like *poop* coming from him. In day-time they ſeldom make any great noiſe, unleſs the ſky is covered. But the night is their croaking time; and, when all is calm, you may hear them, though you are near a mile and a half off. When they croak they commonly are near the ſurface of the water, under the buſhes, and have their heads out of the water. Therefore, by going ſlowly, one may get cloſe up to them before they go away. As ſoon as they are quite under water, they think themſelves ſafe, though the water be very ſhallow.

'Sometimes

' Sometimes they ſit at a good diſtance from the pond; but as ſoon as they ſuſpect any danger, they haſten with great leaps into the water. They are very expert at hopping. A full-grown *bull-frog* takes near three yards at one hop. I have often been told the following ſtory by the old Swedes, which happened here, at the time when the Indians lived with the Swedes. It is well known that the Indians are excellent runners; I have ſeen them at Governor Johnſon's, equal the beſt horſe in its ſwifteſt courſe, and almoſt paſs by it. Therefore, in order to try how well the bull-frogs could leap, ſome of the Swedes laid a wager with a young Indian, that he could not overtake the frog, provided it had two leaps before hand. They carried a bull-frog, which they had caught in a pond, upon a field, and burnt his back-ſide; the fire, and the Indian, who endeavoured to be cloſely up with the frog, had ſuch an effect upon the animal, that it made its long hops acroſs the field, as faſt as it could. The Indian began to purſue the frog with all his might at the proper time: the noiſe he made in running frightened the poor frog; probably it was afraid of being tortured with fire again, and therefore it redoubled its leaps, and by that means it reached the pond before the Indian could overtake it.

' In ſome years they are more numerous than in others: nobody could tell whether the ſnakes had ever ventured to eat them, though they eat all the leſſer kinds of frogs. The women are no friends to theſe frogs, becauſe they kill and eat young ducklings and goſlings: ſometimes they carry off chickens that come too near the ponds. I have not obſerved that they bite when they are held in the hands, though they have little teeth; when they are beaten, they cry out almoſt like children. I was told that ſome eat the thighs of the hind legs, and that they are very palatable.'

We are ſtill however left at a loſs as to the ſize of this alarming animal, unleſs we turn to Linnæus or Cateſby, to which he refers for the characters. It ſhould ſeem as if this was the frog that gave the idea to the fabuliſt, of making him endeavour to emulate the *ox* in ſize, as he already does in voice.

We cannot pretend to trace Mr. Kalm in his tour. neither is it neceſſary. He gives us a deſcription of the inhabitants of Montreal in theſe terms:

' The difference between the manners and cuſtoms of the French in Montreal and Canada, and thoſe of the Engliſh in the American colonies, is as great as that between the manners of thoſe two nations in Europe. The women in general are handſome here; they are well-bred, and virtuous, with an innocent and becoming freedom. They dreſs out very fine on Sundays; and though on the other days they do not take much pains with other parts of their dreſs, yet they are very fond of adorning their heads, the hair of which is always curled and powdered, and ornamented with glittering bodkins and aigrettes. Every day but Sunday, they wear a little neat jacket, and a ſhort petticoat which hardly reaches half the leg, and in this particular they ſeem to imitate the Indian women. The heels of their ſhoes are high, and very narrow, and it is ſurprizing how they walk on them. In their knowledge of œconomy, they greatly ſurpaſs the Engliſh women in the plantations, who indeed have taken the

the liberty of throwing all the burthen of houſe-keeping upon their huſbands, and ſit in their chairs all day with folded arms. The women in Canada on the contrary do not ſpare themſelves, eſpecially among the common people, where they are always in the fields, meadows, ſtables, &c. and do not diſlike any work whatſoever. However, they ſeem rather remiſs in regard to the cleaning of the utenſils, and apartments; for ſometimes the floors, both in the town and country, were hardly cleaned once in ſix months, which is a diſagreeable ſight to one who comes from amongſt the Dutch and Engliſh, where the conſtant ſcouring and ſcrubbing of the floors, is reckoned as important as the exercife of religion itſelf. To prevent the thick duſt, which is thus left on the floor, from being noxious to the health, the women wet it ſeveral times a day, which renders it more conſiſtent; repeating the aſperſion as often as the duſt is dry and riſes again. Upon the whole, however, they are not averſe to the taking a part in all the buſineſs of houſe-keeping; and I have with pleaſure ſeen the daughters of the better ſort of people, and of the governor himſelf, not too finely dreſſed, and going into kitchens and cellars, to look that every thing be done as it ought.'

What work the French Canadian women find abroad to compenſate for their filthy houſes at home, we cannot conceive; imagining that the men might ſuffice for out-door buſineſs, while the women might be employed more uſefully within, to keep their family œconomy in a decent train: at leaſt this is conformable to Engliſh notions, as our Author confeſſes in the compariſon itſelf. But we ſhall produce another paſſage here which is not altogether conſiſtent with the preceding; and this we do with the greater pleaſure, as it will operate ſtill more to the juſtification of our fair ſiſters on the other ſide the Atlantic.

'The ladies in Canada are generally of two kinds: ſome come over from France, and the reſt natives. The former poſſeſs the politeneſs peculiar to the French nation; the latter may be divided into thoſe of Quebec and Moutreal. The firſt of theſe are equal to the French ladies in good-breeding, having the advantage of frequently converſing with the French gentlemen and ladies, who come every ſummer with the king's ſhips, and ſtay ſeveral weeks at Quebec, but ſeldom go to Montreal. The ladies of this laſt place are accuſed by the French of partaking too much of the pride of the Indians, and of being much wanting in French good-breeding. What I have mentioned above of their dreſſing their head too aſſiduouſly, is the caſe with all the ladies throughout Canada. Their hair is always curled, even when they are at home in a dirty jacket, and ſhort coarſe petticoat, that does not reach to the middle of their legs. On thoſe days when they pay or receive viſits, they dreſs ſo gayly, that one is almoſt induced to think their parents poſſeſſed the greateſt dignities in the ſtate. The Frenchmen, who conſidered things in their true light, complained very much that a great part of the ladies in Canada had got into the pernicious cuſtom of taking too much care of their dreſs, and ſquandering all their fortunes, and more, upon it, inſtead of ſparing ſomething for future times.

They

They are no less attentive to have the newest fashions; and they laugh at each other, when they are not dressed to each other's fancy. But what they get as new fashions, are grown old, and laid aside in France; for the ships coming but once every year from thence, the people in Canada consider that as the new fashion for the whole year, which the people on board brought with them, or which they imposed upon them as new. The ladies in Canada, and especially at Montreal, are very ready to laugh at any blunders strangers make in speaking; but they are very excusable. People laugh at what appears uncommon and ridiculous. In Canada nobody ever hears the French language spoken by any but Frenchmen; for strangers seldom come thither; and the Indians are naturally too proud to learn French, but oblige the French to learn their language From hence it naturally follows, that the nice Canada ladies cannot hear any thing uncommon without laughing at it. One of the first questions they propose to a stranger is, whether he is married? The next, how he likes the ladies in the country; and whether he thinks them handsomer than those of his own country? And the third, whether he will take one home with him? There are some differences between the ladies of Quebec, and those of Montreal; those of the last place seemed to be generally handsomer than those of the former. Their behaviour likewise seemed to me to be somewhat too free at Quebec, and of a more becoming modesty at Montreal. The ladies at Quebec, especially the unmarried ones, are not very industrious. A girl of eighteen is reckoned very poorly off, if she cannot enumerate at least twenty lovers. These young ladies, especially those of a higher rank, get up at seven, and dress till nine, drinking their coffee at the same time. When they are dressed, they place themselves near a window that opens into the street, take up some needle-work, and sew a stitch now and then; but turn their eyes into the street most of the time. When a young fellow comes in, whether they are acquainted with him or not, they immediately lay aside their work, sit down by him, and begin to chat, laugh, joke, and invent *double-entendres*; and this is reckoned being very witty. In this manner they frequently pass the whole day, leaving their mothers to do all the business in the house. In Montreal, the girls are not quite so volatile, but more industrious. They are always at their needle-work, or doing some necessary business *in the house* *. They are likewise cheerful and content; and nobody can say that they want either wit, or charms. Their fault is, that they think too well of themselves. However, the daughters of people of all ranks, without exception, go to market, and carry home what they have bought. They rise as soon, and go to bed as late, as any of the people in the house. I have been assured, that, in general, their fortunes are not considerable; which are rendered still more scarce by the number of children, and the small revenues in a house. The girls at Montreal are very much displeased that those at Quebec get husbands sooner than they. The reason of this is, that many young gentlemen who come over from France with the ships, are captivated by the ladies at Quebec, and marry them; but as these

* Vid. the preceding extract for this.

gentlemen

gentlemen ſeldom go up to Montreal, the girls there are not often ſo happy as thoſe of the former place.'

One more paſſage reſpecting the inhabitants at Quebec will fully reconcile us to the Engliſh American ladies.

'The civility of the inhabitants here is more refined than that of the Dutch and Engliſh, in the ſettlements belonging to Great Britain; but *the latter*, on the other hand, *do not idle their time away* in dreſſing, as the French do here. The ladies, eſpecially, dreſs and powder their hair every day, and put their locks in papers every night; which *idle* cuſtom was *not* introduced in the Engliſh ſettlements. The gentlemen wear generally their own hair; but ſome have wigs. People of rank are uſed to wear laced cloaths, and all the crown-officers wear ſwords. All the gentlemen, even thoſe of rank, the governor-general excepted, when they go into town on a day that looks likely for rain, carry their cloaks on their left arm. Acquaintances of either ſex, who have not ſeen each other for ſome time, on meeting again *ſalute with mutual kiſſes.*'

It may be ſo, and we admit that our *civility* is ſo *unrefined* that we ſhould be content with kiſſing the American beauties, and leave the French gentlemen to beſtow their fulſome kiſſes on each other as much as they pleaſe, without longing for a participation in them.

On the whole, though we cannot enter farther into particular inſtances, we think Mr. Kalm has ſufficiently anſwered the intention of his miſſion, by his many deſcriptions of the natural productions and animals of the American continent; which will not fail to entertain thoſe who deſire information reſpecting them, eſpecially in Sweden, the country for which the performance was written and calculated.

ART. VII. *Ecliptical Aſtronomy* reſtored to its *natural Simplicity*, in Theory and Practice, upon *Moſaic* Principles; whoſe Uſes are alſo ſpecified in Navigation. By James Hurly, B. A. Maſter of the Grammar-ſchool, and Curate of St. James's, in Taunton. 8vo. 3s. Law, &c. 1771.

WHOEVER reads the title of this ſingular piece, and the Author's preface, will, we apprehend, have little inclination to proceed any further. We are ſorry to find a work of this kind profeſſedly undertaken upon *Moſaic principles*; becauſe, if the Author had not informed us that he was a clergyman, we ſhould have been ready to apprehend that his ſyſtem, which he ſtiles the *Moſaic philoſophy*, was intended as a burleſque on Moſes and the Bible. If this Author has fairly ſtated the ſcriptural principles of philoſophy, there ſurely never were any more abſurd and unintelligible: and yet they are propoſed with an air of confidence and triumph. The Aronomer-royal and others are ſummoned to attend his deciſion, and the Author is perſuaded that they will ſee 'that the modern aſtronomer has

 a world

a world of errors to correct of his own, at this period of time, notwithstanding the pitch to which astronomy is supposed to be brought by the fancied superiority of modern knowledge above what was revealed in the days of Moses.' If his conjectures are true, our most eminent astronomers have been radically wrong ' in the whole *farrago* of their *hypotheses.*' But we are of opinion that the work before us, whatever ridicule or compassion it may excite, will produce little of that conviction for which it is intended. However, that neither the Author nor our Readers may condemn us for prejudging in the case, and determining without examination, we shall lay before them the leading principles of this chimerical performance.

The Author presumes, on what foundation let his Readers determine, that it is needless ' to apologize for preferring the principles which Moses has delivered to us from a divine revelation, before the principles invented by any human ingenuity. Nor (says he) am I at all afraid of being charged with arrogance, for setting up a system deduced from revealed principles above the most admired system that has been given us by any philosopher whatsoever. Revelation will speak for itself to those that will give attention: and if such do not extol a theory built upon a sure foundation above the *vile hypotheses* of philosophy, I shall be greatly disappointed.'

We cannot but wish that Mr. Hurly had been a little more diffident; and that, for the honour of revelation, he had not charged it rashly with absurdities too glaring and notorious to escape the most superficial enquirer. We are persuaded that the *vile hypotheses* of philosophy will still maintain their ground, notwithstanding the violence of his attack, and to his great *disappointment* and mortification. And, we hope, that neither Moses nor any of his successors in the line of inspiration, are to stand or fall with the principles of the *new ecliptical astronomy.*

The first whim which this curious work presents, we have in the following passage. After some sly hints as to the insufficiency of the method of determining the sun's distance by his parallax, the Author observes, ' that the effects, which philosophers attribute to the difference of central and superficial observers, are nothing else but the *effects of refraction inverted.*' He attempts to prove this strange position by observations, which are partly false and partly nothing to the purpose: and from which our Readers would derive no great satisfaction, if they were transcribed for their perusal.

Our Author sets out, in his next chapter, like a man who had shaken off some heavy incumbrance; and he triumphs in the destruction of *parallactic absurdities.* ' The parallactic absurdities, which were condemned in the first chapter, have no place in Mosaic astronomy. In the revealed system, the sun and moon

moon are set, both of them, in the sphere of the fixed stars, which astronomers place at an almost immense distance from the earth.'

But if we pursue the *ingenious* Author's investigations, and consult his diagram, we shall soon find out the mistake:

'There is no philosophical distance of their orbits to cause the difference of parallaxes, which is founded by philosophers upon that distance, as before-mentioned.' Then comes a new method of estimating the distance of the sun; and had the Author favoured the world with his discovery a few years sooner, it would have saved much labour and expence. This method he grounds on a passage of scripture: *And God set them in the firmament of heaven, to give light upon the earth.* 'If we find (says he) at what distance the sun can enlighten the *whole earth* from pole to pole, we can pretty nearly determine the distance. But the distance, at which the *whole earth* may be enlightened by the sun, may be mathematically demonstrated.'

We will not insist on the inaccuracy of this expression, nor the obscurity and unintelligibleness of many others, but proceed with Mr. Hurly to his *decisive* calculation. The whole depends on the solution of one plain question. 'At what height above the surface will an eye command a prospect of 4000 miles, the extent of the semidiameter of the earth?' The result of the enquiry, deduced by a method not the most accurate, is this, 'that the height of the sun, in the equinoctial line, requisite to look over the whole earth, is one mile and one-sixth part of a mile.' This conclusion, so contrary to all the notions that have prevailed on this subject, is merely speculative.—But there are other mistakes in the *hypothetical philosophy* '*which concern the lives of many people*;' and therefore our Author, like a true friend of his species, has gone a little out of his way, in order to expose and correct them.

'According to Sir Isaac Newton, the earth must be higher at the equator than at the poles. (And lest any should doubt that this is the Newtonian doctrine, here is a quotation to prove the point.) Now if the north pole be lower than the equator, a cross passage for ships might be looked for from the *Atlantic* to the *Pacific* Ocean, about the north pole, as well as by the straits of Magellan in the south. But such a passage has never been sought without many disasters, and loss of lives; and would never have been attempted, if Mosaic astronomy had prevailed in the opinions of men, above the fanciful conjectures of modern astronomers. *And God said, Let the waters under the heaven be gathered together unto one place; and let the dry land appear: and it was so. And God called the dry land earth; and the gathering together of the waters called he seas.* Gen. i. 9, 10.

In

In this philoſophy the earth *emerges* from the ſeas, leaving her roots in the boſom of the deep, which we know to be in the ſouth; therefore that part of the earth round the north pole, which is the oppoſite part to the '*waters beneath the earth*,' is much higher than the equator. Suppoſe an iſland or mountainous rock, in a deep ſpacious water: it may be conſidered as the world in miniature. . A veſſel may ſail round it, but cannot croſs it at the top.'—With much more to the ſame purpoſe. We are glad that the Author 'can touch but lightly on any intermediate occurrences.'

The fourth chapter contains nothing new or ſingular. It ſtates the exact quantity of the *ſynodical* month, and ſhews how to deduce from it the mean motion of the moon in her periodical courſe. However, the Author does not condeſcend to proceed far in a beaten track. He very ſoon ſoars above the regions of common ſenſe and experience, to which Newton and ſuch groveling aſtronomers were confined. He opens upon us with a new ſyſtem of philoſophy, which at once obviates all the difficulties attending the lunar motions, and ſtates the cauſe of their variety beyond all contradiction or diſpute. Strange! that none ſhould have ſtarted the lucky hint before; but that it ſhould have been left to this Author to diſcover, that the variety, which has ſo long puzzled the ſagacity of aſtronomers 'altogether depends on the peculiar and oppoſite qualities of the two luminaries.' But as Mr. Hurly has lately found out, that it is only a ſtep to the moon, he may perhaps have paid it a viſit: and it muſt have been a pleaſant ſight to have ſeen the icicles hanging about him on his return from that dreary planet.

'That the ſun is the fountain of *heat* is evident to our ſenſes; but that the moon is *cold*, as the ſun is *hot*, may appear ſtrange to many who have imbibed the philoſopher's doctrine, that all the celeſtial bodies are *earths*; and that "*the ſun is a* GREAT EARTH *vehemently hot*." It was a doctrine, however, apparently known to Moſes; who 'places the moon at the ſame diſtance from the earth as the ſun and the ſtars; whereas if we judge of the diſtance by our ſenſes, the moon is *viſibly* nearer than the ſtars. What can produce this effect? Why we know very well that objects are *viſibly* nearer as they are ſeen through a denſer medium: and the *cold* moon condenſing the medium by which it is encompaſſed, cauſes it to appear ſo much nearer to us as the medium is more condenſed, through which the *light* of the moon paſſes. So an horizontal object appears larger, and conſequently nearer, in the heavens, than it appears afterwards, when it is got above the denſer air encompaſſing the ſurface of the earth. And thus the moon will be more refracted than other objects, and will appear alſo more depreſſed through a glaſs, or as having a greater parallax than the other planets.

Moreover,

Moreover, the *cold* quality of the moon is alſo an object of ſenſe: and any perſon poſſeſſed of a good teleſcope may make the experiment, who may plainly diſcover, that from the time of the new moon to the full, an envelopement of *ice* ſpreads gradually over the moon's ſurface; and after the full, the *ice* is thawed and diſperſed, as the moon returns to the ſun. Hence the very cold ſtate of the air during a very dark eclipſe is eaſily accounted for.' Such philoſophy needs no comment.

Our Author, having ſo well eſtabliſhed his principles, 'that the ſun is *hot* and the moon *cold*,' is able to furniſh us with the *true theory* of the motions of the moon. But before this can be thoroughly underſtood, it is neceſſary to attend to his preliminary account of the moon's revolution in her orbit. 'The moon appears to be continually going out of her way. From the new moon to the firſt quarter, or quadrature, ſhe riſes above the path in which ſhe firſt ſet out; and from the quadrature ſhe deſcends, and is in her way again at the full moon; then ſhe aſcends again, until ſhe has attained her ſecond quarter; and from thence deſcends towards her old path, where ſhe is found at the new moon ſeaſon, as in the beginning.

'These ſeeming irregularities of the moon in her revolutions are very eaſily explained upon the principles before eſtabliſhed. In the *quadratures* the moon is almoſt, if not altogether, out of the power of the ſun; whoſe rays are full againſt the region poſſeſſed by her, at the oppoſition, or full moon. In the quarters therefore the medium is condenſed, which encompaſſes the moon, in the higheſt degree; and according to the laws of refraction, the moon appears higher than at any other time. When it is new moon, ſhe is ſubject to the power of the ſun's rays, by the conjunction of the two bodies, as ſhe was before affected by the diſplay of his heat againſt her at the oppoſition. Wherefore in both theſe caſes, that is, in the *ſyzigies*, the natural condenſing quality of the moon is deſtroyed by the ſuperior power of the ſun, which dilates the medium by his heat, as the moon condenſes it by her cold.' This is a brief view of the Author's theory, for the ſatisfaction of the curious.

We ſhall not trouble our Readers with the Author's calculations, nor with the frequent references he has made to *Tacquet* and *Whiſton* on this ſubject: our attention being rather called to what is new and curious in this performance.

He begins his chapter 'concerning an eclipſe of the moon' with a leſſon of humility to aſtronomers:

'Aſtronomers are wont to boaſt much of their knowledge in the nature of eclipſes, as they can foretel them with a good degree of accuracy. But there is no foundation for glorying in this reſpect. Their leſſons are good ſo far only as they are founded upon *obſervations*: all the *hypothetical* part of their doctrine

trine is a delusion.' He briefly states the common method of accounting for this phænomenon, and then proposes his own explication. 'If we proceed one step further, and restore *light*, where *darkness* has usurped its place, in the *cone* (one would have thought there would have been an end of the eclipse) we shall have a complete *theory of lunar eclipses*. Experience may convince us, that an eclipse cannot be caused by the moon's entering into a dark shadow of the atmosphere: for we often and familiarly see the moon uneclipsed, and well defined, through a cloud. Now if a cloud itself doth not cause an eclipse, the *shadow* of a cloud cannot produce it. Yet the atmosphere, at the most, is no more than a cloud, and that not opaque, since the heavenly bodies are clearly seen through it, wherefore the eclipse is not caused by a dark shadow.

'The *light* and heat of the sun raises a thick cloud on the surface of the moon, whereby its lustre is taken off, and the moon ceases to be visible, or is eclipsed. It was proved in my 'Essay,' that '*the moon is a composition of cold, as the sun is a fire*;' which cold freezes the ambient fluid, and invelopes a full moon in a covering of ice. The eye of an unprejudiced person may *very clearly see* the process of an icy covering commencing with the new moon, and growing gradually over the old moon, which is oftentimes perceived with the new, till at the time of the full moon the covering is completed. The moon being therefore invested with a covering of ice, the same phænomena must attend the moon, when exposed to the sun's rays, as are observable on the surface of ice when exposed to heat.—When the faces of the sun and moon are opposite, and the sun's rays issue with full force against the moon's surface, the solar heat excites this "*aqueous vapour*," or cloud, which, according to the different proportions of its density, may quite obscure the light of the moon, or leave it more or less perceptible, agreeably to the different effects of different clouds passing over the planet. The cold of the moon also, condensing that part of the atmosphere which she assumes at the full, causes an attraction of the sun's rays that way, tending to a focus, and therefore conical.'

Our Author is no less dissatisfied with the astronomic doctrine concerning an eclipse of the sun, than with that of the moon, and he pronounces it almost totally unintelligible. He acknowledges that the hypothesis of the conic shadow is tolerable, when we consider an eclipse of the sun as caused by the interposition of the moon between the sun and us. But, says he, it often happens that *the moon is not between the sun and us* at the time of a solar eclipse, and then the hypothesis totally fails. Whenever the moon has *south* latitude, that is, when the moon in her path is *south* from the sun in his path, the sun is necessarily between the moon and us. And at other times when the moon has north latitude, the opposite inhabitants to us in the south have the sun at that time between the moon and them.—Upon our principles the difficulty vanishes. We say and prove, by the evidence of sight, that the moon is a cold body, condensing therefore the liquid medium in which it exists, and which consequently attracts the rays of the sun towards these parts in which the cause of the condensation operates. As the heat of the sun goes with the rays of light, when these are drawn from us the heat is also drawn from us, and the positive cold of the moon also is perceivable in a greater or less degree as the cold planet is nearer to the earth and the sun more remote; *as the sun is nearest to his apogee, and the moon to her perigee* *.'

In a subsequent chapter the Author repeats what he had more than once advanced before, 'that the notion of the moon's being nearer to the earth than the sun is certainly false. For as the orbit of the moon extends five degrees and more beyond the ecliptic, northward and southward, it evidently takes in, or *comprehends*, the orbit of the sun, and cannot possibly be included within the ecliptic.'

He moreover informs us, that the common *solar spots* are small parts of the original firmament, which, although created as hard as adamant, was not created for an eternal duration.

He then proceeds to shew 'that the *flux* of the sea *is not produced by the moon, but by the sun*; and that the tides of the sea are *checked* by the *moon*.'

Our Author is fully convinced that eclipses are incompetent for the discovery of the longitude; and he has dropped two or three illiberal reflections on that subject, which could not escape our notice, and would deserve literary animadversion, were they capable of doing any injury.

The Author of this whimsical performance is no inconsiderable publisher; we have therefore been more diffuse in giving an account of this article than indeed it deserves, as we hope

* The Author's curious theory of eclipses puts us in mind of the vulgar doctrine of the *Chinese*. They fancy that in heaven there is a prodigious great dragon, who is a professed enemy to the sun and moon, and ready at all times to eat them up. For this reason, as soon as they perceive an eclipse, they all make a terrible rattling with drums and brass kettles, till the monster, frightened at the noise, lets go his prey. While the astronomers are on the tower to make their observations, the chief Mandarines belonging to the Lipou fall on their knees in a hall or court of the palace, looking attentively that way, and frequently bowing towards the sun, to express the pity they take of him, or rather to the dragon, to beg him not to molest the world, by depriving it of so necessary a planet.

See Le Comte's Memoirs, p. 70, 71.

it

it will be a full diſcharge from all obligation of expoſing his future reveries. A month's reſidence in the moon, and the exerciſe of a journey of little more than a mile, might not hurt our Author. It would, perhaps, reconcile him to think and write on philoſophical ſubjects in a manner more worthy the notice of the public, and the criticiſm of candour.

ART. VIII. *A ſhort Comment on Sir Iſaac Newton's Principia.* By W. Emerſon. 8vo. 3s. ſewed. Nourſe. 1770.

SIR Iſaac's *Principia* is the *Bible* of philoſophers: hence they derive that intimate acquaintance with the laws and operations of Nature, which is neceſſary to juſtify their title and character. A philoſopher ignorant of the *Principia* would be the ſame kind of *phænomenon* as a divine wholly unacquainted with his *Bible.* And the alluſion may be carried ſtill further, as the *one* has employed the ſkill and labour of commentators and critics, to reconcile ſeeming contradictions, to explain paſſages that are obſcure and difficult, and, after all, requires ſome preparatory knowledge, and no ſmall degree of application, in order to be underſtood; ſo the *other* does not lie level to every common capacity: a conſiderable ſhare of previous mathematical knowledge is neceſſary to render it intelligible, and withal ſome outward inſtructions and aſſiſtances may be very acceptable and uſeful.

The path itſelf is ſafe and pleaſant, though it is not eaſily found, nor can it be purſued without toil and danger. Happy are they who are under the direction of a ſkilful and faithful guide, that will aſſiſt them in removing obſtacles as they ariſe, and thus encourage their progreſs and perſeverance. Many, without doubt, have been deterred from the arduous taſk, through the want of ſome able companion and inſtructor, who ſhould give them ſuch hints as might be *incentives* to their own ingenuity and application, without *ſuperſeding* them.

There have been ſeveral laudable attempts of this kind, under various forms, ſince the firſt publication of the *Principia.* But moſt of theſe have been confined to ſome particular part of this admirable work; nor have they been intended ſo much to illuſtrate the ſeveral ſteps of the Author's reaſoning, as to convey the ſubſtance of his diſcoveries, in a ſtyle, and under a form, better adapted for general conception. The ſtudent, whoſe aim was to derive his knowledge from the fountain itſelf, and to underſtand the Author's own demonſtrations and concluſions, has ſtill been at a loſs. Should it be ſaid that, even in this view, the celebrated Jeſuits have provided him with the aſſiſtance he deſires; we may anſwer, that this admirable performance, though in its plan and execution it is *inſtar omnium,* is too voluminous to answer the purpose; not to add, that by being written in *Latin*, it can be of no use to the mere *English* reader.

A short comment, which might serve the student as a "*vade mecum*" was still wanting. With this view we recommend the work before us. And the Author's own modest account of it prevents those reflections which otherwise we might have been disposed to offer. 'This little treatise, says he, was written many years since; for when I studied the *Principia*, I was frequently at a stop, which obliged me to make calculations here and there, as I went on; and when I had done, I set them down as notes upon *these* places; wherein I only meddled with these (those) places that appeared difficult to me. These notes, collected together, are the subject of the following comment. And I have revised the whole, and added several things that seemed wanting: yet I believe there are some things still behind, which are not sufficiently explained by any commentator, and especially such as are there laid down without their demonstrations.'

To this *short Comment* the Author has added a 'defence of Sir I. Newton against the objections that have been made to several parts of the Principia, optics and chronology.' We are sorry to be obliged to say, that the Author's zeal in defence of Sir Isaac sometimes transcends the limits of decency and liberality. Mr. Emerson is too much of a philosopher to need being told, that hard names are no arguments; and that, however provoking to the admirers of Newton, the ignorance, envy, and abuse of his adversaries may be, bad language is a kind of retaliation, which the honour of truth and the liberality of science absolutely prohibit and condemn. The reputation of this illustrious Author, and the merit of his discoveries, rest on a basis, which the malignity and rudeness of censure and cavil can never overturn. Upon the whole, we approve of our Author's vindication, though it has evident marks of haste and negligence; and we could have wished that it had been debased by no single expression unbecoming the dignity of true philosophy. We are disposed however to pardon the overflow of a laudable zeal, and we heartily concur with the Author in every generous attempt towards humbling the pride, and restraining the petulance of the ignorant and censorious.

Our Author's defence consists of three parts. In the first, he vindicates the *Principia* from the objections of J. Bernouilli, Euler, and Leibnitz. He enlarges most on the Newtonian doctrine of the tides, in answer to Euler, and some other foreigners, who have expressed their dissatisfaction with it. We shall make an extract or two from what he has said under this head.

 'Sir

' Sir I. Newton's explanation of the tides (Prop. 24, b. iii.) does not pleaſe *Euler*, though he accounts for every circumſtance thereof. He thinks aſcribing theſe effects to the actions of the ſun and moon, is recurring to *occult cauſes*, and therefore he had rather recur to *Vortexes* for the explanation thereof; the notion of which has been confuted over and over. He denies the gravitation of bodies towards one another, becauſe he cannot diſcover the cauſe of gravity; and therefore he will not allow it to have any thing to do with the matter, as being an occult quality. But he recurs to a principle that is more than occult, his incomprehenſible vortices, which he thinks the tides are raiſed by; though he has not attempted to explain in what manner his vortices can do it.—This gentleman tells us, that Newton's method is erroneous, by which he found the ſea to riſe to the height of near two feet, by the ſun's force only. And ſays, that Newton found out this enormous effect, by comparing the ſun's force with the centrifugal force of the earth. But certainly this gentleman knows little about the nature of forces, if he does not allow that two equal forces, of however different kinds, will always have equal effects; and proportional forces, proportional effects, eſpecially in their naſcent ſtate: for it is not the *kind*, but the *quantity* of force that is to be regarded: therefore Newton rightly found the ſolar tide near two feet, and the lunar tide 8½ feet, agreeable to experience. But to ſhew you what ſort of a theory this gentleman works by, he finds the ſolar tide only half a foot, and the lunar tide 2¼ feet, in all not three feet; which all obſervations confute, and with it his erroneous method of computation.

' He alſo tells us, that Newton found out the forces of the ſun and moon by help of the tides, but he has not done it accurately. And yet Newton took in every circumſtance that could any way affect it; as may be ſeen in prop. 37, b. iii.

' It has alſo been objected by ſome perſons, that the two examples of Newton for finding the tides are ill choſen. But however he had no more to *chooſe on*, and, by their near agreement, it ſhews they were well choſen *Euler* tells you, that at *Havre de Grace*, the greateſt and leaſt tides are as 17 to 11; and therefore the ſun's force to the moon's, will be as 17—11 to 17+11, or as 6 to 28; or as he makes it, as 7.13 to 28, which is about as 1 to 4, a proportion not very different from Newton's. *Dan. Bernouilli* ſays, that at *St. Malo*'s, the greateſt height to the leaſt is as 50 to 15, which makes the ſun's force to the moon's as 35 to 65, or as 7 to 13, not ſo much as 1 to 2; a concluſion utterly inconſiſtent with all other obſervations; which argues, that the obſervation has not been made with ſufficient accuracy. However, this is certain, that if any place can be improper for ſuch an experiment, this place is, by rea-

 ſon

ſon of the very extraordinary tides: for here the tide being hurried up a long channel, growing continually ſtraiter, it is forced up to an unuſual height.——

'There are ſome people that object againſt this method of finding the ſun and moon's forces, by the tides, and reckon it very precarious, and ſubject to many obſtacles and intervening cauſes, by which the tides are perpetually influenced and diſturbed, as if every thing had not its difficulties; the only diſturbing cauſe is the wind. Yet they can tell us of no other method, but what is more precarious and more impracticable, and leſs exact.'

In the ſecond part, 'concerning the optics,' our Author anſwers the objections of Leibnitz againſt the account which Sir Iſaac has given us of the original and conſtitution of the world, and of the Deity.

In the latter part, relating to the chronology, he gives us an account of the numerous inconſiſtencies contained in the objections made by the Rev. Dr. Rutherforth, Regius Profeſſor of Divinity in the Univerſity of Cambridge, againſt Sir Iſaac Newton's account of the Argonautic expedition; and concludes with ſome curſory remarks on Dr. Bedford's chronology.

We will only obſerve, upon the whole, that this defence is fitly connected with a comment, intended for the uſe of 'young beginners' in philoſophy. The Author does not enter minutely into the diſcuſſion of the ſubjects in diſpute between the advocates of Newton and his opponents. He has not allowed himſelf ſufficient compaſs to do full juſtice to the arguments upon which the defence is grounded: but every ſtudent will derive ſatisfaction from the hints which are here offered, and will be prepared for peruſing larger works of the ſame kind, with pleaſure and advantage.

MONTHLY CATALOGUE,

For SEPTEMBER, 1771.

MISCELLANEOUS.

Art. 9. *A Letter to the Members in Parliament on the preſent State of the Coinage:* With Propoſals for the better Regulation thereof. 8vo. 6 d. Browne. 1771.

THE Author of this performance lately publiſhed a pamphlet under the title of *Schemes ſubmitted to the Conſideration of the Public, &c* *. The univerſal complaints relating to the coinage of this kingdom has induced him, we are told, to appear again in print.

The ſcarcity of ſilver, which is now become ſo real an inconvenience and diſadvantage, this Writer attributes to two cauſes; one

* See Review, laſt volume, p. 88.

of

of them is the *real* ſcarcity of ſilver, which ariſes, partly, from its high price; ſo that the government, he ſays, muſt loſe near three halfpence out of every ſhilling they coin; partly, from the method which the dealers have of melting down the good and full weight ſilver as faſt as they get it into their hands, ſince they gain as much by deſtroying it, as the government loſe by coining it. The other cauſe of this evil, it is ſaid, is an artificial ſcarcity, proceeding from many perſons hoarding up the ſilver coin, in order to get a premium for it: ' I think, ſays this Writer, the preſent courſe of exchange is 2d. in the pound, or 8 s. in 50 pounds. This is a ſcandalous trade, and ſtrictly forbidden by law; and yet it is a trade that thouſands in this metropolis carry on: and it is not long ſince I heard a clerk in one of our public offices ſay, " That he did not care how plenty halfpence was, but that he hoped ſilver would never be plenty." Here he ſtopped, without ending his ſpeech by ſaying, " Becauſe I and my brother clerks make a premium of it." Our gold coin, it is here obſerved, was never ſo deficient in weight as at preſent, and; what is remarkable, the guineas of his preſent majeſty are found to be more defective than the old guineas. The true reaſon of which is ſaid to be, that our guineas and half guineas are ſent to Holland and France, and there filed, and then returned to perſons who find their account in this way of trading. The ſilver coin is known to be bad indeed; three-fourths of the ſhillings now current, this pamphlet tells us, are baſe and counterfeit, and their real value about eight-pence halfpenny, beſides which there are a ſet of people called *Whiteners*, who whiten a piece of baſe metal of the ſize of a ſhilling or a ſix-pence, ſo that it can paſs through a dozen or ten hands before it is diſcovered. The copper coin, this Writer remarks to be in as bad a ſtate as that of the ſilver, though there has been a new coinage, and twenty tons he is told already delivered to the public, and yet he ſays we ſee but few of them; which he ſuſpects to be owing to their being deſtroyed by the makers of counterfeit halfpence, who have but little proſpect of ſucceſs in putting off theirs, while there is plenty of good coin. This Letter-writer therefore propoſes that all the acts relative to the coin of this kingdom ſhould be repealed, and a new one made, ſeveral heads of which he offers to conſideration: Such as, that all perſons counterfeiting, diminiſhing, or deſtroying the coin, ſhould ſuffer death, and be hung in chains, with an inſcription denoting their offence: that a diſcoverer of ſuch perſons ſhould have one hundred pounds reward: that no perſon ſhould impreſs gold, ſilver, or copper, with the heads of our kings, or with the arms of the kingdom, &c. that any perſon who ſhould give or receive any premium for change, ſhould forfeit the ſum they gave, or received a premium for, to the informer: that no coin ſhould paſs current farther back than that of King George the Second, and all former coins be called in: that all ſhillings coined in future ſhould weigh but ten-pence, and ſix pences but five-pence: that all perſons ſhould have a right to cut in two any baſe coin offered to them, and then return it to their owners.

He recommends this to the conſideration of parliament, as when the whole community are oppreſſed by the villany of a few individuals, they muſt always look up to the legiſlature for redreſs. ' There has

has lately been people, says he, who have made it their business (from what motive I am not to determine) to possess the people with an ill opinion of the present legislature: the opinions of the people just now in regard to government seem, to use the definition of a celebrated lexicographer, to be upon the *alternate preponderation*: the repealing in a manner the *privilege-act* last session, wrought much effect upon the minds of the people in favour of government, and brought their opinions rather upon the *poise*; one more popular act *turns the scale* in favour of the legislature, and I know of none that would more please the public than this I have proposed relative to the coinage.'

Art. 10. *Instructions for collecting and preserving Insects*; particularly Moths and Butterflies. Illustrated with a Copper-plate, on which the Nets, and other Apparatus necessary for that Purpose, are delineated. 8vo. 1 s. Pearch. 1771.

The Author appears to be well skilled in the art which is taught in this little treatise; to the publication of which, he was induced, from the following considerations:—'Most of the English, says he, as well as Foreign insects, in the collections which I have lately had opportunities of observing, have been either spoiled in the catching, or, for want of properly knowing how to preserve them, rendered imperfect, and of little or no value.' He regretted, he adds, that so much time and labour should be spent to so little purpose; and for that reason he was induced to make these instructions (which were originally drawn up for the use of a gentleman going to reside abroad) more generally known.

The attention of a connoisseur, to this part of the creation, is certainly very amusing; and our only objection to it, is what common humanity must dictate to every reflecting mind; viz. the cruelty, not to say ingratitude, of gibbeting, and impaling alive, so many innocent, little, beautiful beings, in return for the pleasure they afford us, in the display of their lovely tints and glowing colours!

Art. 11. *The History of the Theatres of London, from* 1760, *to the present Time.* Being a Continuation of the annual Register of all the new Tragedies, Comedies, Farces, Pantomimes, &c. that have been performed within that Period. With occasional Notes and Anecdotes. By Mr. Victor, Author of the two former Volumes. 12mo. 3 s. Becket.

Mr. Victor's two former volumes, on this subject, were published in 1761, and our Readers will find so full an account of them in the Review for July, in the same year, that a reference to the article there given may suffice on the present occasion. The Author has here continued his register to the year 1770, inclusive.

Art. 12. *The Dramatic Censor; or, Critical Companion.* 8vo. 2 Vols. 12 s. Boards. Bell, &c.

This work was published about a year ago, in periodical numbers, and these two volumes are supposed to comprehend the whole of the Author's design. He has given a critical investigation of above 50 of our most considerable *acting* plays; with remarks also on the performers who have appeared in the principal characters of those plays. He seems to be intimately conversant with theatrical affairs; to have formed a just estimate of the respective merits of the actors; and to have

have offered many judicious criticisms on the writings of our principal dramatic poets.

Art. 13. *An Address to Dr. Cadogan, occasioned by his Dissertation on the Gout, &c.* 8vo. 1 s. Almon.

The Addresser is an advocate for the meats and drinks proscribed by Dr. Cadogan, and he arms himself with the Bible in defence of the bottle. Need we add that the man is not serious, and that he only means to sell a few pamphlets?

Art. 14. *The Female Monitor.* To which is annexed, a Treatise on Divorces; containing very seasonable Advice to both married and single Ladies. By a Clergyman of the Church of England. 12mo. 1 s. 6 d. Dixwell.

We heartily hope that no clergyman of the church of England, or of any other church, could be the Author of so stupid a performance.

Art. 15. *Miscellaneous Tracts* of the Rev. John Clubbe, Rector of Whatfield, and Vicar of Debenham, Suffolk. 12mo. 2 Vols. 6 s. bound. Ipswich printed, and sold by Hingeston in London.

We have repeatedly introduced this very ingenious Writer to the notice of our Readers. His *Antiquities of Wheatfield* * is an admirable piece of irony; and his tract intitled *Physiognomy* †, is a performance equally ludicrous and laughable. In the present collection there is, beside the two pieces above-mentioned, another humourous production, *viz. Scattered Thoughts on Title-pages, Dedications, Prefaces, and Postscripts:* these make up the contents of the first volume. The second volume exhibits the Author's more serious talents: it consists of, I. *A Letter of Free Advice to young Clergymen.* II. *A Sermon preached before the Sons of the Clergy at Ipswich.* III. *Infant Baptism considered under the great Probability, if not absolute Certainty, of its Practice in the first Ages of Christianity.* Most, if not all, of these have been separately published.

MATHEMATICAL.

Art. 16. *Four Propositions, &c.* shewing not only that the Distance of the Sun, as attempted to be determined from the Theory of Gravity, by a late Author, is, upon his own Principles, *erroneous*; but also that it is more than probable this *capital Question* can never be satisfactorily answered by any Calculus of the Kind. 8vo. 1 s. Newcastle printed, and sold in London by Johnson and Payne. 1769.

To determine the sun's distance with any degree of certainty and precision, is a very important subject of astronomical enquiry. Could this fundamental point be satisfactorily settled, it would be easy to ascertain the dimensions of the whole solar system, and the science of astronomy in general would derive great improvement from the discovery. Many ingenious and laborious attempts have been made towards the solution of this interesting problem; and we have the satisfaction to think that they have not been altogether unsuccessful. The late transits have been of singular service for this purpose; and to these astronomers have directed their attention and wishes, from the days of *Horrox* to this distinguished period. What is the result of

* See Rev. vol. xix. p. 309.

† ——— vol. xxx. p. 482.

the

the laſt obſervations has not yet appeared. Theſe phenomena however are ſo rare, and attended with ſo many contingent circumſtances, that aſtronomers have been deſirous of inveſtigating the ſun's diſtance from other *data*, beſide the parallax: and ſince the *theory of gravity* has been eſtabliſhed on the moſt inconteſtible principles by the *immortal Newton*, ſome have imagined that this might furniſh the ſolution ſought for. Profeſſor Machin has given us a hint to this purpoſe in his *Laws of the Moon's Motion according to Gravity*, annexed to the Engliſh edition of the Principia by Mr. *Motte*: but the ſubject has been ſince proſecuted more largely by Dr. Stewart, Profeſſor of Mathematics in the Univerſity of Edinburgh. His calculations, our Readers may recollect, were publiſhed ſome years ſince; and his concluſions differed conſiderably from the ſentiments which had been commonly adopted by aſtronomers. The principles, upon which his reaſoning was founded, were never formally examined, till the ingenious Author of the pamphlet before us, 'prompted by curioſity and a natural inclination to theſe ſtudies, amuſed himſelf in the peruſal of the *Doctor's Tracts*; and preſuming that his calculations were wrong, and his principles very unſatisfactory, thought it incumbent upon him, as a lover of truth and a well-wiſher to the ſciences, to lay his objections before the public.' The pamphlet itſelf, by ſome miſtake or other †, eſcaped our earlier notice: and it is ſufficient to ſay, on a ſubject which is now *ſub judice*, that the objections here urged are very formidable and well deſerving the Profeſſor's attention. Should his concluſions be 'erroneous on his own principles;' ſhould it be 'more than probable that this *capital queſtion* can never be ſatisfactorily anſwered by any *calculus* of this kind;' his well-intended labour muſt be miſapplied, and the expectations of the public, in the iſſue, diſappointed.

Art. 17. *Animadverſions on Dr. Stewart's Computation of the Sun's Diſtance from the Earth.* By John Landen, F.R.S. 4to. 1 s. Nourſe. 1771.

The deſign of this publication is to expoſe the fallacy of Dr. *Stewart's* calculations. The *Doctor* maintains, that he has "aſcertained the ſolar force affecting the gravity of the moon to the earth, and from that has calculated, *very accurately*, the mean diſtance of the ſun from the earth." This Author tells us, that he has examined what the *Doctor* has done; and having found, not only his principles very exceptionable, but alſo his calculation egregiouſly erroneous; he cannot, as the ſubject is of importance, unconcernedly obſerve *error* promulgated as *truth*, but muſt, as a friend to ſcience, take up his pen, and point out the faults he has diſcovered. And he obſerves, that a concluſion different from the *Doctor's* may be obtained by following his own method, varying the ſteps a little, yet taking none but ſuch as will undoubtedly bring it as near the truth as thoſe taken by him. We need only obſerve, that if the learned Profeſſor's concluſions had been more agreeable to obſervations, it would have yielded only a preſumptive proof of the accuracy of his computation; but as the ſun's diſtance, determined by his method of eſti-

† Probably from its not being ſo generally advertiſed in the London papers, as is uſual with regard to new publications.

mating

mating it, differs widely from the result of the best observations that have yet been made, this circumstance alone may perhaps be a sufficient reason for rejecting his theory as false. Whoever impartially attends to what the Author of this article has done, will find that no great precision can be expected from the *Doctor*'s method.

POETICAL.

Art. 18. *A poetical Essay on the Providence of God.* Part III. By the Rev. W. H. Roberts, Fellow of Eton College. 4to. 1 s. 6 d. Wilkie.

Mr. Roberts found this subject more capable of poetical embellishment than the two former parts, and there is more to praise and less to blame in the present than in either of the preceding pieces. The following description of Winter is tolerably animated and picturesque:

Stern Winter chills the world. From snow-topt hills,
Hæmo, and Rhodope, the sharp North blows,
And drives the naked Thracian to his cave.
Or from those rocks of thick-ribb'd ice, where roams
The shivering *Savoyard*, with intenser cold
Sweeps o'er *Grenoble*'s champain to the streams
Of Isere and the Rhone. Now to his sledge,
Where Lapland *confines* on the Chronian main,
The blighted native yokes his rein deers; they
O'er many a league of snow run panting on
From Kola to Warsuga. To the wind
The crackling forest roars: the *leafless* elm
Spreads o'er the frozen stream her *bare* broad arms;
And that tall oak, which on the mountain's brow
Three hundred summers stood, beneath whose shade
Fathers, and sons had led the rustic dance,
Falls ponderous down the riven precipice
Uptorn———

All these poetical essays abound with inaccuracies. In this short quotation there are three or four exceptionable expressions. To make verse of two of the lines, we must pronounce the words *Savoyard* and *Grenoble* in a manner different from the common pronunciation. The word *confines*, used as a verb, is hardly justifiable, particularly as the same word is differently pronounced, and has its proper meaning, from which it ought not to depart. To give both an active and a neutral signification to verbs is the pest and perplexity of every language. The word bare, applied to the elm, which had before been called *leafless*, is an utter redundancy.

Art. 19. *The Debauchee*; a Poem, in six Cantos. With an Elegy on the Death of a Libertine. By Francis Bacon Lee. 4to. 2 s. Cooke.

No language can characterise this poem so properly as the Author's:

"In the absurdest follies shew your skill.
Will you do all these things? *I will, I will.*"

Art. 20. *The Wedding Day*; a Poem. 4to. 2 s. Flexney.

A horrible story, told, we imagine, by some callow school-boy; who may, perhaps, do better when his wings are fledged.

Art. 21. *The Doctor Dissected; or, Willy Cadogan in the Kitchen.* By a Lady. 4to. 1 s. Davies.

A burlesque on the famous gout-dissertation; awkward, hobbling, and frivolous:—as for example:

"*Salt, mustard,* and *pepper,* ay! *vinegar* too,
Are quite as unwholesome as pudding, I vow;
And bread," *the main staff of our life,* he does call,
No more nor no less—than "the worst thing of all."

Art. 22. *Water Poetry;* a Collection of Verses written at several public Places; most of them never before printed. 8vo. 1 s. 6 d. Pearch.

Every thing in this collection that has the least shadow of merit has been already printed. But the book, as the GUARDIAN says, may be of use with the waters.

DRAMATIC.

Art. 23. *The Magnet;* a musical Entertainment. Performed at Marybone Gardens. 4to. 1 s. Becket.

A trifle.

POLITICAL.

Art. 24. *A Letter to the Earl of Bute.* 8vo. 1 s. 6 d. Almon. 1771.

The commotions, which now agitate the kingdom, are ascribed, in this performance, to the unpopular nobleman to whom it is addressed; the ministry is conceived to be under his influence; and he is directly accused of having formed the design of overturning the constitution and the laws. In what manner these charges are supported, will be differently decided by those who style themselves the King's friends, and those who stand forth as the advocates and champions of the people.—But whatever truth or falsehood there may be in the allegations of this Writer, we have this reflection left to console us, that when statesmen have excited the jealousy of a nation, and roused its attention, they have certainly lost the critical moment for accomplishing any scheme they may have formed to the prejudice of its rights or liberties.

MUSIC.

Art. 25. *Lettera del Defonto, &c.* A Letter from the late Signor *Tartini* to Signora *Maddalena Lombardini* (now Signora Sirmen) Published as an important Lesson to Performers on the Violin. 4to. 1 s. Bremner. 1771.

For the appearance of this short but excellent lesson, in this country, and in our language, the public is indebted to the ingenious Author of the *Present State of Music in France and Italy;* who has likewise given the original Italian on the opposite page of his translation. It contains several fundamental precepts on the articles of tone, bowing, shifting, and shaking, delivered with simplicity and precision; the knowledge and practice of which are essential *to a just* and masterly execution on the violin. Nothing further need be added in recommendation of this little work, when it is considered as containing the instructions of such a master as Tartini, to such a pupil as Signora Sirmen.

Art.

BOTANY.

Art. 26. *The Universal Botanist and Nurseryman, &c.* By Richard Weston, Esq. Vol. II. 8vo. 5 s. 3 d. Boards. Bell. 1771.

In our Review, vol. xliv. p. 130, we gave a brief sketch of the design of this valuable system of botany, &c. to which we now refer for a general idea of the undertaking. This second volume contains the *herbs, flowers*, and *bulbous roots*; to which are added,

I. A catalogue of curious ranunculusses, of the year 1769, describing above 1100 different sorts, with their names, colours, manner of blowing, and prices.

II. A priced catalogue of hyacinths.

III. Ditto of tulips.

IV. Ditto of the polyanthus—narcissus, crocus, colchicum, iris, jonquil, lily, crown imperial, cyclemen, and frittillary tribes.

V. A catalogue of the principal botanical Authors and their works, for above 2000 years, from Theophrastus to the year 1770.

VI. A translation of Adanson's curious chronological table of botanical Authors; with additions and corrections; by which we may see, at one view, what nations have produced most botanists,—the Authors who have copied from others,—and those who have most extended the science, down to 1763. Mr. Weston, in his preface, assures his Readers, that the 3d and 4th volumes are in the press.

MEDICAL.

Art. 27. *Considerations on the Means of preventing the Communication of Pestilential Contagion, and of eradicating it in infected Places.* By William Brownrigg, M. D. F. R. S. 4to. 1 s. 0 d. Davis. 1771.

These Considerations contain some very sensible and useful observations on the laws of quarantine, the establishment of bills of health, the practice of shutting up infected houses, and the means of preventing all communication between the places visited by the plague, and those that are free from the contagion. As these are points of the highest consequence to the security and even to the very existence of mankind, it is with the most sincere satisfaction we see them so ably and amply treated in this truly valuable and important publication.

Art. 28. *A Treasure of easy Medicines, briefly comprehending approved and specific Remedies for almost all Disorders of the human Body.* Extracted from the most celebrated Writings both of the Ancients and Moderns, and digested in alphabetical Order. Licensed and recommended by the Royal College of Physicians. Published originally in Latin, by John Cruso, Pharmacop. To which are now added, large Annotations, with a Glossary and General Index. 12mo. 3 s. bound. Faden, &c. 1771.

This is a compilation in which we find numberless virtues attributed to remedies which never existed but in the imaginations of their Authors.

The diseases are ranged alphabetically, as are, likewise, the medicines, which are all taken from the vegetable kingdom.—The following may serve as a specimen:

MORBI

MORBI CUTANEI.

CUTANEOUS DISEASES.

' *Lepathum Acutum*, SHARP-POINTED OR COMMON DOCK. A ſtrong decoction of the root, uſed either as a waſh or fomentation, is ſurprizingly ſerviceable. *Etmuller*.

MORSUS CANIS RABADI.

BITE OF A MAD DOG.

' *Alyſſum Dioſcorid*, MADWORT OR MOONWORT OF DIOSCORIDES. Uſed any way, it is commended againſt the Hydrophoby by *Sennertus*.

' *Carduus Mariæ*, LADIES THISTLE. Give two drams of the ſeeds pulverized, in wine, and let a ſweat be promoted. *Lindanus*.

' *Cæpa*, AN ONION. *Ruta*, RUE. An onion, maſhed together with rue, ſalt, and honey, is very ſerviceable. *Morriſon*.

' *Centaurium minus*, LESSER CENTAURY. The tops and flowers, well-dried and pulverized, or a decoction of the ſame, ſpecifically cure. *Ray*.

' *Cynorrhodon*, DOG-ROSE. The root of this is a certain remedy. *Baricellus*.

' *Pimpinella*, BURNET. The herb given any way for ſome days together, cures. *Maroldus*.

' *Salvia*, SAGE. I cured a certain perſon of ſixty, who had been bitten by a mad dog in the upper part of the hand, by the following method;

' Take one handful of red ſage; maſh it with a little ſalt and vinegar to the form of a pultice, which is to be applied to the part affected.

' By repeating this twice he got well, without any other remedy.

—SERPENTUM. OF SERPENTS.

' *Allium*, GARLIC. Taken inwardly, or bruiſed and applied outwardly to the part, it is an experienced remedy for the bite of vipers.

' *Fæniculum*, FENNEL. A decoction of the ſeeds, drank, cures. *Morriſon*.

' *Galega*, GOATS-RUE. The juice drank, and the herb bruiſed and applied, is a ſure remedy. *Idem*.

' *Marrhubium*, HOREHOUND. Let the bruiſed herb be outwardly applied, and a ſpoonful or two of the ſyrup taken inwardly. *Boyle*.'

RELIGIOUS and CONTROVERSIAL.

Art. 29. *Propoſals for an Application to Parliament for Relief in the Matter of Subſcription to the Liturgy and Thirty-nine Articles of the eſtabliſhed Church of England*. Humbly ſubmitted to the Conſideration of the learned and conſcientious Clergy of the ſaid Church. 4to. 6 d. White, &c. 1771.

Ever ſince the publication of the free and candid Diſquiſitions, a ſpirit hath been ſpreading among the clergy, in favour of a farther reformation in the church of England. This ſpirit has been promoted, from time to time, by a ſucceſſion of valuable performances, and eſpecially by the celebrated Author of the Confeſſional, and his worthy and learned aſſiſtants. At length, ſome of the clergy are entering into an aſſociation for endeavouring to obtain parliamentary relief in the matter of ſubſcription. That their numbers were larger, and that they had a greater proſpect of immediate ſucceſs, will be wiſhed by every friend to religious liberty. However, we think that good effects will ariſe from keeping the object continually in view; and we hope that the period is not far diſtant in which the upright and conſcientious miniſters of the eſtabliſhed church will be freed from the burthen now lying upon them.

As to the propoſals here offered to the public, it is ſufficient to ſay of them, that they are drawn up with modeſty and judgment.

Art. 30. *Thoughts on our Articles of Religion, with reſpect to their ſuppoſed Utility to the State.* 4to. 6 d. Townſhend, &c. 1771.

The deſign of this piece is to promote the ſucceſs of the ſcheme mentioned in the preceding article. As the grand argument for continuing religious impoſitions has been their imagined uſefulneſs to the ſtate, that argument is here conſidered; and the Author hath clearly ſhewn that the reaſons taken from public utility, to ſupport the ſubſcription to our eſtabliſhed articles of religion, have no reaſonable foundation. This ſmall tract is written with remarkable conciſeneſs, ſpirit, and knowledge of the world, and is evidently the ſketch of a maſter.

Art. 31. *Familiar Epiſtles to the Rev. Dr. Prieſtley.* In which it is ſhewn, I. That the Charges brought by him againſt the Orthodox, are applicable to none but People of the Doctor's own Perſuaſion. II. That, notwithſtanding his endeavours to deſtroy the Doctrines of Chriſt's Divinity, and the vicarious Puniſhment of Sin, the Doctor has eſtabliſhed both, even to a Demonſtration. III. That what the Doctor calls *Rational Religion*, has, according to his own Account, been productive of the moſt unhappy and irrational Conſequences. IV. That the Doctor's religious Pamphlets are a full and complete Refutation of themſelves. By the Author of the Shaver's Sermon on the Oxford Expulſion. 8vo. 1 s. 6 d. Keith, &c.

Dr. Prieſtley is here fallen into the hands of a ſmart Writer, who, having attacked certain of the members of our national church, is now diſpoſed to make trial of his abilities with ſome of the Diſſenters. He gives a ſufficient view of his deſign in the above long title-page. The particular performance which gave riſe to theſe letters, we are told, is a pamphlet, intitled, *A free Addreſs to Proteſtant Diſſenters on the Subject of Church Diſcipline, with a preliminary Diſcourſe concerning the Spirit of Chriſtianity, and the Corruption of it by falſe Notions of Religion*; though there are alſo ſome other publications of Dr. Prieſtley's which occaſionally engage the Shaver's notice. He is a lively antagoniſt, who knows how to improve the conceſſions or unguarded expreſſions of his opponent, and to plead his own cauſe with a ſhew of truth and juſtice. But if we farther obſerve that he is prone to take unfair advantages, to indulge at times a kind of low or flippant humour, and to uſe too freely, for his own credit we mean, the weapon of ridicule, we apprehend it will not be thought, by unbiaſſed judges, upon the whole, any falſe repreſentation. But whatever are his excellencies or his faults, we muſt conſign him to the care of Dr. Prieſtley (ſhould he chuſe to enter the liſts upon the occaſion) who, amidſt his ſeveral productions, has, no doubt, ſometimes afforded opportunities for animadverſion, and has likewiſe in ſome inſtances, which this Author takes notice of, to his honour, diſcovered

discovered a readiness to correct what, upon convincing evidence, has appeared to him to have been wrong in his former publications; for a proof of which our Shaver particularly mentions the additions which were made to the *Address on the Lord's Supper*; the noticing of which, as an indication of the Doctor's regard to truth, must be acknowledged to be so far candid and ingenuous in the present Writer.

SERMONS.

I. *The Spirit of the Gospel, neither a Spirit of Superstition nor of Enthusiasm*—Before the Synod of Aberdeen, April 9, 1771. By George Campbell, Principal of the Marishal College, Aberdeen, and Author of the Essay on Miracles. 1 s. 6 d. Cadell, &c.

II. *The careless Professor's Danger, and the true Believer's Safety, with respect to the unpardonable Sin*—At the Rev. Mr. Maxfield's Chapel in Rope-maker's Alley, Little Moorfields, July 14, 1771. By Benj. Russen, Assistant Preacher to the Rev. Mr. Maxfield. 6 d. Keith, &c.

III. *Murder lamented and improved*—At Kidderminster, June 2[illegible], 1771, on Occasion of the Death of Mr. Francis Best, who was robbed and murdered by John Child. To which is added, a Narrative, &c. By Benj. Fawcet, M. A. 6 d. Buckland.

CORRESPONDENCE.

To the MONTHLY REVIEWERS.

GENTLEMEN,

IN your account of Mr. Addington's piece on Infant Baptism, after quoting the following among other passages, "We have not met with one text in which Christ commanded his ministers to baptize believers much less believers only;" you add, "In what particular sense the Author understands *believers* in the above passage we know not."—But the justice and propriety of his observation does not seem to depend upon any particular sense of the word Believer. The writers on the other side of the question require the Pædobaptist to produce an express command *totidem verbis* for baptizing children; he has in this passage only returned the challenge concerning believers. They ask, where has Christ said to his ministers in so many words, "Baptize children?" This Author replies, neither has *he* said, Baptize believers and believers only. And if they assert that Christ has said enough to authorize the baptism of believers, it is proved, in other parts of this treatise, that Christ has said enough to authorize his ministers to baptize children; but not a word to countenance them in confining baptism to believers (whether by such be meant only those who have received the Christian faith in opposition to Pagans, Jews, &c. or such as have believed to the saving of the soul) much less has he said, "Baptize believers again, upon making a profession of their faith in adult years, who were baptized in their infancy."

*** Stone's "Discourses on some important Subjects," will appear in our next Month's Review. As will, also, a Letter to the Reviewers, relating to Cawthorn's Poems.

ERRATUM in our last.

P. 117, paragraph 7, line 7, for 'Pelagius, who was born in England, &c. r. '*who was born a Briton.*' Vid. Bede, Hist. Eccl. L. 1. c. 10.

THE
MONTHLY REVIEW,
For OCTOBER, 1771.

ART. I. *The Roman History, from the Building of Rome to the Ruin of the Commonwealth.* By N. Hooke, Esq. Vol. IV. concluded.

IN our Review for the last month we attended Mr. Hooke from the rise of the civil war to the assassination of Cæsar. We shall now accompany him through the sequel of his performance, and shall offer our opinion of his merit as an Historian.

Brutus and his associates fancied that they had restored the commonwealth when they had killed Cæsar; but they had only removed the tyrant. The Romans were incapable of receiving liberty; and it was necessary that they should stoop to another master. The consternation with which this event filled all ranks of men, the feeble conduct of the conspirators, who had formed no plan of action, the artful management of Antony, who thought to arrive at empire, the cautious and concealed policy of Octavius, and the revival of the civil wars, are well described and unfolded by our Historian. He then treats of the siege of Mutina, of the success of Brutus in Macedonia, of that of Cassius in Syria, and of the two successive battles in which Antony was defeated, and in which the consuls Hirtius and Pansa lost their lives.

In narrating these transactions, our Author has slightly touched on the singular importance of the Roman ladies, during this period, with regard to public affairs. To an ancient Roman it would have appeared in the highest degree absurd, that a woman should have aimed at obtaining a sway over the deliberations of a Roman senate, or that she should have mixed her counsels with those of the most penetrating statesmen. But Brutus and Cassius, while they held a select conference of their friends at Antium, were not ashamed to require the assistance of Servilia, Porcia, and Tertulla; and other ladies had likewise their ſhare in the politics of thoſe times. The power and conſideration to which they had attained might, doubtleſs, give occaſion to much curious inquiry; and it is ſurpriſing that thoſe who have treated of Roman affairs ſhould have attended ſo little to this ſubject.

The ſituation of parties, after the death of the conſuls Hirtius and Panſa, is ſtated with great perſpicuity by our Hiſtorian. The removal of theſe able magiſtrates ſeems to have ſuggeſted to Octavius the idea of the ſecond Triumvirate. After the victories obtained at Mutina, he was in a condition to have purſued and deſtroyed Antony; but, if he had effected this meaſure, the republican party would have been too ſtrong for him and Lepidus; and while Antony's power was low, and his own conſiderable, he could procure what terms he pleaſed in the partition of the empire. He therefore treated ſecretly with Lepidus and Antony, and ſent a deputation of his officers to demand the conſulſhip. He then proceeded to impeach and condemn the conſpirators; the law againſt Dolabella was repealed; and Cicero was put to death.

The views and conduct of the Triumvirs, and of the generals of the commonwealth, now engage the attention of our Hiſtorian. He relates the reduction of the Lycians and the Rhodians; and while he deſcribes the two battles at Philippi, with their conſequences, he combats, and with good reaſon, the opinion of Monteſquieu, which ſuppoſes that Brutus and Caſſius killed themſelves with a precipitation not to be vindicated. He has ſhewn, in oppoſition to this celebrated Writer, that their defeat was irreparable. They could not depend upon their armies, the provinces were not diſpoſed to ſupply them with money, and they had no place to fly to but Sicily, whither they would immediately have been followed by all the forces of the Triumvirs.

We muſt here however remark, that Mr. Hooke has drawn, with much partiality, the character of Brutus. When he impeaches the honour and the virtue of this celebrated Roman, he ought to have explained the facts, which induced him to form ſo ſevere a cenſure. Tyrannicide was viewed by the Romans in a very different light from what it appears in at preſent; and it is not, by the ideas of our own times, that we are to judge of the heroes of antiquity. According to modern manners, Brutus was guilty of the higheſt ingratitude by killing Cæſar, who had been his benefactor; but in the opinion of the ancients this circumſtance rendered his act the more glorious. By diſregarding favours done to himſelf, he ſhewed the greater attachment to his country. We are not diſpoſed to commend, very highly, his ability; but his inflexible regard to juſtice, and to liberty, are worthy, we ſhould think, of univerſal admiration;

miration; and, perhaps, of all the distinguished personages of antiquity, he best deserves to be considered as the model of a virtuous citizen. The letter which he wrote to Cicero, on his having interceded for his pardon with Octavius, perfectly marks his character; and, as it is an excellent contrast to the views and principles of modern patriots, we shall venture to transcribe it for the entertainment of our Readers.

BRUTUS to CICERO*.

"I have read a part of your letter, which you sent to Octavius; transmitted to me by Atticus. Your zeal and concern for my safety gave me no new pleasure: for it is not only common, but our daily news, to hear something which you have said or done with your usual fidelity, in the support of my honour and dignity. Yet that same part of your letter affected me with the most sensible grief which my mind could possibly receive. For you compliment him so highly for his services to the republic, and in a strain so suppliant and abject; that—What shall I say?—I am ashamed of the wretched state to which we are reduced—yet it must be said,—you recommend my safety to him; (to which what death is not preferable?) and plainly shew, that our servitude is not yet abolished, but our master only changed. Recollect your words, and deny them, if you dare, to be the prayers of a slave to his King. *There is one thing*, you say, *which is required and expected from him, that he will allow those citizens to live in safety, of whom all honest men, and the people of Rome, think well.* But what, if he will not allow it? Shall we be the less safe for that? It is better not to be safe, than to be made safe by him. For my part, I can never think all the Gods so averse to the safety of the Roman people, that Octavius must be intreated for the life of any one citizen; I will not say for the deliverers of the world. It is a pleasure to talk thus magnificently; and it becomes me surely to those, who know not either what to fear for any one, or what to ask of any one. Can you, Cicero, allow Octavius to have this power, and be still a friend to him? Or, if you have any value for me, would you wish to see me at Rome, when I must first be recommended to the boy, that he would permit me to be there? What reason have you to thank him, if you think it necessary to beg of him, that he would grant and suffer us to live in safety? Or is it to be reckoned a kindness, that he chuses to see himself, rather than Antony, in the condition to have such petitions addressed to him? One may supplicate, indeed, the *successor*, but never the *avenger* of another's tyranny; that those who have deserved well of the republic may be safe. It was this weakness and despair, not more blameable, indeed, in you than in all; which first pushed on Cæsar to the ambition of reigning; and after his death determined Antony to attempt to seize his place; and has raised this boy so high, that you judge it necessary to address your prayers to him, for the preservation of men of our rank; and that we can be saved only by the mercy of one, scarce yet a man; and by no other means. But, if we had remembered ourselves to be Romans, these most infamous men would not be more daring to grasp at dominion, than we to repel it: nor would Antony be more en-

* Mr. Hooke has given this celebrated letter from the translation of Dr. Middleton.

couraged by Cæsar's reign, than deterred by his fate. How can you, a consular, and the avenger of so many treasons, (by suppressing which, you have but postponed our ruin, I fear, for a little time) reflect on what your have done, and yet approve these things; or bear them so tamely, as to seem at least to approve them? For what particular hatred had you to Antony? No other, but because he assumed all this to himself; that our lives should be begged of him; our safety be precarious, from whom he had received his liberty; and the republic depend upon his will and pleasure. You thought it necessary to take up arms to prevent him from tyrannising over us: But was it your intent, that, by preventing him, we might sue to another, who would suffer himself to be advanced into his place; or that the republic might be free and mistress of itself? As if our quarrel was not, perhaps, to slavery, but to the conditions of it. But we might have had, not only an easy master in Antony, if we would have been content with that fortune, but whatever share with him we pleased of favours and honours. For what could he deny to those whose patience, he saw, was the best support of his government? But nothing was of such value to us, that we would sell our faith and liberty for it. Would not the very boy, whom the name of Cæsar seems to incite against the destroyers of Cæsar, think it worth any price, if there was room to traffick with him, to be enabled, by our help, to maintain all that power, which he now enjoys? Since we have a mind to live, and to be rich, and to be consulars? But then Cæsar must have perished in vain. For what reason had we to rejoice at his death, if after it we were still to continue slaves? Let other people be as indolent as they please; but, as for me, may the gods and goddesses deprive me sooner of every thing, than the resolution of not allowing to the heir of him, whom I killed, what I did not allow to the man himself; nor would suffer even in my father, were he living, *to have more power than the laws and the senate*. How can you imagine that the rest of you can ever be free under him, without whose leave there is no place for us in that city? Or how is it possible for you, after all, to obtain what you ask? You beg, *that he would allow us to be safe*. Shall we then receive safety, think you, when we have received life from him? But how can we receive it, if we first part with our honour and our liberty? Do you fancy, that to live at Rome is to be safe? It is the thing, and not the place, which must secure that to me: for I was never safe while Cæsar lived, till I had resolved with myself upon that attempt: nor can I in any place live in exile, as long as I hate slavery and insults above all other evils. Is not this to fall back again into the same state of darkness; when he who has taken upon him the name of the tyrant (though in the cities of Greece, when the tyrants are destroyed, their children also perish with them) must be intreated, that the avengers of tyranny may be safe? Can I ever wish to see that city, or think it a city, which has not the power even to accept liberty, when offered, and even forced upon it; but has more dread of the name of their late King, in the person of a boy, than confidence in itself; though it has seen that very King taken off in the utmost height of power, by the virtue of a few? Do not recommend me, therefore, any more to your Cæsar: nor yourself indeed, if you will hearken to me. You set a very high value on the few years which remain to you at that age,

age, if for the ſake of them you can ſupplicate that boy. But take care, after all, leſt what you have done, and are doing, ſo laudably againſt Antony, inſtead of being applauded as the effect of a great mind, *be not charged to the account of your fear*. For if you are pleaſed with Octavius ſo, as to petition him for our ſafety, you will be thought, *not to have diſliked a maſter, but to have wanted a more friendly one.* As to your praiſing him, for the things that he has hitherto done, I entirely approve it; for they deſerve to be praiſed, provided that he undertook them to repel other men's power, not to advance his own. But when you adjudge him, not only to have this power, but that you yourſelf ought to ſubmit to it ſo far, as to intreat him, that he would not deſtroy us; you pay him too great a recompence: for you aſcribe that very thing to him, which the republic ſeemed to enjoy through him: nor does it ever enter into your thoughts, that, if Octavius be worthy of any honours, becauſe he wages war with Antony; that thoſe, who extirpated the very evil, of which theſe are but the relics, can never be ſufficiently requited by the Roman people; though they were to heap upon them every thing that they could beſtow. But ſee how much ſtronger people's fears are than their memories, becauſe Antony ſtill lives and is in arms. As to Cæſar, all that could and ought to be done is paſt, and cannot be recalled. Is Octavius then a perſon of ſo great importance that the people of Rome are to expect from him what he will determine upon us? Or are we of ſo little that any ſingle man is to be intreated for our ſafety? As for me, may I never return to you, if I ever either ſupplicate any man, or do not reſtrain thoſe, who are diſpoſed to do it, from ſupplicating for themſelves: or I will remove to a diſtance from all ſuch, who can be ſlaves, and fancy myſelf at Rome, wherever I can live free; and ſhall pity you, whoſe fond deſire of life neither age nor honours, nor the example of other men's virtue, can moderate. For my part, I ſhall ever think myſelf happy as long as I can pleaſe myſelf with the perſuaſion, that my piety has been fully requited. For what can be happier than for a man, conſcious of virtuous acts, and content with liberty, to deſpiſe all human affairs? Yet I will never yield to thoſe who are fond of yielding, or be conquered by thoſe who are willing to be conquered themſelves; but will firſt try and attempt every thing, nor ever deſiſt from dragging our city out of ſlavery. If ſuch fortune attends me, as I ought to have, we ſhall all rejoice: if not, I ſhall rejoice myſelf. For how can this life be ſpent better, than in thoughts and acts which tend to make my countrymen free? I beg and beſeech you, Cicero, not to deſert the cauſe through wearineſs or diffidence. In repelling preſent evils, have your eye always on the future, leſt they inſinuate themſelves before you are aware. Conſider, that the fortitude and the courage, with which you delivered the republic, when conſul, and now again, when conſular, are nothing without conſtancy and equability. The caſe of tried virtue, I own, is harder than of untried: we require ſervices from it as debts; and, if any thing diſappoints us, we blame with reſentment, as if we had been deceived by it. Wherefore, for Cicero to withſtand Antony, though it be a part highly commendable, yet, becauſe ſuch a conſul ſeemed, of courſe, to promiſe us ſuch a conſular, nobody wonders at it. But if the ſame Cicero, in the caſe of others, should waver at last in that resolution, which he exerted with such firmness and greatness of mind against Antony, he would deprive himself, not only of the hopes of future glory, but forfeit even that which is past: for nothing is great in itself but what flows from the result of our judgment: nor does it become any man, more than you, to love the republic, and to be the patron of liberty; on the account either of your natural talents, or your former acts, or the wishes and expectations of all men. Octavius, therefore, must not be intreated to suffer us to live in safety. Do you rather rouse yourself so far as to think that city, in which you have acted the noblest part, free and flourishing, as long as there are leaders still to the people, to resist the designs of traitors:"

After the victories at Philippi, the Triumvirs made a new partition of the empire. Octavius then led the veteran troops into Italy, to put them in possession of the lands that had been promised to them; and Antony prepared to extort money from the eastern provinces. A league, however, entered into by men who were ambitious, and enemies to each other, could not be of long continuance. The Perusian war broke out; and Octavius's success in it obliged Antony to turn toward Italy. But the veterans being unwilling to fight against him, a reconciliation was produced between the two competitors, by the interposition of Cocceius Nerva, Pollio, and Mecenas. The transactions of Octavius against Sextus Pompey are next detailed by our Historian; and from these he turns his attention to Antony's inglorious expedition against the Parthians, and to Pompey's behaviour in Asia. In the account he has given of the connection of Antony with Cleopatra, he has ascribed to it, with the generality of historians, the ruin of that commander. But modern Authors, while they have insisted at great length, on the follies and immorality of Antony, ought not to have forgot, that, in these respects, the more illustrious of his contemporaries were no less liable to exception. 'The feast of the gods,' celebrated by Octavius, while it displayed no ordinary scenes of intrigue and licentiousness, must be considered as the grossest insult that ever was offered to the popular religion of any country. The moral perfections of Tully have been highly extolled by Dr. Middleton; but has not this Roman been reproached with having entertained a criminal passion for his daughter Tullia? The generosity and the policy of Mecenas have been topics of praise; but do the amusements in which he engaged with his friends in the chapel that he had erected to a certain obscene deity, deserve commendation?

The last objects which employ the learning and the reflections of Mr. Hooke, are the rupture betwixt Antony and his competitor, the decisive battle of Actium, and the settlement of the empire on Octavius; and these he has explained and illustrated with his usual precision.

The

The moſt commendable circumſtance in the volume before us is the uſe that is made of Cicero's familiar letters, and of thoſe to Atticus. The materials derived from them are extracted and arranged with a ſpirit of ſyſtem which does honour to our Author. It is alſo to be obſerved, that, in this volume of his work, he has been careful to guard againſt the art with which Cæſar has written his Commentaries; and that in conſulting Appian and Dio Caſſius, he has had an eye to their prejudices, and to the times when they wrote.

In relation to his merit in general, he deſerves not, in our opinion, to be claſſed with the higheſt rank of hiſtorians. His judgment is better than his taſte, and his knowledge better than his judgment. Accuracy and preciſion in the detail of facts are his chief characteriſtics. We perceive in him the ſcrupulous exactneſs of a compiler, not the important views of a penetrating hiſtorian. His narration is ſufficiently clear and perſpicuous; but it is neither diverſified nor lively. Of the characters of his actors, his religious prejudices have not always allowed him to ſpeak with enlargement; and in the order and diſpoſal of the parts of his work, there is little art. With all its imperfections, however, his performance, we muſt remark, is the beſt Roman hiſtory, that has yet been offered to the public.

Art. II. *A new Introduction to the Study and Knowledge of the New Teſtament.* By E. Harwood, D. D. Vol. II. 8vo. 6 s. bound. Becket, &c. 1771.

WHEN Dr. Harwood publiſhed what he called a *liberal tranſlation* of the *New Teſtament*, he accompanied it with another volume, as an *introduction* to the ſtudy of that book, and promiſed ſtill farther to proſecute the ſame deſign; accordingly a ſecond part of this *introduction* is here offered to the public, in which the Author had at firſt imagined his purpoſe would have been completed; but, we are told, he has found the ſubject ſo complicated and extenſive, that he is obliged to defer to a *third* volume, the illuſtration of the ſtyle of the ſacred writers, the explanation of emphatical words and phraſes, parallel paſſages, and ſeveral other particulars, which will finiſh his primary intention.

The preſent publication contains an account of the cuſtoms and uſages of thoſe times mentioned or alluded to in the New Teſtament. Theſe have, indeed, been frequently noticed, and applied to elucidate ſeveral paſſages of the ſcriptures, by various authors; and will generally be found to have had ſome regard paid to them in our beſt commentaries. It will then hardly be expected, that many obſervations ſhould be met with that are entirely new, either to learned men, or to readers who are much converſant with expoſitions, or with other Engliſh works relative to ſacred literature. It is to be farther conſidered, that remarks of this nature are occaſionally ſcattered in ſuch a number of different volumes, on various ſubjects, that they are not often to be attained without difficulty; beſide which, moſt of our commentaries are too bulky for the generality of readers; and thoſe few which are more conciſe, cannot admit of many reflections of this kind. The collecting them, therefore, in a proper manner, and exhibiting them under one view, is a very uſeful labour, eſpecially when directed by an author who has that conſiderable acquaintance with ancient learning, writers, and cuſtoms, which Dr. Harwood evidently appears to have attained.

This volume conſiſts of twenty-five ſections; from a few of which we ſhall ſelect ſuch obſervations and paſſages as may convey ſome farther notion of the Writer's purpoſe, and of the manner in which it has been executed.

In the third ſection, which contains *alluſions in the New Teſtament to a Roman triumph*, it is obſerved, 'The ſecond paſſage, whoſe beautiful and ſtriking imagery is taken from a Roman triumph, occurs, 2 Cor. chap. ii. *Now thanks be unto God, who always cauſes us to triumph in Chriſt, and maketh manifeſt the ſavour of his knowledge by us in every place. For we are unto God a ſweet ſavour of Chriſt, in them that are ſaved, and in them that periſh: To the one we are a ſavour of death unto death; and to the other of life unto life.* In this paſſage, God Almighty, in very ſtriking ſentiment and language, is repreſented as *leading the apoſtles in triumph* * through the world, ſhewing them every where as the monuments of his grace and mercy, and by their means *diffuſing* in every place the odour of the knowledge of God——in reference to a triumph, when all the temples were filled with fragrance, and the whole air breathed perfume:—And the apoſtle continuing the alluſion, adds, That this odour would prove the means of the *ſalvation* of ſome, and *deſtruction* of others.—as in a triumph, after the pomp and proceſſion was *concluded*, ſome of the captives were *put to death*, others *ſaved alive*.'

In the next ſection, which mentions ſome images ſuppoſed to be borrowed from the theatre, the words of St. Paul, 1 Cor. vii. 31. *The faſhion of this world paſſeth away*, are in this view particularly noticed, as in the theatre the ſcenery is frequently ſhifting, ſuddenly changed, and exhibiteth an appearance to-

* Θριαμβευοντι ημας, *cauſeth us to triumph*, rather, *leadeth us about in triumph*. Εθριαμβευθη και ανηρεθη. He was *led in triumph* and then put to death. *Appian*. p. 403. *Amſl*. 1670.

tally

tally different. But ſome learned writers have rather thought this paſſage to be an alluſion to the *pageants* in a public proceſſion, which were gaudily adorned, continually in motion, and preſently diſappeared. Either illuſtration ſeems to have great propriety, elegance and ſtrength.

In this ſame ſection, for elucidating a very ſtriking paſſage in 1 Cor. ch. iv. ver. 9. it is obſerved, as has been alſo done by others, ' that in the Roman amphitheatre, the *Beſtiarii*, who in the *morning* combated with wild beaſts, had armour with which to defend themſelves, and to annoy and ſlay their antagoniſt. But the LAST who were brought upon the ſtage, which was about noon, were a miſerable number, quite naked, without any weapons to aſſail their adverſary—with immediate and inevitable death before them in all its horrors, and deſtined to be mangled and butchered in the direſt manner. In alluſion to this cuſtom, with what ſublimity and energy are the apoſtles repreſented to *be brought out* LAST *upon the ſtage*, as being devoted to *certain* death, and *being made a* PUBLIC SPECTACLE *to the world, to angels and men*.'

On comparing what is ſaid by this ingenious writer in the ninth ſection, which treats concerning the *domeſtic cuſtoms of the Jews*, with what he adds in the fourteenth, the ſubject of which is *their oratories*, we apprehend there is a *ſeeming* inconſiſtence. In the former, he obſerves, ' The Jews had no manufactures and no fleet, and they maintained no commercial intercourſe with foreign climes. Judæa flouriſhed only in the peaceful arts of agriculture, and its riches principally conſiſted in corn and paſture.' In the other ſection, when ſpeaking of the *proſeuchæ*, or oratories, which were common in Judæa, it is added,—' They abounded in Alexandria, which was then a very large and populous city, flouriſhing in learning and commerce, and inhabited by vaſt numbers of Jews. There being in theſe times an univerſal toleration of all religions, we find this people, ever addicted to traffic, migrating to the utmoſt boundaries of the Roman empire, diſdaining no employment, however ſordid or deſpicable, from which the moſt trifling and miſerable lucre might accrue,—forming themſelves into little communities, and ſettled in all the conſiderable places of the known world. The calamities of their country have *now* diſperſed them into all nations. But in the *Auguſtan* age we find Jews in very conſiderable numbers in all the eminent and flouriſhing towns and cities throughout the Roman dominions.'

Each of theſe accounts may be true, though to a common reader they may appear to be ſomewhat contradictory; and certainly they might have been expreſſed with greater exactneſs. The Jews, as to the larger part of the people, in our Saviour's time, may be ſuppoſed to have been in great meaſure confined

4 to

to the arts of agriculture; but numbers of them, no doubt, had also intercourse and commerce with other nations, and the natives of different countries often appeared on such accounts among this people, many of whom also frequently visited various parts of the earth.

The tenth section gives an account of Jewish weddings, in which the parable of the *marriage-feast* naturally falls under observation; and here, we apprehend, our Author seems rather to infer the use of some particular customs, on these occasions, from the parable, than to illustrate the parable, as might have been wished, by proving that these usages were according to the manners of those times. *From* this parable, he observes, we learn, that all the guests were expected to be dressed in a manner suitable to the splendour of such an occasion; and that before the guests were admitted into the hall where the entertainment was served up, they were taken into an apartment and viewed, that it might be known if any stranger had intruded, or if any of the company were apparelled in raiment unsuitable to the genial solemnity they were going to celebrate. From the knowledge of these customs, it is added, that some passages in the parable receive great light. But we could have wished that he had produced some other authorities by which it might appear that such forms were generally regarded at these times.

There is a difficulty attending this allegory, which Dr. Harwood has not attempted to remove. It was undoubtedly customary for persons at these festivals to appear in a sumptuous dress, but how could it be expected that travellers, pressed into the entertainment, as those were who are here mentioned, should be provided with it?

Other writers have attended to this question, and have concluded that the persons who were called together at such times, were often furnished with suitable dresses from the wardrobe of the master of the feast, and that a robe had been offered to the guest, against whom so great resentment is expressed in the parable, in which he had refused to appear. Among others Dr. Macknight, who is referred to by our Author in this place, has noticed this difficulty, supposing particularly that it was a frequent practice at such public festivals to furnish some of the guests with a change of raiment; and he has produced some instances from ancient writers which favour such a supposition. It is rather remarkable that Dr. Harwood should not have added some observations of this kind, especially as in another part of the work he mentions the large wardrobes which in distant ages were often collected by the great: 'We find, says he, the illustrious and opulent among the ancients were employed not merely in accumulating *gold* and *silver*, but in amassing a prodigious number of sumptuous and magnificent *habits*, which they regarded

regarded as a neceſſary and indiſpenſable part of their *treaſures.*—Hence in the detail of a great man's wealth, the numerous and ſuperb ſuits of apparel he poſſeſſed, never fail to be recorded. *Garments* are generally mentioned along with *gold* and *ſilver*, being *then* eſteemed to be as eſſential in the *diſplay*, and in the *idea* of opulence, as we now deem a ſplendid *equipage* and coſtly *furniture.*' After producing inſtances of this kind, he adds,—' In alluſion to this, our Lord, when deſcribing the ſhort duration and periſhing nature of terreſtrial *treaſures*, repreſents them as ſubject to *moth.*—So alſo St. Paul : I have coveted no man's *gold* or *ſilver*, or *apparel.* St. James, likewiſe, juſt in the ſame manner as the *Greek* and *Roman* writers, when they are particularizing the opulence of thoſe times, joineth *gold*, *ſilver* and *garments*, as the conſtituents of riches.'

We ſhall cloſe this article by preſenting here ſome extracts upon different ſubjects, which may entertain, and perhaps inform, ſeveral of our readers.

In one part of the eighteenth ſection, which conſiders *manufactures*, *ſciences*, *arts*, &c. alluded to in the New Teſtament, among other things is the following remark concerning the Temple of Diana at Epheſus.

' It is well known that this Temple was one of the moſt ſuperb and magnificent edifices which hiſtory hath tranſmitted to us. On account of the grandeur and ſtatelineſs of the pile, and the decorations and ornaments which diſtinguiſhed it, it was reputed one of the ſeven wonders of the world. Antient authors are laviſh in their deſcriptions of the grandeur and majeſty of this wonderful ſtructure, and make us form the moſt exalted ideas of it. I mention this in order to acquaint the reader in what the occupation of *Demetrius*, and of the artiſts whom he employed, conſiſted, from which the ſacred writer informs us *no ſmall gain* accrued to them. Our verſion ſays, *Demetrius was a ſilverſmith, who made ſilver ſhrines for Diana.* This interpretation ſeems to be inaccurate. No clear ideas can be collected, from it. The original is, *who made temples of Diana in ſilver*, which informs us what his employment was. He caſt little ſilver models in miniature of the temple of Diana. From this ingenious art, in which he employed a number of hands, great advantages were derived. As Diana was a goddeſs, *whom all Aſia and the world worſhipped*, as Demetrius told his manufacturers, theſe ſilver miniature temples would have a very rapid and extenſive ſale. The mention of ſuch temples in miniature frequently occurs. Sometimes they were made of *gold.* They were greatly honoured by the *ancients.* In the ſame ingenious occupation with *Demetrius and his craftſmen* are many of the *Latin*, *Greek* and *Armenian* monks in the holy land now engaged. They make very beautiful models in miniature

of

of the church of the holy ſepulchre at Jeruſalem. I have ſeen a very ſuperb and elegant one, inlaid with mother of pearl, a very valuable preſent, if I miſtake not, from a lady, to the academy in which I was educated.'

In the ſame ſection we have the following remarks: 'In military expeditions, a number of perſons who precede the army, are employed in *levelling* the road, filling cavities, removing obſtructions, making the irregular path direct, and the rugged ſmooth. Joſephus giving an account of the incurſion of the army under Veſpaſian into Galilee, deſcribes the uſual manner in which the Romans conducted their marches.—A body of light-armed auxiliaries and archers advanced before the army.—Theſe were followed by a company of heavy-armed Roman troops.—After theſe marched ten men drawn out of every *hundredth*, carrying their baggage, &c.—After theſe the *pioneers*, whoſe buſineſs it was to make the *irregular road direct*, to level what was rough and rugged, and to cut down any woods that interpoſed, that the army might not be obſtructed and moleſted in their march *. So did *Xerxes* in his oſtentatious expedition into *Greece*. He levelled mountains, ſays the hiſtorian, and made an equality of ſurface over the deep and rugged vallies †. To this employment of *pioneers*, who *preceded armies* and facilitated their march, there is a beautiful alluſion in ſcripture. *John* the *Baptiſt* was raiſed up by providence to be the *harbinger* of the Meſſiah, to anounce his advent, and to prepare the Jews for the worthy and virtuous reception of him. How ſtriking, therefore, is the imagery, when conſidered in this light, and how ſingularly happy and emphatical that figurative language, in which his office, as the *precurſor* of the *approaching* Meſſiah, is deſcribed. O! *prepare* the way of the *Lord*, make his paths *ſtraight!* Every *valley* ſhall be *filled:* every *mountain* and *hill* ſhall be *brought low:* the *crooked* ſhall be made *ſtraight:* and the *rough* ways ſhall be made *ſmooth.*'

From this ſection alſo we will extract the following paſſages:

'St. James, deſcribing the infinite beneficence and immutability of God, ſays, *That every good and every perfect gift is from above, and cometh down from the father of lights, with whom is no variableneſs, neither ſhadow of turning.* James i. 17. In this paſſage are ſeveral aſtronomical terms. God is repreſented as the *father of lights*, in alluſion to the glorious lamp of day, the ſource of light to the whole ſolar ſyſtem. The word παραλλαγη, or *parallax*, is not here employed in that acceptation in which *modern* aſtronomers uſe it,—but denotes the continually *mutable*

* Joſeph. Bel. Jud. lib. 3. c. 6. p. 229. *Havercamp.*

† Juſtin. lib. 2. c. 10. p. 209. *Edit. Gronovii.*

and

and different situation in the heavens which the sun every day apparently observes. In *opposition* to which, God the supreme source of light and love is described as subject to *no* variation, but *immutably* and unchangeably the same. By τροπη, *tropic*, at *one* of which the sun arrives on the *shortest*, at the *other* on the *longest* day, on his arrival at each, in his annual course, visibly *turning back*, as the word imports, the Apostle denotes that the divinity is not liable to any such mutation and variableness as affecteth this luminary. And as it is well known the inhabitants of the earth were by the *ancient* geographers distinguished into the *Ascii*, *Amphiscii*, *Heteroscii*, denominations which arose from the *shadow*, at noon, in *various* climates, having *various* directions and falling different ways, the Apostle by employing the technical term αποσκιάσμα, by which this variety of shadow was denoted by geographers and astronomers, intended to indicate to his readers that the pure and ineffable glory of the Almighty is not subject to any such *shade* or obscurity, to any the least darkness or diminution.'

'The Apostle James holds up to every christian a faithful and useful mirrour, in which he may see the detestable form and features of slander and defamation. In that description, which can never sufficiently be admired, he draws a just and striking portrait of the heinous wickedness and innumerable evils of that garrulity and diabolical inclination to asperse and traduce characters, which men are so prone to indulge and gratify. He expatiates on the fatal and extensive mischiefs which *that little member the tongue* scattereth in society. The tongue was a WORLD *of iniquity* in miniature—it was a *fire*, and this fire was first lighted from infernal flames. *It is set on fire of hell.* The poison of asps was under it—and though so little and inconsiderable, it was replete with aconite that infested and *defiled the whole body.* Among other particulars he saith, *That it setteth on fire the course of nature.* The *original* is very beautiful, and is a very elegant allusion to a *wheel* catching fire, as not infrequently happeneth, by its rapid motion, spreading its flames around, and at last involving the whole *machine* in fatal destruction. The true version of the passage is this. *It setteth on fire the* * WHEEL *of human life*, and thus finally destroyeth the *whole body.*'

'— It is an excellent and judicious remark of *Cornelius Nepos* in the *preface* of his history, where speaking of the dissimilitude of *Grecian* and *Roman* manners, he observes, That different modes and usages obtain among different nations: that what is deemed in one country a *polite* and *useful* accomplish-

* *James* iii. 6. Φλογιζουσα τον τροχον της γενεσεως. Τροχος signifies a *wheel.*

ment,

ment, is in another reputed *disgraceful* and *dishonourable*, and that it betrays great ignorance in any one to treat with ridicule and contempt any modes and customs, because not consonant to the manners of the country in which he was educated. With what scorn and petulance have some puny infidels affected to deride our Saviour's *riding on an ass*, and amidst the shouts and acclamations of an immense multitude of people, who spread their garments in the road, and pierced the air with crying and repeating *Hosannah!*——advancing toward the capital in this triumphal procession——and entering the metropolis, mounted on so contemptible an animal. It is only proclaiming our own egregious folly and ignorance to pronounce every thing *reputable* or *disreputable* by the standard of our own national manners. In *eastern* countries this usage *now* obtains, and is not accounted dishonourable, or in any respect degrading. This circumstance which in *European* manners, and ideas of decorum, is the last disgrace, is *there* esteemed to be no discredit to authority and greatness. Persons of distinction and character are thus accommodated. All books of *modern* travels into the *east* are replete with instances. These *recent* accounts corroborate what is related in the sacred records, and wipe away from the scriptural characters that *infamy* and *reproach*, which, from the most *minute* and trivial occurrences, infidelity would rejoice to infix on them. Thus in the song of *Deborah*, we read of persons who rode on white *asses*, *the governors of Israel, those who sat in judgment*. Thus also 2 Sam. xvi. 1, 2. And when David was a little past the top of the hill, behold Ziba the servant of Mephibosheth met him with a couple of *asses* saddled.—And the king said unto Ziba, what meanest thou by these? and Ziba said, The *asses* be for the *king's houshold* to ride on.'

In the twentieth section, the *forms of politeness and civility mentioned in the New Testament* are considered: and here it is remarked;

'—In all countries the modes of *address* and *politeness*, though the terms are expressive of the profoundest respect and homage, yet through constant use and frequency of repetition, soon degenerate into mere *verbal* forms and *words of course*, in which the *heart* hath no share. They are a frivolous unmeaning formulary, perpetually uttered without the mind's ever annexing any idea to them. To these *empty insignificant forms* which men *mechanically* repeat at *meeting* or *taking leave* of each other—there is a beautiful allusion in the following expression of our Lord in that consolatory discourse he delivered to his apostles when he saw them dejected, and disconsolate, on his plainly assuring them, that he would soon *leave* them and go to the Father. My *peace* I leave with you: my *peace* I give unto you:

you: *not as the world giveth* *, give I unto you. Since I must shortly be torn from you, I now bid you adieu, sincerely wishing you every happiness—not as the world giveth, give I unto you—not in the unmeaning ceremonial manner the world repeats *this* salutation; for my *wishes* of *peace* and *happiness* to you are *sincere*—and my *blessing* and *benediction* will derive upon you every *substantial* felicity.'

We shall only farther observe, that Dr. Harwood's collections and remarks are accompanied and supported by a variety of quotations and illustrations from ancient writers.

Art. III. *Institutes of Botany; containing accurate, compleat and easy Descriptions of all the known* Genera of Plants: translated from the Latin of the celebrated Charles Von Linne, professor of Medicine, &c. &c. To which are prefixed, 1. A View of the ancient and present state of Botany. 2. A Synopsis, exhibiting the essential or striking Characters which serve to discriminate Genera of the same Class and Order; as likewise the secondary Characters of each Genus, &c. By Colin Milne, Reader on Botany in London, Author of the Botanical Dictionary. 4to. 6 s. Boards. Griffin, &c. 1771.

NO enquiries seem more congenial to the nature of man, than those which relate to husbandry, gardening, botany and others of a similar kind: they are innocent in themselves; they are also instructive and improving to the mind, and if properly directed may be greatly beneficial to society. The subjects of botany are so exceeding numerous and various, that though mankind could not avoid paying a considerable attention to this science in all ages of the world, it was nevertheless involved in great irregularity and confusion. It has been found almost incredibly difficult to reduce so complex a branch of knowledge to some order, and fix it on such a methodical arrangement as might be intelligible, exact and applicable to

---

* *John* xiv. 27. *Peace* I leave with you; my *peace* I give unto you; not as the world giveth, give I unto you: let not your heart be *troubled*, neither let it be *afraid*. The words of the philosopher are an excellent and striking paraphrase on this passage of scripture. Ορατε γαρ ὅτι ειρηνην μεγαλην ὁ Καισαρ. κ. λ. You see what a great and extensive peace the emperor can give the world: since there are *now* no wars, no battles, no association of robbers or pirates, but one may in safety, at any time of the year, *travel* or sail from east to west. But can the Emperor give us *peace* from a fever, from shipwreck, from fire, from an earthquake, or from thunder? Can he from love? He cannot! from sorrow? No! from envy? No! from none of these things! The principles only of Philosophy promise and are able to secure us *peace* from all these evils. *Arriani Dissert. Epist. lib.* 3. p. 411. *Edit. Upton.* 1741.

general

general advantage. Some attempts have been made in former times to effect this purpose; in later years it has been pursued with great diligence; and botany is now brought into the form of a regular study; particularly under the direction of the celebrated Swedish professor.

It is remarkable, if it is fact, as there appears some reason to believe, that while such considerable improvements have been made in natural history, and several methods invented to facilitate enquiries into the distinct properties and uses of plants and herbs, yet at the same time, the knowledge of this kind, among the generality of people, has greatly declined: it has been usual, formerly, for heads of families, and others, to be acquainted with the remedies which nature furnishes near at hand, and to apply them in some proper manner for common diseases and accidents; but now it is become almost universally necessary in these cases to have recourse, (often with great expence, and at considerable difficulty and hazard) to those who are supposed to be regularly qualified to give the suitable assistance. It is indeed objected, that in the former method, the detriment was nearly equal to the benefit; and upon this supposition, the practice has been condemned; but the argument has prevailed too far, and mankind, ever prone to run into extremes, have almost laid aside, as to general use, their endeavours to preserve or gain that degree of knowledge in this particular branch which might be easily attained, and prove very serviceable, at the same time that they are quite ignorant of any scientific system: for though some mistakes no doubt were made, yet it is most certain they were very often successful; nor can we suppose a more regular assistance to be entirely free from failures and errors. As forms of government in state and church, however well planned and intended, may have some tendency to what is arbitrary and oppressive, and therefore require a watchful guard; so it has fared with systems of botany and medicine; they have formed a kind of monopoly, taking out of the hands of the people the means of helping themselves, and suppressing a proper inclination to, and care about it. But as it would be very weak to conclude in the former instance, that therefore forms of government are not absolutely necessary to the well-being of mankind, so would it be to imagine that the latter are not very important both in the view of entertainment and utility.

The present undertaking is truly commendable and valuable, as we have no reason to doubt of Mr. Milne's ability and disposition to perform the work to the best advantage. It is somewhat surprizing, that in an age so distinguished as the present for improving natural knowledge, a translation of the GENERA PLANTARUM, notwithstanding the great reputation of its ingenious

genious Author has not hitherto been attempted in our own language, nor, we are told, in any other. For though to the learned and classical reader, every purpose of information for which it was intended may be answered in its original form, yet to the illiterate and unclassical, (who, by the way, observes our Author, constitute the bulk of those whom inclination or chance have directed to the study of plants) *that form* proves an unsurmountable obstacle. It deserves likewise to be mentioned, that many ladies who would apply with indefatigable attention to the science of plants, are denied the pleasure resulting from such a study, for want of proper assistance in a language which they understand. For these reasons the translator thought that an English version of the *Genera* would prove acceptable to the public. To render which, in some measure, more compleat, he has presented the Reader with a prefatory *view of the ancient* and *present state of botany*, including a particular analysis and illustration of every plan of arrangement which has appeared since the origin of the science. It is this essay which employs the volume now before us, and only a part of that is now delivered, in four sections, two others being reserved for a farther publication.

The first section has this title, *characteristical distinctions of the three kingdoms of nature:* the subject of the second is, *the extent of botany, its advantages, and the obstacles that have retarded its progress*. Here the utility of botany falls under consideration. After the general and obvious reflection, that an acquaintance with nature 'furnishes one of the strongest arguments for the existence of a supreme intelligent being,' and leads us to meditate upon and adore his perfections; which is certainly a sufficient proof of the importance of such enquiries; Mr. Milne proceeds to a farther view of the benefit which the study of botany may yield to mankind; concerning which, we find the following remarks:—' A distinctive knowledge of the several orders of plants,—the most intimate acquaintance with the various resemblances and contrasts upon which those orders are founded, are of little importance considered by themselves. A man possessed of such knowledge, without applying it to any useful purpose, has, indeed, spent a great deal of time ingeniously upon trifles, which might have been more honourably devoted to the good of society, and the exertion of genius.—With propriety, therefore, is botany divided into two great parts; the first, respecting the knowledge of the several parts of vegetables, and their various assemblages, as connected by resemblance, or distinguished by contrast; the second unfolding their properties, virtues and medicinal powers. The relation between these parts is mutual and dependent.—The reality of this mutual dependence betwixt the two grand objects of botanical knowledge may be inferred from the want of success which has accompanied every attempt to disunite parts so closely connected. The ancient botanists, particularly Aristotle, seem to have paid very little attention to the resemblances on which a distinctive knowledge of plants is founded; their aim was, to possess themselves of the useful part of the science, without encountering its difficulties. The event, however, has shewn, that they were egregiously mistaken; and that, by endeavouring to ascertain the powers of vegetables, without a previous knowledge of vegetable arrangement, they, in effect, laboured to attain an end, without using the proper means to accomplish it.'

'Sensible of the inconveniencies to which this error had subjected the several departments in natural history, the moderns have bestowed their attention principally on description, and systematic arrangement; and, from an excess of refinement, too common in modern times, have hurried into an error of much worse tendency than that which they laboured to avoid. A nice and scrupulous attention to the minutiæ of science is the characteristic distinction of the present age; and in no science is this minutely discriminating spirit so conspicuous, or so detrimental, as in botany. Not that to discover resemblances, even the most trifling, is in itself hurtful to science:—but it is to be feared, that, in proportion as these minute resemblances engross the attention, we shall lose sight of the great object of our pursuit; and, involved in fancy and chimæra, stop short at the means, without having either inclination or ability to attain the end. In fine, we shall rest in a bare knowledge of vegetable productions, without applying it to those purposes which alone determine its utility.—But from all this it were quite unphilosophical to conclude that natural history in general, or botany in particular, is an useless study. The very best things are liable to be abused. But is such an abuse to be employed as a solid argument of their futility or uselessness? By no means. The same science which has been disgraced by a butterfly-catcher, or a hunter after cockle-shells, is immortalized by the labours of a Bacon, a Boyle, and a Linnæus.'

In the remaining part of this section, the botanist is informed of the apparatus with which he ought to be furnished for the more easy and accurate examination of plants; which leads him to speak of the language, or scientific terms, particularly as new-modelled by Linnæus. 'These terms, says he, by reason of their number, and the great confusion that obtains among them, give no small discouragement to the beginning botanist. In a science of such minute investigation as botany, and where the subjects to be examined are so remarkably similar,

milar, the necessity of the utmost precision is obvious. Till very lately, however, the nomenclature of this science was exceedingly defective in this respect. Linnæus has totally reformed the language of botany, and indeed, in great measure, introduced a new language into the science. The Linnæan terms, notwithstanding, are far from being unexceptionable. Of Greek original, they cast an air of obscurity, and even mystery, over a science, which, of itself, is simple and perspicuous. Many of them are totally unclassical; few convey the meaning readily; not to mention the great number of synonimous terms, than which there can be no greater imperfection in scientific language. The source of this error is to be traced in the bad arrangement of the terms themselves.'

In the third section, *natural and artificial methods* are *distinguished*; and the fourth, which constitutes the greater part of this volume, considers, *the progress of method and systematic arrangement, from its simplest rudiments in botanical writings.* Mr. Milne regards what he terms the historical æra as opening with Theophrastus, styled the father of botany. 'The greatest part, says he, of Aristotle's two books on plants has perished in the general wreck of time; and the little that has escaped its undistinguishing fury, has been so mangled and torn by the unskilful, under the specious pretext of supplying its defects, that we have only to lament that the original work was not either totally preserved, or totally lost.' Theophrastus is known to have been the disciple of Aristotle, and flourished in the third century before the christian æra: His history of plants, is executed, this Author observes, in a truly philosophical manner.—It originally consisted of ten books, one of which is lost. In the remaining nine, vegetables are distributed into seven classes or primary divisions, which have for their object the generation of plants, their place of growth, their size as trees and shrubs; their use as pot-herbs and esculent grains; and their lactescence; which last circumstance respects every kind of liquor, of whatever colour, that flows in a great abundance from plants, when cut.—The diction is remarkably elegant, and withal so perspicuous and easy, that a strict perusal of the original cannot be too warmly recommended to botanists who have studied the Greek language; I say, the original, because there are many inaccuracies and errors in the best translations, owing to an ignorance in the translator of the terms of botany.' Dioscorides is next mentioned in the list, concerning whom we have these particulars, among others, 'That the science was still in its infancy, appears from this remarkable circumstance, that, although near four hundred years posterior to Theophrastus, and professedly a collector, Dioscorides has not been able to enumerate above six hundred plants,

 five

five hundred of which were described or mentioned by the father of botany.—His style is simple, plain, and devoid of ornament. The descriptions, nevertheless, although imperfect, are preferable to those of the other, because the characters which they collect are more numerous and invariable. Plants were arranged by this Author, into four classes, which are thus designed; aromatics, alimentary vegetables, or such as serve for food; medicinal, and vinous plants.' Pliny the elder is thought scarcely to merit a place in the Review here intended: However it is observed, that 'the botanical part of his voluminous undertaking is included in fifteen books, which besides the plants of Theophrastus and Dioscorides, contain descriptions of several new species, extracted, in all probability, from works which would have been totally lost, but for the laudable industry of this indefatigable compiler:—it gives descriptions or names of upwards of a thousand species of plants: so that about four hundred species are mentioned by Pliny, which are not to be found in the writings of Dioscorides; an increase which seems amazing, when it is considered, that the interval betwixt the Greek and the Roman could not have exceeded thirty years.' Several other writers are mentioned, till the time of "Ætius Amydenus, Paulus Ægineta, and Alexander Trallian: the two first compilers; the latter a man of a more free and liberal turn; but the science was in disrepute, and not even a Trallian could revive its drooping head. The limited botany of the ancients, adds Mr. Milne, and its rapid decline from the time of Pliny to that of the authors just mentioned, can only be attributed to a neglect of systematic arrangement, which, in facilitating the knowledge of plants, prepares for an investigation of their powers and virtues. It was not till near the close of the eighth century, that the cimmerian darkness which had diffused itself over this science began to dissipate, and botany, as well as the other departments of natural knowledge, reassumed its pristine form. The scene of this first restoration of the ancient botany, lies in Arabia.—On the revival of letters in the beginning of the sixteenth century, the botany of the ancients was restored a second time.—Hieronymus Bock, or Bouc, a German, is the first of the moderns who has given a *methodical distribution* of vegetables. In his history of plants, published in 1532, he divides the 800 species there described into three classes, founded on the qualities of vegetables, their habit, figure and size.—In 1560, Conrad Gesner, who imbibed his knowledge in the mountains of Switzerland, turned his eye to the flower and fruit, and suggested the first idea of a *systematic arrangement.*' The Author distinctly unfolds, and remarks upon, the different schemes; and here ends, with Conrad Gesner, what he terms the *historical*

 æra,

æra, which name he assigns to the above period, because, 'arrangement, we are told, lay either totally neglected, or founded upon insufficient principles,—and the knowledge which was inculcated, being confined to the names, number and virtues of plants, was, professedly of the historical kind.' Though Gesner had suggested the idea of an arrangement from the parts of the flower and fruit, he established no plan upon this principle, he left the application to be made by others; 'and it was not, adds Mr. Milne, 'till 1583, that Dr. Andrew Cæsalpinus, a physician of Pisa, and afterwards professor of botany at Padua; availing himself of the ingenuity of his predecessor, proposed a method which has the fruit for its basis; and thus gave origin to systematic botany, the second grand æra of the history of the science.' Here therefore we are presented with an explication of and remarks upon the scheme of Cæsalpinus, and of various other writers who followed and improved upon his plan, or struck out into different ones:—but for more particulars we must refer our Readers to the book itself.

ART. IV. *The Philosopher, in three Conversations.* Part III. Dedicated to the Bishop of Gloucester. Small 8vo. 1 s. 6 d. Becket. 1771.

OF the first part of these Dialogues we gave some account in the Review for January; the second, which did not afford us equal satisfaction, was mentioned in June. The argument of the piece before us is the old subject, of a coalition between the church of England and the Dissenters, by means of mutual concessions; an event which, (however desirable for the sake of uniformity in religious worship, and its consequent advantage, the promotion of cordiality in the communion of civil life) we may venture to say, without affecting the spirit of prophecy, will hardly ever come to pass: unless, indeed, what happens in the natural course of things, both with respect to religious and political divisions, that the weakness of one party suffers it to be insensibly drawn into the vortex of the other. But this is not likely to be the case for many centuries to come.

This Philosopher has, therefore, in all appearance written his colloquial essay to as little purpose as he has dedicated it. The spirit and temper of his dedication we cannot but condemn. He calls upon the Bishop of Gloucester to assist in the great work of the coalition, and at the same time treats him with the most sarcastic severity. If he was serious in his invitation, he took the most effectual method to render it vain. If he was *not*, it was, on so serious a subject, an ill placed mockery. He says that he pitied the Bishop, whilst he was under the vigorous stroke of Churchill; but who knows not that Churchill's satire on the prelate was the lowest and vilest ribaldry? And that it excited emotions very different from pity both in those who had, and in those who had not a regard for the learned Bishop.

The interlocutors in this dialogue are a Philosopher, a Courtier, a Whig, a Clergyman of the established Church, and a Presbyterian Minister. After some indecisive discourse on the connection between the civil and ecclesiastical establishments, the conversation turns on the popular topic of subscriptions to the articles, &c. 'The evil of creeds and of articles, says the Philosopher, have at this time the worst effect upon the principles and morals of the country.

'*Clergyman.* You know, no man is enjoined to believe them; that belief is made only the condition of certain advantages: if any man will sacrifice his integrity to the prospect of them, the fault is in the man, and not in the articles and creeds.

'*Philosopher.* I do not pretend to excuse the man who will act so dishonest a part; and I blame the creeds only, as they furnish a temptation which some men, of integrity in every other case, have not been able to resist. When a man has spent the early and best part of his time in an education which will suit only the profession of a clergyman, he has the alternative, to starve, or to violate his honour. When he has taken one step out of the way, and has involved himself in the connections and cares of a family, if a provision offers; I do not wonder that he proceeds; I greatly pity the man, and am tempted to curse the institution that makes it almost necessary that he should lose his peace to obtain his subsistence.

'*Courtier.* I believe you need be under no such concern. The gentlemen of that order are as easy about subscriptions, as if they thoroughly understood, and believed every thing enjoined them. In the university, they are accustomed betimes to take oaths, and write their names to, they know not what; and it is an easy step to what they do not believe.

'*Philosopher.* Supposing what you have said to be true, I rather pity than censure the candidates: but I can hardly think, with patience, of the institutions under which they are educated. It is a maxim in morality, that the mind of a young person will take almost any direction you may chuse to give it. Persons have been led by education, to think vice virtue, and virtue vice, in many material instances. It is not strange, therefore, that in a gay and thoughtless time of life, they should be led to suppress their curiosity, and do, they know not what, to be entitled to a subsistence or to affluence.

'*Whig.* What think you of the fashionable principle of submitting to the tenets and creeds of a church, as articles of peace?

'*Philosopher.* Consult your Bible; consult any moral writings; consult even plays and farces, and, if you find such a conduct countenanced, I will never say a word more against the church, I will swear and subscribe to any thing, and turn clergyman myself. All the sophistry of a fallen angel, will not reconcile to honesty and honour, your, the conduct of a man who swears and subscribes to what he does not believe.

'*Clergyman.* I cannot suffer several of my friends, whom I know to be men of honour and integrity, to lie under the imputation which is couched in your last words. They say, that some of the doctrines to which they subscribe, cannot be understood; and others, they do not believe. These things are known. The governors of the church require them outwardly to subscribe to its institutions; and they do so for form, and are often understood so to do; they are not guilty of any fraud, or any concealed dishonesty.

'*Philosopher.* Suppose I was to say, they are guilty of open dishonesty; how would you contradict me with any appearance of reason? Indeed, the more this matter is enquired into, the worse it appears: you had better therefore be content with what I had said, that it is a reproach to a religious establishment, that it leads many of its members out of the plain path of integrity and honour. In matters of conscience, there is never any difficulty; things instantly appear fit or unfit; and sophistry, and even reasoning, is seldom wanted to direct the moral conduct of an honest man. When I am required to do any thing *bona fide*, or *ex animo*, in order to obtain an advantage, and I do it only for form or for peace, I obtain the advantage, without fulfilling the condition. I may adduce circumstances that may palliate and excuse my conduct, but it will be judged morally wrong, as long as men retain their sense of good and evil.

'*Clergyman.* You seem to have had your mind prepossessed by the many virulent things which have been lately written against the church and the clergy.

'*Philosopher.* You are much mistaken I assure you. I have never read more than one book on the subject; and that, as a matter of curiosity, and in a cursory way. I see by the papers, that not only the Dissenters keep up the bustle with you, but that they are aided by some of your own sons. I have not, as I told you, read any of the controversy, ancient or modern; for I have observed, in other cases, that when divines are antagonists, they are more abusive than other men, and draw out their disputes to such a length, that hardly any patience can bear them. Perhaps your suspicion arose from the similarity of my sentiments to some of those which have been lately advanced. If you have any opinion of my judgment, this adds something to their authority.

'*Clergyman.* But give me leave to observe, that you, as well as the writers we now talk of, beg the question in this argument. You take for granted what you ought to prove, that the clergy do not believe the articles and creeds of the church.

'*Philosopher.* It is not said, I suppose, that all of them have departed from the original principles of the establishment; but it is known that many of them have. Their conversation, their preaching, their writings prove it beyond a doubt.

'*Clergyman.* In every profession there are, and ever will be, some who are not honest; but it is uncandid to condemn the whole for the faults of a part; much more is it to attribute those faults to institutions which give them no countenance.

'*Philosopher.* I am sorry to find you so much mistaken. I have not censured the order, in the present affair. I greatly esteem every honest clergyman, who has entered on his office with a clear conscience; who preaches and lives according to those institutions, to which he has vowed and sworn obedience, though his sentiments and mine may be as different as possible. I pity the man who taints his innocence to obtain orders; who has not the resolution to preserve it, and to submit to poverty, and to see his family want; but I cannot think his conduct morally honest.—I have said that the English church, at its institution, was the best that could well have been contrived: the fault I find with it, is, that it has not undergone alterations, even as the state has done; and is not suited to the principles of religion, morality, and policy, which now prevail among us.

'*Whig.* Your sentiments are very candid; and I think no man can be displeased at them.'——

'*Clergyman.* Would you have no subscription at all; and every man who chose it, suffered to undertake the office?

'*Philosopher.* If you could point out any service that subscription can be of, I would wish to have it required. I never could see any thing but mischief arise out of it.

'*Clergyman.* Men of the most profligate principles would then come in.

'*Philosopher.* And do articles shut them out? Are you freer from such men than the Dissenters, where the profession is open to any one who will undertake it, as long as his character is decent, and his capacity and abilities are such as qualify him for his office?

'*Clergyman.* But do not the Dissenters require subscription; or what is equivalent, a confession of faith?

'*Philosopher.* They have required it at what they call the ordination of the minister; and, I am told, the old priests among them are now unwilling to relinquish this apparent compliment to them, from young candidates. But a minister would not be set aside for not complying with this custom; and many have been actually ordained without it. However this may be, it cannot affect my opinion, that subscriptions, articles, and creeds, have done great mischief to religion, lessened the influence of the clergy, and injured the principles and morals of the people.'

We apprehend there are few of the more liberal part, even of Churchmen, who will not conclude with the Philosopher, that there are grievances, with respect to subscriptions, which ought to be removed: but we believe, too, there are few who will not smile to hear him impute the general prevalence of vice and immorality to subscriptions and the book of Common-Prayer. Let us hear the conversation on the latter.

'*Whig.* Take care what you say of the book of Common-Prayer. It is held sacred by the people; and the clergy extol it as the model of devotional composition.

'*Philosopher.* I do not wonder that the people hold it in great veneration. It was formed on a system which they have implicitly believed to be true; and it has a warmth and simplicity which engages

gages the affections. Its incoherence and tautologies are so far from offending them, that it favours that solicitation and importunity of which they are fond.

'*Clergyman.* I believe you are singular in your opinion that it is not a well-composed service. Persons of the best taste have admired the simplicity of its style, and the warmth of its devotion: every attempt to compose a better has failed: and the Dissenters, after all their complaints of the restraint it has laid on the improvement of devotional services, exhibit nothing in theirs to be compared to it.

'*Philosopher.* I am one of the persons who admire the style and devotion of the Common-Prayer, in many parts: but I think that many of the principles which run through it are so generally disbelieved; there is so much confusion from having several services jumbled into one; and so many obsolete, low and indecent expressions, that it greatly wants revisal:

Non equidem insector, delendave carmina Livi
Esse reor;———
——— *Sed emendata videri,*
Pulchraque, & exactis minimum distantia miror.

'*Clergyman.* Well, Sir, as you treat us so candidly as well as freely, I should do wrong in not confessing, that many of the most learned and sensible of our clergy, are much of your opinion. But what are we to do?—To undertake an alteration would be too daring; and in the opinion of many, would be attended with danger; for it would be encountering prejudices which are deeply rooted; and by changing and modernizing what the people have so great a veneration for, we should destroy their regard for public worship.

'*Philosopher.* I am quite of another opinion; and I have attended to the public disposition on this subject with as much care as most people. Some very considerable alterations in the Common-Prayer, would be so far from disagreeable, that it would please the people in general who think at all on subjects of devotion: those who do not, a few excepted, would look on any change with great indifference; and would go to church as they now do, because they are told it is one of the things they must do, in order to go to heaven.—Public worship is now much neglected by the middle rank of people, as well as by persons of fashion. They generally endeavour to imitate their superiors; they adopt their manners, and as much as possible the reasons on which they proceed; and it is now no strange thing to hear a man openly ridiculing many parts of those services which he sometimes attends. He is seldom so cautious as to refrain before his children or his servants, who eagerly catch at any thing like a reason against an attendance and a restraint which is seldom to their taste. In this manner an indifference, if not dislike to public worship is increasing its hurtful influence. This every good man acknowledges to be an evil. It would be so in a great degree, if it was considered only as a loss of that method of moral restraint and religious improvement which are so conducive to the welfare of every state. But there is another light in which it must be viewed; and which to me, I confess, has been often shocking. It is, among other things, at the bottom of that profaneness and irreligion which seem to distinguish our times.

'*Clergyman.*

'*Clergyman* Hold, hold, Sir;—what the book of Common Prayer, the cause of our profaneness?

'*Philosopher.* The faults which are suffered to disgrace it, are among its principal causes. People in general, high as well as low, attend only to that religion which is offered to them. If that is good, they are obliged to revere, however they may practise it. If that is not good, they seldom seek for any other; and they furnish themselves from it as much as possible with encouragements to the vices which they chuse to indulge. We see in fact, that when men leave off going to church, they soon drop all religious pretences; and even a regard to God, the great preservative of conscience and honour, is, in a little time, evidently lost. Who can estimate the mischiefs of such consequences?

'*Clergyman.* But if people disapprove of the liturgy, they are at liberty to have recourse to a better form of worship; and their not doing so, is a presumption that their objections are only pretences to cover a real infidelity.

'*Philosopher.* That does not fairly follow. If the state take upon it to provide a form of worship for the benefit of the public, and that form does not answer the end; what signifies saying, that the people are at liberty to provide for themselves? They reason probably in this manner:—"Here is a book of public service that has the sanction of the legislature and the apparent approbation of our spiritual and learned guides; we suppose it to be the best they can furnish on the subject of religious worship; the best is so bad, that we may almost as well not worship at all." Others perhaps may not reason in this manner, and may have a faint conception that a better form might be obtained; but they cannot tell how; and to desert the church appears to them a less evil than to assemble in opposition to it, with a service ever so much to their taste. You might, therefore, almost as well say, that if people do not like the laws, they may make better for themselves, as that if they do not like the liturgy they must procure a better: they in general conceive themselves to have as much power and right to do the one as the other.

'*Whig.* I fancy they cannot, as they see the Dissenters practising with impunity a method of worship very different from that of the church.

'*Philosopher.* I believe in general they have a notion of crime in dissenting. If not, the fashion would keep them nominally in the church.

'*Clergyman.* You seem to me to make the people ridiculous and important at the same time.

'*Philosopher.* That is not my intention. I ascribe the general disregard to public worship, in a great measure, to the imperfections in the public service. You may say that the people are to blame in suffering such reasons to have such a consequence: they are so. You may think that the best form would not have preserved the religion of such a people. I believe it would. While a man is not actually vicious, and is deliberating on the part he is to chuse, it is easy not only to keep him from vice but to lead him to goodness. The same people who are now irreligious and prophane, might have been religious and decent, if it had been the object of the legislature not only

only to preserve the public worship above contempt, but to improve it into a rational and sublime entertainment.

'*Clergyman.* I cannot help admitting the truth of many things you say; and yet I think you wrong in attributing the decline of religion so much to the inattention of our governors about the improvement of the public service.'

The Philosopher's observations on extemporaneous prayer are very masterly, just, and rational.

'*Presbyterian Minister.* We are certainly entitled to credit in our pretensions as well as other people. We find our devotion is excited and preserved by free prayer; and we join in the several parts with the readiest assent, and with great advantage.

'*Philosopher.* I do not dispute your credit, or the sincerity of your pretensions; but I cannot help thinking, however, that if your method was well calculated for the purposes of devotion, it would have succeeded in the hands of so many able men as you have had; and your numbers, instead of decreasing, would have increased; especially, as the service of the church is so imperfect, and so disagreeable to the principles and taste of the greater part of the people.

'*Presb. Min.* It has succeeded in the hands of many of our ministers; particularly in those of the late Dr. Foster. There are many now living who will declare, they never attended public worship with equal pleasure, as when he conducted it; nor have ever seen greater marks of public devotion.

'*Philosopher.* I fancy you will not find among those, any one who constantly attended his ministry. I am well informed that it was the complaint of those who did, that he varied so little in his prayers, that the first effects of them were lost, in a great measure, on those who were his constant hearers. At his lecture, or on his journeys, where his audiences were, for the most part, persons who had never, or but seldom heard him; a well-composed form as his was; committed to memory; and pronounced with the peculiar advantages of his voice and manner, must have had a great effect. But you see this case is not at all to your purpose. I therefore repeat my opinion, that your method is not well calculated for the purposes of devotion. When I have attended any of you, and have been pleased with the composition and piety of a good prayer; I cannot say that I felt in myself, or could observe in others, any symptoms of a social devotion. My feeling was generally that of admiration; sometimes that of private devotion. I could perceive a sensible difference between giving my heartiest assent to what you say, and the pleasure I had of offering up, as my own, and in union with others, the unexceptionable parts of the public service. I never, in your places, could well conceive myself as one of a multitude of my fellow-creatures, joining in a common action, and expressing, as from one heart, the noblest and most affecting sentiments. I am apt to think, Sir, if you were a hearer, you would be of my opinion. Ministers cannot easily change places with their people. You have a pleasure in expressing your own conceptions, which you cannot fully communicate to them; when a new thought occurs to you, and you form an unusual sentiment of the divine character, it may delight you; it may appear odd to them; they will certainly not have the pleasure

pleasure you have. When you plead, therefore, for free prayers, you consider only yourselves; for you only are free in them; you attend to the pleasures you feel, and some of you perhaps to the importance you are of, when you speak in your own words, and not in those of another. You forget that while you may be delighted, your poor people may be inattentive, looking about them for something to employ their thoughts, and wishing now and then you were come to the end of your service.

'*Presb. Min.* The force of your objection seems to lie against our prayers, as not being immediately offered up by the people; you say that therefore our congregations do not pray. Do those of the establishment pray any more than the Dissenters, except in the responses, which are only a small part of the service?

'*Philosopher.* They certainly do. The service is before them; by following the minister, they make every act of worship their own; which to my apprehension, is very different from giving the heartiest and readiest assent to prayers delivered without book.

'*Presb. Min.* Will you say, that pious affections may not be excited by an extempore prayer, well expressed, and properly delivered? If this be denied, it must be denied at the same time that the power of oratory is any thing; that a speech in the house of commons, or at the bar, never communicated to the audience the sentiments and affections intended to be communicated by the speaker; or that Mr. Garrick's power over you, depends upon your being perfect before-hand in the parts which he is to act.

'*Philosopher.* I never meant to say that pious affections may not be *excited* by extempore prayers; but that to have them excited by a minister, and to express them ourselves in conjunction with a congregation, are very different things. If this distinction were to appear of no great importance in itself, it would be otherwise, when it was considered that there are but few in any age, that can excite those affections in the common services of their whole lives, by free prayers; and that every congregation may express and exercise its devout affections for ever, in the use of a well composed liturgy. You see then I do not deny the power of oratory; I acknowledge it in the fullest manner; I acknowledge it in the influence of a good extempore prayer, under the advantages of novelty and a good delivery: but I maintain it is different from the effect of joining an assembly in an act of public worship: in the one case I am acted upon; in the other I act for myself. Mr. Garrick's powers I have felt in the highest degree; and the more for not knowing the part he was to act. But I did not make his sentiments my own; I very often entirely detested them. Or perhaps he raised in me, pity, terror, love, when I could see he felt himself none of those passions; he was distressed, or brave, or virtuous. Even in expressions of devotion, which I have seen in the highest perfection on the stage, I felt the powers of the actor, and the truth of the sentiments, exactly as I should those of a dissenting minister who had the same advantages:—this assent is certainly a kind of worship, but it is inferior greatly to that, in which we actually bear a part. If this be true, of free-prayer, under all its advantages; what shall we say of the state of public worship among you, when, to say the least, the ministers in general

general muſt be incapable of conducting it, ſo as to give it the effect it ought to have? Thoſe who are not looſe, deſultory, and indecent, are confined to one or more forms, which they have committed to memory, which they repeat as a ſchool-boy does his leſſon; and in that conſtrained manner, and unnatural tone, which they acquired under the difficulty of learning them. In ſhort, gentlemen, between the incoherences and improprieties of the liturgy, and the languid, unaffecting or ridiculous prayers of the Diſſenters, real devotion is almoſt baniſhed the land, and the principles and manners of the people are profligate to the higheſt degree. I do not mean that theſe are the only cauſes of our corruption, but they are very important and very ſhameful ones.'

Towards the concluſion of this work, the defects of the Preſbyterian worſhip are pointed out with great impartiality; the moral advantages of uniting in ſocial devotion are enlarged upon; and, on the whole, we recommend this converſation as manly, ſenſible, elegant, and candid.

ART. V. *Elements of the Hiſtory of England, from the Invaſion of the Romans to the Reign of George* II. Tranſlated from the French of Abbé Millot, Royal Profeſſor of Hiſtory in the Univerſity of Parma, and Member of the Academies of Lyons and Nancy, by Mr. Kenrick. 8vo. 2 Vols. 8s. Boards. Johnſon, &c. 1771.

ART. VI. *A Tranſlation of the ſame Work*, by Mrs. Brooke. 12mo. 4 Vols. 10s. ſewed. Dodſley, &c. 1771.

IT is a matter of curioſity to know the ſentiments of a learned foreigner on the important periods of our hiſtory; and, independent of the pleaſure reſulting from this circumſtance, in the preſent caſe, it muſt be obſerved, that Abbé Millot has executed his taſk with great accuracy and attention. The merit of his Tranſlators is different. Eaſe and freedom, and the dignity of hiſtorical narration have been aimed at by the one. The verſion of the other is faithful, but feeble, and too much in the ſtyle of converſation. A compariſon of the following extracts, with the correſponding paſſage of Millot, may entertain our Readers, and will fully enable them to decide for themſelves concerning the reſpective value of the preſent tranſlations.

Mr. Kenrick's tranſlation.

Of England, under the Romans.

'Great Britain was but little known before Cæſar undertook to conquer it. Till that period,

Mrs. Brooke's tranſlation.

England under the Romans.

'Great Britain was little known before Cæſar formed the deſign of ſubduing it. The only

L'Angleterre ſous les Romains.

'La Grande Bretagne etoit peu connue avant que Céſar entreprît de la ſubjuguer. Tout ce qu'on en ſait d'intéreſſant, c'eſt que les Bretons,

Mr. Kenrick.

period, we are informed of no circumstances more interesting concerning it, than that the Britains were of Gaulic or Celtic origin, that they enjoyed the advantages of a free government, and were remarkable for their ferocity and barbarism. Those of them, however, who inhabited the south-east parts of the island, had become acquainted with agriculture, and were advancing towards refinement. The other inhabitants maintained themselves by pasturage, removed perpetually their seats, and raised temporary huts in their forests and marshes. The Britains, addicted to war, and jealous to extreme of their liberty, were divided into small nations, under the government of kings, or rather of chieftains, who possessed a precarious authority. Their priests, whom they called Druids, enjoyed the greatest influence in their states. The ascendant they obtained, they had procured by the terrors of superstition. Exempted from taxes, and from military service, intrusted with the education of their youth, the arbiters of all con-

Mrs. Brocke.

only interesting circumstance known to us is, that the Britons, descended from the Gauls or Celtes, lived free in the most profound barbarism. Those who inhabited the country situated to the south east, already practising agriculture, were more disposed to civilization. The other inhabitants, ignorant of all but the care of their flocks, led a wandering life in the midst of their woods and marshes. This warlike nation, extremely jealous of its liberty, was divided into small communities, under kings, or rather chiefs, of a very limited authority. The priests called Druids presided in the government. They ruled the minds of men by the terrors of superstition. Exempt from taxes and military service, entrusted with the education of youth, arbiters of all disputes, judges of

Bretons, Gaulois ou Celtes d'origiue, vivoient en peuple libre dans une profonde barbarie. Ceux qui habitoient les pays situés au sud-est, pratiquant déja l'agriculture, avoient plus de disposition à être civilisés. Les autres ne connoissoient que leurs troupeaux, menoient une vie errante, se retiroient au fond des bois & des marécages. Cette nation guerriere, extrêmement jalouse de sa liberté, étoit divisée en petits peuples, sous des rois, ou plutôt sous des chefs dont l'autorité étoit fort restriente. Les prêtres, nommés Druides, présidoient au gouvernement. Ils dominoient sur les esprits par les terreurs de la superstition. Exempts de taxes & du service militaire, chargés de l'éducation de la jeunesse, arbitres de tous les differens, juges

Mr. Kenrick.

controversies, whether among states or individuals, the judges of all matters, whether civil or criminal, respected as oracles, and equally formidable to the people with their deities, they punished the refractory by an excommunication so terrible, that death, in the opinion of many, was preferable to the penalties it inflicted. Human sacrifices, and other barbarous rites, made a part of the religion they inculcated; and in the doctrine of the immortality of the soul, so necessary to inspire men with the love of virtue, and to deter them from the commission of crimes, they found a fruitful source of dominion. That the superstition of the Druids was of singular force, we may easily conceive, since the Romans employed against it the rigour of penal laws; a severity that infringed upon the general system of toleration, which they had adopted.

'It was the love of glory that impelled Cæsar to attempt the invasion of this unknown country. The conqueror of Gaul

Mrs. Brooke.

of all affairs, as well criminal as civil, respected as oracles, and feared almost equally with their gods, they punished the disobedient by a kind of anathema so terrible that death itself appeared often preferable to the consequences of this chastisement. Human sacrifices, and several barbarous superstitions, made part of their religious worship; and the doctrine of the soul's immortality, so necessary to inspire virtue, or deter from vice, was in their hands a powerful weapon to enforce submission to their orders. The religion of the Druids must have been very dangerous, since the Romans employed the rigour of penal laws against it, in spite of that system of toleration which they had till that time always followed.

'No motive but the desire of glory could have tempted Julius Cæsar to an invasion of this unknown country. The con-

juges de toutes les affaires tant criminelles que civiles, respectés comme des oracles, redoutés presque comme leurs Dieux, ils punissoient les réfractaires par une sorte d'anathême si terrible, que la mort même paroissoit souvent préférable aux suites de ce châtiment. Les sacrifices de sang humain & plusieurs superstitions barbares faisoient partie de leur culte; & le dogme de l'immortalité, si nécessaire pour inspirer la vertu ou pour éloigner du crime, étoit entre leurs mains une arme puissante pour soumettre tout à leurs ordres. Il falloit que la religion des Druides fût bien dangereuse, puisque les Romains employerent contre elle la rigueur des lois pénales, malgré le systême de tolérance qu'ils avoient toujours suivi jusqu'alors.

'Il n'y avoit qu'un motif de gloire qui pût faire tenter à Jules César une invasion dans cette contrée inconnue. Le vainqueur des Gaules

Mr. Kenrick.

Gaul must likewise subject Great Britain to his arms. He embarked for this island fifty-five years before the birth of Christ, and obliged the Britains to a promise of submission, which they violated the moment that his departure allowed them an opportunity to resume their courage. The year after his first invasion, he returned with a greater army, passed the Thames in the presence of the enemy, who were prepared to receive him, and exacted from them new acknowledgments of their inferiority and obedience; but his success was rather splendid than effectual. It was not till the reign of Claudius, that the Romans possessed any real dominion over the Britains. Two of the generals of this emperor obtained several victories over them, and he himself made a journey into Britain, to receive the homage of several states, who, having fixed possessions, and practising agriculture, were disposed to sacrifice their liberty to the advantages of peace. The Britains, mean while, were far from being reduced to subjection. Suetonius Paulinus,

Mrs. Brooke.

conqueror of the Gauls aspired to be also the conqueror of Great Britain. He landed there in the year fifty-five before Christ, and obliged the Britons to enter into engagements, which they broke as soon as his departure had restored their courage. He returned the following year, passed the Thames in their sight, and in appearance subdued them. But even to the reign of Claudius, the Roman dominion of Britain was little more than a name. Two generals of this emperor successively defeated them, and he came himself to receive the homage of those who, possessing and cultivating lands, with less reluctance sacrificed liberty to the advantages of peace. Suetonius Paulinus, general of Nero,

Gaules voulut être aussi le conquérant de la Grande Bretagne. Il y débarqua l'an 55 avant Jesus Christ, & força les Bretons à des promesses qu'ils violerent dès que son départ les eût rassurés. L'année suivante il retourna dans leur ile, passa la Tamise sous leurs yeux, & les soumit en apparence. Mais jusqu'au regne de Claude, la domination Romaine fut pour eux un nom sans effet. Deux géneraux de cet empereur les battirent successivement, & il alla lui-même recevoir l'hommage de ceux qui, possédant & cultivant des terres, devoient sacrifier plus aisément la liberté aux avantages de la paix. Cependant la nation n'étoit rien moins qu'asservie. Suétonius Paulinus,

Mr. Kenrick.

linus, under the reign of Nero, gave them a terrible blow, by attacking Mona, now Anglesey, the principal retreat of the Druids. He found the priests and the women, intermingled with the soldiers, in a situation to dispute his landing on this island. Their imprecations, however, their cries, and their savage gesticulations, obstructed not the progress of the Romans. They destroyed their altars and their consecrated groves; and, by a triumph over the superstition of the Britains, they thought to open the way to future conquests; but Suetonius had not removed to a great distance, before they returned to hostilities, under the conduct of Queen Boadicea, a heroine, whom the indignities offered to her person by the Romans had stimulated to revenge. London was then a considerable colony: she reduced it to ashes, and put the inhabitants to the sword. Seventy thousand persons are said to have perished in it. Suetonius, in his turn, gained a decisive

Mrs. Brooke.

ro, gave them a terrible blow by attacking the isle of Mona, now Anglesea, the principal retreat of the Druids. He found these priests, and even the women, intermixed with the soldiers, to resist him. Their cries, their savage leaps, their imprecations, did not deter the Romans from pursuing them. They destroyed the altars and consecrated groves: they hoped to secure their conquest by this triumph over the superstition of the barbarians. But the conqueror was no sooner at a distance than they took arms again under the conduct of their Queen Boadicea, a heroine who breathed nothing but vengeance. London was already a considerable colony: it was destroyed by fire and sword. Seventy thousand men were there cruelly massacred. Suetonius gained in

linus, général de Néron, lui porta un coup terrible, en attaquant l'île de Mona, aujourd'hui Anglesey, principale retraite des Druides. Il trouva ces prêtres & les femmes mêlés avec les soldats pour le repousser. Leurs cris, leurs sauts, leurs imprécations n'empêcherent pas les Romains de les poursuivre. On détruisit les autels & les bois sacrés: on crut assurer la conquête par ce triomphe sur la superstition des barbares. Mais le vainqueur ne fut pas plutôt éloigné, qu'ils reprirent les armes sous la conduite de la reine Boadicée, héroïne qui respiroit la vengeance. Londres étoit déja une colonie considérable: ils la mirent à feu & à sang. Soixante & dix mille hommes y furent massacrés cruellement. Suétonius remporta à son

tour

Mr. Kenrick.

cisive victory; and Boadicea, that she might not fall into his hands, put an end to her life.

'The glory of subduing the Britains was reserved to Julius Agricola, of whom Tacitus has immortalized the virtues and the talents. This great man, having subjected to his arms the more southern parts of the country, advanced northwards, driving before him all the fiercer tribes: he even defeated them in a great battle; and, having chased them into the mountains of Caledonia, or Scotland, he erected a rampart to set bounds to their violent incursions. The other parts of the island he reduced into the form of a Roman province, and employed his attention in civilizing their inhabitants. He introduced among them the arts of peace, reconciled them to more cultivated manners, and instructed them in the sciences; and, by these infallible means, he prepared them for the yoke and servitude, which he meant to impose upon them. The Britains lost by degrees their love

Mrs. Brooke.

in his turn a decisive victory, and Boadicea, by a voluntary death, preserved herself from falling into his hands.

'The glory of subduing the Britons was reserved for Julius Agricola, whose eminent talents and virtues Tacitus has rendered immortal. This great man conquered the southern parts of the island, drove the most ferocious of the inhabitants northwards, defeated them in a battle; and after having forced them into the mountains of Caledonia, or Scotland, raised a rampart against their incursions. The rest of the country, now become a Roman province, was civilized by his cares. He introduced there arts, politeness, sciences; an infallible method of forming a people to the yoke which a master wishes to impose. The Britons lost by degrees the love of

tour une victoire décisive, & Boadicée se donna la mort pour ne pas tomber entre ses mains.

'La gloire de soumettre les Bretons étoit réservée à Julius Agricola, dont Tacite a immortalisé les talens & les vertus. Ce grand homme assujettit les parties méridionales de l'ile, poussa vers le nord les peuples les plus féroces, les défit même dans une bataille; & après les avoir chassés dans les montagnes de la Calédonie ou de l'Ecosse, il opposa un rempart à leurs violentes incursions. Le reste du pays, devenu province Romaine, fut civilisé par ses soins. Il y introduisit les arts, les mœurs, les sciences, moyens infaillibles de façonner un peuple au joug qu'on veut lui imposer. Les Bretons perdirent

Mr. Kenrick.

love of independance, and contracted a relish for the sweets and the conveniencies of life. Adrian, Antoninus, and Severus, added new fortifications to the wall of Agricola; and this province, enjoying an uninterrupted peace, during a long period, its inhabitants never once thought of recovering their ancient liberty.

'The Roman empire had, by this time, grown feeble under the weight of its conquests. A deluge of barbarians pouring from the North, attacked a power, which oppressed the world. Italy and France were overflowed by an inundation of warriors. It was necessary on this occasion to recal the legions, who were defending the frontier provinces; and the Picts and Scots, no longer confined in Caledonia, broke over the wall of *interruption*, ravaged the fields of their effeminate neighbours, and made them dread the total loss of those advantages, for which they had exchanged their freedom. The Britains implored the

Mrs. Brooke.

of independence, in their taste for the pleasures and advantages of polished life. Adrian, Antoninus, and Severus, added afterwards new fortifications to the wall of Agricola; and this province long enjoyed an uninterrupted peace, without its inhabitants entertaining a thought of their ancient liberty.

'The Roman empire had weakened itself by too many conquests. A deluge of northern barbarians came pouring in on this enormous power which oppressed the universe. Italy and the Gauls were over-run by them. It became necessary to recal from the frontiers, the legions which were stationed there for their defence. The Scots and Picts, confined in Caledonia, now passed the wall of separation, ravaged the lands of their enervated neighbours, and gave them cause to fear the intire loss of those possessions which they had preferred to a free condition. The Britons implored the succour of Rome.

perdirent peu à peu l'amour de l'indépendance, en goûtant les douceurs & les avantages de la vie civile. Adrien, Antonin & Sévere ajouterent dans la suite de nouvelles fortifications au mur d'Agricola; & cette province jouit long-temps d'une paix inaltérable, sans que les habitans pensassent à leur ancienne liberté.

'L'empire Romain s'étoit affoibli par trop de conquêtes. Un déluge de barbares du nord vint fondre sur cette énorme puissance qui accabloit l'univers. L'Italie & les Gaules en furent inondées. Il fallut rappeler des frontieres les légions qui veilloient à leur défense. Alors les Pictes & les Ecossois confinés dans la Calédonie franchirent le mur de séparation, ravagerent les campagnes de leurs voisins amollis, & leur firent craindre la perte totale de ces biens qu'ils préféroient à un état libre. Les Bretons implorerent le secours de Rome.

 On

Mr. Kenrick.

the protection of the Romans, who sent them a single legion. This force was sufficient to disperse the enemy; but, immediately on its departure, they returned to distress the Britains. It was again necessary to apply for relief, and another legion was sent, which was equally successful in repelling the invaders. But the Romans had now something more pressing to engage their attention, than the condition of this province; and resolving entirely to abandon it, they encouraged the Britains to defend themselves, and bid them a final adieu; after having been masters of the most considerable part of their island during the course of near four centuries. Before they left them, however, they assisted them to rebuild the wall of Severus; an undertaking, which, at that time, they had not artisans skilful enough to execute; so far removed were they from that excess of luxury, to which the monkish historians have ascribed their destruction. Can luxury prevail among a people where the most useful and necessary arts are unknown or neglected? 'The

Mrs. Brooke.

Rome. They sent them one legion. The enemy, at first dispersed, returned to the charge, after the departure of the legion. They sent a second, which found as little resistance. But the Romans had affairs more pressing. Resolved to abandon for ever Great Britain, where their government had subsisted about four hundred years, they exhorted their subjects to defend themselves, and bid them a last adieu, after having assisted them to rebuild the wall of Severus; an enterprize which the Britons had no workmen capable of executing, so far were they from that luxury to which the monkish historians have ascribed their defeats. Luxury must be unknown where even the necessary arts fail of being cultivated.

'The

On leur envoya une légion. Les ennemis d'abord dissipés, revinrent à la charge dès que la légion fut partie. On en fit marcher une seconde, à laquelle ils ne résisterent pas mieux. Mais les Romains avoient d'autres affaires plus pressantes. Résolus d'abandonner pour toujours la Grande Bretagne, où ils dominoient depuis environ quatre cents ans, ils exhorterent leurs sujets à se défendre eux-mêmes, & leur dirent le dernier adieu, après les avoir aidés à rétablir le mur de Sévere; entreprise que les Bretons n'auroient pu exécuter, faute d'ouvriers assez habiles, tant ils étoient eloignés du luxe qui, selon les historiens moines, étoit la cause de leurs défaites. Il ne peut y avoir de luxe où les arts nécessaires ne sont pas même cultivés.

'Les

Mr. Kenrick.

'The pusillanimous Britains; for to their cowardice we must ascribe their misfortunes; became soon a prey to the ferocious rapacity of the Scots and Picts. In vain they applied to Ætius, whose valour, at that time, protracted the fall of the empire. "The barbarians," said they, in the letter they addressed to him, "drive us towards the sea; the sea throws us back upon the barbarians; and we have only the hard choice left us of perishing by the sword, or by the waves." Their complaints and supplications had no effect with this commander, who was fully occupied in opposing the arms of Attila. Reduced to despair, and incapable of any generous effort, they abandoned the cultivation of their lands, and sought an asylum in their forests. The retreat of the enemy, who began at length to experience the miseries of famine, in a country which they had plundered, gave them an opportunity to repair their losses. An attention to agriculture restored to them their former

Mrs. Brooke.

'The cowardly Britons (for to their cowardice all their misfortunes are to be attributed) saw themselves soon a prey to the ferocious rapacity of the Scots and Picts. They applied in vain to the celebrated Ætius, whose courage supported the empire on the brink of ruin. "The barbarians, said they, drive us to the sea, the sea drives us back to the barbarians; and we have only the choice of perishing by the sword or the waves." Their complaints and supplications had little effect on this general, too much occupied with the war against Attila. Reduced to despair, incapable of any generous effort, they abandoned their settlements, and sought an asylum in the woods. The retreat of the enemy, who, in a ravaged country, were soon exposed to the miseries of famine, put them in a state to repair their disasters. Agriculture restored abundance. They thought

'Les lâches Bretons (car c'est à leur lâcheté qu'on doit attribuer ces malheurs) se virent bientôt en proie à la féroce rapacité des Ecossois & des Pictes. Ils recoururent en vain au célebre Aétius, dont le courage soutenoit l'empire sur le penchant de sa ruine. *Les barbares,* lui écrivoient-ils, *nous poussent vers la mer; la mer nous repousse vers les barbares; & nous n'avons que le choix de périr ou par le fer ou dans les flots.* Leurs plaintes & leurs supplications toucherent peu ce général, trop occupé contre Attila. Réduits au désespoir, incapables de généreux efforts, ils abandonnerent leurs terres, & chercherent un asyle dans les forêts. La retraite de l'ennemi qui éprouva enfin la famine dans un pays ravagé, les mit en état de réparer leurs désastres. L'agriculture leur rendit l'abondance. Ils ne pensoient

Mr. Kenrick.	*Mrs. Brooke.*
former ease and conveniencies; and these they enjoyed without any foresight of future disturbance, and without making any preparations for their security. Their neighbours, always greedy of plunder, soon threatened them with a new invasion. But occupied by the theological disputes, which their countryman Pelagius had introduced among them, and which had divided them into parties; and exposed to another source of disunion from the want of concert in their states; they were not inclined to depend upon themselves; and following the advice of Vortigern, one of their princes, they imprudently resolved to send for assistance into Germany. With this intention they dispatched an embassy to the Saxons, and invited over into their island, a people that were soon to enslave them.'	thought only of enjoying it, without forecast, without precaution against inevitable dangers. Their neighbours, always avid of prey, did not wait long to menace them anew. Theological disputes, occasioned by their countryman Pelagius, gave birth to pernicious divisions. Want of harmony in the government became a source of dissentions. Vortigern, one of their princes, unhappily engaged them to seek assistance in Germany. They sent with this design an embassy to the Saxons; and invited over the people by whom they were to be enslaved.'

pensoient qu'à jouir, sans prévoyance, sans précaution contre des perils inévitables. Leurs voisins toujours avides de rapines ne tarderent point à les menacer de nouveau. Les disputes théologiques occasionées par Pélage leur compatriote, firent naitre des divisions pernicieuses. Le défaut d'harmonie dans tout le gouvernement devint une source de discordes. Vortigern, un de leurs princes, les engagea malheureusement à chercher des secours en Germaine. Ils envoyerent dans cette vue une ambassade aux Saxons, & attirerent le peuple qui devoit les asservir.'

It might have been thought that we departed from our usual candour and impartiality, if, in characterizing the translations before us, we had shewn, by a minute criticism, the advantages of the one over the other. By expressing our sentiments in general terms, and, by submitting the foregoing specimens to our Readers, we exempt ourselves from any censure of this kind.

For a farther idea of this work, the Reader is referred to the Appendix to our 41st volume, in which the Abbé Millot's performance, in the original French, is introduced and criticised as a *Foreign Article*.

Art. VII. *The complete English Farmer, &c.* Concluded, from the last Month's Review.

Part II. Chapter 1, of Wheat.

WE have always thought that the bounty for exportation of corn requires great and various distinctions to reconcile it to true policy; but our *practical Farmer* thinks it sufficient to vindicate this measure indiscriminately, by saying, that 'the more money the merchant receives on this account, the more money he brings back.' Yet it should be considered whether the money he receives, in some circumstances, does not more *harm* to many *individuals*, and consequently to the public, than the money he brings back does good to the public. This is a subject certainly not to be discussed in narrow limits.

He tells us, that 'Mr. Tull placed his chief dependance on wheat.' No wonder, therefore, that he grew not rich by drilling; for most impartial men now own, that 'this plant suits not hoeing.'—[See Mr. Dossie in the second volume of his Memoirs.] The practical Farmer owns that the wind and rains bend the stalks, and loosen the roots of wheat so much, at a critical time of hoeing, that he was justly afraid of introducing the horse-hoe; and although he flatters himself, from Mr. Tull's *silence*, that this untoward circumstance was *peculiar* to his wheat, yet all fair experimenters will assure him that it is, and must be, a *common* one.

He thinks the circumstance of ease, with which blighted ears may be clipped off in the drill culture, a favourable one; but it is at best one of *small* consequence, otherwise Mr. Tull would have insisted on it.

Our Farmer thinks the great crops which have been gained by *extraordinary pulverisation*, a confirmation of Mr. Tull's principles; but we think it none of his practice. All those experiments only prove that pulverisation will do much, and this truth was long ago known; yet they do not prove that pulverisation alone will yield such a profit as to make the expences of drilling rational, but the contrary.

As to the proper season for sowing wheat, Mr. Young, in the course of his experiments, has done much to ascertain it; but of these experiments our complete Farmer here takes no notice.—We refer him to what we have observed on the subject.

But is our practical Farmer either *candid* or *just*, when he appears to condemn Mr. Young for carrying *summer ploughing* to excess? His design in recording the experiments alluded to, is to shew that no corn can pay for 12 or 13 ploughings: the very thing which our Farmer seems to blame him for not teaching!

 Our

Our practical Farmer hopes that, after publication of this work, no farmer will throw away so much seed as he usually does. But here he perhaps *flatters* himself; for Mr. Young seems to have proved, by experiments, that the generality of farmers have been advised, by the Tullians, to sow far *too little* seed.

Our practical Farmer represents the giving more seed to *poor* land than to *rich*, as an 'absurdity of the first magnitude;' and compares it to stocking a poor field with more cattle than a rich one.

We are amazed to meet with such a mistake as this (well-known to every sensible farmer) in one who undertakes to compile 'the *complete* English Farmer.' We will not waste our own and the Reader's time in proving the *rationale* of the practice which he condemns as an absurdity, but refer him to what Mr. Young has written on the subject, in his course of experiments, and to Mr. Peters in his *Winter Riches* *.

On the practice of sowing half of the seed *under* furrow, and half *above*, the practical Farmer observes, that 'it is a *tacit confession* that half the seed is *sufficient*.' We do not take on us the defence of this practice, but must observe, that it only proves that, in the opinion of these husbandmen, it is better to have *two chances* for an *half crop*, however the year prove, than *one chance* for a *full* crop.

Our complete Farmer asserts, that a *sprinkling of soot* on the wheat land '*doubles the expence.*' Some readers might think that he means, '*is equal to all the other expences.*' But this cannot be his meaning! He must, we suppose, have intended to say, that 'it does twice as much good as the expence of it.' But what an improper expression of his sentiment has he made use of!

Our Author imagines that he has *said enough* against the *infamous* practice which Farmer Ellis recommends, of laying 40 or 50 bushels of stone-lime on an acre of wheat land. But whatever cause may have occasioned a want of success in using stone-lime on our practical Farmer's land, he can never say enough to dissuade sensible men, who have experienced its usefulness on various lands, to forego it. He thinks, however, that 10 or 15 bushels of lime will warm and cherish the land. We own that quantity will do good, but is seldom nearly sufficient †.

And now our practical Farmer comes to recommend what he calls, in the title-page, '*a new method of tillage, partaking of*

---

* A work just published; of which we shall speedily give a farther account.

† *Winter Riches* recommends 160 bushels per acre.

the

the simplicity of the old husbandry, and all the advantages of the new.' When we read only the title-page, we were flattered by hopes of some really useful new scheme. But how are we disappointed to find the whole only a proposal to sow every alternate land! Well might his honest sensible ploughman represent to our Farmer the wildness of this scheme. [See p. 212] His plea is *the expence of manuring*. But surely he who assumes to be a *complete* Farmer, should know that there are several fallow crops, such as buck-wheat, &c. to be ploughed in, which answer the end of manure; and the saving the space of the furrows, and giving air to the corn, are such trifling advantages as cannot come in competition with a crop.

On the method of mowing wheat, our practical Farmer observes, 'I do not apprehend that all that is saved in cutting, is *clear gain*,' p. 217. Here we would observe, that an objection to the neatness of the method comes with very ill grace from him who appears not ever to have seen the North of England, where the practice is attended with the greatest neatness.

The not cutting of wheat till it is fully ripe, is a wasteful method. But our practical Farmer is one of the first who ever told us, that wheat is worse for standing till fully ripe, has a *thicker* and *tougher* coat, and contracts a browner colour of the meal *. Just the contrary is the assertion of philosophy and experience.

In chap. 2, on *rye*, our Farmer shews that he knows not much about this valuable crop, which often produces 50 and 55 bushels by the acre, and sells sometimes for 4 s. 6 d. and 5 s. per bushel †. In short, it is frequently a better crop than a good one of wheat; and when it is cultivated as it ought, few would eat it off in spring, in order to sow down turnips.

The pretence that this grain is much addicted to the *blast*, is a mistake; and as to the other pretence that *horned* rye rots off the limbs of those who eat it, no such instance is known in all the North of England, where rye-bread is made in the utmost perfection, so as actually to be sent to court.

How little our Farmer knows about the value of a northern crop of this corn, may be seen by any experienced man, in his assertion that, for an *harvesting* crop, it should be sown even as late as April.

His advice to sow rye with peas seems not well founded.

---

* If wheat stand till it is more than fully ripe, the meal may possibly suffer in colour by more sun than is needful; but how the skin should grow thicker and tougher by more sun, is inconceivable.

† This very year, Mr. Peters informs us, rye sold within 9 d. of wheat.

Our

Our Farmer thinks Ellis's 10, or even 5, bushels of salt, on an acre of rye, a *sure* prescription for barrenness. We wish the experiment tried ‡. See Peters's Winter Riches, p. 159.

The practical Farmer begins his 3d chapter, on *barley*, with a great mistake, viz. that the barley sown in the South is hardly known in the North; whereas in reality the barley generally cultivated in the North of England is the very same as this in the South, and *bear*, or *bigg*, is seldom sown there.

He gives one of the best proofs of his friend Mr. Tull having a mind open to conviction, when he assures us, that he more often sowed his barley broad-cast. Indeed Mr. Young gives so picturesque a description of drilled barley hanging in all directions, that Sir Digby Legard's persevering in drilling this grain does him no honour: and our practical Farmer mentions the tillering of fresh stalks from the roots of drilled barley as an *unanswerable* objection to the practice. See p. 227.

We will pass over his repeated declamation in favour of a small allowance of seed, both of barley and clover, of which latter he allows but a pound to an acre. We join him against Mr. Miller, who would have no seeds sown with barley: but we entirely dissent from him as to leaving the mown barley in swath. It should be neatly bound in sheaves or gaits, and may safely be mown before it is ripe.

In his 4th chapter, on *oats*, our Farmer assumes the character of a prophet of evil tidings:

He asserts, that 'the growth of wheat is become the object of attention not only to Europe but America, which, at this hour, chiefly supplies Italy, Spain, and Portugal; and that France makes such improvements in agriculture that she will soon have an overplus, which (with the *superabundance* of Sicily, and accumulated produce of our colonies) will make wheat so cheap that our merchants cannot go to market without *double* of that bounty which we now complain of.' He adds, that 'we now pay half a million yearly for oats imported.' His conclusion is, that we ought to turn our attention to the culture of oats, for *which* the demand will soon be the greatest, as importation of them must be prohibited. We can only say in this place, "*Dii meliora!*"

But our practical Farmer (now that he is in the way of prophesying) pours forth liberally his evil tidings. In his sad series stand *Plenty*, *Murmuring*, *Poverty*, *Bankruptcy*, *Seizure for Rent*, *Decay of Trade*, *Imprisonment*, *Beggary*.—Rents sinks, interest rises, gentlemen rent lands nominally their own. On this sad prospect we have only one question to ask, "Why would this practical Farmer make *complete* Farmers of us all?"

‡ *Four* have been tried, with great success.

In chapter 5, on *buck-wheat*, our Farmer complains that he does not underſtand Mr. Young's calculations, and thinks the expences throughout much undervalued. Juſtice requires us to ſay that having carefully examined the work of Mr. Young's here referred to (viz. his courſe of experiments) we think this complaint ill founded, and that our Farmer ſhould have given inſtances to juſtify ſuch an heavy cenſure of that Writer*.

In the 6th chapter, on *peas*, our Farmer aſſerts that the Tullian method for them is good. But the practice of *drilling* peas is of much older date than Mr. Tull, and is only tranſferred from the garden to the field. What renders drilling of peas a good method in the garden, is the *rodding* them; but this part is thought too troubleſome and expenſive to be copied in the field; and without this rodding, drilling is ineffectual; for the vines cover the intervals, and are deſtroyed by the horſe-hoe, as any perſon may eaſily imagine, and as Mr. Young, in his experiment, aſſerts; inſomuch that he juſtly looks on the drill huſbandry for this plant as moſt ridiculous.

The *ſuccedaneums* for rods, viz. *oats*, *beans*, or what our Author thinks better than both, *rye*, ſeem indefenſible; and Mr. Young rightly judges that a broad-caſt crop of peas is beſt in value for the ſeed, and beſt prepares the land for wheat.

Amid that great variety of courſes of crops which takes place, and not improperly, in an equally great variety of ſoil, &c. our Farmer ſeems to advance a good *general* rule, which may be applied to them all, viz. that 'every crop which lies *long* in the ground ſhould be ſucceeded by one which lies *not long*;' as *wheat* by *barley*, ſays our Farmer, or by turnips, *ſay we*. We would recommend another general rule, viz. that "exhauſting crops be ſucceeded by meliorating ones;" as *barley* by *clover*.

On chapter the 7th, of *beans*, we muſt obſerve, that this is the vegetable which ſeems to ſucceed beſt in the drill culture, but had poſſeſſion of their culture in the garden long before Mr. Tull, and is only transferred to the field. Our Farmer ſpeaks with juſt reſpect of Mr. Young's method of making them a crop *after* wheat, not *before* it, as is uſual.

But the Friend of Mr. Tull ſeems miſtaken when he ſays, that there is no innovation in the kind ſown in the field. We

---

* We are well aſſured that a *certain* gentleman objected to the truth of Mr. Young's account of expences in his courſe of experiments, that he charged ploughing only at 1 s. per acre. The bookſeller juſtly anſwered, "The ſhilling is only the pay of the ploughman's labour; the charge of the draught is made elſewhere." This is the very fact; and it is no wonder that, when men read thus careleſly, they do not underſtand the calculations which Mr. Young's experiments exhibit, and think his charges much below truth.

apprehend

apprehend that Mr. Young recommends the *tick-bean*, of a middle ſize betwixt the common horſe and large Windſor bean.

In chapter 8, our Farmer repeats his fancy about rye ſown with vetches to ſupport them. His deſcription of a *ſhiem*, or *ſkim*, to hoe weeds, ſeems ſimple and uſeful.

In chapter 10, he recommends, in order to ſave turnips from the fly, the ſowing of ſome ſeed *under* furrow and ſome *above*, that if one ſprouting be deſtroyed by the fly, the other may eſcape; alſo the ſowing of part new ſeed, and part of old, as theſe come up at different times. He owns, however, both methods ſometimes ineffectual, and adviſes to ſcatter new flak'd lime on the turnips beginning to ſprout. The mixing of radiſh ſeed with that of turnip he alſo mentions, and Mr. Miller's hungry poultry, for the deſtruction of the caterpillar.

Our Farmer allows Mr. Miller a very moderate ſhare of *theoretical* knowledge of huſbandry, and accuſes him of manifeſt want of *practical*, and of want of candour towards his friend Mr. Tull, whoſe drilling of turnips he conceals.

In chapter 11, on *carrots*, our Farmer judiciouſly notes, as a matter worthy of obſervation, that, according to Mr. Billing's account, cabbages were more than doubly profitable, compared with carrots, and carrots doubly profitable compared with turnips; alſo that Mr. Billing ſhould have noted whether carrots can be kept in the ground in winter without damage.—We apprehend, they cannot.

In our Farmer's account of *potatoes*, in chapter 12, it deſerves notice, that the earlieſt ſort are the *Iriſh purple*, which, well-managed, afford two crops. But our Farmer is miſinformed when he aſſerts that bread made of them is more wholeſome than that which is made of *wheat and rye*, which is, probably, the wholſomeſt bread imaginable. Potatoe bread is however eatable, and not *unnouriſhing* or *unwholeſome*.

He entertains no high opinion of Mr. Miller as an huſbandman; and indeed he has given us ſome ſpecimens not much to that gentleman's honour, in that character. He adds one, in this chapter, of the ſame tendency, viz. that excellent gardener's aſſertion, that by propagating potatoes by *ſeed* we ſhall have them two months after planting. This aſſertion muſt appear to every reader, as it did to our Farmer, moſt improbable! However, by diligent enquiry into practice, he has found that potatoes are procured as early as Midſummer by ſeed; but then it is by planting them as ſoon after Candlemas as the weather will permit, and when they have been trained *two whole years* before. It muſt be owned that our Farmer has Mr. Miller (whom he conſiders as envious of his old friend Mr. Tull) at great advantage here. ' Mr. Miller ſhould have explained the ſeeming

seeming wonder, if he knew it. If he did not, he confirms our Farmer's idea of the mediocrity of his knowledge in husbandry.

Our Farmer begins his 13th chapter, on *clover*, with an extract from a book, whose title he gives not; but affirms that it was in *no small repute* at the time of its publication, the beginning of this century, in which it is predicted that clover will prove of *mischievous consequence* to the public by the *plenty* it will *create*. Our Author justly laughs at this prophet. Yet we hear people, on just as good grounds, declaim against inclosures.

Mr. Tull receives no credit from his prejudices against clover; and the memory of Sir Richard Weston should be dear to the English husbandman.

We agree with our *complete Farmer* that the clover-seed of a *dry good* year is preferable, when two or three years old, to new seed of a *cold* year; and we think with him, that it is probable, the naturally-brown seed, as best ripened, vegetates best: but we dare not affirm, with him, that one quart of seed, however good, is better than four for an acre; nor know we how large bare patches can be covered without fresh sowing.

He rightly advises to sow clover over barley when in blade, just covering the ground, that it may not hurt the barley crop; and, on the same principle, to sow it quickly after oats, lest they destroy it.

The sowing of clover over wheat is a matter of delicacy. If sown in February, it may overtake and damage the wheat: if later, it will frequently fail, the ground being surface-bound by the heats, &c.

Our Farmer's objection to sowing of clover on what he calls wheat *fleaches* or *ridges*, because the crop growing in the furrows cannot be mown, is trifling. Any practical farmer knows, that when a meadow lies in ridges (as is frequently necessary) the mowers go across the ridges.

Our Farmer well advises to keep the clover, when mown, in windrows till dry; and he justly notes the risque of getting a crop from seed, on account of rains, mists, &c.

Mr. Miller has strenuously advised to sow clover in autumn, on this principle, viz. " the proper time of *sowing* is the precise time of *seeding*." Here our Farmer shrewdly observes, that ' *clover* is not a *native* of this country, but *naturalized* to our climate, and its proper time of *seeding* is May or June; that is, the end of May or beginning of June.' He also observes, not less shrewdly, that, in consequence of Mr. Miller's rule, the time of sowing *barley*, *oats*, &c. would be autumn. He gives also a reason against Mr. Miller's time of sowing, which seems to us unanswerable, viz. that ' clover sown in *autumn* has not time to gather strength to resist the winter's cold.' He has another good observation, viz. that, ' by sowing in autumn, the

the farmer muſt loſe his crop of wheat.' Mr. Miller will hardly ſay, that the wheat may be alſo ſown; for if the clover ſucceed, it will greatly *injure* if not *deſtroy* the wheat. Our complete Farmer is ſevere upon Mr. Miller as going out of the road of his profeſſion, *gardening*; and he corrects Mr. Dickſon, a Scotch clergyman, for blaming *all* Engliſh authors for recommending autumn as the proper ſeaſon for ſowing clover, whereas only Mr. Miller and a few of his pupils recommend it. We wiſh that he had been more particular on the *fly* which deſtroys clover.

We approve our Farmer's advice of *emptying by the hand*, or, as it is uſually called, *raking*, the inteſtines of an *hoved beaſt*, as equally *effectual*, and *ſafer* than inciſion.

On our practical Farmer's 14th chapter, on *white clover*, we have to remark, that any one who doubts that this plant is a native of Great Britain, need only look on lanes and commons in a dropping year, and he muſt be convinced that no plough ever came there.

We have ſome doubt about the truth of our Farmer's aſſertion, that white clover thrives *beſt* on *cold ground*. On the contrary, we have obſerved it to thrive beſt on dry ground; and we think, that when dropping weather combines, with warm manures (of which kind are the coal-aſhes) this excellent plant thrives beſt on grounds generally dry.

We agree ſo thoroughly with our Farmer in his opinion that 'this plant has ſcarce an equal for breeding ſheep,' that we doubt not but its uſual name in the North, '*lamb-ſuckling*,' was derived from obſervation of its uſe to lambs.

On chapter 15, on *ſaintfoin*, we obſerve, that Mr. Tull appears to have gained credit by his cultivation of this plant; and we think that the practical Farmer has done himſelf no leſs by his candid manner of warning his readers againſt what he thinks the miſtakes of his old friend.

Thus Mr. Tull informs us that *one* acre of drilled *ſaintfoin* is worth *two* of ſown. But our Farmer notes, that Mr. Tull himſelf acknowledges that 'ſown ſaintfoin, if kept clean the two firſt years, will thrive as well as the drilled.'

Mr. Tull tells us, that ſaintfoin, though ſo thin the firſt year as ſcarcely to be worth mowing, will in two or three years cover the ground. But our complete Farmer aſſures us, from experiment, (and we believe him) that this is not the effect of new ſhoots from the old plants, but of new plants from the ſcattered ſeed.

In the *old* huſbandry from four to ſeven buſhels of ſeed are ſown on one acre; but in the *new* from *two* to *ſeven* gallons.

Our Farmer obſerves, it is better to hoe out the *overplus* than to want plants. We are ourſelves of opinion that it is ſcarcely poſſible

possible to sow too much saintfoin seed; for the thickness of the plants will keep down the weeds, and the strong plants will often kill the weak ones without hoeing.

Mr. Tull advises to make the saintfoin hay, when dry, into cocks; but our Farmer judges him much mistaken, and advises to windrow and then carry it. He observes, that heavy rain will run through the largest cocks of saintfoin hay (or any that lies light) and spoil it with must. He therefore exhorts (and we think rightly) to stack it as soon as dry, and carry up a tunnel. On the same principle he advises to thatch the stack *immediately*.

On the method of preserving the seed in the hay, our Farmer observes that vermin are fonder of it than of corn. On the other method of preserving it when threshed, Mr. Tull directs to prevent its sweating too much, by laying layers of wheat-straw and of saintfoin seed alternately.

Mr. Tull is very ample in his encomiums on saintfoin. Our Farmer allows them, in general, to be just; but he observes, rightly, that although Mr. Tull magnifies the profit of this plant beyond that of clover, it can never be so general an improvement, as it disagrees with clay lands, which are three-fourths of this kingdom.

In his 16th chapter, on *lucerne*, our Farmer observes, from Mr. Tull, some curious things of this grass, viz. first, that superstition has banished it from the Roman territories, where, secondly, it was cultivated by the old Romans at a vast expence; and, thirdly, held in such veneration, that iron must not touch the place on which it grew. In France it is said to produce on one acre ten tons! The greater heats of the sun, and less rain in that country than ours, may reasonably be supposed to make it suit better to that climate, as its enemy, *natural grass*, less prevails there.

Mr. Tull affirms, that lucerne was *never* known to flourish in England above three years in the old husbandry; but our Farmer, on his own experience, contradicts this assertion. He thinks also that Mr. Tull, who recommends *hot gravelly* soils for its culture with us, was led into his mistake by a neglect of the difference of climate*; and that two or three pounds of seed are sufficient for an acre; but the seedsmen recommend treble the quantity. In this advice we apprehend them to be influenced by a prospect of their own immediate advantage.

We agree with our Farmer that, in the drill husbandry of this plant, it must suffer from horse-hoeing in narrow intervals; and that, in wider, more ground is lost.

---

* But are not hot gravelly soils more necessary in a climate which has less sun?

On

On the whole, we apprehend that hand-hoeing muſt be a neceſſary, though expenſive, culture for it.

We know, by experience, that *tranſplanted* lucerne is preferable to the *untranſplanted.* The elegant Author of this improvement reckons only as much green food on an acre, thus managed, as will keep two horſes, and allow a cutting for hay. We apprehend *lucerne* hay, when moſt ſucceſsfully made, to be a mere bauble; and we fear that the produce in green food, according to Mr. Hart's eſtimate, will not leave generally much profit.

Where ground lets very dear, as near cities and great towns, and a gentleman has ſervants at leiſure to attend the hoeing, we apprehend that lucerne may anſwer as a ſummer food, which it would be very expenſive to bring from a conſiderable diſtance for horſes in conſtant uſe for the coach or ſaddle.

Our Farmer thinks that three acres of drilled lucerne will fully employ a man, and that they will keep in ſummer ſix or eight horſes. Let him then who propoſes to cultivate this plant, calculate whether, in his ſituation, this expence of a man, and the rent, will exceed his expence of keeping the horſes otherwiſe. The profit muſt depend on circumſtances.

On chapter the 17th, of *burnet*, we have little to obſerve, only that Mr. Miller ſeems as unreaſonably partial againſt, as Mr. Rocque was for, this graſs.

The ſpecies of this plant we know to be as numerous as thoſe of almoſt any kind. They are all correſpondent to their different ſoils. Some deſerve all that Mr. Miller ſays againſt *burnet* in general, and others all that its warmeſt advocates have ſaid for it. To hope that a *good* ſpecies of burnet will be produced on *bad* ground, is folly; and to inſpire that hope is generally the effort of knavery!

In the 18th chapter, on *graſſes*, our Farmer thinks that none of the graſſes recommended by Mr. Stillingfleet is preferable to *rey-graſs*, unleſs it be the annual meadow graſs.

We agree with him, intirely, that rolling is a great advantage to new-ſown graſſes, and therefore is adviſeable, as it compacts the ſoil.

We alſo think that what our Farmer obſerves, with regard to the graſſes preferred by Mr. Miller to rey-graſs, has great force, viz. that, 'if once reduced to common field culture, they will grow *ranker*, *coarſer*, &c.'

His method of deſtroying ants in graſs grounds, viz. 'by tobacco leaves ſteeped in urine,' is, we dare ſay, effectual and adviſeable, if not found too troubleſome.

On chapters 18 and 19, concerning the *turnip-cabbage*, and *turnip-rooted-cabbage*, we would obſerve, that the produce of the former is ſaid by Mr. Baker to be 35 or 36 tons per acre, and

and that of the latter, by Mr. Reynolds, to be only 34. The former was said to be impenetrable by frost, but the fact was disproved: the latter is said to be so, and we wish that the fact may not have been disproved by last winter.

On chapter 20, of *cabbages*, we have only to remark, first, that our Farmer seems to prove that *one* ounce of seed will produce more plenty than enough to plant one acre; and, secondly, that seed sown early in spring will produce plants fit to set out in the end of May or beginning of June.

In chapter 21, of the *cole-seed*, our Farmer thinks the Flanders method of transplanting for seed *manifestly* better than the common English one of *sowing*; of which preference, however, we have our doubts.

In chapter the 22d, our Farmer explains, from a Writer in the *Musæum Rusticum*, the whole process of the *teazle*. He supposes that, as its use is applied to the woollen manufacture, it will travel with that, and may perhaps have found its way to the North. We can inform him, that it has been some years cultivated about Wakefield, in Yorkshire.

He justly observes a defect in the Editor of the *Musæum Rusticum*, who, having observed that the head of the teazle must arise to a *certain* size to be useful, has neglected to describe what that is. He is the more blameable for this defect, as he notes that the *hooks* of heads greatly above this size become coarse, and injure the manufacture. Beside, it is evident, from the sequel of the narrative, that the *largest heads* are called *kings*, and reckoned of the greatest value. It appears that the growing on middle stems, or as side heads, distinguishes the teazles into first and second sorts.

In the 23d chapter, of *hops*, our Farmer introduces his account of their whole management, by a doubt whether the *planter* or *factor* gains more by them. He affirms, however, (and, as we apprehend, with truth) that the planter's gain always depends more on his *skill* in *failing* years than on *plenty* in favourable ones. He concludes, that the general culture is of great consequence to the public, as the duty is a considerable branch of the revenue, and the price of the commodity is saved to us at home.

On chapter the 24th, of *saffron*, we find several things which would deserve notice; but the review of the work before us being already of sufficient length, we must not enlarge upon the contents of this chapter, although the subject is little known, and very amusing.

At present, therefore, we shall only observe, first, that nearly four hundred thousand sets go to plant an acre, and yet the price of setting and covering that quantity of ground is only 1 l. 6 s. So greatly does *habit* contribute to expedition!

 Secondly,

Secondly, The nicety of drying the saffron cakes is such, that if the greatest attention is not observed, the saffron will scorch and be utterly spoiled. Surely it deserves the attention of the ingenious to find, if possible, a *safer* and *easier* way of drying them.

Thirdly, Mr. Montague estimates the value of an acre of saffron at 20 l. and Dr. Douglas only at 5 l. Our Farmer observes, that sometimes saffron sells for 1 l. 10 s. per pound, and sometimes for double that sum.

Fourthly, Our Farmer notes a general error of the cultivators of saffron, viz. suffering weeds to over-run the beds, and cattle to graze them: whereas he affirms, that hoeing the weeds, and mowing the grass, would greatly increase their profit. We wonder that such common operations should be neglected!

Fifthly, He asserts, that a whole family is frequently maintained by cultivating one or two acres of saffron, as that quantity finds employment for young and old, during a considerable part of the year.

On the 25th chapter, of *flax*, we have only to notice the manner in which our Farmer introduces his account of its culture.

He observes, that we pay immense sums to Russia, and other foreign states, for flax and hemp, and yet he has been assured, by a manufacturer of undoubted credit, that our *home-raised* commodities are intrinsically better than the *imported*.

He observes, that a want of conveniency for watering flax and hemp seems to retard their cultivation in this kingdom; and, to support this assertion, he notes that our rivers are shut up from this operation for fear of destroying our fish; whereas all rivers abroad are open; that springs of water to fill canals are often not at hand, and that ordinary ponds are very unfit for the purpose. We apprehend that proper attention would, in a great measure, remedy the want of canals filled by springs.

In chapter the 26th, of *hemp*, our Author assures us, that every manufacturer of English sail-cloth laments the backwardness of the English farmer to raise hemp.

Our complete Farmer seems really eloquent in his remonstrance to administration for suffering us to depend on Russia for the materials of our cordage and canvas. He observes, that she may have such an increasing demand at home for these materials, or by policy be led to such a prohibition of the exportation of them, as may leave us in great distress. He adds, that we could not then blame Russia, nor our climate, &c. but our negligence. He concludes with an assurance, that a worthy manufacturer of Gainsborough in Lincolnshire made it a part of the business of a long life, to turn the attention of successive

ſucceſſive adminiſtrations to the encouragement of this important branch of Engliſh manufacture, by convincing them of the ſuperiority of Britiſh hemp, both as to ſtrength and facility of working, over that which is imported. We can only ſay, "Peace to his ſhade!"

In chapter 27, the Author repreſents *weld* as a valuable crop, which requires *little culture*, and will grow on any *barren*, *dry*, *warm* land: for all this he produces authorities; but he is very deficient in not acquainting us with the price of the produce of an acre to the dyers, without which knowledge no one can judge of the profit of it. We apprehend that the vulgar name by which *weld* is known, at leaſt in ſeveral countries, is *woad*.

In chapter the 28th, our Farmer (from Dr. Hill) repreſents *woad* as a plant of eaſy culture; and yet it ſeems agreed, that the ſecret of manufacturing it (that is, reducing the leaves to powder for fixing of colours) is confined to the undertakers, who travel in gangs, and rent the land dear, and that the manufacturing is a *laborious* and *expenſive* proceſs. However, ingenious men might learn the method, and then the public might judge of the profit of the growth of this plant.

On chapter 29, of *madder*, we ſhall obſerve, that our Farmer, like moſt of his brethren, ſeems *unconſcionably ſevere* and *illiberal* on the clergy. He repreſents them as *oppreſſive* in exaction of tithe for this plant, and as neceſſitating the legiſlature to reduce that tithe to 5 s. per acre for 14 years, from 1768.

As *we* are noways concerned in receiving or paying tithe for this plant, we may, therefore, reaſonably be ſuppoſed impartial; and on this occaſion we think it our duty to ſtate the caſe fairly; which will be a full vindication of that reſpectable body of men the clergy, many individuals of whom contribute largely to the improvement of agriculture.

The *general* law of tithes, as ſettled among us, gives a tenth part of the produce of the ground, when reaped, to the rector, &c. The produce of madder was well underſtood to be very profitable; and the clergy, perhaps, expected to have a tenth part of it. Of this the grower of madder complained, becauſe in this caſe the parſon had the tenth part of his labour, &c. not conſidering that the like caſe happened in regard to wheat and other valuable crops. He called it an *arbitrary impoſition*, as our Farmer does; and ſo violent was his prejudice againſt, and oppoſition to, this payment, that he ſeemed likely, through obſtinacy, to loſe nine parts of his profit rather than pay one.

In this critical ſituation, the legiſlature came in to aid the public. In order to encourage the obſtinate grower of madder, they reduced the tithe to a ſmall payment indeed; and did juſtice to the clergy, by confining that reduction to a short term, within which it may reasonably be supposed that the growers of madder will be better acquainted with their own interest than to give up its culture, for being obliged to pay a sum much nearer the value of one-tenth of the produce, and the clergy will have a fair chance of being re-admitted to their original rights. No doubt the legislature have a right to diminish the legal claims of individuals for the good of the public.

Hence it appears, that the tithe of madder was not reduced on account of any *arbitrary imposition* of the clergy, but on account of the stupid obstinacy of a set of men, whom our Farmer joins in their *illiberal* abuse of the clergy.

On chapter the 30th, of *liquorice*, we have only to observe, that as this root requires a soil of *prodigious* depth and richness, the culture of it must be very confined, and as the demand for it cannot be great, it must be more confined still; insomuch that it seems already sufficiently known: especially as few of the planters are said to grow rich.

The Author's conclusion is an epitome of the second volume of Memoirs of Agriculture; of which we have lately given an ample review.

Our complete Farmer's style is not the subject of criticism: but we believe his heart to be *benevolent* and *patriotic* *.

ART. VIII. *Conclusion of the Account of Mr.* Farmer's *Dissertation on Miracles.* See Review for July.

WE come now to the principal part of Mr. Farmer's ingenious and elaborate performance, the design of which is to shew, that the scriptures, both of the Old and the New Testament, strictly corresponding with right reason, always represent miracles as the peculiar works of God; and never attribute them to any other beings, unless when acting by his immediate commission. This subject is considered in its full extent, and our Author is necessarily led by it into a variety of learned and critical enquiries, which we could not abridge, or give a sufficient account of, without extending the present article to an improper length. We must, therefore, in many cases, content ourselves with barely noticing what has been done; referring our Readers to the work itself for more ample satisfaction and entertainment.

---

* Should this work come to a second edition, we would advise the Writer, in the *most serious* and *friendly* manner, to give the sense of Authors from whom he compiles, more exactly than he has done in this first edition, and to refer to books and pages, that the Reader may examine his reports.

The

The first section of the third chapter considers the view which the scripture gives us of angels, both good and evil, and of the souls of departed men; and is designed to shew that this view of them is inconsistent with their liberty of working miracles. As to good angels, they are never represented as capable of performing miracles at their own pleasure. Of whatever dignity, they are only *ministring spirits*, the servants of Jehovah, *doing his commandments, and hearkening to the voice of his word*, without having themselves any power over mankind, or over those laws by which the system to which we belong is governed. Now if this be the case with regard to good angels, what reason can there be for ascribing such dominion to evil angels, who are fallen under the divine displeasure? The scripture never ascribes to the devil the ability of revealing secrets, foretelling future events, or working miracles; never guards mankind against being deceived by the outward effects either of his miraculous power or inspiration, necessary as such a caution would have been, had he been able to inspire prophecies and work miracles; and earnestly as it warns us against a less danger, the pretences of men to divine miracles and inspiration, when they were not sent and assisted by God. It has, indeed, been supposed, from Dan. x. 13, 20, and Ephes. ii. 2, that fallen angels preside over distinct regions of the world, and that they have a power of changing the constitution of the air; but it is proved by Mr. Farmer that no such doctrine can be reasonably grounded on these passages. He has shewn, likewise, that the souls of deceased men have no intercourse with the material creation, at least not with this lower world; that the idea entertained of them by Christians, both in ancient and modern times, has been borrowed from the Pagans; and that the miracles ascribed to departed saints, are branded as impostures by St. Paul.

The next section contains an accurate and curious enquiry into the representation which the scripture affords of the nature and claims of the Heathen divinities. Our learned Author here shews, that the Heathens deified all the parts and powers of nature, and that they believed the existence of demons, who were considered as the distributors or dispensers of good and evil to mankind. It was the opinion of many, that the celestial gods did not themselves interpose in human affairs, but committed the entire administration of the government of this lower world to these subaltern deities; and hence these subaltern deities became the grand objects of the religious hopes and fears of the Pagans, of immediate dependence and divine worship. As it has often been said, that the demons of the Heathens were spirits of a higher origin than the race of man, Mr. Farmer enters into an examination of the reasons commonly assigned for this notion; and has clearly proved, by the testimony of the ancient historians, poets, and philosophers, and by uncontroverted facts, that the more direct objects of Pagan worship were such departed human souls as were believed to become demons. After this he goes on to confirm the same point from the authority of the Old Testament writers; considers the use of the word demon in the Septuagint translation, in Philo, in Josephus, and in the New Testament; introduces some remarks on the late controversy between Dr. Sykes and his antagonists; and refers us to the evidence both of Heathens and Jews, to shew that the spirits of wicked men were thought to become wicked demons. The opinions of the Christian Fathers upon the subject are also particularly considered, and then our Author proceeds to the following judicious and important observations.

'If the foregoing account of the Pagan gods be just, there will be no difficulty in vindicating the censures past upon them in the sacred writings. With regard to the parts and powers of nature, which the Heathen world deified, they are represented in scripture as the creatures of God's power, and the passive instruments of his decrees. Even *the sun, and the moon, and the stars, and all the host of heaven,* however revered by the Pagans as the chief deities, *the Israelites are forbidden to worship and serve, because Jehovah, their God, placed them in the firmament of heaven*; not for the use of any one particular nation, but *for the common benefit of the whole human race.* It is extraordinary that Moses, at a time when the world was universally regarded as animated and divine, and the elements and the heavenly bodies were thought to possess an internal power to exert themselves in all their admirable effects; it is very extraordinary that Moses, at this time, should discover, publish, and (by suitable miracles) confirm the opposite doctrine. His doctrine is perfectly agreeable to the modern philosophy, which represents the whole natural world as a merely material, inert, inactive thing, without any wisdom or power of its own, and resisting any change of state, whether of rest or motion; and which must therefore be continually upheld and directed by the power of God, to whom the whole train of natural causes and effects is to be ascribed. The doctrine alone of Moses, so remote from the sentiments and philosophy of his age, and so agreeable to truth, creates a strong presumption of his having received it by immediate revelation.

'As to the other gods of Paganism, whether they were such human souls as became demons, or (as some apprehend) created spirits of a superior order, we have already seen that the scripture gives us such a view of them, as is inconsistent either with their inspiring prophecies or working miracles. And it will be shewn in the sequel that all supernatural effects are referred to God alone by the sacred writers. Is it possible for them to contradict themselves, as they must do, if they ascribe such effects to the Heathen gods? But so far are they from doing this, that they constantly represent those gods as utterly impotent and insignificant; either as having no real existence,

or

or no more power than if they did not exist. They call them *vanities*, things of no kind of value or efficacy. Nor is this censure confined to a part only of the Heathen gods: it is extended to all, without a single exception. *They are* ALL *vanity.* ALL *the gods of the nations are idols*, or *nothings:* not powerful evil spirits, but mere nullities. In this manner the ancient prophets of God spoke of the Pagan deities; and the apostles of Christ used the same language: *we know that an idol is nothing in the world.* This is not to be understood of the mere images of the gods: for the Heathens did not regard those images, in themselves considered, as real gods. They believed them to be the representatives and the receptacles of their gods. and in this view they spoke of them as gods, and the objects of divine worship, and it is in reference to the divine powers supposed to reside in them, that the scriptures affirm, that they are nothing. On all occasions the sacred writers deride these pretended residences of the Heathen deities, as mere earthly materials, polished by the hand of the artificer, and the deities themselves as equally void of understanding, or rather as being nothing distinct from those senseless materials, and existing only in the imagination of their deluded worshippers. *The stock is a doctrine of vanities. Their idols are silver and gold, or wood and stone, the work of mens hands, which neither see, nor hear, nor eat, nor smell.* Agreeably hereto the scripture represents the votaries of these divinities as persons utterly lost to reason, and without a shadow of excuse. *They are altogether brutish and foolish*, and discover no more understanding than the idols they make.

Oracles, prophecies, prodigies were ascribed by the Heathens to their demons, and on their favour the good or evil state of mens lives was thought to depend. This persuasion was the ground of their worship: and the proper point in dispute between idolaters and the prophets of the true God, was, whether that persuasion was supported by *facts*. We find the messengers of God challenging idolaters to justify the worship of idols, and the idol gods themselves to give proof of their divinity, by a display of knowledge, or by some exertion of power, such as was either hurtful or beneficial to mankind; and even admitting, that by such a display of their power or knowledge, the Heathen deities would have established their claim to divinity, and their title to the homage of mankind. *Produce your cause, saith the Lord, bring forth your strong reasons. Let them shew the former things what they be, that we may consider them, and know the latter end of them:* produce your ancient oracles, that we may judge whether they were fulfilled by correspondent events; *or, now declare to us things for to come. Shew us things for to come hereafter, that we may know that ye are gods; yea, do good, or do evil, that we may be dismayed*: that it may appear ye have, what your votaries assert, a title to the reverence and worship of mankind. *Behold, ye are nothing, and your work of nought*, and therefore there can be no shadow of reason for paying you homage. How very different is this language of the ancient prophets from that of our learned moderns, who tell us, that idolatry cannot possibly be justified by any miracles, however numerous or splendid; and that whatever power over mankind the Heathen gods might possess, they could have no right to

 worship

worship? The prophets would have allowed their title to worship, had they admitted their power. Their utter impotence is the only reason of the scripture's remonstrating against paying them homage. I add, that these remonstrances of scripture, which are frequently repeated, are confirmed by facts, by many striking testimonies of the utter inability of the Heathen deities to interpose either for the conviction of gainsayers, or for the benefit of their worshippers, or in vindication of their own honour. They could not interpret Nebuchadnezzar's dream, nor the hand-writing upon the wall of Belshazzar's palace; nor were they able to answer by fire, in the public trial between their own prophets and the prophet of Jehovah, though on these several occasions, but especially the last, all their credit was at stake. Nor did they oppose (how much soever it might be their interest to do it) any miracles of their own, to those either of Moses or the Messiah, as we hope to shew in the sequel.'

In opposition to all this evidence, it has been asserted, that the system of Pagan idolatry was supported by prophecies and miracles, delivered and performed, not by the fictitious deities of the Heathens, but by *devils*, or wicked demons of a higher order than mankind. It has been farther asserted, that these wicked spirits were, properly speaking, the gods of the Heathens, rather than those imaginary beings, whom they seemed to themselves to worship; and, in support of these assertions, appeal is made to the writings of the Fathers, and the authority of scripture. It must be owned, that these extravagant opinions are clearly contained in the writings of the Fathers; but they are only asserted there, not proved, and perhaps were never really believed by the very persons who maintained them, and upon whose authority alone they have been received in succeeding ages. As, however, it is a matter of no great importance what sentiments the Fathers entertained on the subject, Mr. Farmer (in addition to the general reasons he had already suggested) proves, that the scripture never represents the Heathens as worshipping devils, and considers the meaning of the several words rendered *devils* in the Old Testament, and the signification of *demons* in the New.

Our ingenious Author examines, in the third section, the character and pretensions of the magicians, diviners, and sorcerers of antiquity; lays before his readers the scripture account of them; and refutes the various pleas alledged by Christians, in support of the credit and efficacy of the ancient magic. The magicians undertook to interpret dreams, to foretell future events, and to accomplish many wonderful things, by their superior knowledge of the secret powers of nature, of the virtues of plants and minerals, and of the motions and influences of the stars.—Divination was a science in which they thought themselves sure of success, if they proceeded according to certain established rules. Nor are we hence to infer, as some have done,

done, that the ancient magicians, or priests, were mere naturalists and astrologers. There have, indeed, been Atheists and Christians, who have been much addicted to divination and astrology; but these arts among the Pagan nations were founded in their system of theology.—The scripture, however, without paying regard to the principles the magicians went upon, or the different characters they assumed, brands them all as shameless impostors, and reproaches them with an utter inability of discovering or accomplishing any thing supernatural. The prophet Isaiah, having foretold the destruction of Babylon, so famous all over the world for divination and astrology, thus proceeds to insult that proud city: *Stand now with thine enchantments, and with the multitude of thy sorceries, wherein thou hast laboured from thy youth; if so be thou shalt be able to profit, if so be thou mayest prevail. Thou art wearied in the multitude of thy counsels. Let now the astrologers, the star-gazers, the monthly prognosticators, stand up, and save thee from those things which shall come upon thee*, from that destruction, which, he tells them, with their various methods of divination and sorcery, they would be unable either to foresee or prevent.

But notwithstanding the clear decision of the point by the divine oracles, many Christians have contended for the supernatural power and efficacy of Pagan divination and sorcery. This point was maintained by the Fathers in particular, who ascribed the efficacy of magic to evil demons; as some of the Heathen philosophers also did. It was a very prevailing opinion in the primitive church, that magicians and necromancers, both among the Gentiles and heretical Christians, had each their particular demons, perpetually attending on their persons, and obsequious to their commands, by whose help they could call up the souls of the dead, foretel future events, and perform miracles. Mr. Farmer, therefore, in farther opposition to these sentiments, proceeds to shew, that the supernatural power of magic cannot be inferred, either from the scripture's describing diviners by their usual appellations, or as persons having a *familiar spirit*, and a *spirit of divination*; nor from the laws of Moses against divination and witchcraft; nor from the credit in which these arts were said to be held. Indeed, this credit was not so great as hath sometimes been represented; for it appears, from many passages and testimonies of ancient writers, that magic and divination were treated with general contempt in enlightened ages.

In the fourth section, which relates to the false prophets as spoken of in scripture, are explained, 1. The celebrated warning of Moses, Deut. xiii. 1—5. 2. The prophecy of Christ, Matth. xxiv. 24. 3. Several passages in the Epistles, with regard to the false teachers in the apostolic age. 4. St. Paul's prophecy concerning the Man of Sin, *whose coming is after the working of Satan, with all power, and signs, and lying wonders.*

And

And, 5. St. John's prediction concerning the person, *who was to do great signs, and make fire come down from heaven.* Part of what is said upon our Saviour's prediction, *There shall arise false Christs, and false prophets, and shall shew great signs and wonders,* cannot be unacceptable to our Readers.

'Our Lord is not here warning his disciples against admitting the *divinity* of unquestionable miracles, but against hastily crediting the *truth* of those pretences to miracles, which would be made by the persons of whom he is speaking. This appears, as well from the natural import of this prophecy in its original language, as from the history and character of the impostors to whom it refers. Christ does not say, "False prophets shall *shew*, that is, really *exhibit* and *perform*, great signs," but (as the original word should have been rendered) "they will GIVE, that is, appeal to, promise or undertake to produce such signs, using the very language of the Jewish legislator explained above, who represents a prophet as *giving* (that is, proposing and appealing to) a sign or wonder, whether it did or did not come to pass. The phrase itself does not determine whether the sign given, be it the promise of a miracle or the prediction of an event, would be confirmed or confuted, when it was expected to be accomplished. It might be engaged for, and yet never be exhibited. And every circumstance of the prophecy contained in this context, serves to prove, that the persons here foretold would only undertake to shew great signs, without performing what they undertook. But I shall argue chiefly from the history of those persons, in whose appearance and pretensions this prophecy received its completion, and which must be allowed to be the best key to the interpretation of this prophetic warning.

'Our Saviour here refers to those impostors, who sprung up in Judea in the interval between the delivery of this prophecy, and the destruction of Jerusalem. As early as the 45th or 46th year of the Christian æra, one Theudas, who called himself a prophet, persuaded great numbers to follow him to Jordan, by telling them that he would, by his own command, divide the river: but this confident boast ended in his own destruction, as well as that of many of his followers. About nine or ten years afterwards Judea swarmed with these deceivers, who led the people into the wilderness, and *undertook to exhibit divine wonders.* One who came out of Egypt promised to cause the walls of Jerusalem to fall down; but the deluded multitudes who followed him were dispersed or destroyed by the Romans, *suffering* (to use the language of Josephus) *the just punishment of their folly.* The nearer the Jews were to destruction, so much the more did these impostors multiply, and so much the more easy credit did they find with those who were willing to have their miseries soothed by hope. Even during the conflagration of the Temple, a false prophet encouraged the people with miraculous signs of deliverance: nor did the total destruction of the city cure this madness, as appears by the conduct of an impostor at Cyrene, who *promised to shew them signs and apparitions.*'

The fifth section is employed in proving, that the scriptures represent the one true God as the sole creator and sovereign of the world, which he governs by fixed and invariable laws; and that

that to him they appropriate all miracles, urging them as demonstrations of his divinity and sole dominion over nature, in opposition to the claims of all other superior beings.

'How very different a view of miracles is this,' says our Author, after having fully established his point, 'from that given us by those learned moderns who assert, that they argue only the interposition of some power more than human; that the lowest orders of superior intelligences may perform great miracles, and higher orders of beings greater miracles still; that no miracle recorded in scripture can be pronounced beyond the power of all created beings in the universe to produce; and that in no case whatever can the immediate interposition of God be distinguished certainly by the works themselves? When the adversaries of revelation use such language, with a view to destroy its evidence, they speak in character. But what raises our wonder is, its being held by some of its ablest votaries and advocates, notwithstanding that revelation strongly asserts the sole dominion of Jehovah over Nature, and every deviation from the laws of Nature, (that is, every miracle) to be in itself a demonstration of his being its Creator and Lord. Which of these two opinions is most consonant to reason, is a point discussed in the second chapter. We only observe here, that they cannot both be true. Can those works be the sole prerogatives of Jehovah, and a proof of his sole and unrivalled sovereignty, which *others* besides him, and even when acting in opposition to him, have a power of performing as well as he? And can we successfully maintain the argument from miracles in favour of revelation, if we do not adhere to the use which revelation itself makes of miracles?'

As the most able of our modern writers seem not to have attended to the true state of the ancient controversy between the prophets of God and Idolaters, that matter is considered by Mr. Farmer; after which he proceeds to the sixth and last section of the third chapter. The design of this section is to shew that the scriptures uniformly represent all miracles as being, in themselves, an absolute demonstration of the divinity of the mission and doctrine of the prophets, at whose instance they are performed, and never direct us to regard their doctrines as a test of the miracles being the effect of a divine interposition. Besides taking some notice of the miracles of Moses and the prophets in this view, our Author here distinctly examines the miracles performed by Christ and his apostles, and refutes an objection that may be drawn from Matth. xii. 26, 27. The Pharisees did not ascribe the miracles of our Lord in general to the assistance of demons, nor did Jesus refer them to his doctrine, in order to determine the divinity of his works.

'It is to little purpose, therefore, to plead,' says Mr. Farmer towards the close of the section, 'as the advocates of Christianity are apt to do, that the nature of the doctrines which miracles are designed to confirm, will serve to point out the Author of the works, inasmuch as this can do no service to Christianity; for the divinely authorized teachers of it did not, and, considering the prejudices of the first converts, could not make this use of its doctrines. Had there been

been any ambiguity in the proof from miracles, it would have been rejected by those to whom it was at first proposed. In latter ages learned men have adventured (such is the presumption and weakness of human reason, in many persons endowed with the largest measure of it) to demonstrate *à priori*, that it became God to interpose for the reformation of the world, just at the time, and in the manner related in the gospel; and hence they infer the divinity of its miracles, and very often even their truth. But it is certain, that in the age in which the gospel was published, nothing seemed more incredible than its grand doctrine, that Jesus of Nazareth is the Messiah. And Jesus and his apostles won men to the belief of this article, by the evidence of prophecies and miracles, without once appealing to the internal credibility of it, or entering into any metaphysical reasonings and disquisitions concerning the dispensations of providence.

'Indeed, setting all prejudice aside, the Messiahship of Jesus of Nazareth is a doctrine which natural reason cannot, of itself, discover to be either true or false. It is a doctrine which admits of no other proof than the testimony of prophecies and miracles, and yet can never itself serve to manifest their divine original.

'A late celebrated writer seems to have been sensible of this when he said *, "that we are to distinguish between the doctrines we prove by miracles, and the doctrines by which we try miracles; and that they are not the same doctrines." With what a number of subtle distinctions have the learned perplexed the evidence of the gospel, such as render it very unfit for being (what it was, by its gracious Author, designed to be) the religion of the poor and illiterate? If miracles are common to all superior beings, is it evident to an ordinary capacity, that they necessarily argue the immediate interposition of God, when performed by a person who teaches lessons of morality, though at the same time he alledged his miracles in confirmation of claims and powers quite distinct from, and superior to, that of a teacher of morality, such as his being the Messiah and Son of God? Besides, if the purity of Christ's moral precepts be a necessary test of the divinity of his works, wrought to establish his extraordinary pretensions and character, how comes it to pass that neither Christ nor his apostles have given us any information concerning this matter? As they have no where told us what those doctrines are by which we are to try their miracles, if there be such doctrines, are they not chargeable with the most criminal omission? An omission which no human wisdom or sagacity can supply. Nay, upon the sole evidence of miracles, they demanded faith in Christ as the Messiah, *before* they instructed men in any other doctrines, and therefore certainly without submitting them to previous examination; which would have been very unreasonable, if those other doctrines are a necessary test of the divinity of their miracles.

'The plain matter of fact, as it appears to me, is this: they never taught men to try their miracles, either by the doctrine they were immediately designed to confirm, or by any other; but, on the contrary, taught men to judge of their doctrine by their miracles. The very *purity* of the Christian doctrine, as well as the nature of

* Sherlock's Disc. vol. i. p. 303, 304.

Christ's

2

Christ's personal claims, rendered this conduct necessary. The Jews in general, and the Pagans more especially, were plunged into the deepest corruption. The latter were not only idolaters, but worshipped their gods by acts of uncleanness, such as were suitable to their apprehended natures. Would not the purity of the gospel create in such persons a prejudice against its miracles? What could engage them to embrace a doctrine that contradicted every sentiment and affection of their hearts, but such works as were in themselves, and according to the genuine sentiments of nature, certain and evident proofs of a divine interposition? Those therefore who endeavour to prove, that miracles alone are not a sufficient criterion of a divine mission, do not attend to the nature of the Christian dispensation, nor to the state of the world when it was first erected. They likewise impeach the conduct of Christ and his apostles, and labour to destroy (though without designing it) the very foundation on which Christianity is built. We have shewn in general, that if miracles are ever performed in support of falsehood, they can never afford certain evidence of a divine commission: least of all, then, can they serve to establish the divine mission and authority of Christ, which he requires us to acknowledge upon the account of his miracles, as in themselves a complete and sufficient evidence.'

The design of the fourth chapter is to shew, that the scriptures have not recorded any instances of real miracles performed by the devil. Our Author, in considering this part of his subject, has examined the objections that may be drawn from the case of the magicians in Egypt, and from the appearance of Samuel, after his decease, to Saul. In order to prove that the magicians did not perform works really supernatural, nor were assisted by any superior beings, the following points are discussed at large, with great accuracy and judgment; 1. The character and pretensions of the magicians. 2. The true intention of Pharaoh in sending for them, and the absurdity of the intention commonly ascribed to him. 3. The motives which might induce the magicians to attempt an imitation of the works of Moses. 4. The acts done by Moses, and the principles on which he acted. 5. The language in which Moses describes the works of the magicians. And, 6. The nature of the several works done by them. The case of Samuel's appearance to Saul at Endor, is considered with equal attention, and Mr. Farmer favours the opinion, that God did either raise up Samuel, or present a likeness or image of him before Saul, to denounce the divine judgment against him for the crime he was committing, in applying to a reputed sorceress. Our Saviour's temptations in the wilderness, fall within this part of the Author's plan; but he has formerly examined them in a distinct treatise *.

The fifth and last chapter of the work before us, is taken up in shewing that miracles, considered as divine interpositions, are a certain proof of the mission and doctrine of a prophet; and

* See Review, vol. xxv.

in pointing out the advantages and necessity of this proof, in confirming and propagating a new revelation. At the beginning of the chapter, Mr. Farmer states the circumstances under which miracles prove the divinity of a prophet's mission and doctrine; and guards his readers against two extremes, that of considering miracles as proofs only of power on the one hand, and on the other, that of representing them as proofs of the universal and perpetual inspiration of the person who performs them. After this he goes on to evince, in a very satisfactory manner, that the proof from miracles, of the divine commission and doctrine of a prophet, is in itself decisive and absolute; that this proof is natural, and agreeable to the common sense of mankind in all ages; that it is easy and compendious; that miracles constitute a powerful method of conviction, without being violent and compulsive; that they are necessary to attest a divine commission, and to confirm and propagate a new revelation, such especially as contradicts mens prejudices and passions; that they serve to revive and confirm the principles of natural religion, and to recover men from the two opposite extremes of Atheism and Idolatry; and that the evidence of miracles, whether of power or knowledge, is the fittest to accompany a standing revelation, because it may be conveyed to distant ages and nations.

We have no hesitation in pronouncing this treatise to be the most important and masterly performance we have ever yet seen on the nature, origin, and design of miracles. The former writers upon the subject, who may be thought, in some respects, the most to coincide with our Author, will be found to differ from him, and to be inferior to him in several very considerable points. They are mistaken in their descriptions of the nature of miracles; they ascribe an undue power to evil spirits; and are silent or defective with regard to a number of questions fully examined by Mr. Farmer. No one, in particular, can be compared with him, for the extensive, learned, and judicious manner in which he hath discussed and confuted the system of demonism, or for the perspicuity and strength wherewith he hath stated the certain evidence that miracles afford of the divine commission and doctrine of a prophet.

Were we to recommend, to a young person, a proper method of study, with relation to the subject of miracles, we should advise him to begin with this book. Having thus laid a right foundation, he would proceed with great advantage to the valuable productions of Douglas, Adams, Campbell, Claparede, and the other ingenious writers who have considered the positive testimony in favour of the Jewish and Christian miracles, and endeavoured to remove the difficulties, and to answer the objections which have been raised against this testimony, by the enemies of revelation.

ART.

ART. IX. *Observations on Reversionary Payments, Annuities, &c.* By Richard Price, D. D. F. R. S. 8vo. 6 s. bound. Cadell. 1771.

THERE are few modern publications, which have so many urgent claims on the public attention, as that which is now before us. Whether we consider it in its *design* or in its *execution*, we may venture to say, that it is an honour both to the *ingenuity* and to the *humanity* of its Author; and that none can peruse it, without deriving from it very considerable pleasure and advantage.

If we regard this work, as the production of genius and labour, and as containing many particulars in that department of science, of which it treats, that are *new* and *interesting*, it will naturally excite the curiosity and attract the notice of all, who have any taste for mathematical disquisitions and calculations: but considered in its immediate intention and application, it strongly recommends itself to all, who have any regard either for their species or their country. It is undoubtedly a very excellent, and, we hope, will prove an equally useful antidote against the *contagion* of forming annuity schemes, which too generally prevails. It will be a means of opening the eyes of the public on that ruin in which all such connections, entered into without sufficient examination, and continued without amendment, *may* involve some of the present members, and necessarily *must* involve posterity.

Equity and humanity forbid our enriching ourselves at the expence of our children and successors; and we trust that the managers of all such societies will be disposed to retreat, and to reform their respective plans, before it is too late. With this view we anxiously recommend the present work to their notice, and to the notice of all, who either actually are, or propose to become, members of such associations. Prudence requires that some provision be made in the earlier period of life, and by those whose industry may avail to this end, for a season of growing infirmities and wants. But for God's sake, let it be such a provision as is likely to answer the end proposed by it, and as shall be equitable to others, as well as advantageous to ourselves.

'A tradesman, who sells cheaper than he buys, may be kept up many years by increasing business and credit, but he will be all the while *accumulating* distress; and the longer he goes on, the more extensive ruin he will produce at last.' The allusion is just and forcible, and ought to lead us to consider, that, though our plan may be sufficiently durable to relieve ourselves, the bankruptcy *delayed* will fall the heavier on our descendants: and it is shocking to humanity to reflect, how they will despise and execrate our memories, for engrossing to

our

our own use all the benefits of an institution, in the wreck of which they must perish, without the possibility of relief.

It is with pleasure we are informed, that the Author's calculations, for the accuracy of which time and experience will be the best vouchers, have prevented some from accomplishing a design they had projected, and induced others to plead strongly, we hope not altogether without success, for a reform in societies that are already established. The book itself, we apprehend, is, or at least, will soon be in *very many* hands. It contains a valuable collection of rules, examples, and tables, which render the business of calculation, in all kinds of annuities, plain and easy; besides many curious and useful observations on similar subjects. It corrects the errors of the most approved writers on the subject of annuities; and, in short, may be pronounced the most complete work of the kind extant. The mathematical demonstrations are thrown into the Appendix; and the Author has annexed such remarks and illustrations to those passages, that are the most obscure and difficult, as will render the whole intelligible and entertaining to all those who have a tolerable acquaintance with vulgar and decimal arithmetic.

For the satisfaction of those who have not yet had an opportunity of perusing this work, and as a specimen of what they may expect to meet with, when it falls into their hands, we shall make the following extracts; and shall endeavour so to connect the Author's principles and reasoning, as to do no injustice to the work itself, whilst we are desirous of giving some information to our Readers. We shall, in this article, select those calculations and observations, that relate to some of the most considerable societies for the benefit of widows, and for the relief of age. The seventh and eighth questions in the first chapter contain the calculations, which are largely applied in the three first sections of the second chapter, and are intended to point out and to rectify the errors in the plan of the societies for the benefit of widows.

The calculations are easily made by all who will take the necessary pains, according to the rules and examples proposed by the ingenious Author, and by the assistance of the tables with which he has furnished them.

It is necessary to premise, that 'the value of an annuity, on the joint continuance of any two lives, subtracted from the value of an annuity on the life in expectation,' gives the true present value of an annuity on what may happen to remain of the latter of the two lives after the other.

'Question VII. The present value is required of an annuity to be enjoyed by one life, for what may happen to remain of it beyond another life, after a given term; that is, provided

both

both lives continue, from the present time, to the end of a given term of years. Answer. Find the value of the annuity for two lives greater, by the given term of years, than the given lives. Discount this value for the given term; and then multiply by the probability, that the two given lives shall *both* continue the given term; and the product will be the answer.

' Example. Let the two lives be each 30. The term seven years. The annuity £. 10. Interest 4 *per cent*.——The given lives, increased by 7 years, become each 37. The value of two joint lives each 37, is (by Table VII. taking $\frac{2}{5}$ of the difference between the value of joint lives of 35 and those of 40, and subtracting it from the value of the former) 10.25. The value of a single life at 37, is (by Table VI.) 13.67. The former, subtracted from the latter, is 3.42, or the value of an annuity for the life of a person 37 years of age, after another of the same age, by the general rule premised. 3.42 discounted for 7 years (that is, multiplied by 0.76, the value of £. 1, due at the end of 7 years, by Table I.) is 2.6. The probability that a single life at 30 shall continue 7 years, is (by Mr. De Moivre's hypothesis *) $\frac{49}{56}$. The probability, therefore, that two such lives shall both continue 7 years is $\frac{2401}{3136}$, or, in decimals, 0.765. And 2.6 multiplied by 0.765, is 1.989, the number of years purchase which ought to be given for an annuity, to be enjoyed by a life now 30 years of age, after a life of the same age, provided both continue 7 years. The annuity then being £. 10, its present value is £. 19.89. By similar operations it may be found, that supposing the term one year, and the ages and the rate of interest the same, the present value of the same reversionary annuity is £. 32.4; and that if the term is 15 years, the value is £. 9.7.—For two lives each 40, these values are £. 30.33.—£. 17.44.—£. 7.3. The term being 1, 7, or 15

* The hypothesis here referred to is that of an *equal decrement of life* through all its stages till the age of 86, which Mr. De Moivre considered as the utmost probable extent of life. See Review for Feb. 1771, p. 136, *seq*.—According to this hypothesis, 56 persons being supposed alive at 30, one will die every year. At the end of 7 years then, the number of the living will be 49, and $\frac{49}{56}$, or the odds of 7 to 1 (for the numerator expresses the chances of living so long, and 56 all the chances for and against this event—7 therefore will express the chances of its failing; and the proportion will be as 49 to 7, or 7 to 1) is the probability, that a life aged 30 will continue 7 years; and this fraction, multiplied by itself, is the probability, that *two* lives of this age shall both continue 7 years: and these fractions, subtracted from unity, will give the respective probabilities that they will not continue so long: the sum of both probabilities being always unit; for it is *certain*, that every event will either happen or fail.

years.——For two lives each 50, the ſame values for the ſame terms, are £. 28.2.—£. 13.86.—£. 4.34.'

Theſe values, according to the London obſervations, and Mr. Simpſon's tables of the values of ſingle and joint lives, which are conſiderably leſs than thoſe in any other place where obſervations have been kept, are

'For 2 lives at 30—£. 32.05.——£. 18.62.——£. 7.66.
at 40—£. 30.7.——£. 15.6.——£. 5.45.
at 50—£. 29.36.——£. 12.33.——£. 3.24.'

N. B. It is demonſtrated in the Appendix, that this ſolution of the queſtion is right.

'*Queſtion* VIII. Let the ſcheme of a ſociety for granting annuities to widows, be, that if a member lives *a year* after admiſſion, his widow ſhall be entitled to a life annuity of £. 20. If *ſeven* years, to £. 10 more, or £. 30 in the whole. If *fifteen* years, to another additional £. 10, or £. 40 in the whole. What ought to be the annual payments of the members for the ages of 30, 40, and 50, ſuppoſing them of the ſame ages with their wives, and allowing compound intereſt at 4 *per cent?* Anſwer. According to the hypotheſis, already mentioned; and, very nearly, according to the tables of obſervation for *Breſlaw, Norwich,* and *Northampton*—£. 8.44.—£. 8.69.—£. 9.05. —According to the *London* obſervations, £. 9.41.—£. 10.17. —£. 10.92.

'Theſe values are eaſily deduced from the values in the laſt queſtion; *e. g.* The value of £. 10 *per annum* for life to 40 after 40, provided the joint lives do not fail in *one* year, is, according to the *hypotheſis,* £. 30.33. The value of £. 20 *per annum,* in the ſame circumſtances, is therefore £. 60.66. In like manner, the value of £. 10, after 7 years, is £. 17.44. And of £. 10 after 15 years £. 7.3. Theſe values together make £. 85.4, or the value of the expectation, deſcribed in this queſtion, in a *ſingle preſent payment*; which divided by 9.82 (the value by Table VII. of two joint lives at 40) gives £. 8.69. the value of the ſame expectation in *annual payments,* during the joint lives. In the ſame manner may be found the anſwer in all caſes to any queſtions of this kind.

'Theſe calculations ſuppoſe, that the annual payments do not begin till the end of a year. If they are to begin *immediately,* the true *annual payments* will be the *ſingle* payments, divided by the value of the joint lives increaſed by unity; and in the preſent caſe they will be, by the *hypotheſis,* £. 7.75.—£. 7.9.—£. 8.07. By the *London* obſervations, £. 8.52.—£. 9.06.—£. 9.51.

'By the method of calculation now explained, may be eaſily found in all caſes, ſuppoſing the annual payments previouſly ſettled, what the reverſionary annuities are, correſponding to them

them in value. Thus, the annuities being the ſame with thoſe mentioned in this queſtion, the *mean* annual payments for all ages between 30 and 50, are nearly £. 8, according to the *higheſt* probabilities of life; £. 9, according to the *loweſt*, and 8 guineas the *medium*; intereſt being at 4 *per cent.* and the firſt payment to be made immediately. If the mean annual payments, beginning immediately, are fixed to 5 guineas, the correſponding life annuities will be nearly (by the *hypotheſis*) £. 12, if the contributor lives a year, and £. 24 if he lives ſeven years; or by the *London* obſervations £. 12, if he lives a year, and £. 20 if he lives ſeven years.'

If the rate of intereſt is lower than here ſuppoſed, and wives are younger than their huſbands, which is generally the caſe, the annual payments ought to be increaſed.—' The value of the expectation, according to the conditions of the queſtion, ſuppoſing married men 40 years of age, and their wives 30, is, in a ſingle payment, £. 113. In annual payments beginning immediately £. 9.88, by the *hypotheſis*: and £. 107—and £. 10.93 by the *London* obſervations.'—And the Author further remarks, that *yearly* payments which begin immediately, are more advantageous than *half-yearly* payments which begin immediately; and the difference of value is a quarter of a year's purchaſe in favour of the former.

' The ſcheme mentioned in this queſtion is nearly that of the *London Annuity* Society. The *Laudable Society* is alſo formed on a ſimilar plan. In both, the *annual contribution* of every member is five guineas, payable half-yearly; and for this a title is given to an annuity of £. 20 to every widow during widowhood, if the huſband, after admiſſion, lives *one* year according to the firſt ſcheme; or *three* years according to the *ſecond*; of £. 30 if the huſband lives *ſeven* years, according to both ſchemes; and £. 40. according to the *firſt* ſcheme, if he lives 15 years, or 13 years, according to the *ſecond*. In both ſchemes alſo, there is no other premium or fine required, than five guineas extraordinary, at admiſſion, from every member, whoſe age does not exceed 45. The *Laudable Society* admits none above 45, and the *London Annuity* Society obliges every perſon between 45 and 55 to pay, at admiſſion, five guineas extraordinary, for every year that he is turned of 45.

' Theſe are the main particulars in theſe ſchemes; and, therefore, both of them, were the annuities to be enjoyed for life, would receive (ſuppoſing the members all under 46 at admiſſion, and of the ſame ages with their wives; and money at 4 *per cent.*) but little more than three-fifths of the true value of the annuities; or about one-half, ſuppoſing wives, one with another, 10 years younger than their huſbands, as appears from Queſtion VIII.

'It appears farther in that question, that, supposing the annuities to be *life* annuities, and men and their wives of equal ages, the expectation to which an annual payment of five guineas beginning immediately, entitles, is nearly £. 14, if the contributor lives a year; £. 18 if he lives *three* years; and £. 20 if he lives seven years; taking the medium between the *London* and the other tables of observation.' And the ingenious Author has observed, 'that the addition which ought to be made, on account of excess of age on the man's side is, taking the nearest and the easiest round sums, about a guinea and a half in the single payments, for every year as far as 17 years; or, in the annual payments (supposed five guineas) half a guinea *per annum* for five years excess, and half a guinea more for every four year excess beyond five years, till the excess comes to be 17 years.

'It is likely (says the Author) that many persons will be very unwilling to believe, that these schemes are so deficient as they have been now represented. I will, therefore, endeavour to prove this, in a way, which, though less strict, is sufficiently decisive, and may be more likely to be intelligible to persons unskilled in mathematical calculation.'

According to the *London Annuity* scheme, between which and that of the *Laudable* Society the differences are inconsiderable, 'all that live 15 years in the Society will be entitled to annuities of £. 40 *per annum* for their widows. Suppose the whole Society, at admission, to be men of 40 years of age, taken one with another. A person of this age has an even chance of *living* 23 years; and he has an even chance of continuing with a wife of the same age (that is, of continuing in the Society) 13½ years †. Not much less, therefore, than half the members will continue in the Society 15 years; and, consequently, not much less than half the widows that will come upon the Society will be annuitants of £. 40 *per annum.* These widows, however, being older than the rest when they commence annuitants, will continue on the Society a shorter time; and, therefore, the number constantly in life together, to which they will in a course of years increase, will be proportionably smaller. Putting every thing as favourably as possible, let us suppose that, out of 20 annuitants constantly on the Society, *five* will be annuitants of £. 40, *six* of £. 30, and *nine* of £. 20. To 20 annuitants then the Society will pay £. 560 *per annum*, or the 20th part of this sum, that is £. 28 to every annuitant at an average. But such an annuity for a life at 40, after another equal life, provided both survive one year, is

† According to Mr. *De Moivre*'s hypothesis, explained in the preceding note.

worth

worth (by Question VII.) in a single present payment, £. 85 nearly, according to the *London*, and all the tables of observations, interest being all along supposed at 4 *per cent.*

'It cannot appear improbable to any one that this should be the true value of such a reversion. It is not credible that there is any situation in which the decrements of life are such as can make it a tenth part more or less.—£. 85 in present payment is the same with 3 *l.* 8 *s.* *per annum* for ever. But is an annual payment of five guineas, which must cease as soon as either of two lives, each 40, fails, equal in value to such a perpetuity? Every one must see that there is a great difference.—A set of marriages between persons all 40, will, according to the probabilities of life in Dr. *Halley*'s table, last, one with another, 15 years; and an annual payment beginning immediately, during the joint continuance of two persons of this age, is worth 10 years purchase. The comparison then, in the present case, is between 3 *l.* 8 *s.* *per annum for ever*, and five guineas *per annum for* 15 *years*; or between an annuity of 3 *l.* 8 *s.* worth 25 years purchase, and an annuity of five guineas worth only 10 years purchase.'

The Author places this subject in another light, and suggests several observations of great importance. From which it appears, that, in a society beginning with 200 members, at 40 years of age, and limited to that number, 'the annual income of the society, at the end of 20 years, and before a third part of the highest annuitants would come upon it, would begin to fall short of its expences. About that time, then, it would necessarily run aground; and, long before the number of annuitants could rise to 100, it would spend its whole stock, and find itself under a necessity of either doubling the annual payments of its members, or of reducing the annuities one half.'——If such a society is allowed to increase, 'it may continue a longer time, and, for this reason, a society that wants half the income necessary to render it permanent, may very well subsist, and even prosper for 30 or 40 years. Thus, the *Laudable Society*, was it to keep to its present number of members, might possibly feel no deficiencies for 20 or 30 years to come; but if it should continue to increase at the rate of 70 or 80 every year, it would, at the end of that time, possess a balance so much in its favour, as might enable it to support itself for 20 or 30 years more. But bankruptcy would come at last, and with the more terrible weight the longer it had been deferred. The calculation to prove this Society's capacity of supporting itself, is founded on the supposition (and the Author fears he shall not be credited when he declares it) that a hundred married men, whose common age is 36, will leave but *one* widow every year, though at the same time it is supposed that two of them will

 die

die every year. This mistake has made the whole calculation one half wrong. Nothing can be plainer than that, if the death of a married man does not leave a widow at the end of every year, the reason must be, that both himself and his wife have happened to die in the year. But it is always very improbable that this should happen.

'The rule in the *London Annuity* Society, which obliges every person between the ages of 45 and 55 to pay, at admission, 5 guineas extraordinary for every year that he exceeds 45, is an advantage to it; but it is a very inadequate, and also a very unequitable advantage. For at the same time that it obliges a person 55 years of age, to give *more* than the value of his expectation, it takes *above* two-fifths *less* than the value from a person who is 45 years of age.'

Our Readers may be ready to object, that 'the preceding observations have gone on the supposition, that the reversionary annuities are to be for life.' Our Author has anticipated and obviated the objection. 'What difference (says he) in favour of these Societies arises from the circumstance, that the annuities are to be paid only for *widowhood*, cannot be exactly determined.—Were even one-half of the widows to marry, still the schemes I have been considering would probably be insufficient. But in the circumstances of these Societies it cannot be expected, that above 1 in 10, or perhaps 1 in 20, will marry. The persons most likely to enter into them, are such as have not the prospect or ability of making competent provisions for their widows in other ways. The widows left, therefore, will in general be unprovided for, and being also left with families of children, it is quite unreasonable to expect, that any considerable proportion should marry. This is true of such as may happen to be left young; but when a Society has subsisted some time, the *greater* part will not be young when left, and these, at the same time that no advantage can be expected from their marrying, will be in general the *highest* annuitants, and therefore the *heaviest burdens*. Moreover, the prospect of the loss of their annuities will have a particular tendency to check marriage among them. For all these reasons it seems to me likely that the benefit, which these Societies will derive from marriage among their annuitants, will not be very considerable: or at least not *so* considerable as to be equal to the advantages I have allowed them, by calculating on the suppositions, that the money they receive will be *always improved perfectly, without loss or delay, at the rate of 4 per cent. compound interest*; that the probabilities of life among males and females are the same, and all husbands likewise of the same ages with their wives, and that consequently the *maximum* of widows on such societies can amount to no more than half the number of marriages.

marriages.—It must be added, that I have made no account of any expences attending the execution and management of the schemes of these Societies. Some such expences there must be, and some advantages should be always provided in order to compensate them.' What then are we to think of those who squander away, in needless expences, that money, which, with the utmost prudence and œconomy, will not be sufficient to enable them to do justice to their expectants? Such profusion may give a present credit to their establishments; the unskilful or the unthinking may be misled by parade and ostentation; the number of their members may be daily increasing, and their wealth may flow in upon them so fast as to intoxicate them; but a period will arrive when they will regret their present waste, and wish they had industriously applied the most trifling sum they now heedlessly expend, to the purpose of providing against their future necessities. We hope there are none entrusted with the conduct of such Societies, who care not what becomes of posterity, provided they can secure themselves.

Should it be said, in defence of these Societies, 'that the deficiencies in their plans cannot be of much consequence, because their rules oblige them to preserve a constant equality between their income and expences, by reducing the annuities as there shall be occasion; and that hereby they can never be in danger of bankruptcy.' It is answered, 'that the time when they will begin to feel deficiencies is so distant, that it will be too late to remedy past errors, without sinking the annuities so much, as to render them inconsiderable and trifling. All that is given too much to *present* annuitants is so much taken away from *future* annuitants. And if a scheme is *very* deficient, the first annuitants may, for 30 or 40 years, receive so much more than they ought to receive, as to leave little or nothing for any who come after them. Deficient schemes, therefore, are attended with particular injustice; and this injustice will be the same, if, instead of *reducing* the annuities, the annual payments should be increased; for all the difference this can make will be, to cause the injustice to fall on *future contributors*, instead of *future annuitants*. Besides this, when the annuities have been for some time in a state of reduction, or the contributions in a state of increase, it will be seen that these Societies have gone upon wrong plans, and, therefore, they will be deserted and avoided; the consequence of which will prove still greater deficiencies in their annual income, and a more rapid desertion and decline, till a total dissolution and bankruptcy take place.'

After all that has been said by so great a master of the subject, in order to point out the insufficiency of the plans that have been already adopted, we may reasonably expect an immediate reformation. If those who have concerted such schemes proceed on any principles or calculations, which can bear the public inspection, they are under an indispensable obligation of communicating them to the world; if on the contrary, and as is most probable, they have hitherto been deceived, it is incumbent on them to submit to the evidence of truth, and to the calls of justice and humanity, and to save those with whom they are connected from impending ruin. With the assistance to be derived from this valuable treatise, they may easily make the necessary amendments; but they must set about them without delay. The longer they continue in their present state, the greater will be the confusion and mischief attending a reformation. Dr. Price is no enemy to *all* schemes of this kind; he has proposed several plans for providing annuities for widows, that are both safe and advantageous. ' Institutions (he says) for providing widows with annuities would, without doubt, be extremely useful, could such be contrived as would be *durable*, and at the same time *easy* and *encouraging*. The natures of things do not admit of this, in the degree that is commonly imagined.—From Question VII. and VIII. it may be inferred that (interest being at 4 *per cent.* and the probabilities of life as in Mr. *De Moivre*'s hypothesis, or the *Breslaw*, *Norwich*, and *Northampton* Tables) for an annual payment beginning immediately of *four* guineas during marriage; and also for a guinea and a half in hand, on account of each year that the age of the husband exceeds the age of the wife, every married man, under 40, might be entitled to an annuity, during life, for his widow, of £. 5 if he lives a year, £. 10 if he lives *three* years, and £. 20 if he lives *seven* years.——If such a Society chuses that those who shall happen to continue members the longest time, shall be entitled to still greater annuities, six guineas, additional to all the other payments at admission, would be the full payment for an annuity of £. 25, and 12 guineas for an annuity of £. 30, if a member should live 15 years.

The Author farther observes, that, in conformity to the scheme of the *London Annuity* Society, ' all batchelors and widowers might be encouraged to join such a Society, by admitting them on the following terms: *four guineas* to be paid on admission, and *three guineas* every year afterwards, during celibacy; and, on marriage, the same payments with those made by persons admitted after marriage; in consideration of which £. 1 *per annum*, for every single payment before marriage, might be added to the annuities, to which such members would have been otherwise entitled.—In this case, the contributions of such members as should happen to desert, or die in celibacy, would be so much profit to the Society, tending to give it more strength and security.

' This (says the Author) is one of the best schemes that I am able to think of, or would chuse to recommend. There are,

are, however, others no leſs ſafe and encouraging:' but for the account of theſe we muſt refer to the work itſelf.

We ſhall conclude this article with a brief abſtract of what the Author has advanced with reſpect to the ſocieties for the relief of age; whence it muſt appear to every impartial enquirer, that 'they are all impoſitions on the public, proceeding from ignorance, and encouraged by credulity and folly.'

'Queſtion VI. A perſon, 35 years of age, wants to buy an annuity, for what may happen to remain of his life after 50 years of age. What is the value of ſuch an annuity in *ready money*, and alſo in *annual payments*, till he attains to the ſaid age; that is, in annual payments for 15 years, ſubject in the mean time to failure, ſhould his life fail?

'Anſwer. The preſent value of ſuch an annuity is the *preſent* value of a life at 50, in money to be received 15 years hence, and the payment of which depends on the contingency of the continuance of the given life 15 years: that is, it is equal to the value of a life at 50, multiplied by the preſent value of £. 1 to be received at the end of 15 years, and alſo by the probability that the given life will continue ſo long. A life at 50, according to Mr. *De Moivre*'s valuation of lives, and reckoning intereſt at 4 *per cent.* is worth 11.34 year's purchaſe. The preſent value of £. 1 to be received at the end of 15 years, is, by Table I. 0.5553. And the probability that a life at 35 will continue 15 years, is, according to the *Breſlaw* obſervations $\frac{346}{490}$. (The *numerator* being the number of the living in Dr. *Halley*'s Table oppoſite to the *given age*, and *denominator*, the number oppoſite to the preſent age of the given life.) And theſe three values, multiplied by one another, give £. 4.44, or the number of years purchaſe that ought to be given for the annuity.—The annuity then being ſuppoſed £. 50, its value in preſent money is £. 222.

'In order to find this value in *annual payments*, while the given life is attaining to 50, it is neceſſary to find the value of an annuity for 15 years, ſubject to failure on the extinction of the given life. And the value of ſuch an annuity is, evidently, the laſt value ſubtracted from the value of the given life; or, in the preſent inſtance, £. 4.44, ſubtracted from £. 1397 (ſee Table VI.) that is, £. 9.53. £. 222 then, being the preſent value of an annuity of £. 50 for the remainder of a life now 35, after attaining to 50; and 9.53 being the number of years purchaſe, which ought to be given for an annual payment to laſt 15 years, if a life now 35 laſts ſo long, it follows, that the value of the ſame annuity in annual payments till this life attains to 50, is £. 222 divided by 9.53, or £. 23.3.

'This calculation ſuppoſes, that the firſt of the annual payments is not to be made till the end of a year. If the firſt payment is made immediately, the value will be, the *ſingle payment*

ment divided by the value of the life for the given term increased by unity; that is, in the present case; £. 222 divided by 10.53; or £. 21.08.

'If the value of the annuity is required in a single payment, over and above any given annual payment; deduct the value of the annual payment from the whole value in a single present payment, and the remainder will be the answer. Thus, let 5 guineas, in the present instance, be the given annual payment for the assigned term; and let the enquiry be, how much more in present money the supposed annuity is worth. By what has been just said, 9.53 multiplied by 5 guineas, that is, £. 50 is the value of the annual payment; and this sum deducted from £. 222 leaves £. 172 the answer. If the annual payment begins immediately, its value is 10.53 multiplied by 5 guineas, and the answer comes out £. 166 75.'

It is to be observed in all cases of this kind, 'that it is the *title* to the annuity that will commence at the end of the given term, and that the first payment is not to be made till a year afterwards.'

Upon these principles is formed the following table, which very much eases the labour of such calculations.

Values of £. 1 *per ann.* for life, after 50, to persons whose ages are,	Values in *one present payment*, interest 4 *per cent.*	Interest 3 *per cent.*	Values in *annual payments*, till 50, to begin at the end of a year, interest 4 *per cent.*	Interest 3 *per cent.*
10 - - -	1.235	2.015	.0789	.113
15 - - -	1.583	2.444	.106	.143
20 - - -	2.028	2.989	.146	.193
25 - - -	2.594	3.644	.203	.259
30 - - -	3.369	4.508	.297	.366
35 - - -	4.446	5.667	.466	.559
40 - - -	5.953	7.232	.822	.950
Values of the same annuity after 55, to ages				
30 - - -	2.114	2.937	.167	.211
35 - - -	2.722	3.632	.241	.297
40 - - -	3.732	4.708	.394	.464
45 - - -	5.088	6.115	.703	.803
Values of the same annuity after 60, to ages				
35 - - -	1.667	2.290	.135	.168
40 - - -	2.234	2.923	.2[illegible]3	.245
45 - - -	3.043	3.811	.327	.384
50 - - -	4.255	5.061	.600	.679

'The

'The numbers in the 2d and 3d columns of this Table, multiplied by any annuity, will give the value of that annuity in a *single* payment, to be enjoyed for life, by the ages corresponding to those numbers in the 1st column, *after* the age mentioned at the head of that column; and, in the same manner, the numbers of the 4th and 5th columns will give the values in *annual* payments. Thus, the value of £. 44 *per annum*, to be enjoyed for life, after 50; by a person now 40 (interest at 4 *per cent.*) is 5.95 multiplied by 44, or £. 261.9 in a *single* payment; and .822, multiplied by 44, or £. 36.16, in *annual* payments till 50, the first payment to be made at the end of a year.

'In order to find the same values, partly in *annual* payments, and partly in any given *entrance* or *admission money*; say, 'as the value of the *given annuity* in a *single* payment (found in the way just mentioned) is to the given *entrance money*, so is its value in *annual* payments to a fourth proportional; which, subtracted from the value in *annual payments*, the *remainder* will be the annual payment due, over and above the given entrance money.'

'Example. Suppose a person now 40, to be willing to pay £. 200 entrance money, *besides* such an annual payment for 10 years as shall, together with his entrance money, be sufficient to entitle him to a life annuity of £. 44 after 50, What ought the annual payment to be? Answer, £. 8.55.—For 261.9 is to £. 200 as £. 36.16 to £. 27.61; which, subtracted from £. 36.16, the remainder is £. 8.55, or 8 *l.* 11 *s.*'

'The conditions of obtaining this annuity, according to the tables of the *Laudable Society of Annuitants for the Benefit of Age*, are 76 *l.* 17 *s.* in *admission money*, and 6 *l.* 14 *s.* in *annual payments.*—According to the tables of the Society of *London Annuitants for the Benefit of Age*, the conditions of obtaining the same annuity are £. 30 in *admission money*, and £. 10 in *annual payments.*—The *Equitable* Society of Annuitants requires, for the same annuity, 38 *l.* 10 *s.* in *admission money*, and £. 13 in *annual* payments. The true value is, over and above the *admission money* just mentioned, an *annual payment* of 30 *l.* 17 *s.* (interest reckoned at 4 *per cent.*) or an *annual payment* of 36 *l.* 15 *s.* interest reckoned at 3 *per cent.*—The *London Union Society for the comfortable Support of aged Members*, promises an annuity of no less than 50 guineas for life, after 50, to a person now 40, for 40 *l.* 10 *s.* in admission money, and £. 7 in annual payments. —The *Amicable Society of Annuitants for the Benefit of Age*, promises an annuity of £. 26 *per annum*, for life, to a person now 40, after attaining to 50, for 28 *l.* 16 *s.* in *admission money*, and £. 6 in *annual payments.* The true value of this annuity is 28 *l.* 16 *s.* in *admission money*, and 17 *l.* 8 *s.* in *annual payments*

ments (interest supposed at 4 *per cent.*) or the same sum in *admission money*, and 20 *l.* 18 *s.* in *annual payments*, interest supposed at 3 *per cent.*—The *Provident Society for the Benefit of Age*, promises an annuity of £. 25 to a person now 40, after attaining to 50, for 34 guineas in *admission money*, and 8 guineas in *annual payments*. The true value is, 34 guineas in *admission money*, and 15 *l.* 12 *s.* in *annual payments*, interest at 4 *per cent.* or, the same sum in *admission money*, and £. 19 in *annual* payments, interest being at 3 *per cent.*'

Our Author concludes this section, with suggesting the following plan of a provision for old age. 'Let 13 guineas be given as *entrance money*; and let besides £. 1, £. 2, £. 3, £. 4, &c. be given at the beginning of the 1st, 2d, 3d, 4th, &c. years, as the payments for these years respectively; and let the last payment be £. 16 at the beginning of the 16th year. All these payments put together will, according to the probabilities of life in the 3d, 4th, and 5th Tables (interest being at 4 *per cent.*) entitle a person, whose age was 40 when he begun them, to an annuity, after 15 years, beginning with £. 15, and increasing at the rate of £. 1 every year, till, at the end of 15 years more, or when he has attained to 70, it becomes a standing annuity of £. 30 for the remainder of his life. If the addition of *three* guineas is made to the *entrance money*, for every year that any life between 30 and 40 falls short of 40, the value will be obtained nearly, of the same annuity to be enjoyed by that life, after the same number of years, and increasing in the same manner, till, in 30 years, it becomes *stationary* and *double*.—This plan is particularly inviting, as it makes the *largest* payments become due, when the *near* approach of the annuity renders the encouragement to them *greatest*, and as, likewise, the annuity is to increase continually with age, till it comes to be highest, when life is most in the decline, and when, therefore, it will be most useful. It is farther a recommendation of this plan, that less depends in it on the *improvement* of money than in most other plans.'

The labouring poor have not escaped our Author's benevolent attention; and he has proposed the following plan of a society for their benefit. 'Let the society, at its first establishment, consist of 100 persons, all between 30 and 40, and whose mean age may therefore be reckoned 36; and let it be supposed to be always kept up to this number, by the admission of new members, between the ages of 30 and 40, as old members die off. Let the contribution of each member be four-pence *per* week, making, from the whole body, an annual contribution of 85 *l.* 17 *s.* Let it be further supposed, that seven of them will fall every year into disorders, that shall incapacitate them for seven weeks.—30 *l.* 12 *s.* of the annual contribution will be be just sufficient to enable the society to grant to each of these 12 *s. per* week during their illnesses; and the remaining £. 55 *per annum*, laid up and *carefully* improved, at 3½ *per cent.* will increase to a capital that shall be sufficient, according to the chances of life in Tables III. IV. and V. to enable the society to pay to every member, *after* attaining to 67 years of age, or *upon* entering his 68th year, an annuity, beginning with £. 5, and increasing at the rate of £. 1 every year for 7 years, till, at the age of 75, it came to be a standing annuity of £. 12 for the remainder of life. Were such a society to make its contribution *seven-pence per* week, an allowance of 15 *s.* might be made, on the same suppositions, to every member during sickness; besides the payment of an annuity beginning with £. 5 when a member entered his 64th year, and increasing for 15 years, till, at 79, it became fixed for the remainder of life at £. 20.'

Our limits will not allow our making any extracts from this ingenious Writer's remarks on the association among the *London* clergy, and the ministers in *Scotland*, for providing annuities for their widows, nor on the Amicable Society for a perpetual Assurance Office, and the Society for equitable Assurances on Lives and Survivorships. We must refer our Readers, who may be desirous of information with respect to these particulars to the valuable work itself. And we trust, they will require no apology for our extending this article to an unusual length.

[*To be concluded in our next.*]

ART. X. *Discourses on some important Subjects.* By the late Rev. Edward Stone, M. A. formerly Fellow of Wadham College, Oxford. Revised and corrected for the Press by the Author before his Death; and published by his Son, the Rev. Edward Stone, M. A. Rector of Horsenden, Bucks, and late Fellow of Wadham College. 8vo. 5 s. Rivington. 1771.

THIS Writer is already known to the world by several publications, particularly his Remarks on the Life of *Reginald Pole* *, and also by a tract for explaining and illustrating the whole Doctrine of Parallaxes by an arithmetical and geometrical Construction of the Transits of *Venus* and *Mercury* over the Sun †, &c. He appears in somewhat of a different capacity in these Discourses, which, we are told above, he had himself prepared for the public view.

The Discourses are eight in number, but some of them are divided into two, three, or four parts. The subjects of them

---

* See Review, vol. xxxiv. p. 478.

† See Review, vol. xxix. p. 478.

are, Universal Benevolence, social Justice, Self-interest, Reason and Reflection on religious Subjects, Conscience; beside which, the seventh sermon considers *Matth.* x. 34. *Think not that I come to send peace on earth, I came not to send peace, but a sword.* The eighth, another text in *Matth.* vii. 12, and the first, which consists of three parts, has this title, "No such thing as absolute chance, or natural or moral evil in the works of the creation: preached before the University of *Oxford*, 1767." The Discourses are sensible and practical; they discover the preacher to have been a man who did not rest upon the surface of things, but endeavoured to investigate, with accuracy and precision, the important truths which came under his notice, and to recommend them to a serious and careful regard, by fixing them on a firm and sure basis.

The title of the first sermon mentioned above is, we think, too generally and indiscriminately expressed. It seems to assert that there is no such thing as *moral evil*, though certainly the Author does not intend to mean that there is no such thing as vice or impiety in the world. Indeed, he speaks not of *moral evil* abstractedly considered, but of the inequality observable in the distribution of temporal blessings, according to the different characters of men; and this it is plain is what he intends here by the phrase.

His text is in Psalm civ. 24. After having proved that the preparation and disposition of things in this earth, for the comfort and welfare of the different creatures which inhabit it, and particularly that of mankind, must be ascribed to an all-perfect being, he proceeds to a farther conclusion, which he immediately draws from the instinct observable in animals: this he had before particularly considered as the direct impulse or inspiration of the Deity; and 'since, he adds, the Supreme Lord and Governor of the world condescends to act in this visible manner, in and for the meanest of his creatures, it may be justly inferred that the whole course of Nature is under his special superintendency and direction; that his providence is universal, not only in respect to place, but in respect to time, and that there is no contingency admitted, no irregularity or error suffered to creep into his works; but every thing continues to be done either immediately in himself, or mediately by his second causes, through the whole duration of the universe, in the *wisest and best* manner possible.'

From this conclusion he is led to consider the scheme of some who are fully persuaded of the reality of natural and moral evils, and yet believe in God the Creator of the universe, and acknowledge him to be endowed with infinite perfections. 'These persons, he says, with an air of superior wisdom, form systems for solving these difficulties, and, with a specious shew of argument,

ment, labour to support them, and impose upon themselves and the world.' They, he goes on to observe, suppose that the Almighty instituted general laws for the direction and order of the creation,—that these laws are very excellent in themselves, and as perfect as such laws could be, but from the nature of generality it was impossible for them to be applicable to every case, and subject to no inconveniences.—' Upon these principles, we are told, they argue, that errors, both of the natural and moral kind, may creep into and be suffered in the works of an unerring being, as the unavoidable effects of a general dispensation; and from thence they infer, that as these natural defects are beneath the notice of the Deity, our observation upon them will be as little regarded by him: and that the disorders in the moral world, when considered abstractedly from their future recompences, may be as freely spoken of, and represented as present irregularities, without any reflection upon the author of them.'

This our Author considers as an ' hypothesis big with atheistical consequences, betraying innocent persons into an unwarrantable liberty with the works of the Almighty, and directly tending to vindicate the most impious murmurings, and blasphemous invectives, against the Most High.' He acknowledges that there are general laws; that these laws and causes are excellent in themselves; and farther asserts, that in every case where they are enforced, they are absolutely perfect: ' For, says he, why may not general rules be without exception, and applicable to every particular case under them? Where is the impossibility, or what is there in the nature of universality, that at all times necessarily subjects it to inconveniencies? General rules are made use of in the works of providence, not because they are general, but because the least deviation from them would be erroneous, and the reason is exactly the same, for particular methods being preferred, when a general one would be defective. Where general secondary causes are not equally applicable to every case, and will induce some inconveniencies or improper effects, however rare or trivial they may be, they never can be admitted into the works of an infinite being, and will always require a particular interposition: where errors may be as easily prevented as admitted, there can be no reason assigned for their admission, nay, as they are errors, there is always an obvious reason against it.

' It is almost impossible for us to detach our imagination entirely from our own frailties, or not to consider an infinite subject in a finite manner. In our contemplations on the Deity, we cannot help resembling him in some measure to ourselves, and intermixing our failings with his perfections: this is very evident in the case before us; here it is alledged that it is much

better

better to put up with some occasional disorders, and to bear for a time with others, than to be continually breaking upon these general establishments, and for ever rectifying every minute error as oft as it arises.

'Here I ask, why is it supposed to be much better? Is it not for this reason, because it requires less attention and less attendance, and seems to be more easy and concise? But are we not here unwittingly supposing that these must be recommendations to the Deity, because they are such to us? Easy and difficult are only relative terms appropriated to finite beings, and not in the least applicable to an indefinite power. All things come alike to an omnipotent Being; and as he is omnipresent and omniscient, he is always and equally attendant upon, and attentive to, all his works, and therefore it is as little troublesome or difficult, if I may so express myself, and takes up no more of his time to act in a particular than in a general manner, and consequently neither of them can have the preference to the other on this account; and when it pleases the sovereign Creator of all things to appoint a general method, or depute subordinate agents, he doth it, not that he might withdraw himself, and leave them to act without him; but because this proceeding is most agreeable to his infinite wisdom, and any other would not be so perfect: hence, as I observed before, there can be no possible reason assigned, why any defects should be suffered to creep into his works; and there is always a most palpable reason why they should not be suffered: for, if they were, he would be acting inconsistently with his divine attributes; and nothing surely can be more absurd, than to suppose an error to proceed from an unerring Being.—We have inferred that the great Superintendent of the world vouchsafes to distinguish himself in the most singular manner, for the preservation of the feathered kind; that he inspires them with his knowledge, and acts in them through the whole process of their breeding, their nurturing and rearing their young. Since then it is evident that the Almighty hath not here committed his influence to any secondary causes, and is directly and immediately interposing in this particular case, or is directly and immediately acting in and through these animals, it is a very natural and obvious conclusion, that his divine Providence extends itself over all his works, and that he is no where wanting, no where absent; that he doth not oblige himself to observe any general rules or laws, but when it is fittest and best to observe them, and that every natural occurrence, whatever it may be, proceeds either directly from himself, or indirectly from some deputed cause. However marvellous things may then appear to us, it follows that they cannot be monstrous or mis-shapen in themselves; and whatever charm the phrase *Lusus Naturæ* may carry with it, yet

yet when it comes to be thoroughly examined, it will be found to be most delusive, as it implies, that God wantons in the production of his creatures, and sports with deformities and errors: some things, such as eclipses and comets, which were heretofore looked upon as real defects, or erratic things, have been discovered to be as natural and regular as the more common subjects of our knowledge: and, in like manner, earthquakes, inundations, volcanos, tempests, pestilences, dearths, and such like phænomena, however unaccountable they may at present appear, yet we may venture to assert that they are in themselves, and to prophecy that hereafter they will be found to be, events issuing from the decrees of unerring wisdom, foreseen and foreordained by the Sovereign Disposer of all things, and as useful, and as necessary in the order and administration of the world, as any ordinary occurrences in nature, as the vicissitudes of day and night, as the revolution of the seasons of the year, or as summer and winter, seed-time and harvest: I know, says the preacher, that *whatsoever God doth, it shall be for ever, nothing can be put to it, nor any thing taken from it*, Eccl. iii. 14.—The promiscuous distribution of external things, the prosperity of the wicked, and the adversity of the righteous, with the apparent contingency of events, are not in the least proofs of any real disorder or irregularity in the moral world: it may indeed be extremely difficult for a finite being to point out the particular reasons for the unequal division of this world's goods; an equal allotment of them might perhaps have thrown us into the same station, and been inconsistent with that order and subordination which the constitution of the world might require: or perhaps the disposition of mankind into these infinitely various classes and scenes of life, for the exertion of their different talents, and the display of virtues peculiar to each scene, may be best suited to a probationary state.—Some may be offended with the prosperity of the wicked and the adversity of the good, and may fancy that they see an error or iniquity in this dispensation; but what are adversity and prosperity? Or what influence have they upon the mind? May not the evil person be miserable in the midst of his possessions? And may not his conscience frown when the world smiles upon him? May not the good man likewise be supported with that inward consolation which nothing without can destroy? May not these precarious and volatile things, however glaring they may appear to us, be inconsiderable in themselves? Or lastly, may it not be the design of the Supreme Governor of the world to place the wages of virtue and vice at some distance from them; to bear for a while with the failings of his creatures, and at some future time and place to recompence them according to their deeds.—Whether these, or any of them, may be the reasons why

why the Deity hath set out the world in this manner, we know not; but this we know, that the just Judge of all the earth hath done right; that he hath his reasons, though we have them not, and that the world is best as it is, and would have been wrong had it been otherwise: whatever may appear as contingencies to us, are only relatively so to our finite capacities; there is no such thing as absolute chance, or natural or moral evil in the works of the creation; but every event hath its cause fixed by infinite wisdom, and every thing is extreamely good and beautiful in its kind: transported therefore with this knowledge, may we join with the heavenly quire, and sing, that *great and marvellous are thy works, Lord God Almighty; just and true are thy ways, thou King of Saints.*'

The third part of this discourse is concluded by a rational and devout soliloquy, excellently calculated to form the mind to gratitude and humility, to submission, contentment, or diligence, in whatever circumstances and station a person may be placed.

In the fourth discourse, which treats of self-interest, from Job. i. 9. *Doth Job fear God for nought?* Our Author endeavours to recover religion and virtue from the charge of selfishness, so far as it is supposed to imply any thing ungenerous and unworthy, and to prove that the principle of a true self-interest is a proper ingredient in every principle of virtue. This he illustrates and supports, by considering those virtues which seem to have some apparent connection with self-interest, and then by examining those which appear to be farther removed from it, or to be the least consistent with it: these are piety and benevolence. A particular account of what he says upon this subject we cannot lay before our Readers, and therefore shall only just extract part of a note which we find when he is speaking concerning benevolence, and in which he refers to a very celebrated writer; it is as follows: 'An ingenious author seems to express himself in a very inaccurate and unguarded manner, when he says, that "it seems undeniable, that there is such a sentiment in human nature, as disinterested benevolence; that nothing can bestow more merit on any human creature, than the possession of it in an eminent degree." *David Hume*, lib. iv. sect. 2, of benevolence, page 29.

'By disinterested benevolence, I suppose, he means only a benevolence without any direct impulse of the affection of self-love, and without the least thought or consideration of self-interest: but should he mean a benevolence entirely free from every instigation of present pleasure or pain, and from any joint view of mutual interest with the object of his benevolence, it may be fairly questioned, whether there can be such a disinterested benevolence. And, if it may be, it is unreasonable and

and unnatural, because it is a principle not raised from the affection of benevolence; for if it was, it must be accompanied with present pleasure or pain; neither is it raised from the the sense of the union of our interests, for this would include our own; but it must be raised from the opinion of another's interest, being either unconnected with, and separate from, or contrary to our own, which is unnatural and absurd.'

The sixth sermon is entitled, Conscience, and consists of four parts: the text is in Acts xxiv. 16. *Herein do I exercise myself to have a conscience void of offence towards God and towards men.* The Author very judiciously distinguishes between the conscience and the understanding, and with strength and perspicuity considers and reasons upon the subject in different views: we cannot present our Readers with any extracts from that part of his discourse, but we shall select a few reflections which he makes towards the close, when speaking of an evil and a good conscience.

' When, says he, the gay flattering scenes of vanity are passed away and succeeded by infamy and distress, then the prodigal begins to reflect upon his past conduct, his sins fly in his face, and his conscience comes forth like a strong man awakened from his trance:—the conscious wretch is haunted with the spectres that his troubled imagination conjures up before him; he startles at every noise; thinks every whisper is fraught with the tale of his wickedness, and that the finger of scorn is continually pointing at him; every thing also seems to be hung with the gloominess of his soul, while his understanding serves, like a glimmering taper, only to shew the dismal scene, and render its horrors more visible.

' The story of *Bessus*, a native of *Pæonia*, in *Greece*, comes as well authenticated to us as any thing in ancient profane history, and hath always been received as an indisputable fact *. It is this in short:

' His neighbours seeing him one day extremely earnest in pulling down some birds' nests near his house, and passionately destroying their young, could not help taking notice of it, and upbraided him for his ill-nature and cruelty; to which he replied, that he could not bear them, they were always twitting him with the murder of his father. This execrable villany had lain concealed many years, and never been suspected; and, in all probability, would never have come to light, had not the avenging fury of conscience, by these extraordinary means, drawn a public acknowledgment of it from the parricide's own mouth.

* Plut. de Numinis vind.

'As there is no bearing an evil conſcience, ſo there is no flying from it: when it ſeizes us, ſhould we ſay to it, *Haſt thou found me, O my enemy?* It will anſwer, as Elijah did to Ahab, *I have found thee, becauſe thou haſt ſold thyſelf to do evil.*

'And again, there is no ſhaking off this viper of conſcience; it lays faſt hold of us; it lies down with us, and ſtings us in our ſleep; it riſes with us, and preys upon our vitals: hence ancient moraliſts compared an evil conſcience to a vulture feeding upon our liver, and the pangs that are felt under the one to the throws of the other; ſuppoſing, at the ſame time, the vulture's hunger to be inſatiable, and this entrail to be moſt exquiſitely ſenſible of pain, and to grow as faſt as it is devoured. This, truly, muſt be allowed to be as ſtrong a repreſentation of the moſt lingering, as well as the moſt acute corporeal pains as can be drawn; yet ſtrong as it is, it falls greatly ſhort of the anguiſh of a guilty conſcience; and, indeed, it is not in the power of the imagination, when at reſt, to conceive the horrors which itſelf, when troubled, can raiſe, or the tortures it can put us to.

'But it is now time to turn from this dreary ſcene, to the more pleaſing view of a good conſcience.—When conſcience ſmiles, all nature ſympathizes with it, and ſeems to dance for joy; *a good man is ſatisfied from himſelf*; he hath an inexhauſtible fund of contentment, which ſweetens every condition of life; though he appears to have nothing, yet he maketh himſelf rich, and poſſeſſeth all things, and out of the good treaſures of his heart he can furniſh himſelf with a continual feaſt.

'What are external honours but empty titles and ridiculous pageantries, if there be no internal worth, and we are vile in our own ſight?—Though ten thouſand tongues ſhould chaunt our praiſes, they would ſound unharmonious in our ears, if conſcience join not in the choir!

'Wealth, ſtrength, and proſperity are relative goods, and dependant upon the ſtate of the mind; if this be ſickly and poor, they will be like delicious dainties to a diſtempered perſon; they will offend the loathing ſtomach, and mock the vitiated palate.

'But when the mind is luſty and ſtrong, when it hungers and thirſts after righteouſneſs, then it hath a true reliſh of things, and is filled with good; a good conſcience is the ſalt which ſeaſons all other bleſſings, and gives us a true taſte or zeſt to them.'

From theſe few extracts ſome competent idea may be formed concerning the preſent publication. The Author appears to have employed conſiderable attention on the ſubjects he here treats, and to have been himſelf rational, candid, and liberal in his ſentiments. It will by no means depreciate theſe diſ-

6 courſes

courses just to add, that it would be an unhappy mistake should our clergy imagine that very close reasonings or philosophical dissertations were generally to be attended to in their addresses to Christian assemblies. It is to be remembered that their auditories generally consist of numbers who have few opportunities of receiving instruction, in respect to the truths of religion and virtue, except what they may gain from pulpit discourses, and therefore the more plain, the more affecting, in a rational way (which indeed is very possible) these discourses are rendered, the more likely will they be to impress the hearer's heart, and to influence and regulate his conduct; and certainly persons of superior knowledge, if they are men of any real worth and virtue, will with pleasure attend to addresses which are calculated for such substantial benefit, though they might, in some respects, be much inferior to their learning and taste.

MONTHLY CATALOGUE,

For OCTOBER, 1771.

MATHEMATICAL.

Art. 11. *The young Lady and Gentleman's New Guide to the Elements of Astronomy and Geography*, &c. By J. Seally. 12mo. 3 s. bound. Roson. 1771.

TEACHERS in every department have a peculiar attachment to their own mode of instruction; and, perhaps, this attachment is not altogether the effect of vanity or humour. Every man conveys his own ideas with the greatest readiness and clearness in his own language. But were it otherwise, we cannot much blame those, who are tutors *ex officio*, for these little artifices in support of their own credit and importance. This circumstance gives birth to many *New Guides* to astronomy, geography, arithmetic, &c. while too often they have little more than their novelty to recommend them. We are entirely of opinion with our Author, that the instructions of many writers on this subject, however eminent and respectable their names, are not so well adapted to the young capacity as could be wished. 'To men of extraordinary abilities every thing appears so very easy, and whatever they propose, be it precept or example, they can place the same into so many points of view, that they are apt to conclude it to be equally easy to be understood by others.' The sentiment this paragraph conveys is unquestionably just, though we would not propose it as a specimen of the Author's general style. There is danger at the same time, lest in avoiding the extreme of prolixity, a writer should run into the other of being superficial and inaccurate. Whether our Author has steered clear of this extreme, we leave, with him, 'to the determination of the impartial reader;' while we express our opinion, that there is still room to render this work 'more worthy the approbation and encouragement of the public.' Young ladies and gentlemen may perhaps be charmed into the study of astronomy and geography by the melodious strains of ancient and

and modern poets; and whatever they may think of their lecture on these sciences, they cannot but be pleased with those abstracts of poetry with which it is generally enriched. We hope, the Author's '*utile dulci*' will recommend these studies to the attention of those for whose use this short and familiar introduction is intended.

Art. 12. *The Sea Officer's Companion:* Containing *New Tables* for accurately obtaining the Latitude of a Ship at Sea, and the Variation of the Needle, *by the* MOON: Also *New Tables* to obtain the Latitude, by four different Methods, *by the* SUN, &c. &c. By R. Waddington. 4to. 2 s. Nourse. 1770.

It is sufficient to observe, concerning this article, that it contains several tables and problems which may be of considerable service to seamen. They are the unquestionable result of care and labour, and must answer the purposes of accuracy and dispatch to all who are concerned in determining the *variation* of the *needle*, the *latitude*, and other requisites in navigation. It will be no improper *companion* to those on whom the business of calculation is devolved: but the *Nautical Almanack*, with the *requisite tables*, has in a great measure superseded the necessity and use of such publications. This, however, contains some observations and examples, which, though not of great importance, are not to be met with in any other treatise of the same kind.

POETICAL.

Art. 13. *An Englishman's Remonstrance:* Inscribed to the Right Hon. Brass Crosby, Lord-Mayor of London. By William Sharp, jun. 8vo. 1 s. Almon. 1771.

Wilkes scribbles news-paper squibs and paragraphs, for British liberty! Junius cuts up our ministers and statesmen, for British liberty! Crosby gets into durance vile, for British liberty! and Buckhorse chalks N° 45, on bulks and window-shutters, for British liberty! —The mischief's in it if British liberty is not safe enough! Let Bute, and Mansfield, and Double-fee, and all the rest of 'em, therefore, do their worst!

EAST-INDIES.

Art. 14. *Authentic Papers concerning India Affairs*; which have been under the inspection of a great Assembly. 8vo. 2 s. sewed. Richardson and Urquhart. 1771.

The Editor assures his Readers, that the papers here published, are transcripts faithfully made from authentic copies of original letters. They contain, as he observes, representations of weighty matters, made by rival parties, while contending for power in India; and therefore may be respectively considered, abstractedly from all the direct information which they furnish, as useful comments on each other; so that they will serve, in no inconsiderable degree, to ascertain the comparative talents, principles, practices, and views, of violent antagonists, in their discharge of such public trusts as were highly interesting to all men, while they demonstrate the nature of our territorial connexions with Hindostan, which are now of such infinite importance to the Company and the State.

The pieces here communicated to the public, are,

I. A letter from Lord *Clive*, to the Court of Directors of the East-India Company; dated at *Calcutta*, Sept. 30, 1765.

II. A

II. A letter from Lord *Clive*, and the rest of the *select Committee*, at Fort William in Bengal, to the Court of Directors, &c. of the same date.

III. A letter from Mess. *Ralph Leycester* and *George Gray*, Members of the Council at Fort William, to the Court of Directors, &c. dated Sept. 29, 1765; with a *postscript*, of the 14th Jan. 1766. This last is written in opposition to Lord Clive, &c.

NATURAL HISTORY.

Art. 15. *A Catalogue of the Animals of North America*. Containing an Enumeration of the known Quadrupeds, Birds, Reptiles, Fish, Insects, &c. many of which were never described before. To which are added, short Directions for collecting, preserving, and transporting all Kinds of natural Curiosities. By John Reinhold Forster, F. A. S. 8vo. 1 s. White.

Mr. Forster had hinted, in the preface to the 3d volume of his Translation of Kalm's Travels *, that he could publish but an imperfect and small catalogue of North American animals; for which reason he then declined giving it. 'Since that time, says he, I have been pressed, by some worthy friends, to publish that catalogue, such as it is; and what is still more, I have been favoured with ample materials by a gentleman who is forming a collection for a natural history of North America; and hopes by this to incite the inquisitive and learned, resident in that country, to transmit to their friends in England, the productions of their several provinces.—The zoology of the first four classes of animals in Great Britain, has been very accurately and completely published; that of the country of the descendents of Great Britain ought, with most propriety, to follow.—These reasons had great weight with me; and I offer this small catalogue merely as an essay towards forming a more complete natural history of that extensive continent. To instruct the collectors, I have added to this list, some directions for the best method of preserving and transporting the various subjects of natural history.'

Prefixed to this catalogue, we have a print of a very elegant little falcon, drawn from a fine specimen lately brought over from North America.

Art. 16. *Flora Americæ Septentrionalis*; or, a Catalogue of the Plants of North America. Containing an Enumeration of the known Herbs, Shrubs, and Trees, many of which are but lately discovered. By John Reinhold Forster, F. A. S. 8vo. 1 s. White, &c.

As some Readers might suppose a mere catalogue of American plants, &c to be of little use, and even superfluous, after the publication of Dr. Gronovius's *Flora Virginica*, Mr. Forster justly pleads, in behalf of the present tract, that he has given the English names to the several subjects; that he has added several articles discovered since Gronovius wrote; and also mentioned the œconomical and medical uses of some plants, which is a very material addition.—The industry of this gentleman, in contributing so much to enlarge the stock of natural knowledge in this country, by importations from various parts of the world, certainly deserves commendation.

* See page 213 of last month's Review.

Art. 17. *A Synopsis of Quadrupeds.* 8vo. 9s. Boards. Chester printed, and sold by White in London. 1771.

We are indebted for this publication to the ingenious Mr. Pennant, Author of British Zoology ‡, and other valuable pieces of natural history, which have been mentioned in this Review, as they have severally issued from the press.

This Synopsis, Mr. P. informs his Readers, 'was originally intended for private amusement, and as an index for the more ready turning to any particular animal in the voluminous history of quadrupeds by M. De Buffon; but as it swelled, by degrees, to a size beyond his first expectation, he was, in the end, determined to fling it into its present form, and to usher it into the world.'—With respect to his plan, he follows Mr. Ray, in some respects, in others he copies Mr. Klein, and the great Linnæus: and he gives his reasons, in a judicious preface, for every instance in which he has adopted, or departed from, the methods of his learned predecessors in this branch of study. His plates are well engraved, and a considerable number of his descriptions are new.

LAW.

Art. 18. *The Statutes at Large*, from the *fifth* Year of the Reign of George the Third, to the *tenth* Year of the Reign of George the Third, inclusive. To which is prefixed, a Table of the Titles of all the public and private Statutes during that Time. With a copious Index. 4to. 1l. 1s. bound. Strahan, &c. 1771.

This publication makes the *tenth* volume of the edition of the Statutes at Large, in *quarto*; of which the preceding *nine* were compiled by the late ingenious and indefatigable Owen Ruffhead, Esq. The favourable reception which the public hath given to this important work, precludes all necessity of our enlarging any farther on its merits.

MEDICAL.

Art. 19. *A Philosophical Enquiry into the Nature, Origin, and Extent of Animal Motion.* By Samuel Farr, M. D. 8vo. 6s. bound. Becket. 1771.

We have attentively perused this metaphisico-physiological Enquiry, and are sorry to observe, that we have met with little which can contribute to the advancement of real knowledge or sound philosophy.

Art. 20. *A Treatise on Female Diseases:* In which are also comprehended those most incident to pregnant and Child-bed Women. By Henry Manning, M. D. 8vo. 5s. 3d. Boards. Baldwin. 1771.

The nature of this work renders it improper for us either to enter into a minute detail, or to form any abstract of its contents. We must observe however, in justice to the Author, that, upon the whole, this treatise is well drawn up, and contains many useful, though not many new observations.—The impropriety, in the title, of *female* diseases, is, perhaps, too trivial to be regarded.

‡ This undertaking is now completed, by the publication of the second part of the 4th volume, in 8vo. For an idea of this work, see Review, vol. xxxix. p. 403.

POLITICAL.

Art. 21. *A short Essay upon Republican Government.* In a Letter to a Friend. 8vo. 6d. Blyth. 1771.

In republics, where the talents and the virtues of men are best unfolded, and where the opportunities of exerting them are most frequent; where their natural rights are secured on the most solid foundation, and where certain and known laws preserve their properties from infringement and violation; this wise Author finds nothing but disorder and confusion. In governments, where the administration of affairs is invested in a single person, and where every thing, most sacred and valuable, is subject to his folly and his passions, he finds order, security, and happiness. His performance is replete with ridiculous and absurd sentiments, supported without ingenuity, and dressed out in aukward and inelegant expressions.

MISCELLANEOUS.

Art. 22. *The Life of Joseph, the Son of Israel.* In Eight Books. Chiefly designed for the Use of Youth. 12mo. 3s. Keith, &c.

The pleasing and affecting story of Joseph, is a subject well suited to the nature of *sacred romance*; a species of writing lately brought into vogue among us (with female readers particularly) by the success of Gesner's * *Death of Abel*; in which TRUTH is gaudily equipped with the ornaments of INVENTION.—This history of the young Hebrew, so celebrated for his chastity, his wisdom, and the vicissitudes of his fortune, may be exhibited as a fit companion for Mr. Gesner's performance. In his *prefa e*, which we like better than the work to which it is prefixed, the Author informs his Readers, that 'should the Life of Joseph be acceptable to those for whom it is designed, he is not certain that he shall not send something more of the same kind abroad into the world.'

Art. 23. *A Letter to the Citizens of London, on a very interesting Subject.* Addressed to the Court of Aldermen, &c. 8vo. 1s. Bladon.

A very severe attack on the character of one of the candidates for the place of Upper City Marshal, which was lately vacant. It is not an anonymous stab, of which the press produces but too many; for the Writer has fairly subscribed his name, Robert Holloway, to a dedication of his Letter, to Mr. Crosby, Lord-Mayor of London.—The person whose character is here so strongly impeached, seems to be one Mr B. who did not obtain the place; which has since been sold to a less exceptionable purchaser.

Art. 24. *The Pupil of Nature*; a true History, found among the Papers of Father Quesnel. Translated from the original French of Monf. de Voltaire. 12mo. 2s. sewed. Carnan. 1771.

Another ‡ translation of *L'Ingenu*, of which we gave an abstract, from the original, in our Appendix to Review, vol. xxxvii. The *Pupil* of Nature is a better translation of the title than ours.

---

* We speak of this work as it appears in its English fustian dress; the original being a *poem*.

‡ A former translation of this satirical performance was noticed in p. 161 of our 39th volume.

Art. 25. *Reflections on the too prevailing Spirit of Dissipation and Gallantry*; shewing its dreadful Consequences to *public Freedom*. By the Author of a Review of the Characters of the principal Nations in Europe, &c. 8vo. 1 s. 6 d. Dilly. 1771.

In our Author's *Account of the Characters and Manners of the French**, with occasional observations on the English, some reflections were made on the notorious and scandalous *infidelity* in the *marriage state*, prevailing in France. '*That* evil, the Author thinks (we wish he had less foundation for his opinion) is now become alarming to the *English* nation; which has induced him to consider it more at large, and to submit to the public what has occurred to him upon so weighty a subject; the experience of *last winter* having shewn that dissipation and gallantry, so far from losing ground, were never, perhaps, known to have made, in so short a space of time, such a rapid and dangerous progress in this island: such a progress, indeed, as threatens, if not timely and powerfully resisted, to overwhelm, in the end, the morals of the whole British community.'

We have already given our opinion of the merits of this Writer, both in the review of the work referred to in the note, and in our account of his *Review of the Characters of the principal Nations in Europe*: see Review, vol. xliii. p. 329.

Art. 26. *Copies of the Depositions of the Witnesses examined in the Cause of Divorce*, between Lord Grosvenor and Lady Grosvenor his Wife. 8vo. 3 Parts. 5 s. Sold in Pater-noster-Row.

Those who have imagined, if any such there are, that proof of the lady's *actual transgression* was wanting, may be thoroughly convinced of it, by the testimony of the Countess D'Onhoff, and of Mrs. Reda, from *ocular demonstration*, and a *number* of instances: the shameful particulars of which are recited at large, and in the plainest terms. There is no doubt of the authenticity ‡ of these papers, which, however, certainly ought not to have been published †, not only because of the immodest passages, but as the cause is yet *sub judice*.

Art. 27. *A Journal of a Voyage round the World*, in his Majesty's Ship ENDEAVOUR, in the Years 1768, 1769, 1770 and 1771, undertaken in Pursuit of Natural Knowledge, at the Desire of the Royal Society. Containing all the various Occurrences of the Voyage, with Descriptions of several new discovered Countries in the Southern Hemisphere; Accounts of their Soil and Productions, and of many Singularities in the Customs, Manners, Policy, Manufactures, &c. of their Inhabitants. To which is added, A Concise Vocabulary of the Language of *Otahitee*. 4to. 6 s. sewed. Becket and De Hondt.

Every Reader of this account will be convinced, from its own internal evidence, of its authenticity; notwithstanding its Author (for

---

* See Review, vol. xliii. p. 255.

‡ The depositions were taken by Mess. *Lushington* and *Heseltine*, Proctors.

† An *Appendix* is added, containing the libel exhibited by Lord Grosvenor against her Ladyship, and *her allegations* in support of her *recrimination*.

obvious

obvious reasons) has not given it the sanction of his name. It is, undoubtedly, the Journal of a person who made the voyage, and his narrative and observations afford abundant matter to gratify curiosity. We could with pleasure have made some extracts from it, but we shall reserve the particulars of the discoveries * in this famous circumnavigation, till the appearance of the account advertised to be published by authority from the Board of Admiralty.

NOVELS.

Art. 28. *The unfortunate Lovers*; or, The genuine Distress of Damon and Celia. In a Series of Letters, &c. 12mo. 2 Vols. 6s. Dodsley, &c.

Although we have classed this publication with those works of invention usually ranged under the denomination of *Novels*, it contains nevertheless a recital of facts relating to the unhappy Author, William Renwick, a young apothecary, formerly a Surgeon's mate in one of our regiments, but at present reduced to the humble station of a journeyman, in a shop at Wokingham.

Mr. Renwick's first patron was the late worthy General Crawford: after the General's death, and the reduction of his regiment at the conclusion of the peace, our Author was turned adrift in the world. In this unfavourable situation the unfortunate Damon had the imprudence to marry the amiable Celia, the heroine of these Memoirs, and the partner of his distresses. He had, at this time, flattered himself with expectations from Sir John Hussey Delaval, on the foundation of services rendered to that gentleman at an election for Berwick, the place of Mr. Renwick's nativity. If we may believe our Author, (and we see no reason to question the truth of his narration), he had a *promise* of being provided for by the Delavals, in consideration of his vote and interest at this election, in which Sir John was successful. When the affair was over, however, and the Author came to *want* some proof of his *representative's* gratitude and generosity, his services, he found, were *forgotten*, and he could not, without the utmost difficulty, obtain even the favour of admittance to the presence of Sir John. His request was a commission in the army.

He now began to experience all the miseries of attendance and dependance. Sir John continued to shun him, and even plainly declared he could not serve him. Poor Damon, however, persevered in his solicitations, till at length he was reduced almost to starving; and, to add to his distresses, his beloved Celia brought him a son.

At length, finding that his *patron* would do *nothing* for him, not even send him a guinea, when he was brought so low by sickness and poverty, as to subsist upon small collections made for him by his friends, —he formed the resolution of *telling his story to the public*, in the hope of raising a trifle by a subscription to two little volumes. These vo-

* The Author does not pretend to give a minute description of the subjects of *Natural History*, because, as he handsomely observes, in a note, p. 67, 'Mr. Banks and Dr. Solander, (gentlemen of great erudition, who undertook this voyage for the sake of natural knowledge, and who in almost every place were successful, as well as indefatigable in their researches), will hereafter abundantly gratify the curiosity of those who delight in the study of Nature.'

James

lumes are now before us; and, as far as the distresses of our fellow-creatures are interesting to humane and generous minds, they will not fail to engage the Reader's attention. They are frequently enlivened by occasional pieces of poetry, in which the Writer appears to possess a very agreeable vein; and he has inserted, also, a few letters from General Crawford, and Sir John and Sir Francis Delaval, which at least serve to make a figure in his title-page and advertisements. But the best part of the work consists in his own and his wife's correspondence, particularly the letters from the unhappy Celia, which shew her to be a person of excellent parts, and the most exemplary conjugal virtue.

Art. 29. *The Tutor*; or, The History of George Wilson, and Lady Fanny Melfont. 12mo. 2 Vols. 5 s. sewed. Vernor. 1771.

The benevolent and virtuous sentiments which abound in this performance, are a great recommendation of it. They soften the severe brow of the critic; and, while they induce him to respect the heart of its Author, they excite in him a regret, that he cannot express the highest admiration of his genius.

RELIGIOUS and CONTROVERSIAL.

Art. 30. *Sermons on Several Subjects*. By Thomas Secker, LL. D. late Lord Archbishop of Canterbury. Published from the original MSS. by Beilby Porteus, D. D. and George Stinton, D.D. his Grace's Chaplains. Vols. V. VI. and VII. 8vo. 15 s. bound. Rivington. 1771.

In the xliiid volume of our Review, p. 192. *& seq.* we gave an account of the three preceding volumes of Archbishop Secker's posthumous sermons, and on that occasion we delivered pretty fully our opinion of his Grace's peculiar turn as a preacher, and of the general characteristics of his discourses. To *that* article we now refer; and it will be necessary only to add here, a transcript of what the Editors have themselves said of the present publication, in their prefatory *advertisement, viz.* 'That the three volumes of sermons now offered to the public, are the last of Archbishop Secker's works which they intend to print. Of these the fifth and seventh consist of miscellaneous sermons, not at all inferior, as they conceive, to the former volumes. The sixth contains a series of discourses on scripture, on the English liturgy, and against Popery, some of which they once doubted whether it would be advisable to make public; but several of the Author's friends, who had heard them preached, and received great satisfaction from them, were extremely desirous to have them all collected into one volume, and added to the two others. This induced the Editors not only to give these discourses a second and more careful examination, but to submit them to the perusal of a person of high rank in the church, and acknowledged abilities, who thought them much too useful and instructive to be suppressed, especially as both the nature of the subjects and the manner of treating them, gave them some affinity to the *Lectures on the Catechism*. On these grounds the Editors now give them to the world, and have little doubt but that these concluding volumes will meet with the same approbation which the preceding ones have received from all ranks of people.'

The

The admirers of Dr. Secker may perhaps be glad of the following complete List of his works:

I. Nine Sermons on the War and Rebellion, now reprinted, with the addition of his Anſwer to Mayhew *, and Letter to Walpole†. 8vo.

II. Fourteen occaſional Sermons ‡, 8vo. 1766.

III. Lectures on the Church Catechiſm ‖, 8vo. 2 Vols.

IV. Charges §, &c. 8vo.

V. Sermons, 8vo. 7 Vols. The whole making 12 volumes.

ART. 31. *Sermons to Young Men.* In 3 Volumes. By William Dodd, LL. D. Prebendary of Brecon, and Chaplain in Ordinary to his Majeſty. 12mo. 10 s. 6 d. Cadell. 1771.

In the Dedication of theſe ſermons to Philip Stanhope and Charles Ernſt, Eſquires, Dr. Dodd acknowledges, 'That the thought of this publication was ſuggeſted by the "Sermons to Young Women," whoſe ingenious author certainly deſerves great praiſe from the public, for his well-judged and well-executed deſign. I have not,' the Doctor adds, 'attempted to imitate his manner, for you know my opinion on the ſubject of imitation. Every man certainly ſhould be left to his own mode. That of the author of the Sermons to Young Women is peculiarly his own, and they would hazard much, in my mind, who ſhould attempt to copy it. Beſides, there is a wide difference between ſermons compoſed for the preſs, and for the pulpit. Mine were written principally for the latter; many of them long before the publication of the Sermons to Young Women, for I always thought a peculiar attention due to the younger part of my congregation. But on reading thoſe ſermons, it occurred to me, that a ſet of plain practical diſcourſes to young men might be uſeful and acceptable. I collected therefore and reviſed what I had before written, and ſupplying what was neceſſary to complete my plan, here, my young friends, I commit them to the world, under your protection and patronage. Conſcious of the rectitude of my purpoſe, and of my ſincere wiſhes to promote the cauſe of virtue and piety, I feel no ſolicitude reſpecting their reception; but, with our favourite ROMAN (Cicero) ſhall always think I act a proper part, by applying my little abilities to the inſtruction and improvement of our youth, in duties of the greateſt moment to themſelves and others.'

It is only neceſſary for us to obſerve farther concerning theſe ſermons, that we apprehend them to be well fitted to anſwer the end propoſed, of advancing the trueſt intereſt of young perſons, and we wiſh that the youth of the preſent age may carefully and ſeriouſly attend to them. The Author has judged very properly in ſelecting a number of anecdotes from ſeveral writers, ſuitable to the different ſubjects he conſiders, ſome of which are added at the end of every diſcourſe, and have a tendency both to gain the greater attention of

* For an account of Dr. Mayhew's notable performance, entitled, *Obſervations on the Charter and Conduct of the Society for propagating the Goſpel*, ſee Review, vol. xxx. p. 45. And of Dr. Secker's anonymous *anſwer* to theſe Obſervations, *ibid.* p. 284.

† Rev. vol. xli. p. 220. ‡ Ibid. vol. xxxiv. p. 344.

‖ Ibid. vol. xl. p. 129. § Ibid. vol. xli. p. 316.

young

young perſons, and to make the more laſting impreſſion on their minds.

Art. 32. *Sermons to Doctors in Divinity.* Being the ſecond Volume of Sermons to Aſſes *. 12mo. 3s. Robinſon and Roberts.

This Satiriſt, whoever he is, finds his ſubject ſo prolific, that he has produced a ſecond volume for the edification of the public, and tells us, in the cloſe, of a *third*, which is to make its appearance, but whether any others are to follow *that*, we are not informed. It is happy for an Author, if he knows when it is proper to ſtop, and this is never more true, than in regard to ſubjects of wit and humour; ſince, by ſtretching them too far, a writer may not only ceaſe to entertain, but may even deſtroy the force of his former attempts, and loſe all the credit which he might have gained from them. This Preacher, however, ſeems to keep up the ſpirit of his work throughout moſt parts of his ſix ſermons, though there are ſome paſſages in which he appears to flag, or to deſcend too near to anger and ſcurrility. Some expreſſions in the work intimate that the Author is a North Briton; and he has taken care, with ſome degree of clearneſs, to mark out one celebrated Scotch Doctor: but the Engliſh doctors, of different denominations, alſo come in for their ſhare, and none of them entirely eſcape the laſh of his pen. But we leave them to defend themſelves, as they are able, againſt this troubleſome ſermonizer.

Art. 33. *The Inefficacy of Preaching*; or, Government the beſt Inſtructor. Being an Attempt to prove, in the Teſtimony of paſt Ages, and the Experience of the preſent, how little either Poets, Hiſtorians, Philoſophers or Divines, have ever contributed to the Reformation of Mankind. To which is ſubjoined, A ſhort Plan, offered to the Conſideration of Legiſlators, for the more effectual Suppreſſion of Vice, and Encouragement of Virtue. Tranſlated from the Original of a celebrated French Author. Small 8vo. 3s. bound. Wilkie. 1771.

The work, of which this is a Tranſlation, was publiſhed a few years ago at Paris, and an account was given of it, under its proper title *(De la Predication)*, in the Appendix to our xxxivth volume, p. 538—547. The tranſlation appears to be executed with tolerable fidelity.

This ingenious Writer has advanced ſome melancholy truths. He allows, that, by the various means, which he includes under the term *Preaching*, ſome barbarous prejudices have been overcome; but he thinks, that all the vices that can infect enlightened nations, ſtill ſubſiſt, and that their poiſon continues to circulate through all ranks of men, from the Court to the Cottage.

It is, however, very queſtionable, notwithſtanding what our Author advances, whether GOVERNMENT would prove, as he apprehends, a true and effectual preacher. The means employed by the Magiſtrate are different indeed from thoſe uſed by the Poet, Philoſopher or Divine, whoſe chief aim is to amend and form the heart; which, could it be always effected, would certainly produce good order and virtuous manners: but the methods employed by Government muſt, and ever ſhould, chiefly regard the exterior deportment of the ſubject.

* See Rev. vol. xxxix. p. 100.

There

There are, in all civilized countries, particularly in our own, proper laws and regulations for preserving and securing the harmony and welfare of the community, although there may be just reason to complain of remissness in the execution of those laws. It is also undeniable, that many alterations, and better provisions may yet be made for punishing and restraining those vices which interrupt the order and welfare of society; but is it not to be feared that the institution of CENSORS over a certain number of families (as this Writer proposes), to superintend the behaviour of all ranks of people, would soon be perverted, and, by throwing too great a power into the hands of those who are placed at the head of public affairs, have a most dangerous tendency towards slavery and despotism? Is it not, moreover, probable, that these censorial officers, either through indolence or corruption, would soon learn to connive at, and neglect, the disorders that required their attention? These objections [and more might be offered] are not, we apprehend, unworthy the consideration of this very able and ingenious Writer.

Art. 34. *Short Meditations* on select Portions of Scripture, designed to assist the serious Christian in the Improvement of the Lord's Day, and other Seasons of Devotion and Leisure. By Daniel Turner, M. A. 12mo. 2 s. 6 d. Johnson, &c. 1771.

Pious and sensible Reflections on different parts of the sacred writings, calculated to awaken and cherish a spirit of devotion, and promote a suitable conduct in life. The Author appears, as he professes, to have no view to party-interest, but to advance practical religion; and as his design is undeniably good, he hopes that the veil of candour will be drawn over any imperfections which may be observed, at least so far as not to obstruct the usefulness of these compositions.

To the Meditations are added, *Considerations on the Custom of visiting on Sundays*; which were communicated to this Writer, we are told, ' by a particular friend, from a pious and worthy clergyman of the established church, with a desire of their being published with these meditations, as particularly agreeable to the design of them.' Accordingly Mr. Turner has given them a place by way of appendix, and he expresses his earnest wish that they may answer the valuable purposes which the pious Author had in view.

SERMONS.

I. At the Parish Church at Barking, in Essex, Sept. 23, 1771, on Occasion of opening the said Church (after an expensive Repair) and a new Organ therein, given by one of the Parishioners. By Robert Antony Bromley, Preacher at the Foundling Hospital, and Lecturer of St. John, Hackney. 1 s. Wilkie.

II. In the Chapel of the Foundling Hospital, Dec. 23, 1770, recommending that Institution to the Benevolence of Mankind, and intended as a full Vindication of the System and Purposes of that Hospital. Sold for the Benefit of the Charity. Wilkie, &c.

III. *St. Paul's Exhortation, and Motive to support the weak or sick Poor*—Preached in the Cathedral Church of Salisbury, before the Governors of the General Infirmary, at their Anniversary Meeting, Sept. 27. 1771. By James Stonehouse, M. D. Rivington, &c.

COR-

CORRESPONDENCE.

To the AUTHORS *of the* MONTHLY REVIEW.

It is requested that the Gentlemen concerned in that work will cause some notice to be taken of the following in their next Review:

Sept. 20, 1771.

"The Gentleman who superintended the edition of Mr. Cawthorn's Poems, having thought it incumbent on him to take notice of an anonymous charge of foisting-in a piece which was not the production of Mr. Cawthorn, the anonymous Writer desires leave still to insist, that the poem in question was really written by Mr. Pitt. It was published by that gentleman, in his collection of Poems printed in the year 1727, and the copy inserted in Mr. Cawthorn's Poems bears every mark of being an extract from a printed book,—an hasty and imperfect extract: having two lines, toward the conclusion, omitted. To confirm this charge, the writer of this Letter, who, at present, is at some distance from London, intends, at his return, to leave Mr. Pitt's Poems with Mr. Becket, your publisher; that any person doubting the reality of his assertion, may be satisfied that his accusation of neglect in the Editor was not made but upon the most solid foundation. In the mean time, he cannot but lament that the works of a person so respectable as an author, and so deserving as a man, should be presented to the public without any information concerning his life, family connections, or even the times and places of his birth and death. The Editor would also have done right in preserving such pieces of his Author as were published by him in his life-time: more than one are omitted; and even the celebrated epistle of Abelard to Eloisa appears not to be printed from the original edition, about the year 1746; some introductory verses addressed to a lady prefixed to that edition, not being retained, as they ought to have been, before that excellent performance."

††† Possibly the Writer of the above, somewhat misapprehends the argument of the Gentleman's letter, which was extracted and published at the end of our last Month's Review, The Editor of Mr. Cawthorn's Poems did not appear positively to deny that the piece in question was Pitt's; he only declared his having known nothing of the matter, previously to the publication of Mr. C.'s Poems; and, consequently, that if the poem proved to be Mr. Pitt's, the insertion of it among Mr. C.'s pieces, was a circumstance very different from an *Intentional* Plagiarism.

T. Z. will find the sermon he mentions, at a Quaker's Meeting, in our Catalogue for June. The other performance which he recommends to our notice, will not be overlooked.

ERRATUM in our last.

☞ The Reader is desired to correct the notable *erratum* in the account of *Dr. Burney's Present State of Music* *, &c. in our last number, p. 169, l. 20.

For [we have in no instance, &c.] read, "We have, in *every* instance, conducted ourselves irreproachably."

---

* The sequel of our account of this work was finished too late for insertion this month, but it will certainly appear in our next.

THE

MONTHLY REVIEW,

For NOVEMBER, 1771.

ART. I. CONCLUSION *of Dr.* Burney's *present State of Music*, &c. from our Number for September last, page 161.

WE join company with our amusing and instructive musical traveller at Padua, in a part of his tour marked with a recent event highly afflictive to the musical world;—the death of that great theorist, composer, and performer, the celebrated Tartini, whose loss our Author feelingly laments, and in which all those who cultivate the violin in particular, and who are acquainted with the natural and truly vocal melodies, set off and enforced by a simple and expressive harmony,—or, in other words, with the *Sons raisonnés* of that exquisite and original composer, must sincerely sympathize with him. He visited—he could now do no more—'with all the zeal of a pilgrim at Mecca, the street and house where he had lived; the church and grave where he was buried; his bust, his successor, his executor, and every thing, however minute and trivial, which could afford him the least intelligence concerning his life and character.' Though the particulars which the Author has collected concerning this great master are, by his death, rather become proper subjects for his future history, than for the *present state* of music, the Reader is here gratified, by anticipation, with some interesting anecdotes relative to his life, and with a short sketch of his character as a composer and performer. Considering him in the first of these lights, the Author observes, that 'he was one of the few original geniuses of this age, who constantly drew from his own source; that his melody was full of fire and fancy, and his harmony, though learned, yet simple and pure.' Considering him as a performer, the Author adds, that 'his slow movements evinced his taste and expression, and his lively ones his great hand. He was the first who knew and taught the power of the bow; and his knowledge of the fingerboard is proved by a thousand beautiful passages to which that alone could give birth. His scholar, Nardini, who played to me many of his best solos, as I thought, very well, with respect to correctness and expression, assured me that his dear and honoured master, as he constantly called him, was as much superior to himself in the performance of the same solos, both in the pathetic and brilliant parts, as he was to any one of his scholars.'

He has bequeathed his MS. music to his Excellency Count Torre Taxis of Venice, his scholar and protector; and to his friend, Father Colombo, the professor of mathematics in the university of Padua, he left the care of a posthumous work, of which the theory of sound makes a considerable part, and in which he proposed to remove the obscurity, and explain the difficulties of which he is accused in his former treatises.

The musical establishment at the church of St. Anthony in this city is in the highest degree superb. It consists of four immense organs, all of them fine toned instruments, the front pipes of which are so highly polished, as to have the appearance of burnished silver. These formerly were all played at once; but Father Vallotti, one of the first composers for the church in Italy, who is the present *Maestro di Capella*, has, on account of their totally overpowering the voices, by degrees dropped the use of two of the number. There are likewise employed in the service of this church, on common days, forty instrumental and vocal performers;—eight violins, four tenors, four violoncellos, four double bases, with four wind instruments, and sixteen voices, eight of which are *castrati*; among whom is Signor Gaetano Guadagni, 'who for taste, expression, figure, and action, is at the head of his profession.' His appointment is 400 ducats a-year, for which he is required to attend only at the four principal festivals. The first violin of this select and magnificent band has the same salary, and on the same easy conditions. Signor Tartini occupied this place near 50 years; and so great, we are told, was the fervor of his zeal for the service of St. Anthony, 'that he seldom let a week pass without regaling his patron saint to the utmost power of his palsied nerves.'

The Author's account of the state of music in Venice is highly interesting; and more particularly that of the celebrated *Conservatorios* or musical schools established here, and his animated description of the excellent performance of the young females who receive their education in these seminaries. He was here introduced to the Abbate Martini, an able mathematician, composer, and performer, and one of the best judges of every part of music, ancient and modern, that he had yet met with. This gentleman had travelled into Greece, in order to make observations on natural history, &c. but being unable to satisfy himself as he expected, he did not chuse to publish any of his remarks or discoveries. Among other curious objects of enquiry, he attended particularly to the music of the modern Greeks, in hopes it would throw some light upon that of the ancients. After discussing the Author's plan, article by article, he gave him a very obliging proof of his approbation of it by presenting him with his MS. papers concerning the modern Greek music. We afterwards find that M. Diderot likewise entered, with equal zeal, into the Author's views respecting the history of an art, in which this deservedly celebrated genius interests himself very much, by presenting him with a number of his own MSS. sufficient for a volume in folio, on the subject, with an unlimited permission to make use of them in the course of his intended work, as his own property. Notwithstanding this legal transfer, the Author, with proper delicacy, and with a just sense of the value of the present, declares himself accountable for these papers, not only to M. Diderot, but to the public. We meet, in the course of this work, with many other instances of favour shewn to the Author, which do honour to the parties conferring them, and reflect credit upon him and his undertaking.

The description of the state of music at Bologna is enriched with an account of two very extraordinary persons who reside in that city; the learned Father Martini, and the celebrated Signor Farinelli: the first of whom 'is regarded by all Europe as the deepest theorist, and the other as the greatest practical musician of this, or, perhaps, of any age or country.' He was well received by both, and by the former particularly with the greatest kindness and cordiality; which must have been the more grateful, as this learned churchman has long been engaged in the same design with the Author, which he has in part executed, by the publication of the first volume of a General History of Music, about 14 years ago, in folio and in quarto. This volume is chiefly employed on the history of music among the Hebrews: the second (which, we are informed, has been very lately published) and the third will comprise that of the ancient Greeks; the fourth, the Latin or Roman music, together with that of the church. The fifth and last volume alone is to be appropriated to modern music, and is intended to contain an account of the lives and writings of the most famous musicians. The slowness however with which this immense work has hitherto advanced, together with the great age and infirmities of the good Father, afford too much reason to apprehend that he will hardly have life and health sufficient to complete this voluminous undertaking.

The confidential and even brotherly intercourse between the present and the future historian of music, was such as is not of-

 ten

ten to be found between two persons engaged in the same pursuits. On this occasion however the Author observes that, though they are the same with regard to the object, they differ with respect to the way; and that as the same object may be approached by different routs, and be seen in various points of view, so two different persons may exhibit it with equal truth, and yet with great diversity. 'I shall avail myself,' he very appositely adds, 'of Father Martini's learning and materials, *as I would of his spectacles:* I shall apply them to my subject, as it appears to me, without changing my situation; and shall neither implicitly adopt his sentiments in doubtful points, nor transcribe them where we agree.'

Many curious and interesting particulars are here given, relating to Signor Farinelli, whose almost supernatural powers were long the admiration of Europe, and of this country in particular, which he left in 1737, with a design however of returning to perform at the opera the following season: but Philip V. of Spain, on hearing his astonishing performance, instantly appropriated his talents wholly to his own particular amusement, by settling a pension upon him of upwards of £. 2000 sterling a year; which was continued to him by his successor Ferdinand VI. who added to it the dignity of the order of Calatrava. At the commencement of the present reign, after having resided in Spain, an unobnoxious chief favourite of two succeeding kings, during the space of 24 years, the Cavalier Farinelli was obliged to quit the kingdom; but still enjoys his former pension, and a good share of health and spirits, at a house built by himself, and splendidly fitted up, at the distance of a mile from Bologna.—'This extraordinary person, says the Author, possessed such powers as never met before, or since, in any one human being; powers that were irresistable, and which must subdue every hearer; the learned and the ignorant, the friend and the foe.' Out of the anecdotes here given we shall select one, which furnishes a very striking proof of the justice of this character; at least, of a part of it: premising only that the vocal powers of Farinelli were, in this instance, most conspicuously exerted on a rival.

'He confirmed to me, says the Author, the truth of the following extraordinary story, which I had often heard, but never before credited. Senesino and Farinelli, when in England together, being engaged at different theatres on the same night, had not an opportunity of hearing each other; till, by one of these sudden stage-revolutions which frequently happen, yet are always unexpected, they were both employed to sing on the same stage. Senesino had the part of a furious tyrant to represent, and Farinelli that of an unfortunate hero in chains: but in the course of the first song, he so softened the obdurate heart

heart of the enraged tyrant, that Senesino, forgetting his stage character, ran to Farinelli, and embraced him in his own.'—— This anecdote, while it displays the powers of one of the parties, does almost equal honour to the sensibility of the other.

We pass over the observations which the Author made at Florence and elsewhere, in his way to Rome; where his views and expectations with regard to the principal object of his journey were gratified to the utmost, by a free access to the Vatican library, granted to him by Cardinal Albani, together with an unlimited permission to have copies or extracts taken from the inedited materials relating to ancient music, contained in that celebrated repository, as well as from the archives of the pontifical chapel; in which church music, in particular, had its first rise, or at least received its first refinement, and was brought to its highest perfection. He here likewise received all the light that could be thrown on the subject of his enquiries, from the best remains of antiquity, and many other original and useful materials for his intended work, through the kindness and activity of several distinguished persons, whose essential services he here acknowledges. Among other curious matter contained in this part of the work, an account is given of the musical œconomy of the Pope's, or Sistine, Chapel, together with several particulars, interesting to the lovers of church music, relative to the celebrated *Miserere* of Allegri; which, for upwards of 150 years, has been annually performed there on the Wednesday and Friday in Passion Week, by select voices alone: no organ, or instrument of any kind, being ever employed in that sanctuary of pure vocal harmony.

This composition, the Author informs us, was formerly held so sacred, that it was imagined excommunication would be the consequence of an attempt to transcribe it. Father Martini told the Author that there were never more than two copies of it made by authority;—(the Author afterwards mentions a third, made for the Emperor Leopold the First) one of which was for the late King of Portugal, and the other for himself. This last he permitted the Author to transcribe at Bologna; and Signor Santarelli, *Maestro di Capella* to his Holiness, favoured him with another copy, pretty exactly agreeing with it, from the archives of the Pope's Chapel, together with many other compositions of Palestrina, Benevoli, &c. and with all those likewise which are performed there during Passion Week; the publication of which would, we imagine, be peculiarly grateful to the admirers of pure and simple harmony.

We meet with complaints made a century ago that almost every part of the regions of science had long since been explored and cultivated; and that the fields of description and sentiment, in particular, had so long been pre-occupied, by a succession of able

able cultivators, that the soil was absolutely exhausted:—in short, that almost every species of modern composition furnished instances of identity or resemblance to the ancient productions. It has since been felt and acknowledged, by those extensively conversant in the productions of the art, that even music, the tones of which, together with their different modifications, appear at first sight sufficiently numerous to constitute an inexhaustible fund of novelty and variety, by the multiplicity and diversity of their combinations, is by no means exempt from this reflection; notwithstanding the very modern date of its earliest productions known to us. On this last-mentioned account the *Harmonic Muse* might naturally be considered as the youngest of the whole sisterhood, and as still fresh and in her bloom: and yet Polyhymnia, it seems, is already represented as little better than a battered old harridan, and particularly reproached with betraying frequent and deplorable symptoms of one of the well known infirmities of old age—that of muttering the same tale over and over again.—We premise these reflections as a proper introduction to a conversation which the Author had at Rome, with Rinaldo di Capua, an old and excellent Neapolitan composer, who carries this complaint, with regard to his own art, to a whimsically extravagant length. We cannot better convey his opinion to our Readers, than by giving the whole of it in the words of the Author; and we are sorry to observe that, even from our limited acquaintance with musical productions, there appears to us to be too much foundation for the reproach.

'Rinaldo di Capua is very intelligent in conversation; but though a good-natured man, his opinions are rather singular and severe upon his brother composers. He thinks they have nothing left to do now, but to write themselves and others over again; and that the only chance they have left, for obtaining the reputation of novelty and invention, arises either from ignorance, or want of memory, in the public; as every thing, both in melody and modulation, that is worth doing, has been often already done. He includes himself in the censure, and frankly confesses, that though he has written full as much as his neighbours, yet out of all his works, perhaps not above *one* new melody can be found; which has been wire-drawn in different keys, and different measures, a thousand times. And as to modulation, it must be always the same, to be natural and pleasing; what has not been given to the public being only the refuse of thousands, who have tried and rejected it, either as impracticable or displeasing. The only opportunity a composer has for introducing new modulation in songs, is in a short second part; in order to *fright* the hearer back to the first,

first, to which it serves as a foil, by making it comparatively beautiful.'

No part of the Author's work affords more information and entertainment, than the observations included under the article Naples; which city was the boundary of his excursion. We resist however the temptation of enriching our journal with the many specimens with which the variety of agreeable and interesting matter contained in this part of his performance would furnish us; and shall content ourselves with only extracting the substance of his account of the vulgar or national music of this country, which is of a very singular species. It is as wild in modulation, and as different from that of all the rest of Europe, as the Scots, and probably as ancient: being among the common people merely traditional. The modulation and accompaniment are equally extraordinary; the performers passing from the fundamental key into others the most extraneous and unexpected imaginable; and, after a series of very excentric excursions, almost insensibly returning to the original key, without offending the ear, or affording it any clue to discover by what road the return to it was effected. Some of these street musicians, for instance, after playing a long symphony in *A*, on a violin, a mandoline, and a species of guitar with two strings tuned fifths to each other, accompanied a singer, who began his song in *F*, and stopped in *C*, which is not uncommon or difficult: but, after another ritornel, from *F*, he got into *E flat*, and closed in *A natural*. After this, there were transitions even into *B flat* and *D flat*, without giving offence; the singer returning, or rather *sliding*, always into the original key of *A natural*, and the instruments moving the whole time in quick notes, without the least intermission.

We shall here, though somewhat unwillingly, take our leave of a performance which has afforded us much agreeable information, and which we apprehend to be the first of its kind upon the subject. The design itself, and the manner in which it is executed, must render the work peculiarly pleasing to the *dilettanti* in particular; and not unacceptable to every reader of taste, who interests himself in the state or progress of the fine arts in general, though he may labour under the misfortune (to use the Abbé du Bos' expression) *d'avoir l'oreille tellement eloigné du cœur*, 'of having his ears placed at such a distance from his heart,' as to be rather cool to the charms of that pleasing art in particular, of which it principally treats, and consequently not highly inquisitive concerning matters that relate to it. To the learned and curious in that science it conveys a circumstantial and satisfactory account of the present state of the various musical establishments and exhibitions, in the countries through which the Author passed, and many judicious

 remarks

remarks on the styles and manners of the different masters, accompanied with occasional general observations relative to the art, which indicate the depth, taste, and sensibility of the Observer: while the novelty of the matter, the animated style of the Author, and his perspicuous and feeling manner of describing performers and performances, in a narrative totally divested of pedantry, and well diversified, notwithstanding the sameness of the subject; may render this performance not wholly uninteresting, and scarce any where unintelligible, even to the unmusical Reader.

We should add that, at the end of the work, the Author, after a short and general mention of the materials with which his former researches, and the urbanity of foreigners, have furnished him, towards the composition of his intended *History of Music*, requests the assistance of those ingenious persons in our own country, who are in possession of any curious materials, the communication of which may be conducive to the perfection of his future work. He speaks of the completion of his extensive undertaking, as an event which must necessarily be yet at a distance. 'Respect for the public, for the art about which he writes, and even for himself,' he properly observes, 'will prevent precipitate publication:' afterwards adding that 'to select, digest, and consolidate materials so various and diffused, will not only require leisure and labour, but such a patient perseverance, as little less than the zeal of enthusiasm can inspire.'—Of this zeal, the spirited enterprize which furnished the matter of the present publication, and almost every page of the work itself, shew the Author to be possessed of a very competent share: nor will the intelligent Reader of this specimen of his abilities, entertain much doubt of his possessing likewise the other requisites to the proper execution of an undertaking, which undoubtedly demands the united talents and acquirements of the scholar, the man of science, and the practical musician.

ART. II. *Observations on Reversionary Payments, Annuities, &c.* By Richard Price, D. D. F. R. S. concluded: See Review for last Month.

THE *national debt* is a subject of great consequence to every individual in this kingdom. The welfare of every member is intimately connected with that of the community to which he belongs; and though this connection may not be distinctly observed and universally acknowledged, a period may arrive, in which experience, that infallible teacher of wisdom, may represent it in characters too plain to be disputed, and too alarming not to be deplored. The evil is not felt till it is almost too late to apply a remedy. It is a disease, which first seizes the vitals of the body politic, and is gradually conveyed to to the extreme members. We complain, without being able to trace our disorder to its spring. We are loaded with heavy burdens, without perceiving the hand which lays them upon us, and we seldom think of throwing them off, till we are sinking under their enormous weight. Taxes are multiplied without number, and continued without the prospect of relief. Some new scheme or expedient is contrived, one year after another, to raise fresh supplies; and they are sunk, as soon as raised, in that *vortex*, from the eddy of which there is no escape. It is true, the *interest* of the debt, with which the nation is oppressed, is regularly discharged; but the *principal* remains, very little diminished, a monument of the wretched defect of true policy in our public councils: for every sum, which is funded without any contemporary provision for its payment, is borrowed at an *infinite* disadvantage. We are disposed to ascribe this injudicious management of our national interests rather to want of necessary prudence than to want of integrity. However, it is too obvious to escape the most superficial attention, that the *national debt* is the main pillar of ministerial influence and corruption; and what might occasionally serve an *upright* minister, is a very dangerous weapon in the hands of the *unprincipled* and *designing*.

We are willing to hope, that some of our ministers have honesty and public virtue enough, to give up this power of extending the prerogative, of oppressing the subject, and involving the kingdom in ruin, for the sake of the national security and welfare. 'To settle some plan for putting our debts into a regular and certain course of payment,' would raise the reputation of those who had skill and integrity enough to concert and carry into execution a measure of this kind, high as that of those venerable ancients, who sacrificed themselves to save their country. They will find in the treatise before us many observations which claim their peculiar attention. Nor would it be any degradation to the first minister of the kingdom to adopt, for this purpose, one or other of the schemes which our Author proposes, and the advantages and inconveniencies of which he particularly states and examines. 'At the *Revolution* (says Dr. Price) an æra in other respects truly glorious, the practice of raising supplies by borrowing money on interest, to be continued till the principal is discharged, begun. Ever since, the public debt has been increasing fast, and every new war has added much more to it than was taken from it during the preceding period of peace. In the year 1700, it was 16 millions. In 1715, it was 55 millions. A peace, which continued till 1740, sunk it to 47 millions; but the succeeding war increased it to 78 millions; and the next peace sunk it no lower than 72 millions. In the *last* war it rose to 148 millions; and, at a few

few millions leſs than this ſum it now ſtands, and probably will ſtand, till another war raiſes it perhaps to 200 millions. One cannot reflect on this without terror. No reſources can be ſufficient to ſupport a kingdom long in ſuch a courſe. 'Tis obvious, that the conſequence of accumulating debts ſo rapidly; and of mortgaging poſterity, and funding for eternity, in order to pay the intereſt of them, muſt in the end prove deſtructive.'

We ſhall lay before our Readers as comprehenſive an abſtract as our limits will allow, of the ingenious Author's remarks upon this ſubject; and in order to enable them to examine their truth and accuracy, we ſhall premiſe the queſtions which are annexed to the tables in the Appendix.

'*Queſtion* I. To what *ſum* or *annuity* will any given *ſum* or *annuity*, now to be laid up for improvement, at a given rate of compound intereſt, increaſe, in a given number of years?

'*Anſwer*. Divide the given *ſum* or *annuity* by the value of £. 1, payable at the end of the given number of years, and the quotient will be the anſwer.

'*Queſtion* II. To what *ſum* will a given *annuity* amount, in conſequence of being forborne and improved, at a given rate of compound intereſt, for a given number of years?

'*Anſwer*. From the *increaſed* annuity, found by the laſt queſtion, ſubtract the *given* annuity; and multiply the *remainder* by the *perpetuity*, and the *product* will be the anſwer.—It ſhould be remembered, that the *perpetuity* is 33.33, 28,57, 25, 20, or 16.666, according as intereſt is reckoned at 3, $3\frac{1}{2}$, 4, 5 or 6 *per cent.*' or it is the value of the *fee ſimple* of an eſtate found by dividing £. 100 by the rate of intereſt: and that the *annuity* meant in all theſe queſtions is an annuity, the firſt payment of which is to be made at the end of a year.

'*Queſtion* III. In what number of years will a given *ſum* or *annuity* increaſe to another given *ſum* or *annuity*, in conſequence of being improved at a given rate of intereſt?

'*Anſwer*. Divide the *original ſum* or annuity by the *increaſed ſum* or *annuity*; and look for the *quotient*, or the number neareſt to it, in Table I. (exhibiting the preſent value of £. 1, to be received at the end of any number of years, not exceeding 100) and the number of years correſponding to it will be the anſwer.

'*Queſtion* IV. In what time will any given *annuity* amount to a *given ſum*, in conſequence of being forborne and improved, at a given rate of compound intereſt?

'*Anſwer*. Divide the given *ſum* to which the annuity muſt amount by the *perpetuity*. Add the given annuity to the quotient; and by the quotient ſo increaſed, divide the given annuity; and this ſecond quotient, found in Table I. will ſhew the anſwer.

'*Queſtion*

' *Queſtion* V. In what time will a *given principal* be annihilated, by taking out of it, at the end of a year, a given ſum, and after that, the ſame ſum annually, together with its growing intereſts?

' *Anſwer.* In the ſame time plainly in which an equal annuity would amount to the *given principal.*'

As this abſtract may fall into the hands of ſome, who are not furniſhed with ſuch a table as is here referred to, though it may be met with in moſt of the books that treat of compound intereſt and annuities, we would juſt obſerve, that it may be eaſily ſupplied by the help of *logarithms.* The preſent value of £. 1, for any number of years, is found by dividing 1 by £. 1 together with its intereſt for one year, raiſed to a power whoſe index is the number of years. Suppoſe the rate of intereſt 4 *per cent.* and the number of years 18, the preſent value of £. 1 is equal to $\frac{1}{\overline{1,04}|^{18}}$, or ,4936. But when the preſent value and rate of intereſt are given, and the number of years is required, divide 1 by the preſent value, and the *logarithm* of the quotient divided by the *logarithm* of £. 1, together with its intereſt for one year, will give the anſwer. Thus, $\overline{1,04}|^{n} = \frac{1}{,4936} = 2,02$. And $\frac{0,3053514}{0,0170333} = n = 18$.

The firſt ſcheme which our Author propoſes is that of borrowing money on annuities, which are to terminate within a given period. ' Were this practiſed there would be a *limit* beyond which the national debts could not increaſe; and time would do that *neceſſarily* for the public, which, if truſted to the œconomy of the conductors of its affairs, might poſſibly never be done.'

But on this plan, the *preſent* burdens of the ſtate would be increaſed in conſequence of the greater preſent intereſt, that muſt be given for the money borrowed. This objection our Author conſiders as of no great weight. For an annuity for 100 years is, to the views of men, nearly the ſame with an annuity for ever; and in calculation, its value, at 4 *per cent.* would be 24½ years purchaſe, and therefore only half a year's purchaſe leſs than the value of a *perpetuity.* If the ſtate can borrow money at 4 *per cent.* on annuities for ever, it requires only an advance of 1 *s.* 7 *d. per cent.* (this being the intereſt of £. 2, or half a year's purchaſe) to limit them to 100 years: but were this advance a *quarter*, or even *half per cent.* the advantages ariſing from a neceſſary annihilation of the public debts, by time, would more than overbalance theſe additional burdens. The Author ſuggeſts, that in this way of raiſing money, it might be beſt to offer an higher intereſt at firſt, which ſhould fall to a lower, at the end of given intervals. Thus, though 4½ for 100 years is equal in value to 5 *per cent.* for 17 years,

years, and after that 4 *per cent.* for 83 years, yet the latter might appear more inviting. Besides, it is not necessary that the period of the annuities should be so long as 100 years. Any surplus monies might be employed, before the expiration of this period, in extinguishing part of the annuities, by purchasing them at the market price; and the prudent application of the most trifling sum in this way would aid the operations of time. This scheme has been adopted by government; but, instead of extending and continuing it, it was retracted in the year 1720, when the nation was put to the expence of three millions, in order to reduce several long and short annuities, then subsisting, into redeemable *perpetuities*. This, however, is not the best plan the state can pursue. We would only observe, that the *slowness* of its operations may perhaps be more than compensated by its *certainty*. It is no inconsiderable advantage, that the discharge of the national debt is constant and uninterrupted, and, in a great degree, independent of the management of the public finances by ignorant or unfaithful servants.

There is another method of gaining the same end, which is, on many accounts, preferable to the former; that is, 'by providing an annual saving, to be applied invariably, together with the interest of all the sums redeemed by it, to the purpose of discharging the public debts; or, in other words, by the establishment of a permanent *sinking fund*.' This plan has been also adopted by government; but, though capable of producing the *greatest* effects in the *easiest* and *surest* manner, it has never been carried into execution. The following calculation will evince the truth of this observation. Suppose the annual saving to be £. 100,000. This sum, applied now to discharge an equal debt, bearing interest at 4 *per cent.* will transfer to the public, from its creditors, an annuity of £. 4000. At the end of a year then, there would be a saving of £. 104,000, which would transfer to the public another annuity of £. 4,160, and make the saving, at the end of two years, to be £. 108,160. Thus, the original fund would go on increasing, at the same rate, with money improved at 4 *per cent.* compound interest; so that, at the end of 95 years, it would be, by Question I. £. 4,151,138. At the expiration of such a term, the nation might be eased of above 4 millions *per annum* in taxes; and above 100 millions of its debts would be discharged, gradually and insensibly, at no greater expence than £. 100,000 *per annum*; and without interfering with any of the resources of government, or making any other difference, than causing *funds* to be engaged, for a course of time, to the *public*, that would have been otherwise necessarily engaged to its *creditors*, and which, therefore, must have been entirely useless to it. Nor

is

is it of any great consequence, on this plan, what interest the state pays for money; for the higher the interest, the sooner will such a fund pay off the principal. Thus, 100 millions, borrowed at 8 *per cent.* and bearing an annual interest of eight millions, would be paid off by a fund, producing annually £. 100,000 in 56 years; that is, in 39 years less time than if the same money had been borrowed at 4 *per cent.* Reductions of interest, when the principal is put into a regular course of payment, are no great advantage to a state. They only lighten the evil by protracting it. But if no plan be adopted for discharging the public debts, or if it be not faithfully executed, reduction of interest is really hurtful. It furnishes more money to supply the deficiencies arising from bad management; and by only *retarding*, without *preventing* the increase of the burdens occasioned by the public debts, the affairs of the state must necessarily come to a *crisis*, and the danger, attending such a period, be in proportion to the reductions of interest that have been made. Suppose the whole debt a nation can bear, to be that, whose annual interest is five millions. Let it be further supposed, that it has some resources left, which will enable it to bear this and every additional burden for 23 years to come; and that at this time the state, urged by the fear of an approaching bankruptcy, resolves on some effectual measures for preserving itself. In such circumstances, no measure can be *so* effectual as the establishment of a *sinking fund*, and the faithful application of it, in the manner already explained. Let this fund be such as produces a million annually. If all the debts bear interest at 6 *per cent.* this fund would pay off three-fifths of them, within the period of 23 years, and the state might be saved. But if, in consequence of reductions, they bear interest at no more than 3 *per cent.* the same fund would not give the same relief in less than *double* that time; and, therefore, a bankruptcy might prove unavoidable. In some kingdoms a spunge might be applied, or the funds be one-half reduced by an act of despotism, without occasioning any great convulsions; but such a compendious method of retrieving the errors of bad management is not possible in this free country; and, it is to be hoped, never will be possible.

These observations are too applicable to the state of this nation. The interest of the public debts has been reduced, at different periods, from 6 to 5, and from 5 to 4, and 3 *per cent.* but still they have grown with rapidity; and we now see ourselves overloaded, and in no way of gaining relief. Had there been no reductions of interest, we should, indeed, have been in the same condition sooner; but we might have been relieved also sooner, and with less difficulty and danger.

Our

Our Author obſerves, that conſiderable advantages might be derived from *lotteries*, in paying the public debts; but he adds, *lotteries* do great miſchief in a ſtate, by foſtering the deſtructive ſpirit of gaming. It is wretched policy to make them familiar, by recurring to them in the ordinary courſe of government. There are great occaſions on which they may be neceſſary, and for ſuch occaſions they ſhould be reſerved. Let our Readers apply this juſt reflection.

After ſpecifying ſome of the obvious advantages attending a regular payment of the public debts, and ſuggeſting that ſo ſmall a ſum as £. 200,000, faithfully applied from the beginning of the year 1700, would long before this time have paid off above 80 millions of them, and propoſing *celibacy* as one of the moſt proper objects of taxation for the purpoſe of raiſing this annual ſum, our Author proceeds to ſhew, that the diminution and extinction of the national debt might be effected, by *particular* funds, with ſmall ſurpluſſes, appropriated to *particular* debts. In the wars of King *William* and Queen *Anne*, 6 *per cent.* intereſt was given for all loans. It would have been eaſy to have annexed to each loan a *fund* producing a *ſurplus* of £. 1 *per cent.* after paying the intereſt; and ſuch a *ſurplus* would have been ſufficient to annihilate the principal of every loan in 33 years. Had this plan been followed, the diſengagement of the public funds, and the relief attending it, would have begun 50 years ago; and the debts contracted during the reigns of King *William* and Queen *Anne*, would have been all cancelled near 20 years ago, without any of that trouble, tumult, and diſtreſs, which have been occaſioned by reductions of intereſt, and by the various ſchemes which have been tried for leſſening the debts. The ſums to be laid out would, in this caſe, be ſo ſmall at firſt, that it would be proper to employ them in purchaſing part of the loan to be annihilated, at the prices in the public market; and this, as far as it can be carried, is the moſt eaſy, and quiet, and ſilent way poſſible of extinguiſhing the public debts. A fund, yielding £. 1 *per cent.* ſurplus, annexed to a loan at 5 *per cent*, would diſcharge the principal in 37 years; at 4 *per cent.* in 41 years; at 3 *per cent.* in 47 years.—— *N. B.* This ſurplus is to be conſidered as an annuity, and the amount of it to be determined by Queſt. IV.

Thus we ſee what *might* have been done, had a right plan been purſued from the firſt. But every lover of his country will anxiouſly enquire, whether any thing can be done to relieve us in our *preſent* ſtate? Our circumſtances, though juſtly deplorable, are not abſolutely deſperate. Some have thought that a good method might be found out of diſcharging the national debt, by life annuities. Our Author has fully proved, that this

 expedient,

expedient, though preferable to that of redeemable *perpetuities*, is by no means eligible. Suppose £. 33,333,000 is to be paid off, by offering to the public creditors life annuities, in lieu of their 3 *per cents.* A life at 60, interest being $3\frac{1}{2}$ *per cent.* and the probabilities of life, as in the *Breslaw* Tables, is worth 9 years purchase. A life at 30 is worth $15\frac{1}{2}$ years purchase. No scheme would be sufficiently inviting which did not offer 8 *per cent.* at an average to all subscribers. Suppose, however, that no more than $7\frac{1}{2}$ is given, and that there are 33,333 subscribers, at £. 1000 stock each, for which a life annuity is to be granted of £. 75, or for the whole stock subscribed, two millions and a half. A million and a half extraordinary must, therefore, be provided towards paying these annuities.

It is demonstrated, in the Appendix, that it will be 30 years, at least, before a number will die off (in the particular circumstances here specified) equal to the whole number of annuitants; that is, before 33 millions of debts will be annihilated. But had the extraordinary million and half, provided for paying these annuities, been employed during this time, in paying off so much of the debt at *par* every year, extinguishing at the same time every year an equivalent tax, 45 millions would have been paid. And had the savings also been employed in the same manner, 71 millions would have been paid: for a million and half, considered as an annuity, and improved at 3 *per cent.* compound interest, will be found, by Question II. to amount to more than this sum. Hence it appears, that the nation must lose greatly by every scheme of this kind; and yet they are so specious, that we should not wonder to see them adopted. The following pages contain a fuller explication of this subject. And it is clearly demonstrated, that in paying off a million, raised by annuities on a set of lives, all at 30 years of age, the public would sustain a loss of £. 455,000, or *waste* a sum nearly equal to half the principal borrowed. Persons at such an age have (by the Tables annexed) an *expectation* of 28 years; and they will be entitled, supposing interest at 4 *per cent.* to £. 7 *per annum*, for every £. 100 advanced. For a million then the public must make 28 payments of £. 70,000. Instead of this method of discharging such a debt, let the fund producing this annual sum be engaged to pay the principal and interest of a million borrowed on *redeemable* perpetuities, at 4 *per cent.* At the end of the first year there will be a surplus of £. 30,000. Find, by Quest. IV. in what time this annuity will amount to a million, interest being at 4 *per cent.* and in the same time, or $21\frac{1}{2}$ years, such an annual surplus would annihilate the whole debt. The loss to the public will be $6\frac{1}{2}$ years purchase of the annuities, or 70,000 multiplied by $6\frac{1}{2}$, which is equal to £. 455,000. By similar deductions it may be easily found, that

that the loss in *younger* lives is greater; in *older* lives less; but never inconsiderable, except in the *oldest* lives. This, however, though so wasteful, is a more frugal way of procuring money than by borrowing on perpetuities, without putting them into a course of redemption; for in this case (if a spunge is not applied) the loss must be *infinite*.

The same observations are applicable to all the ways of raising money by the sale of reversions. The public might procure a million, by offering for it a fund, that will be disengaged at the end of 18 years, and then produce £. 80,000 *per annum* for ever. This would be the same, interest at 4 *per cent.* with offering *two* millions, 18 years hence, for *one* million now; and a private man, or an *office* for the sale of reversions, might gain by such a transaction; because the money advanced, in consequence of being improved, might, in 18 years, be more than doubled. But, as the *public* always borrows for immediate services, and never lays up money, it would necessarily lose a sum equal to the whole sum borrowed. And the same money might have been borrowed on a fund, producing £. 50,000 *per annum*; which would not only pay the interest, but discharge the whole principal in 41 years; for in that time the surplus, or £. 10,000, would amount to a million.

By raising money on life annuities, the *present members* of a state take a heavier load on themselves, in order to exempt *posterity*; and there would be a laudable generosity in this, were it not for the *folly* of it; the same exemption being equally practicable at *half* the expence. On the other hand, by borrowing on *reversionary* grants, the *present* members of a state exempt themselves entirely, by throwing the load *doubled* on *posterity*; and there is a cruelty and injustice in this that nothing can excuse.

Upon the whole, it appears, that no money which the nation can spare, applied so as to bear only *simple* interest, is capable of doing us, in our present circumstances, any essential service. If our affairs are retrieved at all, it must be by a fund increasing in the manner above explained. The smallest *fund* of this kind is, indeed, *omnipotent*, if it is allowed time to operate. A single penny, improved at 5 *per cent.* compound interest from our Saviour's birth, would, by this time, have increased to more money than would be contained in 150 millions of globes, each equal to the earth in magnitude, and all solid gold. But as we cannot, in this case, be allowed much time, our fund must be proportionably *large*. Suppose then, that the nation, besides all its other burdens, can provide a fund that shall yield a *million* and *half annually*, for 20 years to come. If it cannot do this, we have nothing to do but to wait the issue and tremble.

Such

Such a fund, together with the savings accruing from the reduction of the consolidated 4 *per cents* in 1779, would increase to three millions *per annum* in 20 years. At the end of this term, the nation might be eased of the most oppressive taxes, to the amount of a million and a half; and if there should be a war in the mean while, the nation would be reinstated nearly in its present circumstances. But if there should be no war, the national debt and taxes charged with it would be reduced a third below the sums at which they now stand. The remaining million and half would, in 23 years, increase again to three millions *per annum*; and then, so much more of the public taxes would be set free; 50 millions more, or 93 millions in all, of the public debts would be discharged, and the difficulties of the nation would be, in a great measure, conquered:—By taking advantage of the low price of the public funds, and with a little management, the annual million and half might be made to increase to another million and half, in less time than has been assigned. Should there be a war in a few years, the 3 *per cents* would probably fall below 75; and if it lasted eight years, the fund would double itself in 18, instead of 20 years; or, if the government should go on to pay off this stock at *par*, the advantage would be the same: for, in that case, money might be borrowed for the public service on proportionably better terms. War, therefore, would accelerate the redemption of the public debts; and it would do this the more the longer it lasted, and the higher it raised the interest of money.—The stocks would be always kept up by the operations of the fund; and, in proportion to the sums yielded by it, the public would be able to borrow money more advantageously, and less would be added to its burdens.

The *sinking fund*, in its present state, and after supplying the deficiencies of the peace-establishment, yields, it is supposed, a considerable part of the million and half required. An annual lottery, though by no means a desirable expedient except in circumstances of absolute necessity, might easily raise £. 200,000 more.—Were there indeed no way of providing the whole, or any part, of this sum, but by creating new funds, or imposing new taxes, it *ought* to be done, because it *must* be done, or the nation be ruined.

Many are the evils and dangers attending an *exorbitant* public debt in this country, and they are so great, that they cannot be exaggerated. It increases the dependance on the crown; it occasions execrable practices in the alley; it renders us tributary to foreigners; it raises the price of provisions and labour, and consequently checks population, and loads our trade and manufactures. It restrains the exertions of the spirit of liberty in the kingdom; and exposes us to particular danger from foreign as well as domestic enemies, by making us fearful of war, and incapable of engaging in it, however necessary, without the hazard of bringing on terrible convulsions by overwhelming public credit.

All these are evils which must increase with every increase of the national debt; and there is a point at which, when they arrive, the consequences must be fatal. 'I am now writing, proceeds the Author, under a conviction that I am doing the little in my power to preserve my country from this danger; I have shewn, that an annual supply of a million and a half for 18, or at most 20 years, may be made the means of restoring and saving us. This, therefore, is our remedy; and it ought to be applied *immediately*, lest it should not be applied time enough.'

The ingenious Author concludes this *very interesting* chapter with some further observations, that demand particular notice. No plan can be effectual for the redemption of the state, unless it be allowed to operate, *without interruption*, a proper time. There must be a *sacred* and *inviolable* application of the fund already described, together with all its produce, otherwise the national debt can never be extinguished, nor indeed much reduced. But how can this be secured? How can an object, that grows continually more and more tempting, be defended against invasion and rapine? 'I might here (says the Author) mention the superintendency and care of the representatives of the kingdom, the faithful guardians of the state, to whom ministers are responsible for the use they make of the public money. But experience has shewn that we cannot rely on this security. The difficulty, therefore, now mentioned is the very greatest difficulty the nation has to struggle with in the payment of its debts.'

The *sinking fund* was established in 1716, when the public debts were little more than a third of what they are now; and yet they were then thought alarming and dangerous. It was intended as a *sacred deposit* never to be touched; and was to be applied to the payment of the debts incurred before the 25th of *December*, 1716; *and to no other use, intent, or purpose whatever.* The faith of *parliament*, therefore, as well as the security of the kingdom, seemed to require that it should be preserved carefully and rigorously from alienation; but, notwithstanding this, it has been *generally* alienated. The exigencies of the state have consumed its produce; and it has been usually pleaded, that, when money is wanted, it makes no difference whether it is taken from hence, or procured by making a new loan. There cannot be a worse sophism than this. The difference between these two methods of procuring money is no less than *infinite*. Suppose a *million* wanted for any public ser-

 vice.

vice. If it is borrowed at 4 *per cent.* the public will lose, by the payment of interest, £. 40,000 the first year, and the same the second year, and the same for ever afterwards. But if it is taken out of the *sinking fund*, the public will lose £. 40,000 the first year; £. 41,600 the second year; £. 80,000 the 18th year; a *million* the 85th year: for these are the sums that would, at these times, have otherwise necessarily reverted to the public. It loses, therefore, the advantage of paying, in 85 years, with money of which otherwise no use could have been made, *twenty-five millions* of debt. By thus employing the *sinking fund*, the state, in order to avoid giving *simple interest* for money, alienates that which otherwise *must* have been improved at *compound interest*, and would, in time, have *necessarily* amounted to *any* sum. Had only one *third* of the produce of this fund been faithfully applied from the first, near *three-fourths* of our present debts might now have been discharged; and in a few years more, the *whole* of them might be discharged. This observation is more particularly explained and demonstrated in the Appendix. Can it be possible then to think, without regret and indignation, of that misapplication of this fund, which, with the consent of parliaments, always complying, our ministers have practised? 'I find it difficult here, says Dr. Price, to speak with calmness.—But I must restrain myself. *Calculation*, and not *censure*, is my business in this work. I must believe, that the grievance I have mentioned, has proceeded more from inattention and mistake, than from any design to injure the public.'

The Author has added four essays on different subjects in the doctrine of life annuities and political arithmetic. The first was published in volume 59 of the Philosophical Transactions, and an account was given of it in the Review for February, 1771. It is now improved by several valuable additions. The *postscript* is wholly new, and contains many important observations on the present state of *Edinburgh*, *Paris*, and *Berlin*, with respect to healthfulness and number of inhabitants. The Author expected to have found the probability of life in Edinburgh, from its moderate bulk and particular advantage of situation, nearly the same with those at *Breslaw*, *Northampton*, and *Norwich*; but was surprised to observe that this was not the case. During a period of 20 years, from 1739 to 1758, only one in 42 of all who died at *Edinburgh*, reached 80 years of age; whereas one in 40 lives to this age in *London*. The probabilities of life are much the same, through all its stages, with those in London; only, after 30, they are rather lower at *Edinburgh*. This fact affords a striking proof of the pernicious effects arising from uncleanliness, and crouding together on one spot too many inhabitants. One house, as is well known, consists of many *families*; in 1748, the whole number of *families* in the city and liberties of Edinburgh was 9064;

 and

and the proportion of *inhabitants* to *families*, in the parish of *St. Cuthbert*, according to an estimate made in the year 1743, was $4\frac{1}{10}$ to 1; and if this is the true proportion for the whole town, the number of inhabitants will be $4\frac{1}{10}$ multiplied by 9064, or 37,162. And, as the yearly medium of deaths for eight years was 1783, one in $20\frac{4}{5}$ died annually. Mr. *Maitland* expresses much surprize that the number of males should be less than the number of females, in the proportion of 3 to 4. But this is by no means peculiar to *Edinburgh*.

In *Paris*, the number of houses, comprehended by an injurious policy within very confined boundaries, is reckoned to be 28,000, or 30,000 (some say 50,000). But the number of inhabitants, supposing a 20th part to die annually, cannot be much less than 480,000, or 16 times the number of houses.

The inhabitants of *Berlin* were numbered by order of the King of *Prussia* in 1747, and found to be 107,224. In 1749, they were increased to 110,933. Their number, therefore, compared with the annual burials, the *medium* of which for 5 years, ending at 1751, has been 4,092, was as 27 to 1; a higher proportion than might be expected in so large a town, and so crouded as, at an average, to have 16 inhabitants in every house. This the Author accounts for by the rapid increase of this town from the year 1700; for in 50 years it quadrupled itself. The ingenious *Susmilch* makes the proportion of people who die annually in *great* towns, to be from $\frac{1}{24}$ to $\frac{1}{28}$; in *moderate* towns, from $\frac{1}{28}$ to $\frac{1}{32}$; and in the *country* from $\frac{1}{40}$ to $\frac{1}{50}$. But our Author states these proportions as follow: *great* towns, from $\frac{1}{20}$ to $\frac{1}{23}$ or $\frac{1}{24}$; *moderate* towns, from $\frac{1}{23}$ to $\frac{1}{28}$; the *country*, from $\frac{1}{30}$ or $\frac{1}{35}$ to $\frac{1}{50}$ or $\frac{1}{60}$. This, however, must be understood with exceptions.

The second essay contains remarks on Mr. *De Moivre*'s rules for calculating the values of *joint* lives. The third essay is published in the last volume of the Philosophical Transactions, and to that we refer for the account of it.

The fourth essay contains observations on the proper method of constructing tables for determining the rate of human mortality, the number of inhabitants, and the values of lives in any town or district, from bills of mortality, in which are given the numbers dying annually at all ages. The Author has added two new tables for *Norwich* and *Northampton* to those that had been already constructed by Dr. *Halley* for *Breslaw*, and by Mr. *Simpson* for *London*. We could with pleasure attend our Author through this *Essay*; it is difficult to determine, what to reject or where to desist; but our limits, on which we have already too much encroached, will not allow us to proceed any further. We take our leave for the present, indulging the hope of another interview in a little while.

ART. III.

Art. III. *An Enquiry into the Nature, Rise, and Progress of the Fevers most common in London, as they have succeeded each other in the different Seasons for the last 20 years. With some Observations on the best Method of treating them.* By William Grant, M. D. 8vo, 5 s. Cadell. 1771.

THE intent of this Enquiry is to point out the several diseases which are produced by, and partake of the reigning constitutions which succeed each other in the circle of the year; their various complications with each other; and the different intentions of cure.

The *spring* season includes these three constitutions: the inflammatory, humorrhal, and catarrhous, with their various combinations.

The disease which most generally prevails in *summer*, is the *synochus putris*, or *typhus*; which Sydenham calls the Variolous Fever, because he observed, that the constitution which produced it, promoted and exasperated the small-pox.

Autumn changes the putrid constitution into the bilious.—The diseases of this season consist of the cholera morbus, bilious dysentery, bilious fever, and the bilious erysipelas.

In *winter* the bilious constitution is succeeded by the atrabilious, which takes place in November, December, and even January, if the winter be soft and open; and produces the *morbus hypochondriacus cum materia*, the *mæstitia sine causa* in men, and one species of the *morbus hystericus* in women; the *peripneumonia notha*, *guttæ rosaceæ*, *impetigo*, herpes, lichen, &c.

With respect to agues, our Author says, 'we seldom meet with agues during the height of either the inflammatory, or the putrid constitutions; but they are very frequent in spring, during the phlegmatic constitution, and during the bilious and atra-bilious constitutions of the latter season; when the colluvies collected in the stomach and intestines obstruct the excretions of the *viscera* of the *abdomen*. The agues of the spring almost always give way to the month of July; perhaps, because the phlegm being attenuated, does not at that season so much obstruct those excretions.

'The agues of the bilious constitution, if they are stopped before the bilious morbid lentor is evacuated, bring on a continual fever, in the same manner as the spring agues, when they are stopped before the phlegm or pituite is removed: but after the phlegm is evacuated in spring, or the bilious matter in harvest, the ague will commonly yield to the bark, given in a proper quantity between the fits.'

As a specimen of this work, we shall give our Readers Dr. Grant's

Recapitulation of the Spring Diseases.

 1. 'The

1. 'The inflammatory fever, or fever from ſizy blood, which I have ventured to call Καῦσος, or ardent, or burning hot, if left to Nature, always terminates by the formation of pus in the veſſels, which is afterwards evacuated by the common emunctories, if in a moderate quantity, and is what forms the moſt perfect ὑπόστασις in the urine. But if the quantity is very conſiderable, and the progreſs of the fever rapid, then phlegmons are formed, or certain depoſits, to which Nature directs ſome part of the pus, and there evacuates it by an ulcer upon ſome of the external or internal ſurfaces of the body, which co-operates with the hypoſtaſis in the urine.

'As ulcers are frequently formed in or near vital organs, whoſe functions they may deſtroy, it is better to prevent this formation of phlegmons, and, early in the diſeaſe, to evacuate the offending matter, by the *open orifice of the vein*, (as Sydenham calls it) without waiting for coction and expulſion; of the ſucceſs of which expedient, I have ſeen numberleſs inſtances.

'This fever may be produced in vigorous, healthy people, young or old, at any ſeaſon of the year, particularly in high and dry countries, where the people live much on bread and vegetables; but it is moſt frequent in this city from Chriſtmas to the month of June incluſive; that is, after the winter cold has ſubſiſted long enough to brace the ſolids and condenſe the fluids of our bodies; and therefore, the moſt genuine inflammations, as well as the moſt violent, happen in the months of February and March; particularly if the barometer is high, and the wind blows from any point between north-weſt and eaſt; conſequently, all fevers of what ſpecies ſoever, which happen between Chriſtmas and June, will be complicated with inflammation more or leſs, according to the idioſincraſy, and other circumſtances, and will require an antiphlogiſtic treatment in proportion. Hence we find, that the catarrhous fever, and the humorrhal fever, both happening during theſe five months, are partly inflammatory, and yield, in a great meaſure, to the antiphlogiſtic regimen; nay, are ſometimes cured by it, and always exaſperated by an oppoſite treatment.

2. 'The humorrhal fever, or *ſynochus non putris* of the ancients, which Sydenham calls the moſt frequent of all fevers, the great fever of Nature, or the deputatory fever, may happen at different ſeaſons of the year in ſome particular conſtitutions; but we do not meet with it often till the day lengthens conſiderably, and the ſpring or vegetation is far advanced. Beſides the inflammation which this fever has in common with the former fever, there is a fluxion of tough phlegm, which Nature depoſites upon the ſtomach and bowels at this ſeaſon, which muſt be evacuated; ſo that after the inflammatory part of the complaint is partly conquered by bleeding and cooling diet, the matter contained in the ſtomach and bowels muſt be evacuated as often as the ſymptoms of turgidity in either denote its exiſtence.

'This will often remove the whole ailment; but ſometimes part of the morbid matter may remain, which requires a longer digeſtion in the veſſels, and will not paſs off properly, by any other outlet than the ſkin. There is indeed ſcarce any of the common fevers, in which kindly moderate ſweats are, through the whole courſe, more beneficial;

beneficial; but if these sweats are promoted before the siziness of the blood is subdued, the inflammation will be exasperated; and if, before the turgid matter in the bowels is evacuated, the quantity of morbid matter will be attenuated and exalted; then reabsorbed, and mixed with the blood, so as to bring on an irregular, dangerous, and miliary fever, which, if the patient lives long enough, frequently terminates in a very bad kind of dysentery.

'This fever remits almost from the beginning, and if properly treated, the remission becomes daily longer and longer, till at last it comes to a real intermission, or the disease goes quite off: it therefore greatly resembles some sorts of the spring ague; and all the spring fluxes partake of its nature.

'When the fluxion of tough phlegm falls upon the bowels without a purging or considerable degree of fever, it occasions indigestion and obstruction, obstinate constipation, dry belly-ach, or jaundice, according to the idiosincrasy of each individual: all these disorders are very frequent at this season, and, having a similar cause with the fever, are cured nearly by the same means, as daily experience shews.

3. 'The other great spring complaint, is the catarrh, or a fluxion of thin acrid rheum on the *membrana sneideri* and lungs, attended with sneezing, coriza, angina, and cough. With respect to this fever also, two things are to be considered: first, The degree of inflammation, and then the quantity and acrimony of the fluxion: this fever seldom happens before Christmas, most commonly in February, and gives rise to the true consumption, or *phthisis* of the lungs; it is of a tedious nature, and frequently lasts to the end of June: during its course, it is sometimes complicated with the humorrhal fever, and relieved by the same vomits and purges necessary for that fever; but when single, it has its natural crisis, chiefly by expectoration: nor does it require repeated vomits and purges, except there should be evident signs of turgid matter in the stomach or bowels.

'But the fluxion of morbid matter upon the *membrana sneideri*, which happens in this fever, is not a true phlegmon that discharges pus; but rather resembles a phlegmonoides, which discharges a thin, acrid lymph; for which reason, perhaps, it has been found in some degree malignant and contagious to young people.

'When a true peripneumony comes, after coction, to a plentiful spitting, the fever subsides every day, and the patient spits a thick, white, laudable pus, plain or streaked with blood, like that from the bursting of an impostume; but in the catarrh, after frequent bleeding, and a cooling regimen, there comes on a vast discharge from the lungs and fauces, of a clear, acrid pituite, fretting and tickling wherever it touches, and the quickness of the pulse continues, notwithstanding the great discharge from the parts affected; so that acrimony seems to have a considerable share in this fever, and therefore many of those who are most subject to it, are also subject to heats, pimples, and tetters upon the skin, previous to the pulmonary complaint, and the return of these eruptions is a sign of recovery; many have brought on a catarrh by endeavouring to remove them. And here let me observe, that if a spring erysipelas, in a young person

son be repelled, a catarrh will also probably follow; whereas dysentery, for the most part, will be the consequence of repelling an erysipelas in harvest.

'To conduct the catarrh, during the violence of the inflammation, besides the common evacuations, the most thin diet is required; such as the juice of ripe fruit, barley-water, infusions of bread, of apples, and the like; but when the hardness of the pulse is abated, soft food of the more nourishing kind, succeeds better; such as cucumbers, lettice, all kinds of seeds, grain, bread, sweet roots, dry fruits, rennette-whey, and butter-milk. I have sometimes thought, that the bad practice, which does so much mischief in this disease, was owing to a notion, that it was of the same nature with the *peripneumonia notha* of the month of November; or rather with that cough and fever which Sydenham calls the winter fever.

'Ignorant people, having observed the great advantage of blisters in these complaints, have expected a like effect from them in the true catarrh, and have been much surprised to find, that, by a single blister unseasonably applied, which they thought at least an innocent remedy, they had exasperated both the inflammation and acrimony to such a degree, as to render the catarrh almost incurable. But if these diseases are compared, they soon appear to have opposite causes.

'The *peripneumonia notha* is the disease of gross and bloated habits, after forty years of age, succeeds the bilious constitution, is complicated with the *humor atrabilarius*, and the lungs are loaded with a tough, viscid, cold phlegm, without much inflammation; whereas the catarrh is the disease of young, plethoric habits, under thirty years of age, succeeding the inflammatory constitution, and complicated with it, the *membrana sneideri* being inflamed as with an erysipelas, and discharging a thin, acrid lymph; so that every incisive medicine, which does good in the one, must do mischief in the other.

'After many days, a digestion is performed in the vessels, as appears by the change in the urine; and the pus thus formed, is discharged by the common emunctories, and the expectoration of concocted matter; but if, instead of this, a large imposthume is formed on the lungs, and the pus is there deposited; or if many small phlegmons, called tubercles, are formed on their internal surface, then the complaint changes its appearance, and an hectic fever is the consequence, which is attended with peculiar symptoms: first, Of the *vomica tecta*, well known and described by authors: and, secondly, Of a real open ulcer, discharging pus, and difficult to be healed; owing partly to the structure of the lungs, partly to the perpetual motion and continual contact with the open air, to which that part is necessarily exposed: hence arises the great difficulty, and almost impossibility of curing this disease in that stage.

'But in most cases, when things are properly conducted, coction and crisis gradually come on, and the whole disease is totally conquered by the month of July, leaving only a weakness and relaxation of the compages of the lungs: this consequence of the disease is curable only by the same air, exercise, diet, and medicines, which are found to be most effectual in the *febris debilis et laxa*, viz. a dry, light

light air, riding on horseback, dry nourishing diet of the antiseptic kind; chalybeate waters, bark, and cold bathing: all which ought to be persisted in during the months of August, September, October, November, and December, and so on to the end of the catarrhous constitution; it being necessary to use all possible means to harden the constitution, without producing a plethora; for without these precautions, relapses are, for the most part, certain in young people, and in our climate, as soon as the catarrhous constitution returns. But though strengthening remedies become necessary when the fever is totally subdued, to prevent relapses, it must ever be remembered, that during the fever they are pernicious, and that the air of Holland will then be more salutary than the air of Montpelier; but the most certain method I have yet been able to discover for preventing a relapse in this dangerous disease, is a residence in the West India islands till the patient passes the age of twenty-five years.'

Upon the whole, this Enquiry is a kind of commentary on the epidemic constitutions of Sydenham: in which the Reader will meet with many excellent practical observations, some crude and inconclusive theories, and some old doctrines earnestly supported and inculcated.

ART. IV. *Observations on the Prophecies relating to the Restoration of the Jews. With an Appendix in Answer to the Objections of some late Writers.* By Joseph Eyre. 8vo. 2s. 6d. Cadell. 1771.

THIS Author's design is to prove that the conversion of the Jews and ten tribes, and their restoration to their own land, is plainly and expresly predicted in several parts of the sacred writings: and the doctrine of the *millenium* he regards as immediately connected with this; a doctrine, he observes, that has been very unfashionable for these last fourteen centuries; but, he adds, it were very easy to show, that it was generally believed in the more early ages of the church, especially in those nearest to the apostolic age. In support of which assertion he offers a few passages in the preface, as a specimen of what might be produced to this purpose, from ancient Christian writers. He avoids a minute enquiry how this primitive, and, as he says, scriptural doctrine came to be so universally rejected in the later and more corrupt times, as the digression would be too long; but he remarks, that ' since such a state of *righteousness* and *purity* as the *millenium* is described to introduce, did imply such a previous corrupt state of the church, as it would require a divine interposition to reform, it is no wonder that a church, which could see no necessity for any reformation at all (meaning the church of Rome) should reject it as useless aud unnessary.—But why they of the reformation, who admit the almost universal corruption of the church for so many centuries, should be opposers of this doctrine, is not so easily to be accounted for. For my part, I much fear that their opposition proceeds from the

the same principle with that of the church they have reformed from; namely, that they look upon their own particular sects and opinions, as too pure and free from error to need any farther reformation.'

To this, he adds, that the ridiculous opinions which some who believed this doctrine, both in ancient and modern times, have superadded to it, have likewise greatly tended to discredit it. And might not we offer a farther observation to those which this Writer has made—that the great obscurity and uncertainty attending some parts of scripture here alluded to, will and must frequently render thinking and judicious persons doubtful at least upon the subject, and unable to determine, with any great degree of satisfaction, what are the particular truths designed to be conveyed?

Mr. Eyre pays great regard to what our learned countryman Mr. Joseph Mede has advanced upon these subjects: he appears also himself to be a man of sense and learning; and qualified for the discussion of the points he has undertaken. He has various quotations from the above-mentioned writer; and the nature of his work required him to insert many passages from the sacred writings, which indeed constitute a considerable part of the pamphlet; yet we find but few critical remarks upon our English translation, excepting sometimes a comparison of it with *Tindale's* version, which, in some instances, he prefers to that in present use. One observation of this kind we may here insert, as tending, in some degree, to obviate a particular difficulty. It relates to Haggai ii. 9, where it is said, *The glory of this latter house shall be greater than of the former.* Tindale's version of the text is, "The glory of the *last* house shall be greater than the *fyrste*:" and our Author has the following note concerning it; 'The *latter* and the *former* house, as our translation has it, seems to imply that there were to be but two houses or temples; that destroyed by *Nebuchadnezzar*, and that which they were then building; but the *first* and *last* house does not confine us to only those two temples.' This may not improperly be attended to by those who find some objection to the prophecy, from considering that the temple which was standing in the time of Christ had been built by Herod, and was entirely new and distinct from that which had been erected after the captivity in Babylon, and which gave rise to the prediction: but we should observe that Mr. Eyre supposes the phrase, *the last house*, in this text, to refer to a temple which is yet in some future period to be erected at Jerusalem.

After presenting to his readers several prophecies from those books which are called canonical, our Author proceeds to the apocryphal books, from whence he extracts two passages, the one *Esdras* xiii. the other *Tobit* xiv. 3, &c.; as to the former of these

ıeſe books, at leaſt, he ſeems to have no doubt but that it ught to be admitted into the canon of ſcripture; in his reflec-ons upon them he has principally had recourſe to what has een ſaid by Dr. Lee and Mr. Mede.

Some *few* extracts, ſuppoſed to be favourable to his deſign, re added from the New Teſtament, with ſeveral pertinent re-ıarks: after which, in the cloſe of the treatiſe, we find a uotation from Sir *Iſaac Newton*, which, though known to ome of our Readers, we ſhall here ſelect, as in this connection appears worthy of particular attention.

'Before I conclude (ſays this Writer) it may be expected y ſome that I ſhould ſay ſomewhat concerning the time when nis reſtoration is to take place; to whom I anſwer, in the vords of our Lord, that *it is not for* us *to know the times and the eaſons which the Father hath put in his own power.* All that we an be certain of in relation hereto, is, that *Jeruſalem ſhall be rodden down of the Gentiles, until the times of the Gentiles be ful-lled*, as our Saviour tells us, *Luke* xxi. 24. What is meant by he times of the Gentiles being fulfilled, is, according to the noſt judicious expoſitors, when the times appointed for the du-ation of the dominion of the four monarchies ſhall be completed. We now live under the laſt ſtate of the fourth monarchy, after he diviſion of it into ten kingdoms, repreſented to *Nebuchad-nezzar* by the feet and toes of the image which he ſaw in his lream; but the preciſe time when the ſtone cut without hands hall ſmite the image *upon his feet* that were of iron and clay, or artly ſtrong or partly brittle, as the angel interprets it, is not perhaps now diſcoverable by us. There are certain periods of time, appointed by the providence of God, for the diſcovery of ſeveral of the prophetic viſions, before which they are cloſed up and ſealed, *i. e.* not to be underſtood. That the time of this reſtoration is one of theſe ſecrets of divine providence, ap-pears from the 12th chapter of *Daniel*, ver. 4—9.——Sir *Iſaac Newton*, in his diſſertation upon this prophecy, p. 251, ſays, " that it ſhould not be known before the laſt age of the world, and therefore it makes for the credit of this prophecy that it is not yet underſtood. The folly of interpreters has been to fore-tel times and things by this prophecy, as if God deſigned to make them prophets; by ſuch raſhneſs they have not only ex-poſed themſelves, but brought that part of ſcripture into con-tempt. The deſign of God was much otherwiſe: He gave this, and other prophecies, in the Old Teſtament, not to gratify men's curioſity, by enabling men to foreknow things, but that, after they are fulfilled, they might be interpreted by the event; and his own *providence*, not the interpreter's, be then fulfilled— that as many as will take pains in this ſtudy, may ſee ſufficient inſtances of God's providence. Among the interpreters of the laſt

last age, there is scarce one of note who has not made some discovery worth knowing; and thence I gather that God is about opening these mysteries: an encouragement this, to be more particularly attentive to these things."

The appendix to this work, consisting of between thirty and forty pages, is intended to remove some objections which have been raised against that explication of the scripture prophecies which this Writer has embraced. The late ingenious and learned Dr. Gregory Sharpe, in a pamphlet intitled, *The Rise and Fall of the holy City and Temple of Jerusalem,* opposes this notion of a future restoration of the Jews. Mr. Eyre speaks of Dr. Sharpe in the most respectable terms, and observes that the character which he has deservedly borne in the literary world, would render him inexcusable if he was wholly to overlook the objections which the Doctor has brought against his opinion. He proceeds therefore in a candid manner to point out the passages in which he apprehends the Doctor to have been mistaken, and to add those scripture grounds and reasons which oblige himself to take a different side.

ART. V. *Elements of the History of France, translated from the Abbé Millot, Confessor in Ordinary to the French King.* By the Translator of Select Tales from Marmontel, and Author of Sermons by a Lady. 12mo. 7 s. 6 d. Dodsley, &c. 1771.

IT is an inconvenience attending all extensive and voluminous histories, that they suit only those who have leisure and a taste for enquiry. Short and comprehensive views of the transactions of different nations have, therefore, been compiled for the generality of readers. The abridgment before us, of the history of France, contains a rapid and accurate narration of the most important and interesting events which have happened in that kingdom. The learned Author has, at the same time, been careful to point out the variations which took place in the manners and government of his countrymen, in the successive periods of their monarchy. His work, though concise, is by no means obscure; and, with regard to the omissions he has made, it may be remarked, in general, that they relate to matters of mere curiosity, or of trivial import. It is our duty, however, to observe, that his partiality to his country is excessive; and that, though he does not seem to be a bigot to the Romish faith, he yet treats it with a distinction and favour that may frequently be prejudicial to the unguarded English reader.

The extracts we shall transcribe from his performance, will exhibit a sufficient specimen, from which an opinion may be formed of the manner and merit of its execution, and will, at the same time, prove both curious and entertaining.

H

He gives us the following particulars concerning Louis XI.

This monarch affected in his drefs a fordid and indecent fim- :ity. In an interview between him and the King of Caftile in ›3, he appeared in a habit of coarfe cloth, his head covered with old hat, ornamented with a leaden figure of our Lady; while the ftilian fparkled with the greateft magnificence. This contraft made n defpicable in the eyes of the Spaniards; but he had gained their nifters by bribery, and affured himfelf of fuccefs in his defigns. e chief expence of his houfehold was for his table; from 12,000 res he carried it to 37: he not only invited the lords of his court eat with him, in order to attach them the more ftrongly to him, t even ftrangers from whom he could gather any thing: fometimes :rchants; for he gave a particular attention to commerce. A mer- ant named Mafter John, flattered by this diftinction, determined afk of him letters of nobility: the King granted them; but from at time took no farther notice of him. Mafter John teftified his rprize: "Go, Mafter Gentleman, faid Lewis to him, when I made n fit down at my table, I looked on you as the firft of your clafs; ›u are now the laft, and it would be an injury to others if I ftill did ›u the fame favour." An excellent leffon this to thofe who prefer in titles to perfonal merit.

' He was often feen to mix with the citizens, and, to inform mfelf of their affairs, had his name infcribed in the companies of e artizans. His anfwer which he made when he was reproached ith not fupporting his dignity was this: "When pride goes before, ame and misfortune follow very near." A defire of keeping people high birth under fubjection (which was a principal object of his olicy) was, without doubt, a reafon why he preferred thofe who ere low born to offices, that he might deftroy them by a word. He ad the addrefs, according to the expreffion of Francis I. of raifing ages above kings: but this was more owing to his cruelty than any ther method; and he fometimes feverely proved how dangerous it as to give his confidence to mean and bafe fouls, who were capa- le of intrigue and deftitute of honour, and who flattered him only › deceive him. He was often miftaken in his finefle. It was a fre- uent expreffion with him, that he who knew not how to diffem- le, knew not how to reign. "If, fays he, my hat was confcious f my fecret, I would burn it." By repeating too often this maxim, e, according to the remark of Mr. Duclos, loft the fruit of it.

' We cannot think, without horror, of the cruel executions which rovoft Triftan the hermit (who was honoured with his friendfhip) erformed by his orders; of the iron cages, enormous chains, and he moft cruel tortures, which became fo common in the laft years f his reign. Tyranny can never be allied with true grandeur; however, this piece of juftice muft be rendered him, that he made very one fulfil the duties of his office. Having one day taken a eview of the officers of his houfehold, and finding the equipages not n good order, he diftributed to each of them efcrutores, faying, fince they would not ferve them with their arms, they fhould with heir pens." This kind of correction had more effect on them than he odious cruelties which he fometimes ufed. He would have de- erved commendation for preferring treaties to war, if it had not been his

his constant system to deceive in negociations. It must, however, be confessed, that he shewed real prudence in always carefully avoiding quarrels at a distance. Genoa having submitted itself to France under Charles VI. this unsteady people, after frequent rebellions, again offered to acknowledge Louis XI. for their sovereign. He replied, "You give yourselves to me, and I give you to the devil." The continual infidelity of the Genoese justifies this answer. When we consider that this perjured and wicked prince was the first of our kings who always bore the title of Most Christian; when we see him delivering himself to all the practices of a popular devotion, making pilgrimages, wearing in his cap images of pewter and lead, giving the county of Boulogne to the Holy Virgin, demanding of the Pope the right of assisting at the holy office with surplice and a mass, establishing the custom of reciting the angelus at mid-day, &c. we know not how to reconcile so many marks of religion with so many vices, which humanity shrinks from; but we often see in nature strange contrasts. He had an odd-turned mind, and a bad heart. "This oddity, says Father Daniel, made him neglect the essential part of devotion, and content himself with exterior practices. It rendered him scrupulous in trifles, when he hesitated not in things of the greatest importance." One of his superstitions was, that he would never swear by a certain cross of St. Leo, which, it was said, had the faculty of striking those with death within a year who perjured themselves on it; but it was his constant practice to oblige others to swear by this very cross.

'Superstition and credulity always go together. He entertained astrologers at his court; but irritated against one of these impostors, who had foretold the death of his mistress, he sent for him, resolved without doubt not to spare him: "Thou who seest into futurity, says he, tell me when thou shalt die." The cunning astrologer saved himself by this reply, "I shall die three days before your majesty." They from that time took care of his person.'

The picture which our Historian exhibits of Henry the Great, is extremely engaging, and delineated with much impartiality.

'Henry IV. says he, being a model for men as well as for kings, the design of this work permits us to add some strokes to the abridgment of his reign. He united to extreme freedom, the best directed policy; to the most exalted sentiments, the most charming simplicity of manners; and, to the courage of a soldier, an inexhaustible fund of humanity. Every thing in him seemed the expression of an amiable soul. Often he conversed familiarly with his soldiers and the people, in such manner as still to acquire fresh respect. His greatest ambition was to render his subjects happy. The Duke of Savoy one day demanded of him at what he valued the revenues of France. "It is worth what I please, said he, because that, having the hearts of my people, I can do what I will. If God gives me life, the time shall come, when there shall not be a labourer in my kingdom who has it not in his power to have a fowl in his pot; and if so, added he fiercely, I shall still continue to be able to support my soldiers in subjecting those to reason who would deprive me of my authority."— The Spanish ambassador one day testified some surprize at seeing him surrounded by a crowd of gentlemen: "If you had seen me in a day

day of battle, said he to him, they would have pressed about me still more."

'His goodness did not degenerate into a weak complaisance: he knew how to refuse on proper occasions, and would make them see the justice of his refusal. A man of rank once demanded mercy for his nephew, who had been guilty of murder. His reply was that of a good prince who was desirous of pardoning, but who could not excuse himself from punishing where it was deserved. "I am very sorry that I cannot grant what you ask; it becomes you to be the uncle, but me to be the king: I excuse your request, do you excuse my refusal."

'If he was sometimes prodigal to ill-disposed noblemen, and rerecompensed less generously the services of his faithful captains; if he established *paulette*, a kind of imposition which perpetuates in families those places which ought to be the reward of merit; if he suffered many abuses to subsist; if he did not do all the good which might have been done in other times, it was less his fault than that of his particular circumstances. Every thing was to be reformed, every thing was to be renewed; but he conquered and pacified his kingdom; he stifled the league and religious wars; re-established order in his finances; made himself beloved by France, and respected by foreign powers; in fine, he reigned gloriously in spite of many obstacles, many disorders, and many enemies, and was a prodigy which nothing in history can equal. One of the greatest objects of his policy, conformable to the principles of Sully, was the enlivening the provinces by agriculture, the true source of riches. An enemy to luxury, which has always more inconveniencies than advantages in it in a vast monarchy, he discredited it by his example and discourses. He incited the noblemen to retire to their estates, "teaching them, says Perifexe, that the best dependance they had was from good management." He rallied those who carried their mills and their high forests of trees on their backs, which was one of the *knaveate* expressions of this great king. The simplicity of his own habit was a lesson sufficient of itself. From the time of his abjuration, he had always appeared sincerely attached to the church. The clergy having made him remonstrances, in 1598, on divers abuses, especially in the nomination of benefices, he replied, "that this abuse was real; that he had found it established; that he hoped to reform it, and put the church again into a flourishing state; but, continued he, do you, on your side, contribute a little towards it; set good examples, that the people may be incited to follow them; and that you going before, they may be turned to the right way. You have exhorted me to my duty, I will exhort you to yours. Let us mutually do well at the desire of each other." Unfortunately he did not always find in the ecclesiastics that love for virtue which establishes itself better by example than by words; and he would sometimes say, "I know very well what they preach; but they do not think that I know what they do."——

'His system was to gain people's minds by mildness, giving for a reason, that you might gain more mouths with a spoonful of honey, than with a ton of vinegar,

'He

'He is justly reproached with an excess of passion for women, and for play. These are the blemishes of a great soul. It is rare to find great virtues without some mixture of vice. Happy the people whose prince makes them forget his faults by his humanity, the wisdom and the glory of his government.'

To these portraits we shall add the following passage from our Author's account of the reign of Louis XIV.

'What principally immortalized Lewis XIV. was the flourishing state of science and letters under his reign, and through his protection. The greatest talents disclosed themselves; the most shining works of all kinds were then published, and the age of Augustus appeared renewed. Corneille, Racine, and Moliere, eclipsed the glory of the Greek theatre. Despreaux gave rules and examples of good taste: sublime eloquence broke forth in Bossuet: Bourdaloue united the force of reason with the profound truths of the Evangelists: Fenelon, with the charms of his style, rendered the austere lessons of morality amiable: the French language, till then vulgar and unformed, rose to perfection; and crowds of good writers employed themselves in the same things of which the scholars seemed to have preserved the knowledge to themselves. Every body read their works. The whole nation became enlightened. Three literary academies brought together in Paris those geniuses who were born for the instruction of the world. Now that men of letters were no more debased by a shameful abuse of their talents, they became much more respectable, as they served not only for the glory but the happiness of society. Knowledge and politeness spread themselves in the depth of the provinces. Though pedantry still reigned in the schools without the burlesque proclamation of Despreaux, the parliament, deceived by false reports, would have renewed the prohibition of teaching any other philosophy than that of the peripatetics. Such is the empire of old established prejudices. Self love, interest, weakness, change of principle, and fear of novelty, pushed beyond their bounds, often prevail over useful truths, which time has not yet made us approve; but when the door is opened to true study, the progress of philosophy necessarily follows that of taste.'

It does not appear to us, that the Translator of the present work deserves great commendation for the manner in which she has executed her task. She has not always been able to render the sense of her Author with sufficient perspicuity: she no where attains his elegance; and her version, instead of 'facilitating the accomplishment of her sex *,' may have a contrary tendency.

It is always with pain that we find ourselves under the necessity of censuring the literary efforts of a lady: but the province in which we have engaged requires impartiality; and the respect that we owe to the public will not allow us to manifest our politeness at the expence of our veracity.

* Translator's pref. p. vi.

ART. VI.

ART. VI. *Principles and Power of Harmony.* 4to. 7s. 6d. Baker, &c. 1771.

THOSE who principally cultivate music as a science, as well as those who follow it as a profession, and are laudably inquisitive concerning the principles on which their art is founded, are greatly obliged to the learned and ingenious Author of this performance, who has here undertaken to introduce to their acquaintance the many new and curious, speculative as well as practical, doctrines, delivered in a work of the late celebrated Signor Tartini, intitled, *Trattato di Musica secondo la vera Scienza dell' Armonia.* He has indeed not only the merit of having naturalized a part of the work of this illustrious foreigner, but that likewise of having considerably enriched it, by an explanation of the principles contained in it, and by the addition of many new and ingenious observations, accompanied occasionally with free but candid criticisms on particular passages. In short, our Commentator has added so much of his own to the original work, that the present publication may very justly be considered as the joint property of Tartini and of his Translator.

It is to be wished that one so excellently qualified for the task, had thought proper to favour the public with an entire translation of this capital performance. This was not however the design of the Author, who has accordingly translated only such parts of it as he thought might give a just idea of Tartini's principles; referring the musical student to the perusal and study of the original, as the best means of contributing to his improvement in one of the most delightful of all the arts. Though the Author however has cleared up many of the obscurities in Tartini's treatise, these omissions are, in their turn, necessarily productive of others of a different kind, to those who cannot consult the original. To this cause, at least, we are willing to attribute many of the difficulties which occurred to us in the perusal of this performance. The public are nevertheless obliged to the Author for what he has done.

The obscurity with which the writings of Tartini have, not undeservedly, been charged, appears to have been owing to a certain mystical turn of mind, a pursuit of fancied analogies, a love of deducing musical principles from abstract ideas, and particularly an abuse of the mathematics; which in his hands became a perplexing guide, and led him into a labyrinth, where the mathematical reader frequently beholds him bewildered, and out of which he escapes only by catching at the clew of a few accidental coincidences. These excentricities of an enthusiastic and exuberant genius were however accompanied with, and corrected by, 'such important physical experiments, so fine an ear, and such a thorough practical knowledge of his art,' that, in the opinion of the Author, he was seldom misled by these *Ignes Fatui* into false conclusions; but, as Petavius said of Scaliger, *Dum errat docet*, his very errors lead to truth. In speaking further on this subject, we cannot follow a better guide than a late musical traveller *, and admirer of this great man, whose observations on the genius of this particular work we shall accordingly transcribe; referring our Readers for a few further particulars concerning its Author to the first page of the present number.

"That his system" (referring to that contained in the treatise before us) "is full of new and ingenious ideas, which could only arise from a superior knowledge in his art, may be discovered through its veil of obscurity; and his friend Padre Colombo accounted to me for that obscurity and appearance of want of true science, by confessing that Tartini, with all the parade of figures, and solutions of problems, was no mathematician.—He saw more, however, than he could express by terms or principles borrowed from any other science; and though neither a geometrician or an algebraist, he had a facility and method of calculating peculiar to himself, by which, as he could satisfy his own mind, he supposed he could instruct others. The truth is, that, with respect to the mysteries of the science, which he seems to have known intuitively, he is sometimes intelligible, and sometimes otherwise; but I have such an opinion of Tartini's penetration and sagacity in his musical enquiries, that when he is obscure, I suppose it to be occasioned either by his aiming too much at conciseness in explaining himself; by the insufficiency of common language to express uncommon ideas; or that he soars above the reach of my conceptions."

The subjects discussed in this work are so various, and, for the most part, treated in so scientific a manner, both in the text of Tartini, and in the comments of his Translator, that we shall not undertake to give any regular or methodical account of its contents; the perusal of which we heartily recommend to the learned in the science: observing in general, with regard to Tartini's mathematical doctrines above alluded to, that the fundamental notes in music which he, justly indeed, but with a most complicated apparatus, derives from various fanciful proportions, and groundless notions about the circle, (for which he entertained a peculiar predilection) his Commentator, more simply, and certainly more naturally, deduces from the harmonical and arithmetical divisions of the trumpet marine

* See Dr. Burney's *Present State of Music*, &c. page 126.

or ſtring trumpet, and the monochord †. We ſhall however extract the ſubſtance [illegible] few ſuch parts of this excellent treatiſe, as may [illegible] to the curious in general; occaſionally accompanying them with ſome reflections of our own, and beginning with that important and ſingular phyſical diſcovery of the *third ſounds*, as they are called, which we imagine may not be known even to ſome philoſophical muſicians in this country, who are not converſant in foreign publications on the ſubject of muſic. The knowledge of them may likewiſe be of uſe to the practical muſician on the violin, violoncello, &c. in directing him to a juſt and accurate intonation; particularly in uſing double ſtops on theſe inſtruments: as by attending to the *third ſounds* which reſult from particular chords, the performer is led to hit upon the very form itſelf of the intended interval, with all the preciſion of the true ratios; his ears and fingers are formed, and by practice become habituated, to the playing moſt perfectly in tune; and one great requiſite is attained towards the producing a good tone.

The *harmonic ſounds*, or the twelfth and ſeventeenth above the principal (as well as ſome others, as we have lately obſerved *) have been long known to accompany every fundamental ſound; and may naturally, and in general, be ſuppoſed to be produced by the partial or ſeparate vibrations of the ſtring or ſonorous body, ſpontaneouſly dividing itſelf, according to a determinate law, into three, five, or other aliquot parts of the whole, conſidered as unity. But Tartini was the firſt who obſerved a *phenomenon*, not ſo eaſily to be accounted for, and of which he makes great uſe in his ſyſtem, produced on the ſounding two notes at the ſame time, on the ſame or two different inſtruments; on which occaſion a third ſound is heard, which is almoſt always graver than the loweſt of the two tones that generated it, and is their proper fundamental baſe.

The experiment may be made by ſounding the perfect interval of a third, fourth, or fifth, &c. either on two ſtrings of the ſame violin; or on two violins played upon at the diſtance of about 30 feet, with a ſtrong bow, and holding out the notes; or with two trumpets, hautbois, or German flutes: the hearer,

† In this the Author follows the excellent advice given by Pythagoras to his diſciples, on his death-bed; as we are told by Ariſtides, one of the ſeven Greek writers upon muſic. *Quare & Pythagoram aiunt, cum ex hâc vitâ abiret, amicos adhortatum,* UT MONOCHORDUM PULSARENT. Vid. Antiq. Muſic. Auct. 7 Edit. Meibomii. p. 11[illegible]. Muſic may indeed be ſaid to owe its exiſtence, as a ſcience, to this inſtrument, by which the fleeting modifications of ſound are fixed, and become the objects of numbers and calculation.

* See Appendix to our 44th volume, p. 553, 554.

in the laſt-mentioned inſtances, placing himſelf in the middle of the interval between the two inſtruments. For want of notes we ſhall mark a few of the intervals, and the third *ſounds* produced by them, by letters. Thus, for inſtance, the interval *C e*, or a major third, produces *C*, the octave below the lower note: *C ſharp e*, a minor third, produces *A*, a tenth below the graver tone: *B e*, a fourth, gives *E*, the octave of the upper note: *B f ſharp*, a fifth, produces a uniſon to *B*: *B g*, a ſixth, generates the double octave below the upper note; and *B flat g*, or the major ſixth, produces *E flat*, the fifth of the lower note. We ſhall only add theſe two general obſervations of the Author, that if any adjoining two ſimple intervals in the harmonic ſeries, $1, \frac{1}{2}, \frac{1}{3}, \frac{1}{4}$, &c. be ſounded, the third ſound will always be that of half the ſtring; and that the ſmaller the interval is, the farther diſtant is the third ſound: ſo that, for example, the third ſound to the interval of the ſemitone minor *G G ſharp*, is the twenty-ſixth below *G natural*.

It appears much more difficult to offer any plauſible conjectures concerning the phyſical cauſe of theſe third ſounds, than of the harmonical notes above-mentioned; as all thoſe of the latter kind, being more acute than the principal, or generating tone, are, for that reaſon, capable of being actually and immediately produced by the vibrations of certain portions of the ſtring or other ſounding body: whereas, in the third ſounds, a tone is heard, always (except in the caſe of the fifth) and often conſiderably, below the pitch of either of the bodies whoſe vibrations it accompanies, and which conſequently cannot *immediately* proceed from either of theſe bodies. To take the firſt of the above-mentioned intervals, that of the greater third, for an example: a third ſound is here heard, ſuch as would be produced by the *actual* vibration of a ſtring of the ſame diameter and tenſion with, but of double the length of, that which produced the loweſt note of the interval. As no ſuch ſtring however is employed in the experiment, we are obliged to ſeek for the cauſe of this new ſound in the air or other medium of ſound, or in the organ of hearing, or in ſome internal modification of the ſenſitive faculty. Our Readers will excuſe us for making a ſhort excurſion or two, on this occaſion, into the ſpacious regions of conjecture; and firſt we ſhall ſuppoſe that the third ſounds derive their origin from ſome hidden properties of the air.

As the immenſe variety in our ſenſations of colour is juſtly ſuppoſed to be produced by an equal diverſity of coloured particles of light, each ſingly qualified to excite one particular ſenſation, and no other: ſo ſome have ſuppoſed that our numerous and diverſified ſenſations of muſical tones are not produced by the undulations of the air, conſidered in its whole maſs; but by aerial

aerial particles ſpecifically different in ſpring; (to which we may add magnitude, figure, and other properties or affections) each capable of exciting, by its motions or other modifications, the idea of only one determinate tone. It is well known that innumerable elective congruities, or affinities, uſually called chemical, ſubſiſt among the minute particles of matter. The philoſopher can only obſerve and mark their effects; for notwithſtanding their multiplicity, he is ignorant of the cauſes which produce them, or of the general laws by which they are regulated, and is content with claſſing the particular appearances under general heads. Following his example in the preſent inſtance, we might ſay that the two orders of particles which give the tones *C* and *e*, either by an harmonical congruity in their ſpring with that ſet of particles which give the *third ſound C* below, or by ſome other peculiar affinity to them, are qualified, by their joint action on theſe laſt-mentioned particles, to give them that particular modification, by which they are enabled to excite in us the ſenſation of that ſpecific tone, to which they are adapted. Or further, why may we not conceive in general (for the analogy will not hold in particular between the objects of two ſenſes ſo different) that a mixture of two given tones may excite the idea of a third and different ſound, in ſome ſuch manner as two given colours, blue and yellow, for inſtance—nay, the paſt impreſſions of theſe colours †,—excite the idea of green, different from both of them?

But the matter perhaps is tranſacted in the organ of hearing itſelf alone. In that caſe, anatomy may poſſibly furniſh us with ſome more plauſible ſpeculations on the ſubject. From a conſideration of the ſpiral and conical ſtructure of the *cochlea*, ſome phyſiologiſts have been tempted to imagine that the branches or filaments of the auditory nerve, after paſſing out from the *nucleus* or axis of the *cochlea*, are ſtrained upon the ſpiral plates, like the radii of a circle, and become gradually ſhorter and ſhorter towards its *apex*. It may be ſuppoſed likewiſe that of theſe nervous ſtrings, the longeſt, which are in the baſis of the *cochlea*, are adapted to receive the tremors or other impreſſions, and convey to the mind the ideas, of grave tones; and the ſhorter nervous chords, fixed more towards the *apex* of the cone, thoſe of acute ſounds. This being allowed, and taking the former interval *C e*, for an example, we would ſay that the tone *C*, beſides acting on the nervous chord appropriated to excite the idea of that tone, muſt act likewiſe on another nervous chord, of double its length, ſituated towards the baſis of the *cochlea*, and which is naturally adapted to receive, and tranſmit to the mind, *C*, the octave below; but which the upper tone

† Appendix to vol. xli. p. 508.

C, now divides into two equal parts, each giving tones unison to the said note *C*. The tone *e*, in like manner, will excite five equal vibrations in each of the halves of this nervous chord; all which likewise produce sensations unison with itself. These *phenomena* at least are invariably observed to be produced in musical strings. Hitherto however we have got only the unisons to *C* and *e*; but further, the last-mentioned chord thus vibrating in two and in ten parts, and *from one extremity of it to the other*, may fairly be supposed (as, there is reason to believe, happens to musical strings, under the like circumstances) to vibrate likewise in its *totality*, or in its whole length; in which case it must excite in the mind the idea of its own fundamental tone, the *third sound*, *C*, an octave below the first of these notes, and a tenth below the latter.—Granting us our anatomical *postulata*, we here find at least the principal *desideratum*, in the organ of the percipient, and which is not to be found in the musical instruments employed;—a chord capable of giving the grave sound which we have been enquiring after.—But enough of conjecture, in these dark matters.

In the second chapter our ingenious Commentator, after observing that Tartini's deductions from the circle and the square, give the true physical system of sounds, though derived from thence in an arbitrary, exceptionable, and illegitimate manner, gives his own more simple theory, founded on the tones produced by the trumpet marine, occasionally employed as a monochord, and stopped at each division of the harmonic intervals. By considering it in both these views, he obtains all the notes of the common octave; which, as he observes, is generally considered as natural, and not requiring much thought to settle. Almost every one who has an ear can readily run it over, and, as he thinks, naturally: but there were many divisions of it proposed, before that was invented which is now in use. Though it is here deduced from physical or natural principles, yet its first formation was undoubtedly artificial, and the result of much and profound thought. 'However paradoxical, says the Author, it may seem, yet it is certainly true, that harmony is more natural than the notes of the octave; for a string cannot be sounded, either as a trumpet marine, or as a monochord, *i. e.* in the common way, without producing harmony; whereas the notes of an octave never appear but in highly civilised countries.'

The scale of sounds above mentioned, though regularly deduced, it is well known, is not perfect in every possible relation of the notes which compose it. Huygens long since remarked *, that no voice or perfect instrument can always proceed by just

* Huygenii Cosmotheoros. lib. 1. p. 77.

intervals,

intervals, or those of this scale, without erring from the pitch first assumed. If the notes *C f D g C*, for instance, are sung by perfect intervals, rising from *C* to *f*, and afterwards alternately falling and rising from *f* to *D*, &c. he observed that this last *C*, which ought to be unison to the first, would be lower than it in the ratio of 80 to 81; and consequently that, if the notes were repeated nine times, the singer would have fallen near a major tone, in the ratio of 8 to 9, below the original pitch.

It is the interval *D F* which, in the preceding passage, falls short of a third minor, in the proportion of 80 to 81; and this deficiency, says the Author, constitutes the famous musical *comma*, which has caused so much dissention among those who have written on music; which has produced the *temperament*; which last has in its turn given rise to many treatises filled with science and ingenuity, but containing systems very different from each other. However the writers of these treatises, he adds, 'may disagree with one another, in bringing this arduous matter about, they all agree to disfigure the fair form of harmony.' The Author (we still mean our Translator) owns that 'Huygen's observation is undoubtedly true; but his conclusion from thence——that the voice therefore uses a temperament,——cannot be allowed of; for to use a temperament is to deviate from the true proportions *required by nature*: Now here the proportion 27 : 32, which represents the interval *D F*, is fixed by nature; for *F* is a fourth to *C*, and a note of the hexachord, and therefore necessarily settled; and *D*, is a fifth of the harmony we are going into, and therefore as necessarily settled. From whence it follows, that the interval *D F*, *pro hic & nunc*, is just what it ought to be.'

What is here said of the true proportions of *D* and *F*, and their just relations to the key, &c. is undoubtedly true; but the difficulty does not appear to us to be in any degree cleared up by this reasoning. This celebrated musical stumbling-block seems still to stand just where it was,—where nature seems to have placed it,—and where Tartini accordingly leaves it, without attempting its removal: nor do we apprehend it can be removed, without raising up others in its room. The proportion 27 : 32, the Author says, is fixed by nature. If we apprehend the the Author right, we suppose he means that *D*, represented by the first of these numbers, is a *perfect* 5th of the harmony of *G*; and *F*, 32, a *perfect* 4th to *C*, 24, the key note. We allow this; but we say nevertheless that *D F*, 27 : 32, is not a *just* minor third; such as is *required by nature*; or such at least as she gives us in other parts of the scale; nor such an one, as the Author himself deduces from the monochord, at page 23, § 37: whose ratio is 5 : 6, and not 27 : 32; but 27 : 32$\frac{2}{5}$.

 —In

—In short differing from the former precisely by a comma, the very deficiency complained of; for 80 : 81 :: 32 : 32$\frac{2}{5}$. And it appears to us to be no explanation of the matter, to say that the two notes which form this defective interval, 'are just what they ought to be,' considered in their relations to two *other* notes; while they constitute an imperfect interval between *themselves*. We should add however that the Author afterwards proceeds further, and endeavours to shew, how justly or satisfactorily must be left to his readers, that *D* is in this place a *discord*, and is resolved as all other discords are: but we cannot render the passage intelligible without notes.

In confirmation of the observation above mentioned, 'that to use a temperament is to disfigure the fair form of harmony,' the Author afterwards adds, 'They only know what true harmony means, who have heard a well-composed piece performed by a set of musicians, who keep perfectly in tune with one another. I never heard such music but once, and the effect was wonderful. It was performed in the Pope's chapel, during passion-week: It seemed to come from one single voice, and that the chords were only the resonances naturally belonging to it; or rather, the music did not seem to be produced by any human voice or instrument; but that spirits were diverting themselves, and trying, like Ariel in the Tempest, the powers of harmony over the human frame. It may be looked upon as whimsical, but I will venture to say, that he who has not heard such music as I have described, may get a better idea of it by listening to Æolus's harp, than by any other way I can think of. Could we but add air and time to it, it would be the most perfect of all musical instruments.

To return to Huygens's celebrated passage, we still cannot avoid thinking, with the proposer, that in executing it, the justest singers are obliged to use occasionally imperfect intervals, which the Author calls *discords*, in order to return to the pitch first assumed. We would ask, on this occasion, whether the most accurate singer in the Pope's chapel, after repeating this melody nine times, would find himself got into the key of *B flat?* It will be allowed on all hands that, if he sings *perfect* fourths, *minor thirds*, and fifths, such must be his situation at the end of the experiment. Though we suspect, that he would in fact sink, we rather imagine that he would still be found in the very near neighbourhood of *C*. Be that as it may, we would reduce the matter to this *dilemma*:—If he descended to *B flat*, we say he could not have used the interval 32 : 27; but 32 : 26$\frac{2}{3}$: (supposing always 5 : 6 the *true* and constant ratio of a minor third) If he remained in the original key, we then say he must have jumped over, or rather stepped short of, this stumbling-block, or must have used a management of some kind or other;—in other words, have used a temperament.

The

The celebrity of this musical question has induced us to discuss it thus largely. We shall dwell a little longer upon it, in order to propose an experiment, the idea of which now first occurs to us. We apprehend that it is new; and it has the appearance of being decisive: so far, at least, as to indicate what are the true intervals that *nature* gives in the intonation of this passage, and how far they agree with the diatonic, particularly in the contraverted part of the scale. An appeal is here made, not to an ear habituated to an *artificial*, and perhaps vicious, mode of intonation; but to *Nature* herself. Let us listen to her voice on this subject.—At least it presents a commodious and accurate way of trying Huygens's experiment: as the performer is kept steady in sounding the true intervals, as they are indicated by nature, without being liable to be drawn aside from them, either by the power of habit, or the remembrance of the key. It is this:

Let the interval *C f* be sounded on the 2d and 1st string of a violin; and the justice of the intonation be ascertained by attending to the *third sound*, which will be *F*, the octave below the upper note. Keeping the first finger fixed on *f*, let the third finger be directed to the true interval *f D*, by the performer's hearing the proper third sound, *B flat*. Keeping *D* fixed, let the 4th *D g*, be ascertained with equal precision, by means of its *natural sign*, the third sound *G*; and lastly, let the 5th *g C* be sounded; for the accuracy of which the ear alone may be trusted; especially as its third sound is not so easily distinguished, being the unison of *C*. Let the passage, thus played by double stops, be repeated a sufficient number of times; nature giving her sanction to the perfect tune of the two parts, by singing herself a base to them, and converting the duet into a *trio*. Should the third sounds invariably conduct the performer back to his original key, the experiment may present us with a method of discovering the proportions of those natural, pleasing and perfect intervals, by which the return to the key was effected. But if, as we rather suspect, the performer descends a major tone in nine repetitions, it would follow that a good singer, who after a few repetitions of the passage still continues in or near the original key, must somewhere have used intervals different from those indicated by nature, and from those called *perfect* in the diatonic system, and consequently that he must have *tempered*, that is, altered, some of them.——To make the experiment with the greatest, and perhaps the necessary accuracy, a moveable fret to each of the strings would be preferable, in the stopping them, to the fingers; as the position of the latter is liable to imperceptible alterations from many causes, during the course of the experiment.

[*To be concluded in our next.*]

Art. VII. *The Farmer's Tour through the East of England, being the Register of a Journey through various Counties of this Kingdom, to enquire into the State of Agriculture, &c.* By the Author of the Farmer's Letters, &c. 4 Vols. 1 l. 1 s. bound. Nicoll, &c. 1771.

WE have always thought the professed design of Mr. Young's several Tours (viz. to communicate the good and bad practices in agriculture, that the one may be imitated and the other avoided) highly useful; and we think this Eastern Tour executed better than the rest.

Here we have a great variety of very useful matter, and not a few judicious observations upon it. In order to convince our agricultural Readers, how well their money will be employed in the purchase of these volumes, we will lay before them a state of the principal articles of intelligence.

Carrots. Average quantity per acre is 18 tons, 12 cwt.—Average value per ton is 1 l. 7 s. 5¼ d. or 8¼ d. per bushel.—But Mr. Stevens's carrots, when boiled and given to hogs, proved worth 4 l. per ton, or 2 s. per bushel; and Sir J. Mills', when given to them raw, proved worth 1 l. 6 s. 8 d. per ton, or 8 d. per bushel.

This root, when given to fatting oxen, or to horses, proves worth 1 l. per ton, or 6 d. per bushel.

In winter, one average acre fattens three large oxen, allowing each half a stone of hay *per diem* *. It will also fatten 18½ weathers, weighing 30 lb. per quarter. But they must have 4 cwt. of hay per week to 20, for twenty weeks.

One acre will winter four horses intirely, without hay or corn.

A cow eats one ton and a half per month, or nine tons in six months; value about 12 l.

Best soils on which carrots grow in these experiments are worth 3 l. or 4 l. per acre; but those valued only at 14 s. 2 d. give a product as high as 25 l. 8 s. 8 d.

The average expence is 7 l. 17 s. 7 d. consequently of ten acres 78 l. 15 s. 10 d. Cattle bought to eat the carrots will cost about 35 l. per acre.

The average product in cash is 22 l. 16 s. per acre, and the average profit by the carrots themselves is 14 l. 15 s. 6 d. But as the average profit by the dung is 4 s. per ton, the whole average profit is 18 guineas.

Here Mr. Y. extends the idea, and raises *two thousand pounds a year* from 100 acres under carrots!

He judiciously observes that few persons can make the high profit of carrots which rises from feeding of oxen, because they cost so much money; and that keeping cows, especially dry

* These three oxen will cost about 40 l.

ones,

ones, with what will feed oxen, muſt be unprofitable; but that the maintaining teams of horſes on them is a profitable application. In all theſe points we agree with him; but huſbandmen will generally think that the maintaining the ſtock which they happen to have, is the preſent beſt uſe of carrots.

POTATOES. The ſoils are chiefly loams; the average rent a guinea per acre; the average product 427 buſhels; the average value 26 l. and the average profit is 11 l. 17 s. But we think that the moor ground, which, at 4½ d. rent per acre, produced 60 l.'s worth, ſhould not be taken into the average.

Boiled, the potatoes *alone* fatten porkers, and mixed with meal (from one-third to one-tenth) they fatten any large hogs.

They keep milch cows well; but Mr. Y. ſeems right in his opinion, that whatever will feed any animal, is too good winter food for cows that go long dry. We except particular circumſtances.

It deſerves obſervation, that one acre of this crop raiſes, by home conſumption, dung ſufficient to manure two acres.

MADDER. The average profit of three crops appears to be 13 l. 10 s. per acre per annum; but Mr. Reynolds's loſs reduces it to 6 l. 9 s. 7 d. Mr. Y. juſtly obſerves, that this loſs 'ought to come into the account, as there does not, from his minutes, appear any *error* or *miſconduct* in the caſe.' We heartily wiſh that he may be always ſo careful in drawing up averages. He notes that the profit of madder appears from theſe experiments to be 47 per cent. High indeed; but that on carrots is 240 per cent.

Mr. Y. is very candid on this article. In his Courſe of experimental Agriculture he had given a diſcouraging account of madder, and here he ſeems ready to allow it every fair advantage.

BURNET. Mr. Y. is praiſe-worthy for endeavouring to reconcile the contradictory accounts which this Tour ſupplies of this plant, by cauſes which very much contribute to reconcile them, viz. the high price at which Rocque propagated it, the diſappointment of many of his cuſtomers, the natural deſire of its firſt encomiaſts to appear defenſible, the difference of the plant when young and when ſeeding, the confuſion with reſpect to its hay and ſtraw, and the profit by the ſeed. To theſe cauſes we beg leave to add two, which, we believe, with Mr. Y.'s, will fully reconcile theſe contradictions, viz. the difference of ſoils, which makes this plant as different in its ſpecies as can well be imagined, and the power of time to reconcile cattle, of all ſorts, to a ſpecies of food, the bitter oil of which is at firſt diſagreeable.

Mr. Y. notes, that the minutes of this Tour are, on the whole, favourable to this plant, particularly for being well eaten by horſes and ſheep, and generally liked by cows and oxen.

oxen. He thinks it beſt as green food for ſheep in ſpring, and to mix with other graſſes in laying down fields. His true obſervation that 'burnet is common in many highly valued meadows,' confirms the ſecond cauſe which we juſt now aſſigned for contradictory accounts of this plant.

SAINFOINE. Land at the average rent of 8 s. 5 d. per acre, yields two tons of this hay worth 4 l. and after-graſs, at a low valuation, worth 8 s. 8 d. which alone is more than the rent; and Sir John Turner's is only 10 s. per acre, yet yields clear profit 3 l. 15 s. 6 d.

The average profit is 3 l. 6 s. 3 d. and the average duration 15 years.

Col. St. Leger's land is the only one manured. Soot, or aſhes, 10 s. per acre, may be well allowed now and then; though it is remarkable that Sir C. Wray found no benefit from aſhes.

The informations which this work affords, that ſainfoine thrives beſt where the bottom has no rock, but loam or clay; that dryneſs only is requiſite; that the deepeſt and fineſt loams pay well under this graſs; and that harrowing clears it well of weeds and natural graſſes, (its great and only enemies in point of duration) are of real importance.

LUCERN. The minutes of this Tour ſhew the average expence of this noble graſs, per acre, to be 3 l. 8 s. 9 d. the product 10 l. 18 s. 8 d. conſequently the profit nearly 7 l. 10 s. This, however, is an average of various methods of culture, viz. of the broadcaſt and drilled, at different diſtances.

Mr. Y. rightly excludes Mr. Ramey's as kept clean only two years. We repeat our wiſh, that he may be as careful in all other averages to exclude what cannot be properly included.

But the point which Mr. Y. here principally directs his readers to obſerve, is, that an acre keeps, in the ſtable, four horſes nearly 23 weeks, which food, at 2 s. 6 d. per head per week, amounts to 10 guineas. But then he judiciouſly notes, that in order to diſcover how much of their profit *may* ariſe from the *manner* of eating the lucern, we ſhould compare it with clover thus eaten; and he ſhews that three horſes were ſoiled with one acre of clover 19 weeks; which food, at the ſame rate, amounts to 7 l. 2 s. 6 d. and having compared another inſtance, he finds the average of both to be 8 l. 2 s. 3½ d which is to the profit of lucern, thus uſed, as four to five. One of theſe Experimenters judges that his three horſes would have deſtroyed nine acres in the field, while one laſted them in the ſtable. From hence Mr. Y. juſtly recommends the practice of ſoiling in the ſtable; but wiſhes that the real value of the plant may be determined by feeding ſheep or ſmall beaſts. It muſt, however, not be forgot, that whatever profit may be made of lucern otherwiſe employed,

employed, it is worth ſo much to the horſe-keeper, as it ſaves him in ſoiling.

Clover. The average rent 14 s. the product 64 cwt. and the value 5 l. 4 s.

Mr. Y. ſhews, from a table, that out of nine places, the inhabitants of five, think mowing a better method of preparing clover land for wheat than feeding is, and he refers to the ſecond volume of his Courſe of experimental Agriculture, p. 372, for the grounds of his own aſſent to this opinion.

Cabbages. Average product per acre of the true Scotch is 42 tons, the value of which is 4 l. 8 s. 9 d. that of cabbage turnips is 36 tons, as valued by Mr. Reynolds at 7 l. 8 s. 6 d. that of ſeveral ſorts is 17 tons, the value 3 l. 18 s. 5 d. From this laſt miſcellaneous article Mr. Y. rightly concludes, that 'any kind of cabbage is profitable.'

But Sir R. Burdett's North American cabbage, on land of 1 l. per acre rent, gives 70 tons, worth 36 l.

In order to ſhew how little we know of the true value of this plant, Mr. Y. well obſerves, that Mr. Wharton's cabbages are valued at 1 s. per ton, and Sir R. Burdett's at 10 s.—What a difference within the limits of this tour!

We muſt applaud an excellent obſervation which our Author makes, viz. that 'cabbages planted in ſpring, and begun to be eaten at Michaelmas, while all their leaves are uſeful, muſt be moſt profitable; for a quantity weighing 50 tons at Michaelmas, may not weigh above 20 in ſpring.'

Mr. Y. thinks cows unprofitable conſumers of cabbages, for a reaſon ſuggeſted above in the articles *carrots* and *potatoes*. This fact may be a true one. But on what cheaper food would Mr. Y. maintain them? 'On ſtraw,' he will anſwer. But is it not to be apprehended, that ſtraw alone will cauſe them to ſink in carcaſe, and not *neat well*, that is, not *milch well* at calving?

Turnips. The average of rents per acre of turnip land through this Tour is 14 s. 1 d. That of the value of the product, when *unhoed*, is 1 l. 16 s. 9 d. but of the *hoed* 2 l. 3 s. 10 d. a difference of 7 s. 1 d. per acre, although they are ſcarcer in countries which do not hoe, and therefore ſhould ſell dearer. This difference is not ſo great as might reaſonably be expected, eſpecially when the expence of hoeing is taken into the account: but the good done to the ſoil by hoeing is conſiderable.

Mr. Y. draws an average of *hoed* and *unhoed* turnips; but we are unable to diſcover the uſe of ſuch average.

Hops. Average rent of hop land is 1 l. 18 s. 10 d. per acre. The expences of which amount to above 19 l. and the product to above 8 cwt. the value of which exceeds 43 l. and gives a pro-a profit above 29 l. as Mr. Y. asserts, but (as it appears to us) only about 24 l.

The profit of an acre of bog, under hops at 5 l. per cwt. gives 30 l. Certainly this bog, at the rent of only 3 s. per acre, should have been excluded from the average!

DRILLING. The comparison of drilling with broadcast was thought so important a matter as to be recommended by the Dublin Society as preferable to every other. Mr. Y. thinks many other subjects of ten times the importance. We cannot here agree with him. He judges, however, the drill to deserve no inconsiderable notice, and accordingly draws out pretty largely the evidence which this Tour supplies; and he is commendably ingenuous on this subject, as he deduces a more favourable idea of drilling, in some circumstances, than his Course of experimental Agriculture afforded. We will review, with attention, that evidence which this Tour suggests.

BEANS. Drilled they afford, on an average, 4 qrs. 4 bush. per acre; an excellent crop. Yet Mr. Anderdon's only experiment gives 20 bush. 1 peck more per acre by broadcast *.

PEAS. Drilled, afford 3 qrs. 5 bush. per acre; an excellent crop. Yet Mr. Anderdon's two experiments give the balance in favour of broadcast. In one, the drilled exceeds by 3½ bush. and in the other, the broadcast by 7 bushels. Yet these are the crops in which drilling may be expected to succeed best.

WHEAT. Average crop of drilled is, per acre, 3 qrs. 1 bush. which, we believe, we may venture to assert is not superior to the average of broadcast among good husbandmen; and such only should be admitted to comparison.

But let us examine the table from whence this average of drilled crops of wheat is deduced. In nine instances there are only two which amount to 4 qrs. and, on the contrary, in four instances (almost half of the whole) the quantities are 2 qrs. 7 bush.—2 qrs. 5 bush.—2 qrs. 4 bush.—1 qr. 4 bush. so that this table consists of quantities very favourable (in deducing an average) to drilling; and it deserves particular notice, that the crops of Mr. Arbuthnot, (that excellent husbandman, and justly a favourite with Mr. Y.) amount only to 2 qrs. 7 bush. although he pretends not to the continual crops of wheat which

* Mr. Y. justly calls the weeding of beans, through the vale of Aylesbury, by sheep, execrable! Such mismanagement should never be brought to discredit the broadcast husbandry in general. There is one piece of important knowledge which Mr. Y. presents his Readers with from these minutes, viz. that by hoeing of beans 1 l. 9 s. per acre is saved, and by hoeing of peas 1 l. and hoed beans and peas are a fallow, whereas unhoed ones are succeeded by a fallow.

Mr.

Mr. Tull boaſted of, but alternate ones; uſes manure liberally, and has a ſoil naturally good. Let us add, that in the only two comparative experiments of Mr. Arbuthnot, recorded in the table of page 214, the broadcaſt exceeds the drill. In Mr. Anderdon's only two experiments, in the ſame table, the events are contrary, and the drill exceeds broadcaſt only by 1¾ buſhel. In Mr. Cowſlade's ſingle experiment, the broadcaſt is ſuperior by a whole quarter and a half: ſo that here is ſmall room for the drillers to triumph.

Mr. Reynolds's getting 6 buſh. more by the drill may ſeem conſiderable. But let us examine the caſe, and we ſhall find it ſo remarkable as to give little advantage to the drillers.

This gentleman's ſoil is a poor, thin, chalky one, heretofore deemed nothing worth. Rent, tithe, and town-charges amount only to 10 s. On ſuch ſoils it ſeems, on an average, only 14 buſhels of wheat can be got by broadcaſt; but by the extraordinary labour of *hand-hoeing*, *hand-weeding*, and *twice horſe-hoeing*, 6 buſhels more are obtained, which, when the price of wheat is 6 s. per buſhel, leave rather better than a guinea and half more than the broadcaſt does. This is certainly an object to the farmer of ſuch poor ſoils, eſpecially when he has plain, ſtrong inſtruments, ſuch as Mr. Reynolds and his neighbours have; but can affect nobody in another ſituation. On his account we muſt however obſerve, that his charge of 1 s. only for twice horſe-hoeing an acre ſeems unreaſonably low.

Mr. Reynolds boaſts of the improvement of their wheat crops by ſowing after clover, trefoil, and ſainfoine. It is a curious and important enquiry, 'Can they get no more than 14 buſhels per acre broadcaſt by this improvement?'

Barley and Oats. Average of drilled crops, per acre, 4 qrs. 4 buſh. But thoſe of Mr. Arbuthnot are as low as 1 qr. 7 buſh. and although in Mr. Anderdon's ſingle experiment of oats the drill excels the broadcaſt by 5¼ buſh. yet in his and Mr. Arbuthnot's experiments of barley, the drill is exceeded by the broadcaſt 2 buſhels; and, to cloſe the whole, Mr. Reynolds, after the experience of 40 years, declares that, for both barley and oats, broadcaſt equals the drill. Finally, although Mr. Y. thinks that drilling and horſe-hoeing in Kent, with their ſtrong ſimple inſtruments, are moſt advantageous in cloſe rows, he owns, 'the broadcaſt much exceeds the Tullian ſyſtem of wide intervals,' and that, 'on ſoils that are ſo heavy or wet as to require ridge-work (and how ſmall a part of the arable in the kingdom does not?) I am clear, from theſe minutes, that (beans excepted) the broadcaſt mode will be found much the moſt profitable.'

As to Mr. Y.'s tables of averages of products and profits in the two methods in which all kinds of crops are thrown together,

gether, we cannot (with all due deference to Mr. Y.) ſee that they are of the leaſt uſe.

Averages, when rightly inſtituted, are indeed what Mr. Y. calls them, the *quinteſſence of experiments*, and averages of averages are the *quinteſſence of quinteſſences*. To be rightly inſtituted, they muſt have *uniformity* and *variety*; the former in the main points (or baſis) the latter in the incidental ones. As Mr. Y. chooſes to repreſent himſelf as not underſtanding what we mean, in our review of the *Courſe*, &c. by a *regular*, *uniform* plan, we will here explain clearly what is meant by thoſe terms, and at the ſame time juſtify our criticiſm on ſeveral of Mr. Y.'s averages in his Courſe of experimental Agriculture, and this Eaſtern Tour.

Every novice in agriculture knows, in general, that ſoils, methods of culture, kinds of crops and manures, quantity of ſeed, time of ſowing, &c. are *extremely different*; but the ſkilful huſbandman wiſhes to know particularly what are the effects of all theſe in various combinations. This knowledge, good books of experiments, and averages built upon them, ſupply; and the knowledge is either of the *abſolute* or *comparative* kind.—We will give inſtances.

When the ſoil is *given*, the experiments ſhew what is the crop (both as to product and value) of a given kind of corn, in a given ſeaſon, by a given method of culture, as to manure, ploughing, hoeing, ſeed, ſeaſon, &c. When ſeveral experiments of the ſame kind are made in the ſame year, there will be incidental varieties in the effects, from unforeſeen or unforſeeable cauſes, and the average of theſe effects, or the middle number which repreſents the product or value, will be the true average of the experiments of that ſort in that year, or the *quinteſſence* of them. And when the ſame experiments are repeated in another year, and the average is obtained, by taking the average of both averages, the *quinteſſence of quinteſſences* is obtained; and their uſefulneſs is heightened by the increaſe of the number of experiments of any one year, and of the number of years. So when experiments are made of any other kind of culture of the ſame kind of crop, on the ſame ſoil, the averages of the different effects of the different cultures compared, ſhew the preference of one method of culture, whether it be of the drill huſbandry to the broadcaſt, or *vice verſa*; of manuring to non-manuring, or *vice verſa*; of deep ploughing to ſhallow, or *vice verſa*; of an horſe draught to oxen, or *vice verſa*; of turnips hoed, or *vice verſa*; carted off, or *vice verſa*.—When theſe experiments are repeated on a different ſoil, and the averages obtained, theſe, compared with the former averages, ſhew which ſoil is better adapted to ſuch a crop, and ſuch a method of culture.—Again; when different kinds of crops are tried on the ſame

5

ſame ſoil, the averages compared, ſhew which kind of crop and culture ſuits beſt with ſuch a ſoil.—Further: when different courſes of crops are tried on the ſame ſoil, the averages compared, ſhew which courſe ſuits that ſoil beſt. And thus, by drawing and comparing averages, and averages of averages, rightly inſtituted, we learn ſome of the moſt uſeful truths in agriculture as a ſcience: but then there muſt be *uniformity* as the *baſis*, and *variety* only in the *incidental* points.—Where *errors* and *miſconduct* are committed in the experiment, the irregularity, which will be the effect, ought never to be admitted into the average, *ex. gratia*, If Mr. Ramey keep his lucern clean only two years, and the two firſt years lucern gives a poor crop, his crops ſhould not be admitted into the average; and Mr. Y. *rightly* rejects them. But if Mr. Reynolds loſe by madder, and no error or miſconduct appear in his management, his crops ſhould come into the average, and Mr. Y. *rightly* inſerts them, as an abatement of the profit which a man may reaſonably expect from the culture of madder on a like ſoil.—But if Mr. Y. have *poor worn out* ground, and no manure to enrich it, his crops of wheat, &c. in this irregular culture, ſhould not enter into the average, which is to ſhew what may reaſonably be expected by *common* good management. If he plough 11 or 12 times, and lay on ſo much manure as to make him a loſer after the rate of 100 l. or 200 l. per acre, ſuch crops ſhould come into no average.—Again; experiments of the effects of hoeing turnips, or not hoeing them, are very uſeful; and the various averages, and average of averages, on this comparative culture, deſerve great praiſe; but an average of hoed and unhoed turnips thrown together, cannot poſſibly have any uſe. Averages of drilled and broadcaſt crops in wheat, barley, oats, beans, and peas, have their uſe when ſeparately compared; but when all kinds of crops are thrown together, they only waſte paper, and deceive the public.

From this juſt explanation it appears, that (as we aſſerted in our review of the Courſe, &c.) "regular culture upon one regular plan," can *alone* afford foundation of uſeful averages. When therefore Mr. Y. enumerates, in the Appendix to this Eaſtern Tour, wheat in one round manured, in another unmanured, turnips in one round procured by purchaſed dung, in another by home-made; in one courſe carted off, in another fed off; wheat in one round ſucceeding clover, in another fallow; clover in one courſe fed off, in a ſecond mown twice for hay, in a third once for hay and once for ſeed, he betrays a *total ignorance* (which he is pleaſed to charge on us) of averages; for, although the ſeveral averages of theſe ſeveral crops, when compared with each other, may be *very uſeful*, yet when thrown into one heap they become *entirely uſeleſs*.—After enumerations

merations of these various crops, and various managements, he cries, 'What great variations in the expences are here in common crops, and in common hands!' Who doubts it? He might have made these variations still greater. But what common farmer, if he is a man of sense, would ever think of jumbling all these inconsistent crops into one average? 'A difference of 5 l. per acre (concludes he) will often be found among common farmers.' In this variety of crops there will, perhaps. But what judicious farmer ever thought of discovering the most profitable method of managing *any one* crop on a given soil, by jumbling together *all* crops?—Five pounds may be a good general expression of the expences of an acre of wheat in common management. But what a monster of an average will result from taking into the account experiments in which there is a difference of 5 l. per acre, or even of half that sum?—This inaccurate Reasoner asks, 'Who but these Reviewers will assert that such an average is *useless*, because the sums from which it is drawn are *various*?' The Reader now sees the foundation of this miserable quibble. We do not assert, that *any* average is useless because the sums from which it is drawn are *various*; but because they are *so various* as to be the effects of *different*, *irregular*, and *inconsistent* cultures on different plans and subjects.

[*To be continued.*]

ART. VIII. *A general History of the British Empire in America: Including all the Countries in North America and the West Indies, ceded by the Peace of Paris.* By Mr. Wynne. 8vo. 2 Vols. 10 s. Boards. Richardson and Urquhart. 1770.

THE British colonies in America, from very unpromising beginnings, have now risen to a greatly extensive and, in many respects, flourishing empire. Several accounts have been published of this part of our globe, and particularly of those countries which have fallen to the lot of the English government; but none of them have been so circumstantial and satisfactory as to preclude the necessity of any farther publications of the same nature.

Although the Author of this history of the new world gives us his name, we find no information concerning the manner in which his work has been conducted; nor any direct references to those authors to which, in such an undertaking, it must be necessary to have recourse; excepting that the names of Mr. Neale, and one or two others, are occasionally mentioned.

Several parts of these volumes appear to be collected from what has been written in other accounts of these countries; and sometimes we apprehend the Author's abridgement has been rather negligently formed; as in one or two instances we have observed part of a sentence to refer to some fact which, we imagine,

imagine, had been related in the account from whence the passage is taken, but which is here omitted. It is true, that these facts are not essentially necessary to the history; but allusions to what has not been before particularly mentioned, gives the performance an imperfect appearance. To this we must add a complaint of carelessness in the original copy, or in the revisal of the press, since the punctuations are often wrong placed, and, in some instances, words are omitted, by which the expression is rendered obscure. We must nevertheless acknowledge, that we have perused these volumes with pleasure. One considerable advantage attending them is, that while they present us with a brief view of the origin, progress, and present state of our American colonies, these particulars are intermixed, and the narrative enlivened by the Author's judicious observations and reflections, particularly as to the importance of our settlements, and our controversies with them; some of which might, perhaps, be read with advantage by those whose immediate business it is to conduct the public affairs relating to those parts of our dominions.

In those remarks, which are delivered as the Author's own, he generally appears as a man of abilities, of knowledge of the world, of humanity, and of candour; we were therefore sorry for the contemptuous manner in which he sometimes ridicules the first settlers in New-England, though he admits the injustice with which they had been treated. They had, no doubt, their weaknesses and their follies; (and what denomination of men, or of Christians, shall we find entirely free from them?) but they manifested a noble and worthy spirit, and shewed a high regard to truth and conscience, notwithstanding they might, in some respects, be mistaken in their views of religious subjects.

We now proceed more directly to the work itself, from which we shall select such passages as we apprehend will be acceptable to our Readers.

Mr. W. begins his history with a short review of the first discoveries of America, including the Spanish conquests; from whence he proceeds, more particularly, to the discovery of North America by the English; gives an account of the several different adventurers thither, and adds some proper reflections, till he is more directly brought to treat of the respective settlements, in their due order.

In his account of New-England, after relating different emigrations thither, during the contentious and unhappy reign of Charles the First, he takes notice of the restraint which was laid upon the subjects of Great Britain, in this respect.

'Sir Arthur Haseirig, Oliver Cromwell, and others, says he, were prevented from trying their fortunes in New-England, by an embargo

bargo laid upon the ſhipping by Charles I. whereby eight veſſels were prevented from ſailing to thoſe parts.—Let us view this meaſure in what light we pleaſe, the abſurdity of it is equally ſtriking; it was no leſs impolitic than unjuſt; and by it that unhappy prince ſealed, as it were, the warrant for his own death. If theſe men were become troubleſome to the church and ſtate, where could a fairer opportunity be found to get rid of them? At home they were malcontents; abroad it was evident they might be of ſervice to their mother-country. It would therefore have been the wiſdom of government to have given them aſſiſtance in their emigrations, rather than to have reſtrained them; but ſuch methods of educing good out of evil, were meaſures unknown to this unfortunate reign.'

From among other particulars and obſervations relating to the government of New-England, we ſhall ſelect the following:

'The general aſſembly of New-England is the ſupreme legiſlative body. In concurrence with the governor, it impoſes taxes, makes grants, enacts laws, and redreſſes grievances of every kind. It conſiſts of the magiſtrates, and a certain number of repreſentatives, which form two chambers, ſo nearly reſembling our lords and commons, that the conſent of the majority of both is neceſſary before any bill can be preſented to the governor for his aſſent. There are three charter governments, of which the chief is the province of Maſſachuſet-Bay, commonly called New-England; the conſtitution whereof is of a mixed nature, the power being divided between the king and the people, in which the latter have much the greateſt ſhare: for here they do not only chuſe the aſſembly, but the aſſembly chuſes the council, and the governor depends upon the aſſembly for his annual ſupport; which has too frequently laid the governors of this province under temptations of giving up the prerogative of the crown, and the intereſt of Great Britain.

'Connecticut and Rhode Iſland are the other charter governments, or rather corporations, where almoſt the whole power of the crown is delegated to the people, who make an annual election of their aſſembly, their council and their governor likewiſe; to the majority of which aſſemblies, councils and governors reſpectively, being collective bodies, the power of making laws is granted; and as their charters are worded, they can and do make laws, even without the governor's aſſent, and directly contrary to their opinions, no negative voice being reſerved to them as governors in the ſaid charter: and, as the ſaid governors are annually choſen, their office generally expires before his majeſty's approbation can be obtained.

'These colonies have the power of making laws for their better government and ſupport, provided they be not repugnant to the laws of, nor detrimental to, their mother-country; and theſe laws, when they have regularly paſſed the council and aſſembly of any province, and received the governor's aſſent, become valid in that province, yet remain repealable by his majeſty in council, upon juſt complaint, and do not acquire a perpetual force, unleſs they are confirmed by his majeſty in council. But there are ſome exceptions to this rule in the proprietary and charter governments.——

'Adultery, blaſphemy, and ſtriking or curſing a parent, are here puniſhed with death; as is perjury where life may be effected. No

perſon

person can be arrested if he has the means of making any satisfaction. Quakers, Jesuits, and popish priests, are * *liable to suf*fer death. Great care is taken by their laws, of the morals of the Indians, and to prevent drunkenness, swearing and cursing; and one of their laws, which they much boast of, is that Christian strangers, flying from tyranny, are to be maintained by the public, or otherwise provided for †.'

We cannot avoid asking here, how is the commendable humanity of the last institute consistent with the severity of the decree against the Quakers? But we are willing to suppose that it is now an obsolete law, framed at a time when the persons mentioned occasioned much vexation and disturbance, and that it is not at present enforced.

Our Author farther observes, concerning these colonists, that 'The police of the inhabitants of New-England, with regard to their morals, is as rigid as that of any in the world. Every town of fifty families is obliged to maintain a school for reading and writing, and of one hundred families a grammar school for the instruction of youth. Thus vices that are common in all other parts of the world, might be unknown in New-England, if the increase of power and riches had not introduced them. Their children being early habituated to industry, could otherwise have no ideas of expensive pleasures or enervating debaucheries; their constitution in church and state confirming them in this sobriety of habit. They have no holidays but that of the annual election of the magistrates of Boston, and the commencement at Cambridge. Thus an uninterrupted course of industry and application to business prevails all the year round.'

In the account which Mr. Wynne gives us of Pennsylvania, he informs us that 'it is inhabited by full 250,000 people, half of whom are Germans, Swedes, or Dutch. Here, says he, you see Quakers, Churchmen, Calvinists, Lutherans, Catholics, Methodists, Menists, Moravians, Independents, Anabaptists, and Dumplers; the last being a sort of German sect, that live in something like a religious society, wear long beards, and a habit resembling that of friars. In short, the diversity of people, religions, nations and languages, is prodigious, and the harmony in which they live together no less edifying. For, though every man who wishes well to religion, is sorry to see the diversity which prevails, and would, by all mild and honest methods, endeavour to prevent it; yet when once the evil has happened, when there is no longer an union of sentiments, it is glorious to preserve at least an union of affections;—it is

* The words and letters here marked in italics are not found in the book, but we have ventured to supply them. There are other instances of such negligence and obscurity. The law here mentioned appears very harsh, at least, certainly with regard to the Quakers; if this short account be just.

† Our Readers may here be referred, for many other curious particulars, relating to the constitution and laws of New-England, to our account of Governor Hutchinson's History of the Colony of Massachusets-Bay, in the 3?th vol. of our Review, p. 185—201.

 a beau-

a beautiful prospect, to see men take and give an equal liberty; to see them live, if not as belonging to the same church, yet as to the same Christian religion; and if not to the same religion, yet to the same great fraternity of mankind. I do not observe that the Quakers, who had, and who still have in a great measure, the power in their hands, have made use of it in any sort to persecute; except in the single case of George Keith, whom they first imprisoned, and then banished out of the province.—This little sally into intolerance, as it is a single instance, and with great provocation, ought by no means to be imputed to the principles of the Quakers, considering the ample and humane latitude they have allowed in all other respects.'

After taking a view of some other of the British settlements, our Author proceeds to give some account of the Indian nations, as introductory to the history of Canada. He agrees with most other writers in the character he draws of the Indians, though we cannot but suppose that there may be a great number of particular exceptions to this general account.

'The North American natives, he says, are in general a wild and a faithless set of men. Their manners are a complication of ill-chosen customs, savage, ridiculous, and barbarous. Whatever some may say of their genius it is certainly not equal to that of the inhabitants of our world; and America is in this sense justly styled the younger sister of Europe. The pains taken to instruct these savages in the laws and religion, have been mostly thrown away, and so bigotted are they to their own manner of living, that some of them who have been regularly bred, cloathed and educated, have thrown away their cloaths, run into the woods, forsaken society, and returned to their own barbarous manners, preferring what they foolishly termed liberty, among their savannahs and vast forests, to all the benefits enjoyed in a well ordered state.'

We suppose our Author, in this last account, intends to speak of savages who had been in some earlier part of life removed from their own country, otherwise we cannot so greatly wonder that prepossessions in favour of their own soil, families, customs, connections, freer manner of living, &c. should sometimes prevail against what may appear to us more engaging considerations. We will not dispute the justice of the observation, which may without doubt have been verified in several instances. But we will oppose to it a relation which is given in this work, of some Frenchmen who had been taken prisoners, by an Indian tribe called the Tsonnonthouans: one Joncaire, we are informed, who had been adopted, or acknowledged for a friend and relation, by these savages, was sent to obtain their release:

'Their liberty, it is said, was immediately granted. What followed was somewhat extraordinary. Most or all of those prisoners had been adopted likewise; and the life of a savage was, in their eyes, so much preferable to that of a French Canadian, that they refused to return to their country. This circumstance may be thus accounted for: amongst the savages they enjoyed, in full extent, not only that freedom which they could not find under French government; but, if they were industrious, more abundance; because what they

they acquired by hunting and sowing was their own, without paying taxes or imposts; and the civil and military duties among the French, were beside more irksome and laborious than among the savages. Some of those captives, therefore, rather than they would follow Joncaire, concealed themselves, while others plainly told him they would remain with the Indians.'

The Indian tribe called the Illinois, is one that is spoken of in the most favourable manner. The relation of their dances, in honour of the Calumet, may amuse some of our Readers:

'The Calumet, it is said, is the most extraordinary thing in the world. The sceptres of our kings are not so much respected; for the savages have such a deference for this pipe, that they seem to think it the god of peace, and war, and the arbiter of life and death. One, with this calumet, may venture among his enemies, and in the hottest engagements they lay down their arms before the sacred pipe. Their calumet of peace is different from that of war. They make use of the former to seal their alliances and treaties, to travel with safety, and receive strangers; and the other is to proclaim war. It is made of a red stone like our marble; the head is like our common tobacco pipes, but larger; and it is fixed to a hollow reed to hold it for smoaking. They adorn it with fine feathers of several colours, and they call it the Calumet of the Sun, to whom they present it, especially when they want change of weather, thinking that that planet can have no less respect for it than men have, and therefore that they shall obtain their desires. They dare not wash themselves in rivers in the beginning of the summer, or taste the new fruit of trees, before they have danced the calumet.

'This dance of the calumet is a solemn ceremony amongst the savages, which they perform upon important occasions, to confirm an alliance, or to make peace with their neighbours. They use it also to entertain any nation that comes to visit them; and, in this case, we may consider it as their ball. They perform it in winter time in their cabins, and in open fields in the summer. They chuse for this purpose, a set place among trees, to shelter themselves against the heat of the sun, and lay in the middle a large matt as a carpet, setting upon it the god of the chief of the company who give the ball; for every one has his peculiar god, whom they call Manitoa: it is sometimes a stone, a bird, a serpent, or any thing else that they dream of in their sleep; for they think that this manitoa will prosper their undertakings, as fishing, hunting, and other enterprizes. To the right of their manitoa, they place the calumet, as their great deity, making round about it, a kind of trophy with their arms. All things being thus disposed, and the hour of dancing coming on, those who are to sing take the most honourable seats under the shade of the trees, or the green arbours they make, in case the trees be not thick enough to shade them. Every body sits down afterwards round about, as they come, having first of all saluted the manitoa, which they do by blowing the smoke of their tobacco upon it; afterwards every one of the company, in his turn, takes the calumet, and holding it with both his hands, dances with it, following the cadence of the songs.

'This *præludium* being over, he who is to begin the dance appears in the middle of the assembly, and having taken the calumet, presents it to the sun, as if he would invite him to smoke; then he moves it into an infinite number of postures, sometimes laying it near the ground, then stretching its wings as if he would make it fly, and then presenting it to the spectators, who smoke with it one after another, dancing all the while. This is the first scene of this savage ball. The second is a fight with vocal and instrumental music, (for they have a kind of drum, which agrees pretty well with the voices). The person who dances with the calumet, gives a signal to one of their warriors, who takes a bow and arrows, with an axe, from the trophies already mentioned, and fights the other, who defends himself with the calumet alone, both of them dancing all the while. The fight being over, he who holds the calumet makes a speech, wherein he gives an account of the battles he has fought, and the prisoners he has taken, and then receives a gown, or some other present, from the chief of the ball: he then gives the calumet to another, who having acted his part, delivers it to a third, and so to all the others, till the calumet returns to the captain. who presents it to the nation invited unto the feast, as a mark of their friendship, and a confirmation of their alliances.'

So much for the Illinois ball, the relation of which we find is translated from Father Marquette, a French writer, by whom we are also told, that the word Illinois, in the language of this people, signifies Men, as if they regarded the other savages as beasts; and it may be confessed, it is added, that they are not altogether in the wrong.

We are now brought to the history of Canada, which employs a very considerable part of this first volume; beginning from the first discovery of this vast extent of country by Cabot, the famous Italian, under a commission from Henry the Seventh of England; whose frugal maxims prevented his making any regular settlement there. We have a more particular account of the proceedings of the French in their discoveries and settlements in these parts from towards the beginning of the sixteenth century. The relation appears to be an abridgement of some French writers and missionaries, and is often done in rather an inaccurate and negligent manner, but will nevertheless be acceptable and entertaining to those who love to know the origin and progress of such plantations in those wild and distant regions. Our Author, in one part, takes notice of a happy reformation which took place for a season at least, at a time when a very dissolute and debauched spirit had greatly prevailed both among the savages and the French people, in consequence of terrible tempests, hurricanes, and earthquakes, with which Canada was visited; frequent evidences of which the face of the country affords unto this day. We meet with some reflections upon this event; whether the writer's own or not we cannot determine, as the whole paſſage is diſtinguiſhed from the reſt by being placed between crotchets. But we obſerve, that after remarking the benefits which afflictions often produce to mankind, and that the notion of a *particular* providence has, in ſome caſes, contributed to work wonderful reformations, it is boldly added concerning this latter opinion, that impartial conſideration muſt convince any perſon of its abſolute abſurdity. This aſſertion appears hazardous in itſelf, and dangerous to the morals of mankind. Beſide that it will, in the general, admit of debate, a believer in revelation muſt allow that it directs us to think and act under this perſuaſion, however unphiloſophical it may appear; and as to the difficulties which may occur upon the ſubject, to the enquiring mind, it is truly rational, as well as properly modeſt, to ſuppoſe that they may be chiefly owing to our ignorance, and our very limited abilities and views.

We ſhall only add, for the preſent, an account of a conference between ſome deputies from the Iroquois cantons, and Montmagny, at that time the French governor of Canada, in order to conclude a treaty of peace. We ſhould obſerve, that Montmagny, to forward this buſineſs, had releaſed an Iroquois captive, but had ſent him back to his own country without any attendants; the ſavages likewiſe were diſpoſed to releaſe ſome French priſoners, among which was one Couture, whom an Iroquois chief had adopted, to replace his nephew who had been killed in the wars, and they took care that Couture and the other captives ſhould not traverſe that wild country by themſelves, but ſent them, accompanied by the five deputies who were to finiſh the treaty; theſe circumſtances are ſtrongly alluded to in the following relation:

'At this conference the ſpeaker of the Iroquois cantons having preſented Montmagny with one of the belts of wampum, accompanied it with a ſpeech to this effect: "Ononthio, (ſo they called the French governor) lend an ear to my voice: all the Iroquois ſpeak by my mouth; my heart harbours no bad ſentiments, and all my intentions are upright. We want to forget our ſongs of war, and to exchange them for ſongs of joy."

'He then began ſinging, and throwing himſelf into a thouſand ridiculous attitudes, walking about, and frequently looking upon the ſun: at length, in a calmer manner, he proceeded as follows: "The belt, my father, which I here preſent thee, thanks thee for having reſcued my brother (the priſoner who had been ſent home) from the tooth of the Algonquin: but how couldſt thou let him return home by himſelf? Had his canoe been overſet, who was to aſſiſt him to bring it to rights? Had he been drowned, or periſhed by any other accident, thou wouldſt have heard no word of peace from us, and wouldſt perhaps, have imputed to us the fault committed by thyſelf."

'When the orator had finiſhed this ſpeech, he hung the belt on the cord; then taking another, he fixed it to Couture's arm, and turning

turning again to Montmagny, he thus addressed him: "My father, this belt brings thee back thy subject; but I was far from saying unto him, Nephew, take a canoe, and return home:—never could I have been easy till I had certainly heard of his safe arrival. My brother, whom thou hast sent us back, suffered a great deal and underwent many perils: He was obliged alone to carry his own bundle; to swim all day, to drag his canoe against the falls, and to be always on his guard against surprize." The orator accompanied this speech with the most expressive action, which represented a man sometimes pushing forward a canoe with a pole, sometimes paddling with an oar; sometimes he seemed to be out of breath, and then resuming his spirits, he appeared more calm. He then seemed as if he had hurt his foot against a stone in carrying his bundle; and halting along, as if he had been wounded, he thus continued his discourse: "Hadst thou but assisted him in surmounting the most difficult parts of his journey.—Really, my father, I know not what became of thy understanding, when thou sentest us back in this manner one of thy children, without an attendant and without assistance. I did not serve Couture so. I said to him, Come along, my nephew, follow me, I will restore thee to thy family at the peril of my own life."

'The other (seventeen) belts were disposed of in the same manner as the two preceding, and each of them had a particular allusion to the terms of the peace in agitation, which was explained by the orator in a very picturesque manner; he continued this fatiguing scene for the amazing space of three hours, without appearing to be heated; for he afterwards led up a dance, and joined in the singing and feasting, which concluded the conference.'

The history of Canada in this volume is continued to about the year 1748 or 1749. Some account of the second volume of this work will hereafter be given.

Art. IX. *Georgical Essays: in which a new Compost is recommended, and other important Articles of Husbandry explained, upon the Principles of Vegetation.* Vol. II. Small 8vo. 2 s. 6 d. sewed. Durham. 1771.

THE public are already acquainted with the design and execution of the first volume of these Agricultural Essays, which was published in 1769, and contained *four* tracts. To these, *five* others were added in a second edition, which appeared the following year*. The present collection consisting of *nine essays*, were, (as we are informed by the dedication to Charles Turner, Esq; and subscribed A. Hunter,) read before a society, of which that gentleman's improvements in husbandry render him a distinguished member. We shall pass over the first of these tracts, which contains a short and general recommendation of the study of nature. The subject of the second Essay is, *The Rise and Ascent of Vapours*, the Author of which, Mr. William White, after declaring his opinion that the true cause of evaporation

* See Monthly Review, Vol. xl. June 1769, page 472; and Vol. xliii. December 1770, page 500.

poration 'hath not *yet* been discovered, or at least enough at-'tended to,' adds, that, having frequently of late given some attention to the subject, he is inclined to believe that 'by 'considering it in a *new* point of view, some light may be 'thrown upon it.' After recapitulating, and shewing the insufficiency of, the most generally received hypotheses on this subject, he proposes the following, which, he very justly presumes, will be found less exceptionable than any of those before-mentioned. For reasons which will immediately appear, we shall give no further *account* of this theory, than that the Author attributes the rise and suspension of vapours 'to the 'power of the air, as a *menstruum*, capable of dissolving, suspend-'ing, and intimately mixing the particles of water with itself.' We think proper, however, to give a short *history* of this opinion, which is by no means *new*, as this gentleman every where supposes throughout this Essay: and this we shall do without the most distant design of mortifying the Author, but merely as a part of our duty, and for the information of our philosophical readers.

The former attempts to explain the nature and cause of evaporation having been found inadequate and unsatisfactory, a very ingenious and well-supported hypothesis was published by Dr. Hugh Hamilton of Dublin, first in the 55th volume of the Philosophical Transactions for the year 1765, and afterwards, with some improvements, in a collection of *Philosophical Essays* published apart by the Author, in the year 1767; in which that natural operation was considered as a solution of water in air, or of the same kind with that of salt in water, or of other substances in their proper menstrua. Our readers will meet with a general account of this hypothesis, and some pretty large extracts from the first publication of it in the Philosophical Transactions, by consulting the preceding volumes of our work, to which they are referred below †.

We should observe, however, that, previous to either of these publications, a paper written by Dr. Franklyn, intitled *Physical and Meteorological Observations, &c.* had been read before the Royal Society, which evidently contained the germ of this theory; though having been casually mislaid, it was not published, till the reading of Dr. Hamilton's paper, above mentioned, revived the memory of it; and it was accordingly, together with it, printed in the volume of the Transactions above referred to, and afterwards in Dr. Franklyn's collection of *Letters and papers on Philosophical Subjects* ‡. We mention these facts

† See Vol. xxxv. November 1766, page 379, and vol. xl. May 1769, page 392.

‡ See Monthly Review, Vol. xlii. March 1770, page 199.

for

for the sake of such of our readers as may wish to peruse what has been already written on this subject; and not without some surprise at the singular coincidence in opinion (which pleads strongly in favour of the plausibility, at least, of this hypothesis) between these writers and the present Author; who every where offers his solution as a new idea, and appears unacquainted with their hypotheses: although we observe him sometimes referring to, and quoting, both the last mentioned work of Dr. Franklyn, and the Philosophical Transactions. With regard to the article of priority or property in this discovery, we could yet name, though indeed from memory only, a fourth claimant: as we recollect to have met with this very hypothesis, proposed in a paper written by M. Le Roi, and published in the Memoirs of the Royal Academy of Sciences at Paris, about twenty years ago. Without entering any further into this part of the subject, we think it sufficient to add, that this ingenious theory is here very well supported by many observations and arguments, which are likewise to be found in the preceding performances; and by a few proofs and illustrations peculiar to the Author.

We shall mention, however, another coincidence, which is *certainly* an accidental one, between the Author and ourselves, in our respective methods of accounting for a singular meteorological *phenomenon*, related by Dr. Heberden, in the last volume of the Philosophical Transactions. From repeated experiments the Doctor found that a much smaller quantity of rain fell on the surface of the ground, than on a place more elevated. We offered some conjectures on the probable cause of this difference, in the Review for April last, page 321, which were founded on this very theory of evaporation; and we are glad to find them in some degree confirmed, from a particular observation here mentioned by the Author, with a view to ascertain the cause of this *phenomenon*; viz. that a small drizzling rain, accompanied with a thick mist, has been observed at York, in the streets *below*; at the same time that no rain has fallen upon the *top* of the cathedral at that place.

In the third of these Essays, an account is given of a new species of grain, called Siberian or *Haliday* barley, very lately introduced into this kingdom, and which appears to possess qualities that intitle it to particular consideration as an object of importance in agriculture. The history of its introduction is as follows: A pint of it was presented about four years ago by a foreign nobleman to the Society of Arts, from a member of which Mr. Haliday received a moderate wine glass full, half of which he sowed in 1767 in his garden. From a quart hence produced, and sown in May 1768 in drills, partly in his garden, and partly in a potatoe field, he procured near a bushel, which

he

he sowed in April 1769, in drills drawn by a plough; from which he reaped thirty-six bushels of clear corn.

Having thus established the fecundity of this grain, and procured a stock on which he could afford to make experiments, in order to ascertain its merit as a bread corn, and as proper for malting, he caused two quantities of it to be ground and malted. The flour of the former made excellent bread, peculiarly retentive of moisture; and the ale brewed from the other quantity proved of a fine colour, flavour, and body;—*grato tam sapore, quam effectu, se commendans*, as Dr. Lochster, in his dissertation, *De Medicamentis Norwegiæ* feelingly characterizes it, speaking of it under the denomination of *Hordeum cæleste*, vulgo *Himmelbyg*; Heaven's corn, or Thor-barley, as it is called by Pontoppidan.

These are the chief particulars of Mr. Haliday's three years experience of this excellent grain, from which he is convinced of its superior utility to any other spring corn. He continues to prosecute the cultivation of it; and we are told that about twenty bushels of his last year's crop were, in the summer of 1770, under skilful culture in the several counties of Kent, Surry, Essex, Middlesex, Hereford, Stafford, Chester, Derby, York, Durham, and many parts of his own county; as likewise in two or three counties in Wales, six or seven in Ireland, and some in Scotland: from all which he entertains hopes of its becoming soon as universally esteemed as known.

In the fourth Essay, some observations are given on the culture of the potatoe, founded on experience, and on a consideration of the manner in which that plant grows, above and below ground. The Author considers the potatoe itself, not as the root of the plant, but as a fruit growing upon branches under ground, and maintained by the real roots, which do not produce fruit, but are destined, together with the leaves, which extract nutriment from the atmosphere, to feed both the potatoe below and the apple above. The two fruits are of the same nature; though, living in different elements, they assume different appearances.

The drill culture of turnips is described in the fifth Essay, and recommended to those gentlemen, who wish to be considered as correct husbandmen, and are not to be deterred by considerations of trouble or expence. In the sixth, the Author recommends the residuum left after the extraction of the oil from whale blubber, as a manure undoubtedly capable of being reduced, by putrefaction, into a rich vegetable food. The seventh gives an account of an experiment made by J. S. Morritt, Esq; made to ascertain the utility or oeconomy of employing carrots in the fattening of hogs. The difference between the result of the Author's and of Mr. Young's experiments on this head, is very remarkable. Mr. Young gets near 18 stone of hog's flesh for 3*l.*; while 33 stone ftone 10lb. coft the Author above 38 *l.*; that is, upwards of 23 *s.* per ftone. He pofitively concludes from the whole 'that carrots alone are of no value for fattening of hogs.'

In the eighth Effay the Author, or rather Mr. Harald Bark *, to whom he refers, recommends to the hufbandmen the profecution of an ingenious idea, fuggefted by Linnæus; of confulting nature annually, with regard to the proper time of fowing different grains, by making the foliation of trees and fhrubs his callendar; inftead of turning to the fun and ftars, or, in other words, confulting the almanac, or the practice of laft year, for the particular day and month; neglecting the more precife information to be obtained from the vegetable tribe around him. Certainly the fame ftate of the earth, air, &c. which brings forth the leaves of trees, in any particular foil, fituation, feafon, or climate, conftitutes a natural and univerfal *fign*; the more juft on account even of its annual variations. He advifes the hufbandman therefore to make a table of the time of budding, leafing, and flowering, of different trees and fhrubs; and to mark in another the days on which his refpective grains were fown: fo that, from a comparifon of the two tables, he may afterwards be enabled to form a *natural calendar* for his fpring corn. He refers to Mr. Stillingfleet's correct obfervations on the firft of thefe two heads, contained in his *Calendar of Flora* for Norfolk, which the reader will find in the volume mentioned below, p. 289. Our Author quotes largely from Mr. Young's experiment, on the article of feed-time.—His quotations are indeed rather too frequent and too copious, for fo very fmall a volume.

The work is terminated by a fhort account, given by Mr. Roebuck, of an unfuccefsful experiment made with the oil compoft, recommended in the firft volume †; and with a fubfequent and more fuccefsful trial, from which the neceffity appears of meliorating this compoft, by expofing it for a length of time to the action of the air, 'in order to abate the heat, and neutralize the acrimony of the falt.'

ART. X. *The Religious Eftablifhment in Scotland examined upon Proteftant Principles:* A Tract, occafioned by the late Profecution againft the late Rev. Mr. Alexander Fergufon, Minifter in Kilwinning. 8vo. 4 s. fewed. Cadell. 1771.

THIS work may, we think, be juftly regarded as the *Confeffional* for the church of Scotland. It is written with as much fpirit as the Englifh *Confeffional*, and with greater perfpicuity

---

* See Mr. Stillingfleet's *Mifcellaneous Tracts*, p. 133. 2d. edit.

† The chemical theory on which this compoft is founded, and its particular compofition, may be feen in our 40th volume, June 1769, page 473, &c.

ſpicuity of ſtyle; though it cannot, perhaps, be conſidered as equal in all reſpects to that celebrated performance.

As the publication before us was occaſioned by a proſecution carried on againſt Mr. Ferguſon, the riſe and progreſs of that proſecution are here related, at large, in the preface; and the ſtory is told in a manner which is peculiarly lively and entertaining.

Mr. Ferguſon is now no more. 'He is, ſays our Author, beyond the reach of his enemies. He died as he lived,—honeſt and open, a friend to truth, and a determined enemy to hypocrites. He has now received his ſentence. His upright ſpirit is happy. While he reſided on earth, he was above diſſimulation, and that expoſed him to the attacks of craftineſs. He is now exalted to his place, and looks down, with pity, on our miſerable politics. Magnanimous Spirit! I am looking for thy fellow. Tell me, ye zealous for the Lord! do you think that, when Mr. Ferguſon appeared in heaven, his Creator aſked him whether he was a Socinian or a Calviniſt?'

The Author, at the concluſion of his preface, ſpeaking in the name of the republican clergymen of Scotland, ſays with great confidence: "We will ſet the example of religious liberty to England." If in this reſpect he is a true prophet, we ſincerely pray that his prediction may be ſpeedily accompliſhed.

The work itſelf is divided into three parts. The firſt contains a number of ſolid, and, indeed, unanſwerable arguments againſt religious ſubſcriptions in general. In the ſecond, the writer particularly examines the conſtitution of the church of Scotland, and diſplays much learning upon the ſubject. Many of his obſervations and reaſonings are here, undoubtedly, curious and important; but yet this is not the part of his tract that hath afforded us the greateſt pleaſure. He appears to have carried his refinements too far, in attempting to give a reaſonable ſenſe to the ſubſcriptions and formulas of the Scotch eſtabliſhment; and eſpecially to the formula of 1711. Perhaps he thought that his countrymen were not yet capable of bearing the full exhibition of the truth. In the third part, our examiner urges additional arguments in favour of a farther reformation; and concludes with pathetic addreſſes to the zealouſly orthodox clergymen of the church of Scotland, and to thoſe who are more liberal minded, but are too timid to engage in any attempt for aboliſhing ſubſcriptions.

It is much to be lamented, that the perſons who ſolicit religious alterations and improvements, have not *the bigots* alone to contend with. The principles and reaſonings of bigots may be confuted, and they themſelves may, in time, be convinced. But there is another ſet of men whoſe oppoſition is more formidable. We mean thoſe who are ſufficiently *enlarged* in their

private

private ſentiments, but who are influenced by worldly views, and political motives. It is to be feared that ſuch men will ever be unfriendly to ſchemes of reformation.

Upon the whole, we are of opinion, that this maſterly performance will be read with great pleaſure by the lovers of religious liberty, and that it ought to excite a general and very ſerious attention among the miniſters and members of the church of Scotland.

MONTHLY CATALOGUE,

For NOVEMBER, 1771.

RELIGIOUS and CONTROVERSIAL.

Art. 11. *A Paraphraſe on the eleven firſt Chapters of St. Paul's Epiſtle to the Romans.* By Thomas Adam, Rector of Wintringham in Lincolnſhire. 8vo. 4 s. ſewed. Rivington. 1771.

THIS appears to be the performance of a ſenſible man, who deſires to deliver the true ſenſe of ſcripture as far as he can attain it, and to advance the cauſe of piety among men. His method is to lay a ſmall number of verſes before the reader at one view, in which are inſerted a few words to illuſtrate and explain them, and then he adds ſeveral obſervations upon the ſenſe of the paſſage, with ſome practical remarks. 'I did not,' he tells us in one part of his work, think myſelf at liberty to ſit down and imagine what anſwer the Apoſtle ſhould have returned to the important enquiries concerning the nature of ſin, and the means of deliverance from the curſe and power of it; but judged it to be my duty to follow the guidance of his light, under a firm perſuaſion that it came from Heaven, and to receive information from him in points of which I was ignorant, and about which I could never have ſatisfied myſelf. If I have miſtaken or miſrepreſented him, the good Lord pardon me, to whom I dare make no proteſtations of perfect ſincerity or freedom from prejudice.'

The Author does not embrace thoſe explications of ſome terms and phraſes in this epiſtle which ſeveral learned men have choſen, but rather inclines to a ſenſe agreeable to the articles of our church, or to a Calviniſtical interpretation; though he differs from them in what he advances in his paraphraſe upon the eighth, ninth, and eleventh chapters of this epiſtle, the two laſt of which relate to the rejection of the Jews,—where he ſays, 'That the divine decree does not relate to the election or reprobation of particular perſons, as the ſtated method of God's proceeding with mankind under every diſpenſation, but to the general calling of the Jews at one time, of the Gentiles at another, to be a ſacred people to God, we have ventured to affirm is the doctrine of St. Paul, and produced the reaſons of our opinion as we are able. Farther we dare not ſearch into this myſtery, and heartily wiſh that all, inſtead of pretending to know what God has reſerved to himſelf, and letting their thoughts looſe into a wide field of lawleſs conjectures, would ſtop where the apoſtle does, and ſay, with a humble ſubmiſſion of their underſtandings to what is written, and profound adoration of the divine counſels—*O the depth!*'

In

In another place, upon one of the above-mentioned chapters, he says, 'What I have offered is the real sense of my own mind, founded on the nature and express purpose of the apostle's argument, and clearly pointed out by himself, which was to vindicate the divine providence in calling the Gentiles to be partakers of the gospel, and refute the vain pretensions of the Jews to an exclusive right in the favour of God and the promise of the Messiah. They, it seems, were strict predestinarians; and it can hardly be supposed that the apostle, in arguing the point with them, combats their error by establishing it upon the whole, as he certainly does if he is here pleading the cause of predestination, only with this difference, that whereas they confined it to their own nation, he admits of the nation only with respect to a small number of them, and, at the same time, extends it to some others, comparatively few, among the Gentiles. It must be confessed, that many of the defenders of this doctrine have been ornaments to the Christian profession.'

Our Author apprehends that the apostle had 'no respect to a predestination, or election of particular persons, with a bar to all the rest of mankind.'

Farther, in regard to this doctrine of a particular personal election, he says, that 'as it is repugnant to our natural notions of the Deity, uncomfortable in itself, and very hard of digestion, so every attempt to reconcile the passages seemingly tending to it with the general tenor and express declarations of scripture, pleads its own excuse.'

Mr. Adam thinks that the offer of salvation is as extensive as it is free, and that the apostle is so far from putting a bar in the way of any,—that he has guarded as fully as words can do, against any such interpretation of his meaning. At the same time this Writer acknowledges, that were the contrary a clear and express declaration of scripture, he should not hesitate a moment to submit to its authority.—On the whole, this Paraphrase, not abounding in criticism as some might expect, appears however to be a candid, well-meant, practical, and useful performance, even though the Author should, in some respects, be mistaken in his explication.

Art. 12. *An Appeal to the good Sense of the Inhabitants of Great Britain* concerning their religious Rights and Privileges. 8vo. 1 s. 6 d. Bladon.

The Author of this Appeal traces the *infringements of human power*, in matters of *religion*, through different periods. Religious opinions, he observes, are of such a kind, that no earthly power can controul them: the absurdity of any attempt to do this, he endeavours to expose by adding, 'It would seem exceedingly ridiculous for any human government to interfere in medical opinions, and to ordain with the same pomp and solemnity which have been affected in religious matters, that particular disorders should be cured by those medicines alone which whim and caprice might approve.' It would, indeed, be exceedingly ridiculous for government to interfere in favour of *whim* and *caprice*, on *any* subject or occasion whatever!

The second section briefly considers the state of Christianity, to the days of the Emperor Constantine, when 'the zealous, or rather the ambi-

ambitious, were willing to yield the pre-eminence in religious affairs to him.' This appeal to human authority, he endeavours to ſhew, 'muſt be derived from bad principles of the heart, much more than from any *polemical* diſputes which might happen among Chriſtians.'

With this influence of the civil magiſtrate as a ſource of religious oppreſſion, he does not fail to unite the early eſtabliſhment of a prieſthood, which he more particularly conſiders in the third ſection, and which he terms 'that golden opportunity to a worldly-minded man.' In the following ſections he confines himſelf 'to the hiſtory of religion in theſe kingdoms, and to the many inconveniencies which at preſent ariſe from a political eſtabliſhment of it in this land of liberty.' From the whole ſurvey of which he boldly infers, that 'every eſtabliſhment, in whatever country it is ſettled, is unjuſt, and every government, by ſupporting it, is guilty of an act of oppreſſion. Let me then, ſays he, with all the reſpect which is due to a powerful as well as good prince, but with as much confidence as is natural to a Britiſh ſubject, call upon the firſt magiſtrate in this kingdom, to relinquiſh that right which has devolved to him from his anceſtors, but of which, as a religious man, he can no longer avail himſelf. Let me call upon both houſes of parliament, the repreſentatives of our wants, and the ſecurity of our properties, to reſcind thoſe acts by which an unnatural authority has been uſurped over the conſciences of men, and reſtore the profeſſors of religion to all the freedom which is allowed them by its Author. Let me call upon the venerable bench of biſhops, and every ſubordinate power under them, to ſearch the ſcriptures, and ſee upon what grounds their authority is ſupported, and, as diſciples of Jeſus, to yield to their fellow-creatures, whatever is derived from human, and not from divine original. Let me call upon our univerſities, to lay aſide *ſubſcriptions*, which can have no influence upon young and unformed minds, but to deſtroy the firſt principles of *truth*, and of *ſincerity*. Let me call upon the inferior clergy who are deprived of their neceſſary ſubſiſtence, and yet are bound to articles, contradictory to their conſciences, to aſſert the ſpirit of free enquiry, and a juſt participation of their lawful dues. Let me call upon every diſſenter to remonſtrate againſt the oppreſſion levelled againſt him in the teſt act, and the reſtrictions by which he is unjuſtly puniſhed.—In fine, let me call upon every man who is an inhabitant of theſe realms, to ſtudy the ſcriptures of truth, and to pay no greater reſpect to worldly authority, than what is warranted by them: let me call upon him particularly to read the precepts, and to obſerve the character of our divine Maſter, and if in nothing which he has ſaid, he can obſerve the traces of the eſtabliſhment of a clergy, the power of a biſhop and church cenſures, let me call upon him to diſclaim this unnatural authority, and endeavour, as much as poſſible, to effect a revolution, which may free him from theſe ſhackles, reſtore the cauſe of reaſon to his mind, ſet his conſcience at liberty from oppreſſion, and juſtify the rights of the Author of his religion.'

The above may ſuffice for a ſpecimen of the zeal and the ſtyle of this Writer.

Art.

Art. 13. *A Letter to the Rev. James Ibbetson*, D. D. occasioned by a Third Edition of his Plea, for the Subscription of the Clergy to the Thirty-nine Articles of Religion; in which the present Scheme of petitioning the Parliament for Relief in the Matter of Subscription, is occasionally defended. By a Clergyman of the Church of England. 8vo. 1s. 6d. Bladon. 1771.

The present laudable attempt of some of the clergy, to procure a deliverance from the burthen of subscription, seems to have excited no small degree of attention, and even alarm, among a number of their brethren. Dr. Ibbetson hath shewn himself one of the first in opposing the scheme, by republishing his plea for subscription; and this has given rise to the letter before us, in which the Author hath pursued the Doctor through his windings, and detected his sophisms, with sagacity and spirit. The following extracts will afford a proper specimen of the perspicuity and good sense with which the subject is treated:

'Whatever ideas of convenience might have induced the first protestant churches to deviate from their own principles, into those of their adversary, by *establishing* confessions of faith, all such ideas must be brought into the present debate, about the *right* and *utility* of subscriptions, very improperly——or brought merely as *apologies* for the conduct of the reformers, not as *justifications* of it.

'If their enemies slandered them by the imputation of impious and extravagant opinions——the proper answer would have been, an appeal to the conduct of their lives, and a solemn declaration that they admitted of no standard of opinion but the sacred Scriptures. For when their confessions were published, the scandal still continued, and the articles contained in them were still condemned as impious and extravagant. So that they weakened the protestant party by dividing it——they gave the Romanist an opportunity of attacking them upon their own principles——and this, without avoiding the abuse, which offended orthodoxy is ever ready to discharge.

'But whether the first reformers were right or wrong is nothing to the present question about subscriptions. Granting them to have acted wisely in publishing their opinions for reputation's sake——yet the question concerning their *right* to *establish* these opinions, upon the oath or subscription of those whom they admitted as preachers of religion, still remains——And even giving up this——we may further question the propriety of making the doctrines of men, just emerged from ignorance, the standard of belief to the present clergy.

'For the dispute about *subscription* contains two different questions. 1st. Can *any* subscription to *human* articles of religious belief——be defended? 2d. Can subscription to those of the church of England be justified? Many who would not hesitate to answer in the negative to the second, would yet, perhaps, be scrupulous about the first, although 'tis impossible to discuss the second without establishing the true and negative answer to the first. For while there is manifest and apparent error, we should proceed to correct it——and error, manifest or apparent, there will be in every set of propositions, which are neither demonstrative, nor inspired. If it be said, that such an acknowledgment of the impossibility of avoiding error, is a good

 apology

apology for not revising the present articles——I answer, No;——for every step towards truth makes the next much easier——and this particular step would convince the people of what thousands are scarce aware of——that articles and liturgies are mere human compositions, which may and ought to be improved——This would induce them to transfer their zeal from them to the bible; which will then be read as a fixed standard, by which to correct any successive improvement, until we come to inspired truth expressed in Scripture language.

'Indeed the certainty that all human systematical explications of Scripture doctrine *may* be wrong——is so far from an apology for our continuance in the present forms, that it is an unanswerable reason against it. For if they *may* be wrong, why make *them* the tests of our orthodoxy——while the plain words of Scripture are at hand, which we know *must* be right.'

We could wish that our letter-writer, in his future publications, would be more sparing of his *Italicks*, and especially his *long strokes*, or *dashes*. A frequent use of them is disgustful to most persons who are habituated to good composition, and can be of little service to any reader, of tolerable understanding. The present Author has no need of such helps, in order to render his meaning clear and emphatical.

ART. 14. *Remarks upon certain Proposals for an Application to Parliament*, for Relief in the Matter of Subscription to the Thirty-nine Articles, &c. 8vo. 6d. Rivington. 1771.

This remarker is not a little displeased with that part of the clergy, who are engaged in the scheme for obtaining relief with regard to subscription. Accordingly, he has endeavoured to vindicate subscription as one of the chief pillars of our excellent establishment; as necessary even to its very existence; and the subject is treated by him with a confusion of sentiment and reasoning happily suited to the cause he hath undertaken. It is pleasant to observe the manner in which the advocates for religious impositions have been obliged, of late years, to change their modes of expression. They dare not to deny the right of private judgment. To evade, therefore, the force of any argument that may be drawn from it against them, the ecclesiastical establishment, fenced around with its civil sanctions, is erected into a single person; and then truly the poor lady is not to be deprived of the liberty of exercising her right of private judgment, in imposing what terms she pleases, however coutrary to the genius of the gospel, or to the nature of a protestant church. In the same way, might the church of Rome pretend to vindicate all her persecutions.

Another thing we cannot help smiling at, in the present performance, is the alarm which the Author is in, lest the removal of subscription should expose us to be swallowed up by popery. Who could have expected that popery would be promoted by a scheme, the very aim of which is, by bringing the church of England to the purest protestant principles, to place it at a still farther distance from the church of Rome? Are not papists excluded by the oaths of allegiance and supremacy? Can nothing be contrived to prevent their admission

admiſſion into the eſtabliſhment, except the impoſition of a ſubſcription which is itſelf contrary to the true grounds of proteſtantiſm?

It is inſinuated, at the cloſe of theſe remarks, with a deſpicable meanneſs and malignity, that the oppoſition now made to the ſubſcribing to human articles of religion, proceeds from the licentious humour of the times. But we are perſuaded that it hath no connection with our political diſſentions, and that it ſolely ariſes from a laudable deſire of obtaining relief in a matter of great importance to the rights of conſcience.

Art. 15. *A further Defence of the preſent Scheme for petitioning the Parliament for Relief in the Matter of Subſcription*, occaſioned by a Pamphlet called *Remarks upon certain Propoſals*, &c. [See the preceding Article.] By the Author of a Letter to James Ibbetſon, D. D. 8vo. 1 s. Wilkie. 1771.

Though the Author of the tract deſcribed in the preceding article, has urged no arguments in favour of ſubſcription, but what have been repeatedly confuted, it hath been thought proper to honour him with a diſtinct reply. It is, indeed, irkſome, to be obliged to repeat the anſwers already given to every thing he has been able to produce: but perhaps, ſays the preſent writer, the fault is not ſo much in this gentleman, who may be acting under command, as in the policy of our adverſaries, who have drawn up a front of wretched ſoldiers as food for our powder, while the beſt of their troops reſerve their fire, to do more heavy execution.

The Remarker having affected to triumph over the petitioning clergy, as being *few*, a *contemptible few*: this hath drawn from the defender of them the following animated expreſſions, in the concluſion of his performance:

'Whatever be our names, our ſtations, or our numbers, we are men, freemen, chriſtians, proteſtants: and theſe are no contemptible characters. We are united, and determined by truth. Our proceedings and views, whenever they are more fully laid before the world, will exculpate us from the injurious charge which this writer has dared to bring againſt us without the ſlighteſt evidence, the charge of bring licentious men.

'With the preſent ſtate of party we have not——we will not interfere. I repeat it; ours is a proteſtant deſign, and whoever repreſents it otherwiſe, ſhould have given the reaſon of his ſuſpicions.

'We have long wiſhed for, we ſtill hope for, the countenance of our venerable ſuperiors in the church: but let it be remembered that the deſign of aboliſhing ſubſcription is not a merely clerical deſign. The laity are involved in the grievance, and no doubt will aſſiſt vigorouſly in its removal. Having long enjoyed a more juſt and generous legiſlation in the ſtate than we do in the church, they are a century before many of us in their notions concerning their rights as Engliſhmen and proteſtants, and will, of courſe, exert themſelves proportionably in the preſent enterprize.

'But beyond the ſupport of man, we look up to the great Author of our religion for aid. We know the unconquerable and progreſſive nature of his truth; and we call to mind thoſe periods of Britiſh hiſtory, in which ſome of the moſt important points of religious liberty

liberty were gained, under Providence, not by counting the votes of the clergy, but by a rational and juſt legiſlature.'

Through the whole of this defence, the erroneous reaſonings of the Remarker, are clearly and convincingly refuted.

Art. 16. *Free Thoughts on the Subject of a farther Reformation of the Church of England*; to which are added, the Remarks of the Editor. By the Author of *a ſhort and ſafe Expedient for terminating the preſent Debates about Subſcription.* Publiſhed by Benjamin Dawſon, L. L. D. Rector of Burgh. 8vo. 2 s. 6 d. Wilkie. 1771.

These Free Thoughts are the production of the late excellent Mr. Jones, whoſe uſeful writings, and laudable endeavours to promote the cauſe of religious liberty, and to obtain a farther reformation in the church of England, are well known to many of our readers. The contents of the ſix numbers, of which the preſent publication chiefly conſiſts, are as follows. 1. *Modern Church Policy*: containing articles of opinion and ſubſcription, formed upon the plan of the *alliance* between church and ſtate, and more particularly collected from the ſermon of Dr. *Balguy* upon the ſubject. 2. Seaſonable mementos tendered to Dr. *Balguy*, on occaſion of his uncandid reflections on the Authors of ſome late writings addreſſed to the governors of the church of England. 3. Concurring ſentiments of ſeveral learned and judicious perſons concerning the right of private judgment in matters of Religion. 4. Some *Specimens* of the learning and other qualifications of our principal reformers, for drawing up articles of theology, to be the ſtandard of the doctrines of the church of England. This number is very curious, and affords a deciſive proof how ill-qualified archbiſhop Cranmer, in particular, was, to compoſe a ſyſtem of belief which ſhould be binding upon poſterity. 5. Thoughts on ſubſcriptions required from the clergy. 6. Candid ſentiments in favour of dutiful applications for a review.

The Author has introduced, under theſe ſeveral articles, many important reaſons for aboliſhing ſubſcriptions; and his ingenious and worthy Editor hath added a number of notes, moſt of them tending to advance the ſame valuable deſign.

Art. 17. *An Addreſs to Presbyterians and Independants*; or a Letter to a Friend, in Defence of religious Liberty: occaſioned by ſeveral Miniſters being denied the Benefit of the Independent Fund, for refuſing to ſend in ſatisfactory Confeſſions of Faith. 8vo. 6 d. Johnſon. 1771.

It is greatly to be wiſhed, that the worthy perſons, who ſuffer from the rigid principles on which the independent fund is ſaid to be conducted, had met with an abler advocate than the preſent writer.

Art. 18 *A free and plain Expoſition of the 9th and 10th Verſes of the 2d Chap. of Titus*: addreſſed to Servants profeſſing Godlineſs. With a Preface addreſſed to Maſters and Miſtreſſes. 8vo. 6 d. Whiſton, &c.

As the religious principles and moral conduct of ſervants are of the higheſt conſequence, not only to themſelves, but alſo to thoſe under whom they are in ſubordination, their minds cannot be too carefully cultivated and informed. This little tract affords good and important advice,

advice, both to ſervants and to the heads of families; prudently and piouſly exhorting them ſo to conduct themſelves, in the diſcharge of their reſpective duties, as may beſt promote their mutual intereſt and ſatisfaction: "Adorning the doctrine of God, our Saviour, in all things."

Art. 19. *A Vindication of the Hebrew Scriptures*; with Animadverſions on the Mark ſet on Cain, the Giantſhip, Wizardry, and Witchcraft, mentioned in the Pentateuch and the Prophets. Alſo Strictures on Samſon's Accoutrement of his hoſtile Foxes, the Woman of Tekoa, Job, and on various other Paſſages of Scripture, as they relate to Divinity, Philoſophy, Law, Goſpel, Gentiliſm, or Chriſtianity. With a Preface to juſtify the Ways of God to Men, addreſſed to Eccleſiaſtics and Philoſophers. By John Dove. 8vo. 2 s. Norris. 1771.

If any of our Readers are diſpoſed for an half hour's laugh, let them run over this curious performance of the renowned John Dove. The title-page affords ſome ſpecimen of the honeſt man's pedantry and confidence. He is himſelf ſo enamoured with the Hutchinſonian method of reading and explaining the Hebrew Scriptures, that he hardly gives any quarter to thoſe who are willing to purſue a different courſe: indeed he brings a general charge againſt the eccleſiaſtics, as well as the philoſophers of the preſent age, that they are ignorant of the Hebrew language. He profeſſes not to write with rancour, but with a wiſh to promote the peace and happineſs of mankind, even of his worſt enemy: However this may be, he does heartily and freely laſh and abuſe philoſophers, commentators, churchmen and others, who do not fall in with his ſyſtem. He acknowledges a great neceſſity for a new tranſlation of the Scriptures, but at the ſame time expreſſes his apprehenſion, that as things are now circumſtanced among us, this new verſion would be even worſe than that we have at preſent. He offers ſome inſtances of ſuppoſed errors in the Engliſh Bible; but we imagine it is not neceſſary to apply to Mr. Dove to learn that a different account might be given of the *mark ſet upon Cain*, or of *Samſon*'s hoſtile *foxes*, as this Author calls them, and of other particulars.

Among others who fall under Mr. D.'s cenſure, the Reviewers come in for their full ſhare; and he aims at them ſomething about *brazen-heads*, which may be very ſmart and clever, for aught that ſuch dull fellows may think to the contrary.

Art. 20. *Two Diſcourſes*. I. On the Sufficiency of the Scriptures, and the Right of private Judgment. 2. On the Doctrine of the Trinity. Both lately preached in the Country. By a Friend to Truth and Liberty. 8vo. 1 s. Evans, &c. 1771.

Theſe diſcourſes are declamatory, and, as is to be expected in ſo narrow a compaſs, (for they are ſhort,) rather ſuperficial. But they are, nevertheleſs, agreeably written; they ſhew the Author to be a man of ſenſe; and they may prove ſerviceable to numbers of Chriſtians, who have not leiſure or opportunity to enter into a more cloſe and particular examination of the important ſubjects on which they treat.

The firſt diſcourſe is founded on *Rom*. i. 16. *I am not aſhamed of the goſpel of Chriſt*, &c. Among other things the preacher propoſes the

the following questions; 'While at the head of protestantism stand the sufficiency of the holy Scriptures, and the right of private judgment in religious matters: while these dignify our church with the name of Christian, and declare our members consistent with their pretensions to a separation from the power and influence of the Roman pontiff: while these are our boast and our glory, how is it to be lamented that we do not atchieve the deed? While a further reformation is acknowledged to be necessary, why do we not proceed to the arduous, but great and glorious, the immortal undertaking, the reducing an ecclesiastical establishment nearer to the standard of Scripture, that inexhaustible fountain, from whence flow living waters? As we most happily differ from the Romanists, in having the bible open to all, why do we yet conform to them, in receiving the addition of human explications?'

In the second discourse, the subject of which is, the doctrine of the trinity, we meet with the following passage:

'After all that has been said on this subject within the last 1400 years, notwithstanding the number of pages, I may say the thousands of volumes which have been written, we remain just where we were: we are not one jot wiser, except the knowledge of our ignorance be called wisdom. All parties have alternatively been called heretics; numbers of both have been led martyrs to the stake, when their adversaries had the sanction of the sovereign magistrate. Almost every Christian virtue hath been violated to establish *it*. Charity, patience, perseverance, humanity and benevolence, brotherly-love and good-will towards all on whom the Almighty hath stamped the figure of man, have been turned adrift, and made way for the distinguishing characteristics of furies, rather than of rational beings. "The armour of hell hath," in this case most apparently, "been worn in the cause of heaven." By these means, Christianity hath greatly suffered from the intemperate zeal of mistaken men, if not of venal and interested bigots. Bigotry ever turns a deaf ear to truth; she is active on the side of hell; scarce knowing why she sells herself to the blinded mercenaries of the prince of darkness. Though she cannot convince, she will continue to impose. Indulgent Heaven hath, however, I trust, banished her these kingdoms, though too apparent that indifference hath succeeded her. It is moderation and candour which must ultimately guide us to the glorious mean.'

Art. 21. *The leading Sentiments of the People called Quakers examined, as they are stated in Mr. Robert Barclay's Apology*: with an Answer to what Mr. Phipps has advanced for the Defence of them, in his Observations upon an Epistle to the Author of a Letter to Dr. Formey. By S. Newton, of Norwich. 8vo. 3 s. sewed. Dilly. 1771.

The Writer of this controversial tract was also the Writer of the epistle mentioned in the title-page. The principal motive for the present publication appears to have been, to make a reply to Mr. Phipps, whom our Author considers as an unfair disputant, and charges him with writing frequently in a manner unbecoming the gentleman or the Christian.

In his introduction Mr. Newton observes, that, 'In this age, when enthusiasm and deism, the two extremes, (which, it has often been

been remarked, ſometimes meet in the ſame center) greatly abound; it cannot be thought, with any juſtice, an odious undertaking, though it be not ſo well executed, to endeavour to ſet forth the important difference, which, I apprehend, there is between the ſimple religion of Jeſus and his apoſtles, and that of Robert Barclay and his zealous followers. For if I am miſtaken, Barclay's ſcheme will not be injured, as he has many *fond* votaries, who want neither inclination nor ability to defend him: If upon an examination it ſhould appear I have, upon the whole, the Bible, reaſon, and experience, on my ſide, then not only the Quaker's ſyſtem will be affected, but, that of all other enthuſiaſts, which is founded upon a ſuppoſed ſaving influence of the holy Spirit, without the inſtrumentality of Scripture.'

This Author confines himſelf principally to what he conſiders as the leading ſentiments of the Quakers, ſuch as the *inward call*, *the light within*, &c. and does not conſider other particular tenets and practices by which they are diſtinguiſhed. He ſpeaks of them, in the general, in a handſome and honourable manner, at the ſame time that he endeavours to ſhew the falſity or dangerous tendency of their principles. In one part of his work he labours to prove that the doctrine of election, and reprobation or preterition, is inſeparably connected with the Quakers ſyſtem, and theſe doctrines, from the charge of holding which Mr. Phipps would defend his party, our Author himſelf ſeems in ſome ſenſe inclined to receive and maintain. It is ſufficient for us to add, that, as to the particular points of diſpute which are here conſidered, he appears to have, without doubt, the advantage of his antagoniſt.

Art. 22. *Sermons for the Uſe of Families.* Vol. II. By William Enfield. 12mo. 3 s. 6 d. bound. Johnſon. 1771.

The character of theſe ſermons may be inferred from the account we have given of the preceding volume, ſee Review, vol. xxxix. p. 364. The ſame liberality of ſentiment, and eaſy flow of language, will recommend both, to readers who, to a pious diſpoſition, have added a taſte for elegance in religious compoſitions.

POLITICAL.

Art. 23. *A Letter to the Right Hon. Braſs Croſby, Eſq; Lord-Mayor of the City of London*, reſpecting the preſent high Price of Proviſions. 8vo. 6 d. Payne.

The Writer attempts to aſcertain the true cauſes of the evil here complained of, and to point out the only probable means of removing it. He aſcribes the high price of proviſions to the exorbitant demands of luxury, to which the produce of the country, he ſuppoſes, is by no means equal. He, therefore, thinks that the rich ought to conſume leſs, in order that the prices might fall, and the poor, conſequently, be able to procure a greater ſhare than, at preſent, falls to their lot. He has ſome juſt remarks, and offers ſeveral good hints; but the ſubject is too nice, difficult, and important, to be duly and ſatisfactorily diſcuſſed in a common ſix penny pamphlet.

Art. 24. *Thoughts on our Acquiſitions in the Eaſt-Indies*; particularly reſpecting Bengal. 8vo. 1 s. Becket. 1771.

The intention of this publication is to moderate that ſyſtem of deſpotiſm, which has prevailed for ſome time in the adminiſtration of the affairs of our Eaſt India Company. The plan, which the A

t

thor proposes for this end, appears to be plausible, and is certainly worthy of attention.

Art. 25. *The National Mirror.* Being a Series of Essays on the most important Concerns, but particularly those of the East-India Company. 8vo. 2s. Richardson and Urquhart, &c. 1771.

The following account of this re-publication is extracted from the Editor's previous address to the public:

'These papers,' he tells us, 'were first published separately in the Gazetteer, in the year 1768-9.——The matters of which they treat, are undoubtedly of great consequence, being a very important branch of our national trade, and the preservation and administration of such acquired territories, as would be sufficient to constitute a great kingdom.

'The Author has taken much pains to expose the ignorance and guilt of some past administrations, the venality and subserviency of parliaments, and the frauds and corruptions of East-India Directors, in the many powers of abuse which have been granted on one side, and acquired on the other: insomuch that the constitution has been repeatedly violated; the rights of the people invaded, or sacrificed; the interest of the kingdom mistaken, or betrayed; and, in fine, that property of the state injuriously bargained for, which probably may soon be endangered by the inabilities, or worse, of those who have acquired a power to mismanage it. He likewise points out many imperfections in the constitution of the Company, and also various abuses which have been practised; (as well as others that may rationally be expected,) which, in their consequences, have already produced, and naturally must continue to produce, fatal effects to those countries, as they likewise may do to this kingdom, if adequate remedies be not timely discovered and applied.'

These are, undoubtedly, important matters; and, accordingly, they are here treated in no slight or superficial manner. The Author, however, writes with too much heat and acrimony. Whether this proceeds merely from the laudable principle of genuine public spirit, or from secret motives of private resentment, is best known to himself; but we hope the latter is not the case. He expresses himself, indeed, like a most bitter and exasperated enemy to the Company: strenuously contending that the conquered territories in India, are the property of the crown, and that government should apply their large revenues toward the reduction of our taxes, and the discharge of our enormous national debt.—What he urges, on this capital point, certainly deserves the attention of the public——at the same time that the judicious Reader will make proper allowances for the want of temper in an Author who, however, discovers no want of knowledge.

MEDICAL.

Art. 26. *Some Remarks on Dr. Cadogan's Dissertation on the Gout,* &c. 8vo. 6d. Baldwin.

Who does not know that there are spots in the sun? The sun is, nevertheless, a most glorious luminary!

DRAMATIC.

DRAMATIC.

Art. 27. *The Songs, Choruſes, and ſerious Dialogue,* of the Maſque called, *The Inſtitution of the Garter; or, Arthur's Round Table Reſtored.* 8vo. 6 d. Becket.

From this out-line, people who ſtay at home will have but a faint idea of the finiſhed picture as exhibited at Drury-lane theatre.

In the tranſcript, however, here given, of the *words* of this entertainment, we meet with ſome pleaſing paſſages; and one, in particular, which ought to be inſcribed in golden capitals over the entrance of St. George's Hall; *viz.*

" —— DIGNITIES AND TITLES, WHEN MISPLAC'D
UPON THE VICIOUS, THE CORRUPT, AND VILE,
LIKE PRINCELY VIRGINS TO LOW PEASANTS MATCH'D,
DESCEND FROM THEIR NOBILITY, AND SOIL'D
BY BASE ALLIANCE, NOT THEIR PRIDE ALONE
AND NATIVE SPLENDOR LOSE, BUT SHAME RETORT
EV'N ON THE SACRED THRONE, FROM WHENCE THEY SPRUNG."

Thoſe who recollect ſome of the characters which have been honoured with the enſigns of the order here celebrated, will applaud the ſpirit of the man who could hazard a public recital of the above-quoted lines. Their author was the late ingenious Gilbert Weſt; from whoſe poem on the Inſtitution of the Garter, the greateſt part of this very agreeable Maſque is borrowed.

Art. 28. *The Fairy Prince:* A Maſque: As it is performed at the Theatre Royal in Covent-Garden. 8vo. 1 s. Becket.

This piece, though founded on the ſame occaſion with the entertainment mentioned in the preceding article, is very differently conſtructed; and both have conſiderable merit in their way.

As the Drury-lane Maſque is, for the moſt part, taken from a poem of Mr. Weſt's, ſo the compiler of this is chiefly obliged to Ben Johnſon. He alſo acknowledges himſelf indebted to Shakeſpeare, Dryden, and the ſame Mr. Weſt.

The ſpirit of dramatic amuſement would certainly become languid without the frequent aid of novelty: new compoſitions are as neceſſary in theatrical entertainments, as new faſhions in trade: and as our modern dramas (eſpecially thoſe of the laſt three or four winters) are, for the generality, but indifferent performances, the managers are, conſequently, forced to acquieſce in the reigning and popular taſte for muſic's charms, and ſhewy exhibitions. The improved ſtate of the elegant arts among us, is extremely favourable to ſuch productions: and can we blame an audience for preferring good muſic to dull writing, and brilliant ſhews to unintereſting plays?—But ſo highly do we deem of the public taſte and diſcernment, that we have not the leaſt doubt, were another Shakeſpeare or Dryden to ariſe, that geniuſes like theirs would ſoon baniſh pantomime and pageantry from the ſtage, and victoriouſly

" Chace the charms of ſound, the pomp of ſhow,
For uſeful mirth, and ſalutary woe."

Prologue, ſpoken by Mr. Garrick, at the opening the theatre in Drury-lane, 1747.

POETICAL.

POETICAL.

Art. 29. *An Essay on Education*; a Poem. In two Parts. I. The Pedant. II. The Preceptor. By S. Johnson. 4to. 2 s. 6 d. Baldwin. 1771.

For me, the meanest of the flogging train,
Destin'd for life to drag this galling chain,
Whom no gay prospect of preferment courts,
Nor better view of golden showers supports,
Oh, grant me patience, heaven!——

Thus saith the worthy Author, and we, his brethren of the flogging train, heartily join him in the last clause of his prayer.

Art. 30. *Religion*; a Poem. By G. Mennell, Lieutenant of his Majesty's Ship Namur. 4to. 1 s. Printed for the Author.

Fighting, not writing, is this gentleman's business; what business, therefore, has he with poetry? Marine affairs, we are informed, he *does* understand, and is a very good officer. Let that praise fill the measure of his ambition; especially as we are told, also, by an undoubted judge both of poetry and of human nature, that

"*One* science only will one genius fit."

Art. 31. *The Candid Inquisitor*; *or, Mock Patriotism Displayed*; a Poem. By Oliver James Murray. 4to. 1 s. 6 d. Shatwell.

From this furious attack on the patriots we learn that Oliver James Murray is a young man, and that this poem is his 'first essay.'—For the young man's sake, as well as our own, we heartily wish it may be his last.

Art. 32. *A familiar Epistle from a Student of the Middle Temple, to his Friend in Dublin.* Written in the Year 1759. 4to. 2 s. 6 d. Davies. 1771.

This Epistle is written in an easy and not very inelegant style of poetry. But it is too local to afford general entertainment, and too personal to be generally interesting.

Art. 33. *Fables, Odes, and Miscellaneous Poems.* By Elizabeth Fell, of Saffron Waldon. 8vo. 3 s. bound. Robson. 1771.

We wage no war with women.

MATHEMATICAL.

Art. 34. *The Radix*: A new Way of making Logarithms. In five Problems. By Robert Flower. 4to. 3 s. sewed. Beecroft. 1771.

The name of Lord Neper is justly celebrated in the history of mathematical science, for his admirable invention of logarithms. It is well known, that these artificial numbers are of the greatest use in all mathematical calculations, as they save both time and labour, and prevent many mistakes, incident to the tedious operations of multiplication and division: but the construction of these numbers is much more difficult and laborious than their application. Many attempts have been made to facilitate this work; and the Author of the *Radix* apprehends, that the method he proposes, is the shortest and easiest of any, at present known, for finding logarithms from numbers, and numbers from logarithms, to twenty places of figures. Such exactness may serve very well to amuse those who have leisure, but we are of opinion, that it is hardly necessary in any case, which may

may ordinarily occur. If any one, however, will take the pains to investigate the logarithm of any number in the way here proposed, and by any of the common methods, he will find, that the latter have greatly the advantage, both in certainty and expedition.

To explain the Author's principles and practice at large, would require more room than we can allow to this article. It is but justice to acknowledge, that the work before us is the result of ingenuity, and of prodigious labour; and that every new attempt on a subject of such unquestionable importance as the construction of logarithms, is, in some degree, laudable and meritorious.

NATURAL HISTORY.

Art. 35. *Outlines of the Natural History of Great Britain and Ireland:* Containing a systematic Arrangement, and concise Description of all the Animals, Vegetables, and Fossils, which have been hitherto discovered in these Kingdoms. By John Berkenhout, M. D. In three Volumes. Vol. III. *Comprehending the Fossil Kingdom.* 8vo. 2 s. 6 d. Boards. Elmsley.

The ingenious and learned Dr. Berkenhout has now finished the outlines of Natural History, as he modestly, yet not improperly, styles this work. For the former volumes, see Review for May 1769, and for July 1770.

This compilement will certainly prove very useful to young persons who are engaged in the pleasing pursuit of natural knowledge.

MISCELLANEOUS.

Art. 36. *The History of a Voyage to the Malouine (or Falkland) Islands,* in 1763 and 1764, under the Command of M. de Bougainville, in order to form a Settlement there; and of two Voyages to the Streights of Magellan, with an Account of the *Patagonians.* Translated from Dom Pernety's Historical Journal, written in French. Illustrated with Copper-plates. 4to. 15 s. sewed. Jefferys. 1771.

In the Appendix to our 42d vol. the Reader will find some account of Dom Pernety's work, as a foreign article; to which we now refer: and shall only observe that the English Editor has judiciously omitted the detail of ordinary occurrences which are common to every voyage; retaining whatever seemed in any view peculiar to this expedition. In respect to the plates, some alterations and additions have been made. A general chart, shewing the situation of Falkland's Islands in the Southern Ocean, which was not given in the original, is here inserted. Plans of the islands of St. Catherine, and of Buenos Ayres, are also added; and the birds, fish, &c. are classed in their proper order.

Art. 37. *Reflexions sur le Gouvernement des Femmes.* Par le Colonel Chevalier De Champigny. *A Londres.* 8vo. 3 s. 6 d. sewed. 1770.

We have here none of those reflexions that would occur to a philosopher, when he looks into history, considers the capacity of women for political affairs, and reviews the influence they have had in different ages and nations. The Chevalier has more gallantry than wisdom; and if his book finds any readers, it must be among fops, fine ladies, and pretty gentlemen.

Art.

Art. 38. *An Oration pronounced by Order of her Imperial Majesty, at the Tomb of Peter the Great, in the Cathedral of Petersburgh.* By Platon, Archbishop of Twer. 4to. 1 s. Oxford. 1771. Sold by Wilkie in London.

There is not perhaps in history a finer subject for panegyric than the character and actions of the Emperor Peter the Great. In the common course of human affairs, civilization and knowledge make their way among nations by slow and almost imperceptible degrees; but this wonderful man, without any aid from education or science, and by the mere force of his genius, taught refinement and the arts to an immense multitude of savages. By operations, of which the consequences were immediate, he made a country, involved in barbarism, to rise into importance. Every thing gave way to his efforts. He seemed, by a kind of magical influence, to create fleets, to discipline armies, and to diffuse over an extensive empire, the advantages of commerce, and the lights of literature.

In the performance before us, the orator has not been perfectly able to do justice to his hero. He has omitted many of the topics, on which he ought chiefly to have insisted; and he has not had the art to give dignity and value to those which he has selected. He mistakes pomp for eloquence; and possesses no great degree of penetration or genius.

Art. 39. *The History of the English Language*; deduced from its Origin, and traced through its different Stages and Revolutions: In which its Excellence and Superiority over the other European Tongues are evidently demonstrated, as well as the Source of those Revolutions: Being very interesting for Persons ignorant of the Infant State of their own Country and those Revolutions; and for the Benefit of those who aspire to the perfect Knowledge of their Mother Tongue. By V. J. Peyton, Author of the Elements of the English Language. 8vo. 1 s. Bladon. 1771.

Mr. Peyton has unfortunately stumbled on a Subject, with which he is very little acquainted. He presents us, of consequence, with mean, desultory, and uninteresting observations. The labours of Lloyd, and of Hicks; of Elstob, Somner, and Bullet, offered to him an ample share of rich materials; but he does not seem to have ever heard of these writers. As we can see nothing in this performance but imperfection, it is impossible for us to speak of it with that tenderness for the Author, which we could wish to shew to every writer, who is in any degree qualified to do justice to the subject which he undertakes to treat upon; however mistaken he may be, in too fondly estimating his own abilities.

Art. 40. *An Essay on the Revolutions of Literature.* Translated from the Italian of Sig. Carlo Denina, Professor of Eloquence and Belles Lettres in the University of Turin. By John Murdoch. 12mo. 3 s. sewed. Cadell.

Nothing can be more interesting to men of letters than the History of Literature: and though every learned man must, from the course of his studies, necessarily become acquainted with the greatest part of that history, yet it must be both useful and agreeable to see it drawn up in a regular form. Such is the work before us, wherein brevity appears to be the greatest fault. Sig. Denina, a man of taste

7 and

and extenſive erudition, has given a ſhort account of the revolutions of literature, from the earlieſt to the preſent times, with diſtinct views of the progreſs of letters in Italy, Spain, France, England, and Scotland. But to do all this effectually in 300 12mo pages was impoſſible. Had the Author extended his work to three ſuch volumes, it would have been infinitely more uſeful, and not ſurely too hard a reading-taſk, even to the mere polite ſcholar. We have lately given a ſufficient ſpecimen of this Writer's abilities, in our account of his *Revolutions of Italy*: ſee Appendix to Review, vol. xliii. and likewiſe our Number for February laſt.

Art. 41. *A Letter to John Wilkes*, Eſq; Sheriff of London and Middleſex; in which the Extortion and Oppreſſion of Sheriff's Officers, with many other alarming Abuſes, are exemplified and detected; and a Remedy propoſed: The infamous Practice of Attornies clearly pointed out; and many other real Grievances which the common People have long groaned under without Relief, &c. &c. By Robert Holloway, Gent. of Gray's Inn. 8vo. 1 s. Bladon.

In a country where the laws are ſo perfect, it is ſhameful that the execution of them ſhould be attended with abuſe and oppreſſion. The evils here complained of, while they are in the higheſt degree illegal, imply a cruelty and wantonneſs which reflect a diſgrace on humanity: the patriotic Sheriff, therefore, to whom this performance is addreſſed, will, doubtleſs, exert himſelf in order to remedy ſuch deteſtable grievances. In doing ſo, he will not only prove himſelf a friend to his country, but to human nature.

Art. 42. A *compendious* and *perfect* Accidence of the French Tongue for the Improvement of Engliſh Proficients in that univerſal Language. 12mo. 1 s. Ridley. 1771.

This treatiſe is ſufficiently *compendious*, and may have its uſe; though we cannot allow that it exhibits a very *perfect* Accidence of the French tongue. Nor can we conceive the ſtrict propriety of the term *universal*, when applied to that particular language.

Art. 43. *An eaſy, comprehenſive, and familiar French Grammar*; with a Spelling book prefixed. The whole compoſed agreeable to the Sentiments of Reſtaut, Author of the Rational French Grammar, univerſally uſed in France, of Locke on Education, and of Dr. Watts on Grammar: in pure natural French, with all the modern Improvements; likewiſe the uſeleſs Accents and Letters are laid aſide. With a Preface, containing the beſt Method of teaching or learning the French Language. For the Uſe of Schools. By G. Maſſon. 12mo. 2 s. bound. Nourſe. 1771.

We have here a very laudable attempt to accommodate the knowledge of the French grammar to pupils of the meaneſt underſtanding, and in the loweſt claſſes.

Art. 44. *A Treatiſe on the Copal Oil Varniſh*; or, what in France is called *Vernis Martin*. Together with the undoubted Receipt for making that excellent Varniſh, and the Method of laying it on Wood, Metal, or *Papier Machée*, and highly poliſhing the ſame. 8vo. 5 s. (a pamphlet of 38 pages.) Crowder, &c.

Thoſe only who have prepared the elegant *Vernis Martin* according to the method here preſcribed, can pronounce with certainty of the genuineneſs of this anonymous receipt. To us, however, it appears to deserve the public attention. The Author declares that he purchased the secret at an high price; but the question will be, *Who is the Author?*—He may, however, have sufficient reasons for suppressing his name; which, after all (in a matter of this sort) is not indispensably requisite. If he has given to the public the real process, the public is, undoubtedly, obliged to him: but, if his receipt is not true, the fallacy will be soon detected, by those who make trial of it. In the mean time, we scruple not to declare, that we have no suspicion with regard to the Author's veracity; as he really expresses himself like an honest man, who only means to further the progress of the fine arts in his own country. At the close of his pamphlet, he makes some observations on the impositions of coachmakers, in the article of painting, &c. which seem to merit the notice of those who chuse to be at any considerable expence in the decoration of their equipages, and who wish to have the work executed with true taste and elegance, by real artists, and not by wretched hands, employed at the pitiful rate of five shillings a-day.

SERMONS.

I. At the Consecration of St. Aubyne's Chapel, Plymouth Dock, Sept. 17, 1771. By Edward Bridges Blacket, LL. D. Rector of Stoke-Demerel, Devon. 6 d. Nicoll.

II. At the Consecration of the Hon. and Rev. Father in God Brownlow Lord Bishop of Litchfield and Coventry, Sept. 8, 1771. By John Lynch, LL. D. Rector of Adisham, in Kent. 6 d. White.

III. Before the Governors of the Ratcliff Infirmary, at St. Mary's, Oxford, July 3, 1771. By Robert Lord Bishop of Oxford. To which is annexed, an Account of the Establishment of the Infirmary. Dodsley, &c.

IV. At St. Nicholas's Church, at Newcastle upon Tyne, July 27, 1771, before the Governors of the Infirmary. By John Rotheram, M. A. Rector of Houghton le-Spring. Sold for the Benefit of the Charity. 1 s. Robson, &c.

V. *The Glory of the second Temple superior to that of the first*; or, the Edification of Christian Societies promoted: *Two* Sermons at the first Opening of a new Meeting house in Mare-street, Hackney, Oct. 13, 1771. By Samuel Palmer 6 d. Buckland.

VI. Before the Lord Mayor and Court of Aldermen of the City of London, at St. Laurence, Sept. 28, 1771. By the Rev. Robert Evans, M. A. 1 s. Almon.

VII. On the Death of Dr. John Gill. By Samuel Stennet, D. D. With Mr. Wallin's Address at the Interment. 1 s. Keith.

VIII. On the Death of Mrs. Poole, Mr. Poole, Mrs. Martha Poole, and Master Poole, who all died in the space of five Days; preached at the Old Jewry, Oct. 27. 1771. By N. White. 6 d. Buckland.

CORRESPONDENCE.

N. V. is assured that Whitaker's valuable History of Manchester is not '*forgotten*,' although the account of it has been unavoidably delayed. We hope it will soon appear in our Review.

ERRATUM.

In the Review for *September*, p. 164, l. 24. for 13th century, read 11th century.

THE

MONTHLY REVIEW,

For DECEMBER, 1771.

ART. I. *The Nature and Institution of Government; containing an Account of the Feudal and English Policy.* By William Smith, M.D. 8vo. 2 Vols. 12 s. bound. Owen. 1771.

IN the reign of the elder James, it was first discovered that monarchy was of divine institution, and that the subject owes to the prince the most unlimited and unreserved obedience. These detestable doctrines were agreeable to monarchs who aimed at despotism; and the clergy, during the administration of James, and still more during that of his unfortunate successor *, were zealous to inculcate them. For this purpose the scriptures were tortured, laws were misinterpreted, and records were falsified. The Revolution brought along with it more enlarged sentiments. The nature and ends of civil government had been inquired into, and were understood; our constitution was properly defined; the limits of the regal prerogatives were ascertained; and the rights of the subject were confirmed and established. While the prince directs himself by the laws, the people are engaged to obey and to respect him; but when he insolently presumes to disregard their force, it is their duty

* About the beginning of Charles's reign, Dr. Manwaring maintained from the pulpit, 'That the king was not bound by the laws of the land, not to impose taxes or subsidies without the consent of parliament, and that when they were so imposed, the subjects were obliged in conscience, and upon pain of damnation, to pay them; which if they refused to do, they were guilty of disloyalty and rebellion.' About the same time a sermon by Dr. Sibthorp was licensed by Dr. Laud, which affirmed, 'That it was the king alone that made the laws, and that nothing could excuse from an active obedience to his commands, but what is against the law of God and Nature: and that kings had power to lay pole-money upon their subjects heads.' See Bibl. Polit. Dial. 1.

to resist his authority. An Englishman is a part of the legislature of his country, and disdains to bow to a master.

But, notwithstanding the abhorrence into which the doctrines of passive obedience, and the divine right of kings have deservedly fallen, our Author has ventured to pronounce their panegyric. He presses upon his readers, with a petulant obstinacy, arguments and reasonings that confute themselves. With the mind and the sentiments of a slave, he would degrade others to the same situation. Such is his rage for kinghood, that he even seeks for it in the wilds of America! Among men, who are scarcely removed from the state of freedom and of nature, he finds chains and despotism. The chieftain, who rises to distinction by his valour or his wisdom, and who exercises a precarious jurisdiction over his tribe, he converts into a sovereign, appointed by the Deity, and invested with an authority, which it is not lawful to controul. The members of a free association, where the individual goes in arms to give his voice in the senate, he considers as subject to the caprices of a tyrant.

The account which he has given of the feudal polity, is less exceptionable than his eulogium on royalty; but it has not merit sufficient to entitle it to approbation. The feudal arrangements, so favourable to liberty at one period, and so oppressive at another, form an object too complicated for the understanding of our Author. For, notwithstanding the masterly reflections, which several ingenious men have lately communicated to the public on this subject, he has not been able to exhibit a tolerably distinct and systematical idea of it.

In the observations he has made on the nature and history of the English parliament, he returns to his monarchical principles, and seems to have conceived an utter contempt for the testimony and informations of our most intelligent historians.

Destitute of every claim to recommendation and applause from his matter and his reflections, our Author has been no less unfortunate with regard to the manner in which he expresses himself. Without taste, capacity, or erudition, he has yet thought that he could enlighten and entertain the present age, and posterity.

But that our Readers may form for themselves some judgment of his merit, we shall present them with the following extracts from his performance:

' It may seem absurd, says he, to maintain that the fatherhood has not lost its right of governing, and that kings now are, as they were at the first planting and peopling of the world, the fathers of their people or kingdoms, since experience shews the contrary. It is true all kings are not the natural parents of of their subjects; yet all kings that now are, or ever were, either were the next heirs or usurpers of the right of those first progenitors, who were at first the natural parents of the whole people, and in their right succeed to the exercise of supreme power; for every man is by nature either a king or a subject. The obedience which all subjects pay to kings, is but paying that debt which is due to the supreme fatherhood; for the heirs, as lawful successors of the first progenitors, are not only lords of their children, but also of their brethren, and of all others that were subject to their fathers.

'If it please God, for the correction of the prince, or punishment of the people, to suffer the right heir to be removed and dispossessed, and another to be placed in his room, either by the factions of the nobility, or the rebellion of the people; in all such cases the judgment of God, who hath power to give and to take away kingdoms, is most just; yet the ministry of men, who execute God's judgments without commission, is sinful and damnable. God doth but use and turn men's unrighteous acts to the performance of his righteous decrees; and in such a case, the subjects' obedience is not due to the usurper, but to the lawful exiled king, who has a just title, and the other an unjust possession, which obliges him to repentance and restitution: and certainly no man can have a true right to what he is bound to restore; nor can others be obliged to maintain him in it. Good men indeed submit to a prosperous invasion as to torrents and inundations, when they cannot be resisted; but certainly it is a crime of the deepest dye for subjects to begin a war with their prince, and throw a nation into blood and confusion. And none can place himself on the throne of these kingdoms, when others who have a nearer relation to it by descent are living, without much blood and perjury: and I challenge any one to produce a precedent where the true heir hath been laid aside, where there was not a long chain of wickedness, perjury, rebellion, invasion, deposition, murder, slavery, and oppression: and kings set up by faction, without an hereditary title, never answered the people's expectations in the preservation of their laws and liberties.

'It is true, indeed, God may and can give kingdoms to whomsoever he will; I know it: he can make a new world on purpose for them, or take the forfeiture of the whole, and dispose of his own creation as he pleases; but then it must appear to be his will; and he must send a new revelation into the world, with such a high favoured prince, to every man that is to be his subject: and this extraordinary revelation ought to be as clear and as distinct as Abraham's was for the sacrificing his son; for it is as contrary to all the settled rules of right to dethrone a lawful king, as it is to destroy an only son: and yet the

the command was only intended as a trial of Abraham's obedience; neither would God suffer it, that there should be a precedent of an inhuman sacrifice in the world, though at his own bidding.

'It is not enough for an usurper to wrong a prince of his crown, but this must be hallowed by false prophets, and said to be done in God's name; and this proved by no better argument than Mahomet's miracle of success and settlement. If, therefore, a pretended prophet tells me that I am to own an usurper as God's choice, and by divine right, and therefore he is no usurper, I must needs answer, that the title is far fetched, and comes a great way; therefore I must desire to see some proof in point, and shall always call for miracles for what is said to come from heaven. Shall I believe that Mahomet was a true prophet by his miracle of success and settlement? No true Christian, I believe, will desire that; neither will any true Christian believe that usurpation is lawful government, or ought in conscience to be obeyed, though firmly settled: and it is a plain and undoubted usurpation, without manifest revelation from God, confirmed by miracles, to preclude any person of the royal family, much more the next heir, from succeeding to the crown, to whom alone God hath given it. And usurpation is of the devil, who is the father, promoter, assister, and supporter of it; and they are his agents and tools who are employed in it; and as they are all of one flock, so they will at last have one fold, even hell; which is the kingdom where rebellion reigns and rebels burn.

'The spirit of resistance is an unchristian spirit; it is so far from favouring of God, that it savours strongly of the devil, who fought against God; and as it would be an injury that such company in iniquity as rebels should be separated, I verily believe they will rest together. For if we ought to be subject for conscience' sake, and if our obligation is bound upon us by the hand of God himself, then we may very fairly infer, that both the doctrine and practice of resistance comes from the devil. If that may be truly accounted a devilish sin which opposes God's declared will with resolution and impudence, then, because rebellion against a lawful prince does so, we may well reckon it to come from the devil.

'Rebellion, and what it drives at, is a Pandora's box, fraught with all sort of evils to a nation, worse than plague, pestilence, and famine; it is so heinous a sin, so hateful in the sight of God and every good man, that it draws an odium upon those that are guilty of it that succeeding generations cannot wipe out. When I find God himself call it as the sin of *witchcraft*, which, like it, is seldom repented of; for me to speak against it, by endeavouring to aggravate the iniquity, would be of small purpose

pose to any ingenuous man; yet though hell itself will be its reward, it hath not wanted daring and knowing patrons, and it is very remarkable that few of them, very few rebels ever repent.

'Resistance against the supreme magistrate (under any lawful government) and that even to the wresting the sword out of his hands, and abolishing the fundamentals of the constitution, is, as I said before, according to the dictates of religion, a damnable sin; and though the adhering to this maxim should, in the course of human revolutions, involve the church and her members in manifold inconveniences, yet there is no help for it; these must be borne as well as we can, for Christianity is the doctrine of the Cross. Our duty obliges us to a firm reliance on the wisdom and goodness of his providence, however surprising some things may appear, when considered separately from the whole, or examined, or judged of by what falls only within our short view and narrow apprehension of things. On whom can we more wisely and safely rely, than on him who has infinite knowledge to guide, power to protect, and mercy to save? Therefore let us do our duty, for, in this particular, we can be at no loss to know it. I know, indeed, no commandments more positive than what our blessed Lord and his apostles have given for our obedience to kings, even to heathen kings; and the command is inforced by the most dreadful of all penalties, not imprisonment, not confiscation of goods, not death, but damnation: where there is a right in the supremacy, there obedience in inferiors becomes a duty; and where the supremacy is just, there subjection is necessary; therefore it is no hard matter to determine to whom it is that our subjection is due: and a revelation sent on purpose from heaven, and preaching from the clouds, in place of pulpits, cannot oblige us to be subjects to any usurper under that notion; because it is a notion of wrong, and God himself cannot make wrong to be right: and our Saviour hath forbid us to give assent to any other doctrine but what himself hath taught, even though it should be delivered by an angel, and sure one must forget all the Old and New Testament, and what is the foundation of both, even the law of moral and natural honesty, that approves of rebellion; and it is a manifest contradiction to suppose a government not rightful and lawful, and yet allegiance to be due to it; and if an angel was to come down from heaven and preach any other doctrine, if I believed that doctrine, I should think myself guilty of a greater transgression than that prophet who turned in, and did eat bread and drink water with his brother prophet, contrary to God's command.

'Shall such a wretch bid us swear to be faithful to an acknowledged wrong, and to be false to an acknowledged and

 unex-

unextinguished right? for a rightful title is as immoveable as the pillars of the earth, and an usurped crown is a stolen crown: it is the crown of blood; and that power which is purchased by crimes is seldom durable.'——

'If the king will pervert the great ends for which God made him king; if he will not act as becomes God's vicar; if he will obstruct or pervert the laws, and govern tyrannically, yet there is left no remedy to his subjects by the law but tears and prayers; for the laws imperial of this realm, of ancient date, have formerly declared the king to be free, unconditional, and independent sovereign, and exempted him from all action and force *.

'The reason why a king cannot be punished is, not because he is exempted from punishment, or doth not deserve it, but because there is no superior to judge him, but God alone to whom he is referred. If the king does any thing wrong, the subject is to beg for redress by petition, which if he will not hear, it is a sufficient penalty for him, that he is to expect punishment from the Lord.

'Among the many securities the subjects have, though they may not take arms against their sovereigns, this is none of the least, that God is the judge and governor of the world. Shall it be thought a sufficient restraint to the exorbitancy of a father's power over his children, that if he becomes unnatural, the earthly judge can both vindicate them and punish him, though children be not allowed, when they think fit, to beat and kill their father? And shall not the judgment and authority of God over princes be thought valuable and considerable, when he is more righteous, and more able to help the oppressed, than any other judge upon earth? If ever it be our misfortune to live under an unjust prince, we ought to embrace the temper of David's spirit, in his words concerning Saul, 1 Sam. xxvi. 10, 11.

'Many are ready to say, that it is a slavish and dangerous condition to be subject to the will of any one man, who is not subject to the laws; but such men consider not that the prerogative of a king is to be above the laws, for the good only of them who are under the laws, and to defend the people's liberties; and, indeed, the case of the subject would be desperately miserable without it.

---

* This bold assertion is ill supported by the following law of Edward the Confessor: Rex, quia vicarius summi regis est, ad hoc est constitutus, ut regnum terrenum, et populum domini, et super omnia sanctam veneretur ecclesiam ejus, et regat, et ab injuriosis defendat, et maleficos ab ea evellat, et destruat, et penitus disperdat. *Quod nisi fecerit, nec nomen regis in eo constabit, verum nomen regis perdit.*—See Wilkins, Leg. Angl. Sax. p. 200.

'Nay,

'Nay, some are so bold as to say, that to make a king by the standard of God's word, is to make the subjects slaves for conscience' sake; a hard saying! and I doubt whether such a censure can be excused from basphemy. It is a bold speech to condemn all the kings of Judah for tyrants, or to say all their subjects were slaves. Bracton tells us, "that all are under the king, and he under none but God only; if he offend, since no writ can go against him, the remedy is, by petitioning him to mend his fault; which if he shall not do, it will be punishment sufficient for him to expect God as a revenger: let none presume to search into his deeds, much less oppose him *." It is not indeed right for kings to do injury, but it is right for them to go unpunished by the people if they do it; and subjects must in all things obey him †, except the laws of God forbid it; for there is no other law but God's law to hinder their obedience.

'There are some that say, that the first invention and institution of laws was to bridle and moderate the over-great power of kings; but the truth is, laws were first devised for the ease of kings: a proof unanswerable for the superiority of princes above laws, seeing there were kings long before there were any laws.

'For a long time the word of a king was the only law; and that which gives the very being to a king, is the power to make laws: without this power he is but an equivocal king, and there is no sovereign majesty in him; and if the nature of laws be advisedly considered and weighed, the necessity of a prince's being above them will be manifest.

'We all know that a law is the command of a superior in power; for there cannot be laws without a supreme power to command or make them. In all governments that ever were, or can be, the supreme power, wherever it is lodged, is, and must be, uncontroulable and irresistible: that is a truth included in the notion of authority or power; so as, the one granted, the other follows as plainly as two and three make five. Government resistible is no government, and those who say the contrary are no more to be talked to than sceptics in philosophy. If any man finds us out such a kind of government, wherein the supreme power can be without being free from human laws, he should first teach us that; but if all sorts

* We could have wished that our Author had here cited the original words of Bracton; for that writer has expressed himself in very different terms, in the following passage: *Habet rex*, says he, *superiores in regno, comites et barones, qui apponuntur regi, ut si rex sine pœno regeret, pœnum sibi imponerent.* *Lib.* 2. *c.* 16.

† Them.

of

of popular governments that can be invented, cannot be one minute without an arbitrary power freed from all human laws, then we may safely infer the absolute necessity of an uncontroulable power lodged somewhere in the state. The laws, indeed, in any kind of government, in time of peace, may govern, and each magistrate may discharge his duty, and see the laws put in execution, without knowing where the supreme uncontroulable power is lodged; but immediately when that scene changes, and wars, rebellion, invasions, &c. take place of the quiet and peace which the kingdom enjoyed before, then they find a necessity to seek for and apply to the supreme, absolute, uncontroulable power for relief and direction. And, upon duly weighing the subject, you will be forced to confess, that it is impossible for any government to be in the world without any arbitrary power. It is not power except it be arbitrary. A legislative power cannot be without being absolved from human laws; neither can it be shewed how a king can have any power at all but an arbitrary power. The laws, as I said before, may govern and direct people in time of peace and quiet, when nothing opposes the execution of them; but these very laws can neither be made nor revoked but by a supreme uncontroulable power.'

There are but three subjects, in the opinion of our Author, that can properly engage the attention of a wise man. These are, government, physic, and religion; and having now delivered his sentiments upon each of them *, we should hope that he is no longer to contend for literary honours. He should, by this time, be fully convinced that an inclination to scribble is very different from genius; and he should forsake a pursuit in which nature never designed that he should be successful.

ART. II. *Interesting historical Events relative to the Provinces of Bengal, and the Empire of Indostan. With a seasonable Hint to the Directors of the East India Company. Also the Mythology and Cosmogony, Fasts and Festivals of the Gentoos: And a Dissertation on the Metempsychosis.* By J. Z. Holwell, Esq; Part III. 8vo. 3 s. 6 d. Becket and De Hondt. 1771.

MR. Holwell, if we remember right, appears, in his second volume of this work, to regard the Gentoo *Scriptures*, (as he terms the Shastah) as the most ancient writings in the world; at the same time that he professes himself a zealous subscriber to those writings which are received as sacred among christians; so far as they are pure and original. But he apprehends that the

* See our Review for September and October, 1768; for September and October, 1769; and for August, 1770.

Supreme

Supreme Being may in different methods, suitable to the various dispositions of mankind, have revealed his will to the different parts of this habitable globe. ' It is not becoming us, says he, to doubt, the authority and divinity of *any original religious system*, unless it *evidently* is repugnant to the idea of a just and omnipotent God.'

This third part of his work consists of his dissertation on the *Metempsychosis*, the notion of which he rather thinks the *Egyptians* obtained from the *Chartah Bhade Shastah* of Indostan, than that the inhabitants of this country, obtained it from the *Egyptians*. He hopes to prove that this doctrine of the *Bramins* ' is not repugnant to the doctrines of christianity.' For the more orderly discussion of his subject, he reduces it under five general heads, as agreeable to the essential parts of the doctrine promulged by *Bramah*, whom he calls the great legislator, prince, and high-priest of the Gentoos: This *prophet and divine legislator*, as he elsewhere terms him, ' taught, he says, not only the *four great fundamentals*, of the unity of the Godhead, his providence, the immortality of the soul, and a future state of rewards and punishments, but also every other divine and *primitive truth*, necessary for man's knowledge in his present state of miserable existence; and these he taught, not *as mysteries* confined to a *select few*, but as public religious tenets known and received as such by *all*: And so forcible and efficacious was the influence of these doctrines upon the people, that they strictly adhered to them, and kept them inviolate for the space of one thousand years, and until they were perverted by their own priests, and led to new modes of worship.'

The general heads into which our author divides his essays are: I. The existence of angelic beings. Their fall. Their expulsion from the heavenly regions. Their punishments. II. The universe formed by God, for the residence, and imprisonment of the apostate angels. III. Mortal organised bodies formed for their more immediate, or closer confinement. Their transmigrations through those mortal forms. The human form their chief state of probation. IV. Liberty given to the apostate angels to pervade the universe. Permission given to the faithful angelic beings to counteract them. V. The seven regions of purification, wherein the fallen angels cease from their mortal transmigrations. The dissolution of the universe.

From the above particulars collectively considered, Mr. Holwell forms one general conclusion as the basis, he says, of this ancient doctrine of the Metempsychosis, ' viz. *That the souls or spirits, of every human or other organised mortal body, inhabiting this globe, and all the regions of the material universe, are precisely the remainder of the unpurified angels, who fell from their obedience in heaven, and that still stand out in contempt of their Creator.*'

Under

Under the first head of his division, we have in one place, the following remarks: 'As the gospel dispensation is allowed by our most learned divines, to be *founded upon the angelic fall*, great is the degree of veneration, which every *Christian* owes to the *Gentoo scriptures*, which taught minutely circumstances of that fall, more than three thousand years *a priori*.—How can this gospel dispensation, which *so nearly affects man*, be said with any propriety to be founded upon the *angelic fall?*—unless there is a nearer relation between man and angel, than appears to have been hitherto imagined or adverted to by the professors of christianity?—This (otherwise) incomprehensible difficulty is solved only by the doctrine of the Bramins, which teaches, that the apostate angelic and human souls are one and the same spirit; nor can we upon any other rational principle conceive how the gospel dispensation can be founded upon the angelic fall.'

Under the third general division, this writer labours to reconcile the narration which *Moses* gives of the creation and fall of man, with the doctrine of *Bramah*. He regards the relation given by Moses as an allegory, *typical of the angelical fall*, and in analising this allegory, he thinks, 'that it affords the fullest confirmation of the Bramanical doctrines of the creation of man; that man can be no other than the apostate Angels; and that the Metempsychosis is a well founded truth, necessarily resulting from these premises;—and, farther, that Moses was well acquainted with those doctrines; nay, that it is more than probable that he himself was the very identical spirit, selected and deputed in an earlier age, to deliver those truths free from allegory, under the style and title of *Bramah*.'

Upon admitting the doctrine of the Metempsychosis, we are told, the state and sufferings of the brute creation, which on any other hypothesis are utterly inexplicable, no longer remains a matter of difficulty, nor incompatible with divine justice. From hence the author is led to take notice of the practice which prevails, *not only to murder but to eat these animal beings*. The rise of such a practice, which, instructed by *Bramah*, he deems so iniquitous and cruel, he attributes to the machinations of *Moisasoor* or Satan, who having had experience that the angelic spirits in their superior pre-existent state, had not been proof against his artful seductions, prevailed with those who presided in the ceremonies of religion, to persuade the people to sanctify the murder of these creatures, by offering them up in sacrifice; that the priests at length tasted and rioted upon these sacrifices; and the 'laity observing how their priests *piously devoured them*, began to demur against supplying them with victims, unless they also came in for a share; which at last they obtained.—And thus, adds he, in process of time, both priests and laity, killed and ate the brute creation in common, without even the *pretence* of of religious motives, or indeed any principle at all; a point which Satan foresaw they would in the end arrive at.'

While considering this practice, so opposite, he observes, to the positive injunctions delivered by the mouth and scriptures of Bramah, our author in the rough overflow of his humour, falls into the following curious reflection: 'Let us not, however, in our abundant zeal for the brute creation, be wanting in our due applause to the amazing and unaccountable *moderation* and forbearance of man, in that he has not in *Europe* yet arrived to what most certainly must be the highest perfection of good eating, *the flesh of his own species*; which from the nature of its regimen, and the repletion of animal salts and juices, must yield a much more exalted flavour, and higher enjoyment, than any other kind of *brutal flesh* can possibly afford.' Farther he adds, 'Man's abstinence from this *supreme indulgence* is the more to be honoured, and the more wonderful, as he is not without precedents for the practice, on the authentic records of *America* and other *savage nations*; besides his virtue shines brighter in this great *self-denial*, when he may with propriety urge very cogent *political* reasons that would fully justify his transplanting that *luscious delicacy* and fashion into *Europe*, to wit, the *increasing scarcity* and *high price* of all animal food, both which evils would be effectually and speedily averted from us, by the project of—KILLING AND EATING THE CONSUMERS; from which practice, the two great population of the human species would also be prevented.' Our Author, in this passage, has Dr. *Swift* in his eye, but he professes, that where *Swift* was ludicrous, he is himself quite serious!

This writer is a professed Unitarian; but when speaking of what he calls *primitive truths* which had forcibly been impressed on the mind of man, in the beginning, he adds, 'one of the most important was, the notion of *three prime created celestial beings, either confounded with, or exclusive of and subordinate to the Deity*; *thus the Bramins* have their *Birmah, Bistnoo, and Sieb*; the *Persians* their *Oromazes*, *Mythra*, and *Mythras*; the *Egyptians* their *Osyris*, *Isis*, and *Orus*; the ancient *Arabs* their *Allat*, *Al. Uzza*, and *Manah*, or the Goddesses; the *Phœnicians* and *Tyrians*, their *Belus*, *Urania*, and *Adonis*; the *Greeks* and *Romans* their *Jupiter*, *Olympus*, *Minerva*, and *Apollo*; the *Christians* their *Father*, *Son*, and *Holy Ghost*; the *American's* their *Otkon*, *Messou*, and *Atahauta*, &c. &c.' And we doubt not, he adds, 'but a similar doctrine might be traced among all the different nations of the earth, had we authentic records of their primitive, religious institutes; it was a principle adopted by all the ancient western world, probably introduced by the *Phœnecians*, and confirmed to them by the *Romans*.—To a notion so universal in the first times, we think ourselves warranted in giving the

the title of a primitive truth; which must have had unerring fact, and a divine revelation for its source and foundation, as well as the other primitive truths, of the rebellion, fall and punishment of part of the angelic host, &c.—And that other *great truth*, the necessity of a mediator or mediators, employed either in imploring the divine mercy in behalf of the delinquent angels, or in combating or counteracting the wiles and influence of the arch apostate, and his prime adherents;—hence the *Birmah* of the *Bramins*; the *Mythras* of the *Persians*; the *Orus* of the *Egyptians*; and the *Messiah* of the *Christians*.'

We shall here close our extracts from this extraordinary work, which some of its readers will probably be inclined to class with the Reveries of Jacob Behmen and his followers.

ART. III. *A New Geographical, Historical, and Commercial Grammar, and present State of the several Kingdoms of the World. With a Table of the Coins of all Nations, and their Value in English Money.* By William Guthrie, Esq. Illustrated with a new and correct Set of Maps, engraved by Mr. Kitchin, Geographer. The Astronomical Part by James Ferguson, F. R. S. 8vo. 6s. * Knox. 1771.

IT is remarkable that, in a country where commerce and navigation have been cultivated with the greatest success, the study of geography, which is so intimately connected with them, has yet, till of late, been almost wholly neglected. But it would seem that the ambition of our men of letters to distinguish themselves by invention and discovery has, in general, rendered them averse from ascertaining the advances of knowledge in the different branches of literature. They enjoyed their acquisitions, and thought not of marking the steps by which they attained them. It appeared to them a drudgery, and a prostitution of their talents to explain the first elements of science; and, in a kingdom where education is not a principal object of public concern, this task, though important and difficult, became the province of illiterate teachers, and men of low and inferior capacity.

We must, however, in some degree, exempt the present performance from the general censure too justly applicable to our elementary treatises. It is, without doubt, the completest book of the kind which has hitherto been offered to the public, and on that account is worthy of encouragement. In the descriptions here given of the different quarters of the globe, our Author is tolerably accurate, and very comprehensive; and to

---

* Beside the edition of this work, in one volume, there is another edition, which we deem the most valuable, printed on a larger type, in two volumes, with ten additional whole-sheet maps, by Kitchin, price 12 s. The same, also, with the maps coloured, price 14 s.

these

these he has added, a compendious, and not uninteresting, detail of their history. Nor has he always confined his attention to modern times. His researches frequently penetrate into the remote ages of antiquity. The maps, with which his work is illustrated, will, we apprehend, afford general satisfaction. In the style and composition Mr. G. appears to have been careless and negligent; and he frequently adopts the language of those writers from whom he has borrowed his materials. Hence his book is full of inequalities, which will too obviously appear in the perusal; but, though it is destitute of unity, and is not altogether entitled to the praise of elegance, it is, notwithstanding, sufficiently clear and perspicuous.

His remarks on the origin and progress of religion, will furnish, to our Readers, a proper specimen of the merit of his publication.

'Deity, says he, is an awful object, and has ever roused the attention of mankind. But incapable of elevating their ideas to all the sublimity of his perfections, they have too often brought down his perfections to the level of their own ideas. This is more particularly true with regard to those nations whose religion had no other foundation but the natural feelings, and more often the irregular passions of the human heart, and who had received no light from heaven respecting this important object. In deducing the history of religion, therefore, we must make the same distinction which we have hitherto observed in tracing the progress of arts, sciences, and civilization among mankind. We must separate what is human from what is divine, what had its origin from particular revelations from what is the effect of general laws, and of the unassisted operations of the human mind.

'Agreeable to this distinction, we find that in the first ages of the world, the religion of the eastern nations was pure and luminous. It arose from a divine source, and was not then disfigured by human fancies or caprice. In time, however, these began to have their influence; the ray of tradition was obscured, and among those tribes which separated at the greatest distance, and in the smallest numbers, from the more improved societies of men, it was altogether obliterated.

'In this situation a particular people were selected by God himself, to be the depositories of his laws and worship; but the rest of mankind were left to form hypotheses upon these subjects, which were more or less perfect acording to an infinity of circumstances, which cannot properly be reduced under any general heads.

'The most common religion of antiquity, that which prevailed the longest, and extended the widest, was Polytheism, or the doctrine of a plurality of gods. The rage of system, the ambition of reducing all the phænomena of the moral world to a few general principles, has occaſioned many imperfect accounts, both of the origin and nature of this ſpecies of worſhip. For without entering into a minute detail, it is impoſſible to give an adequate idea of the ſubject; and what is ſaid upon it in general, muſt always be liable to a great many exceptions.

'One thing however may be obſerved, that the polytheiſm of the ancients ſeems neither to have been the fruit of philoſophical ſpeculations, nor of disfigured traditions, concerning the nature of the divinity. It ſeems to have ariſen during the rudeſt ages of ſociety, while the rational powers were feeble, and while mankind were under the tyranny of imagination and paſſion. It was built therefore ſolely upon ſentiment; as each tribe of men had their heroes, ſo likewiſe they had their gods. Thoſe heroes who led them forth to the combat, who preſided in their councils, whoſe image was engraved on their fancy, whoſe exploits were imprinted on their memory, even after death enjoyed an exiſtence in the imagination of their followers. The force of blood, of friendſhip, of affection, among rude nations, is what we cannot eaſily conceive; but the power of imagination over the ſenſes is what all men have in ſome degree experienced. Combine theſe two cauſes, and it will not appear ſtrange, that the image of departing heroes ſhould have been ſeen by their companions, animating the battle, taking vengeance on their enemies, and performing, in a word, the ſame functions which they performed when alive. An appearance ſo unnatural would not excite terror among men unacquainted with evil ſpirts, and who had not learned to fear any thing but their enemies. On the contrary, it confirmed their courage, flattered their vanity, and the teſtimony of thoſe who had ſeen it, ſupported by the extreme credulity and romantic caſt of thoſe who had not, gained an univerſal aſſent among all the members of their ſociety. A ſmall degree of reflection however would be ſufficient to convince them, that as their own heroes exiſted after death, it might likewiſe be the caſe of thoſe of their enemies. Two orders of gods, therefore, would be eſtabliſhed, the propitious and the hoſtile; the gods who were to be loved, and thoſe who were to be feared. But time which wears off the impreſſions of tradition, the frequent invaſions by which the nations of antiquity were ravaged, deſolated or tranſplanted, made them loſe the names, and confound the characters of thoſe two orders of divinities, and form various ſyſtems of religion, which, though warped by a thouſand particular circumſtances, give no ſmall indications of their firſt texture and original materials. For in general the gods of the ancients gave abundant proof of human infirmity. They were

subject

ſubject to all the paſſions of men; they partook even of their partial affections, and in many inſtances diſcovered their preference of one race or nation to all others. They did not eat and drink the ſame ſubſtances with men; they lived on nectar and ambroſia; they had a particular pleaſure in ſmelling the ſteam of the ſacrifices, and they made love with a ferocity unknown in northern climates. The rites by which they were worſhipped, naturally reſulted from their character.

'It muſt be obſerved, however, that the religion of the ancients was not much connected either with their private behaviour, or with their political arrangements. If we accept a few fanatical ſocieties, whoſe principles do not fall within our plan, the greater part of mankind were extremely tolerant in their principles. They had their own gods who watched over them; their neighbours, they imagined, alſo had theirs; and there was room enough in the univerſe for both to live together in good fellowſhip, without interfering or joſtling with one another.

'The introduction of Chriſtianity, by inculcating the unity of God, by announcing the purity of his character, by explaining the ſervice he required of men, produced a total alteration on their religious ſentiments and belief. But this is not the place for handling this ſublime ſubject. It is ſufficient to obſerve here, that a religion, which was founded on the unity of the Deity, which admitted of no aſſociation with falſe gods, muſt either be altogether deſtroyed, or become the prevailing belief of mankind. The latter was the caſe. Chriſtianity made its way among the civilized part of mankind, by the ſublimity of its doctrines and precepts; and before it was ſupported by the arm of power, ſuſtained itſelf by the voice of wiſdom.

'The management of whatever related to the church, being naturally conferred on thoſe who had eſtabliſhed it, firſt occaſioned the elevation of the clergy, and afterwards of the biſhop of Rome, over all the members of the Chriſtian world. It is impoſſible to deſcribe within our narrow limits all the concomitant cauſes, ſome of which were extremely delicate, by which this ſpecies of univerſal monarchy was eſtabliſhed. The biſhops of Rome, by being removed from the controul of the Roman emperors, then reſiding in Conſtantinople; by borrowing, with little variation, the religious ceremonies and rites eſtabliſhed among the Heathen world, and otherwiſe working on the credulous minds of Barbarians, by whom that empire began to be diſmembered; and by availing themſelves of every circumſtance which fortune threw in their way, ſlowly erected the fabric of their power, at firſt an object of veneration, and afterwards of terror, to all temporal princes. The cauſes of its happy dissolution are more palpable, and operated with greater activity. The most efficacious was the rapid improvement of arts, government and commerce, which after many ages of barbarity, made its way into Europe. The scandalous lives of those who called themselves the ministers of Jesus Christ, their ignorance and tyranny, the desire natural to sovereigns of delivering themselves from a foreign yoke, the opportunity of applying to national objects, the immense wealth which had been diverted to the service of the church in every kingdom of Europe, conspired with the ardor of the first reformers, and hastened the progress of reformation. The absurd mummeries established by the Romish clergy in order to elevate their power, and augment their riches, were happily turned into ridicule by men of letters; who, on that account, deserve to be held in everlasting esteem, as they contributed, in a very eminent degree, to that astonishing event, so favourable to the civil as well as to the religious liberties of mankind.'

The branch which, in the work before us, is the most censurable in the execution, regards the manners and the government of different nations. These topics require a force and extent of penetration, and a delicacy of precision, which are never possessed by ordinary men.

ART. IV. Wynne's *general History of the British Empire in America,* concluded: see Review for last Month.

THE second volume of this work opens with the commencement of the last war, and the principal events of it, so far as they regard America, are here concisely related: the Author assures us that he has spared no pains to render the narrative as perfect as the nature of the work would admit; from which consideration, he flatters himself, and we think not unreasonably, that it will prove as entertaining as the subject is interesting to the Reader.

In tracing the origin of this war, after having remarked how impossible it was that the charters, granted by the English and French sovereigns, respecting American lands, should not frequently clash and be inconsistent with one another, he proceeds to observe, that

—' We are neither to seek for the causes of the quarrel, nor to form our notions of the justice or injustice of either side, from any claims founded on these grants, or inferences drawn from them.' All this, says Mr. W. must depend on ' other and more established principles; and considering the matter in the real and only point of view it ought to be viewed in, we hesitate not, without departing from our avowed impartiality, to maintain that the French had long been inspired with intentions of making hostile encroachments upon the

the English colonists, and that they were, in the last war, particularly, the original aggressors.

'When any members of a civilized people leave their native land, to settle in a waste uncultivated country, the natural employment of these emigrants must be agriculture, and a confined sort of commerce. To do justice to the English colonists, it must be confessed, they have never, but when driven by force, varied from that line of action. It has been quite otherwise with the French: almost entirely neglecting commerce, looking upon agriculture as only a secondary consideration, their main politics have been rather to conquer and subdue, than to plant and settle: and instead of mercantile factories, they have erected military forts. It is from this different genius and bent of the two nations, manifested by the uniform series of their conduct pursued for ages, and not from a few particular accidents, nor from flimsy reasoning on the meaning of terms and the extent of boundaries, and the running of imaginary lines in vague and indefinite charters, which undoubtedly would never furnish an object of dispute, unless people were predisposed to quarrel, and only wanted a pretence for proceeding to hostilities, that we are to form our judgment of the justice or injustice of either side, in the commencement of the last war. This is a new point of view in which we have set this important object; and we are persuaded it will be found consonant to truth and reason, and that it does ample justice to the moderation and pacific dispositions of our countrymen. It is certain, that the main object of the English was planting and agriculture; and that they never removed from the sea-coasts and settled up the country, but when they were straitened for room in the places which they originally occupied. They made no settlements, and built no forts, at a distance from the capitals of their respective colonies.—When such was their invariable practice, it was impossible they could be justly charged with making hostile invasions and encroachments on their neighbours the French; and had the conduct of the latter been directed by the same motives, many centuries must have elapsed before the two nations could have been, properly speaking, neighbours to one another, in those almost unbounded territories. But their principles and conduct were quite the reverse: actuated by the same principles in the new world, which had so long, and so fatally distinguished that people in Europe, they have made military establishments, and erected fortifications at an immense distance from one another, and from their two capitals, and in situations where they cannot be even kept up but by unnatural exertions, both of power and politics; and where they could never serve any good purpose of commerce, far less of cultivation and agriculture. Beholding with the jealous and envious eyes of a rival, the slow, but sure advance of the British colonies in population, commerce, and cultivation; mortally dreading the increase of a power, which must be the more confirmed and stable, because it employed no unnatural or iniquitous means for that purpose, they have long determined on measures to stop the growth of the British settlements,—and to confine them within narrow limits, within a few leagues of the sea coast. With this ambitious view, they had connected their two colonies of Canada and Louisiana, by a chain of forts from Quebec to New-Orleans. This, though it could have served no purpose of colonization,

lonization, might have been defensible, had they restricted themselves, in these military establishments, to the banks of the two great rivers, or their neighbourhood: but not contented with this, they made military settlements so very near the English frontier, which had been planted by a natural and regular progress, and, what is still more convincing, at so great a distance from any of their own colonies, with such vast tracts of land, either desert, or inhabited by hostile savages lying between them, that a bare inspection of the map is sufficient to demonstrate, that it could only be done with an hostile intention, and a view of making encroachments.' The most palpable instance they gave of such designs was the building of Fort Frederic, called by us Crown Point, upon Lake Champlain, at a great distance from Montreal, the nearest of their own establishments, and within the territories of the Mohawks, acknowledged, by treaty, to be under the protection of the English. This they effected in the year 1716.—In short, from the whole tendency of the French conduct, it appears almost indisputable, that they had fixed their hearts on possessing themselves of one of the English harbours on the Atlantic ocean; envying their rivals, no doubt, the advantages they reaped, in the way of navigation and commerce, from the most extensive sea-coast in their hands, and regretting their own unfortunate situation with respect to these articles, having no other maritime communication for the immense territory which they claimed as their own, but the mouths of two rivers, the navigation in neither of which was convenient. To conclude, a very superficial reflection on the different foundations of the British and French colonies, and the different temper and character of the inhabitants, will enable any impartial man, without the least hesitation, without having recourse to partial representations of inconsequential, and, at best, doubtful facts, and without lending ear to vulgar prejudices, equally forcible on both sides, to determine the important question, Who were the aggressors in the last war? The British colonies were bounded by sober, regular progressive cultivation; the French by wild, irregular, unconnected enterprize. The British colonists were peaceable farmers and traders; and the French, turbulent freebooters and adventurers.'

The writer has frequent occasion, in the course of his narrative, to celebrate the bravery of the British soldiers and sailors. Among other enterprizes, the siege of Quebec affords a particular opportunity for it: In his account of General Wolfe, he gives the following brief character of that illustrious commander:

'The death of General Wolfe was a national loss, and universally lamented: soldiers may be raised, officers will be formed by experience, but the loss of a genius in war is not easily repaired. By nature formed for military greatness, his memory was retentive, his judgment deep, and his comprehension surprisingly quick, clear, and extensive; his constitutional courage not only uniform and daring, perhaps to an extreme, but he possessed also that higher species of it, a strength, steadiness, and activity of mind, which no difficulties or dangers could deter. Generous, gentle, friendly, affable and humane, he was the pattern of the officer, and the darling of the soldier; his sublime genius soared above the pitch of ordinary minds, and had his faculties been exercised to their full extent, by opportunities

and

nd action, and his judgment been fully ripened by age and expeience, he would have rivalled the most celebrated heroes of antiquity.'

The account of the reduction of Guadaloupe is concluded vith the following anecdote, which we shall transcribe, in hoour of the ladies:

'It ought not to be omitted, to the honour of the inhabitants, that general they exerted themselves very gallantly in the defence of heir country; *Madame du Charmey*, a considerable planter, particuarly distinguished herself, heading her servants and negroes, and cquitting herself in a manner not unworthy of the bravest soldier, n the defence of her property.'

The history of the war is followed by some farther descripions of the British settlements,—Virginia, and North and South Carolina, continued from the former volume; also Georgia, and East and West Florida. The narratives are short, but entertaining; and intermixed with sensible observations.

After several judicious reflections on the present state of the North-American colonies, which deserve serious attention, this Author gives a general account of the Indian nations, and hen proceeds to the inland parts of Louisiana; the description of which is followed by remarks on the trade and late regulaions of the colonies.

He then gives the history of Jamaica, Barbadoes, St. Christophers, Grenada, and the other West India islands. To this he adds a chapter upon the manufacture of sugar, and another on hat of indigo: concerning the last, it is remarkable, that almost the same relation, though with some variation of expression, had been before made in the history of Carolina. This, with some other things of the like nature, gives this work not only the air of a compilation, but also of negligence in the collector of the materials. Notwithstanding which, we must acknowledge, that hese volumes contain a great number of sensible remarks, several of which might, no doubt, (as we have already observed) be applied to public utility, by those whose peculiar province it s to attend to affairs of this kind.

The second volume is concluded by *Thoughts on the Slave-Trade*, and the number and management of negroes in the plantations. This famous, or we should be apt to say, infamous, commerce, Mr. Wynne observes, can only be justified by necessity, which he appears to think must be admitted as a plea n its behalf. These poor slaves, it is observed, are generally prisoners taken in the wars, but then we are at the same time old, that the petty nations on the coast of Africa carry on these wars with one another for this very purpose. It is certain that Africans or their descendants are better able to undergo severe atigue in hot countries than any of European blood, who are ot fitted to endure the climate or the labour, or so to perform t as to be any sort of equivalent to the expence: therefore it is urged, this cruel traffic is *necessary*:

'But, our Author adds, it is an *unfortunate* circumſtance, becauſe no inſtitution is ſo apt as ſlavery to extirpate the milder and more amiable virtues of compaſſion and humanity, and to render men cruel, hard-hearted, and remorſeleſs.—A remarkable inſtance of this in South-Carolina, we have heard well atteſted. The moſt laborious drudgery in that colony is clearing the rice of its huſk. This is now generally performed by machines; but formerly it was done by the hand-labour of the ſlaves, who uſed for that purpoſe a wooden trough, in which the rice is put, and then beat it with a mallet, much of the ſame nature with that uſed by paviors. An eminent planter in that colony, whenever there happened a ſudden demand for rice, uſed commonly to deſtroy five or ſix of his ſlaves in a ſeaſon, by over-taſking them at that drudgery, and coolly juſtified this ſhocking barbarity, by alledging, that he found the extraordinary profit he made by this means of his rice, more than compenſated for the value of the ſlaves he loſt. We are afraid that ſuch barbarians are too often met with in all our colonies.

'Among the bad conſequences of the ſevere treatment of theſe poor creatures, who doubtleſs have an equal claim to all the comforts of freedom with any of their oppreſſors, Mr. Wynne obſerves, one is, the prodigious annual decreaſe of their number, 'which is, he ſays, ſo great, that in the iſland of Barbadoes, where there are computed to be about ſeventy-five thouſand blacks, an annual importation of no leſs than five thouſand is required barely to keep up the ſtock.'—This, he adds, is the more remarkable, ſince Barbadoes is a very healthy climate, quite friendly to their conſtitutions, as much at leaſt as their native country, where they are ſo wonderfully prolific, that, notwithſtanding the immenſe drains annually made by the ſlave-trade, and the loſſes occaſioned by their perpetual wars, their numbers have not ſenſibly decreaſed. If ſuch be the yearly exceſs of deaths above births in Barbadoes, it muſt at leaſt be proportionable in the other iſlands, from whence the ſum of the whole may be eaſily computed. That it is ſolely occaſioned by the ſeverity of their maſters, is evident from the following circumſtance. There are ſome exceptions from this habitual ſeverity of planters, and thoſe who are ſo, find their advantage in it, for inſtead of being obliged to purchaſe ſupplies of new negroes to keep up their ſtock, they are known to turn out into their fields an additional number of working hands every year, born and bred upon their own eſtates. Theſe inſtances, are, however, at preſent ſo extremely rare, that it is to be feared they can never ſerve as an example.'

Here we muſt take leave of our Author, though we could, with pleaſure, have made a greater number of extracts, which, we doubt not, would have been very acceptable to our readers.

ART. V. *The Hiſtory of England, from the earlieſt Times to the Death of George* II. By Dr. Goldſmith. 8vo. 4 vols. 1l. 1s. boards. Davies, Becket, &c. 1771.

THE condition of the Britons, before the Romans arrived in this iſland, claimed naturally the firſt attention of our hiſtorian; but, though many curious particulars may be gathered on this ſubject from ancient authors, he has treated it in

a care-a careless and superficial manner. It is his opinion, that no advantage can result from an acquaintance with nations in their savage and barbarous state; and that it is fortunate for mankind, that the ruder periods in the history of society are the least known. We profess ourselves to be of very opposite sentiments, and are not afraid to affirm, that it is highly instructive and entertaining, to behold the first efforts of a rude community towards government and legislation; and to be informed of the ideas that prevail in it, in relation to property, religion, and the œconomy and arrangements of civil life. Is there no merit or value in the comprehensive and sentimental picture, which the pencil of Tacitus has delineated of the ancient inhabitants of Germany? It is surely inauspicious for an Author, when he introduces his work with a sentiment so inconsistent with good sense and philosophy!

At the time when the Britons were prevailed upon by Vortigern to send a deputation to Germany for assistance against the Picts and Scots, they are represented by our Author as sunk in barbarity and savage rudeness; while their Saxon allies are considered by him, as infinitely superior to them in refinement and knowledge. It were to be wished, that, at the distance of so many centuries, he had produced the evidence upon which he has ventured to contradict the uniform tenor of our history. In the life of Julius Agricola, we are told, that in order to subdue the refractory spirit of the Britons, it was the great object of the policy of that commander, to instruct them in the Roman language and manners; and he was so successful, it is said, in his endeavours to this end, that our ancestors even proceeded to vie with their enemies in luxury and magnificence. They built sumptuous palaces, courted the pleasures of the table, and excelled in the elegance of their baths *. To their excessive refinement too, and degeneracy, has it been ascribed by Gildas and Bede, that the Saxons turned their arms against them, and almost totally extirpated them. These authorities, though they are perhaps to be received with some degree of latitude, are fully sufficient to overthrow what our Author has observed of the rude state of the Britons, at the period in question.

With respect to the cultivation he has imputed to the Saxons at the æra of their establishment in England, we have to observe, that authors, from whose authority in this matter there can be no appeal, have concurred to describe them as the most fierce and barbarous of all the German tribes †. Their subsequent

* *Jam vero principum filios liberalibus artibus erudire, et ingenia Britannorum studiis Gallorum anteferre, ut qui modo linguam Romanam abnuebant, eloquentiam concupiscerent. Inde habitus nostri honor, et frequens toga: paulatimque discessum ad delinimenta vitiorum, porticus, et balnea, et conviviorum elegantiam. Agr. vit. c.* 21.

† *Præ cæteris hostibus Saxones timentur; says Marcellinus, in allusion to their ferocity. See also Zozim. hist. lib.* 3.

hiſtory too, and the laws of their monarchs, furniſh ample confirmations of this opinion. It is not only inconcluſive, but perfectly ridiculous in our hiſtorian to pronounce them refined;—becauſe "their women uſed linen garments, trimmed, and ſtriped with purple; had their hair bound in wreaths, or allowed it to fall in curls upon their ſhoulders;—becauſe their arms were bare, and their boſoms uncovered; and—becauſe theſe faſhions ſeem peculiar to the ladies of England to this day." Not to mention that theſe modes of dreſs prevailed among this people, before they ſallied out from their woods to make conqueſts*, and when they were ſcarcely removed from the ſtate of nature; it may be remarked, that he might with equal force, infer from the erect poſture of the Samoeide and the American, that they were deſcended of the ſame race of men with the old inhabitant of Gaul or of Germany.

When he proceeds to aſſert, 'That the government of the Saxons was generally an elective monarchy, and ſometimes a republic,' he gives his reader another proof of his inattention. In no authentic hiſtorical monument is there the moſt diſtant alluſion to revolutions or fluctuations of this kind in the hiſtory of this people.

If they were divided into tribes, like ſeveral other nations which inhabited ancient Germany, there were, perhaps, peculiarities in government and manners, which might diſtinguiſh *theſe* ‖; but it is by no means probable, that their political inſtitutions would be eſſentially different; and if the Saxons formed only a ſingle nation or community, it cannot, without the higheſt abſurdity, be imagined, that they were in the habit of paſſing from one form of government to another; and were now ſubject to the reſtraint of kings, and now under the direction of a democracy.

It is likewiſe obſervable, that our Author has talked, and with great gravity, of the *ſalaries* of the Saxon commanders, at a period, when the German tribes were hardly acquainted with agriculture, when the metals were not impreſſed with a mark of value, and when war and depredation were the chief ſources of

* *Nec aliud feminis quam viris babitus, niſi quod feminæ ſæpius lineis amictibus velantur. eoſque purpura variant, partemque veſtitus ſuperioris in manicas non extendunt, nudæ brachia ac lacertos: ſed et proxima pars pectoris patet. De Mor. Germ. c.* 17.

‖ The Suevi, for example, were divided into different tribes: and in theſe, there could not fail to be a variety of *peculiar*, as well as *common* circumſtances: Nunc de Suevis dicendum eſt, ſays the Roman hiſtorian, quorum non una ut cattorum Tencterorumve gens: majorem enim Germaniæ partem obtinent, propriis adhuc nationibus nominibuſque diſcreti, quamquam in communi Suevi vocentur. Tacit. de M. G. c. 38.

their

their subsistence. Nor must it be forgot, that he has dogmatically pronounced, that the Saxons were strangers to slavery; though the Authors ‡ that should have directed his decision, as to this particular, have been at singular pains to enumerate the different causes which reduced men to slavery among the German communities, and to explain the different forms of their servitude. Let us confess, however, that in another part of his work †, he has no less boldly maintained, that villenage or slavery was not unknown in England during the Saxon times. We leave the reader to determine the respect that is due to an historian, who can support with equal confidence and facility, opinions totally inconsistent and contradictory.

But it is not solely in the more obscure periods of our annals that this compiler, though a man of genius and taste, as his poetical compositions have demonstrated, discovers a want of penetration and of knowledge. He also carries it into his narration of the transactions of times, when the truth is well ascertained, and when the researches and toils of laborious and intelligent writers, offered to him a copious store of important materials. The curious and constitutional topics, which the reigns of William I. Henry III. and Henry VII. held forth to his observation, he has passed over with the utmost precipitation. One wou'd almost imagine, that he had intended to present the public with whatever is most obvious, or least interesting in the history of England.

In the following passage, there is an error of so capital a nature, that we cannot but lay it before our readers, with a few animadversions.

'*Henry* VII. says Dr. Goldsmith, had all along two points principally in view; one to depress the nobility and clergy, and the other to exalt and humanize the populace. From the ambition and turbulence of the former, and from the wretchedness and credulity of the latter, all the troubles in the former reigns had taken their original. *In the feudal times, every nobleman was possessed of a certain number of subjects, over whom he had an absolute power*; and therefore, upon every slight disgust, he was able to influence them to join him in his revolt or disobedience. Henry, therefore, wisely considered, that the giving these *petty tyrants* a power of selling their estates, which before his time were unalienable, would greatly weaken their interest. With this view he procured an act, by which the nobility were granted a power of disposing of their estates; a law infinitely pleasing to the commons, and not disagreeable even to the nobles, since they had thus an immediate resource for supplying their taste for prodigality, and answering the demands of their creditors. The blow reached them in their posterity alone; but they were too ignorant to be affected by such distant distresses.'

‡ *Heinnec. Antiq. Germ. Potgiesser de Stat. Serv. Montesquieu, &c.*
† *Compare the 35th and the 134th pages of volume* 1st.

We are not to be informed, that several modern writers, as well as our historian, have concurred to describe the ancient English nobility as insupportable and cruel tyrants. This opinion, however, we will be bold to affirm, receives little support from history. The nobles of former ages, it is allowed, had a great deal of influence; but did not this influence consist in the number, the valour, and the attachment of their vassals and retainers? Was it then their interest to treat them with severity? By oppressing men, who constituted their power, they would detract from their own importance; and if they had observed a conduct so weak and impolitic, it is difficult to conceive, how they should have been able to disturb, as they often did, the peace of their country, and to bid defiance to their prince. Their conduct was directed by very opposite maxims: the utmost indulgence and lenity distinguished the treatment of their retainers and vassals: their halls were at all times open to receive them; and they entertained and courted men whom they found so necessary to their grandeur, and their power.

It must be confessed, notwithstanding, that though the barons were humane and tender to their own vassals, they were yet, to the kingdom, a powerful source of oppression and grievance. The great object of their ambition was to excel each other in parade and magnificence; and their attendants and followers naturally entering into their views, felt, and were directed by their passions. Haughty and independent, the slightest circumstances were sufficient to alarm their pride; and their animosities, uncontrouled by government, broke out into acts of open violence. They alternately laid siege to the castles, massacred the vassals, and wasted the territories of each other. It was thus, that the confusion and disorder arose, which authors, inattentive to the times to which their observations refer, have endeavoured to explain, by considering the nobles as oppressive to their retainers.

In the general spirit of the publication before us, we must also remark, that, in our opinion, the historian has leaned with too much partiality to the prerogative of our kings: and in a work, which is evidently addressed to young and inexperienced minds, there cannot possibly be a fault of a more destructive tendency. The first political lessons inculcated on the youth of a free state, ought not, surely, to be dependence and servility.

There is one light, and perhaps but one, in which, if the performance before us is considered, it will appear to have merit. In its style it has a degree of dignity, which is perfectly suitable to historical compositions; and its periods are harmonious and flowing. It must be remarked, notwithstanding, that it is frequently deficient in grammatical precision; and that it sometimes degenerates into the insipid languor and the tawdry prettiness of romance.

The following extract from our Author's account of the reign of Henry II. may enable our readers to form an opinion of his ability, and manner of writing.

'Among the few vices ascribed to this monarch, unlimited gallantry was one. Queen Eleanor, whom he had married from motives of ambition, and who had been divorced from her former royal consort for her incontinence, was long become disagreeable to Henry; and he sought in others, those satisfactions he could not find with her. Among the number of his mistresses we have the name of Fair Rosamond, whose personal charms, aud whose death, make so conspicuous a figure in the romances and the ballads of the time. It is true, that the severity of criticism has rejected most of these accounts as fabulous; but even well-known fables, when much celebrated, make a part of the history, at least of the manners of the age. Rosamond Clifford is said to have been the most beautiful woman that was ever seen in England, if what romances and poets assert be true. Henry loved her with a long and faithful attachment; and in order to secure her from the resentment of his queen, who, from having been formerly incontinent herself, now became jealous of his incontinence, he concealed her in a labyrinth in Woodstock Park, where he passed in her company his hours of vacancy and pleasure. How long this secret intercourse continued is not told us; but it was not so closely concealed but that it came to the queen's knowledge, who, as the accounts add, being guided by a clew of silk to her fair rival's retreat, obliged her, by holding a drawn dagger to her breast, to swallow poison. Whatever may be the veracity of this story, certain it is, that this haughty woman, though formerly offensive by her own gallantries, was now no less so by her jealousy; and she it was who first sowed the seeds of dissention between the king and his children.

'Young Henry was taught to believe himself injured; when upon being crowned as partner in the kingdom, he was not admitted into a share of the administration. This prince had, from the beginning, shewn a degree of pride that seems to have been hereditary to all the Norman succession: when the ceremony of his coronation was performing, the king, willing to give it all the splendor possible, waited upon him at table; and while he offered him the cup observed, that no prince ever before had been so magnificently attended. There is nothing very extraordinary, replied the young prince, in seeing the son of a count serving the son of a king. From this instance, nothing seemed great enough to satisfy his ambition; and he took the first opportunity to assert his aspiring pretensions. The discontent of young Henry was soon followed by that of Geoffry and Richard, whom the queen persuaded to assert their title to the territories assigned them; and upon the king's refusing their undutiful demands, they all fled secretly to the court of France, where Lewis, who was instrumental in increasing their disobedience, gave them countenance and protection. Queen Eleanor herself was meditating an escape to the same court, and had put on man's apparel for that purpose,

purpose, when she was seized by the king's order and put into confinement. Thus Henry saw all his long perspective of future happiness totally clouded; his sons, scarce yet arrived at manhood, eager to share the spoils of their father's possessions; his queen warmly encouraging those undutiful princes in their rebellion, and many potentates of Europe not ashamed to lend them assistance to support their pretensions. Nor *was* his *prospects* much more pleasing when he looked among his subjects: his licentious barons, disgusted with a vigilant government, desired to be governed by princes whom they could flatter or intimidate: the clergy had not yet forgot Becket's death; and the people considered him as a saint and a martyr. In this universal disaffection, Henry supported that intrepidity which he had shown through life, and prepared for a contest from which he could expect to reap neither profit nor glory. Twenty thousand mercenary soldiers, joined to some troops which he brought over from Ireland, and a few barons of approved fidelity, formed the sole force with which he proposed to resist his opponents.

'It was not long before the young princes had sufficient influence upon the continent to raise a powerful confederacy in their favour. Beside the king of France, Philip count of Flanders, Matthew count of Bologne, Theobald count of Blois, and Henry count of Eu, all declared themselves in their interests. William, king of Scotland, also made one of this association, and a plan was concerted for a general invasion of Henry's extensive dominions. This was shortly after put into execution. The king's continental dominions were invaded on one side, by the counts of Flanders and Boulogne; on the other by the King of France, with a large army, which the young English princes animated by their presence and popelarity. But Henry found means to oppose them on every quarter: the count of Boulogne, being mortally wounded in the assault of the town of Drincourt, his death stopped the progress of the Flemish arms on that side. The French army being obliged to retire from the siege of Verneuil, Henry attacked their rear, put them to the rout, and took several prisoners. The barons of Britanny also, who had risen in favour of the young princes, shared no better fate; their army was defeated in the field, and, taking shelter in the town of Dol, were there made prisoners of war. These successes repressed the pride and the expectations of the confederated forces, and a conference was demanded by the French king, to which Henry readily agreed. In this interview, he had the mortification to see his three sons, ranged on the side of his mortal and inveterate enemy; but he was still more disappointed to find that their demands rose with their incapacity to obtain them by compulsion.

'While Henry was thus quelling the insolence of his foreign enemies, his English subjects were in no small danger of revolting from their obedience at home. The nobility were in general united to oppose him; and an irruption at this time by the king of Scotland, assisted their schemes of insurrection. The earl of Leicester, at the head of a body of Flemings, invaded Suffolk, but were repulsed with great slaughter. The earl of Ferrars, Roger de Mowbray, and many others of equal dignity, rose in arms; while, the more to augment the confusion, the king of Scotland broke into the northern provinces

provinces with an army of eighty thousand men, which laid the whole country into an extensive scene of desolation. Henry, from baffling his enemies in France, flew over to oppose those in England; but his long dissention with Becket still was remembered against him, and it was his interest to persuade the clergy, as well as the people, that he was no way accessary to his murder. All the world now began to think the dead prelate a saint; and if we consider the ignorance of the times, perhaps Henry himself thought so too. He had some time before taken proper precautions to exculpate himself to the pope, and given him the most solemn promises to perform whatever penances the church should inflict. He had engaged the Christmas following to take the cross; and, if the pope insisted on it, to serve three years against the infidels, either in Spain or Palestine; and promised not to stop appeals to the holy see. These concessions seemed to satisfy the court of Rome for that time; but they were, nevertheless, every day putting Henry in mind of his promise, and demanded those humiliations for his offences, to the saint, that could alone reconcile him to the church. He now therefore, found it the most proper conjuncture to obey, and, knowing the influence of superstition over the minds of the people, and perhaps apprehensive that a part of his troubles arose from the displeasure of Heaven, he resolved to do penance at the shrine of St. Thomas of Canterbury, for that was the name given to Becket upon his canonization. As soon as he came within sight of the church of Canterbury, alighting from his horse, he walked barefoot towards the town, prostrated himself before the shrine of the saint, remained in fasting and prayer a whole day, watched all night the holy relicks, made a grant of fifty pounds a-year to the convent, for a constant supply of tapers to illuminate the shrine; and, not satisfied with these submissions, he assembled a chapter of monks, disrobed before them, put a scourge of discipline into each of their hands, and presented his bare shoulders to their infliction. Next day he received absolution; and departing for London, received the agreeable news of a victory over the Scots, obtained on the very day of his absolution.

'Having thus made his peace with the church, and brought over the minds of the people, he fought upon surer grounds; every victory he obtained was imputed to the favour of the reconciled saint, and every success thus tended to ascertain the growing confidence of his party. The victory which was gained over the Scots was signal and decisive. William, their king, after having committed the most horrible depredations upon the northern frontiers, had thought proper to retreat upon the advance of an English army, commanded by Ralph de Glanville, the famous English lawyer. As he had fixed his station at Alnwick, he thought himself perfectly secure, from the remoteness of the enemy, against any attack. In this however he was deceived; for Glanville, informed of his situation, made an hasty and fatigueing march to the place of his encampment, and approached it very nearly during the obscurity of a mist. The Scotch, who continued in perfect security, were surprized in the morning to find themselves attacked by the enemy, which they thought at such a distance; and their king venturing with a small body of an hundred horse to oppose the assailants, was quickly surrounded and taken prisoner. His

troops

troops hearing of his disaster, fled on all sides with the utmost precipitation, and made the best of their way to their own country.

'From that time Henry's affairs began to wear a better aspect; the barons who had revolted, or were preparing for a revolt, made instant submission, they delivered up their castles to the victor, and England in a few weeks was restored to perfect tranquillity. Young Henry, who was ready to embark with a large army, to second the efforts of the English insurgents, finding all disturbances quieted at home, abandoned all thoughts of the expedition. Lewis attempted in vain to besiege Rouen, which Henry hastened over to succour. A cessation of arms and a conference was once more agreed upon by the two monarchs. Henry granted his sons much less advantageous terms than they formerly refused to accept: the most material, were some pensions for their support, some castles for their residence, and an indemnity to all their adherents. Thus England once more emerged from the numerous calamities that threatened to overwhelm it, and the king was now left at free liberty to make various provisions for the glory, the happiness, and the security of his people.

'His first care was to make his prisoner, the king of Scots, undergo a proper punishment for his unmerited and ungenerous attack. That prince was content to sign a treaty, by which he was compelled to do homage to Henry for his dominions in Scotland. It was agreed, that his barons and bishops also should do the same; and that the fortresses of Edinburgh, Stirling, Berwick, Roxborough, and Jedborough, should be delivered into the hands of the conqueror till the articles were performed. This treaty was punctually and rigorously executed; the king, barons, and prelates of Scotland did homage to Henry in the cathedral of York; so that he might now be considered as the monarch of the whole island, the mountainous parts of Wales only excepted.

'His domestic regulations were as wise as his political conduct was splendid. He enacted severe penalties against robbery, murder, false coining, and burning of houses; ordaining that these crimes should be punished by the amputation of the right-hand and right-foot. The ordeal trial by water, though it still subsisted, was yet so far weakened, as that if a person who came off in this scrutiny were legally convicted by creditable testimony, he should nevertheless suffer banishment. He partitioned out the kingdom into four divisions; and appointed itinerant justices to go their respective circuits to try causes, to restrain the cruelties of the barons, and to protect the lower ranks of the people in security. He renewed the trial by juries, which, by the barbarous method of camp-fight, was almost grown obsolete. He demolished all the new-erected castles that had been built in the times of anarchy and general confusion; and, to secure the kingdom more effectually against any threatened invasion, he established a well-armed militia, which, with proper accoutrements, specified in the act, were to defend the realm upon any emergency.'

In the task of abridging the history of England, our Author has started with very humble competitors. But we cannot justly remark, to his praise, that he has left them behind him at a great distance.

ART.

ART. VI. *The Farmer's Kalendar; or, a Monthly Directory for all Sorts of Country Business: Containing plain Instructions for performing the Work of various Kinds of Farms in every Season of the Year: Respecting particularly the buying, feeding, and selling live Stock; the whole Culture of Arable Crops; the Management of Grasses; the œconomical Conduct of the Farm, &c.* By an EXPERIENCED FARMER. 8vo. 5 s. Robinson and Roberts.

HE who presents the public with *experiments*, or (in somewhat a more modest style) *experience*, without communicating his name and place of abode, cannot reasonably expect attention and credit.

A *Farmer's Kalendar* seems to us one of those many instruments which are *needless* to an old and judicious husbandman, and *dangerous* to the *young* and *injudicious*.

The first 14 pages of this book are spent in title and contents. The next 16 are *filled*, shall we say, or *thinly spread*, with flimsy excuses for publishing a Kalendar, and shewing a farmer how to keep an account of disbursements and receipts. This introduction ends, however, with a *clear profit* of 173 l. 10 s. per annum from a farm of about 100 acres. And how can the Reader be so ungrateful as to deny our *experienced Farmer*, or his booksellers, what *clear* profit they can make out of 5 s. for instruction how to gain yearly such a considerable sum!

To make a Kalendar a *safe* instrument, continual attention to the difference of *weather* and *climate* is necessary. Our Farmer is indeed so honest as frequently to admonish his young pupil never to go with his plough to the field when the *weather* suits not. But he says not one word (so far as we remember, after an attentive perusal of the whole) about differences of *climate*: so that the same directions are given to the northern and southern farmers. One instance we must mark. In December, he tells his pupil, that his ews begin to lamb: though within a day's ride of London the farmers *prudently* take care that they do not lamb till *April*.

There is a dispute in some parts of the kingdom, Whether it is adviseable to *feed down* turnips in the field where they grow, or *draw* them. Our Farmer thinks that they should be eaten only on lands which are *perfectly* dry. In consequence of which restriction, we apprehend, the greatest advantage of a crop of turnips, as preparative to barley, is lost. He advises to take cows with calf *from straw* only a fortnight before they calve, and affirms that there is *no use* of hay for them. The young farmer, who is his pupil, will soon find, by the bad milking of his cows, and weakness of their calves, that the dams should never have come into the straw-yards; not to mention the danger from the pushing of other beasts, to which, in such a crowd, they are liable.

In

In plashing an hedge, and ditching, he advifes to throw the earth from the ditch on to the bank, and then to plash the hedge. But prudence will dictate juft the contrary, viz. to finifh the plafhing of the hedge firft, and then to throw the earth (in cafes where it is proper) on to the bank; for thus it will ftand, but in the other cafe it will tumble into the ditch while the work of plafhing is performed. He advifes to *water meadows* where water *cannot* be brought on it, &c. We doubt not he means *can*. But we muft think that he chufes a ftrange time for this work, viz. *February* inftead of *April* or *May*. We apprehend that his pupil will hardly find *watering* in February as effectual as *any other manuring*, as he promifes.

He affures his pupil that he will find the advantage of fowing barley in *March* rather than in *April*, to be *cæteris paribus* fix bufhels per acre; but he fhould add, when he has a king's ranfom, a peck of March duft; and we can hardly afford a king's ranfom above once in a century. Speaking of the barley crops fpoiled by the luxuriancy of clover, and the *common prudence* of farmers to prevent this evil, by fowing the clover only before the roller, after the barley is up, he propofes, as a *proper management eafily to remedy this evil*, fuch a method as muft difcredit, except with ideots, all his other advice: *viz.* as foon as the barley *begins to ear*, to mow *all* for hay. Thus would both the crops be deftroyed; for the clover would be too light to pay expences, and the barley a mere nothing.

We will not *affirm abfolutely* that it is better management to fow down clover with a fecond crop of white corn, than with the firft, after turnips or fallow; but we muft treat with contempt the farmer who pretends to dictate that, after a fallow and wheat, a crop of oats muft be *very trifling*, fee p. 62. On the contrary, noble crops may be thus obtained; and, as oats are a crop without which the farmer can feldom keep his teams, this is often good management. But the farmer who decides thus *peremptorily*, feems to forget that clover fown with oats brings a man back to the courfe which our *Kalendarian* thinks the fole profitable one. If a fallow, with manure, will not give one crop of white corn after wheat, it gives nothing.

Our Farmer recommends, for potatoes, a neat horfe-hoe, which *turns* no *furrow*, and only *cuts* the *furface* of the *ground*. But we cannot conceive the benefit of fuch an horfe-hoe on this or fimilar occafions. Where rain, or the juices of manure, or any liquids are to be communicated to the roots of corn or grafs, fuch an horfe-hoe as only *cuts the furface* may be very ufeful; but as the *turning up a new furface* to the influences of the fun, air, &c. appears a principal benefit of drilling, whatever inftrument turns no furrow, appears almoft entirely ufelefs.

He

He exhorts his *pupil* to have horſekeepers for mere attendance on the teams. But we apprehend that if the young man have any *prudence* or *common ſenſe*, he will make two objections to this advice, viz. firſt, that the expence of a team will be *prodigiouſly augmented*; and, according to him, it is already very high; for (in p. 12 of the introduction) he ſtates the winter and ſpring keeping at 10l. per head;—and, ſecondly, the ploughmen, when willing to work a bad day's work, will always have the horſekeepers to complain of.

Our Farmer aſſures his pupil that one good acre of lucerne will keep five horſes from May-day to the end of *October*. We have an high opinion of this plant; but fear that the encomiums on it have been carried too far. Mr. *Baldwin*, in a piece lately publiſhed and republiſhed, has endeavoured to ſhew the world that he has exceeded the beſt *French* and *Iriſh* cultivators of this admired plant in the drill culture, and yet that he can only keep five horſes on an acre 21 days. But our *experienced* Farmer promiſes to keep them on it during ſix whole ſummer months; that is, *nearly* 9 times as long!

Our Farmer tells us that rye is a *moſt paltry* feed, and never pays expences. From many paſſages we learn that he is a ſouth-country *man*, we do not ſay a *farmer*; for, probably he has farmed *no where*. But if he knew any thing of *northern farming*, he might know that rye is, when properly managed, an excellent crop, and *frequently* ſuperior to wheat; and that it affords an admirable ſpring feed for ſheep, nay, (if prudently managed, without damage) with benefit to the crop.

He informs his pupil that the turnip-cabbage will laſt till the middle of May: but he ſhould have added, "when the winter is *not ſevere*;" for experience ſhews, that a ſevere one kills, that is, rots it long before *May*.

He has mentioned rollers of 50l. a-piece. 'Tis pity that he has not dignified his page with the names of thoſe *modeſt* gentlemen who trade for public good, in theſe cheap inſtruments.

This ſagacious Farmer pretends to ſtate the diſpute betwixt the different partiſans for *mowing*, and *reaping by ſickle*, a wheat crop. How unequal is he to the *moderatorſhip* on this ſubject! He *ſuppoſes* the crop *weedy*; and, from the deductions on this ſort of crop, concludes generally on crops of an oppoſite kind. On his own premiſes, however, his concluſions would not hold good for the particular ſpecies of crops which he inſtances.

He pretends that an *horſe-rake* on barley ſtubbles will work againſt 20 men with *dew-rakes*. This is an horrible exaggeration! When the high price of his horſe-rakes (viz. *four guineas and an half*) and the frequent ſtops neceſſarily made to unburthen

burthen the rake, and the neceffity of a *man* to *drive* an horfe, for a boy cannot well unburthen them, or the addition of a man for this work folely, are confidered, no prudent perfon will wonder that fo many farmers retain their *dew-rakes*.

He tells us that lucerne has produced above 40 l. an acre. Anonymous experimenters have no credit with rational people. What fays Mr. Baldwin? See fecond volume of Memoirs of Agriculture, Art. I.

He advifes his pupil at once to reject a farm from which tithes are gathered; and afferts, that *no profit* arifes from poor foils, though the rent be ever fo low. What extravagance!

We need fay nothing on his direction to *water* meadows in December: nor need we comment on his affertion that good dry walls are but a *temporary* fence, and *afford not* fhelter; and therefore hedges, which are diverted of leaf during all winter, *muft be raifed*. His method of putting down the *old ant-bills*, (p. 367) is a wretched one. The plough affords the only effectual cure.

We will conclude with a *few fhort* obfervations on our Farmer's *manner* and *matter*. As to language, we do not expect that of writers on agriculture to be *elegant*, nor even *exact*: but we may reafonably expect that, like other people who profefs to inftruct, they fhould endeavour to be *intelligible*; and, to this end, that they fhould obferve the common rules of grammar in the language which they pretend to write: yet of the want of this, we Reviewers have often fufficient caufe to complain. We will give only one inftance (and it is a fhort one) of a deficiency of this kind in our *Kalendarian*: 'You may manure *moffy* ground often, before you deftroy *it*; but the treading of the fheep at the fame time that the dung and urine are drupt, completely deftroys *it*.' P. 354. Secondly, we have briefly noticed much exceptionable matter: "Is all or moft of the reft fuch?" it may be afked. By no means! There is, on the contrary, much fenfe and knowledge of agricultural affairs in this Kalendar; but then it is *ftolen* from others, and particularly from Mr. *Young*, whofe fields the Kalendarian has robbed without mercy, efpecially his *Farmer's Guide*, his *Experiments*, &c. and without acknowledgment of any kind. He once fpeaks of a *late Author*. Thirdly, he not only commits plagiarifms, but repeats them: his mode of *Kalendar* affording him ample opportunies for this impofition, under different months. To fell another man's property, as though it were our own, is bad enough; but to fell it again and again, is execrable!

ART.

ART. VII. *Medical Observations and Inquiries.* By a Society of Physicians in London. Vol. IV. 8vo. 5 s. Cadell. 1771.

THE first article in the fourth † volume of this valuable collection, contains a singular history * of a diseased leg. A healthy girl of six years, received a slight hurt on the outside of the leg, a little below the knee. In a few days a painful tumor began to form; and in six months this tumor increased to such a size, and put on such appearances, that amputation was judged necessary. Soon after the operation the child died, and, on examining the diseased limb, it appeared, that there were no bones, but a few bony *lamellæ* interspersed through the substance of the tumor; the tumor itself was like a spunge, with its cells distended with coagulated blood: the substance of the *tibia* and *fibula* was dissolved to within half an inch of the articulation at the knee, and to within an inch or two likewise of the articulation of the ankle: and the whole appeared one confused mass of coagulated blood and mucus, without distinction of bones, membranes, or muscles.

Article II. *Experiments relative to the Analysis and Virtues of* Seltzer Water. *By* Richard Brocklesby, *M. D. Fellow of the Royal Society, and of the College of Physicians of* London.

From Dr. Brocklesby's experiments he draws the following conclusions with respect to the ingredients with which the Seltzer water is impregnated:

'By the result, says he, of the foregoing experiments, doth it not seem probable, that Seltzer mineral water contains, beside the mere elementary water, a very small quantity of calcarious earth, and a much greater portion of a native mineral *alkali*, together with some acid retained a while within the water, but which either evaporates into the open air, or else is combined with the mineral *alkali*? And is it not farther probable, that the active virtues of Seltzer water depend more on this elastic matter or fixed air, which it contains in such uncommon abundance beyond other mineral waters, than on any combination of its saline and earthy contents, which indeed were found in such small quantities, that I cannot deem them capable of any material service, and yet, from experience, I am satisfied this water is exceedingly beneficial?'

These waters are recommended as particularly useful towards the end, as well as often in other stages, of several acute and some chronic diseases.

We have three histories in which they were successful.—The first was in the case of a lady, who was much reduced by con-

† For an account of the preceding volumes, see Review, volumes xiv. and xxvii.

* By Mr. Balfour, Surgeon at Edinburgh.

ſumptive complaints, accompanied with hectic and calcarious concretions in the lungs.—In the ſecond caſe, they were given towards the end of a long continued fever, attended with repeated crops of the miliary eruption.—In the laſt caſe, there was a lingering obſtinate feveriſhneſs, accompanied with ſome ſingular appearances.

Art. III. *Remarks on the* Hydrocephalus internus, *by* John Fothergill, *M. D. F. R. S.*

This paper contains ſome accurate obſervations on the internal hydrocephalus, and is written chiefly with a view to point out the characters by which it may be diſtinguiſhed from other diſeaſes, and particularly from the *worm-caſes.*—We muſt refer our Readers to the article itſelf as well worth their peruſal.

Art. IV. *An Account of a Rupture of the Bladder from a Suppreſſion of Urine in a pregnant Woman, by Mr.* Hey, *Surgeon at* Leeds.

The rupture of the bladder moſt probably happened during the labour, and the patient lived till the ninth day after the delivery. On diſſection, fourteen pints of urine were found in the cavity of the abdomen, and an aperture in the ſuperior part of the bladder, large enough to admit a finger.

Art. V. *Of the Cure of the* Sciatica, *by* John Fothergill, *M. D.*

The method of curing this very painful and obſtinate diſeaſe, which is here recommended from experience, is to give calomel in ſuch ſmall doſes as either not at all to affect the mouth, or but very ſlightly; and to mitigate the pains by an anodyne compoſed of the tinctura thebaica and the antimonial wine, in a draught every night.

'I have ſeldom, ſays Dr. Fothergill, met with a genuine *ſciatica* but has yielded to this proceſs in the ſpace of a few weeks, and has as ſeldom returned.

'My inducement to make trial of this method at firſt was, that this kind of pains are deep ſeated in the moſt fleſhy parts of the human body, and to which it is extremely difficult to convey the efficacy of any medicine entire, either given internally, or applied without.

'That mercurials, of all the medicines we are acquainted with, moſt certainly pervade the inmoſt receſſes of the muſcular and tendinous parts, and remove diſeaſes which we know have in their their reſidence.

'That, till theſe could take effect, it was neceſſary to mitigate the pain; for all painful diſorders increaſe in proportion to the irritation attending them.'

Art. VI. *Obſervations on the* Hydrocephalus internus, *by* W. Watſon, *M. D. F. R. S.*

We have here the hiſtory of a caſe which confirms the obſervations of the late ingenious Dr. Whytt; but we meet with nothing which throws any new light upon the ſubject.

3 'Art.

Art. VII. *A Case of the* Locked Jaw, *and* Opisthonotos; *to which are added, some Remarks on the Use of the* Cicuta, *by* William Farr, *M. D. Physician to the Royal Hospital at* Plymouth.

This patient took more than five drachms of *opium* in three weeks, and with success. There was no stupor, neither was the head at all affected through the whole of the disease.

Art. VIII. *A* Hemiplegia, *attended with uncommon Circumstances: Communicated by a Member of the Society.*

The singular circumstances which occurred in this case were the following: that the patient, who survived the stroke near five years, could eat very freely, and especially of animal food, during this time; that there were no *sensible* evacuations proportioned to her manner of living; that for twelve days before her death she took nothing either solid or fluid; that during this time she was perfectly in her senses, and never expressed the least degree of hunger or thirst; but that her breath, &c. &c. became intolerably offensive before death.

Art. IX. *Of the Use of Tapping early in Dropsies, by* John Fothergill, *M. D. F. R. S.*

'I have endeavoured, says Dr. Fothergill, to prevail upon such patients labouring under this disease as have requested my assistance, to submit to it as early as possible, after I found that the quantity of water was such as could not be removed by medicines, without doing great violence to the constitution. There are several persons now living, whom I prevailed on early to submit to this operation. When I found the usual diuretics had no effect, and the more active purgatives did as much prejudice by weakening the whole frame, bringing on thirst, loss of appetite, debility, and fever, as they did service by the evacuation they produced; I desisted from medicine, allowed them to drink as much as thirst required; and, when the fluctuation was so evident as to render the operation safe, it was performed. In one case, one operation alone succeeded: for, by diuretics and corroborants, proper diet and suitable exercise, the urine passed the kidneys freely, and the patient recovered perfectly. This was an evident *ascites*, and came on soon after a lying-in; apparently from the power of absorption being weakened beyond a speedy recovery, and the exhalant vessels being relaxed immoderately; the balance was destroyed and a vast quantity of water was collected in a shorter time than I ever saw. All the *viscera* seemed to be sound, and none of the usual causes of dropsies from intemperance had preceded. Had we persevered with strong purgatives or diuretics much longer, the tone of the absorbent vessels would perhaps have been so far weakened, as to have rendered tapping, or any other means ineffectual.

'Another case was, in a single woman of about thirty-five years of age; the disease succeeded a tedious lingering fever attended with great thirst; and very large quantities of thin liquors had been poured down without discretion.

'Apprehending the distemper proceeded from the diminished power of the absorbing vessels, the redundancy of fluid, the general debility

debility of the whole frame; very few medicines, except cordials were given, till she was full enough to be tapped. This was happily performed; but she soon filled again. The operation was repeated. The medicines ordered for her now began to take effect. The urine was increased, her strength returned, and she left the town perfectly recovered.

'If we consider that this operation is far from being one of the most painful, and that, if the fluctuation is sufficiently evident, and the belly moderately tense, it is one of the safest, it seems to me, that we have nothing to fear, either in respect to ourselves or our patients, if we recommend it as early as possible.

'If I am called to a patient tending to a dropsy, the belly beginning to fill, the urine passing in small quantities, and high-coloured, the appetite falling and thirst increasing, with the loss of flesh in the upper parts of the body; I have recourse to such diuretics, purgatives, and corroborants intermixed, as the state of the case and the nature of its causes indicate. The preparations of squills, the neutral and alkaline salts, the *terebinthinate* balsams, afford many efficacious compositions. The purgatives are known to every one. If, by a reasonable perseverance in this course, no considerable benefit accrues; if the *viscera* do not evidently appear to be obstructed and unfit for the future purposes of life; if the complaints have not been brought on by a long habitual train of intemperance, and from which there seems little hope of reclaiming the patient; if the strength and time of life are not altogether against us; I desist from medicine, except of the cordial restorative kind; and let the disease proceed till the operation becomes safely practicable; when this is done, by the moderate use of the warmer diuretics, chalybeates and bitters, also the preparations of squills in doses below that point at which the stomach would be affected, I endeavour to prevent them from filling again.

'If we recollect what happens in the cure of several incysted dropsies, we shall find the opinion here advanced confirmed. Divers of these are cured by puncture; sometimes once only, sometimes the operation is necessarily repeated. You will remember many cases, I doubt not, of the dropsies of the *testis* or *tunica vaginalis* particularly. I can recollect several within my own knowledge; some that have required but once tapping, others repeatedly, and yet at last have remained perfectly cured.'

To this paper are added some useful observations on a new method of scarification in anasarcous swellings of the legs and thighs.

Art. X. *On painful Constipation from indurated* Fœces *.

Painful and frequent motions to stool, accompanied with liquid evacuations, as in a diarrhœa, often proceed from the irritation of indurated fœces.

---

* Communicated by a gentleman who pleads the privilege offered in the preface to the first volume of these Medical papers, of remaining, if a writer pleases, concealed.

'When

'When this is the caſe, ſays the ſenſible Author of this paper, the patient complains of excruciating forcing pains about the *anus*; but remitting. Some thin excrement is diſcharged, and the pain abates. A freſh ſpaſmodic effort follows, and with the like ſucceſs. It is a kind of ſpontaneous ſpaſm of all the parts in, or connected immediately with the *pelvis*, for the excluſion of this irritating ſubſtance. Should ſuch a thin diſcharge, attended with pain, lead any one to ſuppoſe it a *diarrhæa*, and, in conſequence of ſuch a ſuppoſition, treat it with aſtringents and opiates, it is evident that greater miſchief would enſue.'

The diſeaſe is not to be cured but by removing the irritating cauſe, either by the finger or ſome other convenient means.

Theſe painful motions are eaſily diſtinguiſhed from a *teneſmus*; for they are *previous* to the diſcharge, the *teneſmus* always *ſucceeds* it.

Art. XI. *An Account of the Putrid Meaſles, as they were obſerved at* London *in* 1763 *and* 1768, *by* William Watſon, *M. D. F. R. S.*

This ſpecies of meaſles is deſcribed by Morton and Huxham. Morton calls them the *morbilli maligni*, or malignant meaſles; and Huxham, the *morbilli epidemici*, or epidemic meaſles; to diſtinguiſh them from the common or benign meaſles.

The epidemic, which is here deſcribed, was more fatal in the year 1763 than in 1768.

Dr. Watſon, at the end of this paper, makes ſome obſervations on the ſmall-pox, when they ſucceed the meaſles, and ſays;—I am convinced that the ſmall pox, occurring in any way ſoon after the meaſles, eſpecially the more malignant, are dangerous.

Art. XII. *Obſervations on the Bilious Fever uſual in Voyages to the* Eaſt Indies, *by* James Badenoch, *M. D.*

The pernicious effects of the night air upon the conſtitutions of the Europeans, unſeaſoned to the torrid zone, who ſleep in woods, or in the neighbourhood of marſhes, have been inſiſted on by ſeveral medical writers, and are confirmed by our Author. With reſpect to the cure, it is obſerved, that if the pulſe and ſtrength fail, and there are other ſymptoms of impending danger, the bark is to be immediately given, without waiting for a clear remiſſion.

'During the rage of the Joanna * fever, ſays our Author, I began the cure with evacuants, &c. in expectation of procuring a plain remiſſion or intermiſſion: but I found myſelf much deceived; for it aſſumed the appearance of a continual, with now and then violent exacerbations, under which ſeveral ſunk. Fearing this might be the fate of the greateſt part of thoſe at the ſame time ill of this fever, I, without further delay, gave between thirty and forty patients in the different ſtages of that fever, one drachm of the *pulv. cort. peruv.* in

* Joanna, an iſland in the Oriental Ocean, not far from Madagaſcar.

wine, or in wine and water; and this to be taken hourly.—Several were, at the time of administering this remedy, seemingly within a few hours of their end, with the pulse sunk, and an almost universal coldness of the body, who yet, after a few doses of the bark, were much better, and, by continuing it for a day or two, recovered.'

Art. XIII. *An Account of a new Method of amputating the Leg a little above the Ankle Joint, with a Description of a Machine particularly adapted to the Stump, by Mr.* Charles White, *Surgeon to the* Manchester *Infirmary.*

This paper has already appeared in a volume of *Cases in Surgery*, published by our ingenious Author, and noticed in our Review for March last, page 218.

Art. XIV. *A* Bubonocele, *attended with uncommon Circumstances; with Remarks on the Use of Carrot Poultice. By Mr.* Henry Gibson, *Surgeon at* Newcastle upon Tyne.

This case of an inguinal hernia, is an extraordinary one. With respect to the carrot-poultice, though it is a very simple, yet it promises to be a powerful and useful application; and we think Mr. Gibson is fully authorized, from his own experience, when he recommends it, in all ill-smelling ulcers with large surfaces, whether venereal, scorbutic, scrophulous, or cancerous. He does not say that it will *cure* an ulcerated cancer, but that it will relieve the pain, and very speedily and effectually take away the offensive smell.

Art. XV. *Experiments on the* Cerumen *or Ear-wax, in order to discover the best Method of dissolving it, when causing Deafness, by Dr.* John Haygarth, *at Chester.*

From these experiments it appears, that water is the most powerful solvent of the ear-wax; and that the warmer it is applied, the more effectual, provided it is not so warm as to injure the ear.

If larger syringes, says Dr. Haygarth, were made use of, a little more forcibly applied, and longer persevered in, the success of the operation would probably be more evident.

Art. XVI. *Observations on the* Hæmoptoe, *and upon riding on Horseback for the Cure of a* Phthisis; *by* Thomas Dickson, *M. D. Physician to the* London *Hospital.*

The virtues of nitre, given in small doses, and frequently repeated, are here very highly extolled, and considered as *specific* in the *hæmoptoë*.

Art. XVII. *Some Remarks on the Bills of Mortality in* London, *with an Account of a late Attempt to establish an annual Bill for this Nation.* Anonymous.

The intent of this paper is to point out the advantages which would arise, from obliging not only the parishes within the bills of mortality, but all the parishes in England, to keep exact registers of BIRTHS, BURIALS, and MARRIAGES, instead of *christenings* and *burials* only, as the bills at present are.

' Art.

Art. XVIII. *Case of a fatal Ileus, by* M. Garthshore, *M. D. Communicated by* Richard Huck, *M. D. F. R. S. Physician to* St. Thomas's *Hospital.*

This ileus was produced by a membranous cord, which was formed into a noose, and included a doubling of about two inches of the lower end of the *ileon.*—There are four cases of the ileus, occasioned by the same cause, related in the third and fourth volumes of the Memoirs of the French Academy of Surgery.—Were there any symptoms by which we could distinguish when this was the cause, the operation of *gastrotomy* might be performed with probability of success.

[*To be concluded in our next.*]

Art. VIII. *Philosophical Transactions,* Vol. LX. For the Year 1770. 4to. 15s. sewed. Davies. 1771.

Mathematics and Mechanics.

Art. 24. *Directions for making a Machine for finding the Roots of Equations universally, with the Manner of using it. By the Rev. Mr.* Rowning.

WE are informed, in the introduction to this paper, that the circumstance which gave rise to it, was the perusal of a discourse in the Memoirs of the Royal Academy at Petersburgh, tom. vii. by the learned John Andrew de Segner; containing an universal method of discovering the roots of equations. This Author's method consists in finding several ordinates of a parabolic curve, such, that its abscissas being taken equal to any assumed values of the unknown quantity in the equation, the ordinates corresponding to those abscissas should be equal to the values of all the terms in the equation (when brought to one side,) that is, in other words, in finding several ordinates of a parabolic curve defined by the equation proposed. In such a case, it is well known, that, if a curve be drawn through the extremities of the said ordinates, the points upon the axis, where the curve shall cut it, will necessarily give the several values of the *real* roots of the equation; and the several points, where the curve shall approach the base, but return without reaching it, will shew the *impossible* roots. This learned author expresses his wishes, that some method might be thought of, whereby such curves might in all cases be described by *local* motion, but he considered this as a task too difficult to attempt. Mr. Rowning however was convinced by this hint, that the thing was possible, and therefore determined to make a trial. He soon found, that, if rulers were properly centered and so combined together, that they should always continue representatives of the several right lines, by which the above-mentioned ordinates were discovered, upon moving the first, a point or pencil, so fixed as to be carried along perpendicularly by the inter-

intersection of the first and last rulers, would describe the required curve, let the number of dimensions in the equation be what it will; only the greater that number, the greater must be the number of the rulers made use of. The Author has actually constructed a machine for this purpose, which, he thinks, may not improperly be called an *Universal Constructor of Equations*, though in its present form it extends only to equations of two dimensions. We have here a particular description of this instrument, together with the manner of rectifying it for use; a drawing of it is likewise annexed, for want of which any abstract of the Author's description must be unintelligible to our readers. The original machine is presented to the society for the inspection of those, who may be desirous of having such made. We shall only add, that all instruments of this complicated nature appear better in *theory* than they prove in *practice*. What they save in labour is generally lost in accuracy.

Art. 24. *Observations on the proper Method of calculating the Values of Reversions depending on Survivorships: By* Richard Price, D. D. F. R. S.

The design of these observations is to point out a particular error, into which there is danger of falling in finding the values of such reversions as depend on survivorships; and the ingenious Author, for the sake of perspicuity, proposes the following case. "*A*, aged 40, expects to come to the possession of an estate, should he survive *B*, aged likewise 40. In these circumstances, he offers, in order to raise a present sum, to give security for 40 l. *per ann.* out of the estate *at his death*, provided he should get into possession; that is, provided he should survive *B*. What is the sum that ought now to be advanced to him in consideration of such security, reckoning compound interest at 4 *per cent?*"

Mr. de Moivre in prob. 17 and 20 of his Treatise on Annuities, proposes the following solution. Find first the present sum *A* should receive for the reversion of 40 l. *per ann.* for ever after his death, supposing it not dependent on his surviving *B*.—The present value of such a reversion is the value of the life subtracted from the perpetuity. The value of the life, taken from Mr. de Moivre's tables, is 13.2 years purchase. This subtracted from 25, the perpetuity, leaves 11.8, the value of the supposed estate after the life of *A*; which value therefore is in money 472 l. But (as M. de Moivre observes) the lender having a chance to lose his money, a compensation ought to be made to him for the risk he runs, which is founded on the possibility that a man of the age of 40 may not survive another person of the same age. This chance is an equal chance; and therefore *half* the preceding sum, or 236 l. is the sum which should be advanced now on the expectation mentioned.

This

This solution is so plausible (says the Author) that most persons will be ready to pronounce it right. The authority of so great a master of these subjects as Mr. de Moivre has a tendency to mislead even those, who are particularly skilled in these calculations; and it is therefore the more necessary to guard against deception. The fallacy of the above solution is here evinced by applying it to the following similar question. "*A*, aged 40, offers to give security for 40 l. *per ann.* to be entered upon at his death, provided it should happen before the death of *B*, aged likewise 40. What sum should now be advanced to him for such a reversion, interest being reckoned at 4 *per cent?*" The answer to this question obtained by Mr. de Moivre's rule will be the same with the former; but it is evident that the value of a reversion to be received when a person of a given age dies, cannot be the same, whether the condition of obtaining it is, that he shall die *before*, or that he shall die *after* another person; that is, whether it is provided that a purchaser, if he succeeds, shall get into possession sooner or later. In the latter case the reversion must undoubtedly be of less value than in the former. The Author resolves both these questions into two general questions of the same kind; and, with respect to the *first*, he shews, that the value of the *longest* of the two lives, (or, the value of the two joint lives subtracted from the sum of the values of the two single lives,) should have been subtracted from the perpetuity. But in the *latter* case, the value of their joint continuance ought to have been subtracted from the same perpetuity. The true value, therefore, of the former reversion is 168:4 l. and of the latter 303 l.; so that the error is in the one case above a fifth, and in the other above a third of the true value. In all cases where three equal lives are taken, the errors will be much greater.

Mr. Simpson's method for finding the values of reversions depending on survivorships, proposed in the 28th and following problems of his Treatise on the Doctrine of Annuities and Reversions, is exact only when the lives are equal; but it gives results that are too far from the truth, when there is any considerable inequality between the lives.

The Author has subjoined a strict demonstration of the above solution; and he concludes his paper with a general rule for making assurances on the survivorship of one life beyond another, for a term of years only. Let the age of *A* be 7 years; that of *B*, 30; the term of years, 14; and the given sum assured, 100l. Let the rate of interest be 3 *per cent.*; and the table of observations that of Mr. Simpson, in his Select Exercises, p. 254. Let *a* and *b* represent the numbers in the table of observations alive at the ages of *A* and *B*, divided by the quotient arising from dividing the sum of the differences in the table from these ages respectively for the given number of years, by the said number.

number. "Find (by problem 23, in M. de Moivre's Treatise on Annuities, 4th edition) the value of an annuity on the life of *B*, for 14 years. To this value, add the quotient arising from dividing by 2 *b*, the value of an annuity certain for 14 years, taken out of M. de Moivre's tables in the treatise just mentioned, or out of table iii. in Mr. Simpson's Select Exercises; and the sum multiplied by the quotient arising from dividing the given sum assured, or 100 l. by *a*, will be the required value."

'The sum of the differences or decrements in the table for 14 years from 7 years of age, is 73; which divided by 14 gives 5.2. The number alive at 7 is 430; and this, divided by 5.2, gives 82.6 for the value of *a*. In like manner the value of *b* may be found to be 41.7. The value of an annuity for 14 years on a life of 30, is 9.5. The value of an annuity certain for 14 years is 11.296, which divided by 2 *b* or 83.4, gives 0.13; and this added to 9.5, and the sum multiplied by $\frac{100}{82.6}$ gives 11.66, or 11 l. 13 s. for the value in present payment of 100 l. assured to a person 30 years of age, and payable to him at the death of a child 7 years of age, provided that should happen before his own death in 14 years.'

In the same way may be determined, what sum ought to be paid on any survivorship, within a given term of years, of one life beyond another, in consideration of any given sums now advanced; as in the following example:

"A person aged 30, having in expectation an estate which is to come to him, provided he survives a minor aged 7, before he comes of age, wants in these circumstances to raise 1000 l. What reversion, depending on such a survivorship, is a proper equivalent for this sum now advanced, interest being reckoned at 3 *per cent.* and the probabilities of life being supposed the same with those in the *London* table of observations?" 'Answer. It appears from what has been just determined, that for 11 l. 13s. now advanced, the proper equivalent in these circumstances is 100l. to be paid, in case the supposed survivorship should take place. By the rule of proportion, therefore, it will appear, that for 1000 l. the proper equivalent is 8576 l.'

The subject of this paper is more largely discussed in the Author's *Observations on reversionary Payments, &c.** to which he has added the necessary tables for making the above calculations.

Art. XXXVI. *Some new Theorems for computing the Areas of certain curve Lines. By Mr.* John Landen, *F. R. S.*

The Author here proposes a concise and expeditious method of determining the areas of particular curves. The theorems, which the learned Editor of Mr. Cote's *Harmonia Mensurarum* has given for this purpose, and those, which several other

* For which see Reviews for October and November.

writers

writers have since made use of, are much more complicated than might be wished, and are obtained by resolving the expression for the ordinate, into others of a more simple form: whereas upon Mr. Landen's principles this labour is unnecessary, and the *whole* areas of the curves here specified (when finite) are computed with admirable facility. The three theorems contained in this article are investigated according to the new method of comparing curvilineal areas, inserted in the Phil. Transf. for 1768.

Art. XLIII. *A Letter to James West, Esq; President of the Royal Society, containing the Investigations of twenty Cases of compound Interest. By* J. Robertson, *Lib.* R. S.

It is well known by all who are acquainted with the subject of compound interest, that it was more fully considered by the late William Jones, Esq; F. R. S. than by any other writer. He caused to be engraved, on a copper-plate, more cases in interest than had been exhibed before his time; and the theorems for these cases were inserted by Mr. Jones himself, without their investigations, in the quarto edition of logarithms, published by Gardiner; they were likewise published by Mr. Dodson, with examples to illustrate the use of his antilogarithmic tables. This article contains the investigation of these theorems, and will be acceptable to all who have any taste for such subjects.

Astronomy.

Many of the articles in this class relate to the transit of Venus in 1769; and, as this is a subject which has been before our readers for several years past, we shall only select such remarks or conclusions, as have not been already noticed. *Mr. Dunn*, in art. 9, gives a particular account of several phænomena, which attended the late transits, and made it difficult to determine the exact moment of circular contact; after describing many of these, he observes, "that at 7^h 29′ 38″ he saw the planet as it were held to the sun's limb by a ligament formed of many black cones, whose basis stood on the limb of Venus, and their vertexes pointing to the limb of the sun. These cones put on various positions, and as Venus advanced, they alternately contracted themselves towards the limb of Venus, and expanded themselves towards the sun's limb, performing their undulations always regularly and in the same time, as the planet advanced on the disc, till 7^h 29′ 48″ apparent time. At the end of this interval, the agitation or fermentation was exceeding violent, for the whole limb of Venus would sometimes librate towards the limb of the sun, and sometimes the limb of the sun would turn convex in yielding towards Venus; but the thread of light was not yet formed."—"I carefully examined

mined the sides of those black cones connected with the limb of the sun, and saw the fissures or spaces between them to be filled with a steady illumination, of the colour of twilight, compared with the light of the sun; and whilst I was steadily attending to these circumstances, I saw the pure and genuine light of the sun break in between some of those fissures like streaks of lightning, which made the partial light become, in two or three seconds of time, of the same colour as the light of the sun, yet still the undulating ligament though reduced was not broken."

This partial light Mr. Dunn ascribes to rays scattered by refraction and reflection through that part of the planet's atmosphere where the contact was to happen; and the well-defined streaks of light following it, he takes to have been the sun beams passing between mountains on the surface of Venus's globe. To this paper the Author has annexed several drawings of the appearances in the transit of 1761, and also of the like appearances in the transit of 1769.

Article 29. gives an account of an occultation of the star Tauri by the moon, observed at *Leicester*, by the Rev Mr. *Ludlam*.

Articles 30 and 47 relate to the effect of the aberration of light on the phases of the transit of Venus. As they treat of the same subjects, we connect them together. Mr. Winthrop, the Hollisian professor of mathematics and natural philosophy at Cambridge, New England, in a letter to Dr. Franklin, observes, That Mr. Bliss and Mr. Hornsby, in their calculations, suppose the phases of the transit of Venus to be accelerated by the aberration of light, which amounts to 55″ of time. According to his own idea of aberration, he apprehends the transit would be retarded by it. In order to have his mistake rectified, if the hint he gives should prove such, he familiarly illustrates, by the help of a diagram, the several steps whereby he was led into it. Dr. Price, to whose consideration this paper was referred, makes no doubt of the truth of the ingenious Author's observation. He concurs with him in opinion, that the effect of the aberration of Venus is to retard, and not to accelerate the phases of a transit; and this retardation is 55½″, since this is nearly the time, which Venus, during a transit, takes to move over 3″.7. He further observes, that this is by no means the whole retardation of a transit occasioned by aberration. There is (says he) a retardation arising from the aberration of the sun, as well as from that of Venus. The aberration of the sun, it is well known, lessens its longitude about 20″; and the aberration of Venus increases its longitude at the time of a transit 3″.7. Venus, therefore, and the sun, at the instant of the true beginning of a transit, must be separated from one another by aberration 23″.7; and since Venus then

moves

moves nearly at the rate of 4′ in an hour, it will move over 23″.7 in 5′ 55″. And consequently, from the instant of the *real* beginning of a transit, 5′ 55″ must elapse before it can begin *apparently*. Should it be objected, that the sun's aberration ought not to be reckoned, because the solar tables give his apparent places or longitude with the aberration included; it is answered, that the retardation here mentioned is properly the time that the calculated phases of a transit of Venus will precede the apparent phases, supposing the tables, from which the calculation is made, to give the *true* places of the sun. If they give the *apparent* places of the sun, this retardation, instead of being lessened, will be considerably increased. This is evident, if it be considered, that the geocentric places of the planets are deduced from their heliocentric, on the supposition that the earth is exactly opposite to the sun in the ecliptic; but this supposition is just only when the sun's *true* place is taken. The earth is, in reality, always about 20″ more forward in its orbit than the point opposite to the sun's *apparent* place; and hence it will happen, that in calculating a transit of Venus from tables which give the sun's *apparent* places, a greater difference will arise between the calculated and the observed times than if the tables had given the sun's *true* places. The ingenious Author further explains the reason of this difference by a figure; and plainly shews, that at the time of a conjunction calculated from the apparent places of the sun, Venus will be observed at a distance from the sun equal to an angle of 72″.2, supposing its distance from the earth to be 277, and from the sun 723. To which if we add 3″.7, the proper aberration of Venus at the time of a transit, we shall have 75″.9 for the whole visible distance of Venus from the sun's center at the calculated moment of a conjunction, over which it will move in 19 minutes of time. And this, consequently, will be the retardation of the phases of a transit of Venus occasioned by aberration, on the supposition, that in calculating, the sun's *apparent*, and not his *true* place is taken.

In order to estimate this retardation exactly, allowance must be made for the inclination of the orbit of Venus to the ecliptic; and the aberration of the sun together with the proportion of Venus's distance from the earth to her distance from the sun must be taken as they really are at the time of a transit. Thus, at the time of the last transit of Venus, supposing light to come from the sun to the earth in 8′.2, the abberration of the sun was 19″.8. The distance of Venus from the earth was to its distance from the sun as 290 to 726, and therefore the retardation 18′ 16″.

These observations are new as well as important; and for this reason, the above abstract will be peculiarly acceptable to our readers.

8 Art.

Art. XXXI. *Extract of a Letter from Mr.* Mallet *of* Geneva *to Dr.* Bevis, F. R. S.

This paper contains sundry miscellaneous observations made in the north, and printed in the commentaries of the academy of Petersburgh. The latitude of Ponoi, where the Author was stationed to observe the transit, was determined by several meridian altitudes of the sun and stars to be 67°. 4'. 30"; and by the sun's eclipse of June 4th, the difference of meridians between Paris and Ponoi was found 38°.51' east. With respect to the transit of Venus he observes, that, assuming the nearest distance of the centers of Venus and the sun, as seen from the center of the earth 10' 27", the moment of conjunction was 12^h 46' 21½" apparent time, and the geocentric latitude of Venus for that moment 10' 33".9; but if the nearest distance of the centers be supposed 5" less, the latitude becomes so much less, and the moment of conjunction 1' 28" later. Mr. Mallet made, also a great number of observations for determining the force of gravity, and the length of the simple pendulum swinging seconds. The pendulum he used made 98740 oscillations at Para in 24 hours of mean time, and at Paris 98891 in the same time. At Petersburgh the number of oscillations was 98941; at Ponoi 98946. Whence it follows, that the simple pendulum, which beats seconds at Petersburgh, will be 441,02 lines (Paris measure); that is, $\frac{45}{100}$ line longer than the pendulum which beats seconds at Paris: and the pendulum at Ponoi will be 441,22 lines, that is, $\frac{65}{100}$ line longer than that at Paris. As the excess therefore of the Paris pendulum above that at the equator has been determined 1.50 line; we shall find, admitting the principle of Newton and Huygens, that the increase of gravity follows the ratio of the square of the sine of latitude in approaching the pole, the excess of the Petersburgh pendulum above that at the equator 1.98 lines, instead of 1.95 which is the result of experiments; and 2.24 lin. for the excess of the Ponoi pendulum instead of 2.15 lin. Whence the Author suggests, that the increments of gravity follow a ratio somewhat greater than that of the squares of the sines of latitude, which is confirmed by other experiments. The declination of the magnetic needle at Ponoi was found 1° 20' east; and the inclination, determined both by Dr. D. Bernouilli's machine and Mr. Euler's compass in 1769, 76°.½ at Ponoi; at Petersburgh lat. 59° 55', long. 48°, 73°⅔; and at Kola lat. 68°. 54' long. 49°.45', 77°.¾. It appears further from the meteorological observations made in Lapland, that the mean height of the barometer for four months was 27 inches 6⅓ lin.

Art. 39 contains astronomical observations made in Ireland by Mr. Charles Mason.

Art.

Art. 40 is a letter from M. Pingrè to the Rev. Mr. Maskelyne, giving an account of observations at Fort Royal in Martinico, and Cape Francis in the island of St. Domingo.

Art. 41 contains observations of immersions and emersions of Jupiter's first satellite, made at Funchal in Madeira by the late Dr. *Heberden*, from Dec. 26, 1763 to July 5, 1768. The next article gives an account of the transit of Mercury observed in Pennsylvania, Nov. 9, 1769.

Articles 49 and 50 furnish the observations of the last transit of Venus made in California; the solar paralax is stated in the first of these papers at $8''1$, and the sun's distance greater than it was supposed to be $\frac{7}{31}$, or nearly 6,685,000 leagues; but without the corresponding observations, the problem cannot be completely solved.

[*To be continued.*]

Art. IX. *The History of the Art of Horsemanship.* By Richard Berenger, Esq; Gentleman of the Horse to his Majesty. 4to. 2 Vols. 2 l. 2 s. Boards. Davies, &c. 1771.

THIS elegant work is divided into two capital parts, happily answering its division into volumes.

The first volume contains an history of the art of horsemanship, from the earliest accounts that are to be collected of it from history, and historical monuments; together with a detail of the qualities of horses of different countries, both in ancient and modern times. To these curious particulars are added, a translation of *Xenophon's Treatise of Horsemanship*; a piece that will gratify every intelligent lover of the art: with a *Dissertation on the Ancient Chariot; the Exercise of it in the Race, and the Application of it to real Service in War*; for which contribution Mr. Berenger is indebted to Governor Pownall.

The second volume contains the principles of the art of horsemanship, and a dissertation on the merits of the various kinds of *bits*.

In Mr. Berenger's inquiry into the horsemanship of the ancients, he shews great reading; and appears to have been indefatigable in collecting whatever was to be found in ancient historians and poets, respecting the noble animal which is the object of his enquiries.

In his account of the qualities of horses of the present time, our Author begins with those of Arabia; thus describing both them and their riders:

'Among these *Arabia* stands most eminently distinguished for the excellence of its horses, and the address of its inhabitants in riding them. Historians and travellers unite in the praises of both; yet a person of knowledge in the *art*, will, nevertheless, be somewhat perhaps

haps embarrassed in forming his opinion, and think it necessary to have a fuller and clearer evidence, before he will decree the palm to them. Happy indeed would it be for the *Arts*, if *Artists* only were its *Judges*, and people meddled with nothing but such things as they are qualified to understand: but, unfortunately for the present subjects, among numbers of others, it is not so: unfortunately for us, none of the writers who have touched upon it, have gone far enough into it, so as to open and explain many particulars, with that accuracy and fullness, which alone can enable us to judge of the real merit of these famous riders, and horses; for the accounts given of them are so loose and imperfect, that it is as difficult for a real judge to form any precise opinion concerning it, as it would be for a *Jeweller* to know what to think, if a common *Sailor* were to give an account of the *Diamonds* which he had seen in the mines of India or Brazil; the lustre, the hardness, and other particulars, which solely constitute their merit, are unknown to him; and the jeweller would probably be in danger of being misled, if he should trust to the ignorance of such a reporter.

'Hence the random accounts of Arabian horsemanship, so much boasted and extolled, but related too *superficially* to enable us to form any clear judgment, or know by what means they teach and dress their horses to perform the feats ascribed to them, or what their notions and principles of riding are; no writer or traveller that I could ever consult, being an horseman, and none but an horseman can give a clear and satisfactory account of *Horsemanship*; it is to be suspected, therefore, from this want of *lawful evidences*, that in the feats of Arabian horsemanship so much boasted by writers and travellers, more is to be ascribed to the activity and powers of the horses, than to the knowledge and judgment of the riders; who yet are confessedly very bold and dexterous in the saddle; but who, by working upon false rules, or perhaps without any, never attain that grace, exactness, and certainty, which the principles of the *Art*, if known, would insure to them; principles which have their foundation in nature, and are justified by truth and experience.'

Here however Mr. B. appears to presume too far in decrying the merit of the Arabian horsemen, as, by his own confession, he only wants evidence and information, owing to the deficient knowledge of *our* travellers: this deficiency then is all on our part, and we may as well presume, on the other side, that a nation, so long famous for their horses, for their attention to them, and for the extraordinary feats they perform with them, are not without principles sufficient to produce and support the reputation they have acquired. We may farther suppose, and justice seems to demand it, that if they do not derive their rules immediately from the European manege, they are at least dictated by the nature of their beasts, by the climate they live in, by the soil they tread, and suited to what themselves require of their horses. These local circumstances may perhaps account, in great part, for what our Author says farther respecting them; viz.

'They

'They are reported to have their stirrups remarkably short, which obliges the rider to sit upon his saddle, as if he was in an easy chair: their bridles * are so powerful, as to endanger the breaking of the horse's jaw, if he should resist; the hand being as rough and severe, as the bridles are cruel, and both co-operating to bruise and tear the mouth, and in the end to render it callous and dead: it is a great feat of horsemanship with them to stop *short*; this they effect by mere violence and strength, and as they never previously *make* the mouths, nor supple the joints of their horses, the rudeness of the *stop* so shocks the whole frame, as frequently to spoil and ruin the haunches and other parts. The horse-shoes used by them are large, very heavy, and of a circular form, resembling in shape that sort of shoe, called by us the *Bar-shoe* †. The province of *Sinan* is at present eminent for its race of horses, of which some are near sixteen hands in height, and very muscular and strong; while the breed of the *wandering Arabs*, seldom exceed the measure of fourteen and two inches, probably for the want of more generous nourishment than they can find in their migrations and unsettled condition. The Arabians feel no reluctance to part with their horses in sale, they being a commodity which they breed for that purpose, and the *Imaum* raises a revenue from the duty of horses which are sent out of the country, the tax being about ten pounds sterling paid for each horse.

'The gross and ignorant state in which these people live, their bigotted attachment to their own customs and manners, their little intercourse with the more polished parts of the globe, and their manner of sitting on horseback (which, though sufficient for their purposes, yet does not speak them to be acquainted with the *true* seat, and is aukward and clumsy) seem all to incline us to believe, that this suspicion is not groundless. Nevertheless, it must be acknowledged, that without these advantages, the *Arabs* and their horses deserve the greatest commendations; but the latter seem to be entitled to the *larger* share, while we cannot but lament, that people who have such noble and fine-toned *Instruments*, should understand *Music* no better.

'These horses, by the unanimous allowance of all who have seen them, are reckoned the most beautiful of their kind, larger and more furnished than those of *Barbary*, and of the justest proportions; but as very few have been brought into Europe, it is not possible to speak of them *collectively*, with that justice and accuracy, which would decide their character. There is scarcely an *Arab*, how indigent and mean soever, who is not possessed of some. They usually prefer (like the ancient Scythians) to ride *Mares*, experience having convinced them, that they endure fatigue better, and resist the calls of hunger and thirst longer than horses, not being so inclined to vice, but gentle and willing, nor so subject to neigh as the males. They are so

* They are known in Europe by the name of Turkish bits.

† In a hot climate, and on a loose sandy soil, the foot may require an extraordinary security against being inflamed, and the hoof against being ground away. Ignorant as the Arabs may be, they must have some reason for what appears to *us* so preposterous, and so ill calculated for speed.

accustomed to be together in great numbers, that their owners venture to trust them whole days by themselves, and are under no apprehension of mischief, from their biting or kicking one another.

'The *Arabs* sell such of their horses as they do not like to keep for *Stallions*, and are more scrupulously exact in preserving their *Pedigrees*, even for ages back; so that they know, with the utmost certainty, their parentage, alliances, and genealogy; distinguishing each family, or breed, by different appellations or epithets, and dividing the whole kind into three classes.

'The first is called *Noble*, being the purest and most ancient, without ever having received any stain or mixture, on the side of the sires or dams.

'The second class is composed of horses, whose race, though *ancient*, has been mixed and crossed with *Plebeian* blood, either on the male or female side, which, nevertheless, is deemed *noble*, but *misallied*.

'The third, and last division, is made up of the common and ordinary horses, which are sold at a low price, while those of the first and second class (among the latter of which some are to be found equal to those of the first) command excessive sums of money, when sought in purchase.

'It is a rule with the Arabs never to let a *capital* mare be covered but by a stallion of equal quality. Each breeder acquires a perfect knowledge of their own and neighbours' horses, and of each particular relative to them; and their names, mark, colour, exploits, and age. When an Arab has not an approved stallion of his own, he hires one for a certain sum of his neighbours; *Witnesses* are called to be present at the consummation, who give a solemn certificate of the performance, signed and sealed in the presence of the *Emir*, or some other magistrate. In the instrument of attestation, the names of the horse and mare are mentioned, and their pedigrees set forth. When the mare drops her foal, witnesses are called again, who sign a fresh certificate, touching the birth of the foal, in which they describe each particular, and record the day of the birth. These vouchers stamp a great value upon the animal, and, like the deeds of an estate, are given with it, when sold, or otherwise called in question.

'The lowest-priced mares of the first class, are worth five hundred French crowns; many of them will bring a thousand, and some even four, five, or six thousand livres. As the Arabs have no houses, but live in tents, these tents serve at the same time for stables for their horses, and homes for themselves. Mares, foals, the master, and his wife and children, *lay* together pell-mell, and receive the shelter of the same roof; which

Et pecus et dominum communi clauderet umbrâ. Juv.

In the same cavern, undistinguish'd, sleeps
The humble owner, and the flocks he keeps.

'The young children will *lay* upon the neck, side, or crawl between the legs of the mare and foal, without receiving the least hurt; and it is even asserted, that these animals are cautious how they move, lest they should incommode these little ones, by whom they will permit every playful liberty to be taken. Their masters treat them with the utmost fondness, and perfect good-will and harmony subsists between

between them; they are extremely nice in the care of them, and endeavour to engage them to perform what they require by the gentlest means, seldom chusing to urge them beyond the walk, which is their usual pace; but if they have occasion to give the spur, the animal no sooner feels its side touched by the toe of the *Stirrup*, which is pointed and sharp, so as to answer the intention of a spur, but it springs forward at once with incredible force, runs with amazing rapidity, and leaps over whatever obstructs its way, with the lightness and vigour of a stag; yet is so gentle and attentive to the rider, and so well taught, that if he should happen to fall, it will stop at once, though running at the top of its speed. The Arabian horses generally are of a middling size, neat and clean in their shape and limbs, and of a thin and slender figure. Their keepers feed and curry them morning and night with great exactness, never suffering the least stain to remain upon them, frequently washing their legs, manes, and tails, which latter they encourage to flow at full length, and comb but seldom, for fear of breaking or pulling out the hairs. They never feed them in the day, but allow them to drink two or three times, reserving their meal till sun-set, when they dispense to each horse about half a bushel of barley, well sifted and cleaned, and put in a sack, which they tie upon their heads, where they leave it till morning, that they may take due time to eat their allowance. About March, when the grass is strong and plentiful, they soil them, and devote this season likewise to the work of procreation; observing always to throw cold water upon the mare, the moment the stallion descends from her back. This custom is observed by us, and other European nations, being probably borrowed of the Arabians, as well as that of keeping the pedigrees, and recording the victories of our race-horses. When the spring is past, the horses are taken from the pastures, and kept for the rest of the year without grass or hay, and solely upon barley, with a certain portion of straw. When the colts are about a year and six months old, the Arabs sheer the hair of their tails, to make them grow thicker and stronger.

'They begin to ride the colts at the age of two years, or two and an half at most, rigidly observing never to touch them before this period, and always keeping those horses which they ride, saddled and bridled, and waiting at the doors of their tents the whole day.

'The most ancient and noblest breeds of this country, are said to be sprung from the wild horses of the *Desert*, of which, many ages ago, a stud was composed, which increased the breed, and peopled Asia and Africa with these noble animals. These horses are so fleet as to outrun the *Ostrich*; and the Arabs of the *Desert*, as well as the people of *Lybia*, rear a great number, and devote them solely to the chace, never using them in combat, or upon journies, feeding them with grass, and when that fails, supporting them with dates and camels milk, which contributes to make them active and vigorous, without inclining them to grow fat.

'From these accounts it is to be concluded, that the Arabian horses are, and have been, from all time, esteemed to be the first and best of their kind; and that it is originally from them, that the noblest breeds of Europe, Asia, and Africa proceed, being immediately or remotely

 descended

descended from *Barbs*, descended from Arabians, whose climate is, perhaps, the most favourable and best adapted to the nature of horses of any hitherto known, since, without going elsewhere, in search of horses to *cross* and mend their breed, the Arabians keep it religiously pure from all foreign mixture, and trust solely to their own stock, which affords them a finer, and more generous race, than they could procure by any alliances with other horses. So that if the climate should not in itself be the most friendly and congenial of all others to the nature of horses, yet the inhabitants seem to make it so, by their nice and judicious care, and by never permitting an horse or mare to come together, unless of equal rank, beauty, and merit. By this exactness, scrupulously observed for ages, they have raised and refined the species, and led it up to a pitch of perfection, beyond what mere nature perhaps could have attained, though assisted by the advantages of a better country.'

[*To be concluded in another Article.*]

ART. X. *The History and Antiquities of the Conventual and Cathedral Church of Ely: from the Foundation of the Monastery, A. D. 673, to the Year 1771. Illustrated with Copper-plates.* By James Bentham, M. A. Fellow of the Society of Antiquaries, Rector of Feltwell St. Nicholas, Norfolk, and late Minor Canon of Ely. 4to. Royal Paper. 1 l. 11 s. 6 d. sewed. Cambridge printed, and sold by Bathurst in London. 1771.

TO those who are fond of the study of ecclesiastical antiquities, the publication before us will be highly acceptable. It exhibits, with minute precision, the history of the *Church* of *Ely* in five successive periods. The first commences with the foundation of a church and monastery at Ely by Etheldreda, Queen of the Northumbrians, and describes the state of it under several Abbesses, till it was destroyed by the Danes in 870. In the second, we have the condition of this church, while it continued in the possession of the secular clergy; in the third, the refounding of the monastery for Monks, by King Edgar, with the government of it under the succeeding Abbots; in the fourth, the conversion of the abbey into a bishoprick by Henry I. with the succession of Bishops to the dissolution of the monastery under Henry VIII. The fifth and last period contains the establishment of a Dean and Prebendaries by that monarch, and extends to the present year.

In the course of this long detail, our Author appears to have examined, with much industry and attention, every historical monument and authority that could throw any light on his subject. But, with a zeal that is too common to antiquarians, he has frequently given an importance and value, to trivial and uninteresting circumstances; and he seems to have thought, that he was doing service to mankind, while he was ransacking the refuse

refuse of libraries to collect the private and useless occurrences, which the folly or the fraud of priests has preserved, or invented, concerning saints and abbesses.

Amidst the fictions, however, and the strokes of superstition, with which his work abounds, there is yet to be found in it much curious information; and, if he has not always made the most profitable use of the materials he has collected, they may chance, nevertheless, in their present form, to prove highly serviceable to future writers.

That he might diversify and enlarge his performance, he has prefixed to it a general and succinct account of the introduction and advancement of Christianity in this kingdom, previous to its settlement among our Saxon ancestors; at which æra his history properly begins. These reasons have also induced him to enquire into the origin and progress of *Gothic* architecture; and his observations on this subject, form, in our opinion, the most valuable part of his work.

The temporal jurisdiction of the Bishops of Ely was a matter of too much moment to be passed over in silence; but we must confess, that we could not have expected our Historian to have treated of it with so much parade and ostentation. There is nothing more certain than that the dignified clergy arrogated, in former times, a royal and independent jurisdiction. They appointed judges to try all causes, whether civil or criminal. The inhabitants of their lands they considered as their subjects, and gave laws to them. They made war by their own authority. They stamped and issued money within the bounds of their territories; and they performed every other act of princely power. But is it to be mentioned to the honour of the priesthood, that they neglected the cares and duties of religion, to add to the splendor and dominion of their order, and that they employed the influence derived to them from their office and character, to impose on the common understanding of men, and to violate their most sacred rights?

There is an appendix to this publication, which contains a variety of ancient charters, and other authentic writings; together with several critical disquisitions, by the Author and his friends. Of these last-mentioned papers it is sufficient to remark, that they discover considerable erudition, but they relate not to topics of general curiosity. The plates, with which the work is embellished, are, many of them, elegant, and seem to be executed with accuracy.

Art. XI. Conclusion of the *Farmer's Tour through the East of England.*

IN our last month's Review, we endeavoured to come to a right understanding with our hasty Author, in regard to the doctrine of averages; and we shall now resume our abstract of such points of information as, in our apprehension, will be most acceptable to our agricultural Readers. Accordingly we come next to what is said with respect to

Quantity of Seed.

And here we must again praise Mr. Young's candour *; for he collects from these minutes, conclusions which seem rather contrary to the results of his own Course of experimental Agriculture.

Wheat.		Barley.		Peas.		Beans.	
Seed.	Crop.	S.	C.	S.	C.	S.	C.
2 bush.	- 24 b.	2 b. to 3	32 b.	2½ b. to 3,	23 b.	2 b. to 3,	37 b.
2¼ or ½	- 23	3½ to 4	- 33	3 to 4	- 22	3 to 4	- 29
2¾ or 3	- 22	4½ to 5	- 27	Above 4,	22	Above 4,	26
3¼ or ½	- 21						

† Oats uncertain; but best quantity from 2½ bush. to 3¾ bush.

Mr.

---

* We are glad of this opportunity of doing justice to Mr. Y. and also to ourselves. We declare that we never thought Mr. Y. either the *founder* or *follower* of any system of agriculture; but, on the contrary, that he may say justly with *Horace*,

"*Quo me cunque ferat* TEMPESTAS, *deferor* HOSPES."

I sail before the wind, where'er it blows.

And, on this occasion, we must for a moment remonstrate to Mr. Y. that he has permitted *squint-eyed* Jealousy to suggest to him, effectually, that we designed, in the review of the *Course of experimental Agriculture*, to represent him unfavourably to the public, by using the word *systematiser*, instead of *founder of a system*, in our account of his character of Mr. *Mortimer*: We avow that we meant only an innocent variation of style. But Mr. Y. maintains that '*systematiser* is a *barbarous* word.' Is it so indeed? It is directly from the Greek; and our Author may as well call *critic* a *barbarous* word: but we know who they are to whom the Greeks are *barbarians*; viz. the Goths and Vandals of every age! these enemies of all Mr. Y.'s *virtù*.

† Mr. Y. has decried (in the preface to his Course of experimental Agriculture) the very useful and skilful Mr. *Blythe*, for an assertion that oats, worth 6 l. per acre, may be produced on ground worth *nothing* while uncultivated. We judged this censure severe and unjust, and ventured, in our review of that article, to hint that such crops, on such land, might be obtained by paring and burning. In reply, Mr. Y. with assurance asserts, that 'the man who could quote such management, cannot know his right hand from his left, in farming:' and he maintains that, in order to get the work of paring and burning done early enough in spring for sowing of oats, with

reason-

Mr. Y. observes, that the small quantity of seed for wheat, barley, and oats, is partly owing to his including several places

reasonable expectation of a great crop, it must be performed in *frosts* and *snows*. But we know of no patent which Mr. Y. has obtained to be believed, contrary to the common experience of mankind, and we therefore assert, that there is often, in fine springs, opportunity of getting land, in no small quantity, pared and burned (especially with the help of furze faggots, &c.) early enough in spring to sow *hasty* oats, with just expectation of a better crop than five or six quarters per acre; so that if Mr. Y. will not allow that oats sometimes, in Blythe's days, sold for 20 s. per quarter, yet his crop might amount to 6 l. per acre in value in different ways, viz. either by the crops yielding more than six quarters per acre, or by adding to the value of the oats themselves that of their straw, frequently equivalent to an equal quantity of ordinary hay. But since Mr. Y. is very positive, that no man who quotes the getting good crops of oats immediately after paring and burning, *can* know his right hand from his left in farming, we will mention one who has done this, and yet is in Mr. Y.'s esteem one of the best farmers in England. This is no other than his dear self, who (in Vol. III. p. 131. of this Eastern Tour) informs us, that it is the custom, in a large tract of country, to pare and burn their soil, and that they *immediately* gain from it five quarters per acre of oats; and Mr. Y. must know that in the North are many thousands of acres, which, when pared and burned, and aided by lime, will give better crops of oats than these.

On occasion of these strictures of Mr. Y. on good crops of oats, we are naturally called upon to examine his remarks on some crops of rape. In the preface to his Course of experimental Agriculture, he censures *Beati* as a *conceited* writer; and cites a passage from him, in which he prints the word *cannot* in italics. A man must be a wretched judge of style, indeed, who could apprehend that the Tourist intended not, by this distinction in printing, to censure Beati as a conceited writer. But Mr. Y. being by us admonished of his undue severity, now pretends that he meant a censure of the *fact*, not the *expression*. Yet, alas! the fact admits nothing to be said in defence of his censure, and he has sense enough not to attempt to say any thing. Beati speaks of crops of rape which *cannot* produce less than five quarters per acre. Farmers, in the Fens, often get twice the quantity.

With how ill a grace does the man, who shews himself to have so bad a memory with regard to his own assertions in this work, upbraid us with a single slip of memory, of no consequence to the subject treated of! The candid Reader of the Monthly Review will not expect that we should always have at hand every book *incidentally* mentioned. We well remembered, that a good list of old agricultural writers was given in the *Musæum Rusticum* many years ago, and given *anonymous*. The Author of this article read, with attention and pleasure, although he did not review them, Mr. Hart's Essays; and when we mentioned (in the review of Mr. Y.'s Course of experimental Agriculture) that list, we did not immediately remember places where drilling and hoeing are used. But, we apprehend, that by this confusion the usefulness of these tables is lessened, if not destroyed.

DRAUGHT. Horses, or oxen, 3½ plough an acre *per diem*. —*N.B.* The same average as in the Northern Tour. But here surely Mr. Y. should observe that the horses, in most parts of the North, are small, and probably not above two-thirds in weight of draught to the great black breed in other countries.

He makes 6⅓ of horses the average of this Tour for 100 acres; whereas 9⅓ is the average for the Northern Tour. The consideration of the size and strength of the horses in the two Tours should have great weight.

Mr. Y. makes the average expence of an horse, per annum, through this Tour, 9 l. 4 s. But in two places the decline in value is included, and in one place it is made so enormous as to amount to 7 l. which is the whole real value of a draught-horse in several parts of the kingdom, and probably the half in many more, and a third part in almost any.

Beside, if any allowance is to be made for decline of value in some places, an allowance for improvement of it should be made in many others; nay, in the same places.

This we say merely from a principle of equity, as we are, on the whole, strongly inclined to give the preference to oxen, for draught.

Farmers at Rye reckon the expence of an horse, per annum, 10 l. 15 s. 6 d. of an ox 2 l. 8 s. 4 d. nearly, as Mr. Y. observes, 'four and a half to one.' But it appears not that they make due allowance for the improvement or decline of either animal. This nice point wants to be settled by experiments. However, the minutes of this Tour seem to evince two important points, viz. first, that oxen are greatly superior to horses; and, secondly, that oxen in harness are superior to them in yokes.

Mr. Y. assigns, as two powerful causes of the unreasonable disuse of oxen in draught, the high price of live stock, and the absurd custom of using great numbers of oxen, 10 or 12, in one draught. The former we cannot comprehend.

SHEEP. Mr. Y. shews, very clearly, we think, that in Dorsetshire, where they boast of scarcely any thing but skill in sheep, this article is nearly a losing one; so much grass land do they allot to their flock: and he puts them upon a very rational improvement of their management.

---

member that it had been given as Mr. Hart's. Will any one Reader of sense and candour from hence conclude, either that the Monthly Reviewers reviewed Mr. Hart's Essays, without reading them, or even that we are unfair or incapable reviewers of Mr. Y.'s productions?

We think, with our Author, that a proper breed and management are of much more consequence to the shepherd's success, than richness of land.

The minutes of this Tour assign most contradictory causes of the rot.

Mr. Y. shews how, by purchasing of litter, the annual profit of folding 100 sheep may be made 24 l. 7 s. 6 d. *

The superiority of the fold of ews to that of wethers is much disputed in the course of this Tour; from the minutes of which it appears, that ews may safely be folded during winter, and then their fold will exceed that of wethers, on account of urine.

COWS. Mr. Y. reckons them, in general management, unprofitable to the farmer; and, in order to render them profitable, he proposes first, to keep them in winter, when dry, on straw; and when in milk, on straw and turnips. We ourselves often wonder how farmers, who depend chiefly on a dairy, can make cows pay for their chargeable winter keeping on hay; but we fear they would find, by summer's milking, the imprudence of making straw so principal a part of winter food. Experiments on this head are desirable.

The second thing which Mr. Y. advises is, to save, for hogs in winter, in cisterns, all the wash of the dairy through summer. Mr. Peters, the Author of *Winter Riches*, is in this, as in many other things, so opposite to Mr. Y. that he thinks the farmer may as well throw all his summer wash on the dunghill.

Mr. Y. observes, that in all probability the mongrel breed of cows (such as are in Suffolk) are much better for the pail than the finest, which is twice as large. He apprehends that, by this change, half the expence of keeping may be saved. But then it should be considered what loss to the plough and the butcher might be hereby sustained. The dairy scheme seems to connect milking and breeding, on which latter *feeding* depends.

PROVISIONS. Mr. Y. shews, from the minutes of this Tour, that *bread* is at a pretty equal price through the whole kingdom, and also *cheese*; but that *butter*, and butcher's meat rise towards the capital. For these variations and equalities he assigns obvious reasons, viz. that a good police communicates corn pretty equally through the body of the realm, and also cheese; but that butter and butcher's meat cannot be so easily conveyed without considerable charge; and yet, after all, the cases of cheese and butter are not very different.

LABOUR. From the same source, he shews that the price of labour is nearly sufficient to maintain the industrious, frugal, and temperate poor, comfortably, without parish assistance.

* A point very worthy of attention.

POOR

POOR RATES. Our Author shews that these rates, as managed under the present laws (except where houses of industry are erected) are by no means proportioned to the natural, real, honest wants which they are designed to relieve. He justly inveighs against tea-drinking twice a day by the poor who depend on parish support; and he rightly asserts, that the raising of the price of labour, which is already advanced one-fourth in 18 years (as appears from the minutes of this Tour) will not relieve those who honestly want relief. He very reasonably distinguishes himself from those who want *true rational* humanity for the poor, and justly stigmatises the indiscriminate declaimers for the poor, as real enemies to the landed interest.

MANURES. The view which Mr. Y. gives us of this very important article in the Eastern Tour is extremely useful. We must be particular in our review of it.

LIME appears efficacious in almost all soils, although least so on thin loams, limestones, and old pastures. It is very considerable on poor sands, but most powerful on peat land, particularly in the Peak of Derbyshire, where strong stone-lime, to the amount of 360 bushels (equal to 600 of chalk-lime in Mr. Y.'s estimation) is laid on one acre with amazing success. What will the *complete Former*, whose work we have very lately reviewed, say to this phenomenon, which we were well prepared to receive and believe?

MARLE (including chalks) is very good on light loams and sands; but best on heavy lands. Like lime, it kills weeds, and it fertilizes. Even a third marling is found beneficial. We think, with this Author, that its good effect greatly depends on quantity. In some places it costs from 7 s. to 9 s. per waggon-load at the pit, and yet the farmers find it worth their while to bring it many miles, and lay on seven loads per acre.

CRAG. Of this excellent but scarce manure, 10 or 12 loads are found, in Suffolk, to be equal to 60, 80, or even 100 loads of marle! It lasts very long, and gives necessary adhesion to sands, which it fertilizes.

CLAY. This manure lasts almost 20 years, and is preferred even to marle, by those who experience both.

SEA-OUSE, excellent when mixed with farm-yard dung.

SEA-WEED, equally good, especially when rotted by being used as litter in the farm-yard.

BURNT CLAY. Experiments of its real value are much wanting, as the present seem contradictory.

TOWN MANURE must be excellent: but experiments how far it deserves to be brought, and at what price, are wanting.

ASHES, from Paring and Burning, are a cheap manure, as an acre yields five or six hundred bushels for about 1 l.

D° of Wood and Coal. Excellent for grass lands.

D°

D° of Peat, are so good, that even the small quantity of 10 bushels has great effect. Mr. Y. advises farmers to search for peat in their grounds.

D° of Soap-boilers, are useful, but only when applied in large quantities, as the salts are much washed away.

SOOT, good for both grass lands and arable; but, in order to be lasting, should be laid on in large quantities.

MALT-DUST. Useful, but in no great degree.

SALT. Sufficient experiments of its usefulness are wanting, as the present seem contradictory. The Irish one in Mr. Peters's *Winter Riches* seems very decisive, as far as *one* goes, for its usefulness.

OIL COMPOST. As much of this manure as costs 15 s. 6 d. exceeds 12 loads of rotten dung for a single crop, and does honour to its ingenious prescriber, Dr. Hunter of York.

OIL-CAKE is uniformly excellent.

BONE DUST, CUTLER'S BONES, HARTSHORN SHAVINGS, TANNER'S BARK, and TROTTERS, seem all trifles.

WOOLLEN RAGS. We want experiments how far, and on what soils, they answer the cost.

BUCK WHEAT. Excellent on strong land. We add, on almost any land.

DUNG of RABBITS*, POULTRY of all Kinds, and PIGEONS,

* Mr. Y. (in the preface to his Course of experimental Agriculture) has given, on this subject, a striking specimen of his *justice* and *candour*, and confirmed it in his Appendix to this Eastern Tour. He there abused Adam Speed for a project of raising 2000 l. per annum, by rabbits in hutches; and went so far as to assert, that it was sufficient to ruin *any* man. We judged this censure too severe, and therefore suggested somewhat in mitigation of it. It was obvious that honest Adam must propose a considerable part of his gains from the carcases and skins of his rabbits, but not so obvious that he might hope for no inconsiderable part of it from their dung likewise. We therefore suggested to our Reader that this consideration should certainly be taken into the account, if not of *absolute gain* by the scheme, yet at least in abatement of loss by it. And now what defence does the Tourist make on this topic? Truly he asserts, that 'rabbit dung sells now, when manures are much dearer than in Speed's time, only for 1 s. 2 d. per sack.' And what then? Does it follow hence that old Adam's project *must ruin* even a man of Mr. Y.'s *moderate* fortune, after a loss of 1200 l. by experiments, many of which he knew before-hand could not possibly turn out other than unsuccessful? From the minutes of this Tour he informs us, first, that the dung of rabbits is a very good manure; secondly, that it can be got in considerable quantities only from great cities; thirdly, that wise farmers fetch it at no inconsiderable expence of price and carriage; and, fourthly, that sheep penned make a great quantity of

GEONS †, are very good, especially in such quantity as to create great fermentation.

MANAGEMENT of MANURE. Mr. Y. seems, with justice, to condemn the practice of that excellent farmer Mr. Bakewell, who keeps his farm-dung so long as to be reduced amazingly in quantity †. He fixes on a criterion for keeping it till 50 cubical yards, or loads, can be afforded to an acre: but this appears to be a vague determination.

CONFINEMENT of CATTLE. He advises, not only to confine all the cattle to the farm-yard, but to tie them up, as Mr. Bakewell does; and a man must be a novice in farming who knows not the expediency of this measure; of which stacking all hay, &c. at home is a necessary part.

We doubt not but our judicious and impartial Readers will approve the liberal praise we have bestowed on the Eastern Tour, whose Author, however, will be content with nothing

---

of excellent manure of purchased litter. From all which it follows that rabbits, fed in hutches by old women or children, on green crops suited to them, and growing *near* to or *on* the fields to be manured, may make so cheap a manure as to evince that Adam Speed's project deserves not the name of *nonsense*, which Mr. Y. liberally bestows on it, and that Mr. Y. need not fear the utter ruin of his fortune by trying Adam's experiments *in small*. To be more serious: how utterly destitute of candour must the writer be, who wilfully misrepresents the 'gaining of 2000 l. per annum by rabbits dung,' and 'the rabbits dung contributing to save the projector's fortune from utter ruin,' as the same thing! If this be '*agriculture de cabinet*,' it is 'agriculture de cabinet du Monf. Young.'

† Mr. Y. (in the preface to his Course of experimental Agriculture) censures the very ingenious Mr. Bradley, for two opinions on the subjects here referred to, viz. that the dung of pigeons and poultry should be *diluted* with water, and so used; again, that *manure* should be kept till it *turn* to *earth*. Hereupon we observed, that many sensible farmers were of Mr. Bradley's opinion on both subjects, although we *perhaps* inclined neither to one side nor the other. On this occasion Mr. Y. exclaims, 'if the Reviewers had *any* opinion would they not be more explicit?' We answer: the pains we took in the review of Mr. Y.'s Course, &c. allowed us not to be so particular on many points as we should otherwise have been; and it was, and is, our *real opinion*, that *universal* assertions are frequently wrong on both sides, circumstances deciding the case on this and many other subjects. We think with Mr. Y. that on most soils, and for most crops, manures may prudently be used before they become earth: but for some particular delicate crops they will be more proper when thus reduced. On soils which require warmth, the dung of pigeons, &c. may be used properly in specie; but on soils which are too hot, it is better when diluted. If Mr. Y. would learn to distinguish in matters on which he rashly ventures universal assertions, he would probably often save himself from censure and ridicule.

less

less than *indiscriminate panegyric*, due only to *infallibility* *. But we equally scorn to with-hold praise where due, or to bestow it where undeserved.

* Here we close the account of the Eastern Tour; and as it is inconsistent with the plan of our work to enter into direct controversy with the Author whom we are (by the nature of our engagements to the public) obliged to review, and sometimes to censure, we should pass over all the gross and low abuse which, in the Appendix to *this Tour*, Mr. Y. has thought proper to bestow upon us; but, as he happens to mistake his real friends for enemies, in the Monthly Reviewers of his "Course of experimental Agriculture," we will, in the APPENDIX to the present volume of our Journal, presume to remonstrate a little (under the article of CORRESPONDENCE) with this "angry boy," || on so extraordinary a specimen of his *Politeness* and *Gratitude*.

|| See *Kastril*, in the *Alchymist*.

ART. XII. *On the Principles and Power of Harmony*, concluded. See last Month's Review.

WE concluded the preceding part of our account of this performance, by proposing an experiment relative to Huygens's celebrated passage ‡. Some circumstances which we need not specify, respecting the accurate execution of it on one instrument, prevent us at present from speaking decisively concerning the event of the trials which we have since made. We shall mention however another passage, which may be more conveniently performed, and which we have frequently tried, and can accordingly speak somewhat more confidently with regard to the result of it; in which two minor thirds are taken, in ascending, instead of one in descending, according to that experiment. It is as follows:

Sounding *E*, on the second string of a violin, in perfect unison with *e*, the open first string, proceed to *g* above, the stopping of which last note is not to be trusted to the ear alone, but to be ascertained by hearing distinctly and perfectly *C*, the third sound to the minor third *E g*. Descend a fourth from *g* to *D* †, the place of which is fixed by hearing the *third sound G*. Let the performer then ascend another minor third to *f*, directed by the

---

‡ See Monthly Review, November, page 377.

† On sounding the open third string *D* with the note thus obtained, the latter will already be found not to be a just octave to it, but sensibly sharper. We foresee an objection that may be made to the inference which may be drawn from this circumstance, and therefore proceed further, to procure a note that may be compared with the note of the open first string *E*; the sound with which the melody begins, and to which, as a fixed standard, the final note of the melody may be applied.

third

third sound B; and finally descend a fourth to *C*, ascertaining the interval by the third sound *F*. Or, to give the passage in one view, let him sound the notes *E g D f C*. On repeated trials made with care, we have constantly found that the last note *C* was evidently sharper than it ought to be, compared with, and considered as a major third to, the note *e*. A sensible cacophony and clashing is perceived on these two tones being sounded together, which will not be removed, nor will the proper third sound attending the true interval, viz. *C*, be heard, without bringing the finger higher up the finger-board. Huygens's passage may likewise be thus conveniently tried, but attended with a contrary effect, by changing his final note *C* to *E*; which last note we have always found considerably flatter than the *E* of the open first string, with which it is compared.

We have not room or leisure to add what further occurs to us on this subject, and shall only observe that, granting the truth and accuracy of the experiment, it will follow that a series of the most perfect intervals, such as are indicated by nature, and, which is of still greater consequence, such as are the most grateful to the ear (as those undoubtedly are, which are given by the third sounds) necessarily lead to other intervals that are imperfect and disagreeable, and which do not produce the proper third sounds; and consequently that, in the practice of music, whether by the voice, or on instruments stopped *ad libitum*, some intervals cannot possibly be made perfect, or possess that *resonance* which is given by the third sounds, but at the expence of others.

After selecting and translating or abridging several of the most essential parts in the four first chapters of Tartini's work, illustrating the new principles with which they abound, and adding some excellent occasional observations of his own, our Author proceeds to the fifth chapter, in which Tartini undertakes to discuss a very intricate and interesting subject; the nature of the ancient musical modes of the Greeks, by the means of which and of poetry, they are said to have excited and appeased, at their pleasure, the passions of the human mind. He endeavours to draw a comparison between these ancient and our modern modes; so far as such a comparison can be instituted between two subjects, on one of which so little is known with certainty. This division of the work however is instructive and entertaining. Recommending to the curious a perusal of the original, we shall only extract a few general observations from this interesting chapter.

Tartini first undertakes to prove,—what had indeed often been proved before, but he does it in a new manner, and draws different consequences,—that the musical modes of the ancients were of a very different nature from ours, and particularly that the

the intervals employed in them varied very considerably from those which exist in the present or diatonic scale. For example, Aristides enumerates six of these ancient modes, in all which, according to him, there ought to be the *Enharmonic diesis*; 'whereas our modes neither have, nor can have such an interval; which is entirely unknown amongst us, and which we cannot execute.' He observes that the ancient music was rigorously regulated by the prosody; so that it was impossible to prolong a vowel in singing, beyond its due quantity: whereas we lessen or destroy the proper effect of vocal music, by making the prosody subservient to it; frequently protracting long, and even short vowels, through an extent of several bars. He supposes, however, that a discretionary measure was adopted with regard to the bars, in order to imitate more naturally, and to excite more forcibly the human passions.

After observing that the Greeks were unacquainted with harmony, in our sense of the word, or an union of different voices singing different parts, as base, tenor, &c ‡. he goes still further, and supports an opinion, which, strictly taken, will not meet with universal acquiescence. He affirms, with regard to the principal effect intended by the Greek music, that if simultaneous harmony had even been known to the Greeks, they ought not, nay they could not avail themselves of it, in order to arrive at the end which they had in view; but must employ a single voice, or simple melody, in their songs. He endeavours to shew that harmony, from its very nature, is in a great measure unfavourable to *expression*; and that, though a general affection may be excited, or a tendency towards a certain passion may be produced by it, yet no determinate or specific passion can be completely excited by compositions in different parts, in consequence of the *intrinsic opposition* in the very nature of these parts. In simultaneous harmony, he observes, there is, in fact, a mixture of *grave* and melancholy, with *acute* and sprightly sounds; of slow and languid, with quick and joyous movements; and of the intervals that correspond to mirth, with

‡ His translator is of a different opinion. After quoting or referring to some well-known, but inconclusive passages from some of the ancient writers, he produces a strong passage from Plato, which he had never yet seen quoted, in behalf of his sentiment; and from the whole infers 'that the ancients were acquainted with music in parts, but did not generally make use of it.' The passage from Plato has however been noticed before, and the Author may see some ingenious criticisms upon it, in support of both sides of this qeestion, by consulting the third volume of the *Memoirs of the Royal Academy of Inscriptions*; where M. Burette, particularly, refutes the conclusions drawn from this passage by another academician, in favour of the supposed simultaneous harmony of the ancients.

those

thoſe adapted to excite other and different affections: not to omit the diſtraction which muſt ariſe in the mind of the hearer, who liſtens to theſe various and contraſted tones, movements, and intervals; which muſt altogether form an aſſemblage very unfavourable towards promoting the main intent of the compoſer.

Tartini, in ſhort, ſpeaks of ſimultaneous harmony in ſuch a manner as muſt greatly ſcandalize not only the rigid contrapuntiſt, but even many of thoſe who loudly exclaim againſt the abuſe of it. Though the ſolidity of ſome of his *data* above given might, we think, be queſtioned, or, to take a ſtill ſhorter courſe, though his own *expreſſive* harmonies,—(we will ſtill venture to uſe the term) might be produced againſt him; yet, on the other hand, his reaſonings, nay his mere authority, ought to have great weight on this ſubject; for they are the reflections and opinion of one who, as our Author obſerves, may almoſt be ſaid 'to have led the way in the flowery regions of harmony, and of whom moſt artiſts are but diſtant followers.' When an artiſt, he adds, ſpeaks ſlightingly of an art in which he excels, one may ſafely, he conceives, rely upon his opinion.——We ſhould not, however, omit to obſerve, that a great part of what Tartini advances againſt harmony, is evidently ſaid with a view to the effects which the ancients meant to produce by *their* muſic, which was very different, both in its nature, its concomitants, and its intention, from *ours*; and not with a deſign abſolutely to condemn harmony, as an adjunct to modern muſic, conſidered and cultivated, as it is with us, merely as a pleaſing art, a piece of ſenſual, though refined, luxury, and without reference to any other conſideration whatever.

The extraordinary powers attributed by the ancient writers to the muſic of their times, and of thoſe preceding them, have been conteſted by Wallis and others, and have been aſcribed to the novelty of the art, and the ſtrong natural ſuſceptibility of a Grecian audience; not without ſome derogatory inſinuations reſpecting that extreme latitude of expreſſion, in which, it muſt be owned, the ancient authors too frequently indulged themſelves. Tartini, however, curſorily, and his learned commentator afterwards more diffuſely, ſupport the credibility of theſe accounts. We ſhall not enter the liſts on this occaſion; but ſhall content ourſelves with giving an abſtract of Tartini's relation of a leſs notable, but certainly remarkable, effect of *modern* muſic, of which he was repeatedly a witneſs. We confeſs that it would cut a very inſignificant figure, after a recital of the feats of Timotheus or Terpander: but we ſhall inſert it, as it is ſomewhat better authenticated.

After mentioning Plato and Ariſtotle, whoſe weighty teſtimony in favour of the powers of the Greek muſic, ought to make

make us bow down our heads, Tartini adds, 'if you ask me whether such a dominion over the passions, by the means of music, is possible in nature? I answer frankly, Yes; because I am a witness myself of the possibility of it, from many instances; one of which I will relate. In the year 1714, (if I am not mistaken) in an opera that was performed at Ancona, there was, in the beginning of the third act, a passage of recitative, unaccompanied by any other instrument but the base; which raised, both in the professors and in the rest of the audience, such and so great a commotion of mind, that we could not help staring at one another, on account of the visible change of colour that was caused in every one's countenance. The effect was not of the plaintive kind: I remember well that the words expressed indignation; but of so harsh and chilling a nature, that the mind was disordered by it. Thirteen times this drama was performed, and the same effect always followed, and that too universally; of which the remarkable previous silence of the audience, to prepare themselves for the enjoyment of the effect, was an undoubted sign.

'I was too young to think of preserving a copy of this passage, and have since been very sorry I did not. That the composer, though excellent in his time, knew by principle that such an effect would be produced, I do not believe; but I believe that, being a man of very fine taste, and great judgment, he was led by good sense, and by the words, and had, on that occasion, accidentally hit upon the truth of nature.—The fact is, that, in small movements, and for a little time, a lucky hit of this sort oftentimes happens amongst composers; but there is no rule nor science to attain this end in many movements, and for a considerable time.'

We shall only add two observations of Tartini, in behalf of simplicity; the one relating to harmony and modulation united; the other to the latter alone. He has long, he says, and attentively remarked two things on this subject; and first that, when in our musical compositions, a *tasto fermo*, or single base note occurs, and is held on for many bars together, the modulation continuing in the same key, of which the *tasto fermo* is the first base, one constant effect has been produced by it. The same audience, which had hitherto given little or no attention to the composition, he has constantly observed to be rouzed, and attentive to the melody, thus regulated and supported by the simple harmony of the *tasto fermo*. His next observation is, that every nation has its popular songs, adopted by universal consent, and to which they listen with greater pleasure than to the most exquisite composition, modulated through all the maze of harmony. He observes that these melodies are all extremely simple; as the modulation in them seldom reaches farther than the 5th of the key, which has a natural relation to it, and the transition to which is accordingly easy, and agreeable to human sentiment; and that the most simple of these songs are generally the most in vogue. From hence he would infer, that in our learned modulation we deviate from nature, and consequently from the end at which the Greeks aimed, and which they attained; and that therefore it is not wonderful that we fail of reaching the heart.

This appeal of Tartini to the *Vox populi*, in favour of simple music, is strongly enforced by his commentator, who declares it as his opinion, that most men, if they dared to speak their own feelings, would talk his language; and instead of undergoing the fatigue of silently listening, with a dozing kind of attention, to what they are told is fine, but what they cannot, with all their endeavours, be brought to think agreeable, would boldly call out, with the *Duke* in *Twelfth Night*, Act ii. Scene 6.

> ——————' Give me that piece of song,
> That old and antique song we heard last night;
> Methought it did relieve my passion much;
> More than *light airs*, and *recollected terms*
> Of these more brisk and giddy-pated times.
> ——————*It is old and plain*;
> The spinsters and the knitters in the sun,
> And the free maids, that weave their thread with bones,
> Do use to chaunt it.'

There is truth in this observation, considered in general, and merely as to the matter of fact; but we own that we are surprized to find the ingenious writer afterwards so far over-rating the music in the Beggar's Opera, as to declare that 'there is a greater number of truly affecting songs in *it*, than can be picked out of *many* (he will not say how many) *volumes* of operas:' as we think he cannot be unacquainted with, or insensible to, the chaste, elegant, and affecting simplicity of many of the songs in our modern compositions;—the children indeed of art, but of nature likewise;—the joint offspring of science and sensibility. We own we cannot see Science thus slightingly treated by her own children, and continue silent. With regard, however, to Tartini's observation, we shall briefly remark that he is here supporting a particular system, and accounting for the supposed wonders which the Greek music produced, by its simplicity; and that he recommends simplicity, principally as opposed to *merely learned* modulation: for surely he must have been too conscious of his own powers, and of those of his art, to mean to exhibit the popular melodies in every nation, so various and dissimilar, as standards of musical excellence or energy; melodies which in general possess only a local and exclusive power of pleasing the natives of these particular countries, and are

are heard with coldneſs or contempt by all the reſt: whereas the productions which we would defend are the admiration and delight of the enlightened and feeling part of the human ſpecies diſperſed over the whole earth*. With reſpect to his commentator, notwithſtanding the high opinion which he entertains of the tunes in the Beggar's Opera, we are ſomewhat ſurprized at his conſidering the firſt ſucceſs of that drama, and its continuing to be the 'darling of the nation,' as a mark of its muſical excellence; without attending to thoſe proper and obvious diſcriminations, which he is undoubtedly very well qualified to make on this occaſion.

"*It is old and plain*,"—the good duke's reaſon—who was probably no great adept in theſe matters—furniſhes us with the beſt key to the acknowledged popularity of that piece, (ſo far as the muſic has contributed to it) and to the popularity of all national or vulgar tunes whatever. Indeed, we know not whether thoſe very "*light airs, and recollected terms*," ſo offenſive to the good duke, may not, in fact, be ſome of thoſe identical ſongs which now, mellowed by age, are become the ſettled delight of an audience who have liſtened to them in their cradles, and who reliſh and admire them, merely, or at leaſt principally, becauſe they are plain, and becauſe they underſtand them. We queſtion much whether the *pathos* of Tartini in his *Adagios*, his brilliancy in his *Allegros*—nay even his favourite and acknowledged virtue, ſimplicity, in both, would work upon their callous fibres, and extort a clap---unleſs it were beſtowed upon the hand that executed them.

The value of the applauſe of a mixed aſſembly---and that too an ancient—and a Grecian audience, was otherwiſe eſtimated by a Greek muſician; who certainly did not conſider it as a very competent tribunal in matters of this kind. When a pupil of Hippomachus (according to the anecdote tranſmitted to us by Ælian) had on a public occaſion received the higheſt applauſe from the audience, this ancient muſician laid his cane acroſs the ſhoulders of this favourite of the public, and exclaim-

* The effects formerly recorded of the *Rans de Vaches*, a celebrated Swiſs tune, are wonderful and well authenticated. The playing it among the troops, when in foreign ſervice, was forbidden by the magiſtrates, on pain of death. It produced in them the moſt longing deſire to return to their country, tears, and a degree of grief which ſometimes ended even in death, and often produced deſertion. It is *ſimple*; but we may venture to ſay it will excite no other paſſion, in a perſon of any other country under heaven, than the utmoſt aſtoniſhment that any human being could be thus affected by it; the muſic of it only conſidered.

ed, '*Perperam cecinisti; nam alias hi tibi non applauderent.*' Anglicé, '*Your performance, sir, must have been most abominable; otherwise these gentry would not have clapped you so outrageously.*' ——This Hippomachus was undoubtedly a passionate fellow, as appears from his *manœuvres*; and his inference was certainly too hasty, and perhaps too universal. We who are more temperate, would therefore compromise the whole matter thus:—that *after* a performance or composition, in music or any of the fine arts, has received the approbation of the proper judges; the applause of the multitude may *then* be admitted as adding to the weight of it. But this, it will be said, is a very unsubstantial concession: We reckon their votes, when they are with us; but reject them, when they are against us. It is very true, but we are not inclined to propose any higher terms: if they do not join us, we must continue with the *minority*.

Towards the end of this chapter, the Author investigates the system of the third minor, making use of Tartini's principles, but employing them in a different manner. He next translates a part of the sixth and last chapter of the original, in which Tartini proceeds to the examination of those particular intervals and modulations, which are commonly used in modern music, but which were unknown in the fifteenth century; and adds some ingenious observations of his own. But for these and many other articles treated of in this performance, relating to the more profound and recondite parts of the science, we must refer our learned musical readers to the work itself; which, notwithstanding its mutilations and obscurities, we cannot but consider as a valuable addition to the stock of musical literature in our language.

ART. XIII. *An Essay on national Pride.* Translated from the German of Mr. Zimmermann, Physician in Ordinary to his Britannic Majesty at Hanover. 12mo. 3s. Wilkie. 1771.

THIS writer introduces his subject with some observations on the nature of Pride; which he considers as the most common foible of human nature. 'From the throne to the cottage,' says he, 'every one conceits himself, in some point or other, above his fellow-creatures, and looks down on *all* but himself with a kind of haughty compassion.'—Without stopping to lay down the proper limits, which the Author himself ought to have prescribed to this extravagant assertion (from whence it might be inferred that there is no such thing as humility among mankind) we shall proceed, with Dr. Zimmermann, to his particular examination of the several species of Pride by which men are actuated, and their effects.

By

By amplifying the single observation, that all mankind are proud of something or other*, our Author has ingeniously contrived to spin out an entertaining philosophical miscellany. Pride indeed appears to be a principle implanted, in a greater or less degree, in every animated being; among the human race, it contributes to make weak understandings ridiculous, but it serves as a security against men of sense acting in any manner beneath the dignity of their stations and characters; and proves a stimulus to laudable deeds, where other motives may fail. So that as ludicrous displays of human pride are not likely to eradicate that principle, so neither ought we to wish them to have that effect: and, accordingly, the writer before us, frequently distinguishes the proper from the improper spirit.

It has been hinted, that man is not the only creature which discovers the principle or passion of pride; and when we see the stately attitudes assumed by a spirited horse, peacock, turkey, or swan, animals which occasionally seem to exult in their strength or plumage, we shall be inclined to think that this principle was given to them for some useful end. Man, who is proud of his reason, is to take care how he exerts it, that others may not esteem him less than he esteems himself: for if he sets an exorbitant value upon ridiculous distinctions, he will be sorely mortified by finding that they will not pass current, where he most desires his own value of them to be accepted. A ploughman, the son of a ploughman, possesses as perfect a human frame, as a grandee of the most illustrious house of Spain; the gifts of fortune are frequently possessed by the most worthless beings; and the most arrant fop, with all his adventitious trappings, and fond idea of his own importance, cannot, even with the aid of Signior Gallini, step with the native grace and dignity of a dunghill cock; and can no more bear stripping, than the jackdaw in the fable.

It will be natural that English readers should be curious to know the opinion which a philosophical foreigner entertains of their nation, in this point of view: our Author, who is a Swiss, thus represents us:

'Well-bred people, among the English, make no difficulty of owning, that a contempt for all other nations under the sun, is as it were hereditary in that country; whenever one of those islanders is

* Which may be true, in a *national* sense, although we cannot admit that every *individual* looks down with contempt on *all* but *himself*; for, if this were fact, we should find every poor, harmless wretch [and many such are to be met with, in most neighbourhoods] ridiculously affecting to despise men of the highest characters and ranks in society:—an height of absurdity which would, surely, indicate not so much the natural pride of a man in his senses, as a considerable degree of insanity.

 engaged

engaged in a quarrel with a foreigner, he is sure to let fly a volley of opprobrious epithets against his adversary's country: You are a French braggadocio, an Italian monkey, a Dutch ox, a German hog, are but slight specimens of English contumely. The bare word *French* carries so much indignity with it, that they would not think the foreigner sufficiently vilified by calling him only dog, therefore is *French* added to it by way of amplification. This national prejudice spares not even their fellow-subjects, the two nations who live under the same laws as they themselves, and are fighting for one common cause. Nothing is more frequent in England, that is among the commonality, than, *You beggarly Scot—You blood-thirsty Irish hog-trotter.* In a word, an Englishman, after guttling on pudding and beef, well diluted with strong beer, talks away, of all other nations, as if they had not the same creator.

'But what is to be thought of a current comparison, which these intelligent persons make between them and other nations? "The French, say they, are polite, witty, artful, and vain; withal, a parcel of half starv'd slaves, their time, purse, and person absolutely at the Grand Monarque's command. As for the Italians, they have neither morals, nor freedom, nor religion. The Spaniard, indeed, is brave, devout, and of nice honour, but poor and oppressed; and, with all his boasting of the sun never rising and setting but in the Spanish dominions, he has not a word to say as to freedom, science, arts, manufactures, atchievements, and trade. The Portuguese again are likewise slaves, and so ignorant and superstitious, that it would be a pity they were otherwise. The Germans, if not at war, are repairing the damages brought on them by wars. The Dutch are slow and heavy, have no notion of any good but money; gain is their main spring and ultimate end." Such is the point of view in which an Englishman looks on all Europeans: all nations in the universe are indeed found light, extremely light, when an homespun Englishman weighs them against his countrymen. This contemptuous partiality too plainly shews itself in his coldness and indifference at his first acquaintance with a foreigner.'

These *well-bred* Englishmen must be very *homespun* indeed, whom Dr. Zimmermann here characterizes.—In another passage, however, our countrymen are allowed to be better judges of merit; unless the Author will establish a distinction between our judgment of foreigners and of natives; but he grants rather too much, to have such a charge in reserve against us.

'The English are as eminent in all sciences, and I could almost say in all arts, as men can possibly be, withal it is very apparent that they are highly sensible of the superiority; and the honours which they liberally shew to their distinguished countrymen are a convictive proof how much they value themselves on their merits.

'There is no country on the face of the globe where they so far divest a man of his birth, his rank, and every thing which is not inherent and personal. In Germany, the question concerning a stranger is, *Is he a nobleman?* In Holland, *Is he rich?* But in England it is asked, *What sort of a man is he?* A noble of the first rank complained to Henry VIII, of the painter Holbein having affronted him, to which the

the king answered, *No more of your complaints against Holbein. Of seven ploughmen I can at pleasure make as many lords, but to make one Holbein is beyond my power.* Even a minister of state in England, is a kind of an intermediate Being between angel and beast. My lord Chatham is eagerly deified by some, and as virulently bespattered by others; and yet no where is merit less made a crime of than in England. This people, though so outrageously turbulent on any suspicion of a scheme against liberty; readily lays aside enmity, sect, and faction when great talents are to be rewarded. Under the same roof where are interred their kings, lie their geniuses. The remains of an actress, for whom, in France, a lay-stall would be thought good enough, in England are deposited among the chiefs of the state. Newton whilst living, had extraordinary honours paid him in this nursery of great men; and was interred with regal pomp in the stately repository of fame among the great and the learned, and even among crowned heads. Accordingly, the nobility of this kingdom, invited by the honours paid to eminent geniuses, have, in all ages, interlaced the palm of sciences with their coronets; and in their daily intercourse the most abstruse or important disquisitions are as customary as disputes about a new head-dress or a ragout in France.

'The English are more knowing than other nations, only as being more free; for that spirit of liberty of which most republics have not so much as an idea, prompts the English ardently to apply themselves to the sciences, discuss the interests of nations, to be ever taken up with great objects, and ever doing great things. Their acquirements and their perspicuity dispel detrimental prepossessions, and overthrow all illicit power; it is only a legal authority wisely conducted, which can stand their researches. Most free nations are but superficial thinkers; whilst the English, their wings being unclipped, range at will the infinite expanse of contemplation.'

But can this be the same people, the *well-bred* part of which are represented as such foul-mouthed Billingsgates in the former extract?

This is not the first time we have had occasion to remark inconsistencies in the characters given of the English nation *; and the true reason of this difficulty in drawing our character may be, that we have less of a national character belonging to us, than perhaps any other people in Europe; unless this very want of a national cast is accepted as a positive distinction. Living in a mild climate, under an easy government, both civil and ecclesiastical, the English think more for themselves than other nations; and this mental independency gives a greater scope to natural inclinations, than is to be found among those who yield up their opinions to the dictates of stern authority, which becomes more obligatory and universal, the more mankind give way to it.

---

* See Review, Vol. xlii. p. 179. Vol. xliii. p. 333.

Mr. Zimmermann mentions a charge brought against him by a French critic, for overlooking † the Germans when he was producing instances of ridiculous pride; and he replies in the following terms:

'Too many single instances of pride, I acknowledge, are met with in the German universities, the Imperial cities, the German nobility, and in every thing else in Germany; yet instances of a silly national pride can hardly be said to swarm in a nation which despises the fabrics and works of its own artists, is the first to ridicule its own poets, readily draws its purse-strings at the powerful temptation of a foreign piece of workmanship, and even cannot sufficiently express its admiration of foreign literati, except now and then a flirt at the lumpishness of the Swissers; but who minds so petty a people as they? With what face could I have charged the esteemable Germans with national pride, only on a few appearances of any such thing, and those equivocal, when one of the most learned men of our age taxes them with the want of this useful folly, as a national failing, and not a slender one. This gentleman, in the preface to an *History of the Frogs*, says, "There is in Europe a great nation, outdoing all others for industry and laboriousness, and equally fertile in men of invention and genius; little addicted to voluptuous pleasures; and for valour, rivalling, if not surpassing, the most valiant; yet this same people, with all their endowments and advantages, seems blind to its own worth, despising itself, praising, purchasing, and imitating only what is foreign. It imagines, that in apparel, food, and buildings, there can be no elegance, or exquisiteness, unless cook, wines, taylor, stuffs, and architect be foreign; and, besides the excessive cost, these artizans and materials chiefly come from the country of a natural enemy. This same infatuated nation farther confines its praise to the wit, understanding, erudition and genius of foreigners. Foreign poets, and foreign painters, alone meet with encouragement; and foreign histories, without judgment, stile, or truth, bear the palm; very seldom do booksellers complain of a foreign book being a shop-keeper."

All this may however be true, without depriving the Germans of their share of pride. The English are fond of the fashions and productions of a nation, whose merit in more important articles they nevertheless hold very cheap; and however the Germans may esteem the productions of foreign artists, their pride of family, and scrupulous exaction of punctilios of ceremony, are remarked by all travellers.

However tenderly our Author may treat the Germans, he gives the French no great cause to thank him for the following picture:

'The French, in their own account, are the only thinking beings in the world. They converse with foreigners no farther than is usual with inferior and shallow creatures, and who owe all their im-

† This must refer to one of the former editions of our Author's work.

portance

portance to such condescension, yet in nothing are they more offensive than that farcical compassion and equity of some among them, who deign to allow other nations a pittance of virtue and genius, but in such a manner, that it is plain, this favourable opinion is not due to the merit of those nations, but flows from the indulgent courtesy of French politeness. Let them, if they can, deny their contempt, as barbarians, of all nations who, are either inferior in power, or of less skill and taste in the frivolous arts. They daily betray in their conversation, their gestures, and even their books, a conceit that neither courage, beauty, nor wit, nothing amiable or great, is to be met with out of their country.

'The French think themselves intitled to prescribe laws to the whole universe, because all Europe takes its cue from their milliners, taylors, periwig-makers and cooks. There is not a candid Frenchman who will deny but that his nation accounts itself the principal, the most accomplished in the world. How does Mr. Lefranc storm and vapour in a discourse addressed to the king, at the presumptuous Britons, in pretending to any equality or resemblance to the French; when Patin had pronounced the Britons to be among other nations, like wolves among the beasts? Is it not common among the French, to stile their sovereign, the first monarch in the world, or—the *grand monarch*? Though they account themselves the first born sons of nature, some are so condescending as to look on their neighbours as their younger brothers, and allow them to be laborious, and judicious collectors, and men of thought, even not without some good thinkers. But why is Newton, after all his valuable discoveries, made light of in France, because he has not discovered every thing? Why is Raphael looked on as low and timorous, and his divine piece of the transfiguration, a flat performance? That national vanity, admitting no great man out of France, is well known in numberless instances, which excite the derision of all nations. If we look back into the history of human genius, we find Italy renowned for actors and poets, England's unparalleled Shakespear, and at the very same time France noted for the most paultry versifiers in the world. The French, one and all, undervalue the harmonious, the picturesque, the ethic Pope, as not fit to hold a candle to their superficial Boileau.

'All nations are reduced nearly on a level in self-conceit and contempt of others. The Greenlander, who makes his dog his messmate, despises the Danes; the Cossacs and Calmucs look still with a more disdainful eye on the Russians; and the Hotentots, of all men the most stupid, are excessively vain; and when the Caribbees along the river Oroonoko are asked about their extraction, their constant answer is, *we alone are real men.* Scarce is a nation to be found under the sun, which swarms not with extravagant instances of vanity, pride, and self-conceit. All are more or less a-kin to the Spaniard who said, *it was very lucky that Satan, when he tempted our Saviour in the wilderness, forgot to shew him Spain, as Jesus certainly could not have withstood the temptation*; or to the Canadian, who thought he highly complimented the Frenchman in saying, *he is just such a man as myself.*'

Here

Here the grand point ſeems to be ſettled, and the inference is, that human nature is nearly the ſame every where, and has a greater outline reſemblance, than a reader would ſuppoſe, who derives his notions of his neighbours from books of national characters.

It is amuſing to obſerve how this Author balances accounts with a nation before he leaves it. The French are hitherto celebrated for their ſkill in frivolous arts, and in their contempt of other nations for their inferiority in theſe arts; we will now examine the *per contra* ſide of this account.

'A ſenſe of national merit in the ſciences often ſhews itſelf among the French, and it is what they are moſt juſtly intitled to. We are too much accuſtomed to view them only in a frivolous light, whereas much more matter do they afford for panegyric than for ſatyr.

'The geniuſes of the French, at this time, may be ſtiled tranſcendent; they ſeem formed for every thing becoming man; they meaſure the heavenly bodies, and have a moſt impreſſible ſenſibility; they improve the moſt abſtruſe ſciences, and draw tears from our eyes for imaginary diſtreſſes. All their writings abound in beauties ſcarce imitable. Order and method, energy and nature, perſpicuity and propriety ſhine with mingled rays, nothing ſuperfluous, nothing trivial; every thought is exhibited in its moſt affecting light. As to that moſt valuable ſcience of being at once both ſcholars and men, no nation can be offended at the French being recommended as models; the midnight lamp ſees them at their lucubrations, yet has pedantry no place in them.

'It is the French, particularly, who have decked out the ſciences in Attic elegance. Their drama muſt in the whole be allowed to ſurpaſs every other, and for the moſt agreeable and beneficial of all arts and ſciences, ſociality and good manners, all nations yield the palm to them. They have brought natural hiſtory, politics, commerce, the finances, and likewiſe painting and ſculpture, nearly to their utmoſt point of perfection. The numerous employments and rewards for men of learning of all kinds, give France a very great advantage, as inciting diligence and endeavours after ſuperiority, and thus have been greatly conducive in raiſing France to the pre-eminence in which it ſtands for aſtronomy and the art of war. Philoſophy daily gains ground among them. At preſent, men indeed think on every thing, and the French as much as any men whatever. It were to be wiſhed that their geniuſes did not carry their complaiſance ſo far to a ſex which can give a value to trifles, and ſtamp a ridicule on what is really great; to a ſex which is welcome to the dominion over hearts, if it will but leave us the direction of the mind.

'There is farther another kind of rational ſelf-eſteem, of which, though ariſing from the nobleſt principles, the benefit is very often miſunderſtood and abuſed, yet manifeſtly productive of every thing great, and many advantages. I mean the ſpirit of liberty, which Engliſh writings have transfuſed into the hearts of the French, and impart to a Pariſian philoſopher in his lofty manſion, that juſt and neceſſary pride, which comports with the freedom and dignity of his profeſſion. This ſpirit does honour to mankind, and is a relief, when

uſed

used in a proper manner, to clear the intellectual eye from the motes of prejudices. The English look on the French as a nation of slaves, but this is really ridiculous; a body of French before the throne are not less free than the most free Englishman; and some of the Encyclopedists are as staunch republicans as the generality of the professors of law in Holland and Swisserland; and these heroes are publickly known.

'Farther, the parliaments of France do, with a manly and free eloquence, display and ascertain their monarch's true interest; they lay before the throne, the affections, blessings, and requests of all ranks, that from thence, safety, peace, and prosperity, may the more readily flow down on the palaces of the great, and the cottages of the poor. Their hearts sink not under oppression, their minds are ever employed on great and sublime subjects, and ready to forfeit their personal liberty, their substance and places, rather than betray their zeal for truths of public advantage. This kind of freedom consists in the free use of their knowledge and abilities; it arises from philosophy, and not from the form of government, being much more noble, as springing from a more noble source. Thus a nation can hardly exceed in valuing itself on free-thinking and free-speaking, not as being allowed, but as really being not allowed such freedom.'

The French, after all, are a most ostentatious people, the same lightness of mind that inclines them to make a ridiculous parade of trifles and frivolous arts, governs their more important attempts; and Candour itself must allow, that their real excellence in scientific pursuits, though very considerable, falls very short, on a close examination, of their own pompous accounts.

[*To be concluded in another article.*]

ART. XIV. *Zobeide*; a Tragedy. As it is acted at the Theatre-Royal in Covent-Garden. 8vo. 1 s. 6 d. Cadell. 1771.

ALTHOUGH M. Voltaire's tragedy, *Les Scythes*, &c. is the stock from whence this poetical scion has sprung, yet the transplanter, Mr. Cradock (whose name is subscribed to the Dedication of Zobeide) is totally silent with regard to this capital circumstance; some acknowledgment of which we expected to meet with, in a preface or advertisement;—but it was no secret with the town, and therefore we conclude our Author intended no concealment—of what indeed could not be concealed, and that the omission we have noticed, was only the effect of inadvertence.

In the *Appendix* to our Review, vol. xxxvii. we gave an account of M. Voltaire's *Scythians*, to which article we refer our Readers for an idea of the plan and conduct, with some specimens, of the original of the present tragedy. Mr. Cradock has, indeed, (to the best of our remembrance, for we have not a copy of the French play at hand) made considerable alterations in it, but it has still, for the most part, rather the meagre appearance of an out-line, or sketch, as Voltaire left it, than

than of a finiſhed production; though, perhaps, we may make ſome exception in favour of the fourth and fifth acts, ſeveral ſcenes of which are highly wrought, and contain a variety of noble and ſtriking paſſages.

As it is ſaid to be Mr. Cradock's firſt performance, and as he appears to be a writer who will draw improvement from experience, we would juſt hint to him to be more attentive, for the future, to the harmony of his verſification, and to propriety of diction; and to beware alſo of an error into which young authors are ſometimes apt to fall, from a miſtaken idea that poetical licenſe will warrant their paſſing the bounds of common ſenſe, in the ardour of their purſuit after bold metaphors and ſublime expreſſions. We have obſerved a few defective lines, which we ſhall briefly point out, that the Author, if he pleaſes, may reconſider, and correct them.

The honeſt, plain Scythian, expreſſing his contempt of the rich trappings and ornaments of Perſian luxury, declares that 'poverty is chiefeſt grandeur' in Scythia, p. 2. The Author, no doubt, intended a beauty here; but the paſſage is a ſtriking inſtance of the *falſe brilliant*, and no better than a downright *Hiberniciſm*. Had he, for grandeur (a word which often occurs in this play, and of which all French writers are remarkably fond) wrote *greatneſs*, he had been leſs unfortunate. An Engliſhman's idea of *grandeur* is *ſtate*, *ſplendour*, *magnificence* of appearance, &c. and ſo it ſtands defined in our beſt dictionaries. But to talk of poverty being ſplendour, or magnificence, is to ſay that indigence is wealth, littleneſs greatneſs, or weakneſs ſtrength.

An exact ear, a correct judgment, and taſte, can never tolerate ſuch lines as the following:

'Hircania bow'd her neck *unto* my yoke.' P. 7.

We cannot ſuppoſe that any critic will grant his paſſport *unto* this line.

'Demanded Zobeide as deſpotic maſter.' P. 8.

How this rugged line was ſpoken on the ſtage we cannot imagine, not having been preſent at the repreſentation.

'*Dear father*, he regards us both.'—— P. 38.

Does not this deſcend (eſpecially in the exalted character of Zobeide) too near to the ſtyle of Pamela's letters to her "*honoured father and mother?*"

The *low familiar* is equally conſpicuous in Sulma's expoſtulation with Zobeide: 'What think you? O return, &c.' p. 42, and this in the moment of Zobeide's extreme diſtreſs, when every expreſſion ought to be animated or pathetic.

'*In ſhort*——————————' *Ibid.*

The ſame glaring unfitneſs of language.

'Nor

'Nor force me act a deed yourselves abhor.' P. 72.

* * * *

'Preserve a fond heart, devote to thee alone.' P. 76.

The two last are grossly ungrammatical.

In page 72, we have also

'Laurels which fade not, gems which *can't* decay.'

The vicious and vulgar abbreviation of *cannot*, is surely incompatible with the dignity of the buskin!

We should not have given ourselves the trouble of pointing out the foregoing blemishes, had we not discerned merit enough in many parts of this performance, to render it an object worthy of critical attention.

*** Is there not a mistake in prefixing the Persian SEYFEL's name to the speech, p. 74, beginning, '*All shall be spar'd, &c.?*' This assurance could only come from the Scythians.

ART. XV. *Letters on the French Nation, considered in different Departments; with many interesting Particulars relating to its Placemen.* By Sir Robert Talbot, who attended the Duke of Bedford to Paris, in 1762. Translated from the French. 12mo. 2 Vols. 6 s. sewed. White. 1771.

THE name of Sir Robert Talbot is obviously one of those innocent fictions under the disguise of which, authors have sometimes chosen to conceal their personal identity; such as Isaac Bickerstaff, —— Ironsides, Fitzosborne, Sir Harry Beaumont, and fifty others.

The real Author of these Letters we conclude to have been some ingenious foreigner, who having gained a competent stock of political knowledge, and anecdotes of the times, chose to turn it to what literary advantage he might make of a couple of very *readable** volumes. Not that he confines himself, however, to such moderate limits; for he tells us, in the preface, that he has materials enough to make several volumes more. But whether or not he hath, as yet, made any addition to the quantity here communicated to the *English* reader, is a circumstance unknown to us. The original of the present publication first appeared (as the Translator informs us, in a note, vol. ii. p. 109) at Amsterdam, in 1766, and we wonder that we have not seen it in our own language before.

---

* We have here adopted a phrase which often occurs, in *conversation* among men of letters, but of which we are not over fond, and therefore do not apprehend that we shall be tempted to make frequent use of it; though, really, *we* might expect some indulgence from our Readers, for the sake of a little variety: for, surely, the same eternal round of *learned, judicious, ingenious, instructive,* and *entertaining,* is enough to tire even the patience and perseverance of a Reviewer!

With respect to the nature and merit of the work, we shall briefly observe, that the Writer, whoever he is, appears to be well acquainted with the political state of France, as it stood about eight years ago; and that he talks, and reasons, on a great variety of topics, in a manner which not only shews the man of sense, and the philosopher, but *the man of the world*: not like one of our Grubstreet statesmen, prating, from his garret, on subjects with which it is impossible for him to be personally conversant, and which, consequently, he understands, as well as Mr. Pope's coxcomb-bird understood the scurrilous language which he was taught to bestow, indiscriminately, upon all who passed by his cage.

But these Letters are not all confined to state affairs, or to persons connected with those subjects. Several of them relate to matters of other kinds. The LADIES come in for their share; and the various modes and manners of the times are occasionally introduced. The theatre, too, is not unnoticed. There is one letter particularly addressed to Mr. Garrick, in which, beside the many just compliments paid to our admirable Roscius, we have a curious discussion of the essential differences between the French and English stage.—We have here, also, a very curious letter on the subject of convent education. There is another on the French police, and the insufficiency of the penal laws in England. The expulsion of the Jesuits is a frequent topic; and the pretended Sir Robert seems to know the society well:—perhaps he has the very best grounds for that knowledge.—As to his discussions of English government affairs, and the genius, laws, and manners of this country, we do not apprehend he is here so much *at home*. In short, his historical anecdotes, and portrait paintings, will, by the majority, be deemed the most curious of his performances, and will prove the most generally entertaining.

We must not pass over, in silence, the merit of a translation which is superior to most productions of the kind; and that merit is not a little enhanced by the Translator's judicious notes. There is likewise a copious index: an appendage which, in our estimation, adds considerably to the value of every book which hath in it substance enough to afford materials for that useful citizen of the literary world, an index-maker, to work upon; which, we are sorry to add, is not often the case, in this age of light, empty, frivolous publications.

MONTHLY CATALOGUE, For DECEMBER, 1771.

MISCELLANEOUS.

Art. 16. *Epistolæ Turcicæ et Narrationes Persicæ Editæ ac Latine conversæ, a Joh. Ury.* 4to. 2 s. 6 d. Oxon. Sold by Wilkie in London. 1771.

THIS publication may be of singular advantage to those, who wish to make a proficiency in the Turkish and Persian dialects. It supposes, however, that they are acquainted with the Latin; a circumstance, we apprehend, that is rather unfortunate, as those gentlemen, who have connexions with India, and are the most concerned to profit by it, are not in general very intimately versant in that language. Our learned Editor, therefore, would have done them a much more acceptable favour, if he had presented them with his translations in their own vernacular idiom. The original pieces he exhibits cannot boast, in our opinion, of much *intrinsic* merit; and we think, we perceive, in his latinity more correctness than elegance, and more labour than taste.

Art. 17. *The Lady's Polite Secretary*; or New Female Letter-writer. Containing an *elegant* Variety of interesting and instructive Letters, intended as Models to form the Style on every Point essential to the Happiness or Entertainment of the Sex. To which is prefixed a short but comprehensive Grammar of the English Language. The whole so calculated, that any Lady may, in a very short Time, be enabled to write her Thoughts with a becoming Propriety and Ease. By the Right Hon. Lady Dorothea Dubois. 12mo. 2 s. Coote, &c.

A professed cultivator of language and style should, at least, write grammatically. Lady* Dorothea Dubois does not always acquit herself so happily, in these models of epistolary elegance. One instance of her failing, in this respect, will suffice:—'I never had more inclination to *write you*, p. 2.' If a longing lady had said to her husband, "I never had more inclination to *bite* you,"—or a quarrelsome one, "to *fight* you,"—or a malicious one "*to spight you*,"—it had been English.

The above instance does not arise from an error of the press, for the same phrase occurs in several different places, among her best specimens. We have often seen it in *private* letters; but we could not expect to meet with such a vulgarism ‡, in a work, the writer of which justly remarks, that 'Correctness is necessary in letter-writing;' and that it is an article of 'female education, which she is sorry to observe so much neglected.'

For the rest, these letters, in general, are neither ill-written, nor ill-calculated for the purpose of forming the epistolary style of young

* This lady is an unfortunate branch of the Anglesey family. If we rightly remember, we have already mentioned somewhat of her "Unhappy Tale," on a former literary occasion. She has published *Theodora*, a novel; and a few other pieces.

‡ Perhaps it is a *Scoticism*; or is it of *Irish* extraction?

ladies.

ladies. There are a number of very good letters in the latter part of this collection, taken from authors of reputation, of both sexes.

Art. 18. *Tables for the easy valuing of Estates*, from 1s. to 5 l. per Acre; also the Parts of one Acre, from 3 roods to one perch. By Bernard Scale, Land-surveyor, Topographer, and Valuer of Estates. 8vo. 5 s. sewed. Cadell, &c. 1771.

The obvious utility of tables of the kind above mentioned, to all who are concerned in holding, letting, dividing, or valuing lands, must render any recommendation totally unnecessary. The Author assures us, in his introduction, that 'particular care has been taken in the accuracy of the calculations;' and we see that the whole is arranged in so familiar a manner, as to render the work very acceptable to gentlemen; who cannot, as Mr. Scale observes, but 'be pleased in being saved the trouble of calculations;' and to others (he adds) 'who are incapable of such a task, it must be very important and satisfactory.'

To render his work the more extensively useful, Mr. Scale has added, tables of reduction of English money into Irish, at par, and of Irish into English; of Irish plantation measure into English statute measure, and of English statute measure into Irish plantation measure; of Irish plantation measure into Cunningham, *et vice versa*; and of guineas, from one to 1000, reduced to Irish currency.

Art. 19. *A Report from the Committee appointed* (on the 11th of March, 1771) *to consider how his Majesty's Navy may be better supplied with Timber*. Published by Order of the House of Commons. Fol. 5 s. sewed. Whiston, &c.

A great deal of valuable and curious matter is contained in this publication; enough to set up a score of our political pamphlet-spinners: who may, from hence, in every new '*State of the nation, &c.*' set forth the alarming general decrease of ship-timber in this island, and particularly in the king's forests; the advanced prices of foreign timber; with the causes of both, viz. the great increase of the royal navy; and of the general trade of the kingdom; but, especially, of the E. India company, who, within these 30 years past, have raised the number of (their capital) ships from 30 to 91 *. They will here find, also, some important remarks on inclosing waste and wood lands; on planting; and the various measures necessary for encouraging the growth of timber: together with observations on the savings that might be made of our English oak, by using beach and other timber in some parts of a ship, and on the causes and remedies of the quick decay of ship-timber. There is also a report of the present state of the several forests and chaces, with respect to timber trees fit for navy use; and in the *Appendix*, we have accounts of the stores in his majesty's dock-yards, the shipping of the E. India company, and various other important articles, relative to the general subject of enquiry before this committee.

---

* And all these, going but 4 voyages, to be rebuilt every 12 years,—What an enormous consumption of timber by this company alone, in the space of one century!

Art.

Art. 20. *A New Grammar of the English Language*; or an Easy Introduction to the Art of Speaking, Writing, &c. By D. Fenning. 12mo. 1 s. 6 d. Crowder. 1771.

The Author conceiving that Lowth's and Priestley's Grammars are fitter for men of letters than for youth at school, has adapted this work, chiefly, for the use of English learners; and we think it well calculated for that purpose: as we do not remember to have seen any thing of the kind, delivered in so plain and familiar a manner.

Art. 21. *The London Spelling-Dictionary*—consisting not only of the Words but also of their different Significations. Together with such additional Improvements as the Author, in a Course of 20 Years Study, has been able to furnish. By J. Seally. Small 4to. 2 s. bound. Coote, &c.

We have had several Spelling-dictionaries of the English language; and they may all be useful to the young readers for whom they are intended.

Art. 22. *Free Thoughts on Seduction, Adultery, and Divorce*; with Reflections on the Gallantry of Princes, particularly those of the Blood-royal of England. Occasioned by the late Intrigue between his Royal Highness the Duke of Cumberland, and Henrietta, Wife of the Right Hon. Richard Lord Grosvenor. Also Remarks on the Trial at Law between his Lordship and his Royal Highness, in consequence of that illicit Amour; with Observations on the Depositions since taken, in the Cause depending in Doctors-Commons, between Lord Grosvenor and his Lady. By a Civilian. 8vo. 5 s. 3 d. boards. Bell. 1771.

In this performance, there are many pertinent and acute observations. It is intended to repress the licentiousness of the times; and the correction it applies to the low vices of one of the highest personages in the kingdom, discovers the independent spirit of the Author. The animadversions, which our Civilian makes on the charge of a certain judge to the jury, in the cause between Lord Grosvenor and the Duke of Cumberland, have likewise the merit of being free and spirited; and we are sorry to observe, that they seem to rest on too solid a foundation. But, perhaps, it is not to be accounted surprising, in an age, when virtue is, in some measure, a reproach, and men of high quality are only noted for debauchery, that judges should dispossess themselves of every appearance of integrity, and assume the boldest and most unpardonable latitude in the interpretation of laws.

Art. 23. *A Treatise on Marriage*, being serious Thoughts on the original Design of that sacred Institution, and the absolute Importance of its Solemnization between real Christians, for promoting mutual Happiness. To which are added, Strictures on the Education of Children. By W. Giles. 12mo. 1 s. 6 d. J. Buckland, &c. 1771.

The Author of this tract appears to be a pious, well-disposed man, who wishes to be of service to his fellow-creatures. He was led, we are told, to write upon education, by being placed in a family in which some children were committed to his care; and what he had thus written was, it seems, communicated to the public at different times in a periodical paper. Some of his friends, we are farther informed, who had requested the publication of his thoughts on education, solicited him likewise to write a treatise upon marriage, which was also, by parts, laid before the public, in the same manner with the other: and in compliance with the renewed request of his friends, he has now published them all in this small volume.

In this work Mr. Giles has laid down several useful admonitions and directions for the proper instruction of children, both by precept and example. His observations on marriage are intermingled with the sentiments of Calvinism, and his method will by many be deemed puritanical. Should none enter into the *holy state* but upon his plan, we fear these matrimonial alliances would not be very frequently contracted. The Author's views are, however, benevolent, and his performance ought to be read with a due regard to what he himself proposes in his preface, when he says, 'In any point where the reader may find occasion to differ, I only solicit that right of private judgment, which he thinks himself entitled to. This will effectually secure me from that censure which is apt to steal imperceptibly even into minds naturally the most ingenuous, liberal, and candid.'

Art. 24. *Love-Letters*, which passed between his Royal Highness the D. of C—— and the Hon. Mrs. Horton, &c. 8vo. 1 s. Swan.

Obviously spurious.

Art. 25. *Lettre a Monsieur* A*** Du P*** *Dans laquelle est compris L'Examen de sa traduction des Livres attribués a Zoroastre. A Londres.* 8vo. 1 s. 6 d. Elmsley. 1771.

Wit, ridicule, and reasoning are here employed against Monsieur Anquetil Du Perron. His absurd pretensions to eastern literature are treated with the utmost pleasantry: and we have a full exposition of the total insignificance of those writings which he has impudently ascribed to Zoroaster*. The public in general, and the learned professors at Oxford in particular, whom M. Du Perron has mentioned in his work with the highest disrespect, are indebted for this publication to the ingenious Mr. Jones.

Art. 26. *Fencing Familiarized:* or, a new Treatise on the Art of Sword-play. Illustrated by Engravings, representing all the different Attitudes on which the Principles and Grace of that Art depend. By Mr. Olivier, educated at the Royal Academy at Paris, and Professor of Fencing in St. Dunstan's Court, Fleet-street. 8vo. 6 s. boards. Bell.

In order to criticize a book of this kind, the reviewer must be supposed to understand the subject as well as Mr. *Professor Olivier*, who teaches the art; nay, to correct Mr. Olivier, he must understand it *better*: this, however, none of us can pretend to do. One half of our corps are parsons, who *profess* only to wield the "sword of the spirit;" others are physicians, who *wear* swords, indeed, but not for *use*; and

* More of this in our *Appendix*, which will be published next month.

the

2

the reſt are men who are not ſuppoſed to brandiſh any weapon more terrible than a gooſe-quill.—As, therefore, the points in which our preſent Author deals, are not, with *us*, at leaſt, points of criticiſm, we have only to obſerve, that, for aught we dare ſay to the contrary, Mr. Olivier's book is a very good book, and may help to teach, as much as *books* can teach, the noble *ſcience of defence*; or, as our Author terms it *ſword-play*. But, we imagine, that young gentlemen who wiſh to make a conſiderable proficiency in this polite branch of education, will learn more from a courſe of lectures in St. Dunſtan's court, than from the peruſal of printed leſſons, even with all the advantage of the engravings; in which, however, the various attitudes and poſitions ſeem to be here accurately and elegantly delineated.

Art. 27. *An Hiſtorical Miſcellany.* 12mo. 3s. Cadell. 1771.

This collection of hiſtorical pieces for the uſe of ſchools, is, by much, the moſt valuable, that we have at any time met with. It is admirably calculated for inſtilling into our youth, juſt and liberal ſentiments; for improving their taſte and ſenſibility; and for qualifying them to enter into ſociety with advantage, by forming them to candour, generoſity, and probity. The articles of which it is compoſed, are collected, with a careful and happy choice, from the moſt approved authors of ancient and modern times.

RELIGIOUS *and* CONTROVERSIAL.

Art. 28. *Conſiderations offered to the Public, and to the Subſcribers for Relief againſt Subſcriptions, &c.* Containing ſatisfactory Reaſons to all who deſire to be acquainted with the Affair of Subſcriptions, and Matter ſufficient to remove all Objections againſt ſubſcribing to the Articles and Liturgy of the Church of England. By Samuel Roe, M. A. Vicar of Stotfold, Bedfordſhire. 8vo. 6d. Kearſly. 1771.

If ignorance, bigotry, nonſenſe, and falſe grammar conſtituted the principal excellencies of literary compoſition, to what a great degree of applauſe would Mr. Samuel Roe's production be entitled!

Art. 29. *Free Thoughts on the projected Application to Parliament, for the Abolition of eccleſiaſtical Subſcriptions.* By Auguſtus Toplady, A. B. Vicar of Broad-Hembury, Devon. 8vo. 6d. Gurney. 1771.

This gentleman may well, in a certain ſenſe, call his performance *free thoughts*; for he has treated the perſons he writes againſt with great freedom indeed! It is not, however, the becoming freedom of a gentleman or a Chriſtian, but ſomething very different from the character of either. Mr. Toplady's zeal for Calviniſm is ſo exceſſive, that it renders him totally forgetful of candour, and even of decency, in his treatment of the petitioners for the removal of ſubſcription. He thinks proper to ſubſtitute abuſe for reaſoning; and as to what arguments he makes uſe of, they are ſuch as have been refuted again and again.

But although this Author appears to be ſo bigotted in ſome reſpects, he is enlarged and liberal-minded in others. He is a zealous advocate for the unlimited toleration of proteſtants, wiſhes to have the ſubſcription of the diſſenters removed, and is of opinion that a

 burthen

burthen of this kind ought not to be impofed on thofe of the laity who take the academical degrees in law or phyfic. In thefe inftances, he confiders fubfcription as a real grievance, equally *oppreffive* and *abfurd*.

Thus we fee the inconfiftency of which the human mind is capable, and that the fame perfon who, on one fubject, is wholly guided by the moft narrow prejudices, may, on another, entertain generous and noble fentiments.

Art. 30. *Jefus feen of Angels; and God's Mindfulnefs of Man.* Confidered in three Difcourfes: the Subftance of which was preached in the Parifh Church of Broad-Hembury, Devon, Dec. 25, 1770. By Auguftus Toplady, A. B. 8vo. 1 s. 6 d. Gurney. 1771.

Perfons who are fond of Calvinifm in its higheft ftrain, will be much delighted with thefe difcourfes, which difplay great vigour of imagination, and confiderable powers of language, but which, in our opinion, are very defective with regard to truth and judgment.

Art. 31. *A Treatife on the Walk of Faith.* By W. Romaine, M. A. Rector of St. Andrew Wardrobe and St. Ann Black-Friars, and Lecturer of St. Dunftan's in the Weft. 12mo. 2 vols. 6 s. Worral, &c. 1771.

The genius, learning, and principles of Mr. Romaine are fo well and fo generally known, that we think it entirely needlefs to enter particularly into the merits of this or any other production of his pen; efpecially as any cenfure which we might now pafs on his writings, might be thought rather invidious by his friends and followers, on account of the little bickerings which formerly fubfifted between him and the Monthly Reviewers.

It is certain, that, with refpect to articles of faith, we have the misfortune to differ very widely from this gentleman. We hope, neverthelefs, that Mr. Romaine and the Reviewers will agree, as may well become them, in duly obferving the pious precept* which ftands as the motto to this treatife; and then it will be of fmall confequence whether they accord or not in matters of *fpeculation*.

Art. 32. *A Converfation* between Richard Hill, Efq; the Rev. Mr. Madan, and Father Walfh, Superior of a Convent of Englifh Benedictine Monks at Paris,—held at the faid Convent, July 13, 1771; in the prefence of Thomas Powis, Efq; relative to fome *doctrinal Minutes* advanced by the Rev. Mr. John Wefley, and others, at a Conference held in London, Auguft 7, 1770. 8vo. 6 d. Dilly.

Mr. Hill and Mr. Madan, in a converfation with Father Walfh, at the time and place above-mentioned, were curious to learn the good Benedictine's opinion of our Methodifts, and particularly of fome tenets maintained by Mr. Wefley and his followers, in oppofition to the Calvinifts. They fhewed him an extract of the aforefaid *minutes*; on perufal of which, Father Walfh expreffed his deteftation of the principles they contained, and pronounced Mr. W. to be a *Pelagian*. From hence the Author of this pamphlet [whether Mr. Hill or Mr.

* WALK HUMBLY WITH THY GOD. Micah vi. 8.

[adan does not appear] takes occasion to triumph over Mr. W. whose doctrines, he says, are "too rotten for even a papist to rest upon;" and he adds, that, from a review of all that passed in this conversation, "it may be supposed, that popery is about mid-way between protestantism and Mr. J. Wesley."

But the attack on Mr. W. is carried still farther. An attempt is here made to convict him of the grossest prevarication and inconsistency, with respect to the doctrine of imputed righteousness, &c. Some notable extracts being given, in a contrasted view, from what he has said both *for* and *against* that doctrine, at different times, and in different publications.

The Author declares, that he had, for many years, an high veneration for Mr. W. even though, says he, "I differed from him in those points deemed Calvinistical. But his late Minutes have obliged me to form very different sentiments of him; and these sentiments are so far from being changed into more favourable ones by the late declaration at Bristol*, that I am thereby more than ever convinced of his unsettled principles, and prevaricating disposition."—What will Mr. W. say to these ugly *pros* and *cons*.

Art. 33. *Discourses to the Aged*; on several important Subjects. By Job Orton. 12mo. 3s. 6d. bound. Buckland. 1771.

We have more than once had occasion to mention the works of this pious and worthy Author with due regard: the discourses now before us well deserve the attentive perusal of those for whom they are chiefly intended; they breathe an excellent spirit, and shew an earnest desire in the writer to advance the interests of genuine piety and practical religion.

We cannot give a shorter nor clearer account of his views, in these discourses, than in his own words:——"It seems natural, says he, that persons should read, with special attention and regard, what is particularly addressed to them, and suited to their age and circumstances. It is, no doubt, on this principle, that many volumes of sermons to young persons have been published within the last forty years: and of late, particular addresses have been made from the press, to the poor and the great, and to young persons of each sex, which have been well received, and, I am persuaded, have done much good. But I have not seen nor heard of any sermons immediately addressed to the aged: yet, surely, they highly deserve esteem, compassion, and assistance; and they may expect, among other acts of respect and kindness, to have such advices, encouragements, and consolations, addressed to them, as may, by the blessing of God, contribute to make their old age honourable, comfortable, and useful, and smooth the last scenes of their lives. This is attempted in the following discourses. I am far from pretending to equal the composures of my honoured fathers and brethren, who have addressed to the young. But much accuracy, sprightliness, and elegance, do

* A copy of which is given in this pamphlet. The Author informs us that it was signed by Mr. W. and upwards of fifty of his preachers.

not seem necessary in addressing the aged. What is abstruse, critical and difficult, is here avoided, as it appeared improper and absurd to trouble persons who are in the decline of life with such things; and I have long observed that they are best pleased with what is plain, simple, and affectionate.

"These sermons were delivered in the course of my stated ministry, and most of them on the last Lord's days of successive years; it being my custom, on those days, to address more immediately to my aged friends, to whom they were very acceptable, and I hope beneficial. I was more disposed to employ some time in preparing them for the press, as Providence hath rendered me incapable of being useful in other ways; and as I am myself declining into the vale of years, and, by long-continued daily infirmities, got very far into it, from much experience, therefore, I know how to pity the aged under their infirmities and decays, and desire to be their humble monitor and comforter.

"I hope the subjects of these discourses will be thought suitable to the circumstances of the generality of the aged; and that other infirm and afflicted persons, though not old, may find some things in this volume, which may assist them to bear and improve their afflictions, as becometh Christians. The affinity there is between some of the subjects, occasioned the same thoughts to be repeated, which could not be avoided without injustice to the subjects and the readers. On the other hand, some important thoughts are omitted, or only hinted at, in places where it might be expected they should have been introduced, or largely discussed; because they are inserted and enlarged upon in some other discourses.'

The subjects of the discourses are, chiefly, these:—*The difference between the activity of youth and the infirmities of age.—Barzillai's refusal of David's invitation to Jerusalem.—Caleb's reflection on the goodness and faithfulness of God to him.—The design and improvement of useless days and wearisome nights.—God's promise to bear and carry his aged servants.—Israel's journey through the wilderness, an emblem of the Christian's state on earth.—The outward man decaying, and the inward man renewing.—Joseph's dying assurance to his brethren, that God would visit them.—The honour of aged piety.—The joy of the aged to leave their descendants prosperous, peaceful, and pious.—The hand of God in removing our friends far from us.*

Art. 34. *Two Dissertations on Popish Persecution and Breach of Faith.* In answer to a Book, intitled, "A Free Examination of the common Methods employed to prevent the Growth of Popery." With an *Introductory Discourse*, containing the State of the Controversy, and some occasional Remarks. By D. Grant, M. A. Vicar of Hutton-Rudby, Yorkshire. 8vo. 2 s. 6 d. sewed. Murray. 1771.

In our Review vol. xxxv, p. 4[illegible], and vol. xl, p. 72, we gave some account of the two parts of the *Free Examination*; and we expressed our hope that this doughty champion of the church of Rome might not be suffered to triumph in his bold attempt against the honour and interest of the protestant cause; and our hopes have not been disappointed.

painted. Some considerable writers * have entered the lists against him, and he has been smartly repulsed in several skirmishes; but the learned and able writer of the performance now before us, has totally defeated him in a general engagement.

NOVELS.

Art. 35. *The Elopement*; or Perfidy Punished. 12mo. 3 vols. 7 s. 6 d. sewed, Noble. 1772.

In this novel, there is a degree of vivacity, which supports the attention of the reader, and renders it interesting, though the Author possesses little power over the passions, and though the circumstances, which constitute the story, do not grow naturally out of each other. The conclusion, in particular, is abrupt and unsatisfactory.

Art. 36. *The affected Indifference.* 12mo. 2 Vols. 5 s. sewed. Noble. 1771.

The novel before us, is not void of interesting scenes; and when we reflect on the load of obscene or insipid performances of this class, with which the press abounds, we cannot justly refuse our suffrage to it. In a listless interval, it may furnish a tolerable entertainment to even a cultivated mind.

Art. 37. *The Man of Honour*; or the History of Harry Waters, Esq; 12mo. 2 s. 6 d. sewed. Noble.

This is only the 1st volume of the contemptible history of 'squire Waters: we hope we shall never be troubled with the second.

Art. 38. *The Phœnix*: or the History of Polyarchus and Argenis. Translated from the Latin. By a Lady. 12mo. 4 Vols. 12s. Bell. 1772.

The public is here presented with a new translation of that fine old romance, Barclay's *Argenis*. The original has been well known to the learned these 150 years; and, for the accommodation of the mere English readers, two versions of it, in our language, were given, in the course of the last century; but the style of these is grown too obsolete for the present age.

The unknown lady, who professes to have made a new translation of this work from the original Latin, apologizes for the liberty she has taken in prefixing a new title to Barclay's work, by saying, 'It is published in this manner, partly in compliance with the taste of the times, and partly for reasons of a more private nature, respecting the Editor.'—This is rather mysterious;—and, as we desire to have nothing to do with mysteries, so let it remain.

The Editor, as she chuses to style herself, rather than Translator, has prefixed to the work, a very judicious account of the Author's design, and of the merit of his performance: which is, as she well observes, 'A romance, allegory, and a system of politics. Considered as an investigation of the various forms of government, and of the most proper remedies for the political distempers of a state, it will certainly be thought a work of great merit, if we make due allowance

* Particularly Archdeacon Blackburn, in his Considerations on the State of the Controversy, &c. (See Review vol. xxxix. p. 225) and Mr. Pye, in his *Five Letters*, &c. See Review vol. xxxviii. p. 254.

for the time * in which it was written. But if regarded only as a work of moral entertainment, it will be allowed to ſtand in the foremoſt rank of the old romances, ſacred to chivalry and virtue. In brief, to uſe the words of the ingenious Editor, 'Barclay's Argenis affords ſuch variety of entertainment, that every kind of reader may find in it ſomething ſuitable to his own taſte and diſpoſition: the ſtateſman, the philoſopher, the ſoldier, the lover, the citizen, the friend of mankind, each may gratify his favourite propenſity; while the reader who comes for amuſement only, will not go away diſappointed.'

John Barclay, the Author of this work, was a gentleman of Scotch extraction, born and educated in France. He died in 1621. For further particulars relating to him, we refer to the biographical dictionaries. Being a Roman catholic, he was, in courſe, an enemy to the Hugonots †, to whom he gives no quarter in this work; and on that account, together with his partiality for monarchy, his Argenis, with all its merit, will never be a popular book in this country.

EAST-INDIES.

Art. 39. *Obſervations on the preſent State of the Eaſt-India Company*; and on the Meaſures to be purſued for inſuring its Permanency, and augmenting its Commerce. 8vo. 2 s. Nourſe. 1771.

The chief deſign of this performance is to ſhew, that it is very poſſible for this kingdom to center in itſelf almoſt all the trade to the Eaſt-Indies: and in the reaſonings employed by its Author with regard to the execution of an undertaking of ſo much conſequence, there is an extreme degree of plauſibility. He appears to be intimately acquainted with the ſtate of India, and he ſtates the facts on which he founds his obſervations with great candour and impartiality. The defects in the preſent arrangements there, and the dangerous conſequences that may ariſe from them, he has certainly very fully expoſed: but, while we think that there is much to commend in the plan he has ſketched out for remedying and preventing them, we ſhould ſuſpect that it implies a degree of integrity in the officers of the Eaſt-India company, which will never be found among men who forſake their own country to amaſs wealth under an unkindly climate.

NATURAL HISTORY, GARDENING, &c.

Art. 40. *The Modern Gardener; or, Univerſal Kalendar.* Containing monthly Directions for all the Operations of Gardening to be done either in the Kitchen, Fruit, Flower, and Pleaſure Gardens, as likewiſe in the Greenhouſe and Stove; with the Method of performing the different Works, according to the beſt Practice of the moſt eminent Gardeners. Alſo an Appendix, giving full and

* The reign of James I.

† The Argenis is chiefly founded on the religious civil wars of France, in which Henry IV. made ſo capital a figure. He is the hero of this work, under the name of Polyarchus.

ample

ample Instructions for forcing Grape Vines, Peach, Nectarine Trees, &c. in a new Manner, never before published. Selected from the Diary Manuscripts of the late Mr. Hitt. Revised, corrected, and improved by James Meader. 12mo. 5s. bound Hawes, Law, &c. 1771.

What a number of comely, well-looking children hath Father Miller * begotten! and one generation, we see, always improves on another. Hitt was, undoubtedly, a skilful manager of fruit-trees; and we have more than once commended his book on that subject to the notice of our horticultural readers. The other branches of the gardener's art seem to be here judiciously treated. Much, indeed, is borrowed, as must be expected, from preceding writers, but many things are also added, which appear to be the result of real practice, and rational observation. The plan or form of the work is also, in some respects, more distinct and methodical than that of former kalendars.

Art. 41. *The Eighteenth Volume* of Dr. Hill's Vegetable System. Fol. Royal Paper. Baldwin, &c.

We have, at several times, mentioned the preceding parts of this great and voluminous work, which is now finished, and the whole advertised at twenty-seven guineas and a half in sheets: the coloured sets at 126 guineas. The Doctor observes, in his advertisement, that 'Many books must, in general, be consulted to find a plant;' that 'this needs no reference to any other;' and that 'the history, stature, colours, and description of every plant are here:'—Each volume containing figures of near 200 plants, 'all drawn from nature, as they arise in Bayswater garden, or from specimens faithfully collected, or drawings taken on the spot, by botanical correspondents and others.'

Art. 42. *Novæ Species Insectorum. Centuria I. Auctore Joan. Reinoldo Forstero*, S. A. S. 8vo. 2s. 6d. sewed. Davies, &c. 1771.

The pursuit of natural knowledge is ever to be honoured and respected, except when cruelty attends, and it does not seldom attend, the investigation. Naturalists are always curious, and no passion leads us into contracted paths, or makes us lose sight of the principles of humanity, in general, more than curiosity. Men of more exalted minds will tell us, that

———" the poor beetle which we tread upon,
In corporal sufferance feels a pang as great,
As when a giant dies."———

As to the rest, this work is accurate, ingenious, and entertaining.

Art. 43. *The Naturalist's and Traveller's Companion.* Containing Instructions for discovering and preserving of Natural History. 8vo. 2s. Pearch.

Instructions of this kind may be usefully attended to by travellers, who are laudably inclined to regard and to collect the curious productions of nature peculiar to other climes, but are ignorant of the proper means of preserving them.

* Author of the well-known Gardener's Dictionary, and Gardener's Kalendar.

Art.

Art. 44. *Thomæ Martyn, S. T. B. Coll. Sidn. Soc. Prof. Botan. Prælect. Walk. et Hort. Curat. Catalogus Horti Botanici Cantabrigiensis, Cantab. &c.* A Catalogue of the Botanic Garden at Cambridge, by T. Martyn, B. D. Fellow of Sidney College, Professor of Botany, Walker's Lecturer, and Keeper of the Botanic Garden. 8vo. 3 s. 6 d. White, &c.

Mr. Martyn informs us that about ten years ago Dr. Walker began his botanic garden; that Mr. Charles Miller, son of the celebrated Mr. P. Miller, being chosen manager of the garden, laboured much to enrich it with plants, and to range them according to the sexual system; that himself having nearly finished this work, presents the world with this Catalogue, which would have been more complete, had he not paid greater regard to the request of his impatient friends than to his own reputation; but that he shall be content if his botanic readers be not displeased. He then adds the heads of his botanic lectures, premised to his description of the plants in this Catalogue.

Those heads regard the principal things in botany, and premise some entertaining matter, as the *age* and *size* of trees, the *sleep* of leaves, the *watchings of flowers*; the *history* of *botany*, &c. He enumerates the classes of *Cæsalpinus, Ricinus,* and *Tournefort*, and describes the systems of Magnolius and others. His lectures then explain the sexual system, and consequently Linnæus's classes; and conclude with an appendix, and two indexes, *Latin* and *English*.

TRADE and BUSINESS.

Art. 45. *Tables of the several European Exchanges, &c. &c.* By Phineas Barret, Merchant at Lisbon. 4to. 2 l. 2 s. Blyth.

Beside the courses of exchange, Mr. Barret accurately shews in what money, real or imaginary, merchants' accounts are kept; the manner of drawing bills in most of the capital cities in Europe; with the usances, days of grace, &c. &c.—The utility of publications of this kind, in the mercantile world, is sufficiently obvious; but *correctness* is indispensable: and the merit (in this respect) of any books which are chiefly composed of figures, will best be known to those who try them by the touchstone of experience.

Art. 46. *The Tariff*, or Book of Rates and Duties on Goods passing through the Sound, at Elsinoor, &c. By John Anderson. 8vo. 1 s. 6 d. Robinson and Roberts.

Useful to those who trade to Denmark.

POLITICAL.

Art. 47. *Letters* addressed to the King, the Duke of Grafton, the Earls of Chesterfield and Sandwich, Lord Barrington, Junius, and the Rev. Mr. Horne; under the Signature of P. P. S. 4to. 1 s. Almon, &c. 1771.

These Letters (replete with nothing but *abuse alamode*) originally appeared in the Public Advertiser, and other news-papers. They are now *prefaced* by a *dedication* to the *public*; in which the Author threatens to continue his collections ' in six-penny numbers, according to the political occurrences of the week.' But as the execution of of this noble design is to depend on the degree of approbation which the public shall bestow upon No. I. we may take it for granted that we shall never see No. II.

Art. 48. *Sentiments* offered to the Public, for the Coining of 40,000 Pounds worth of Silver. 8vo. 6d. Evans. 1771.

The great scarcity of silver coin, in this nation, is generally and grievously felt. The Author of this homely pamphlet (for it is very ill written) strenuously urges the immediate coinage of 40,000 or 100,000 pounds worth, all in shillings, as a measure which would prove highly acceptable to the public; and he thinks it might easily be done, by fixing the standard according to the present advanced price of silver, viz. 23 shillings in every four ounces: which, he apprehends, would prevent the mischievous practices of those who make a gainful trade of melting down the coin of the old standard. But this is a subject of such great nicety and importance, as to require the best heads in the kingdom to investigate and determine upon it.

DRAMATIC.

Art. 49. *Amelia.* A musical Entertainment, of two Acts. 8vo. 1s. Becket.

This piece was first acted and published in 1738; and it was mentioned in our 38th volume, p. 335. It is now revived, with some alterations and improvements; but they are not considerable enough to become the subject of a particular detail in the Review *. Mr. Cumberland, Author of the celebrated comedy entitled the *West Indian*, is mentioned in the papers as the writer of this musical entertainment.

Art. 50. *Timon of Athens*, altered from Shakespeare. A Tragedy. As it is acted at the Theatre Royal in Drury-lane. 8vo. 1s. 6d. Becket. 1771.

Mr. Cumberland, the ingenious Editor, has retrenched some extravagances, and lopped off several excrescences which have disfigured the otherwise excellent play of Timon. This performance hath now more regularity and decorum to recommend it to the taste of the present age, than it could boast in the wild and rough state in which it was left by its great Author; yet the manly spirit and vigour of Shakespeare seem not in the least emasculated by the chastisement he hath received from the hand of his bold and adventurous Reviser.

To supply the places of the many rejected parts of this play, the Editor has introduced several new scenes of his own; and this, we think, with as good success as could be expected, in so arduous and difficult an attempt, with the prejudices of the public against him, and all the (we had almost said) *devout* reverence in which even the faults of Shakespeare are generally held.

* Mr. Cumberland also wrote *The Brothers*, and *The Summer's Tale*, two other plays, introduced on the theatre a few winters ago, and mentioned in our Reviews, at the times of their appearance: see vols. xxxiii. and xliii.

Mr.

Mr. Cumberland has much improved the plan and *composition* of the piece, by admitting Love, the favourite passion with the dramatic Muses, to a place in this tragedy. He has given Timon a daughter, with whom the gallant Alcibiades is in love. From hence, in our opinion, the character of this hero rises in importance, and his conduct, subsequent to the ruin of Timon's fortune, becomes more interesting to the generality of an audience, and particularly to the female part of it: to whose tender and sympathetic feelings, the distress of this play (which, hitherto, hath not seemed to have much affected the ladies) is now more naturally and more agreeably accommodated.

POETICAL.

ART. 51. *The Theatres*; a poetical Dissection. By Sir Nicholas Nipclose, Bart. 4to. 3 s. Bell.

We have had a *Rosciad* from Churchill, a *Thespis* from Kelly, and now we have a fresh poetical dissection of theatrical delinquents, from—we know not who.—Nor is it material *who*. The question from the public will be, "*What* has the Author prepared for our entertainment or instruction?" We will endeavour, briefly, to answer this question; and we hope to do it as satisfactorily as the narrowness of our present limits will allow, and as explicitly as the *importance* of the subject may require.

This Author, then, has poured out a great deal of virulent invective against not only the principal performers, but the managers also of the theatres in Drury-lane and Covent-garden. The great reformer of the English stage, the restorer of Shakespeare, is here treated as though we were under little, if any, obligation to him for the reformation (so much wanted!) of our most rational amusement; and he is, moreover, ungratefully and cruelly reproached, for still exerting his admirable talents, to gratify a discerning public, which, by its unremitted applause, continues to manifest a more just as well as more generous sense of his unrivalled and UNEXAMPLED merit!

Mr. Colman, too, is grossly abused for having, according to our Author, shewn too much countenance to pageant and pantomime: with other high crimes and misdemeanors, committed in his managerial capacity.

It would be curious to see in what manner these railers would themselves proceed, were they entrusted with the theatrical direction. Sir Nicholas Nipclose, himself, (who satirizes our present dramatic *writers*, as well as the managers and actors) condemns, in general, the new plays which have been exhibited for some years past: our tragedies are languid, our comedies are dull, and shews and pantomimes are fit only for Sadler's Wells and Bartholomew-booths. What, then, does he want? Would he have none but the old stock pieces represented? He would soon feel the melancholy effects of such management, on the drooping spirit of the theatre, and in the decay of the public appetite for its amusements: every novel mode of diversion would soon prevail, and even *Jonas*, or the Italian *Fantoccini*, would, merely from the love of novelty, triumph over the neglected genius

genius of the stage. Not the immortal Shakespeare's self, that 'god of our' theatrical 'idolatry,' would be able to keep the field throughout the course of one winter's campaign.

But it is idle to argue with these discontented, waspish gentlemen; who may have reasons for provocation, of which the public are ignorant. Perhaps a play, "a most excellent piece!" has been *refused:* VENGEANCE is then the word, and authors (*unhappily* more *successful*) together with the whole world of managers, actors,—nay prompters, treasurers, box-keepers, and all, are involved in the universal wreck, occasioned by the furious tempest raised by an hostile poet,—whose

"—— Great revenge has stomach for them all!"

A few of the devoted crew, however, are saved from this general shipwreck of the stage, viz. Mrs. Abington (to whom the poem is dedicated) Mrs. Barry, Messrs. Woodward, King, Weston, and two or three more. An encomium on Mr. Foote is likewise introduced; and as it will always afford the benevolent mind more pleasure to be instrumental in the diffusion of well-earned fame, than in propagating detraction, we shall select this short panegyric, as a specimen of our Author's poetical abilities.

After decrying the dramatic writings of Goldsmith, Hoole, Bickerstaff, Gentleman, Reed, Franklin, &c. he thus proceeds:

The Muse, at length, with painful censure tir'd,
Meets with an author worthily admir'd;
Rival'd in strength of character by few,
Rich in a fund of humour ever new,
Whose pregnant pencil takes from life each tint,
Whose thoughts are stamp'd in brilliant Fancy's mint;
Who never makes a vain or feeble hit;
Terse in his style, and polish'd in his wit;
Copious in subject, yet compact in scenes,
Dull explanation never intervenes;
Each line, each person, under just controul,
Speaks to the heart, and *beautifies the whole:*
Laughter attends,—Spleen flies the house of joy,
Where Genius, Foote, and Nature never cloy.

We are prevented from affixing our mark of approbation to all the foregoing verses, by the expression printed in *italic*, in the last line but two; which, we think, is far from *beautifying the whole* of our Author's poetical picture of the British Aristophanes.

Art. 52. *The Frequented Village*; a Poem. [illegible] a Gentleman of the Middle Temple. 4to. 2 s. Godwin.

This seems intended both as a companion and contrast to Goldsmith's *Deserted Village*. It displays the pleasing scenery of a *flourishing* village, with its rural *environs*; and describes the innocent and happy lives of the rustic inhabitants.

What Pope modestly said of his WINDSOR FOREST, may, with the strictest truth, be applied to this piece; in which mere *description* holds *the place of sense*. The Author intimates his youth,—perhaps to to bespeak the reader's indulgence for the imperfections of an unfledged muse. But although inexperience, and immature faculties, may be pleaded in extenuation of defects in *writing*, for private amusement, yet this will not excuse an over-forwardness to appear in *print*.

It may be thought somewhat cruel to damp the ardour of a young writer, by the severity of censure; but it would be greater cruelty to encourage a * worthy youth, by fallacious complaisance, to an unavailing perseverance, in a pursuit, wherein the impossibility of his succeeding is but too obviously to be inferred from the imbecillity of his out-set.

Art. 53. *The Patriot's Guide*; a Poem. Inscribed to the Earl of C——m, Junius, and John Wilkes, Esq; 4to. 2 s. 6 d. Wheble.

A satire on the popular party. The best part of it is the last couplet; one half of which is stolen from Swift: speaking of 'the rabble rout,' he says

> 'They rage, believing their seducers true—
> *Madness of many, for the gain of few.*'

There is some spirit in this poem; but it is, on the whole, a crude and boyish performance.

Art. 54. *Galfred and Juetta; or, the Road of Nature.* A Tale, in three Cantos. By the late Thomas Brerewood, Esq; 4to. 2 s. 6 d. Bladon. 1771.

The Editor informs the public, that this poem 'is the work of no hackney or *modern* writer, but was written near *forty* years ago, and is the posthumous work of Thomas Brerewood, junior, Esq; of Horton, Bucks: a gentleman then known, among persons of genius and the best taste, to have possessed peculiar talents in the lyric way of writing; and to have been greatly esteemed and distinguished for his uncommon strain of wit and humour in the descriptive way, in which he characterised and painted Nature, which he strictly followed, in the most strong and lively colours, and with the greatest warmth of imagination.'

This Editor, like most other Editors, has formed too high an opinion of his author. Mr. B's poem is a tedious recital of the low and loose intrigues among the servants, male and female, at Galfred Hall; in which old 'squire Galfred's wanton wife comes in for her share. The incidents are not over modestly related, nor is the versification to be commended for correctness or elegance. The Author appears, indeed, to have possessed a pretty good talent at describing the natural scenes afforded in a country life; and in this, we apprehend, consists his only merit.

---

* There are, in this piece, (which we are sorry we cannot praise as a poem) many indications of an amiable disposition in the Writer; from which we found ourselves the more strongly inclined to deal HONESTLY with him; and he will the more readily give us credit for pure impartiality, as we are utter strangers to his person, and even to his name.

Art.

Art. 55. *An Elegy on the Death of the Rev. John Gill*, D. D. who departed this Life Oct. 14, 1771. By John Fellows. 8vo. 6 d. Robinson.

This pious rhimester seems to charge the Almighty with having, in his anger, slain Dr. Gill; at the same time peremptorily demanding of him, "When his anger will cease?" Is this incredible? take, then, his own words for it:

"How are the mighty fallen! Lord when will
Thine anger cease? The great, the learned Gill
Now pale and breathless lies!——————"

Not to enlarge on the PRESUMPTION of the Writer (whose *intention* may not have been altogether so criminal) let us only remark the FOLLY of his thus lamenting, as though it were an untimely stroke of death, the natural departure of a venerable old man of near eighty! Was this sufficient cause for raising such an outcry in Zion, and calling on her sons and daughters to weep and wail, as if the day of judgment were come?—But we ask our Reader's pardon: the verses of the spiritual bellmen, who usually exercise their talents on these occasions, are not the objects of criticism. We had, however, too much respect for the eminent character of the late Dr. Gill, to behold with indifference so unworthy a tribute paid to his memory.—It is a misfortune to men of learning and merit, such as the Doctor's, that they are not suffered to remove from a bad world to a better, without having their fame burlesqued by incompetent and absurd panegyrists.

Art. 56. *The Love Epistles of Aristænetus.* Translated from the the Greek into English Metre. 8vo. 3 s. bound. Wilkie. 1771.

No such writer as Aristænetus ever existed in the classic æra. Nor did even the unhappy schools, after the destruction of the Eastern empire, produce such a writer. It was left to the later times of monkish imposition to give us such trash as this; on which the Translator has ill spent his time. We have been as idly employed in reading it; and our Readers will, in proportion, lose their time in perusing this article.

Art. 57. *Poems on several Occasions.* By William Dine. 8vo. 1 s. Robinson and Roberts. 1771.

My stock of learning is but small,
As you full well do know;
Yet, poet like, am oft oppress'd
With poverty and woe.

So deep immerg'd in anxious cares,
My mind they so torment,
That when to write I do intend,
They often me prevent.

Such is the poetry of William Dine, clerk of the parish of Chiddingly in Sussex; and such is the sorrowful account he gives of himself. Poor man! we heartily wish his circumstances were better; but we fear that the printing his verses is not the way to mend them.

SERMONS.

SERMONS.

I. *The Causes and Consequences of evil Speaking against Government,* considered—before the University of Cambridge, at Great St. Mary's, on the King's Accession, Oct. 25, 1771. By John Gordon, D. D. Archdeacon of Lincoln, and Chaplain to the Bishop of that Diocese. 4to. 1 s. Beecroft, &c.

*** A very loyal, declamatory, *court* sermon; in which, we think, the judgment of the preacher is less conspicuous than his zealous attachment to the *powers that be.*

II. Two Sermons, *on Stedfastness* in the Christian Faith, and the Union of Charity with Zeal;—before the University of Cambridge. By Thomas Stevens, M. A. Fellow of T. C. C. 6 d. White, &c.

III. *The Rock of Offence the Sinner's last and only Refuge,*—on Rom. x. 3. Wherein the Cause and Consequence of not submitting to the Righteousness of God are considered. By J. Martin. 8vo. 8 d. Buckland.

IV. *The Requisition of Subscription to the Thirty-nine Articles and Liturgy of the Church of England not inconsistent with Christian Liberty:* a Sermon. To which are prefixed, Reasons against subscribing a Petition to Parliament for the Abolition of such Subscription. 4to. 1 s. Flexney. 1771.

††† The Author of this discourse appears to be a man of abilities, but we can neither agree with him in his reasonings, nor approve of the temper with which he writes.

CORRESPONDENCE.

THE long letter from a young man 'who lives on the side of 'a bleak hill, surrounded with moors and high mountains, 'remote from the polite and refined,' is received; but the contents are all foreign from the plan of our Review. With respect to the *recommendations* which he desires, it seems very strange that a person should ask favours, depending on the merit of private character, at the same time that he conceals both his name and place of residence!

*** The writer of the Letter recommending to our notice a pamphlet concerning *Lotteries*, omitted to inform us where that piece was to be met with; so that it was near the end of the month before we could procure it, and too late for any account of it to be given in this number of the Review.

APPENDIX.

TO THE

MONTHLY REVIEW,

VOLUME the FORTY-FIFTH.

FOREIGN LITERATURE.

ART. I.

Histoire de l'Academie Royale des Sciences, &c.—The History of the Royal Academy of Sciences at Paris; together with the Mathematical and Physical Memoirs for the Years 1767, and 1768. 4to. Paris. 1770.

GENERAL PHYSICS.

MEMOIR I. *An Account of some Experiments made on Gunpowder.* By the Abbé Nollet.

WE shall collect the general result of these experiments; recommending the perusal of the memoir itself to those who are more peculiarly interested in the contents of it.

It has hitherto been generally supposed that gunpowder, in an ungranulated state, to which a considerable part of it is reduced, after having been long kept in the magazines, or in barrels, will not do that effectual service, or produce that sudden explosion which is expected from it. This quality is, in some degree, known to those who purposely reduce it to a fine powder, in the preparation of fire-works, &c. on which occasions it produces rather a slow deflagration, than a momentary explosion. It has likewise been supposed that, by long keeping, it is in some measure decompounded: at least, the nitre seems to separate from the other two ingredients; and saline efflorescences are observed on the surfaces of the grains. In both these cases it has been judged to be absolutely unfit for service. The Abbé Nollet however, for reasons which are given in this memoir, entertained some doubts concerning the truth of these opinions, and in order to ascertain the justice of his suspicions, undertook a set of experiments on a large scale; in which he was assisted by several experienced officers of the artillery.

For this purpose repeated discharges were made from mortars and cannon, charged alternately with equal quantities of new granulated powder, and of the two kinds above specified, generally reputed unserviceable; and their different strengths were ascertained by the respective ranges or force of the bombs or cannon balls discharged from them. From the whole of these trials it appears, that pulverised and decompounded gunpowder is not greatly inferior in strength to that which is granulated and fresh; that an adequate compensation for their inferiority may easily be made, by a moderate addition to the charge; and that, at least, they may be usefully employed in public rejoicings, and in besieged places, or on other urgent occasions, in want of better.

MEMOIR II. *On the luminous Quality of Sea Water, particularly in the Lagunes of Venice.* By M. Fougeroux de Bondaroy.

M. Fougeroux balances between, or rather considers a phosphoric matter, luminous insects, and electricity united, as the probable causes of this phenomenon.—But instead of giving an analysis of this memoir, we shall refer our Readers to Mr. Canton's more satisfactory observations and experiments on this contraverted subject, published in the 59th volume of the Philosophical Transactions; or to our account of them in our 44th volume, April 1771, page 329. We shall only add, that some of the observations of the present inquirer confirm Mr. Canton's opinion, that the putrefaction of the many animal substances contained in the sea, is the principal cause of this appearance.

MEMOIR III. *On a Method of preventing the offensive Smells proceeding from Drains.* By M. Deparcieux.

Philosophy, we think, is far from being degraded when she is so condescending as to interest herself in the homely offices in which we view her employed in this memoir;—in extinguishing a stink, and rendering a kitchen or scullery less offensive. A method, equally simple and ingenious, is here given, of preventing the foul and stinking air, proceeding from the fermentation of the various impurities carried off into draining wells, from being driven back, or rising and entering into the lower apartments of a house, so as to render those situated under ground particularly, almost absolutely uninhabitable: an inconvenience which, the Author observes, is very frequently suffered at Paris, to the great annoyance of the whole family.

Though this method cannot be particularly described without the plates, we think it worth while to attempt giving a general idea of the simple principle on which it is founded, by observing that it consists in fixing a stone trough or cistern in the side wall of the waste well or draining well; one side or end of which cistern, viz. that which is next the draining well, is

two

two inches lower than the other three ſides. This trough, the top of which is level with the pavement of the drain, is always full of water, or of the fluid that has been laſt thrown into the drain. A ſtone ſlab fixed perpendicularly over the middle of this ciſtern, forms a partition which accurately cloſes the paſſage of the drain on all ſides, except at the bottom of the trough, which the ſlab does not reach; but at the ſame time its lower edge always dips an inch into the water contained in it. In conſequence of this ſimple contrivance, all communication of air between the draining well and the houſe is completely intercepted: for the ſlab ſhuts up the greater part of the paſſage; and the water, which is always in the ciſtern, performs the office of a ſtopper to the reſt of it: while the liquid impurities paſs freely in the interval between the lower edge of the ſlab and the bottom of the ciſtern, and then run over its lower ſide. This method has been ſucceſsfully applied to ice-houſes; where it prevents a current of the warm external air from entering through the paſſages made for carrying off the water that naturally drains from the ice, and thus quickly diſſolving it.

MEMOIR IV. *On the Cauſe of Water-ſpouts.* By M. Briſſon.

After recapitulating and ſhewing the inſufficiency of other ſyſtems, propoſed with a view to explain the nature and cauſe of this meteor, the Author endeavours to ſhew that it is one of the numerous phenomena in the train of electricity: but he nearly indiſpoſes us againſt his hypotheſis by employing, in his explication of it, the ſimultaneous affluences and effluences of the late Abbé Nollet. M. Briſſon preſents his theory as a new idea; though the *phenomena* of water-ſpouts were long ago attributed to electricity by Mr. Wilke, and much more particularly and ſatisfactorily explained, on electrical *data*, by Signor Beccaria *.

MEMOIR V. *A Diſſertation on the Nature of Water.* By M. Le Roi.

This diſſertation is not publiſhed as one of the memoirs of the academy, but contains the ſubſtance of an hiſtorical account, read by M. Le Roi before that body, of the different opinions which have been entertained by philoſophers concerning water; which is conſidered by ſome, as a ſimple and indeſtructible element, and by others, as a matter actually convertible into other bodies. As the ſettling the rank of an *element* is a matter of no ſmall concern among philoſophers, we ſhall particularly diſcuſs

* See his theory in his *Elettriciſmo artificiale e naturale*, p. 206, &c. or Dr. Prieſtley's account of it in the *Hiſtory of Electricity*, p. 377, &c. firſt edit.

the merits of the experiments brought in ſupport of its ſuppoſed degradation.

Our Readers who are converſant in the philoſophical part of chemiſtry, are not ignorant of the experiments mentioned by Boyle and others, from whence they deduce the actual *tranſmutation* of water into earth, in conſequence of repeated diſtillations. Even Newton adopts and reaſons upon this ſuppoſed tranſmutation in his *Optics*. Paſſing over, however, the incredible reſults of former experiments, which have either been greatly miſrepreſented, or not made with ſufficient accuracy; we ſhall only give the ſubſtance of thoſe of M. Margraaf, in which that great chemiſt took every poſſible precaution, that either ſcience or genius could ſuggeſt, to guard againſt deception. He received rain, immediately as it fell from the clouds, into clean glaſs veſſels, taking care never to collect it till after the rain had fallen ſeveral hours, and might be ſuppoſed to have brought down with it any duſt or other matters floating in the atmoſphere. He likewiſe gathered it in winter only, when the air may be ſuppoſed to be moſt free from ſuch ſubſtances. He collected ſnow with the ſame attention, and diſtilled the water in glaſs retorts made of one entire piece with the receiver; a ſmall aperture only being made, through which he introduced the water, and which afterwards was always accurately cloſed, ſo that not a ſingle atom of duſt could enter into the receiver from without. Nevertheleſs, after repeated diſtillations, he not only procured a ſmall portion of the nitrous and marine acids, but, to the laſt, the water continued to furniſh a quantity of fine calcareous earth; though, it is owned, in ſmaller and ſmaller quantities towards the end of the experiment.

But there is another proceſs, in which water has been ſaid to undergo a tranſmutation. Van Helmont's willow is well known; but we rather chuſe to mention the more accurate experiment of M. Du Hamel, publiſhed in the Memoirs of the Academy for 1748, who brought up a young oak without any other perceptible aliment than pure water, which had been previouſly diſtilled and filtered. It lived with him and continued growing (though not ſo faſt towards the latter part of the time, as an oak planted in earth) above eight years; and at laſt died merely through the neglect of thoſe intruſted with the care of it, while he was abſent upon a journey. Here water appears to have been converted into *wood*.

Notwithſtanding experiments ſo accurately and judiciouſly conducted, M. Le Roi denies, we think with juſtice, the inferences that have been drawn from them. With regard to M. Margraaf's experiments in particular, he affirms that the earth originally exiſted in the rain water; that it roſe with the vapours in their aſcent from the earth, and deſcended with them in rain; and that in these distillations it was only separated from it by the continued action of the fire. He observes that, according to M. Margraaf's own account, rain water of the same purity, exposed only to a simple and long continued agitation, constantly furnished portions of calcareous earth and acids, of the same kind with those which he procured by distillation; and that it might as justly be supposed that the water was, by his successive distillations, *converted* into spirit of nitre, or spirit of salt, as that it was transmuted into earth; merely because small quantities of each of these three substances were still furnished by it.

But we may place this matter in a clearer light than the Author has done, by observing that the most transparent waters are incontestably known to contain a calcarious earth, of the same kind with that procured by the last of M. Margraaf's distillations of rain water, a great part of which may be rendered visible, and separated from them by simple processes; that this earth is held in a state of the most perfect *solution* (a circumstance which M. Le Roi neglects to consider) by some of the acids, or a considerable portion of *fixed air* *; and further, that it is as easy to conceive that water containing earth thus dissolved in, and intimately united with it, may ascend into the atmosphere in natural evaporation, as that it should rise accompanied with the ponderous nitrous and marine acids. Nay, we could produce many instances in which earths, united with other bodies, are actually thus elevated.

But the water, it may be said, continues to furnish fresh portions of earth, after repeated distillations; and therefore there are grounds to believe that it is generated *de novo*. But this proves nothing more than the difficulty of separating the earth from the water; which is increased by the distillation's being performed in close vessels. A chemist will easily perceive how, after the precipitation of the *unneutralized* earth in the first distillations, in consequence of the more early escape of the *fixed air*, which held it in a state of solution, fresh portions of the neutralized earth, or that which had been dissolved and neutralized by acids, will be successively precipitated in each subsequent process, in proportion only as its former acid solvents escape or are expelled from it, by the action of the fire, in the progress of the operation. It appears from M. Margraaf's own experiments that, at the end of his 13th distillation, his water was still found to contain a small quantity of nitrous and marine acid: it contained therefore, we say, the proper solvents

* See the Hon. Mr. H. Cavendish's experiments on Rathbone-place water, in the Philosophical Transactions, vol. lvii. part 1.

of calcareous earth, and at that very time, no doubt, the earth itself; which afterwards appeared on their expulsion, and which it is no ways necessary to conceive to have been manufactured from water in the act of distillation. On the whole, the quantity of water thus supposed to have been transmuted into earth is very inconsiderable: as at the close of the 13th distillation of 3600 ounces of water, only the 14,400th part of its weight of earth was obtained.

M. Le Roi does not consider the growth of M. Du Hamel's oak as any proof of transmutation; attributing the whole of its increase to the earthy and saline parts, which the purest waters have been above shewn to contain. These alone however seem to furnish very slender and scanty *pabulum*. The Author should not have neglected to consider the copious *effluvia* from animate and inanimate bodies, or the various saline sulphureous and other particles continually floating in that chaos, the atmosphere; either condensed by the water, or which are probably still more strongly attracted and imbibed by the plant: for it is evident that vegetables extend their branches, and expand their leaves into the air, partly at least, for the same purposes that their roots penetrate and explore the earth; in order to extract nourishment from both these elements. But we may go further; for the chemical analysis of bodies will countenance the supposition that M. Du Hamel's oak derived its principal increase from the pure water alone; which, together with fixed air, is known to constitute the greatest part of the weight of even the most solid animal and vegetable substances. After all, we are too conscious of our profound ignorance of the laws of Nature to affirm the absolute immutability of water: we only mean to shew, that the experiments above produced do not prove its actual transmutation into earth.

MEMOIR VI. *An Account of a Thunder-storm which struck the Terrace of the Royal Observatory.* By the Abbé Chappe D'Auteroche.

The lightening struck the mast fixed on the terrace of the observatory, while the Abbé Chappe and M. Cassini were minutely observing the appearances and progress of the thunder-storm, at the distance only of 32 fathoms from the mast. The Abbé, whose opinion with regard to the constantly ascending direction of the electric matter we have formerly controverted, in our account of his *Travels into Siberia* *, says that he saw the lightening evidently ascending from the earth, at some distance, in the form of a rocket, and, in the subsequent explosion, proceeding from the bottom to the top of the mast, which was considerably damaged by it. Though his station

* See Monthly Review, vol. xli. December, 1769, page 439.

was

was ſo very near the place of the explosion, he affirms that the thunder did not immediately follow it; from whence a conclusion is drawn that the explosion was made in mid air, on the meeting of the *effluent* matter from the earth, with the *affluent* matter from the cloud.

Among the ſhort phyſical obſervations annexed to this claſs are accounts of two other conſiderable thunder-ſtorms, which happened at Paris in the courſe of this year, the *phenomena* of which in every particular confirm, if that were now neceſſary, the identity of the electric matter and lightening. One circumſtance, however, related in the firſt of theſe accounts appears to be of importance; as it ſhews into what a variety of channels the electric matter divides itſelf, when not collected into one, by means of a proper conductor. The lightening ſtruck a very large ſtack of chimnies, eight in number, ſix of which it entered, and did conſiderable miſchief in the chambers of every one of five floors with which they communicated. One of the moſt ſingular circumſtances attending it in one of theſe rooms was, that it broke a box containing ſeveral iron tools, which bore marks of fuſion in many places, without ſetting fire to half a pound of gunpowder, contained in an open veſſel in the ſame box.

Profeſſor Boze's celebrated electrical *Beatification* * has been realized, and nearly equalled, by a natural *Apotheoſis* of the ſame kind, the relation of which was communicated by M. Jallabert. His ſon travelling with Profeſſor Sauſſure, over one of the higheſt mountains of the Alps, they were catched there by a thunder-ſtorm; and ſoon found themſelves, to their great aſtoniſhment, electrified to ſo high a degree, that, on holding out their arms from their bodies, *ſpontaneous* ſparks darted from their fingers, accompanied with the uſual ſenſation; and frequent and ſtrong ſparks likewiſe proceeded from a metal button in M. Jallabert's hat. In this beatified ſituation they continued during the whole time of the ſtorm, which laſted about a quarter of an hour.

ANATOMY.

MEMOIR I. *On the real Sex of thoſe called Hermaphrodites.* By M. Ferrein.

In giving a particular account of this memoir, we ſhould find ourſelves under a neceſſity of entering into details, fit only to be peruſed in a treatiſe of anatomy, or diſcuſſed in a court of juſtice. The ſubject, indeed, is of ſuch a nature, and is repreſented in ſo very naked a manner in this memoir, that we cannot handle the nudity without wounding the delicacy of a part of our Readers. In compliment however to the reſt, be it

* See Monthly Review, vol. xxxvii. Auguſt 1767, page 103.

sufficient to observe, that M. N. the subject of this memoir, a young noble*man*, as he is here every where called, and whose right to a very considerable inheritance depends on the determination of his sex, appears, like most of the hermaphrodites upon record, to be a female. From M. Ferrein's account he seems, like them, to owe his reputed rank in the male class, chiefly to the *luxuriance*, and partly to the parsimony of Dame Nature, employed in the extension of some parts, and the obliteration of others, by which the two sexes are distinguished. Those who would enter more deeply into this matter, may have their curiosity in some measure gratified by turning to our account of M. Arnaud's memoir on hermaphrodites, in his *Melanges de Chirurgie* †, where some anecdotes are given of one or two of the most celebrated of these anomalous personages.

CHEMISTRY.

MEMOIR I. *Observations on the Nature of the Salts extracted from the Ashes of Vegetables.* By M. Du Hamel.

MEMOIR II. *Analysis of the Salts procured from the Marine Plant called Varech, or Sea Wreck.* By M. Cadet.

In the course of M. Du Hamel's experiments, mentioned in a preceding article, it appeared that plants, brought up in the purest water, furnished the same chemical principles with others of the same kind that grew in the richest soils. From hence it should seem to follow, that the chemical principles of vegetables arise principally from the internal œconomy, or organical structure of their parts; by which they assimulate the nourishment they receive, however simple or various, into their own specific nature. On the other hand it is evident, that fruits and greens often contract a particular taste or flavour from the soil, and that they receive from thence certain principles which, notwithstanding the interior organisation of the plant, retain their respective natures unaltered. The experiments related in the first of these memoirs were made partly with a view to throw some light on this subject, but principally to discover whether the *kali* or glasswort, in particular, from which pot-ashes are procured, which are of such extensive use in many of the arts, might not be cultivated with advantage at a distance from the sea; or whether, if produced in that situation, its principles or chemical produce would be altered. To render what follows intelligible, we should add, that there are two kinds of fixed alcaline salts, the first of which is contained in the ashes of vegetables in general, and which does not chrystalize, but deliquiates in the air: the other, which is the object of these experiments, commonly called the fossil alcali, and which is the basis of sea-salt, chrystallises, and does not deliquiate in the air. It

† See Monthly Review, vol. xlii. January 1770, page 17.

is

is procured from the ashes of kali and other plants which grow near or in the sea, and is brought from Alicant and the Levant, under the name of pot-ashes.

M. Fontana, director of the manufactories of Poictou, having procured some of the seeds of the kali, in order to sow a considerable quantity of it on the borders of certain salt marshes in that province, M. Du Hamel at the same time sowed a parcel of the same seed at Denainvilliers, at a considerable distance from the sea, and in soils of various qualities. M. Fontana's crop furnished pot-ashes consisting of the true fossil alcali, without the least admixture of the common alcali, and of as good a quality as those imported from Alicant. The salt which M. Du Hamel obtained from his plants raised from the same seed, indicated how much this vegetable was affected by situation, and the nature of the pabulum: for a considerable part of it deliquiated in the air, and was in every other respect of the same nature with the common alcali. The plant had, nevertheless, still retained its disposition to furnish the fossil alcali: for on dissolving that part of the salt which did not deliquiate in cold water, he procured from the lixivium, after due evaporation, some large chrystals of the true fossil alcali. Although the experiments were conducted with sufficient accuracy, the singularity of the fact induced M. Du Hamel to repeat them the following year. He accordingly sowed some of the seed of this year's crop, and found the result the same as before: except that the produce of the common or vegetable alcali appeared to be somewhat increased; apparently in consequence of the longer continuance of the plant in an inland country.

Some interesting observations are given in the second of these memoirs on the analysis of the sea wreck, and particularly on the salt extracted from its ashes, with which the pot-ashes of Alicant are frequently adulterated. His experiments prove, that this plant furnishes, in fact, only a small quantity of fossil alcali, mixed with a very considerable portion of sea salt not decompounded. He therefore recommends the cultivation of the kali in proper situations, as a national concern; observing that, according to M. Fontana's observation, the pot-ashes imported from Spain and the Levant, for the use of the manufacturers in glass, soap, &c. cost France two millions of livres annually.

MEMOIR III. *On the Effects of a violent Fire on several Earths, Stones, and metallic Calces.* By M. Macquer.

We shall not enter into any particular detail of the numerous experiments related in this memoir; which were made in a new kind of wind-furnace, constructed for this particular purpose, and well adapted to experiments of this nature. We shall only observe that, by the intense heat produced by it, a variety of apyrous earths and stones or other substances, hitherto

hitherto deemed absolutely refractory, were brought into fusion; and that there is room to expect that, from the mixtures of different substances, several new combinations, of use in the different arts, may be the result of the further prosecution of these trials.

MEMOIR IV. *A chemical Analysis of the mineral Water at the Abbey des Fontenelles, &c.* By M. Cadet.

Passing over the analysis of the water, we shall only notice one singular observation contained in it, in which the Author contraverts the generally received opinion concerning the nature of the selenite, which is found in all waters, and which is generally supposed to be solely compounded of the *vitriolic* acid combined with a *calcareous* earth. He does not deny that some kinds of this terrene salt may be thus compounded; but he takes pains to prove that other kinds of this concrete owe their formation to the other two acids united with sands, or *vitrifiable* earths. He proves, at least, that such a combination is possible; having rendered even *glass itself* soluble in water. He effected this singular dissolution, by previously reducing it, by means of a strong and long continued trituration, to an impalpable powder; so that, on being moistened with a little water, the mass felt between the fingers like a fine paste or soft clay. In this state it was acted upon by all the three mineral acids indifferently; and the compound resulting from their commenstruation, being diluted with water, and then decompounded, furnished selenites, with fine or silky spicula, in every respect resembling each other.

MEMOIR V. *Chemical Experiments on the Human Bile, and that of Animals.* By M. Cadet.

The set of experiments related in this memoir was undertaken with a view to ascertain the constituent principles of this fluid, which is of such great importance in the animal œconomy; and thereby to throw some additional light on its properties, and on the different alterations which it undergoes and produces in the human body.

After a summary recital of the experiments of preceding enquirers, and particularly those of the ingenious Dr. Macbride, in his *Experimental Essays*, the Author relates his own; from whence he deduces that the volatile alcali observed in the bile is only the produce of a spontaneous putrid fermentation, and that it probably did not exist in the living animal. He establishes however the existence of the fossil alcali in this fluid, or the basis of sea salt detached from its acid, in consequence of a decomposition effected within the body. For on adding the marine acid to a portion of fresh bile, chrystals of sea salt were produced; and, on the addition of the nitrous acid, he procured quadrangular nitre; and Glauber's salt, on the addition

tion of the vitriolic acid. This alcali, intimately united with an animal oil, another of its conſtituent principles, forms a natural liquid ſoap. We ſhall only add, that from an admixture of theſe acids with the bile, true ſelenites were produced; which detect the preſence of a calcareous or other earth in this fluid, to which, as a baſis, biliary concretions or gall ſtones probably owe their formation. M. Cadet draws a practical inference from this obſervation, and gives ſome cautions againſt the too liberal uſe of abſorbent earths; after having recited a caſe which, he thinks, furniſhes an inſtance of their having actually produced theſe morbid concretions.

BOTANY.

MEMOIR. *On a particular Motion in a Plant called* Tremella. By M. Adanſon.

The obſervations of modern naturaliſts have brought us acquainted with many individuals, that ſeem to bear an equal relation to the animal and vegetable kingdoms; or which are of ſo anomalous a kind, as to excite doubts to which of them they belong. M. Adanſon, however, conſiders the ſubject of this article as belonging undoubtedly to the ſecond; though if there be a body which really participates both of the animal and vegetable nature at the ſame time, and forms the link which joins the two claſſes, he thinks that it is undoubtedly the *Tremella*. The motions of the ſenſitive and other plants of the ſame kind, he obſerves, are not properly ſpontaneous and intrinſical, or independent of external cauſes, at leaſt ſenſible ones; as he intimates thoſe of the *Tremella* to be, which he qualifies with the epithet of *nearly animal*: and yet afterwards, by the term Spontaneous, he obſerves, that he does not mean to deſign a voluntary motion; for he apprehends, that there is a material difference between the voluntary motions of animals, and thoſe of the plant in queſtion. There is indeed an obſcurity, and a ſeeming contradiction, in ſome of his reaſonings, and in his deſcription of the particular motions of this plant; which are not at all cleared up to us, even by the engravings that accompany this memoir. We ſhall attempt, however, to give a ſhort deſcription of this curious ſubject, and of its ſingular properties, together with a general account of his obſervations upon it.

This vegetable production is that ſpecies of the *Tremella* which is denominated by Dillenius *Conſerva gelatinoſa omnium tenerrima & minima, aquarum limo innaſcens*. It is ſeen only in the ſpring and autumn, when the temperature of the air is between 45 and 55 degrees of Fahrenheit's thermometer, generally at the bottom of water in ditches and cart-ruts, after long rains, in the form of a tender ſlimy cruſt of a deep green colour. It is generally found in pieces extending from two inches to a foot

foot in diameter, and from a quarter of a line to a line in thickness, comprehending the slime which adheres to it. On examining it with a moderate magnifier, it is observed to be entirely composed of short cylindrical fibres, obtuse at each end, and crossed or interwoven with each other in all manner of directions, like the threads of felt. These filaments, which are about thirteen times smaller in diameter than a fine hair, do not exceed three lines in length, and are constantly strait and pretty rigid. Observed with a lens, which magnifies the diameters of objects 400 times, each fibre is seen to consist of articulations, separated by diaphragms or membranes; each joint being equal in length to the diameter of the fibre.

In the subsequent observations, relating to the motion of this plant, we shall, for the reasons already hinted, follow M. Adanson as closely as is consistent with brevity. He says that, 'notwithstanding the apparent rigidity of these fibres, they have a spontaneous lateral motion, by which they approach and separate from each other;—that this motion, which is not very sensible, except towards the edge of this vegetable tissue, is not observable in all the filaments at the same time, nor in the same direction.—Some appear to shorten themselves, (*se raccourcir*,) that is, to go backwards without any sensible contraction, and to interweave themselves with each other, to render the texture of the piece more compact; but the greater number appear to move forwards.' Notwithstanding the different movements which these threads exhibit, he adds, that their various motions compensate each other; so that the fibres (we suppose he means the intire piece) do not upon the whole sensibly change place.

Beside these lateral, progressive, and retrograde motions, which all appear to be spontaneous, they have likewise, he adds, *un mouvement d' accroissement*, or a motion produced by their growth, and by which they are lengthened *near 3 lines* in the space of a night. These observations were made on filaments kept apart in glasses, and the growth of which was always visibly promoted, to a certain extent, by the increased warmth of the air; though, on the other hand, they perished in a heat exceeding 80 degrees. In these glasses he observed their manner of propagation, which is effected by a spontaneous separation into two unequal parts *. The smaller parts soon grow to their proper size, and the filaments thus multiplied approach, and proceed to cross and interlace themselves with each other;

* This mode of propagation reminds us of the similar process performed by some of the animalcular tribe, (particularly the *Volvex* of Linnæus,) as observed by M. de Saussure of Geneva, and of which our readers will find a description in our 44th volume, March 1771, page 210.

still

ſtill perſevering in theſe motions, even after they are thus interwoven, and have manufactured themſelves, if we may be allowed the expreſſion, into this ſingular ſpecies of vegetable felt.

Twice in the year, this ſeemingly animated *vegetable aſſociation* periſhes, at leaſt to all appearance, in conſequence of the heats of ſummer and the froſts of winter. They, however, reappear likewiſe twice a-year, and generally in the ſame places. On this occaſion M. Adanſon aſks, Whether their re-appearance is owing to a *new ſpontaneous creation?* meaning only however by this phraſe, whether their reproduction be owing merely to the genial and temperate moiſture of the earth, and independently of any pre-exiſtent germs, or of ſeeds or other parts analogous to them. The ſtate of his health and of his eyes preventing him from proſecuting the delicate and deciſive experiments neceſſary to the determination of this problem, Mr. Needham has undertaken to communicate M. Adanſon's ideas on this ſubject to that celebrated naturaliſt and microſcopical obſerver, M. Spalanzani; from whom the public may expect ſome further lights concerning this very ſingular production.

[*To be concluded in a following number.*]

ART. II.

Hiſtoire de l'Academie Royale des Sciences, &c. The Hiſtory of the Royal Academy of Sciences and *Belles Lettres* at Berlin, for the year 1767. Vol. XXIII. 4to. Berlin, 1769.

EXPERIMENTAL PHILOSOPHY.

MEMOIR I. *A Relation of the artificial Fœcundation of a female Palm-Tree, performed at the Botanical Garden of the Royal Academy.* By M. Gleditſch.

IT appears from this memoir that the neceſſity of a natural or artificial application of the *farina fœcundans* of the male palm-tree to the flowers of the female, to enable it to produce dates, its proper fruit, and ſeed, has lately been very warmly conteſted by ſome German naturaliſts; notwithſtanding the high antiquity of this opinion, and the well authenticated accounts of the univerſal practice of the inhabitants of the Eaſt, on this ſubject. Experiments nearly of the ſame kind with thoſe here related had likewiſe been twice before tried with ſucceſs upon the ſame tree, which is now old, and is of that ſpecies denominated *Chamærops* by Linnæus. It differs from other trees of the family of the palms in being an *imperfect female hermaphrodite*; poſſeſſing the female organs of generation in a perfect ſtate, while the male parts want the eſſential matter requiſite to impregnate them, and which muſt therefore be furniſhed by the male palm-tree, evidently deſtined by nature for this purpoſe.

The

The tree which was the subject of these and the former experiments, had continued many years in the Royal Botanic Garden, in a state of constant sterility. In the years 1749 and 1750 the Author successively impregnated its female flowers with some dust procured from the flowers of a male palm-tree growing at Leipsic, which was sent to him by the post. In consequence of these operations, it produced in both these years perfect dates, which arrived at maturity; some of which were sown, and the young palm-trees which sprung from them are now growing in the botanic garden. After this, no male dust having been procured, the tree returned to its former barren state, in which it continued 18 years. In May 1767 the Author procured some fresh farina, which was sent to him from Carlsruhe, at the distance of 80 German miles, in a letter; together with some that had been collected the year before. At the proper time he applied the dust, and particularly the fresh *farina*, to three particular clusters of the female flowers, with a small hair pencil. The effect of this application very soon became sensible, by the changes observed in all the flowers thus treated, except those which had received the old *farina*. At the end of seven months, the former bore perfect and ripe dates, undoubtedly capable of producing plants of the same kind with that from which they proceeded, as appeared from the two former experiments; while the remaining flowers, to which the dust had not been applied, produced, as usual, little imperfect fruits, which scarce arrived to the size of chick-pease.—We shall only add, that this process bears a very manifest analogy with the singular operation described in a former volume of these memoirs, as performed by M. Jacobi, in the *fructification* of salmon, by means of the *liquor seminalis* of the male fish brought from a distance; the detail of which may be seen in the *Appendix* to our 40th volume, page 560. &c.

MEMOIR II. *On the Figure of the Ocean.* By M. Lambert.

The Author endeavours to shew in what manner the Alps, the Cordeliers, the other large chains of mountains on our globe, nay the whole habitable earth itself, may have been raised up from the sea (which he supposes to have formerly covered it) by means of explosions produced by deeply-seated and extensive subterraneous conflagrations. He considers the direction of the various currents of water, that must have been formed by these operations; by which were determined the courses of rivers, and the figure of the ocean. This last he considers in the light of an immense river, flowing in the wide extended valleys formed by, and remaining after, these great convulsions. He explains and corroborates these gigantic ideas by a map of the world, in which the branches of this great river, the ocean, are displayed and pointed out. He gives us some

ſome comfort by aſſuring us, that the ſyſtem of our globe is now at laſt happily arrived at a ſtate of permanence, and that no ſuch extenſive concuſſions are hereafter to be apprehended; as ſo many vulcano's or *ſpiracula* are now open in various parts of the globe, which give a free vent to the ſubterraneous fires. Theſe, however, ſtill manifeſt their exiſtence, and exert their activity in other parts of the world, though on a ſmaller ſcale, by throwing up from the bottom of the ſea a new iſland occaſionally, or, in a laſt feeble effort, producing an earthquake.

MEMOIR III. *On the Cauſe of the Colours obſerved in the Shadows of Bodies.* By M. Beguelin.

M. Buffon, the Author obſerves, was the firſt who noticed, or at leaſt publiſhed any account of theſe colours, which may be ſeen ſoon after the riſing, and a little time before the ſetting of the ſun*. At theſe times, the ſhadows of bodies received on a white plane, are ſometimes obſerved to be green, but more generally blue, and frequently of the brighteſt azure colour. M. Buffon did not undertake to explain the cauſe of theſe appearances, though he propoſed to conſider them in a future memoir, which, however, never appeared; nor have the Abbé Mazeas, or others who have ſince attempted the ſolution of this optical queſtion, ſucceeded. M. Beguelin's explication is in ſubſtance as follows:

The ſhadowed part of a white wall, or piece of paper, expoſed to the ſun's rays, he obſerves, receives light at the ſame time from every other part of the atmoſphere. But in a clear ſky this light is always blue. This part of the paper, therefore, from which only the ſun's light is intercepted, reflects to the eye the blue colour which it receives from every other part of the ſky. It will be objected, that when the ſun is more elevated above the horizon, as at noon for inſtance, the ſhadow is dark and not at all coloured, though the blueneſs of the ſky continues the ſame. To this he anſwers, that the ſhadowed part undoubtedly reflects the blue light which it receives from a clear ſky, during every part of the day; but that it is not ſtrong enough to produce any particular ſenſation, when the ſun is conſiderably elevated, on account of the ſplendor of his beams; and that this blue reflected light can only be perceived in the evenings and mornings, when that ſplendor is conſiderably diminiſhed. M.

* See *Memoires de l' Acad. Roy. de Sciences de Paris, Année* 1743, p. 203. edit. in 12mo.—M. Buffon, however, was not the firſt who obſerved or wrote concerning theſe colours. The celebrated Leonard da Vinci, who lived above 250 years ago, deſcribes them very accurately in his *Traité de la Peinture*, chap. 328. and in a conciſe manner aſſigns the very ſame cauſe for their production with that here given by the Author.

Buffon, however, twice obſerved theſe ſhadows to be green, as we have often done :--an appearance not ſatisfactorily accounted for by this hypotheſis ; as the ſky is ſeldom or never of that colour. M. Beguelin ſuppoſes this appearance to have been owing to ſome local cauſe ; poſſibly to ſome yellowneſs, in the wall which received the ſhadow, mixed with the blue light of the ſky, or to ſome accidental reflection from the graſs or other neighbouring bodies.

Some of M. Beguelin's experiments ſeem to prove ſufficiently that the blue colour of theſe ſhadows, in a great meaſure, proceeds from the cauſe which he aſſigns, though not univerſally ; for we have obſerved them at a time when the atmoſphere was covered with whitiſh clouds, and conſequently when there was no blue ſky to produce them. He neglects likewiſe to conſider a very material circumſtance ;—the evident differences in the colour of the ſun's light, at the different times when this phenomenon is, and is not, perceived ; which is uſually yellow or reddiſh in the evening and morning, and white in other parts of the day. There is accordingly another cauſe which, in our opinion, ſometimes wholly produces, and at other times greatly contributes to the appearance. The influence of this cauſe may be ſtrongly preſumed from ſome experiments related by M. Buffon in the memoir above referred to ; in which, however, he does not undertake to ſolve the appearances, nor applies them to this particular caſe. As they are curious in themſelves, and, we think, applicable to the preſent queſtion, we ſhall briefly relate one or two of them, and offer an explanation of them ; which, though neceſſarily ſhort, will be readily underſtood by thoſe converſant in inquiries of this nature.

After looking attentively and ſteadily for two or three minutes, or longer, if poſſible, at a ſmall ſquare piece of paper or cloth, of a bright *orange* or *yellow* colour, placed in the middle of a ſheet of white paper, a border of a bright *blue* colour will begin to appear on one or more of its ſides, eſpecially on giving the eye any motion, which is indeed unavoidable ; and it will conſtantly appear on that ſide to which the eye happens to ſtray. On turning the eye to the blank part of the ſheet, a ſquare of the very ſame ſize will be perceived ; but of a *blue* colour. After long viewing a *red* ſquare in the ſame manner, a border of a pale *green* will appear on the ſides of the figure ; and a *green* ſquare of the ſame ſize will be ſeen, on directing the eye to another part of the paper. With regard to the cauſe of theſe *imaginary* colours, it may, we think, be eaſily conceived, that the nerves of that part of the retina, on which the image of the yellow or red paper has been ſo long received, are blunted, and at laſt almoſt rendered inſenſible to the impreſſions of the rays of thoſe colours. This indeed is rendered evident to to the aching ſenſe, by the gradual dilution and faintneſs of the colour of the cloth, towards the end of the experiment. Theſe nerves nevertheleſs continue perfectly ſenſible, and as it were alive, to the very different impreſſions of all the other rays, contained in the white compounded light reflected from the paper. Now, of theſe rays, thoſe at a diſtance from red and yellow in the priſmatic ſeries, and particularly the green and blue rays, will moſt diſtinguiſhably affect nerves already jaded with the ſenſations of red and yellow. In other words, the inſenſibility of the retina to red or yellow light, will produce the ſame effect as if the red or yellow rays, contained in the white light reflected from the paper, were intercepted; as happens in one of Newton's well-known experiments, where, after the interception of theſe rays in the coloured *ſpectrum*, the remaining light, collected by a convex lens into a focus, appears green or blue.

It is eaſy to apply theſe obſervations to the preſent ſubject; making allowances for difference of circumſtances, and conſidering the white wall or paper as illuminated by the *reddiſh* or *yellowiſh* light of the riſing and ſetting ſun; and the ſhadow (and conſequently that part of the retina on which its image falls) as ſecluded or guarded from it, but, at the ſame time, receiving and reflecting to the eye the common light of the atmoſphere *. In the firſt of theſe caſes, that is, when the light of the ſun is of a *reddiſh* hue, the ſhadow will appear *green*; and in the latter, *blue*. On the whole, M. Beguelin's obſervations united with theſe, ſeem fully to account for every circumſtance attending the *phenomena*. From the cauſe which he propoſes, the blue ſhadows would be painted on the retina of an eye taken out of the head of an animal; as being produced by *real* blue rays reflected from the atmoſphere. From the cauſe which we aſſign, conſidered alone, no ſuch coloured ſhadow would exiſt, either in the living or the dead organ. In the former, however, the colour will be *perceived*, though not painted on the retina; and accordingly the ſenſation of blue, though, in this inſtance as well as in the former, actually produced by blue rays, may be called *imaginary*, or *accidental*; (ſo M. Buffon terms theſe colours;) as depending *ſolely* on a peculiar modification, or the ſenſibility of the organs in a living ſubject. Both, however, we preſume, at different times, either

* We ſhall mention, however, in a few words, the following eaſy experiment, the circumſtances of which correſpond more nearly with thoſe of the ſubject in queſtion. If a piece of paper be viewed, which is painted all over of a bright blue or yellow colour, except a narrow ſtripe, which is left white, and repreſents the ſhadow; this uncoloured ſlip will appear of a greeniſh or bluiſh hue, according as the paper was painted either red or yellow.

fingly or together, according to different circumftances, produce the appearances.

MEMOIR IV. *On the Art of Dying, as practifed both by the Antients and Moderns.* By M. de Francheville.

The firft part of this memoir contains the hiftory of this art, and the latter, many details relative to the practice of it; particularly a defcription of the different drugs and other fubftances which conftitute the *materia tinctoria*, digefted in an alphabetical order. We need fay nothing farther concerning this differtation, than that among thefe drugs we obferve a plant here named *Dividivi*, which was brought from the Caraccas into Spain for the firft time in 1769, and which, in confequence of experiments that have been made upon it at Madrid, is found to be preferable to galls in dying black. The royal council of commerce have taken meafures to encourage the importation of it; his Catholic majefty has given directions for a new fet of experiments on this fubject, and has ordered the refult of them to be printed.

MATHEMATICS.

MEMOIR I. *On a Method of carrying the Object Glaffes of Telefcopes to a higher Degree of Perfection.* By M. L. Euler.

It is well known that images formed by rays differing in refrangibility, and paffing through one or more glaffes, made only of one kind of refracting matter, cannot poffibly be united in the fame focus. In our Review of a *Summary of a general Theory of Dioptrics* *, written by the Author, and publifhed in the Memoirs of the Royal Academy of Sciences at Paris for the year 1765, we gave a general account of the method which he there propofed of conftructing a compound object-glafs of one fpecies only of refracting matter, by which the images formed by the differently coloured rays, though not united in the fame plane, might be thrown into fuch a fituation, as to be all feen under the fame angle, fo as not to produce any colours, or fenfible confufion whatever, to an eye viewing them at a proper diftance, or in the point of concourfe of two lines drawn by the extremities of the different images. For a fhort account of the principles on which this ingenious propofal is founded, we refer the reader to the article quoted below.

In this memoir he profecutes this idea, and fhews the practicability of executing it. He referves for another memoir the particular confideration of the method of entirely deftroying the colorific aberration, where only one fpecies of glafs is employed in the conftruction. In the prefent paper he confiders only the proper method of correcting the aberration arifing from

* See Appendix to our 42d volume, page 506.

the

the aperture or figure; which it is absolutely nec ssary to effect completely, before the precise arrangement of the coloured images above-mentioned, so necessary to the destruction of the colours, can possibly take place: affirming, that all the advantages, which Mr. Dollond has derived from the use of glasses of different refracting powers, may be thus obtained with one species of glass; and declaring, that the mere difference in the refractive powers of glasses is too small to produce these advantages.

M. Euler, however, does not dissemble one apparent disadvantage, arising from the position of his differently coloured images, which are projected in planes situated at different distances from the eye. From hence it may follow, that if the image formed by the mean rays is at the proper distance for distinct vision, that produced by the red rays will be too near, and that produced by the violet rays, too distant, for this purpose. He owns that some degree of indistinctness or confusion may arise from hence; but observes, in the first place, that it is of a very different nature from that hitherto complained of. He affirms, in the next place, that it will be very small, and of little consequence, unless a very great magnifying power is wanted; as the human eye is accustomed to see objects, placed even at very different distances, with a sufficient degree of distinctness. It were to be wished, nevertheless, that even this slight confusion could be removed: but he owns that this can only be effected by employing glasses of different refractive powers. This remedy, however, would give rise to other inconveniencies. The object-glasses for this purpose would not bear an aperture large enough for clear vision, and their focal lengths must be considerable. On the whole, if a very great magnifying power is required, he recommends the construction of a hollow object-glass filled with water, according to the rules and measures formerly determined by his son; in which both the species of aberration might be entirely annihilated.

The three remaining memoirs contained in this class are not susceptible of abridgment. In the two first of them, M. de la Grange treats of the resolution of numerical equations; and, in the last, M. Lambert attempts a general and absolute solution of the celebrated problem of three bodies, by the means of infinite series.

Speculative Philosophy.

MEMOIR I. *Considerations on the principal End proposed in the Formation of Academies, and on the Advantages to be derived from these Establishments.* By M. Formey.

To these institutions the Author principally attributes that astonishing progress which has been made in philosophical and useful knowledge, during the last hundred years: observing that, within that period, the ſtock of real knowledge has received a much greater increaſe, than in the forty centuries which preceded it. The Royal Society, he obſerves, was the firſt that undertook, and that has moſt ſucceſsfully proſecuted the true and proper deſign of theſe eſtabliſhments. He is not equally juſt and accurate in attributing to Deſcartes the great and intereſting revolution produced in philoſophical inquiries, in modern times. He conſiders him as the founder of philoſophy, and as having taught us to think and reaſon for ourſelves. We are ſurpriſed that the Author, ſo well informed in the hiſtory of philoſophy as he is known to be, ſhould, on this occaſion, overlook one, who was not indeed the founder of any particular ſyſtem, nor does his name ſtand at the head of any particular ſect of philoſophers; but who was undoubtedly the father of true philoſophy. We ſcarce need to name the Lord Chancellor Bacon, to whoſe profound and extenſive views and excellent precepts, the laſt and preſent age are wholly indebted for the true and only ſucceſsful method of proceeding in philoſophical inquiries.

In the following paper, M. Beguelin applies Leibnitz's celebrated metaphyſical principle of a *ſufficient reaſon*, to the clearing up ſome doubts; and the reſolving certain queſtions, which have been much litigated by mathematicians, relative to the doctrine of Chances; and in the third and laſt memoir of this claſs, M. Sulzer endeavours to throw ſome light on the origin of language, and treats of the reciprocal influence which the faculties of ſpeech and reaſon have on each other: ſhewing, that in proportion as language is ſucceſſively improved by the reaſoning faculty, the latter, in its turn, is ſtrengthened, and the various operations of the mind are facilitated and extended, by the ſucceſſive improvements made in language.

Belles Lettres.

Memoir I. *On the true Nature and Character of the Beautiful in general.* By M. de Catt.

The Author of this diſſertation takes more pains than are neceſſary, to ſhew that our ideas of the Beautiful are in general excited in us by objects, in conſequence of their being poſſeſſed of an aptitude to give us pleaſure, without reference to utility. He does not, however, enter deep into the ſubject, and in particular neglects to obſerve in how great a number of caſes our ſenſe of beauty derives its exiſtence, either wholly or in part, from real or ſuppoſed utility; though, in other inſtances, it appears to be totally independent of it.

We ſhall only give the titles of the remaining articles of this volume. Theſe are, A Diſcourſe on Senſibility, by M. Touſſaint; a Diſſertation on the Influence of the Belles Lettres on the Progreſs of Philoſophy, by M. Bitaubé; and the Eloge

Eloge of M. Sussmilch. In a kind of appendix, which terminates the volume, an account is given of the transit of Venus in 1769, as observed by M. J. Bernoulli, at Colombes near Paris.

Art. III.

Observations Physiques, &c. Physical and moral Observations on the Instinct of Animals, on their Industry, and Manners. By Hermann Samuel Reimar, Professor of Philosophy at Hamburgh, and Member of the Imperial Academy of Sciences at Petersburgh. Translated from the German, by M. R** de L***. 12mo. 2 Vols. Amsterdam and Paris *.

THE Author of this performance died about three years ago, at Hamburgh, with the character of a profound metaphysician, an excellent naturalist, and a judicious divine. He had been many years employed in selecting, with a view to publication, from the writings of the most celebrated naturalists, the best authenticated and most interesting observations relative to the different instincts of particular animals, together with circumstantial descriptions of their various operations and respective modes of living. The abundance of the materials which he had collected with this view, would, he observes, have rendered the execution of this scheme very easy. He chose, however, to publish first these general observations on animal instinct, and to reserve the particular details for a subsequent publication. Though the completion of his entire plan has been defeated by his death, his translator expresses his hopes that the curious collections made by so judicious a naturalist as M. Reimar, will not be lost to the world.

In our review of the present work, the principal fault of which is, that it is in general written in too diffuse and systematic a manner, we shall endeavour to extract the substance of the more essential and interesting parts of it, divested, as much as possible, of the scholastic distinctions and divisions with which it too much abounds. To perform this properly, it will be necessary to premise a short historical account of the various systems which have been proposed by ancient and modern writers, with a view to explain the principles which produce and direct the spontaneous actions of brute animals. In the course of this exposition, as well as in the entire account of this work, instead of transcribing any part of it, we shall, for the reasons above hinted, shut the book, and endeavour to present the Author's meaning in more plain and popular terms; occasionally interspersing such reflections or illustrations as have occurred to us in the perusal of it.

* See Appendix to our 44th volume.

The greater part of the ancient philosophers have ascribed to brutes an understanding, or a degree of reason, of the same nature with, but more or less differing in degree from, that of man. The Sceptics, according to Sextus Empiricus, absolutely placed them on a level with man; and Pythagoras, Plato, and some other philosophers, attribute their inferiority to him, to the want only of proper and sufficient bodily organs. We shall, on this occasion, add, that even a modern writer, M. Helvetius *, has taken some pains to support the credibility of this opinion, by the enumeration of several physical causes to which he ascribes the inferiority of brute animals. These are, the great difference between their organical structure and that of human bodies, and particularly their want of hands, with which men are enabled to execute so many admirable operations; the general shortness of their lives; their not usually living in society; and lastly, the cloathing with which nature has bountifully endowed the greater part of them, and the possession of which renders the exercise of many arts absosolutely unnecessary among them, which are indispensably requisite to man.

Among the moderns, Cudworth endeavoured to explain the instincts of animals, by means of a certain *plastic nature*, an intermediate being existing between God and the universe; by which, under the direction of the Deity, the bodies and souls of men and animals are excited to the production of certain ends, respecting their well-being and preservation; without any knowledge however of the means, or any sentiment, appetite, or volition whatever concurring to the production of the effect.

This strange and mysterious system was followed by that of Descartes, who thought that all the actions of brute animals might be explained by the simple laws of mechanism. This philosopher considered animals as machines totally devoid of life and sentiment; but constructed by the Creator with such exquisite art, and so highly finished, that the mere impressions of light, sound, and other external agents, on their organs, produced a series of motions in them, and caused them to execute those various operations, which before had been ascribed to an internal principle of life and spontaneity. The absurdity of this opinion must appear evident, on the slightest consideration of the actions and manners of animals, which are totally incompatible with the mere principles and laws of mechanism.

The *pre-established harmony* of Leibnitz, a system formed to elucidate the mysterious union between the human soul and body, has been applied to explain the actions of brute animals. Accord-

* De l'Esprit, tom. 1, p. 2.

ing to this hypothesis, the soul and body have no energy or influence whatever on, nor any physical communication with, each other. The volitions of the one, and the motions of the other, are only cotemporary *phenomena*, or simultaneous but independent modifications of the two substances. According to established laws, by which they are both regulated, they exist together, but do not produce each other; any more than two pendulums of equal length, put in motion at the same time, and vibrating exactly in equal times, and in the same direction, are the causes of each other's motions. According to this system, however, brutes are acknowledged to have a soul, and to be possessed of life and sensibility; but a soul that has no influence in producing or directing the motions of the body, which, on its part, is as much a machine as that of Descartes; though, in one respect, seemingly a more perfect one: as it is a piece of machinery that goes alone, and executes, of its own accord, the various movements to which it is destined, and which exactly correspond and harmonize with the pre-established perceptions and volitions of the soul to which it is united. To a body, however, thus constituted, the soul seems to us an unnecessary appendix.—But we need not dwell any longer on an hypothesis which destroys all physical influence and causation; which leaves every motion of body, and every modification of mind, both in men and brutes, perfectly insulated, and unconnected with each other; and, at one stroke, breaks all the links that unite the physical, moral, and intellectual world together.

According to Malebranche's system, we see all things in God, who is the immediate Author of every motion. This hypothesis seems to have been applied to the present subject by some, who consider the actions of animals as produced by the constant and immediate influence of the divine energy, directing all their inclinations and motions. But this method of treating the question is as unphilosophical, as it would be to say that the soul of the artist resides in the watch that he has made, and actuates its motions. It is mounting up at once to the first cause, without acknowledging, or making any inquiry into the nature of, those intermediate and subordinate causes, which the Creator has undoubtedly placed between himself and his creatures; the existence, nature, and design of which, it is the proper business of philosophy to discover and investigate. Such, however, appears to have been the opinion of Mr. Addison, as may be seen on consulting the second volume of the Spectator.

M. Buffon considers brutes, with Descartes, as merely corporeal machines, without a soul, without notions or imagination, or any faculty that bears even a distant analogy to thinking, or understanding; and consequently without prudence, art, or invention. He differs from that philosopher, however, in granting them life, and the faculty of perceiving and distinguishing between pleasure and pain; together with a strong inclination to the former, and aversion to the latter. By these inclinations and aversions he undertakes to account for all, even the most striking operations of animals; affirming that, in consequence of impressions made on the brain, by means of the sensitive organs, and by the re-action of the brain and nerves on the muscles, these machines acquire a motion conformable to the nature of the animal, and of the impressions of the different objects which act upon their organs, and excite desire or aversion. M. Buffon makes a considerable stride, however, in attributing to the mere *desire* of pleasure, or aversion to pain, the *power* of employing the proper means, nay the best of all possible means, tending to their well being and preservation.

We shall only cursorily mention the opinions of another set of philosophers, who endeavour to explain the actions of brute animals, by mere corporeal feeling, without any assistance of the mind. Among these, Mylius is of opinion, that pain alone produces many of those actions which we attribute to design. He supposes that the caterpillar, for instance, at the time of its metamorphosis, labours under a fit of the cholic, produced by the superabundance of that glutinous liquor, which afterwards forms its *envelope* or case, and which it twists round its body, drawing it into threads in a variety of directions, in consequence of the repeated contorsions caused by the pain it suffers during the time of its exudation. We shall likewise only briefly notice a system proposed by some young philosophers at Leipsic, who published their inquiries in 1745, under the direction of Professor Winckler. These gentlemen suppose brutes to be possessed of an immaterial soul, which has its seat in the brain: and with regard to the curious works of many animals, such as bees, beavers, spiders, &c. in particular, they suppose that, in the brains of these animals, at their first birth, there are proper images, and even geometrical figures, impressed; and that by means of these models, and by their action or impression upon the soul, the latter is both enabled and excited to execute, by means of the proper bodily organs, certain figures analogous to them. The possibility of this they endeavour to prove, or at least to illustrate, by a very notable and singular experiment. If a person, they observe, hold his ear at one extremity of a beam of wood or a bar of iron, while another person strikes the opposite end with a body of a triangular figure, in such a manner that all the three angles, or the whole plane, that is, the flat part of the figure, may strike it at the same time; the ear of the observer will not only convey to to the mind the idea of a triangle, but likewiſe the particular ſpecies of the figure. M. Reimar, on this occaſion, very modeſtly confeſſes the ſtate of his organs, or of his mental faculties, to be ſuch, as to be by no means qualified or adapted to the *hearing of triangles*; and much leſs to the perceiving by the ear, whether they are equilateral or rectangular.

To ſhorten our enumeration of the various ſyſtems that have been offered relative to this ſubject, we ſhall proceed to thoſe in which brute animals are ſuppoſed to be endowed with a certain portion of reaſon and intelligence, directing them in their various operations. When we obſerve many of their actions to be conformable to the moſt exact rules of reaſon, and to be ſuch as we ſhould have executed in the like ſituations, it is undoubtedly very natural to conclude that they are the reſult of the ſame principle by which we conduct ourſelves. Of the many ſupporters of this opinion, M. Condillac may be juſtly conſidered as having given it the higheſt embelliſhments in his *Traité des Animaux*; where he ſuppoſes that brutes poſſeſs, in common with us, though in an inferior degree, the faculty of reaſon; and that the art and addreſs which they manifeſt in many of their operations, is acquired by reflection, and by comparing objects with each other; that they improve their knowledge, in the ſame manner as we do, by exerciſe and experience; and that accordingly they poſſeſs the faculty of invention. Mr. Reimar's objections to this hypotheſis, collected into one point of view, are in ſubſtance as follow:

No art can be invented, or operation executed, which is the reſult of thought or reflection, without experience, either our own or that of others, as a baſis or groundwork. But the operations which brute animals perform, ſo manifeſtly and neceſſarily conducive to their well-being, their preſervation, and that of their ſpecies and progeny, are executed by them previouſly to all experience whatever. The ſpider forms its web, and the lion-piſmire digs its little pit, before the former has yet taſted a fly, or the latter, an ant; and even before they know, or can have been informed, that ſuch inſects exiſt. The caterpillar, at the proper ſeaſon, weaves the caſe for its approaching metamorphoſis into an aurelia, without having had any experience of its own, or having received any light or inſtruction, either from the example or precepts of other caterpillars or butterflies. Further; ſcarce has the young bee completed its metamorphoſis from the aurelia-ſtate, and expanded and dried its wings, but it ſallies forth alone from the hive, alights upon the proper flowers, extracts from them the proper juice, collects their *farina*, kneads it into a little pellet, and depoſites it in the proper receptacles in its feet, returns back to the hive, and delivers up the honey and the wax which it it has collected and manufactured. But what experience can this novice have acquired in a single day, to direct it in these various occupations? Supposing it even to have had time and leisure to have observed most minutely the various transactions passing in the inside of the hive, how does it acquire its knowledge of the appropriated matter which forms the wax, &c. of the places where it is to be found, of the application of the instruments with which it is to be collected and transported, of the right road to the hive, and of the use to which its cargo is to be applied? Certainly not by reason, or observation founded on instruction and experience.

If reason, or even a very moderate portion of that faculty, were the guide which directed animals in their operations, they could not exhibit such instances of ignorance and stupidity, as many of them betray on several occasions. Monkies approach the nearest to men, not only in shape, but in understanding, and are particularly remarkable for their readiness in imitating human actions. Yet when travellers have left a fire, which they had kindled at night, in the woods of Africa, they have seen the monkeys flocking round it with pleasure, in order to enjoy the warmth; but observed, that they had not the sense to keep up the fire, by throwing into it the half-burnt sticks lying on the sides, but retreated from it as soon as it was extinct †. A hen sits upon a piece of chalk, and turns it with the same care and assiduity that she employs in the case of her eggs; though it differs from them in weight, in colour, in form, and the nature of its surface. She hatches the eggs of a duck and her own with equal assiduity, and attends the young ones with equal care, though so different in their figure, in the tone of their voice, their manners, and particularly their propensity to dive, as soon as they are hatched, into an element so different from her own; at which, however, we should observe in her favour, she expresses some alarm. The proceedings of those birds which hatch the eggs of the cuckow, afford another striking proof how little capable brute animals are of exercising some of the essential attributes of reason; that of comparing objects with each other, distinguishing the differences between them, and drawing proper conclusions from the premises: faculties without which men could not proceed a single step beyond the first intuitive principles implanted in their nature.

We shall add a further observation or two on this part of the subject, which we have indeed already in some measure antici-

† Though the Author's observation is just in general, yet the Reader may see the proceedings of the monkeys, in this particular instance, very well vindicated by M. Rousseau, in his *Inegalites parmi les Hommes*. Note 10, English Translation.

pated.

pated. The arts which are exerciſed among mankind undoubtedly owe their origin and improvement to the uſe and ſucceſſive cultivation of the faculty of reaſon. There was a time when even thoſe, which now appear to us the moſt indiſpenſable, were not known. At that time, however, and at all times, brute animals were endowed with the faculties neceſſary to the performance of all their curious operations, and exerciſed their various arts in the higheſt perfection. A very ſenſible difference is obſervable in the ſtate of human arts, between one nation and another, and between the individuals of the ſame nation; where they vary both in kind and degree of perfection: but in thoſe of animals of the ſame ſpecies, not the leaſt ſhadow of a difference is to be perceived. Their operations and productions are all uniform, equally perfect in all climates and countries, and in all the individuals of the ſame ſpecies. Human arts have been multiplied, and received progreſſive improvements, or have been loſt or fallen into decay, in conſequence of the various exerciſe or neglect of the mental powers in different ages; and, with regard to individuals, are acquired only by inſtruction, and by aſſiduous and repeated application. Thoſe of animals, on the contrary, have never ſuffered any variations; they are neither improved, nor do they decline, but are tranſmitted from one generation to another, as the hereditary gifts of nature, diſpenſed to them in ſo bountiful a manner, as to render all inſtruction and exerciſe unneceſſary.

The bees of the preſent age, for inſtance, conſtruct their combs, and collect their honey, preciſely in the ſame manner as in the days of Virgil; nor have the birds or the beavers of the 18th century ſtruck out the leaſt convenience in the ſtructure of their neſts and cabins, which was not to be found in the works of their forefathers, in the firſt ages of the world. Time neither improves the arts of the whole ſpecies, or matures the talents of the individual. The young bee at once ſprings forth from his cell a maſter-workman. On the ſame day that gives him birth, he appears in the fields a complete artiſt in wax and honey; and on entering the hive he diſplays the talents of a finiſhed architect. Thus different are the operations of reaſon and inſtinct. Human wiſdom we may term the accumulated wiſdom of ages: the knowledge of brutes is only that of the preſent hour. The proceedings of one individual, in this country, and to-day, whether it be the firſt or the laſt of his life, are the proceedings of the whole ſpecies, in all places, and at all times.

Having cleared the way by this ſhort expoſition of the preceding ſyſtems, and, in thoſe inſtances where it was moſt neceſſary, ſhewn their apparent inſufficiency, we ſhall now endeavour to give the reader ſuch an idea of M. Reimar's hypotheſis, as can be conveyed within the limits to which we are confined by the nature of our work, and which we find too ſcanty to admit of a clear explanation of a ſubject ſo very complicated and intricate. Under theſe diſadvantages, a ſhort and imperfect ſketch of his ſyſtem is the utmoſt we can undertake to give.

M. Reimar, conſidering the different ſignifications which have been given to the word, Inſtinct, on account of the various modes in which that faculty diſplays itſelf, acknowledges the difficulty of giving ſuch an exact definition of the term, as ſhall comprehend all the ſpecies. By inſtinct, in the moſt comprehenſive ſenſe of the word, he means every natural inclination, accompanied with a power, in animals, to perform certain actions. Taking the term in this general ſenſe, he divides inſtincts into three kinds. The firſt of theſe he chuſes to call *Mechanical Inſtincts*, which belong to the body, conſidered as an organized ſubſtance, and which are exerciſed blindly and independently of the will of the animal. Such are thoſe which produce the motion of the heart and lungs, the contraction and dilatation of the pupil, digeſtion, &c. which are performed independently of the will, and without any interference or even knowledge of the ſoul. This claſs of inſtincts is poſſeſſed in common both by men and brutes, and in ſome meaſure even by vegetables; in which its effects are obſerved more particularly in the ſenſitive plant, the *Dionæa Muſcipula*, &c. as well as in certain parts ſeparated from the bodies of living animals, which ſtill continue to move, or may be excited to motion, after it has ceaſed, by the activity of proper *ſtimuli*.

The ſecond claſs comprehends thoſe which the Author terms *Repreſentative Inſtincts*; which conſiſt partly in the power of perceiving external objects, by their preſent impreſſion on the ſenſes; and partly in the faculty of rendering the ideas of theſe objects preſent to the mind, by the powers of imagination, or of memory, in a lax ſenſe of the word. Theſe likewiſe are common to men and other animals, except in one particular: for though Mr. Reimar acknowledges that brutes poſſeſs equally with us the faculty of imagination, and that they have a confuſed idea of events that are paſt, which is excited by the view, or other impreſſions, of objects that are preſent; yet he denies that they have any memory, or reminiſcence, in the ſtrict and proper ſenſe of the word; or that by any act of their minds, they can bring paſt events before them, or reflect upon them, as connected with each other, or with the preſent repreſentations. He endeavours, indeed, to prove, throughout the whole of this treatiſe, that the knowledge of brutes does not merely differ in degree from that of man, but that it is of a kind totally different from it; that there is an analogy indeed, but no gradation,

4

dation, between the operations of their minds and ours; and particularly, (which constitutes the first discrimination between the minds of men and animals) that they have no real memory or knowledge of the past, *as being past*. They are acquainted, he says, with *to-day*; but *yesterday* is totally unknown to them. In short, as he denies all kind of reasoning to brute animals, he takes great pains to shew that, in those instances in which their conduct appears to be influenced by a remembrance of preceding events, and to be regulated by a retrospect and comparison of them with present impressions, they confound the past with the present: so that when a horse, for instance, endeavours to turn into the gateway of an inn, or stops at a stable, where some years ago he had found good entertainment; he does not do this from a *recollection* that he had formerly been gratified with good provender at that place; but because the ideas of hay and corn, on the view of the stable, become present to his imagination, and excite a desire of enjoying the good cheer. The present and past representations are confounded together, and, as it were, identified, in his sensory, where they appear equally present.—But to explain the Author's meaning somewhat more particularly.

Though it is not perhaps easy, as Dr. Beattie has lately observed *, to define accurately, or to express in unexceptionable terms, the difference between memory and imagination; yet the most ignorant of the human species feels, and has a clear idea of, the very essential difference between these two faculties; and knows at once, whether a certain representation in his mind is only a fanciful exhibition of the imagination, or is attended with a *conscious retrospect* to a past event. According to the Author's doctrine, brute animals do not really perceive this difference. With them, a past transaction, though the idea of it is in the mind, is not *recollected*. In consequence however of a present impression on some of the external senses, the idea of it is renewed and rendered present to the imagination, associated with its former agreeable or disagreeable concomitants and consequences. From this faculty alone they draw advantages, suited to their peculiar modes of life, similar to those which we derive from the use of memory. But even human memory, we shall observe, is, in many instances, not very different from this substitute which the Author here ascribes to the brute creation. To give one instance, which will at the same time illustrate his general meaning: A man has, in the former part of his life, in consequence of an acci-

* Essay on the Nature and Immutability of Truth. p. 100. 2d Edit. 1771.

dental

dental surfeit, acquired a distaste to a certain dish. This distaste may still subsist, though the occasion which first gave rise to it may be now totally forgotten, and is therefore not founded on a particular reminiscence of the transaction, but is a creature of the] imagination, which revolts at the taste or even sight of the offensive viands. What sometimes happens to man in this and other similar instances, according to the Author's system, constantly happens to brutes. Past transactions have a place in their imagination, but not in their memory; and accordingly they cannot reason concerning them, or draw any consequences from them, as we do, to the great extension of our knowledge. A dog runs away at the sight of an uplifted cane: not because he remembers the uneasy sensations which have formerly attended that appearance; but because the ideas of blows and pain spontaneously arise in his imagination, intimately associated with that phenomenon.

The third, and principal class of animal instincts, is that which comprehends all those that the Author calls *spontaneous*. This species of instinct is not, according to him, attended with any power of reflection, determining the animal to decide freely between two different modes of action present to his imagination; nor is it merely corporeal or mechanical. It is put into action by the natural and primitive principle of self-love, implanted in all animated beings; or by a love of pleasure and aversion to pain, producing a voluntary inclination to perform certain actions which tend to their well-being and preservation. To the performance of these actions they are particularly prompted by their present sensations; by imagination, supplying the place of memory; and by a cause, previous to both, hereafter to be mentioned. The wonderful effects produced by these instinctive appetites are further to be attributed to the exquisite mechanism in their bodily conformation, particularly in the structure of the various organs with which they execute their operations; and to the superior perfection and acuteness of their external senses, by which they are quickly and distinctly informed of those qualities of objects which most materially concern them.

But though a very considerable part of the actions of brute animals may in some measure be satisfactorily accounted for, by the perfection of their bodily structure, their exquisite sensibility, and the natural principle of seeking what is useful and agreeable, and of avoiding what is hurtful and disagreeable to them; there are innumerable circumstances relative to them, which are not explicable from these *data*. To give only an instance or two. The mere possession of certain organs, however elaborately formed, or exquisitely adapted to the particular uses for which they are designed, does not convey any knowledge

ledge of the art of employing them. Were we to suppose a human body to be provided, for a certain time, with one of these organs, such as the trunk of a bee for example, the possessor of it would be as little able to apply it to its proper use, as a man, who had all the materials and tools of an optician put into his hands, would find himself in a condition to make a Dollond's telescope: although, to make the cases as nearly parallel as possible, we were to suppose that nature, in order to stimulate him to perfection, had even given him the most ardent and insatiable longing to view Saturn's ring or the moons of Jupiter. But further, it is evident that in the exercise of many of the operations of brute animals, they are far from appearing to be incited to them by the present or immediate allurements of sensual gratification. In the many laborious occupations preceding and attending the incubation of birds, and the bringing up of their progeny, we may see them suffering hunger and thirst, debarring themselves of rest, in short rejecting all the solicitations of present ease and pleasure, and facing the greatest dangers and even death, in defence, not of themselves, or even of their progeny, which in some degree resemble them, but of their eggs, which differ so much in form from themselves, that mere self-love cannot be supposed to be the motive of their actions. But even granting that they found the greatest pleasure in all these operations, many of which are the productions of the most exquisite art, still it is evident, as we have already observed, that the mere *desire* to execute them does not imply or convey the *ability* of performing them.

For such reasons as these, M. Reimar adds two principles to account for the surprising and curious operations of brute animals. These are, first, an internal distinct perception of the precise power and proper use of their various bodily organs, to which should be added, an *innate* knowledge of the qualities of those objects around them, in which they are interested: and secondly, (which constitutes the principal part of his system,) certain *innate and determinate* powers and inclinations, impressed by the Author of nature, *à priori*, on the soul itself; by which they are arbitrarily, and without their knowledge or consciousness, directed and irresistibly impelled to the performance of those various operations which we see them execute with such unremitting industry and art. These *determinate forces* are nowhere so visible and distinguishable, as in that numerous set of instincts which the Author classes under the title of the *Industrious Instincts* of animals. The number of these is so great, and they are so various according to the peculiar nature and mode of living of each animal, that the bare enumeration of the different classes into which he divides them would occupy,

cupy ſeveral pages. We ſhall content ourſelves with giving two or three detached obſervations, ſelected from the Author's more diffuſive deſcription of the properties of ſeveral of theſe *induſtrious inſtincts*, or *innate arts*; obſerving, only that theſe are, in general, poſſeſſed in the higheſt perfection by the moſt contemptible and ſeemingly helpleſs inſects; which in many of their operations mimick human reaſon, and exhibit greater apparent marks of wiſdom, addreſs, nay, of foreſight, than even the quadrupeds which approach nearer to man in the organization of their bodies, and in the number and perfection of their external ſenſes. Of theſe inſtances we ſhall chuſe ſuch as have a more direct tendency to explain and illuſtrate the Author's hypotheſis of *innate determinate powers*; though we have neceſſarily anticipated ſome of them.

We have already noticed with what readineſs and ſeeming expertneſs the new born bee appears on the great theatre of the world; where, at his firſt ſtarting out of his dark cell, he executes, but in one *determinate* manner, the moſt delicate operations, without any previous obſervation, inſtruction, or experience. In the ſame manner, the maggot or worm of the common or domeſtic moth, on his firſt coming out of the egg, begins, in conſequence of an interior ſentiment and a power accompanying it, to make himſelf at once both a coat and a lodgment, out of the ſtuff on which his mother had been inſtructed by nature to depoſite her eggs, in order that her progeny might have at hand both food and the materials for cloathing. In this firſt eſſay, with great ſeeming judgment, he makes it very wide in the middle, that he may not hereafter be under the neceſſity of forming a new garment as he grows larger. He contracts it however towards the extremities, where he leaves a ſmall aperture at each end, from which he can protrude his head and tail. When it becomes too ſtrait in theſe parts, he quickly remedies this inconvenience by ſlitting it at each end, and manufacturing a piece which is neatly ſet in: nor has he any occaſion during the term of his whole life to renew his dreſs; unleſs perhaps ſome curious or waggiſh Naturaliſt deprives him of it, that he may have the pleaſure of ſeeing him fabricate a new and variegated coat, by placing him ſucceſſively on cloths of different colours: in which caſe the animal loſes no time to repair the loſs, and very ſoon appears in the motley ſtriped garb of a harlequin.

Theſe and innumerable other operations, thus timed and circumſtanced, ſeem to be the pure effects of an innate appetite, joined with an innate power, to perform them; both originally infuſed by nature into the mind of the animal, and exerting themſelves independently of all deſign, reflection, or invention. In like manner the water-ſnail, another of nature's early and completely inſtructed pupils, taken even out of the *matrix* of his

his mother, and being thrown into the water, where it sinks, soon rises to the surface; and for this purpose withdraws the farther part of his body from the interior part of the shell, and thereby makes a vacuum that renders the whole lighter than water. When arrived there, he turns the convex part of his shell undermost, thus converting it into a natural canoe, and uses his feet with the utmost dexterity as oars; returning to the bottom, when he thinks proper, by re-occupying the empty part of the shell, and thereby rendering it specifically heavier than water. We scarce need to multiply observations of this kind, by instancing the cases of those animals whose parents deposite their eggs in the sand on the sea shore. These are no sooner hatched by the heat of the sun, than the young brood, leaving the air which they first breathed, and the place which gave them birth, without instructions and without a guide, but possessed of a certain unerring and innate science, move towards the sea, and undauntedly plunge as it were into another world, and into an element perfectly new to them.

Nature, however, it must be acknowledged, does not put all her pupils out of her hands thus completely finished, and qualified to live in the world. Many come into it feeble and ignorant, and absolutely stand in need of the assiduous care of their parents to nurse and educate them. During this time, many of them evidently receive instructions from them; by which they profit, merely in consequence of a principle of imitation. But this nursing and education are never extended beyond the necessary term; for as soon as all the organs requisite to their preservation and well-being have acquired their proper strength, the mother abandons her progeny, who find themselves, both with regard to their bodily organs and the furniture of their mind, completely qualified to provide for themselves. In most animals some of these *determinate instinctive powers* appear, or are developed, only in certain periods of their lives; as in incubation, insects preparing for their aurelia state, &c.

We shall only add on this head, that the instincts of brute animals have not been so specifically determined by nature, as to regulate their entire conduct, or to impel them to a certain regular series of motions, as so many machines, in every circumstance or incident of their lives. Under some circumstances, and in some particular operations, as in the instances above recited, a certain rule of conduct is minutely prescribed to them, which they invariably follow: but on many occasions there is a diversity in their operations, occasioned by external circumstances, and in which the impressions of external objects on their senses, the appetites and passions thereby excited, and the power of their imagination, produce variations in their conduct. These

however

however are all regulated by, and have a general resemblance, and are subservient to, the innate fundamental principles of knowledge and action originally implanted in them. It is in consequence of this latitude that men are enabled to form and train up animals to certain purposes, respecting their own particular use and entertainment, and for which nature did never design them. This they effect by working on their sensual appetites and imagination, and thus directing their natural determinate forces to their particular purpose. Still the primitive instinct of the animal is the foundation of all these acquired arts. Though nature has not given the falcon any appetite for, or knowledge of, the hare or the wild boar; yet the falconer by hunger, watching, deceit and other means, teaches him to stoop at these animals, and thus leads him to the exercise of new arts not natural to him, and which are, as it were, *engrafted* on the *wild stock* of animal instinct.

We know not whether by what goes before, we have succeeded in our attempt to give the reader a clear idea of the precise meaning of the Author's *determinate forces* of nature, by which he accounts for the various operations of brute animals. Were we barely to transcribe his definitions and explanations of these forces, we should probably disgust our readers by the length, as well as the scholastic dryness, of the quotations that would be necessary for that purpose. We shall therefore on this occasion pursue the same method which we have followed in the preceding part of this account, and shall endeavour, in our own manner, to give a general though somewhat incomplete idea of what we conceive to be his meaning. This, we think, may be best effected by appealing at once to the *instincts* of our readers, as to an example more intelligible than a set of metaphysical definitions and distinctions, and which will sufficiently illustrate those, at least, which he calls the *industrious instincts* of animals.—For we too have, and have had, our instincts, as well as the brutes; though not in equal number, or so specifically determined. These last therefore will be most easily explained, by reflecting on those which we feel, or have felt within ourselves.

The innate instinct of a child, in the act of sucking the breast, which M. Reimar cursorily mentions, may be very properly applied to this purpose; as it appears to be of the very same kind with those here called industrious instincts implanted in brute animals. In the performance of this seemingly simple operation (which however is of a very complicated kind, if we attentively consider all the *innate* knowledge and powers which it implies) he is, on his very first appearance in the world, and previously to all observation, instruction, or experience, infinitely more adroit than the wisest philosopher, grown grey in the study of the properties of the air, the nature

ture of fuction, and the motion of the mufcles of deglutition. Without any acquired knowledge of thefe particulars, this young adept burfts into being, not only poffeffed of an appetite for human milk, but perfectly, that is, practically inftructed, and completely accomplifhed in the art of making a *vacuum* in his mouth, by means of his tongue and other organs, and of conveying the liquor that flows into it, with perfect fafety to himfelf, over the dangerous paffage of the wind pipe, into the œfophagus. In the fame manner the young bee, on his firft coming into life, moves his trunk, his feet, and other organs, with which he collects honey and wax, and builds hexagonal cells: for fuch are the appetites and powers with which *he* is endowed. Both execute their refpective operations blindly, that is, without thought, reflecting, or comparing; and yet with fome degree of fpontaneity. Bad weather will prevent the bee from fallying forth; and, with feeming fpontaneity, he will leave a flower that contains *farina* not fit for his purpofe; in the fame manner as the child will voluntarily quit a nipple fmeared with aloes. Nature has however furnifhed the former, and all the individuals of the brute creation, with a greater variety of thefe *innate arts* and practical knowledge, and with a more acute fenfibility, by which they are excited to exercife them. But though nature has thus liberally furnifhed them with a larger ftock of this innate fcience and art, fhe has not given them any means of enlarging the original fund; which they accordingly tranfmit from father to fon, without increafe and without diminution. Human beings, on the contrary, are fent into the world endowed with a more fcanty portion of thefe original powers; but at the fame time are furnifhed with faculties, that of reafon in particular, by which they are enabled to improve and increafe this fmall capital to an almoft unlimited extent.

Actions of the nature above mentioned may be referred to a corporeal inftinct: but we have likewife, in common with the brutes, certain inftinctive principles which belong peculiarly to the mind. Reafon builds upon them as on a foundation; but the foul poffeffes them totally independent on that faculty. Of this kind is our knowledge and conviction of the real exiftence of an external, material world. Of this knowledge and belief all men fince the creation, a few fpeculative philofophers excepted, have been poffeffed: not in confequence of reafoning; for the real exiftence of matter, (as has lately been very clearly fhewn *) is a fubject which from its very nature is incapable of argumentative proof; but from a natural inftinct, or innate principle implanted in the foul, and irrefiftibly compelling this belief. By a fimilar principle, and not by rea-

* See Dr. Reid's *Inquiry* and Dr. Beattie's work above referred to.

soning, men and brutes are equally led to infer the future from the past, and firmly to believe that the same causes will produce the same effects;—that a stone unsupported will fall to the ground, and that fire will burn, to-day, as it did yesterday, and has done in all times past. That this firm and universal persuasion is not a conviction founded on any process of reasoning, Mr. Hume first observed and satisfactorily proved. Not the shadow of a reason can indeed be given for this belief, that will hold universally. It cannot be founded on any reasoning on the stability and regularity of the course of nature: for of such reasoning children, ideots and brutes are certainly incapable; who nevertheless infer the effect from the cause as readily as the acutest philosopher. Experience is indeed the groundwork of this belief; but that informs us only of what is *past*; and no one has had *experience* of the *future*. This knowledge therefore is derived from another instinctive principle, which, like the former, is a part of the original furniture of the mind. We shall not mention any more of those principles, as these, we imagine, will be sufficient to give a general idea of what the Author seems to mean by his *determinate forces of nature*, to which he attributes the various operations of brute animals.

It has been objected to the Author, since the first edition of this treatise, that his *innate arts*, and *determinate natural forces*, infused into the souls of animals, are mere terms, void of meaning, and which do not convey any particular or satisfactory knowledge of the subject intended to be expressed by them. Instead of quoting any part of M. Reimar's metaphysical and elaborate answers to this objection, we shall briefly observe in his defence, that he has the merit, at least, of having clearly shewn the insufficiency or absurdity of many of the former systems; and farther, that it is making some progress in knowledge to reduce different *phenomena* under one class, and to explain them plausibly by one principle; though the precise and specific nature of that principle remains undiscovered. Thus Newton greatly extended human knowledge by shewing that gravity, or the very same power that causes a stone to fall to the ground, and a projectile to describe a parabola, likewise keeps the planets in their orbits; though he did not pretend to ascertain the intimate nature, or assign the cause, of gravity. If the Author has succeeded in proving that brutes are not possessed of the faculty of reason, and that they are directed in their various operations by a set of original sentiments and powers implanted in them; he has certainly added to the stock of knowledge, though the intimate nature of these instinctive powers still remains involved in the greatest obscurity. Nature has set bounds to all human enquiries; and this possibly cannot be extended much further.—On the whole, though

though there is conſiderable merit in this attempt, the work is more commendable for the matter than the form, which, as we have already more than once obſerved, is not ſo inviting as the nature of the ſubject might give us reaſon to expect, when treated by a writer of abilities.

ART. IV.

Memoire ſur la Muſique des Anciens, &c.—An Eſſay on the Muſic of the Ancients, explaining the Principle on which the authentic Proportions aſcribed to Pythagoras are founded; as well as the various muſical Syſtems of the Greeks, Chineſe, and Egyptians: Together with a Compariſon drawn between the Syſtem of the Egyptians and that of the Moderns. By the Abbé Rouſſier. 4to. Paris.

THE learned and very ingenious Author of this curious and profound eſſay attempts to prove and explain, by means of one ſimple principle, the true nature and generation of the moſt ancient ſcales of muſical ſounds; and particularly the muſical proportions known under the title of Pythagorean. His intention indeed is to ſhew, not only that theſe ancient ſyſtems were founded on this principle, but likewiſe that all thoſe which depart from it are falſe and defective. He undertakes to prove the firſt part of this poſition, both from the nature of the thing, and from the remains of antiquity; and appeals to the ear for the truth of the latter part of it. We ſhall endeavour to give the outlines of his ſyſtem in as clear a manner as the nature of the ſubject, and the limits to which we are confined, will admit.

The notes of the common ſcale, or octave, as we have lately had occaſion to obſerve *, however natural that diviſion may appear to be, are undoubtedly artificial, and the reſult of much and profound thought. According to the Author, nothing can be more natural to ſuppoſe than that a ſcale of ſounds was originally formed, by taking a certain perfect, concordant interval as a model or rule; by the ſucceſſive application of which, a ſeries of ſounds would be produced, which being all brought down to, or raiſed up to the ſame octave, according as the progreſſion was taken upwards or downwards, would give all the requiſite notes contained within the compaſs of an octave. The concordant interval which he ſuppoſes to have been employed for this purpoſe by Pythagoras, and the Egyptians his maſters, is the fifth, taken in a deſcending, or its equivalent the fourth, in an aſcending progreſſion: and as a ſeries of numbers in a geometrical triplicate ratio to each other, will expreſs a ſucceſſion of perfect fifths (or rather of perfect twelfths, their octaves)

* In our Review of *The Principles and Power of Harmony*, November 1771, page 374.

affuming 1 to denote the fundamental note, he proceeds in a defcending triplicate progreffion, and thus procures a feries of numbers, expreffing the increafing lengths of a fuppofed mufical chord, and denoting the different founds which it would produce. On this particular progreffion, according to him, as on a fundamental and inalterable principle, the genuine fyftem of the *ancient* Greeks was conftructed. Many of the fucceeding fyftems, naturally, and as it were, of their own accord, arrange themfelves under this fimple and luminous principle, to the difcovery of which the Author acknowledges himfelf indebted for the knowledge of an infinite number of particulars, which throw light on many queftions that have long divided the mufical world on this fubject. We have faid, the fyftem of the *ancient* Greeks; for, according to the Abbé, the knowledge of the principle which he here explains was very early loft; as it was unknown even in the time of Ptolomy, whofe errors have been adopted by all fucceeding writers.

Before we proceed further, we fhall give, in one line, the firft eight terms of this triplicate progreffion, in a feries of defcending fifths (or twelfths) formed by multiplying each preceding number by three; together with the names of the notes expreffed by them. We fcarce need to add that the lower numbers are to be elevated, in a duplicate progreffion, in order to bring them up into the fame octave with any particular note with which they are to be compared. To fave the trouble of calculation, tables are given at the end of the work, in which are contained all the neceffary feries of thefe numbers, in duplicate and triplicate progreffion.

Ift term.	II.	III.	IV.	V.	VI.	VII.	VIII.
1.	3.	9.	27.	81.	243.	729.	2187.
B.	*E.*	*A*	*D*	*G.*	*C.*	*F.*	*B flat.*

Here, according to the Author, Pythagoras and the ancient Greeks clofed the progreffion; probably from an apprehenfion that the chromatic genus, which would be introduced by a further extenfion of the feries, might, from its effeminate nature, prove dangerous to manners: for it is well known that, long after the time of Pythagoras, the Lacedemonians punifhed Timotheus in an exemplary manner, for attempting to introduce that genus among them, by adding four ftrings to the ancient heptachord; as appears from the remarkable *Senatus confultum* iffued on that occafion, and which may be found in *Boethius, lib.* 1mo.

The Author proceeds afterwards to fhew that the Egyptians added four more terms to this progreffion. He endeavours to prove likewife, that the Chinefe mufical fcale of fix founds, of which he treats particularly in an article apart, commences with the laft term of the preceding progreffion; and draws from

from thence concluſions favourable to his hypotheſis. The four added terms are theſe:

IX.	X.	XI.	XII.
6561.	19683.	59049.	177147.
E flat.	*A flat.*	*D flat.*	*G flat.*

The Reader has now before him a ſeries of twelve numbers, which are ſaid to expreſs the value aſſigned by the Egyptians to the notes of their ſcale. They carried on the progreſſion no farther than the twelfth term, for an obvious reaſon. The thirteenth, 531441, he obſerves, which anſwers to *C flat*, in a manner excludes itſelf from the ſeries: as this *C flat* would be lower than the *B natural* (which is the fundamental note of this progreſſion) raiſed up to the nineteenth octave, and which is expreſſed by the number 524288. The difference between theſe two numbers, it is well known, conſtitutes the muſical interval known by the name of the *Comma* of Pythagoras, but hitherto ſuppoſed to be produced by an aſcending progreſſion.

To ſave our muſical Readers the trouble of calculation, we ſhall ſubjoin a regular ſcale of ſounds founded on the preceding deſcending progreſſion, but here given in an aſcending ſeries, and reduced, we believe, to the loweſt terms in which the ratios can be expreſſed without fractions. We ſhall likewiſe place below them the numbers which correſpond to the ſame notes in the modern diatonic ſcale; in order that the difference may be ſeen at one view: we ſhall likewiſe add, between every two notes, the ratios expreſſing the interval between them:

Ancient ſcale	*C*	$\frac{8}{9}$	*D.*	$\frac{8}{9}$	*E*	$\frac{243}{256}$	*F*	$\frac{8}{9}$	*G*	$\frac{8}{9}$	*A*	$\frac{8}{9}$	*B*	$\frac{243}{256}$	*C*
	384.		432.		486		512		576		648.		729		768
Diatonic.	384	$\frac{8}{9}$	432	$\frac{9}{10}$	480	$\frac{15}{16}$	512	$\frac{8}{9}$	576	$\frac{9}{10}$	640	$\frac{8}{9}$	720	$\frac{15}{16}$	768

The Author having, by a variety of arguments and authorities, taken pains to eſtabliſh the preceding ſeries, as the genuine ſcale uſed by the ancients, proceeds to ſhew that this is the only juſt and natural method of dividing the octave; that Ptolemy and all the ſubſequent writers of muſic loſt ſight of this juſt and original principle, that of forming a muſical ſcale by a ſeries of perfect fifths ſucceeding each other; and that all the errors and imperfections of the preſent or diatonic ſyſtem, and the numberleſs diſquiſitions and diſputes to which this ſubject has given birth, proceed from our not having known and adopted this ſimple principle, both in theory and practice. We ſhall now proceed to offer a few obſervations that preſent themſelves on a conſideration of this ſcale; firſt briefly obſerving, in general, that it not only differs, in many parts of it, from the diatonic ſyſtem, but that it is inconſiſtent likewiſe with many of the principles deduced from the experiments made with the ſtring trumpet, the *harmonical ſounds* naturally produced by ſounding bodies, and other phyſical *phenomena*.

 In

In the first place, we shall observe that, on calculating the ratios of the numbers given in the supposed ancient scale formed by a triplicate progression, it will be found, that the fifths are all perfect; that there is only one kind of tone in this scale, and that the major, in the proportion 8 : 9; that the major thirds, in every part of it, consist of two such major tones, and consequently constitute an interval larger than that in the diatonic system, which is expressed by the ratio 4 : 5: that the semitone, on the other hand, is every where less than the diatonic; that the minor thirds are likewise every where the same throughout this scale, and form an interval smaller than the diatonic of 5 : 6. To shew these differences at one view, and in the smallest numbers:—The ratios expressing the present diatonic semitone, major third, and minor third are 15 : 16 (or 240 : 256) 4 : 5; and 5 : 6. In the ancient system the same intervals are expressed by the ratios 243 : 256; 4 : $5\frac{1}{16}$; and $5\frac{1}{16}$: 6. We scarce need to add, as it will appear on the bare inspection of the preceding scale, that the minor tone of the moderns, 9 : 10, is not admitted into this system. This, as well as many other devices, tending to perplex the theory of music, and to disfigure genuine harmony, are here said to be the invention of the modern Greeks.

The inalterability and indivisibility of the tone is strongly and frequently insisted upon by the Author; who affirms that there is not, nor can be, any other tone than the major; which is formed by the two extremes of any three succeeding terms in the triplicate progression, given at the beginning of this article; the first, taken in any part of the series, being raised up into the same octave with the third: as *B* 1, elevated, by a duplicate progression, to 8, and forming with *A* 9, the ratio 8 : 9.

It follows, as a necessary corrollary, from this inalterability of the tone, that the interval of the major third in this system must be larger than the modern interval of the same denomination, which, as is well known, consists of a major and a minor tone, producing the interval 4 : 5; for $\frac{8}{9} \times \frac{9}{10} = \frac{72}{90} = \frac{64}{80} = \frac{4}{5}$. But the major third of this system, the true *Diton* of the ancient Greeks, is produced by taking the two extremes of any five succeeding terms in the above mentioned series, and raising the lowest, *B* 1, for example, six octaves, that is, into the same octave with *G* 81, which gives the ratio 64 : 81 = 4 : $5\frac{1}{16}$, and greater than the former interval by a comma. In short, to give a more familiar instance, it is the interval produced by the extremes of four perfect fifths; between *G*, the open fourth string of a violin, and *B*, the perfect fifth of *E*, the open first string.

After these two examples, we need not proceed farther to exemplify in what manner the minor third, and the semitone, are deduced from this progression. They are both contracted by by this operation. The former which, in the diatonic fcale, is expreffed by the ratio 80 : 96, or 5 : 6, is here reduced, by an operation fimilar to thofe above given, to 81 : 96, or $5\frac{1}{16}$: 6; and the latter, 240 : 256 (or 15 : 16) to 243 : 256. We need not mention the remaining intervals, which depend upon thefe.

Such, according to the Author, was the fcale of founds, by which the ancient Greeks fung and executed their divine compofitions, at a time when mufic was among them the fcience of poets and philofophers: nay fuch, he affirms, are the tones which Nature forces even the modern European to produce, provided his ears have not been debauched to a certain degree, by our arbitrary, fictitious, and falfe proportions; or by having been long accuftomed to the difcordant intervals of *tempered* inftruments. In the ancient fcale, founded on the defcending progreffion of *perfect* fifths, no fuch temperament was neceffary; and had Didymus and Ptolemy known or attended to that fimple principle, the mufical world would not have had their heads confounded with endlefs difputes and calculations, undertaken and inftituted in defence of complicated and erroneous fyftems; nor their ears wounded by falfe and difcordant intervals, the natural offspring of their reveries.

The felection and adoption of our prefent fyftem, which is no other than the *Diatonicon fyntonon* of Ptolomy, out of a great many others prefented by that writer (who feems to have taken a pleafure in fplitting of tones) according to the Author's account, arofe from hence: it found favour, it feems, with Zarlin; has been adopted by all fucceeding theorifts, and acquired the epithet of a *natural* fcale, merely becaufe its concordant intervals *happened* to correfpond with the natural feries of the numbers 1, 2, 3, 4, 5, 6, in arithmetical progreffion. It is true, fays the Abbé, that there is real harmony between the numbers 1 and 2, as they reprefent the octave; between 2 and 3, which give the fifth; and between 3 and 4, which truly exprefs the fourth: but it does not follow from hence that harmony muft be produced from the numbers 4 and 5, or 5 and 6, if they do not actually prefent fuch harmony. What reafon, he adds, can be given for not carrying this progreffion further *? There are the fame grounds to expect harmony from the numbers 6 and 7, 7 and 8, &c. I mean, fays the Abbé, mufical harmony, harmony of founds, in fine harmony for the ear; and not a harmony of numbers, or of quantities proceeding in arithmetical progreffion.

* This has been lately done, certainly to a very extravagant extent, by M. Jamard. A particular account of his arithmetical operations on mufic may be feen in the Appendix to our 44th volume, page 551.

The

The Author pays as little regard to the ſounds furniſhed by the reſonnance of ſonorous bodies, commonly called the harmonical notes, and to others naturally produced by certain inſtruments, as well as to other phyſical phenomena, which have been appealed to in the theory of muſic, but which do not coincide with his ſyſtem. Though they are produced by Nature, it does not, according to him, follow that they are to regulate the ſcale of muſic; if a ſyſtem of ſounds formed upon them ſhould be unpleaſing to the ear. Some of them indeed appear, upon that account, to be inadmiſſible into a regular ſcale. We muſt interpoſe however in favour of the *third ſounds*, againſt which this objection certainly does not operate; as the intervals which have their ſanction are in the higheſt degree pleaſing. We lately appealed to their authority, with regard to the difficulty concerning Huygens's celebrated paſſage †, and which vaniſhes on uſing the proportions of the Author's ſcale: as his contracted minor third which, not only in this, but in every part of the ſcale, is in the ratio of 81 : 96 (or 27 : 32) will bring the performer down from *f* to *D*, in ſuch a manner as to enable him to cloſe finally in *C*, the original key.

Some experiments are propoſed by the Author, to prove that every juſt ſinger, whoſe organs have not been vitiated by our falſe and temperating principles, and every accurate performer on the violin, violoncello, and other perfect inſtruments which are ſtopped *ad libitum*, actually ſing and execute their pieces by the intervals of this ſcale. Theſe experiments however are of ſuch a nature that, we apprehend, they will not univerſally be deemed deciſive; as the major part of them depend only on an *eſtimation* of the diſtances obſervable between certain intervals, on hearing a melody executed by a juſt ſinger or player; which diſtance different perſons will probably *eſtimate* differently. One of them alone is not liable to this objection, and is therefore more deciſive: but the reſult affects only the authority of the harmonic ſounds produced by the forced tones of a wind inſtrument. We ſhall cloſe our account of this work by a ſhort relation of this experiment.

Stopping all the holes of a German flute, let the inſtrument, by a forced blowing, be made to ſound an *harmonical f* ſharp, the ſeventeenth, or the double octave of the major third, to *D*, the loweſt note on that inſtrument. Let the performer then ſound the uniſon to this harmonical note; producing it by ſtopping the flute in the uſual manner. It will be

† See Monthly Review, November 1771, page 374, &c. and for December, page 477.

found,

found, says the Abbé, that the first or harmonical note will be sensibly flatter than this last. But every one acknowleges that it is one of the imperfections of the German flute, that this last note is too flat, as a major third to *D*. The harmonical note, which is still flatter than this, cannot, consequently, be just. No regard therefore is to be paid to the authority of the harmonical sounds.

We have taken some pains to give a general idea of the principal doctrines contained in this memoir. Our limits will not permit us to enquire into the justice of them, or into the circumstances which occasioned the adoption of the present system. For the many other particulars here incidentally discussed, we must content ourselves with recommending the perusal of the entire essay to those who cultivate this agreeable branch of science. They will find in it much philological and musical erudition, and many ingenious remarks both on the ancient and the modern systems of music.

Art. V.

Experimenta, atque Observationes, quibus Electricitas Vindex *late constituitur, atque explicatur, &c.*—Experiments and Observations, by which the Nature and Properties of *Recuperative Electricity* are amply established and explained. By J. Baptista Beccaria. 4to. Turin.

SHOULD the English phrase by which we have found ourselves obliged, for want of a better, to express the Author's *Electricitas Vindex*, appear singular, we desire that his apology, if any should be thought necessary, may be applied, *mutatis mutandis*, to ourselves. '*Si cui nomen hoc aut minus consentaneum videatur, aut minus latinum, is sciat velim, me rebus studere impensius quam vocibus.* On a subject which has been so fruitful in new discoveries, it is necessary to invent or adopt new terms, to which, however singular they may appear at first, custom only can give a sanction.

We would willingly gratify such of our Readers whose curiosity may be excited by the singularity of the title of this essay, by giving an account of some of the experiments contained in it, which were made with a view to discover the nature and laws of the *Electricitas Vindex*; but, as we have not the advantage of figures, this cannot be effected without endless circumlocution: nor is the matter very easy to explain, even with their assistance. We shall however endeavour, in a few words, to give a general idea of this quality of electrical bodies.

On removing one of the coatings, the upper for instance, of a plate of glass charged positively on that side, it loses some part of its electricity. On replacing the coating, and again removing

moving it, it loses a fresh portion, but less than the former. On repeating the experiment, the diminution becomes gradually less and less sensible. This quality the Author terms *Negative recuperative Electricity*. After coating and uncoating the plate 6, 8, 10, or a certain number of times, it no longer loses any of its electricity from this denudation. This point of time the Author terms the *limit of the two contrary electricities*. On continuing however the operation, that is, on repeatedly removing the upper coating, and then replacing it, the plate begins and continues to *recover* each time part of the electricity which it had lost by the former operations: and this it does, in the common manner, even after it has been discharged, by forming a communication between its two surfaces. This quality the Author terms *Positive recuperative Electricity*. On using two plates of glass in contact with each other, the exterior surfaces only of which are coated, and on alternately separating and conjoining them, the phenomena are more manifest and lasting. Other curious appearances likewise present themselves; some of which seem unfavourable to the Franklinian doctrine, but which the Author takes great pains to reconcile with that simple and luminous theory.

We offer this very imperfect and uncircumstantial account, only as an explanatory comment on the title of this work. The name alone of the Author will recommend it to the perusal, we should rather perhaps say, to the study of electricians; as, partly from the complicated nature of the subject, and partly from the obscurity of the language, employed on a matter so new and foreign to it, they will find no small degree of attention, necessary to enable them to make themselves every where masters of his meaning.

ART. VI.

Histoire et Memoires de la Société, formée a Amsterdam en faveur des Noyés.—The History and Memoirs of the Society, formed at Amsterdam, for the Recovery of Persons that have been drowned. A°. 1767. Three Parts. Amsterdam. 1768, 1769, 1771.

THE same element to which the Hollanders are indebted for their wealth and their liberty, is to them a source of loss and calamity. The sea, when it breaks in upon their ramparts, carries destruction along with it; and the frequent canals, with which their country is intersected, are no less fatal and destructive. It is with nations as with individuals; the advantages they possess are ever accompanied with inconveniencies.

The almost incredible number of persons drowned annually at Amsterdam, excited attention and regret; and it having been found, on enquiry, that the majority of these died merely for want

want of affiftance, a Society was formed, which offered premiums to thofe who fhould fave the life of a citizen that was in danger of perifhing by water; and which propofed, from time to time, to publifh the treatment and method of recovery followed in fuch fituations.

The utmoft encouragement was every where given throughout the United Provinces, by the magiftrates in particular, and afterwards by the States General, to fo falutary an inftitution; and, from the fhort memorials before us, it appears that it has been attended with very confiderable fuccefs, and will be productive of the moft beneficial confequences. In a matter of fuch extenfive and important concern, we think it our duty to extract from this interefting work a general account of the fuccefs which has attended the endeavours of this laudable fociety; and of the methods by which it was procured: premifing a fhort *rationale* of the principles to which it is evidently to be attributed.

It is certainly not very eafy, in many cafes, to afcertain precifely that ftate of an animal body which is called Death; and in none, perhaps, more difficult than in bodies which have lain for fome time under water. In thefe cafes the principal, and often the only material change produced in the animal œconomy is, that by the preffure of the water on the *epiglottis*, and the want of air, an entire ftop is put to refpiration; confequently to the free paffage of the blood through the lungs; and, as an effect of that obftruction, to its circulation throughout the whole body: fo that the heart, after a few ineffectual ftruggles and efforts to move the mafs through the ftraitened paffages of the lungs, at laft becomes quiefcent. Neither the vital organs, however, or the animal fluids, have perhaps received any irreparable or even material injury, by this ftate of reft in the one, or ftagnation of the other: and nothing feems wanting to reftore the yet unimpaired machine to the exercife of its accuftomed functions, than merely to put it once more into motion. Former experience has fhewn the juftice of this reafoning, and of the conclufion which we have drawn from it; which is ftill more fatisfactorily evinced by the very large number of well authenticated hiftories contained in thefe three publications.

The moft obvious methods of renewing the fufpended motions of the heart and lungs, on which all the others depend, are, to blow air repeatedly into the laft mentioned organ, and to relieve the heart by leffening the *moles movenda*? the mafs of blood, as quickly as poffible, by bleeding in the jugulars or arm. The other methods may, we imagine, be all nearly comprehended under this one general indication: of applying to the whole body, or to thofe parts of it which are more peculiarly

liarly ſenſible or irritable, the moſt powerful and appropriate *ſtimuli*. Such are thoſe recommended by the members of this humane and truly patriotic inſtitution; as warmth; the blowing common air, or, which is preferable, the ſmoke of tobacco into the inteſtines, either by the chirurgical inſtrument here called a *fumigator*, and which our Readers may find deſcribed and delineated in *Heiſter*'s *Surgery* *; or, if that is not at hand, through a tobacco pipe, or the ſheath of a pocket knife, the point of which is firſt cut off. To theſe expedients muſt be added the application of the moſt pungent volatile ſalts or ſpirits to the noſtrils, or the tickling them with feathers; gentle ſhaking, and continued warm frictions, either dry, or with proper liniments rubbed in, from the neck down the ſpine of the back; the exhibition of ſtimulating clyſters; and afterwards, when the ſigns of returning life begin to appear, the pouring of brandy or other warm and ſtimulating liquors into the mouth, and the adminiſtration of vomiting and purging medicines.

It will give a humane reader pleaſure to be informed, that in this publication the hiſtories are given of no leſs than 109 citizens, who, from the firſt inſtitution of this ſociety towards the end of the year 1767, to the cloſe of the year 1770, have, in the United Provinces alone, been reſtored to their friends and country, by the uſe of ſome or all of the methods above indicated. Of theſe, fifty-five have been thus preſerved in the compaſs only of the laſt year: All of them were univerſally adjudged to be dead by the bye-ſtanders; as they had every ſign or criterion of death, except putrefaction. Many of them were already ſtiff, and in none of them was there the leaſt obſervable pulſation, either of the heart or arteries. Several of them had been half an hour, and ſome an hour, under the water, and even under ice; the heads of ſome having ſtuck, during that time, in the mud of the canals or rivers: and yet all of them were reſtored to life, and the honorary medal of the ſociety, or their premium of ſix ducats, paid to their preſervers. In a very ſmall number of caſes, indeed, the patients relapſed and died: but ſome of theſe had fallen into the water when in a ſtate of intoxication; others had received injuries in the dragging them out, by means of hooks, from the bottoms of the rivers or canals, or from the rough and ill-judged proceedings of the byeſtanders, rolling them upon caſks with the belly undermoſt, and the head hanging downwards: a practice which the ſociety juſtly condemns.

One of the moſt obſervable circumſtances which we remark in theſe hiſtories, and which confirms what we have ſaid above

* Tab. xxxiv. fig. 13.

con-

concerning the ſmallneſs of the injury which the human body may ſuſtain, by being for a conſiderable time immerſed in water, is, that in many of the caſes here recited, we obſerve the ſubjects of them, who formerly would have been numbered among the dead, and moſt undoubtedly been treated as ſuch, walking about the next day, or even in a few hours, to thank their deliverers in perſon. In ſome of theſe inſtances, the *human machine* appears to have ſcarce ſuffered any greater injury, than a clock ſuſtains by having had the motion of its pendulum accidentally ſtopped. Its works are not affected by the accident, and are all in a condition and ready to perform their reſpective movements, the moment that ſome friendly hand gives it a puſh, and renews its vibrations.

We ſhould not omit to obſerve, that thoſe who may find themſelves in a ſituation to put the methods here recommended into practice, ſhould not be diſcouraged at the ſeeming bad ſucceſs of their firſt endeavours. Some of the ſubjects, whoſe complete recovery is related in theſe publications, exhibited no ſigns of returning to life, till a very conſiderable time had been employed in the charitable work. Putrefaction alone, more particularly in caſes of this nature, ſeems, as we have already hinted, to be the only certain criterion that the vital principle is irrevocably fled, and that all attempts to recal it are fruitleſs.

ART. VII.

Traité de l'Electricité, &c. A Treatiſe on Electricity, in which all the Diſcoveries made on that Subject to the preſent Time are explained and demonſtrated. By M. Sigaud de la Fond, Profeſſor of Mathematics, &c. 12mo. Paris. 1771.

THE number and importance of the diſcoveries which have been made in this branch of natural knowledge, induced the Author, who had before publiſhed a courſe of Experimental Philoſophy, to treat of this fruitful and extenſive ſubject, in a volume apart; which, though it may be conſidered as an appendix to the former work, may be had ſeparate. After a ſhort hiſtory of the firſt diſcoveries in this ſcience, he proceeds, in a regular order, to treat of the beſt method of performing electrical experiments, and to deſcribe the moſt important. He every where adopts the ſyſtem of Dr. Franklin, and occaſionally refutes the objections which have been made to it by the late Abbé Nollet. His deſcriptions are in general clear, and his manner of reaſoning juſt and philoſophical. On the whole, conſidered as an introductory manual to the knowledge of electricity, the work is not without a pretty conſiderable ſhare of merit. The account, however, of electrical diſcoveries is not here brought down to the preſent time: as the Author appears to be unacquainted with many curious and important obſervations,

made

made in our own country particularly, which have been published within a few years past.

In an elementary treatise novelties are not to be expected. We shall briefly mention, nevertheless, M. de la Fond's short description of a singular application of electrical attractions and repulsions to music, which may be new to some of our readers; though the Author of it, Father de la Borde, published an account of it (which we have seen) together with a strange theory of electricity, several years ago, in a small treatise intitled *Claveſſin Electrique.* By an ingenious but complicated disposition of bells properly toned, with clappers hanging between each, and communicating with a set of keys, the Father affirms, that, after a few previous turns of his globe, his apparatus was put into a condition to enable him to execute a musical piece of considerable length. The present Author, who does not notice the seeming impossibility of effecting this, by simply electrifying the bells previously to the experiment, declares however, that he has heard him play several airs on this instrument, thus animated by electricity; and which the inventor observes had this advantage over the harpsichord and other instruments of that kind, that the notes given by it could be *held on*; each tone being caused by the quick motions of the clapper vibrating between two bells unison to each other, and thereby producing a uniform and continued sound, as long as the finger was kept upon the key, and which ceased not till it was withdrawn.

ART. VIII.

Le Necrologe des Hommes celebres de France, &c.—The Lives of celebrated Writers and Artists lately dead. By a Society of Gentlemen. 12mo. Paris.

THIS work is consecrated to the memory of those who, in our times, and in France, have been celebrated, or at least have aspired to celebrity, either in the sciences or in the arts. The intention of the writers of these *Eloges* is to give, not a set of anecdotes relating to the private life, but a history of the genius, talents, and productions, of those who have excited the attention and merited the approbation of the public, in the different walks of philosophy, poetry, oratory, and history; painting, sculpture, music, and architecture; or by their performances upon the stage.

The work begins with the *Eloge* of M. de L'Isle, written by M. de la Lande; which is succeeded by those of M. de Premontval; the celebrated physiologist and physician; M. de Sauvages; the Abbé D'Olivet; some particular artists, and various writers whom the Authors have judged to be intitled to this distinction. Some of these articles are well written and inte-

interesting; but many of them are meagre, and the subjects of them persons of no very considerable eminence. The Authors propose to continue these *Fasti* of the French literature and arts; which may be amusing to those who wish to be informed of the characters, and of the circumstances relating to the lives and writings of their cotemporaries, who have distinguished themselves by their literary or other productions.

At the close of this performance, we meet with an instance of that frivolity so generally imputed to our neighbours. At the end of a work consecrated to a display of the various talents of philosophers, scholars, and artists, we meet with some grave and minute information with regard to the *etiquette* established on the important article of mourning; very proper undoubtedly for the perusal and study of Taylors, Mantuamakers, and Milliners. The laws here laid down, on this momentous subject, particularly with regard to the duration of mournings, it seems, admit of no other exception than the following: The established time of mourning for a brother or sister, we are here told, is two months: but should the mourner come into the possession of a good estate by the departure of the defunct, in this case, the afflicted heir must make a parade of the additional load of woe hereby imposed, by displaying this superadded grief, through a regular gradation of all the tints between black and grey, for four months longer.

ART. IX.

Zend-Avesta, Ouvrage de Zoroastre. — Zend-Avesta, a Work of Zoroaster, containing the theological, physical, and moral Opinions of that Legislator, the Ceremonies of the religious Worship he established, and many other Particulars relative to the ancient History of Persia. Translated from the Zendic, with remarks, and accompanied with Discourses in Illustration of the Topics of which it treats. By M. Anquetil Du Perron, Member of the Royal Academy of Inscriptions and Belles Lettres, and Interpreter to the King for the eastern Languages. 4to. 3 Vols. Paris, 1771.

RELATIONS of the travels of candid and intelligent men are full of instruction and entertainment: but how few of those who have visited foreign countries have given a just account, or have been able to make a proper use of what they have observed? The gratification of a restless disposition is, in general, the principle by which they are directed; and, in the mere pleasure which results from enterprize and action, they find a compensation for the dangers and the difficulties they encounter. Their journals, accordingly, are almost always personal, and have little that can amuse or interest.

 Monsieur

Monsieur Anquetil du Perron, whose labours are now before us, must be classed with the generality of travellers. He has not the most distant pretensions to the deep reflexion, or the extended views of a Chardin, or a Bernier. The spirit of adventure he discovers is the only circumstance for which he deserves commendation. The facts he details are trifling and unimportant; his remarks are idle and without solidity; and the reader is perpetually offended with the displays of his vanity.

The Zend-Avesta, which he has translated, he considers as a genuine remain of Zoroaster: but a collection of observations and descriptions which express the greatest folly and enthusiasm, cannot, with any degree of justice, be imputed to that celebrated philosopher and legislator. The following quotation, which we give in the words of the translator, and from the most intelligible part of his translation, will be fully sufficient to satisfy our readers both with regard to the merit and to the authenticity of this publication:

'J'ai donné au chien, ô Sapetman Zoroastre, moi, qui suis Ormusd, son poil pour vêtement; (je l'ai donné) fier, prompt & agissant, ayant la dent aiguë & l'intelligence étendue, (comme il convient) à un Chef du Monde. Moi, qui suis Ormusd, j'ai donné au chien un corps grand & fort. Son intelligence fait subsister le Monde. Lorsqu'il fait entendre sa voix, ô Sapetman Zoroastre, (le Monde) est dans un état brillant. S'il ne (gardoit) pas les rues, le voleur ou le loup, qui en seroit instruit, enleveroit les biens des rues; le loup frapperoit, le loup se multiplieroit, le loup frapperoit & feroit tout disparoître.

'Juste Juge, &c.

'Quel est (le chien) qui frappe le loup avec force, ô saint Ormusd, soit qu'il attaque le loup, ou que le loup l'attaque?

'Ormusd répondit: ces chiens frappent le loup avec force, soit qu'ils attaquent le loup les premiers, ou que le loup les attaque; ces chiens sont supérieurs au loup, lorsqu'ils se collettent avec lui, les Pessoschorouns, les Veschorouns, les Vôhonezags, & les Derekhtô honéres.

'Dés que l'un (de ces chiens) est au Monde, il se répand, cherche à se distinguer; il frappe celui qui dans le Monde aime, cherche le mal: tel est le chien.

'Le loup de même s'éleve, se collette avec (le chien), dès qu'il est né. Lorsqu'il a un an il se répand, cherche à se distinguer; il frappe celui qui dans le monde aime, cherche le mal: tel est le loup.

'Le chien a huit qualités: il est comme l'Athorné, il est comme le Militaire, iel st comme la Laboureur (principe) de biens, il est comme l'oiseau, il est comme le voleur, il est comme,

comme la bête féroce, il est comme la femme de mauvaise vie, il est comme la jeune personne.

' Comme l'Athorné, le (chien) mange (ce qu'il trouve); comme l'Athorné, il est bienfaisant & heureux; comme l'Athorné, il se contente de tout; comme l'Athorné, il éloigne ceux (qui s'approchent de lui): il est comme l'Athorné.

' Le (chien) marche en avant, comme le Militaire; il frappe les troupeaux purs (en les conduisant), comme le Militaire; il (rôde) devant, derriere les lieux, comme le Militaire: il est comme le Militaire.

' Le (chien) est actif, vigilant, pendant le tems du sommeil, comme le Laboureur (principe) de biens; il rôde devant, derriere les lieux, comme le Laboureur (principe) de biens; il rôde derriere, devant les lieux, comme le Laboureur (principe) de biens: il est comme le Laboureur.

' Comme l'oiseau, le (chien) est gai; il s'approche (de l'homme), comme l'oiseau; il se nourrit de ce qu'il peut (prendre), comme l'oiseau: il est comme l'oiseau:

' Le (chien) agit dans l'obscurité, comme le voleur; (il est exposé) à ne rien manger, comme le voleur; souvent il reçoit quelque chose de mauvais, comme le voleur: il est comme le voleur.

' Le (chien) aime à agir dans les ténebres comme la bête féroce; sa force est pendant la nuit, comme à la bête féroce; (quelquefois) il n'a rien à manger, comme la bête féroce; souvent il reçoit quelque chose de mauvais, comme la bête féroce: il est comme la bête féroce.

' Le (chien) est content, comme la femme de mauvaise vie; il se tient dans les chemins écartés, comme la femme de mauvaise vie; il se nourrit de ce qu'il peut (trouver), comme la femme de mauvaise vie: il est comme la femme de mauvaise vie.

' Le (chien) dort beaucoup, comme la jeune personne; il est brûlant & en action, comme le jeune personne; il a la langue longue, comme la jeune personne: il court en avant, comme la jeune personne.

' Tels sont les deux Chefs que je fais marcher dans les lieux, sçavoir, le chien Pesoschoroun & le chien Veschoroun. Les différens lieux que j'ai donnés ne subsisteroient pas sur la terre donnée d'Ormusd, si je n'y avois pas mis le chien Pesoschoroun ou le chien Veschoroun.

' Juste Juge, &c.

' Si le chien vient à mourir, & que sa semence reste sur la terre, (sans qu'il se soit accouplé,) que deviendra le corps (l'espece de cet animal?)

' Ormusd répondit: le monde est sur l'eau, ô Sapetman Zoroastre. Maintenant il y a dans (l'eau) deux (chiens) aquatiques; & des milliers de chiennes, des milliers de chiens (viennent) du mélange de la femelle avec le mâle. Frapper ces (chiens qui ſont) dans (l'eau), c'eſt faire ſécher tous les biens: alors ſortiront, ô Sapetman Zoroaſtre, de ce lieu, de cette Ville, ce qui eſt doux au goût, les viandes bien nourries, la ſanté, la vie longue, l'abondance, la pluie (ſource) de biens, la profuſion, ce qui croît (ſur la terre, comme) les grains, les pâturages.

'Juſte Juge, &c.

'Comment (ferai-je) revenir dans ce lieu, dans cette Ville où je ſuis, ce qui eſt doux au goût, les viandes bien nourries? Comment (y ferai-je revenir) la ſanté, la vie longue? Comment (y ferai-je revenir) l'abondance, la pluie (ſource) de biens, la profuſion? Comment (y ferai-je revenir) ce qui croît (ſur la terre, comme) les grains, les pâturages?

'Ormuſd répondit: maintenant, ô Sapetman Zoroaſtre, ce qui eſt doux au goût, les viandes bien nourries ne reviendront pas dans ce lieu, dans cette Ville; la ſanté, la vie longue n'y (reviendra) pas; l'abondance, la pluie, (ſource) de biens, la profuſion n'y (reviendra) pas; ce qui croît (ſur la terre, comme) les grains, les pâturages, n'y (reviendra) pas, à moins que l'on n'ait frappé, que l'on ne frappe actuellement celui (que aura) frappé les (chiens qui ſont) dans (l'eau), ou que l'on ne faſſe pendant trois jours & pendant trois nuits izeſchné aux ames du Monde, à l'intention de celui qui aura frappé (les chiens qui ſont) dans (l'eau). On allumera pour cela le feu, on liera le Barſom, on mettra le Hom ſur (la pierre Arvis); après cela retourneront dans ce lieu, dans cette Ville, ce qui eſt doux au goût, les viandes bien nourries; après cela la ſanté, la vie longue; après cela l'abondance, la pluie (ſource) de biens, la profuſion; après cele ce qui croît (ſur la terre, comme) les grains, les pâturages, (retournera dans ce lieu).

'L'abondance & le Beheſcht, &c.'

Having had occaſion, before his return to France, to pay a viſit to Oxford, our author was there honoured with the attention of ſeveral learned and valuable men; and we cannot but obſerve, to his diſgrace, that he has made mention of them in his book, in a ſtrain of abuſe which implies the utmoſt unworthineſs and illiberality. Never, in the courſe of our periodical toils, have we met with a work which attempts ſo groſsly to impoſe on the underſtanding of men of letters; or with an author that has ſuch a multitude of demerits.

Art. X.

Trag'dies d' Eſchyle.—The Tragedies of Æſchylus. 8vo. Paris.

THIS tranſlation has very conſiderable merit, both in point of elegance and accuracy. A ſhort account of the life of Æſchylus is prefixed to it; and in his advertiſement the tranſlator makes ſome general obſervations concerning the difference

ference between the Greek and modern tragedies in regard to morality. Some of his remarks are extremely juſt; but the ſubject well deſerves a more ample and accurate diſcuſſion than it has here met with.

ART. XI.

Tableau Hiſtorique des Gens de Lettres, &c.—A chronological and critical Abridgment of the Hiſtory of French Literature, conſidered in its different Revolutions, from its Origin to the eighteenth Century. By M. L'Abbè de Longchamps. Vols. 5th and 6th. 12mo. Paris.

WE have already * given an account of the preceding volumes of this ingenious and entertaining work, and we can with pleaſure aſſure our readers, that the continuation now before us does no leſs honour to the taſte and judgment of the Author than the preceding parts of his performance.

The hiſtory of each century is introduced with a general view of the genius and ſpirit of that century; and theſe introductory views are equally curious and inſtructive. Our Author is now arrived at the twelfth century, and we are perſuaded it will not be diſpleaſing to ſuch of our readers as are fond of literary hiſtory, to ſee a part of what he has here advanced in the introduction.

The reign of barbariſm, ſays he, yet continues; ignorance and ſuperſtition ſtill diſplay their deſpotic power; theſe cruel tyrants of the human mind are ſtill the lords of the world, and the glory of overturning their empire, of breaking their iron ſceptre, is not reſerved for the twelfth century.—The darkneſs of barbariſm, however, begins to diſperſe; the age we are going to delineate is only the dawn of a bright and glorious day; but the light it affords, though faint and glimmering, preſages the infallible return of the arts and of good taſte. Their progreſs, indeed, will be ſlow; but had Francis I. never exiſted, the ſtupidity of his predeceſſors would only have retarded the progreſs of the French genius. The impulſe is given; the human mind muſt neceſſarily awaken from its lethargy; an irreſiſtible propenſity already puſhes it forward to that point of perfection which it will only reach in the ſeventeenth century.

The predeceſſors of Lewis XIV. might, undoubtedly, by a judicious encouragement and protection of letters, have deprived him of the glory of giving the finiſhing blow to barbariſm, and have introduced the reign of light and knowledge

---

* Vid. Append. to our 38th and 40th vols. eſpecially the laſt.

ſeveral ages ſooner; but their indifference, though one of the ſcourges of literature, only ſerved to retard the revolution which was to complete its triumph. Beſides, if the princes who governed France in the twelfth century neglected to encourage men of letters, this title was at leaſt no obſtacle to their favour. The court of *Louis le Gros* was one of the moſt learned courts in Europe, and hiſtory makes mention of ſeveral men of letters whom he honoured with his confidence. It was not their learning, indeed, that procured them the good graces of their maſter; it is true, however, that he obſtructed the progreſs of literature by nothing but his indifference to it.

It was the glory of *Louis le Jeune* to chuſe his miniſters from the moſt enlightened and learned claſs of his ſubjects. The famous Abbé Suger, to whom he truſted the reins of government, aſſociated with himſelf, in his miniſtry, ſeveral other men of letters; they encouraged talents, in the name of a prince, who, for want of genius, deſpiſed them, but who loved his people ſufficiently to favour their progreſs. Their influence upon the public welfare was ſo obvious, that no prince of good diſpoſitions would have dared to proſcribe them. *Louis le Jeune*, however, cannot be ranked among the benefactors of reaſon; he was only pious and juſt; but wanted knowledge and diſcernment to be a good king. The glory of his reign belongs ſolely to thoſe great men whom fortune, rather than his choice, gave him for his miniſters.

Philip Auguſtus loved, protected, and encouraged the arts, but neither he nor thoſe whom he employed were acquainted with the true principles of them. *La metaphyſique des arts et des Sciences*, ſays our Author, *fut un ſecret pour ce prince et pour tous ceux qu'il employa. Son regne eût fait époque dans l'hiſtoire de l'eſprit humain, ſi, ſous ce regne, l'ambition de ſavoir, d'entreprendre et d'exécuter eût été ſubordonnée au beſoin des etudes preliminaires.*

The want of method, due arrangement, and harmony in all the monuments of the age of Philip, was not the only ſign of the barbariſm of his reign. It was under this monarch that poetry and muſic, ſo highly valued in every enlightened age, were proſcribed in France. That kind of inquiſition which Philip eſtabliſhed againſt the *Jongleurs* had undoubtedly a very laudable motive; he wanted to remedy the diſorders which the abuſe of this profeſſion had occaſioned: but could he have ſeen that half the crimes that are committed ariſe from ignorance and idleneſs, he would never have run the riſk of drying up the ſource of all the virtues, in order to check the irregularity and corruption of manners. For the fate of letters was at that time, in reality, in the hands of the *Troubadours*;

dours; and in every nation which is advancing towards civilization, the progrefs of virtue is always in proportion to that of literature.

This profcription, it is true, was only momentary; but the favour which the *Troubadours* regained could not entirely efface a kind of reproach which was fixed upon the cultivation of the moft fublime art by one who was efteemed a great prince. Such is the empire of Prejudice, that the anathema it pronounces againft the abufe of a profeffion remains in full force even after the reformation of thofe who exercife it. It will clearly appear, by what we fhall have occafion to obferve, that the prejudice of Philip Auguftus was founded only upon a miftake, and that the *Troubadours*, at the fame time that they made a profeffion of gallantry, diftinguifhed themfelves, at leaft externally, by the purity of their manners. Such was the decency of their behaviour, that the graveft prelates were not afhamed of affociating with them; princes themfelves looked upon the title of *Jongleur* as an honour, when they had talents fufficient to difcharge the duties annexed to it; every perfon of rank afpired after the glory of deferving it. All were ambitious, at leaft, of having the *Troubadours* in their palaces, and of exercifing the genius of thefe poets upon their favourite fubjects. Ladies, of the firft character for virtue, birth, and literature, and who prefided in the *Courts of Love*, adjudged the prizes to fuch as diftinguifhed themfelves in thefe poetical and gallant exercifes; and this obliged the poets to abftain from fuch obfcene fallies of fancy as would have fhocked the modefty of the fair prefidents. The poetical performances of this age were, accordingly, no lefs decent than ingenious, and Philip was foon convinced that one of the principal means of polifhing and civilizing a nation, is to encourage the arts *de pur agrément*. He recalled the *Jongleurs* whom he had banifhed from his dominions, and, notwithftanding the kind of difgrace which, as we have already obferved, attended this profeffion, they multiplied in all the provinces of the kingdom.

They are generally called the *Provençal* Poets; and it muft be acknowledged that *Provence*, the idiom of which they were particularly fond of, was the moft brilliant theatre of their exercifes; and, thanks to the talents of thefe poets, *Provençal* poetry became fo famous all over Europe, that foreigners, efpecially the Italians, fometimes adopted it. One needs only read the works of Dante, Petrarch, and Boccace, to be convinced that the Tufcan language, in particular, was enriched with the ideas and expreffions of our *Provençal* poets. The Emperor Frederic, after the example of the counts of *Provence*, introduced feveral *Courts of Love* into his dominions, and caufed this fpecies of poetry to be relifhed in Germany too.

It maintained its credit in Spain, under the auspices of several kings of Arragon, who cultivated and encouraged it; nor was it till toward the end of the fourteenth century, after the death of Queen Jane, countess of *Provence*, that it fell into disrepute. Till this period, the *Provençal* muses were highly favoured in every part of Europe that had any regard to literature. But not to anticipate what I have to say concerning the subsequent ages, let me proceed to shew briefly, what, in the twelfth century, was the fate of letters, considered in another point of view.

What has been said of Philip Augustus and his predecessors is sufficient to prove, that the favour they shewed to men of letters was not calculated to quicken the progress of the human mind. If some of their institutions do them honour, as being favourable to genius, posterity will still accuse them of having consulted their humour and caprice more than their judgment in the distribution of their favours. It cannot be too often repeated that this unjust predilection of some monarchs is no less prejudicial to letters than the absolute indifference of the generality of princes. The prosperity of a man of inferior and very moderate abilities is a real injury to superior and distinguished talents when neglected; the favour such a person obtains is a robbery committed upon genius; to enrich a blockhead is to empoverish a man of merit. And as respect and consideration, which all men aspire after, generally follow this kind of injustice, the superior artist, who strives to obtain them, too frequently abandons the path which ought to lead to them, and no longer looks for fame in his own art, but pursues it in the same track with the favourite, who is preferred to him.—A fatal mistake! To make a Dauber our model, and to reduce genius to the condition of a mere Copyer! We need look no farther than this for the principal cause of the decline of arts, sciences, and good taste. If the successors of Augustus had been possessed of this emperor's taste and discernment, Seneca's manner would never have prevailed at Rome;—but Cicero himself would have taken Seneca for his model, if Seneca had been the favourite of Augustus.

Another obstacle to the progress of the human mind, in the twelfth century, was the obstinate madness of the Crusades. In the preceding century, France had felt the fatal effects of these wars, but afterwards this barbarous spirit went much farther. Of the 800,000 men who composed the second Crusade, the greatest part were Frenchmen: How much this tended to depopulate the whole kingdom is obvious! On the other hand, the indulgences that were annexed to these bloody expeditions, rendered the study of morality, of the canons and discipline of the church, almost useless. Other motives, too, contributed

contributed to a neglect of the ecclefiaftical fciences. The defign of the Crufades being not to inftruct but to exterminate Muffulmen; in order to enlarge the boundaries of chriftianity, foldiers were more wanted than divines: accordingly the fchools were thinned to fwell the armies of fanaticifm, and the clergy of France had no other emulation but who fhould fhed moft Mahometan blood.

Profane literature fuffered no lefs from this furious fpirit than theology. The exorbitant taxes that were neceffary in order to fupport the Crufades, were one of the principal obftacles to the cultivation of the human mind. By diminifhing the revenues of men of letters, they were rendered incapable of purchafing thofe helps which the fineft genius cannot do without.

One of the greateft evils of the Crufades, in relation to letters, was the inftitution of the orders of chivalry, to which they gave birth. Thofe who enlifted in thefe military orders had no occafion for any previous ftudy. Parents accordingly neglected the education of their children, in hopes of making a provifion for them independent of any cultivation.

The only advantage which feemed to arife from this pious rage was, that it made the eaft the theatre of thofe wars which till now had defolated the weft; but the dreadful perfecutions that were exercifed in France againft heretics, occafioned torrents of human blood, without gaining a fingle profelyte to the truth. Herefies multiplied more than ever in all the provinces. The fect of the Albigenfes infected Aquitain, Gafcoigne, Dauphinè, Provence, and Languedoc. Inftead of enlightening the ignorance of this ftupid crew, they maffacred them; but the greateft fanatics muft grant that this method of deftroying a fect, fhewed more ferocity than knowledge, in the apoftles of the twelfth century.

The foolifh and ridiculous paffion which poffeffed feveral learned men of the ninth century, who were defirous of being acquainted with all the fciences without being mafters of any, ftill prevailed in the twelfth. The fpirit of criticifm and accurate difcuffion had given place to an eagernefs for knowing every thing without ftudying any thing. They were ftill ignorant that antiquity alone can furnifh us with models in all the different walks of literature. They were fond of fome cotemporary author, and confulted him alone upon every branch of fcience; even thofe which he himfelf was totally unacquainted with. The law to which they had fubjected themfelves, of neglecting the ancients, admitted of no exception but in favour of Ariftotle. The moft famous profeffors were afraid of altering the doctrine of this philofopher, and the dogmas of religion were lefs refpected in this age than the

the reveries of the peripatetics. The abuſe of logic produced a thouſand errors, of which ſeveral of the *Beaux Eſprits* of thoſe times were the moſt zealous apoſtles. The fooliſh rage of determining every point by nice and ſubtle queſtions and diſtinctions was principally owing to the famous Abailard. The ſuperiority of his genius induced the other cotemporary profeſſors to adopt his method of inſtruction, which led the greateſt number of his diſciples into ſcepticiſm, and occaſioned much diſorder and confuſion in the public ſchools. But this confuſion was one of the leaſt effects of the ſpirit of controverſy; it often degenerated into perſonal hatred and animoſity, and gave birth to plots and aſſaſſinations. The humbled pride of a ſcholaſtic divine was never known to forgive; and much blood was ſhed, upon more occaſions than one, becauſe an obſtinate and vindictive profeſſor was obliged, for want of a ſubtle and diſtinguiſhing head, to give up the field of battle to his adverſary.

It is eaſy to conceive what an unhappy influence this ſcholaſtic rage muſt have had upon the ſtudies of the twelfth century; but what prolonged the infancy of all the arts was the manner of teaching in thoſe days. The public maſters ſtill continued to inſtruct their diſciples *viva voce*; they gave them nothing in writing, but ſatisfied themſelves with lecturing in a haſty precipitate manner; their lectures often turned upon abſtract metaphyſical ſubjects, ſo that their pupils could ſcarce remember any part of them, and, beſides, they were obliged to pay for theſe lectures. Abailard reproached himſelf, after his converſion, with having ſold his lectures to thoſe who gave him moſt money for them; he confeſſes ingenuouſly that the art of teaching became, under his direction, a mere mercenary art. The other profeſſors were not more diſintereſted than Abailard; they not only ſold their lectures to the higheſt bidder, but when age and infirmities rendered them incapable of teaching, they ſometimes obliged their ſucceſſors to pay exorbitant ſums by way of gratuity for giving up their trade. This office, ſo noble and honourable in itſelf, was become abſolutely venal; and perhaps it is needleſs to look for any other cauſe of that kind of diſrepute under which it ſtill labours.

An intereſted and avaricious ſpirit had gained ſuch an aſcendant over all the men of letters, that the glory annexed to this title ceaſed to be the principal ſpring of their emulation. Poetry, eloquence, and the other walks of genius, were almoſt forſaken; the *Jongleurs*, and a few Chriſtian orators, were almoſt the only perſons who trod in them with any degree of confidence; and even they were not always free from the ſordid ſpirit of enriching themſelves as ſoon as they had gained any conſiderable degree of reputation. The more lucrative ſciences,

ſuch

such as jurisprudence and medicine, opened to the men of letters, of this age, an easier and much surer road to fortune. Accordingly, physicians and lawyers multiplied to such a degree, that public authority was obliged to interpose, and prohibit the monks from meddling with professions, which, thanks to their ignorance, they could not exercise without the manifest hazard of the lives and fortunes of their fellow citizens. This obliged them to apply to those studies which were better suited to the views of their institution, as a remedy against that languor which always accompanies indolence and inactivity.

The favour which ignorance and the love of gain procured to some inferior professions, and subaltern arts, occasioned literary quarrels and disputes, from which the human mind would have derived considerable advantage, had not barbarism frequently armed the authority of the magistrate against those who had both justice and learning on their side. Hence arose those literary censures, which, under pretence of checking the licentiousness of the pen, fettered genius, intimidated invention, and damped the efforts of fancy. The institution of censures, which begun in the twelfth century, produced salutary effects in after-times, both in regard to manners, religion, and laws; in their origin, however, they were only a barrier opposed by ignorance and envy to the progress of arts and sciences, and were, indeed, one of the most dreadful scourges of literature. This institution was perhaps the most active and powerful engine employed by Barbarism in those days to prolong the duration of her dark empire; and the low state to which letters were reduced at this period, was the effect of this new inquisition.

That literary ardor which, for more than a century, had distinguished France from other nations, visibly cooled towards the end of the twelfth. The generality of our historians have taken notice of the effects of this sudden change and decline of literature, without looking for the cause of it in those events which I have been mentioning, and which they have passed over in silence, or employed merely to fill up their historical gazettes, because they have nothing in them that strike the imagination. But it is upon those events which connect and give birth to revolutions, that a philosophical historian ought to fix the attention of his readers. *Ce ne sont pas des portraits isolés,* says our Author, *des scènes décousues, des volumes de tirades qui peignent la châine des siécles et des nations.*—The philosophy of history consists principally in marking distinctly the central point, the primitive source of the laws, manners, customs, virtues, and vices, of a nation. The influence which letters have

have always had upon the fate of empires, renders it the duty of an hiſtorian to take particular notice of whatever relates to their progreſs; and yet our hiſtories, in general, are far from being literary, and hence it is, in ſome meaſure, that they are neither eccleſiaſtical, civil, nor military.

After conſidering the twelfth century in relation to thoſe obſtacles which barbariſm ſtill oppoſed to the progreſs of literature, our Author proceeds to view it in thoſe comfortable lights which preſaged the infallible return of learning and knowledge. He gives a long account of the moſt celebrated ſchools and academies, together with the character of their maſters, and of ſuch of their ſcholars as made the moſt diſtinguiſhed figure; and then goes on to ſhew what attention was paid to, and what progreſs was made in, claſſical learning, criticiſm, rhetoric, logic, metaphyſics, natural philoſophy, mathematics, morality, theology, hiſtory, and the liberal arts.

He obſerves that the light which the writers of the twelfth century had diffuſed over France was much obſcured in the thirteenth; and in the introduction to his ſixth volume he points out the cauſes and the conſequences of this degeneracy. He gives a particular account of the famous quarrel between the monks and the univerſity of Paris, which was one of the principal cauſes of the darkneſs and ignorance of the thirteenth century. Theological diſputes and quarrels, however, together with the reputation in which *Provençal* poetry was held, kept up, he tells us, a kind of literary activity, and prevented that languor which is ſo fatal to letters. In ſpeaking of the *Troubadours*, he expreſſes himſelf in the following manner:

'Pendant plus de deux ſiécles qu'ills inondèrent toute l'Europe, la république des lettres eut à gemir ſur le mauvais goût qu'ill mirent en faveur, mais la langue françoiſe leur fut redevable de ſes progrès, et comme on l'a dit ailleurs, c'eſt à ces poëtes ſi mediocres pour la plupart, que nous devons le genie qui caractèriſe notreidiôme, qui le rend ſi cher aux nations étrangères, et qui luí promet dans l'avenir le plus éloignè, ce triomphe que le tems et la barbarie n'ont pu enliver aux langues immortelles de la Grèce et de Rome. Oſons le dire, ces Jongleurs ſi dédaignés de nos jours, ſout les peres de notre litterature: ce ſont eux qui ont modifiè nos mœurs, établi nos uſages, égayé nos eſprits, épuré notre galantrie, et garanti la France de cette âpretè de mœurs, que les querelles ſcholaſtiques n'auroient pas manquè de repandre ſur le gros de la nation.

Cette urbanitè qui nous diſtingue des autres peuples devint le fruit de leurs chanſons, et ſi nous ne leur devons pas nos virtus, nous

nous leur devons au moins l'art de les rendre aimables. Ce goût exquis dont nos chefs—d'œuvre sont empreints, leur fut sans doute inconnu; mais ils nous préparèrent à recevoir les impressions du beau, et leurs productions sont les seuls monumens de ce siécle où l'on retrouve quelqu' imitation de la belle nature. Cette imitation, toute imparfaite qu'elle est, plaît encore à ceux qui ont étudiè le genie de ces anciens poëtes, et l'on ne peut s'empêcher d'avouer que, rapprochès des autres Ecrivains contemporains, ils meritent la preséance qu'ils obtinrent sur les autres gens de lettres.'

We are sorry that the narrow bounds to which we are obliged to confine ourselves, will not permit us to accompany the ingenious Author any farther in his researches into this period of the Literary History of France; but we must now conclude with recommending the work before us to such readers as have a taste for this curious subject.

ART. XII.

Histoire de l' Anatomie et de la Chirurgie.—The History of Anatomy and Surgery; containing an Account of the Origin and Progress of those Sciences: With a chronological View of the principal Discoveries in them; a Catalogue of Books of Anatomy and Surgery, Academical Memoirs, Dissertations, &c. By M. Portal, Professor of Medicine and Anatomy, &c. &c. 8vo. 5 Vols. Paris.

IN a work of this kind, containing such a multiplicity of articles, and requiring long and laborious researches, it is scarce possible to avoid mistakes; accordingly the discerning Reader will find not a few in M. Portal's performance. It would be the heighth of injustice, however, not to acknowledge its great merit, and its usefulness to all those who are desirous of being acquainted with the history of anatomy and surgery.

The work is divided into two parts: the first contains the history of anatomy among the Jews, Greeks, &c. down to the celebrated Harvey: the second contains the modern history of anatomy.—M. Portal gives a short account of each celebrated anatomical writer, mentions the different editions of his works, and presents his readers with what is most remarkable in them. He is at great pains to shew, and often shews very clearly, that the moderns value themselves upon many discoveries which they have no title to, and, in this respect, *gives honour to whom honour is due.*—This subject, however, is no where so amply and satisfactorily discussed, as by the learned and ingenious Mr. Dutens, in his Inquiry into the Origin of the Discoveries attributed to the Moderns: see *Appendix* to our 35th volume, page 544, *et seq.*

ART.

Art. XIII.

Histoire des Douze Césars du Suetone, traduite par Henri Ophellot de la Pause.—The History of the Twelve Cæsars, by Suetonius, translated by Henry Ophellot De la Pause; with Philosophical Reflections on different Topics, and explanatory Notes. 8vo. 4 Vols. Paris. 1771.

THE defects of ancient authors are more frequently transfused into modern languages than their beauties. The Du Ryers and the Guthries are more numerous than the Melmoths and the Ablancourts. It almost perpetually happens that the scholar, who is minutely skilled in the languages of antiquity, has no knowledge of his own; and that the man of taste, who knows perfectly his vernacular idiom, and possesses a delicate discernment in the art of composition, has obtained but a slender acquaintance with them. These characters must be blended to produce an accomplished translator. The honours, accordingly, that are due to those who have translated with success are, by no means, contemptible. To render Polybius, or Titus Livius, with precision and eloquence, requires a degree of merit which will qualify its possessor to excel in original composition.

The Translator, whose work is now before us, is entitled to the highest praise. He seems to have perfectly understood his Author, and has very happily imitated his manner. Suetonius, though he has written with the freedom which history allowed him to exercise over tyrants, has yet displayed no traits of indignation and resentment. He aimed not at eloquence, which too frequently leads to exaggeration, and addresses itself to the passions. The perpetration of crimes, the most offensive to virtue and society, and the commission of vices, the most shocking to humanity, he records with fidelity, but with indifference. He is more attentive to instruct than to please; and, if we are sometimes surprized at his want of sensibility, we perpetually admire his candour, and his scrupulous attachment to truth. That coldness of narration, which displeases in other writers, is a merit in this Historian; and his Translator, sensible of this circumstance, has not disfigured his version, by attempting to render it pompous or affecting.

To his translation, M. Ophellot De la Pause has prefixed a life of his Author, written with spirit and elegance. In the notes which he has annexed to each book, there is much erudition, and a happy vein of conjecture; but they are somewhat deformed by an affectation of wit, and an acrimonious censure of commentators and critics. Our Translator has not always been aware that an intelligent reader would perceive, that while he laughs at Muretus, Oudendorpius, and Pitiscus, he has

has been greatly indebted to them for his materials and his learning.

At the end of each of his volumes, under the title of Mélanges Philosophiques, he has entered on the examination of many curious subjects, into which particular passages in Suetonius induced him to enquire. This he acknowledges to be the favourite part of his work; and, for this reason, our Readers will expect that we should lay before them some extracts from it.

The character of Julius Cæsar is perhaps the most distinguished and important that is presented to us in ancient times; and, on this account, it has been very much canvassed and enquired into. The subsequent portrait is drawn for him by our Translator:

'If, after the lapse, says he, of eighteen centuries, the truth may be published without offence, a philosopher might, in the following terms, censure Cæsar without calumniating him, and applaud him without exciting his blushes.

'Cæsar had one predominant passion: it was the love of glory; and he passed forty years of his life in seeking opportunities to foster and encourage it. His soul, entirely absorbed in ambition, did not open itself to other impulses. He cultivated letters; but he did not love them with enthusiasm, because he had not leisure to become the first orator of Rome. He corrupted the one half of the Roman ladies, but his heart had no concern in the fiery ardours of his senses. In the arms of Cleopatra, he thought of Pompey; and this singular man, who disdained to have a partner in the empire of the world, would have blushed to have been for one instant the slave of a woman.

'We must not imagine that Cæsar was born a warrior, as Sophocles and Milton were born poets: for if Nature had made him a citizen of Sybaris, he would have been the most voluptuous of men. If, in our days, he had been born in Pennsylvania, he would have been the most inoffensive of Quakers, and would not have disturbed the tranquillity of the new world.

'The moderation with which he conducted himself after his victories, has been highly extolled; but in this he shewed his penetration, not the goodness of his heart. Is it not obvious that the display of certain virtues is necessary to put in motion the political machine? It was requisite that he should have the appearance of clemency, if he was desirous that Rome should forgive him his victories. But what greatness of mind is there in a generosity which follows the usurpation of supreme power?

'Nature, while it marked Cæsar with a sublime character, gave him also that spirit of perseverance which renders it useful.

6

ful. He had no sooner begun to reflect, than he admired Sylla, hated him, and yet wished to imitate him. At the age of fifteen he formed the project of being Dictator. It was thus that the President Montesquieu conceived, in his early youth, the idea of his spirit of laws.

'Physical qualities, as well as moral causes, contributed to give strength to his character. Nature, which had made him for command, had given him an air of dignity. He had acquired that soft and insinuating eloquence, which is perfectly suited to seduce the vulgar, and has a powerful influence on the most cultivated minds. His love of pleasure was a merit with the fair sex; and women, who, even in a republic, can draw to them the suffrages and attention of men, have the highest importance in degenerate times. The ladies of his age were charmed with the prospect of having a Dictator, whom they might subdue by their attractions.

'In vain did the genius of Cato watch for some time to sustain the liberty of his country. It was unable to contend with that of Cæsar. Of what avail were the eloquence, the philosophhy, and the virtue of this republican, when opposed by a man who had the address to debauch the wife of every citizen whose interest he meant to engage; who, possessing an enthusiasm for glory, wept, because, at the age of thirty, he had not conquered the world like Alexander; and who, with the haughty temper of a despot, was more desirous to be the first man in a village, than the second in Rome?

'Cæsar had the good fortune to exist in times of trouble and civil commotions, when the minds of men are put into a ferment, when opportunities for great actions are frequent, when talents are every thing, and those who can only boast of their virtues, are nothing. If he had lived an hundred years sooner, he would have been no more than an obscure peasant; and, instead of giving laws to the world, would not have been able to produce any confusion in it.

'I will here be bold enough to advance an idea which may appear paradoxical to those who weakly judge of men from what they atchieve, and not from the principle which leads them to act. Nature formed in the same mould Cæsar, Mahomet, Cromwell, and Kouli Kan. They all of them united to genius that profound policy which renders it so powerful. They all of them had an evident superiority over those with whom they were surrounded; they were conscious of this superiority, and they made others conscious of it. They were all of them born subjects, and became fortunate usurpers. Had Cæsar been placed in Persia, he would have made the conquest of India; in Arabia, he would have been the founder of a new religion; in London, he would have stabbed his sovereign, or have

have procured his aſſaſſination under the ſanction of the laws. He reigned with glory over men whom he had reduced to be ſlaves; and, under one aſpect, he is to be conſidered as a hero, under another as a monſter. But it would be unfortunate, indeed, for ſociety, if the poſſeſſion of ſuperior talents gave individuals a right to trouble its repoſe. Uſurpers, accordingly, have flatterers, but no friends; ſtrangers reſpect them; their ſubjects complain and ſubmit; it is in their own families, that humanity finds her avengers. Cæſar was aſſaſſinated by his ſon, Mahomet was poiſoned by his wife, Kouli Khan was maſſacred by his nephew, and Cromwell only died in his bed, becauſe his ſon Richard was a philoſopher.

'Cæſar, the tyrant of his country, Cæſar, who deſtroyed the agents of his crimes if they failed in addreſs, Cæſar, in fine, the huſband of every wife, and the wife of every huſband, has been accounted a great man by the mob of writers. But it is only the philoſopher who knows how to mark the barrier between celebrity and greatneſs. The talents of this ſingular man, and the good fortune which conſtantly attended him till the moment of his aſſaſſination, have concealed the enormity of his actions.

'Becauſe the ſucceſſors of Cæſar adopted his name, we muſt not conclude, that they regarded him as a hero; they only conſidered him as the founder of a monarchy. This name was not the ſymbol of greatneſs of mind, but of power. The ſovereigns of Rome were afraid to aſſume the title of *King* becauſe it had too much meaning in the opinion of the people. They adopted that of Cæſar, which had no meaning, and thus the Cæſars became greater than kings.

'Beſides, the ſovereigns of Rome aſſumed the name of Auguſtus, and we cannot poſſibly imagine, that by doing ſo, they propoſed to do homage to the memory of that deteſtable prince. Could that accompliſhed philoſopher who ſucceeded Antoninus, take Octavius Cepias for the model of his conduct? What relation is there between the ſublime ſoul of a ſovereign, the diſciple of Zeno, and the atrocious mind of a tyrant, whoſe deſtructive policy had made deſpicable ſlaves of thoſe Romans whoſe fathers he butchered? Had he any occaſion for the name of Auguſtus? Had he not that of Marcus Aurelius?

'I reſpect highly genius and talents; but if a Cæſar ſhould ariſe in any of our modern republics, I would adviſe its magiſtrates to lead him to the gibbet. If ſuch a man ſhould appear in a monarchy like France, it would be prudent to confine him in the Baſtile. He ſhould receive no protection but under an abſolute government; and there he might riſe to be an excellent deſpot.'

To this extract, we shall subjoin a specimen of the short memoirs which our translator has given of the men of letters who lived under the Cæsars.

'*Agricola*, says he, one of the greatest commanders that Rome has produced, conquered Great Britain, and gave laws to it. We have lost the journal which he wrote of his voyage round this island; but we have still one of his harangues, from which we may form a judgement of his eloquence *. But, to give a complete eulogium of this great man, it is only necessary to remark, that he was the father-in-law of Tacitus, the friend of Pliny, and fell by the arts of Domitian, who envied his virtues. He was poisoned in the fifty-sixth year of his age, and in the ninety-third of the Christian æra.

'*Arulenus Rusticus*, an excellent citizen, neither flattered tyrants, nor conspired against them. He was condemned to die by Domitian, because he had written the life of Thrasea, a hero, and a martyr to liberty. His book also was ordered to be burnt:' "And in the fire which was kindled to consume it, it was intended, says Tacitus, that the voice of the Roman people, the liberty of the senate, and the consciousness of mankind, should perish †."

'*Cicero* was one of the greatest men that ever existed; if the union of great talents and virtues give a claim to that appellation. His orations have perhaps been too much commended: Our enthusiasm ought to have been reserved for his philosophical works, though the chief lesson they teach is to doubt. He was assassinated forty-three years before Christ, by Popilius Lenas, whose life he had saved some time before: he was then sixty-three years of age.

'*Cornutus* (*Annæus*) wrote discourses on the philosophy of the Greeks, and commentaries on Virgil; but these works have not descended to us. This Author had Lucan and Persius for his disciples; and Nero sent him into exile because the misfortunes of those respectable poets had not deterred him from honouring their memory.

'*Cremutius Cordus*, composed annals of Roman history, and was admired by Tacitus, who, notwithstanding, has written annals. The cruel Tiberius put him to death because he had praised Brutus, and because he had observed, that Cassius was the last of the Romans.

---

* Our translator here alludes to the speech which Agricola pronounced to his soldiers before he gave battle to Galgacus. But the merit of this speech, we suspect, belongs more properly to the historian in whose work it appears, than to the general.

† *Scilicet in illo igne vocem populi Romani & libertatem senatus & conscientiam generis humani aboleri arbitrabantur.* Vit. Agr.

'*Dionysius*

'*Dionysius of Halicarnassus*, a celebrated historian of the Augustan age. He composed in Greek his Roman antiquities, which originally consisted of twenty books; but only eleven of these have come down to us. Is it not singular, that we have lost so much of the writings of Dionysius of Halicarnassus, Titus Livius, and Tacitus, and that we have yet entire such wretched works as the Noctes Atticæ of Aulus Gellius?

'*Diodorus Siculus*, a famous Greek historian, who flourished under Augustus. He employed thirty years in composing the forty books of his Universal History. Of these there remain only fifteen. His authority was very great with the ancients, and is so to this day, except in those places where he talks of prodigies.

'*Dydimus*, a celebrated critic of Alexandria, who lived in the Augustan age. Seneca says, that he composed four thousand treatises on different subjects; a circumstance, however, which is less astonishing than that Lopez de Vega, a writer of the last age, should have composed a thousand pieces for the stage. It has also been observed of this indefatigable critic, that he wrote annotations on Homer.

'*Epictetus*, the most illustrious disciple of the school of Zeno, which produced so many heroes and philosophers. He was born at Hierapolis in Phrygia, lived in slavery, and was comprized in the tyrannical ordinance of Domitian, which banished the philosophers from Italy. His manual, with the offices of Cicero, and the reflexions of Marcus Aurelius, are the finest moral pieces of antiquity. This sage was not the founder of a sect, yet his name, during several ages, has been pronounced with veneration. History has recorded, that a philosopher, in the age of Lucian, purchased, at a great price, an earthen lamp, which had belonged to Epictetus; but we cannot buy the genius of a great man as we can do an utensil that he had possessed.

'*Frontinus*, an author famous for his capacity, and the offices he enjoyed. He was named to the consulship by Vespasian, and made governor of Britain. His works relate to military stratagems, and the aqueducts of Rome. He was versant in Tacitus as well as Polybius; as was our chevalier Folard. He died about the end of the first century.

'*Manilius*, a poet and mathematician, who lived under Augustus, composed in verse a treatise on astronomy, of which we have only five books, which treat of the fixed stars. Natural philosophers have despised his discoveries, and poets his verses.

'*Mæcenas*, the minister of Augustus, whose name is become proverbial to express the protectors of men of letters, composed several works in verse and in prose, which his panegyrists were unable to transmit to posterity. The softness of his manners passed into his style. It was smooth, and even elegant, but it discovered not that genius which gives immortality to books and to Authors. Mæcenas died eight years before the birth of Christ. It is to be observed of him, that he never sullied his power by committing acts of oppression; and it is somewhat remarkable, that every minister who has encouraged literature has been gentle and humane in his manners.

'*Pliny the elder*, one of the finest geniuses that the world has to boast of, was born at Verona ann. 23. He wrote upon all sorts of subjects, and always with success. His life of the tragic poet Pomponius Secundus, his treatise on rhetoric, his annals, and his history of the German wars, have been much extolled. We are only acquainted with his natural history, an admirable monument of his knowledge, and which appears to be the fruit of twenty years labour. He died ann. 79, by approaching with too much curiosity to examine an eruption of mount Vesuvius.'

It only remains for us to observe, that M. Ophellot de la Pause appears, in our opinion, to be more respectable as a translator than as a philosopher. In the latter character, he is too fond of paradoxes, and mistakes vivacity for penetration.

ART. XIV.

Vera Christiana Religio: continens universam Theologiam novæ Ecclesiæ a Domino apud Danielem, cap. vii. 13, 14. *et in Apocalypsi*. cap. xxi. 1, 2. *prædictæ*.—The true Christian Religion: containing the whole Theology of the *New Church*, &c. By Emanuel Swedenborg, a Servant of the Lord Jesus Christ. 4to. Amsterdam, 1771.

IN our Review for June, 1770, we gave an account of a small quarto volume, containing some of Baron Swedenborg's lucubrations; and which was probably intended as an introduction to farther publications of the same kind. In that work, we had some information concerning the family, rank, and office, as also of the peculiar turn and disposition of this extraordinary person. The present much larger performance, containing upwards of 500 pages, presents us with the same enthusiastic reveries, and unaccountable sallies of imagination, of which a specimen was given in the book above-mentioned. We observe in it the marks of natural good sense and ingenuity, as well as of application and learning; but intermixed with so much mysticism, and farther accompanied with such astonishing accounts of what the Author has seen and heard when he was admitted to converse with angels and spirits in the invisible world, that, though his relations are delivered in a plausible a plausible and coherent manner, it is impossible not to conclude that they are the productions of a disordered brain. We meet continually with these *memorabilia*, as they are called, which, it might have been supposed, were only intended as a kind of allegories to diversify his work, and by this means to amuse and more strongly to impress his readers: but he asserts with the greatest coolness and confidence that he has frequently been admitted, during the last twenty-seven years of his life, into the *unseen worlds*, and that the accounts he gives are not chimeras or inventions, but founded on what he has truly seen and heard; and this not in a kind of dream or vision, but when he was fully awake.

The baron has conceived some notion of a great alteration which took place in the spiritual world in the year 1757, when, if we understand him right, the *New Church*, or *Nova Hierosolyma*, as he elsewhere calls it, began to be erected, and the last judgment (*ultimum judicium*) was held in the world of spirits, which, says he, I do attest, because, when I was broad awake, I beheld it with mine own eyes. He tells us that all that is said in the scriptures concerning a new heaven and a new earth, and the second advent of Christ, is to be explained and understood, not literally, but in a spiritual manner.

The doctrine and practice of this new church, of which our Author seems to consider himself as a special messenger, are laid before us in this volume. We observe, that he strenuously asserts the unity of the Deity, although he acknowledges a Trinity; but, at the same time, declares, that this Trinity *was not* till the appearance of Christ, when the Supreme God united himself to the man Christ Jesus. He contends that a trinity *of persons* was not the primitive faith of the church, and that, by the Nicene and Athanasian trinity, the whole Christian church has been perverted. He is a warm advocate for charity and good works, he abhors the notion that faith alone is requisite to salvation, and speaks of the doctrine of predestination as detestable.

His account of the decalogue, of which he gives what he calls the natural, spiritual and celestial meaning, is very imperfect, as the second commandment is omitted, and the tenth divided into two, to form the ninth and tenth: This we have heard has been done in the church of Rome, but we apprehend has not been the practice in Protestant churches.

Concerning the spiritual world which Baron Swedenborg has so frequently visited, he tells us that there are in it lands, plains and vallies, mountains and hills, as in our earth; that there are also fountains and rivers, gardens, groves and woods, houses, palaces and cities, writings, books, offices and employments, gold, silver, precious stones, &c. as there are also

in

in ours; but that all these things are created in an instant according to the ideas and affections which arise among the angels and spirits who inhabit those regions. In the different visits this writer has paid to them, he has conversed, we are told, with many persons of every rank and of all nations and countries. In the close of the present work, he gives a short account of the situation allotted to the inhabitants of different countries or religious professions, and to some of the more remarkable individuals among them. Possibly the curiosity of some of our readers may be excited to hear what is the state of our own countrymen according to the relation of this noble visionary; but we doubt whether the view of it will contribute much either to their edification or amusement. However, we may briefly remark, that he allots a station to the worthier part of the English people in the centre of all the Christian world, for which he assigns as a reason, the share they have of what he calls the *intellectual light*, which, he says, they derive from the freedom of speaking, writing, and thinking, which prevails among them. He says, that they have a great similitude of mind, that they form friendship among themselves, but rarely with those of other countries; that they are very sincere, very ready to assist each other, and still fond of their country, and zealous for its glory. We are farther informed, that there are two large cities, resembling London, into which the greater part of the English, after death, are received; that the chief (*priorem*) of these cities, he has been allowed to see and to walk in; that the middle part of the city, answering to that which in London is called the Exchange, is inhabited by persons denominated moderators; that the eastern quarter is possessed by those who have been eminent for leading a life of charity, and here are magnificent palaces; that in the southern quarter dwell the wise men, (*sapientes*) in which also are splendid buildings; that the northern quarter is inhabited by such who above others indulged a freedom of speaking and thinking; and the western by those who insist upon justification by faith alone. As our Author discovers a particular dislike to those who hold the opinion last mentioned, we should not have been greatly surprized if he had allotted them their place in the other city, which is differently situated and appointed for the reception of those of the English who are internally bad; in the midst of this latter city there is an open communication with the infernal prisons, by which they are in their turns swallowed up.

The state of the first reformers from popery is particularly related: Poor Calvin appears to have but a very uncomfortable situation according to this writer's account; for, after other disagreeable circumstances, the last thing we read is, that he

was

was shut up in a cave destined for the predestinarians, who are doomed to hard labour, and whose pleasure it is to do some injury to each other.

The impostor Mahomet, we are told, did at first preside among his followers in the world of spirits, but as he discovered a proud domineering disposition, he was hurled from his seat, and very seldom afterwards seen, unless when some warm altercation arose concerning him among those who had been his adherents; at such a time, he is just produced to view, faintly saying, 'I am Mahomet,' and then vanishes. On one of these occasions, this Author tells us, he beheld him; when he appeared like *those corporeal spirits who have no interior perception*, his face verging towards blackness: and he just uttered the words above-mentioned.

Although this remarkable production abounds with such amazing conceits and extravagancies, it must be regarded as a curiosity of enthusiasm, and may afford some entertainment to those who understand Latin, and have leisure for the perusal of so large a volume.

ART. XV.

Histoire de l'Aacademie Royale des Inscriptions et Belles Lettres, &c.— The History of the Royal Academy of Inscriptions and Belles Lettres, from the Year 1764 to the Year 1766 inclusive. Vol. XXXIV, XXXV. 4to. Paris, 1770.

IN announcing the appearance of these volumes, which contain a great variety of articles, many of which are both entertaining and instructive, we are obliged, by the very nature of our plan, to confine ourselves to a general view of their contents: were we to enlarge, and give a full and distinct view of them, they would alone furnish matter for several numbers of our Appendix.

The *historical* part of the thirty-fourth volume is introduced with some remarks on the text of Xenophon's Cyropædia. M. Bejot, the Author of the remarks, seems to be well acquainted with Xenophon's works, and is happy in most of the corrections which he proposes; they are, indeed, very much in the style and manner of his Author, who, for purity, perspicuity, and elegant simplicity, is certainly equal, if not superior, to any other of the Greek writers:—his works being justly numbered among the most valuable remains of antiquity.

The corrections which M. Bejot proposes are not supported by the authority of manuscripts; he only consulted those of the French king's library, which were of very little use to him; in order to correct the text of his Author, he had recourse to the text itself, and his observations may be useful

ful to the critical reader, and to those who may undertake a new edition of Xenophon's works.

Mr. Bejot's remarks are followed by a short extract from a *memoir* of the late Count Caylus concerning the temples of ancient Greece.—The ceremonies of Greece and Rome, in general, are presented to our view *sous l'aspect le plus riant*. The elegant architecture of their temples, the master-pieces of sculpture upon their altars, the flowers which adorn the heads of their priests and priestesses, the beautiful whiteness of their garments, the musicians, in a word, the whole apparatus of their sacrifices, embellishes the pictures of our modern artists, and makes the most agreeable impressions upon our minds. The charms of ancient poetry, which celebrates this religious pomp with so much harmony, add to the enchantment. But all this splendour, all this magnificence is viewed through the medium of a long series of ages; the distance of the objects prevents our seeing what was disgreeable and disgusting in them. Count Caylus dissipates part of this illusion; he introduces us into the temples themselves, and points out to us some of the spots and stains which sullied the splendour of superstition. He mentions several altars that were composed of the ashes of their victims, the disagreeable exhalations from the bloody sacrifices, and other circumstances of the like nature. The custom of washing the statues, which superstition covered with a mystic veil, and converted into a ceremony of expiation, was owing, he observes, to the inconveniencies arising from the vapours of the sacrifices, as was likewise the custom of cloathing the statues, several instances of which practice he mentions from Pausanias.

We are also presented with a few observations of Count Caylus upon an ancient marble statue of Minerva, found at Rome during the embassy of Cardinal Polignac. The observations are not very interesting, and relate chiefly to the particular species of marble of which the statue is made. The statue itself, we are told, has nothing remarkable in it in point of workmanship, and is *d'un très-mauvais goût*.

We have next some remarks by M. le Beau *Jun.* upon the Greek romances. Those frivolous tales, though not worthy of much serious attention, may however be read with a degree of advantage, as they contain some remarkable facts, some peculiar usages, which throw light upon the arts and sciences of the ancients. M. le Beau, we are told, intended to give a pretty large work upon this subject, but was prevented by death.

Under the title of romance, he comprehends every ingenious or whimsical fiction, for the purpose of amusement, and tells us that there are only three works of this kind to be found among

among the Greeks before Lucian; *viz.* the Milesian fables of Aristides, the amorous tales of Parthenius of Nicæa, and the metamorphoses of Lucius of Patræ. The first and the last of these works are lost; and, as the tales of Parthenius are far from being interesting, M. le Beau only mentions a few particulars concerning the Authors and their productions.

Miletus, a city of Ionia, was famous for its commerce and its colonies, and no less for the effeminancy of its inhabitants. Every thing had the appearance of love and gallantry; and here it was that those romances, called *Milesian fables*, took their rise; they were imaginary adventures that had love for their object. The person who distinguished himself most in this species of composition was Aristides, who wrote a history of Persia, and another of Sicily, mentioned by Plutarch. When he lived is uncertain; he must have written, however, before Crassus, who was killed in the war against the Parthians, fifty-three years before the Christian æra. Plutarch relates, that Surenas, who conquered Crassus, ordered the Milesian fables of Aristides, which were found in the baggage of a Roman officer, to be brought into the senate of Seleucia, and took occasion from thence to treat the Romans with great contempt, since, even in the midst of arms, they amused themselves with lascivious and obscene writings; for such was the character of these fables, as appears by all antiquity.

Parthenius of Nicæa, in Bithynia, acquired some degree of reputation by his poems, and particularly by his elegies, which were hymns in honour of the Gods, like those of Callimachus. This taste for elegiac hymns, which appears to have had its rise under the Ptolemies, continued long in Greece. Amongst the great number of authors quoted by Parthenius in his amorous tales, and who lived, almost all of them, under the Ptolemies, several are mentioned as writers of elegiac hymns.

Parthenius was cotemporary with Cornelius Gallus, to whom he dedicates his amorous adventures, and it must be acknowledged that he could not have chosen a fitter patron for such a work. But, as M. le Beau observes, there is reason to doubt whether a poet so full of warmth and fire as Gallus could possibly be pleased with the frigid and meagre style of Parthenius, who merely relates facts, without sentiment or embellishment.

The metamorphoses of Lucius of Patræ are only known to us by the testimony of Photius. This learned critic informs us, that he was cotemporary with Lucian, and that the metamorphoses of the former had so much resemblance to the golden ass of the latter, that it could not be determined which of the two had copied the other; he is of opinion, however, that Lucius is the original, and says that Lucian seems to make use of

the

the absurdities of Lucius, in order to turn superstition and Lucius himself into ridicule.

M. le Beau makes a few remarks upon Lucian's *ass*, but they contain little if any thing that is new; he then proceeds to make some observations on Apuleius's golden ass, and some other Greek romances; and concludes with a short account of the authors mentioned by Parthenius. Those who are fond of this kind of erudition will find many particulars which M. le Beau has collected from Strabo, Athenæus, and Suidas, which are not to be found in Vossius or Fabricius.

M. le Beau's observations are followed by a *Memoir* of M. de Burigny, which contains an account of what the writers before the times of Constantine have said concerning the ancient history of India. Such readers as have neither time nor inclination to consult ancient writers, will find, within a narrow compass, a distinct view of what they have said upon a curious subject, together with some pertinent remarks.

This *Memoir* is followed by some reflections of M. de Burigny, on a passage in Plautus, relating to the history of Sicily. One does not expect to find in the poets any important historical facts, that are omitted by the historians; there are, however, some instances of this kind, and the following passage in Plautus is a rem. :kable one:

Non ego novi Menæchmum Moscho prognatum Patre!
Qui Syracusis perhibere natus esse in Sicilia,
Ubi rex Agathocles regnator fuit et iterum Pinthia,
Tertiùm Liparo, qui in morte regnum Hieroni tradidit;
Nunc Hiero est. Menech. act ii. scene iii. v. 56.

Now the kings Agathocles and Hiero are well known; the tyranny of the one, and the wise government of the other, are distinctly related by Diodorus, Justin, Polybius, and Livy, but no mention is made by the historians of Pinthias and Liparo. There was a tyrant indeed named Pinthias, who reigned at Agrigentum, but the Phintias mentioned by Plautus was prince of Syracuse. It would be absurd to suppose that Plautus was mistaken; when he wrote, Sicily was well known to the Romans, and the intercourse between Rome and Syracuse was too great to admit of such a supposition, especially as Plautus and Hiero were cotemporary. What he advances, therefore, in the passage referred to, was publicly and certainly known to the Romans, and there is no reason to doubt of the truth of it. M. de Burigny acknowledges, that he did not recollect this passage when he wrote his history of Sicily; he is of opinion that Pinthias and Liparo governed Syracuse after Pyrrhus left Sicily.

It is the duty of men of letters to celebrate those who have distinguished themselves as friends to learning and science, and

is,

if, through the injuries of time, they have sunk into oblivion, justice and gratitude require, that they should be restored to that renown which they merited. M. Valerius Messala, the friend of Augustus, is entitled to this kind of gratitude; accordingly, M. de Burigny, in a memoir which immediately follows his reflections upon the passage of Plautus, collects all the testimonies of antiquity in his favour.

*** We are sorry that our present limits will not allow us to proceed any farther, at this time, with these *Memoirs*; the *continuation* of which we must, therefore, postpone to a future opportunity.

Art. XVI.

Vie du Cardinal D'Ossat.—The Life of Cardinal D'Ossat. 8vo. 2 Vols. Paris, 1771.

THE Cardinal D'Ossat rose from a low origin to the highest honours *. The possession of rare and useful talents supplied to him the defects of his birth. His knowledge of mankind, his penetration, and his extensive views, admirably qualified him for the scenes in which he acted; and when we consider his importance and merits, we cannot avoid expressing our surprize that the public should have waited so long in the expectation of having a minute and regular history of his life. For, with regard to the memoirs which Amelot de la Houssaye has prefixed to his edition of the letters of this great man, it may be remarked, that they are extremely vague and imperfect.

In the present publication, the actions and behaviour of Cardinal D'Ossat are exhibited in a very circumstantial detail. The Author has endeavoured solely to be useful, and, for that reason, has disregarded elegance, and the graces of composition. His account of one negociation he concludes before he enters upon another; and he has therefore neglected the order of time. But by this method he has guarded against confusion and embarrassment, and has rendered his narration the more interesting. He has laid open the progress of events, of which, in general history, it is esteemed sufficient to mark the bare occurrence; and while he unfolds the secret springs and œconomy of transactions, he offers many valuable lessons of political wisdom.

Let us confess, however, that, in our opinion, his admiration of the Cardinal is excessive. He considers him, in every respect, as a perfect character. His sagacity and discernment, we can readily allow; nor have we the least doubt but that he

---

* In the time of Henry IV.

prepared

prepared for action by deep meditation and ſtudy. It appears to us alſo ſufficiently obvious, that he was intimately acquainted with the intereſts of the different powers of Europe, with the treaties into which they had entered, with the characters of its particular nations, their laws, and the nature of their governments. Thus far, we can go with our biographer. But, when he dwells on the probity and the piety of the Cardinal, we feel an inclination to be ſomewhat ſceptical. Is it poſſible that this prelate could have a capital concern in the ſophiſtry of high and public life, and not infringe on the ſtrict rules of morality and religion? The air of ſanctity he aſſumed was, doubtleſs, equivocal; and, perhaps, there is a duplicity of conduct which is equally inſeparable from the ſtateſman and the eccleſiaſtic.

This Author has likewiſe attempted to prove, that the Cardinal was devoid of ambition; and, by his manner of doing ſo, he very prepoſterouſly inſinuates, that ambition ought to be conſidered as a crime. But, if the Cardinal was actuated by no motives of ambition, for what end did he aſpire after dignities and honours? Why did he enter on the career of glory and of fortune, if his mind was bent on inaction, and the indolent gratifications of a private ſtation?

From theſe circumſtances, and from others which might be collected if it were neceſſary, we may conclude, that this life of Cardinal D'Oſſat is written with extreme partiality. Our candour, at the ſame time, obliges us to obſerve, that, from the many curious particulars it contains, it ought to be accounted a valuable acceſſion to modern hiſtory.

Art. XVII.

Lettre de Brutus, ſur les Chars anciens et modernes.—The Letter of Brutus concerning ancient and modern Chariots. 8vo. 1771.

THE humanity of the Author of this performance, affected with the number of accidents occaſioned by carriages, has induced him to declaim againſt the uſe of them. But, while he paints with much pathetic lamentation the unfortunate condition of the poor man who walks on foot, and endeavours to throw into ridicule, and to laſh the indolence and cruelty of the rich man, who cannot croſs a ſtreet but in his chariot, and who values leſs than his horſes the lower claſſes of mortals; he ſhould have known, that luxury and indulgences of every kind are abſolutely inſeparable from cultivated and refined nations. To repreſs by laws the magnificence and expence of individuals, is to repreſs the trade and the grandeur of a kingdom. The equality of condition which he affects to admire in the citizens of Sparta, can only prevail in a ſmall republic; and he he ſhould not have forgot, that it was the conſequences of inſtitutions which kept them in an unnatural ſituation, that marked out to each of them an equality of property, deprived them of every ſpur to induſtry, confined their powers and faculties, and made them ſtrangers to almoſt every pleaſure and gratification.

Projects, which appear very plauſible in theory, are often moſt abſurd in practice. Recluſe and good-natured men, who judge of human affairs without having any experience of them, are too ready to imagine, that the manners of a people may be modelled into a ſtate of perfection; and they are too apt, from a ſpirit of miſtaken patriotiſm, to communicate their dreams and viſions to the public. Theſe Utopian and ſublime theoriſts never conſider, that vices are no leſs natural to mankind than virtues; that little evils muſt ſometimes be encouraged to prevent the riſe of great ones; and that the laws and ordinances of kingdoms muſt perpetually have a reference to the bad as well as the good diſpoſitions of men.

Though we cannot commend the political ſagacity of this writer, who would humble the pride of the rich by forcing them to make uſe of their limbs, we muſt, however, obſerve, that in his whimſical publication there are many ſtrokes of real eloquence, and ſeveral reſearches which indicate an extenſive erudition. His inquiries and obſervations concerning the antiquity and the forms of carriages in different nations may ſuggeſt ſome valuable remarks to an author who has fewer prejudices and more penetration.

ART. XVIII.

Hiſtoire naturelle de Pline.—The natural Hiſtory of Pliny: tranſlated into French, with critical Notes; and Remarks on the Knowledge of the Ancients, and the Diſcoveries of the Moderns. 4to. Vols. * I. II. III. Paris, 1771.

FEW of the monuments of ability and induſtry that have deſcended to us from ancient times are ſo valuable as the natural hiſtory of Pliny. The immenſe variety of his details, his wonderful erudition and the advantages reſulting from his manner, which diſpoſed him rather to collect and to deſcribe, than to make general reaſonings and obſervations, render it, in the higheſt degree, inſtructive and entertaining. But in an Author of ſuch extenſive genius we are ſorry to perceive ſo many ſtrokes of ſuperſtition, and ſuch a multitude of fables. The tranſlation † of his hiſtory, now before us, ſo far as it goes.

---

* Theſe 3 vols. comprehend the firſt 9 books of Pliny.

† The *original* Latin is given with the French tranſlation.

goes, is faithful and exact, and, in the notes which accompany it, there is learning, good-ſenſe, and philoſophy. Men of letters will expect the ſequel of it with impatience.

ART. XIX.

Eſſais de Poeſies, &c.—Poetical Eſſays. By Mr. D. P. 8vo. Paris. 1771.

IN this collection are free tranſlations or imitations of ſeveral of the odes of Horace: An Author who has the merit of beauties ſo peculiar, that they could never be transfuſed into any modern language; who has ſo often been tranſlated, and ſo ſeldom underſtood. This muſt extenuate the diſgrace which the Author of theſe poems may apprehend from his want of ſucceſs.

Ad PYRRHAM.
Lib. I. Ode V.

Quis multa gracilis te puer in roſa
Perfuſus liquidis urget odoribus
Grato, Phyrra, ſub antro?
Cui flavam religas comam.
Simplex munditiis? Heu, quoties fidem,
Mutatoſque Deos flebit!

TRANSLATION.

Quel eſt, Phyrra, cet Adonis ambré
Qui, dans cet antre aux amours conſacrè,
Sur un lit parſemé de roſes,
Preſſe, d'un doux baiſer ſes livres demi cloſés?
Pour qui tes belles mains ont-elles preparè
De tes cheveux le charmant edifice,
Et ce vetement azurê
Dont la ſimplicité deguiſe l'artifice?
Ah! quel que ſoit cet amant adoré,
Qu'il ſera confondu! &c.

Simplex munditiis, the Reader will perceive is not tranſlated; and it is, indeed, difficult to tranſlate; but all who have attempted this Ode have overlooked the contraſt between *ſimplex*, and the *fidem mutatam* that follows, by which a conſiderable advantage is loſt.

'Simple in ornament but not in heart,' is apparently the idea which the poet means to convey.

On account of ſome obſervations of this kind, which we have to ſubjoin, we ſhall preſent our Readers with the Ode to the courtezan Barine, ſo celebrated for its ſpirit and elegance, together with the French tranſlation, and an Engliſh one from a MS. in our poſſeſſion.

Lib.

Lib II. Ode VIII.

Ad Barinen.

Ulla si juris tibi pejerati
Pœna, Barine, nocuisset unquam,
Dente si nigro fieres, vel uno
Turpior ungui,

Crederem : sed tu, simul obligasti
Perfidum votis caput, enitescis
Pulchrior multo, juvenumque prodis
Publica cura.

Expedit matris cineres opertos
Fallere, et toto taciturna noctis
Signa cum cœlo, gelidaque divos
Morte carentes.

Ridet hoc, inquam, Venus ipsa, rident
Simplices Nymphæ, ferus et Cupido
Semper ardentes acuens sagittas
Cote cruenta.

Adde quod pubes tibi crescit omnis :
Servitus crescit nova, nec priores
Impiæ tectum dominæ relinquunt,
Sæpe minati.

Te suis matres metuunt juvencis,
Te senes parci, miseræque nuper
Virgines nuptæ, tua ne retardet
Aura maritos.

A Barine.

Si, lorsque ta bouche infidelle
Prodigue tant de faux sermens
Tu devenois un peu moins belle
Ou tu perdois quelques amans.
Barine, si lorsque tu mens
Tes attraits en portoient la peine,
Quel cœur gemiroit dans ta chaîne ?
Que deviendroit tes agrémens ?
Mais de tes levres un parjure
A peine s'est il echappé,
Que des attraits de ta figure
On est encore plus frappé,
Et, que, par la même imposture
Chacun voudroit être trompé,
Qu'il te sied bien, d'être perfide,
De violer les noms sacres,
Des fleuves ou Pluton preside,
Et des dieux le plus révéré !

A te parjurer tout conspire;
Venus elle meme en sourit;
La troupes de nymphes l'admire;
Le cruel amour l'applaudit.
L'amour dont les mains menaçantes,
Aiguisent ses flèches ardentes
Sur un grés que le sang rougit.
Dans ses yeux la joie etincelle;
Chaque infidelité nouvelle
Te donne des nouveaux amans
Te soumet tout, te rend plus belle
Et dans tes fers souvent rappelle
Ceux qu' eloignoient tes faux sermens.
Ton luxe, tes mœurs, et tes charmes;
Causent des terrible alarmes,
Aux parens des enfans chéris.
Tu fais trembler, tu rends jalouses,
Les jeunes et tendres epouses.
Dont tu regardes les maris.

To Barine.

Barine, on thy perjured head
Had any god his vengeance shed,
Or, punish'd in a tooth or nail,
Hadst thou but found one lover fail,
The gods, I'd own, might heedful be,
And trust in them, though not in thee.

But thou no sooner art forsworn
Than sweeter smiles thy mouth adorn,
No sooner breath'd thy faithless vows,
Than lower every lover bows.

Attest thy mother's injur'd ghost,
And night's serene and silent host,
And heaven, and all th' immortal train;
For perjury to thee is gain.

To Venus these are things of joy,
The simple nymphs, and savage boy.
The blood stone whets his fatal darts,
Unheedful he of faithless hearts.

Hence thine are slaves of each degree;
The beardless youth but grows for thee.
While, weary of thy wicked reign,
Thy veterans curse, yet keep their chain.

By thy delusive arts undone,
The matron's fear foresees her son.
Thee sparing Age beholds with care
The syren of his thriftless heir:
And, conscious of thy conquering eyes,
The young bride thinks of thee and sighs.

The French Tranſlator has given no interpretation of the word *crederem*, at the beginning of the ſecond ſtanza. Dacier interprets it *Je vous croirois*, I would believe you. But we do not ſee how the viſible puniſhment of Barine for perfidy ſhould become an inducement for the poet's confidence in her. We take CREDEREM here to be a religious term, by which Horace ſignifies, that if he had ſuch proofs of the divine interpoſition, he would, contrary to his Epicurean principles, believe in the moral agency of Providence. The firſt line in the fourth ſtanza ſtrongly confirms this:

Ridet hoc, inquam, Venus ipſa, &c.

'But, *I ſay*, that the gods only laugh at theſe matters.'

There is another expreſſion in this Ode, the beauty of which does not ſeem to be generally, or indeed at all, underſtood: that is the *cote cruentâ*. The following paſſage will explain it: *Optimæ autem cotes*, colore ſanguinem referentes, *interioribus Calabriæ partibus maximé reperiuntur.*

Aul. Gell. ap. Comm. Plin. Nat. Hiſt.

ART. XX.

Opuſcules de Feu M. Rollin, &c.—Miſcellaneous Pieces by the late Mr. Rollin, Rector of the Univerſity of Paris, &c. 12mo. 2 Vols. Paris. 1771.

THE celebrated Mr. Rollin, beſide thoſe more important works that have ſo well eſtabliſhed his reputation in the world of letters, wrote many poetical and rhetorical pieces, which, though they were applauded in the circle of private friendſhip, he never thought of conſequence enough to deſerve the attention of the public. But ſome years after * his much lamented death, both the good and the bad effects of his ſingular virtue diſappeared. The Univerſity, over which he preſided, loſt the powerful and animating example of literary induſtry, but the world had the advantage of thoſe valuable, though not large, remains which his peculiar modeſty concealed.

Theſe two volumes conſiſt of letters between the Author and his friends, orations, diſſertations, charges, and poems. Crevier was left in poſſeſſion of the manuſcripts, and planned that order of publication in which they now appear; but he lived not to execute the plan he had formed; and his own long and uſeful labours may be conſidered as no inſufficient apology.

The letters that are found in theſe volumes have not, indeed, much more to recommend them than that grateful affection we naturally entertain for every thing that falls from the pens of renowned men. The mutual compliments that paſſed be-

* It is extraordinary that it ſhould be almoſt 30 years after his death when the poſthumous works of this great man firſt appeared.

tween Mr. Rollin and the present King of Prussia, and the correspondence on private business between the former and Mr. Rousseau are of that kind.

The style of the orations is much inferior, in strength of genius, to that of the younger Pliny; much inferior in precision and terseness to the language of Quintilian; but it is better than the language of the Provencial writers, and much superior (though it is hardly a compliment so to say) to our college-hall Latin in general.

ART. XXI.

Bibliotheca Medicinæ & Historiæ Naturalis. Tom. I.—*Continens Bibliothecam Botanicam qua Scripta ad rem Herbariam facientia a rerum primordia ad* Tournefortium *recensentur*, Auctore Alberto Von Holler, 4to. Part I. Heydinger, London. 1771.

WE have not yet had time to peruse this valuable body of physic and natural history, (of which only the first part, containing the review of botanical writers, down to Tournefort, is yet published) but our Readers may expect an account of it from us very soon.

ART. XXII.

Recueil d'Antiquités dans les Gaules.—A Collection of Antiquities in Gaul, enriched with Plates, Figures, &c. Being a Continuation of the Antiquities of the late M. De Caylus. By M. De la Sauvagere, Knight of the Royal and Military Order of St. Louis, &c. 4to. Paris.

THE monuments which the Romans left behind them in Gaul, form the subject of this work; and its Author, in describing them, discovers uncommon exactness and erudition. But to what purpose, it may be asked, has he employed so much care and time in exhibiting the remains of a distant age? No reasonings are made from them with regard to arts, manners, or science. The department in the republic of letters, the most ridiculous and frivolous, is that surely, which is filled by the mere Antiquary. He weeps over ruins, which other men behold with indifference; and hastens to perpetuate them in books which attract no curiosity, and are never mentioned but to be condemned. "What benefit is society to reap from my labours?" If our author had put this question to himself, the world would not have been troubled with his industrious but useless researches.

INDEX

INDEX

To the REMARKABLE PASSAGES in this VOLUME.

N. B. *To find any particular* Book, *or* Pamphlet, *see the* Table of Contents, *prefixed to the Volume.*

INDEX.

F

INDEX.

INDIANS

NATURE,

INDEX.

SOCIETIES,

END OF VOL. XLV.

Princeton University Library
32101 064253949

CPSIA information can be obtained
at www.ICGtesting.com
Printed in the USA
BVHW081611220819
556561BV00017B/3613/P